Lecture Notes in Computer Science 16504

Advanced Research in Computing and Software Science

Subline of Lecture Notes in Computer Science

More information about this series at https://link.springer.com/bookseries/558

Elvira Albert · Corina Pasareanu
Editors

Fundamental Approaches to Software Engineering

29th International Conference, FASE 2026
Held as Part of the International Joint Conferences on Theory and Practice of Software, ETAPS 2026
Turin, Italy, April 11–16, 2026
Proceedings

Editors
Elvira Albert
Complutense University of Madrid
Madrid, Spain

Corina Pasareanu
Carnegie Mellon University
Pittsburgh, PA, USA

ISSN 0302-9743 ISSN 1611-3349 (electronic)
Lecture Notes in Computer Science
ISBN 978-3-032-22773-7 ISBN 978-3-032-22774-4 (eBook)
https://doi.org/10.1007/978-3-032-22774-4

This Springer imprint is published by the registered company Springer Nature Switzerland AG
The registered company address is: Gewerbestrasse 11, 6330 Cham, Switzerland

ETAPS Foreword

Welcome to the 29th edition of ETAPS, which took place as an on-site event in Turin, Italy during April 11–16, 2026!

ETAPS 2026 was the 29th instance of the International Joint Conferences on Theory and Practice of Software (ETAPS). ETAPS is an annual federated conference established in 1998, and consists of four main conferences: ESOP, FASE, FoSSaCS, and TACAS. Each conference has its own Program Committee (PC) and its own Steering Committee (SC). The ETAPS main conferences cover various aspects of software systems, ranging from theoretical computer science to foundations of programming languages, tools and algorithms for system analysis, and formal approaches to software engineering. Organizing these conferences in a coherent, highly synchronized conference programme enables researchers to participate in an exciting event, having the possibility to meet many colleagues working in different directions in the field, and to easily attend talks of different conferences. In addition to its four main conferences, ETAPS 2026 also hosted fifteen satellite workshops and two colocated events, which together further attracted many researchers from all over the globe.

ETAPS 2026 received 456 submissions in total, 138 of which were accepted, yielding an overall acceptance rate of 30%. Out of the 138 accepted papers, 16 papers were selected as ETAPS distinguished papers. I thank all the authors of submitted papers for their interest in ETAPS, all the reviewers for their reviewing efforts, the PC members for their contributions, and in particular the PC (co-)chairs for their hard work in running this entire intensive process in a constructive, objective and timely manner. I congratulate all authors of the ETAPS 2026 accepted papers!

ETAPS 2026 featured the unifying invited keynotes by

- Monika Henzinger (Institute of Science and Technology Austria, Austria), delivering a talk about “Guarding Privacy Over Time: Challenges and Solutions in Continuous Data Observation”,
- Einar Broch Johnsen (University of Oslo, Norway), discussing “Formal Methods Meet Digital Twins: Challenges and Opportunities”.

ETAPS 2026 hosted the invited keynote speakers

- Christel Baier (Technische Universität Dresden, Germany) for FoSSaCS, presenting “Verification of Infinite-horizon Properties of Dynamic Bayesian Networks”,
- Guy Van den Broeck (University of California, Los Angeles, USA) for TACAS, introducing “Symbolic Reasoning in the Age of Large Language Models”.

The ETAPS 2026 invited tutorials were provided by

- Mieke Massink (CNR-ISTI Pisa, Italy) on “Model Checking in Space with Applications to Medical Image Analysis”,
- Leonardo de Moura (Amazon Web Services, USA) surveying “The Lean Programming Language and Theorem Prover”.

The ETAPS 2026 programme also featured a lively Ask-Me-Anything session, interactive tool demos, a Diversity, Equity, and Inclusion session, SV-Comp and Test-Comp community building events, and the ETAPS industry day. The goal of the ETAPS industry day is to bring industrial practitioners into the heart of the research community and to catalyze the interaction between industry and academia. The ETAPS 2026 industry day was organized by Giorgio Audrito (University of Turin, Italy), Sean Kauffman (Queen's University, Kingston, Canada), and Nikolai Kosmatov (Thales Research and Technology, Palaiseau, France).

ETAPS 2026 was organized by the Department of Computer Science of the University of Turin, which is the center for coordinating research, teaching, dissemination and technological transfer in computer science in Turin, Italy. The department covers both methodological and application oriented aspects of computer science, and performs research in several interdisciplinary areas. This is reflected in the collaborations with other research centers and companies in many scientific areas and in its participation in national, European and international projects.

ETAPS 2026 was further supported by the following associations and societies: ETAPS e. V. (the ETAPS Association), EATCS (European Association for Theoretical Computer Science), EAPLS (European Association for Programming Languages and Systems), and EASST (European Association of Software Science and Technology).

The ETAPS Steering Committee consists of an Executive Board, and representatives of the individual ETAPS conferences, as well as representatives of EATCS, EAPLS, and EASST. The Executive Board consists of Laura Kovács (TU Wien, chair), Andrzej Wąsowski (IT University of Copenhagen, vice-chair), Thomas Noll (RWTH Aachen, treasurer), Arnd Hartmanns (University of Twente, artifact evaluation coordinator), Barbara König (University of Duisburg-Essen, proceedings coordination), Caterina Urban (Inria, PhD activities), Elizabeth Polgreen (University of Edinburgh, social media), Jan Kofroň (Charles University Prague, organisational support, website), Jan Křetínský (Masaryk University Brno and TU Munich, diversity & inclusion), and Marieke Huisman (University of Twente, blog, awards). Further members of the ETAPS Steering Committee committee are: Robbert Krebbers (Radboud University Nijmegen), Azalea Raad (Imperial College London), Luís Caires (Tecnico ULisboa), Elvira Albert (Universidad Complutense de Madrid), Corina Păsăreanu (Carnegie Mellon University), Erika Ábrahám (RWTH Aachen), Marsha Chechik (University of Toronto), Marie-Christine Jakobs (LMU Munich), Nathalie Bertrand (Inria Rennes), Stefan Milius (Friedrich-Alexander Universität Erlangen-Nürnberg), Alexandra Silva (Cornell University), Joël Ouaknine (MPI-SWS Saarbrücken), Andrzej Murawski (University of Oxford), Sebastian Junges (Radboud University Nijmegen), Guy Katz (The Hebrew University of Jerusalem), Christian Schilling (Aalborg University), Naijun Zhan (Peking University), Joost-Pieter Katoen (RWTH Aachen and University of Twente), Dirk Beyer (LMU Munich), Fabrice Kordon (Sorbonne University Paris), Laure Petrucci (Université Paris 13), Peter Y.A. Ryan (University of Luxembourg), Claudio Menghi (University of Bergamo and McMaster University Hamilton), Mark Lawford (McMaster University Hamilton), Maurice ter Beek (CNR-ISTI Pisa), Ferruccio Damiani (University of Turin), Kim Guldstrand Larsen (Aalborg University), Bernhard Beckert (KIT Karlsruhe), Mattias Ulbrich (KIT Karlsruhe), Reiko Heckel (University of Leicester), Vladimiro Sassone

(University of Southampton), Anton Wijs (Eindhoven University of Technology), and Nikolai Kosmatov (Thales Research and Technology, Palaiseau).

The ETAPS 2026 local organization team consisted of Maurice ter Beek (CNR-ISTI Pisa, general co-chair), Ferruccio Damiani (University of Turin, general co-chair), Barbara Boni (Synesthesia Turin, local organization chair), Vincenzo Ciancia (CNR-ISTI Pisa, satellite events co-chair), Luca Paolini (University of Turin, satellite events co-chair), Maria Tacconi (Synesthesia Turin, satellite events co-chair and publicity co-chair), Francesco Brocero (Synesthesia Turin, web co-chair and volunteers co-chair), José Proença (University of Porto, web co-chair), Gianluca Torta (University of Turin, publicity co-chair and local proceedings co-chair), Lucy James (Synesthesia Turin, sponsor chair), Giovanna Broccia (CNR-ISTI Pisa, local proceedings co-chair), Giorgio Audrito (University of Turin, volunteers co-chair), Riccardo Sieve (UiO Oslo, volunteers co-chair), and Reiner Hähnle (TU Darmstadt, wine chair).

I would like to take this opportunity to thank all authors, keynote speakers, invited tutorial speakers, and attendees. Special thanks goes to the organizers of the ETAPS 2026 satellite workshops and colocated events. ETAPS 2026 is grateful for the generous support of Amazon Web Services, AccessiWay, Camera di Commercio Industria Artigianato e Agricoltura di Torino, the Department of Computer Science of the University of Turin, Springer Nature, and Turismo Torino e provincia Convention Bureau. I thank our general co-chairs Maurice ter Beek (CNR-ISTI Pisa) and Ferruccio Damiani (University of Turin), who made it all happen in Turin, and their local organization team for their enormous efforts to make ETAPS 2026 a fantastic event. I am especially grateful to Barbara Boni, Maria Tacconi, and Lucy James (Synesthesia Turin) for handling the organizational process in a smooth and reliable way. Last but not least, a big thanks to Jan Kofroň for all his help as an ETAPS Fellow and providing online presence support for the ETAPS conferences and the ETAPS Association.

I hope you all enjoyed ETAPS 2026!

April 2026

Laura Kovács
ETAPS SC Chair, President of the ETAPS Association

Preface

FASE 2026, the 29th International Conference on Fundamental Approaches to Software Engineering, was held from April 11–16, 2026, in Turin, Italy, as part of the 29th ETAPS International Joint Conferences on Theory and Practice of Software (ETAPS 2026). FASE serves as a premier venue for researchers, developers, and users to discuss innovations in software engineering.

The topics of interest for FASE include: requirements, design, architecture, and modeling of software systems, applications of AI to software engineering and applications of software engineering to AI-based systems, software quality, model-driven engineering, software processes, as well as software evolution.

There were four submission categories for FASE 2026:

1. Research papers, which clearly identify and justify a principled advance to the fundamentals of software engineering.
2. Empirical-evaluation papers, which evaluate existing software challenges or critically validate current proposed solutions with scientific means, that is, by empirical studies, controlled experiments, rigorous case studies, and simulations.
3. New Ideas and Emerging Results (NIER) papers, which seek to disrupt the status quo with forward-looking, thought-provoking, innovative research on the foundations of software engineering, as well as lessons learned from the past.
4. Tool demonstration and data showcase papers, which present a new tool, a new tool component, novel extensions to an existing tool, or a new dataset.

This year, 68 papers were submitted to FASE. Three papers were desk rejected. The remaining 65 papers were distributed in categories 1–4 as follows: 45 research papers, 9 empirical-evaluation papers, 8 NIER papers, and 3 tool-demonstration and data showcase papers. Each paper underwent a double-blind peer review process, where three program committee members reviewed each submission. The review process spanned 9 weeks, ensuring thorough evaluation and discussion of submissions. It was possible to submit an artifact for evaluation alongside a paper, if made long-term available and declared in the Data-Availability Statement. The program committee extensively discussed the papers and ultimately decided to accept 21 papers included in these proceedings: 15 research papers, 3 empirical studies, 2 NIER papers, and 1 tool paper, resulting in an acceptance rate of 32%.

Artifacts comprise tools, models, proofs, or other data for validating the results of a paper. The artifact evaluation committee (AEC) reviewed the artifacts based on their documentation, ease of use, and, most importantly, whether the results presented in the corresponding paper could be accurately reproduced. As in 2025 FASE offered a joint voluntary artifact evaluation together with ESOP and FoSSaCS to authors of accepted papers. All of the 8 artifact submissions that were linked with accepted FASE 2026 submissions met the requirements for the "Artifacts Available" badge. In addition, 2 submissions were awarded the Artifacts "Evaluated – Functional" badge and 5 submissions the Artifacts "Evaluated – Reusable" badge.

FASE 2026 was proud to host an invited tutorial by Mieke Massink from the C.N.R. –Area della Ricerca di Pisa– Ist. ISTI. These proceedings contain the invited paper supporting the tutorial.

FASE 2026 also hosted Test-Comp 2026, the 8th International Competition on Software Testing. This event evaluated 21 tools for automatic test generation for C programs, where 11 test-generation tools were registered and actively supported by development teams, including one tool that participated for the first time. One coverage validator was run in four different configurations to evaluate the coverage of the test-suites produced by the test-generation tools. In addition, the new test-suite validation tool TestCoCa participated for the first time. The FASE 2026 proceedings contain a competition report by the Test-Comp chair and 5 short papers selected by the competition jury. The short papers describe 5 out of the tools participating with active team support. The 5 short papers were reviewed by a separate program committee (jury); each was assessed by at least three jury members. Two sessions in the FASE 2026 program were reserved for Test-Comp: (1) a presentation session with a report by the competition chair and summaries by the development teams of participating tools, and (2) an open community meeting in the second session, jointly with SV-COMP.

We would like to thank all the people who helped make FASE 2026 successful. First, we thank the authors for submitting their papers. The PC members and additional reviewers did a great job: they contributed informed and detailed reports and engaged in the PC discussions. We thank Reiner Hähnle and Marie-Christine Jakobs, initial and current chairs of the FASE steering committee, and Marieke Huisman and Laura Kóvacs, also initial and current chairs of the ETAPS steering committee, for their valuable advice. Lastly, we would like to thank the overall organization team of ETAPS 2026. We extend our gratitude to Gianluca Torta and Giovanna Broccia, the local proceedings chairs, for their diligent oversight of the proceedings preparation. We also thank the Artifact Evaluation Committee (AEC) for their assessment of submitted artifacts and the Test-Comp 2026 jury members for their evaluation of competition submissions. Additionally, we appreciate the editorial support of Springer Nature, as well as the local organizers of ETAPS 2026 in Turin, Italy, for their efforts in facilitating this event. Finally, we note the Gold Open Access publication of these proceedings in the Lecture Notes in Computer Science (LNCS) series, ensuring unrestricted access to the contributions presented at FASE 2026.

February 2026

Elvira Albert
Corina Pasareanu
Dirk Beyer
Yannic Noller

Organization

Program Committee

Erika Abraham	RWTH Aachen University, Germany
Elvira Albert	Universidad Complutense de Madrid, Spain
Dirk Beyer	LMU Munich, Germany
Artur Boronat	University of Leicester, UK
Tevfik Bultan	University of California at Santa Barbara, USA
Ana Cavalcanti	University of York, UK
Marsha Chechik	University of Toronto, Canada
Priyanka Darke	Tata Consultancy Services, India
Stijn De Gouw	The Open University, UK
Bernd Fischer	Stellenbosch University, South Africa
Gordon Fraser	University of Passau, Germany
Divya Gopinath	NASA Ames (KBR Inc.), USA
Marie-Christine Jakobs	LMU München, Germany
Susmit Jha	SRI International, USA
Martin Jonáš	Masaryk University, Czechia
Sun Jun	Singapore Management University, Singapore
Thierry Lecomte	CLEARSY, France
Ravi Mangal	Colorado State University, USA
Raffaela Mirandola	Politecnico di Milano, Italy
Corina Pasareanu	CMU, NASA, KBR, USA
Luigia Petre	Åbo Akademi University, Finland
Cesar Sanchez	IMDEA Software Institute, Spain
Natasha Sharygina	University of Lugano, Switzerland
Dániel Varró	Linköping University, Sweden and McGill University, Canada
Andrzej Wasowski	IT University of Copenhagen, Denmark
Haoze Wu	Amherst College, USA
Jianjun Zhao	Kyushu University, Japan

Test-Comp Program Committee and Jury

Dirk Beyer (Chair)	LMU Munich, Germany
Kaled Alshmrany	Institute of Public Administration, Saudi Arabia
Max Barth	LMU Munich, Germany

Zhenbang Chen	National University of Defense Technology, China
Marie-Christine Jakobs	LMU Munich, Germany
Martin Jonáš	Masaryk University, Brno, Czechia
Matthias Kettl	LMU Munich, Germany
Thomas Lemberger	LMU Munich, Germany
Christophe Meudec	South East Technological University, Ireland
Marek Trtík	Masaryk University, Brno, Czechia
Henrik Wachowitz	LMU Munich, Germany
Chenfeng Wei	University of Manchester, UK

Additional Reviewers

Mohammad Afzal
David A. Anisi
Aren A. Babikian
Daniel Baier
Anna Becchi
Konstantin Britikov
Matías Brizzio
Margarita Capretto
Boqi Chen
Bharti Chimdyalwar
Achintya Desai
Mara Downing
Grigory Fedyukovich
Attila Ficsor
Dominik Frey
Carolina Gerlach
Marek Jankola
Matthias Kettl
Rick Koenders
Shrawan Kumar
Faezeh Labbaf
Fabrizio Leopardi
Marian Lingsch-Rosenfeld
Kumar Madhukar
Juraj Major
Logan Murphy
Sahar Nasimi Nezhad
Nico Naus
Matthew Peng
Venkatesh Ramanathan
Moeketsi Raselimo
Pedro Ribeiro
Andoni Rodriguez
Chia Sabah
Laboni Sarker
Stefano Schivo
Vincenzo Scotti
Md Shafiuzzaman
Jeroen Spaans
Jan Strejček
Alexandra van der Spuy
Erik Voogd
Henrik Wachowitz
Yiran Wang
Philipp Wendler

Contents

Autonomous Systems and Applications

Testing and Verification

Competition on Software Testing (Test-Comp 2026)

Keynote

Model Checking in Space with Applications to Medical Image Analysis*
Invited Abstract

Gina Belmonte[1], Vincenzo Ciancia[2], Diego Latella[3], and Mieke Massink[2]

[1] S. C. Fisica Sanitaria Nord, Azienda Toscana Nord Ovest, Lucca, Italy
gina.belmonte@uslnordovest.toscana.it
[2] ISTI, Consiglio Nazionale delle Ricerche, Pisa, Italy
{Vincenzo.Ciancia, Mieke.Massink}@cnr.it
[3] Formerly at ISTI, Consiglio Nazionale delle Ricerche, Pisa, Italy (Ret.)
Diego.Latella@actiones.eu

Abstract. Model checking has traditionally focused on the analysis of the *behaviour* of concurrent systems. In this invited abstract, instead, we focus on *spatial* model checking. We briefly motivate its development and its application in the domain of medical imaging, providing a gentle guide to our recent work on that topic and future research lines.

Keywords: Spatial logics · Closure spaces · Spatial model checking · Medical imaging · Polyhedral models

1 Introduction

The purpose of this brief invited abstract is to provide the reader with a concise guide to our recent work on spatial model checking, and, in particular, to its innovative application to medical image analysis. Traditionally, model checking techniques have been developed for the analysis of the behaviour in time of system models. The focus in that context is on the discovery of errors early on in the software development process, in particular software for safety-critical concurrent systems and control systems. Many variants of temporal aspects have been investigated, ranging from discrete and continuous time, hybrid forms combining both, to stochastic time and probabilistic behaviour (see e.g. [4] and references therein). Only recently, spatial aspects and spatio-temporal aspects have received attention from the Formal Methods community. Early examples in the Computer Science literature concern situations in which modal operators are interpreted "syntactically", i.e. against the structure of agents in a process calculus (see [22, 24] for some classical examples). The object of discussion in that research line are operators that quantify, for example, over parallel sub-components of a system, or the hidden resources of an agent. Furthermore, logics for graphs have

* The authors are listed in alphabetical order, as they equally contributed to the work presented in this paper.

E. Albert and C. Pasareanu (Eds.): FASE 2026, LNCS 16504, pp. 3–18, 2026.
https://doi.org/10.1007/978-3-032-22774-4_1

been studied in the context of databases and process calculi (see [23, 40], and references therein). However, the relationship with physical space is often not made explicit, if considered at all. There has been work on studying the influence of space on the interaction between agents in the literature on process calculi using *named locations* (see for example [39]). Variants of spatial logics have also been proposed for the symbolic representation of the contents of images, and, combined with temporal logics, for the analysis of sequences of images [16]. In our current work we use the terminology *spatial logics* in the "topological" sense, starting from a spatial interpretation of modal logics.

In our work we extend the topological semantics of modal logics to *closure spaces*. A closure space (also called *Čhech closure space* or preclosure space in the literature), is a generalisation of a standard topological space, where idempotence of the closure operator is not required. This choice is motivated by the need to treat (general) graphs and topological spaces in a *uniform way* so that we can reason on both discrete and continuous models of space in the same general framework. Closure spaces have also been proposed as an alternative foundation of digital imaging by various authors, in particular Smyth and Webster [52] and Galton [41]. Our work continues that line of research, enhancing it with a logical and a model checking perspective. We have developed the Spatial Logic for Closure Spaces (SLCS) [32, 33], interpreting the diamond operator of modal logics as a closure operator as in closure spaces, and adding a spatial conditional reachability operator to the logic that is inspired by a first brief mention of such an operator for a topological space in the work by Aiello [1] and in that by van Benthem and Bezhanishvili [11]. The latter paper is included in the Handbook of Spatial Logics [2], which formed a further source of inspiration for the introduction of additional spatial logic operators to SLCS such as a distance operator [5, 9], operators for collective spatial logic CSLCS [33, 34] and the combination of SLCS with branching time temporal logic, leading to the Spatial-Temporal Logic for Closure Spaces (STLCS) [30, 29]. In [34] we showed that the well-known discrete variant of the Region Connection Calculus (RCC8D) could be expressed in terms of CSLCS. SLCS also inspired the development of a spatial version of the Signal Temporal Logic (SSTL) [50]. More recently, SLCS was also given a *polyhedral semantics* [12, 15, 14, 13]. This allows for the expression of properties of continuous spatial models, in particular polyhedra. Such spatial models are widely used in the field of computer graphics where they are known as 2D triangular surface meshes or 3D tetrahedral volume meshes.

For all the variants of SLCS we have developed efficient *spatial model checkers*. The first model checker, `topochecker`, is actually a spatio-temporal model checker [30, 33, 29]. It also deals with the collective version of SLCS. `topochecker` has been applied in case studies in public transportation [35, 29]. In [35, 46] it has been combined with a stochastic simulation model of bike sharing systems. The approach has been extended in [36] with statistical model checking, exploiting its combination with MultiVesta [51]. `topochecker` has also been used in first experiments with spatial model checking the medical field [5]. The success of the latter work was one of the reasons to focus on the development of a purely spatial model checker, VoxLogicA [9, 10]. This model checker was built on top of the Insight Toolkit (ITK) [47], which is an open-source, cross-platform software library providing advanced and efficient algorithms for medical image analysis and supported by the National Library of Medicine (NLM) in the United States, which is the world's largest biomedical library. This choice not only considerably improved the efficiency of spatial model checking, but also allowed for the introduction of a suitable image query language (ImgQL), having SLCS as its core logic, extended with (possibly derived) operators that are familiar to domain experts in medical image analysis. Furthermore, VoxLogicA is able to deal with the common NifTy (Neuroimaging Informatics Technology Initiative) format for storing brain imaging data like 3D MRI (Magnetic Resonance Images) scans. A hands-on tutorial for VoxLogicA model checking is provided in [27]. Finally, the third spatial model checker we developed in the context of SLCS is PolyLogicA [12]. This is a polyhedra model checker that can also analyse surface and volume meshes [12, 15, 14, 3] and, in the future, could also play a role in the analysis of 3D meshes of medical images.

To the best of our knowledge, our work is the first to explore the application of (spatial) model checking techniques to the analysis of medical images. This idea emerged in an informal discussion between the co-authors of this abstract trying to find a common ground of understanding of medical image analysis in the clinical practise on one hand, and spatial model checking on the other hand. The discussion took place in the context of the segmentation (contouring, delineation) of High-Grade Glioblastoma (HGG), a very serious form of brain tumours. For the treatment of glioblastomas, neuro-imaging protocols are used before and after treatment of a patient to evaluate the effect of treatment strategies and to monitor the evolution of the disease. Radiotherapy is often part of such treatments and legal aspects about the accountability and justification of particular treatments as well as the quality of life of a patient are all serious issues to be taken into consideration. This makes the accurate contouring of lesions in the brain an important but challenging and safety-critical task, which, in the current practise is also rather time-consuming as delineation is mainly performed manually with the help of computer-assisted drawing tools. Although the actual trend is the use of Deep Learning methods for fully automatic medical image analysis (see for example [49] for a recent overview), the lack of explainability and accountability and a meaningful human control of these methods form a problem in the clinical practise. We have applied spatial model checking on three different case studies in the medical domain: contouring HGG [9, 5, 10], identifying white and grey matter in the brain [8, 10] and contouring potentially harmful lesions of the skin (nevi) [6]. Furthermore, we have studied a neuro-symbolic approach to the contouring of HGG [7, 10].

In the subsequent sections we provide some further details on spatial models and logics, the spatial model checker VoxLogicA and its application to the analysis of medical images, providing relevant pointers to the literature.

Synopsis: Section 2 presents an overview of closure models, the main spatial models used in our work, the *Spatial Logics for Closure Spaces*, and variants thereof. Section 3 presents some further information on the various spatial model checkers, Section 4 gives an overview of the application of `VoxLogicA` in medical imaging. Finally, Section 5 concludes the abstract providing some lines for future research.

2 Models of Space and Spatial Logics

Topological spaces are a foundational framework for, among others, a mathematical representation of physical space and for reasoning about its properties. Central in the theory of topological spaces is the notion of *closure* of a set of points. If a set of points is an open set, for example all points on the line segment between 1 and 2, but without its endpoints, the closure operator adds these endpoints to the set. If the set of points is already closed, i.e. including such endpoints, then the closure does not add any further points, i.e. topological closure is idempotent. This implies that topological spaces are not well suited for the representation of other kinds of "spaces", like, e.g., general graphs — even if some restricted classes of graphs can still be represented as topological spaces.

Closure spaces are a *generalisation* of topological spaces where idempotence of the closure operator $\mathcal{C}$ is instead not required. Furthermore, for a certain subclass of closure spaces, namely *quasi-discrete closure spaces* — that includes finite graphs — it can be shown that there is always a binary relation R on the set of points of the space that characterises the closure operator. More specifically, in this case, it can be shown that, letting X denote the set of points of the space, the function $\mathcal{C}_R : \mathbf{2}^X \rightarrow \mathbf{2}^X$ defined as follows for any $A \subseteq X$

$$\mathcal{C}_R(A) = A \cup \{x \in X \mid a\, R\, x \text{ for some } a \in A\} \tag{1}$$

is a closure operator, according to the axiomatic definition of closure spaces of Čech [25]. Similarly, this also holds for the converse relation R^{-1}, which induces the *converse closure* $\mathcal{C}_{R^{-1}}$.

Mathematical logic, and in particular modal logics, have long been a successful framework for formal reasoning about space. In their seminal paper of 1944, Tarski and McKinsey proposed a topological interpretation of the classical necessity modality and its dual modality, the possibility modality [48]. There, the necessity modality, often denoted by $\Box$, is interpreted as *topological interior* — and the possibility modality, i.e. the $\Diamond$ operator, is interpreted as topological closure. In other words, given a formula Φ and a point x of a topological model — i.e. a topological space enriched with an evaluation function $\mathcal{V}$ associating a set of points to each element of a given set `PL` of *predicate letters* — satisfies formula $\Box\,\Phi$ if and only if x lays in the (topological) interior of the set of points satisfying Φ. Similarly, x satisfies $\Diamond\,\Phi$ if x belongs to the closure of the set of points satisfying Φ. Since then, a flourishing field of research in mathematical logic has been developed that focussed on the study of logical operators interpreted on models of space, namely the field of "Spatial Logics" [2].

In [32, 33] the *Spatial Logic for Closure Spaces* (`SLCS`) has been proposed that includes, besides predicate letters, negation and conjunction, a *proximity* modality $\mathcal{N}$ and a *surrounded* modality $\mathcal{S}$. The logic is interpreted on closure models — a closure model is a closure space enriched with an evaluation function $\mathcal{V}$ as in the case of topological models.

A point x of a closure model satisfies a formula $\mathcal{N}\Phi$ if it lays in the closure of the set of points satisfying formula Φ. Note that in SLCS the closure operator is that defined for *closure spaces* and not necessarily the topological one. For instance, in the case of a Kripke model — seen as quasi-discrete closure model — the closure operator will be that of (1) above, computed with respect to the accessibility relation R of the Kripke model. In particular, idempotence of the closure operator will depend on the structure of the model.

A point x of a closure model satisfies a formula $\Phi_1 \mathcal{S} \Phi_2$ if it lays in a set of points all satisfying Φ_1 that is surrounded by a set of points satisfying Φ_2. In other words, there is no path in the space, starting from x that can reach a point satisfying neither Φ_1 nor Φ_2 without first passing from a point satisfying Φ_2. Of course, the notion of "path" depends of the nature of the closure space one is considering: in the case of continuous spaces a path is a continuous function from $[0, 1]$ to the space whereas for discrete spaces, e.g. graphs, it is a function π from a set $\{0, \ldots, \ell\}$, for some natural number ℓ, such that $\pi(i+1) \in \mathcal{C}(\{\pi(i)\})$ for all i such that $0 \leq i < \ell$.

Several additional operators have been incorporated in SLCS. We will briefly discuss some of them. From the above informal description of the surrounded operator, it should be clear that reachability plays a crucial role in the study of properties of space. For this reason, a specific *conditional reachability* operator ρ has been introduced: a point x satisfies $\rho\,\Phi_1[\Phi_2]$ if a path π exists from x such that the end-point of π satisfies Φ_1 while all intermediate points of the path satisfy Φ_2. The surrounded operator can be expressed using the reachability modality and negation, as follows: $\Phi_1 \mathcal{S} \Phi_2$ is equivalent to $\Phi_1 \wedge \neg \rho \neg(\Phi_1 \vee \Phi_2)[\neg \Phi_2]$. When interpreting the logic on a quasi-discrete closure space, the "direction" of the underlying relation R induces a splitting of ρ into two distinct operators: a direct, or "forward", reachability operator $\vec{\rho}$, and a converse, or "backward" reachability operator $\overleftarrow{\rho}$. The semantics of $\vec{\rho}$ are the same as those of ρ above, whereas x satisfies $\overleftarrow{\rho}\ \Phi_1[\Phi_2]$ if a point y exists that satisfies Φ_1 and from which a path π exists such that the end-point of π is x while all intermediate points of the path satisfy Φ_2. In other words, while whenever x satisfies $\vec{\rho}\ \Phi_1[\Phi_2]$ we have that x *can reach* a point satisfying Φ_1 via points (of a path) all satisfying Φ_2, when x satisfies $\overleftarrow{\rho}\ \Phi_1[\Phi_2]$ we have that x *can be reached* from a point satisfying Φ_1 via points (of a path) all satisfying Φ_2. This difference is quite important when reasoning about space: just think, for instance, of a graph modelling the road system of a city where there are one-way roads. Another example could be the need to express the fact that, from a certain location of a building, via a safe corridor, a rescue area can be reached (forward reachability) that cannot be reached by (backward reachability) smoke generated in another area of the building. Note that for quasi-discrete closure models $\mathcal{N}\Phi$ can be expressed as $\overleftarrow{\rho}\ \Phi[\mathtt{false}]$ and that, whenever R is symmetric, $\vec{\rho}\ \Phi_1[\Phi_2]$ and $\overleftarrow{\rho}\ \Phi_1[\Phi_2]$

coincide: in this case we simply use the notation $\rho\,\Phi_1[\Phi_2]$ [6]. The case of R being symmetric is of great importance in the context of the present paper since digital images, of which medical images are only a special case, are just finite regular grids, which, in turn, can be modelled as finite, thence quasi-discrete, closure models where points are related by a binary symmetric relation — the so-called *adjacency relation*.

When reasoning about space, it is often useful to make reference to the distance between points. For this reason, in [9, 5] variants of `SLCS` have been equipped with a *distance operator* $\mathcal{D}^I$ and are interpreted on distance closure models, i.e. closure models extended with suitable distance functions[4]. A point x satisfies $\mathcal{D}^I\,\Phi$ if the distance of x from a point satisfying Φ falls in the interval I of the real numbers.

In the context of (medical) image analysis, texture analysis plays an important role. For that purpose, in [9] the statistical correlation operator $\triangle\!\!\!\triangle\,\Phi$ is introduced that compares the correlation between the histogram of a given *area of interest* and that of the set of points satisfying Φ with a given threshold; the specification of the histogram of the area of interest as well as the threshold are given as additional parameters, not shown above (see [9, 6, 10] for details).

3 Spatial Model Checking with `VoxLogicA`

The spatial model checker `VoxLogicA`[5] (Voxel-based Logical Analyser) [9, 10] provides a rapid-development, declarative, logic-based approach to image analysis and segmentation and is a free and open source tool. It is particularly suitable to reason at the "macro-level" by exploiting the *relative* spatial relations between regions of interest in multi-dimensional digital medical images. The input language of `VoxLogicA`, the Image Query Language (`ImgQL`), has `SLCS` at its core, but also encompasses several domain oriented operators to accommodate the level of abstract spatial reasoning by domain experts such as neuro-radiologists. Examples of such operators are region growing, region touching and the surrounded operator (all derived from the reachability operator), distance operator and a texture similarity operator, as well as additional operators to specify similarity measures (e.g. Dice, specificity, sensitivity), primitives for images management (loading and saving results) and mechanisms for the definition of new (derived) logical operators. This choice provides powerful building blocks to develop concise, human readable and explainable image segmentation methods. A tutorial on `VoxLogicA` and `ImgQL` can be found in [27].

[4] In the simplest case, a distance function is a real-valued function d such that for all points x and y $d(x, y) = 0$ if and only if $x = y$. Distance functions generalise metric functions.

[5] Available from: https://github.com/vincenzoml/VoxLogicA

4 Application to Medical Imaging

So far we have applied spatial model checking to three different case studies in the medical domain. The first one concerns the contouring of HGG in 3D MRI images from a public dataset of the BraTS (Brain Tumour Segmentation) 2017 Challenge [49]. In these experiments we have been using the spatial model checker `topochecker` for the contouring of the gross tumour volume, consisting of tumour tissue and the surrounding cerebral oedema [5]. The first results with `topochecker` were encouraging as we obtained a similarity (Dice) score of 0.76 with respect to the manual contouring performed by experienced neuro-radiologists. A Dice score of 0.76 roughly means that there is an overlap of 76% between our contouring result and that made by domain experts (providing the ground truth). This number may not look that high at first sight, but one has to take into account that there is a relatively high intra-expert and inter-expert variance estimated between 20(±15%) and 28(±12%), respectively. This means that a similarity score between 80-90% would actually be excellent. With the dedicated `VoxLogicA` spatial model checking approach we have obtained Dice scores in that range. With a 10 lines long `ImgQL` query on the larger BraTS 2020 training dataset considering 276 multi-institutional pre-operative MRI scans of patients affected by HGG we obtained an average Dice similarity score of 0.85(±0.11 standard deviation) [10]. An example of a HGG contouring is shown in Fig. 1.

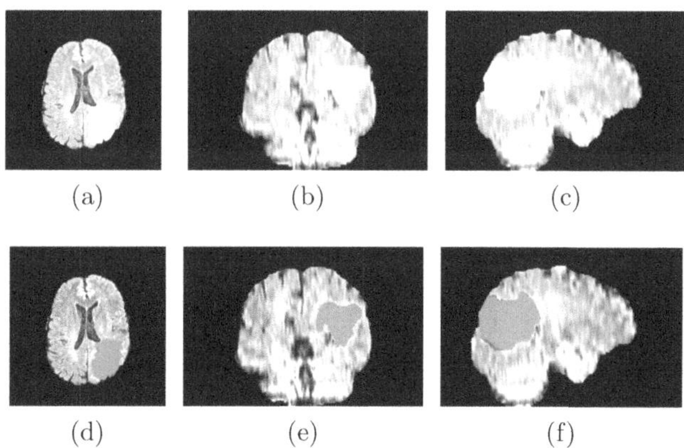

Fig. 1: First row: original MRI images of case BraTS17_TCIA_335 case. Second row: segmentation result of tumour and oedema with `VoxLogicA` (green) and largely overlapping ground truth (red). Images from [10].

The second case study concerned the automatic identification of tissues in the brain. We looked in particular to white matter and grey matter. The analysis with VoxLogicA on the public BrainWeb[6] dataset containing 20 cases of healthy brains (synthetic MRI scans) gave a similarity of 0.93(±0.02 std) for white matter and 0.91(±0.16 std) for grey matter [8, 10]. An example of the identification of white matter in a healthy brain is shown in Fig. 2.

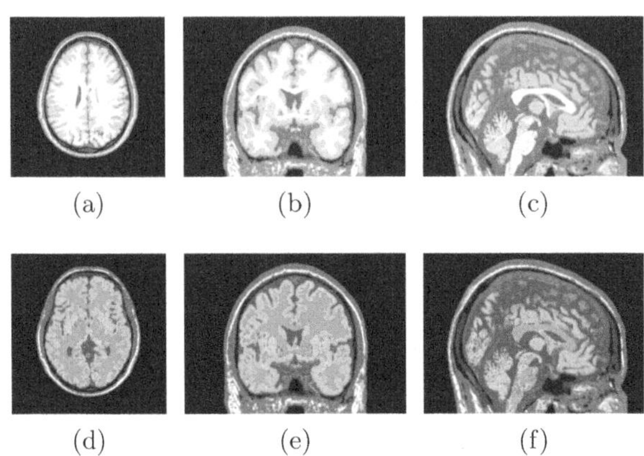

Fig. 2: First row: Original Images for the pat_4 case of the BrainWeb dataset. Second row: white matter segmentation (green) and largely overlapping ground truth (red). Images from [10].

The third case study addressed the contouring of nevi, which are possibly malicious lesions of the skin [6]. The challenges here are the enormous variation in colour and shape and the presence of additional elements such as hairs and ink annotations on the skin that were added by clinicians to indicate the location of a lesion. For the evaluation of the approach we used the ISIC 2016 training and test sets of dermascopic images [45], originally designed for machine learning approaches. We obtained a Dice similarity score of more than 0.8 in 70% of the cases, both in the test set (379 cases) and in the training set (900 cases). Of course, a spatial model checking approach does not require any training or learning phase, but we did use a small sample of the set of images for the development of the logic specification. To analyse the complete test set of 379 cases with VoxLogicA took approximately 30 minutes on an AMD Ryzen 7 2700 Eight-Core processor with 32GB of memory, i.e. 4 seconds per image on average. A few examples of nevi contouring are shown in Fig. 3.

Finally, in [10], we have also proposed a neuro-symbolic approach to the segmentation of HGG glioblastoma. This hybrid approach combines the symbolic VoxLogicA approach to contouring with nnU-Net, a deep-learning technique. The main motivation for that approach was to investigate whether the symbolic approach could provide a high-level, explainable spatial logic based description

[6] See the following link: http://www.bic.mni.mcgill.ca/brainweb/

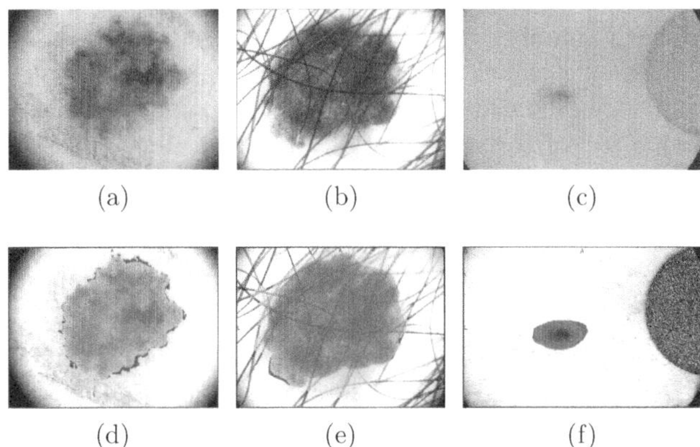

Fig. 3: First row: Original images. Second row: segmentation (cyan) and ground truth (dark blue): Case ISIC_0000002 (3a) resp. (3d), case ISIC_0000043 (3b) resp. (3e) and case ISIC_0004309 (3c) resp. (3f). Images from [6].

for a contouring result obtained using nnU-Net, that showed a sufficient overlap with the spatial model checking result. This would provide two results, obtained with completely different techniques, but in case of sufficient similarity, one could be used as the explanation for the other and having two similar results would increase the confidence in the reliability of the contouring. We used a trained nnU-Net model to estimate two threshold values that were directly relevant for the ImgQL specification. We then used these values in the symbolic model checking procedure and compared the results using the Dice similarity index. If the results were sufficiently similar, we accepted the result. The hybrid approach showed slightly higher accuracy than a symbolic approach alone. This approach can also be used when no contouring by experts is available, such as in the clinical case. In this approach there would also be space for meaningful human control as the two threshold values could be adjusted manually and the result checked visually by neuro-radiologists.

5 Conclusion and Future Research

The various case studies with VoxLogicA in medical imaging show promising results, reaching levels of accuracy that are in line with the state-of-the-art reached with other methods in the literature as published in the leaderboard scores of the various segmentation challenges. This paved the way to many new avenues for research in this field. In the following we briefly mention the currently activities and future challenges.

Concerning the VoxLogicA model checker, work has started to develop a version that exploits Graph Processing Units (GPU) computing [18]. Logic specifications in ImgQL are such that they often consist of many independent sub-formulas. In the CPU-version of VoxLogicA such sub-formulas can be computed in parallel, upto the number of available cores. Adding GPU computing would allow for many more parallel computations and a consequent speed-up of the analysis. It also opens the way to analyse video streams [20]. The challenge here is the transformation of the spatial model checking algorithm problem for the various operators into suitable parallel counterparts. Extensions of SLCS and CSLCS with spatial quantification operators are studied in [21, 19]. The former concerns the existential quantification over points in a space, the latter amounts to a form of quantification over atomic propositions. The development of further case studies and the wider take-up of the approach in medical image analysis would greatly benefit from a suitable Graphical User Interface for VoxLogicA (VoxLogicA-UI) that would neatly fit into and support the workflow of different user classes, such as ImgQL specification developers, clinicians and neuroradiologists. Work in this direction can be found in [17, 53] and a prototype implementation of VoxLogicA-UI can be found online.[7]

Since spatial models, and in particular 3D medical images, can be rather large, work has been carried out on the development of suitable spatial model reduction techniques. In particular, minimisation techniques based on spatial bisimulation [26, 37] have been investigated [31]. More specifically, a notion of "path-compatibility" for quasi-discrete closure models has been proposed that gives rise to a spatial bisimilarity which enjoys the Hennessy-Milner property with respect to (a variant of) SLCS [26, 37]: two points in space are bisimilar if and only if they satisfy the same logic formulas. In [31], it has been shown that an encoding exists of finite quasi-discrete closure models into labelled transition systems such that two points in space are spatially bisimilar if and only if their encodings are branching-bisimulation equivalent [38]. The encoding allows to exploit efficient branching-bisimulation minimisation tools [42, 44] for spatial model minimisation.

A further line of research [43] involving VoxLogicA concerns the definition of a comprehensive benchmark framework designed to systematically evaluate spatial reasoning capabilities in neural networks, with a particular focus on morphological properties such as connectivity and distance relationships. In this context the capabilities of nnU-Net are studied, exploiting the spatial model checker VoxLogicA to generate two distinct categories of synthetic datasets: one relates to maze connectivity problems for topological analysis, and the other addresses spatial distance computation tasks for geometric understanding. Preliminary experimental results demonstrate significant challenges in neural network spatial reasoning capabilities, revealing systematic failures in basic geometric and topological understanding tasks.

Finally, in [12] PolyLogicA[8] is presented that is a model checker supporting SLCS for finite polyhedra models. Thus (a restricted form of) continuous spatial models can be checked against SLCS formulas. The result of polyhedral model checking can be visualised by the visualisation tool PolyVisualizer, an ad-hoc

[7] Available at: https://github.com/VoxLogicA-Project/VoxLogicA-UI
[8] Available at: https://github.com/vincenzoml/VoxLogicA

3D visualiser for polyhedral models. Also for polyhedral model checking notions of spatial bisimulation and minimisation [28, 15, 14] have been developed.

Acknowledgments. We would like to thank all the co-authors of the research on spatial model checking and all the people supporting us on this endeavour (in alphabetical order): Yuri Andriaccio, Nick Bezhanishvili, Luca Bortolussi, Giovanna Broccia, Laura Bussi, David Fernández-Duque, David Gabelaia, Fabio Gadducci, Stephen Gilmore, Gianluca Grilletti, Jan Friso Groote, Manuela Imbriani, Mamuka Jibladze, Michele Loreti, Laura Nenzi, Antonio Strippoli, Erik de Vink. Research partially supported by Bilateral project between National Research Council of Italy and Shota Rustaveli National Science Foundation of Georgia "Model Checking for Polyhedral Logic" (#CNR-22-010); European Union - Next GenerationEU - National Recovery and Resilience Plan (NRRP), Investment 1.5 Ecosystems of Innovation, Project "Tuscany Health Ecosystem" (THE), CUP: B83C22003930001; European Union - Next-GenerationEU - National Recovery and Resilience Plan (NRRP) – MISSION 4 COMPONENT 2, INVESTMENT N. 1.1, CALL PRIN 2022 D.D. 104 02-02-2022 – (Stendhal) CUP N. B53D23012850006. MUR project PRIN 2020TL3X8X "T-LADIES"; Shota Rustaveli National Science Foundation of Georgia grant #FR-22-6700.

Disclosure of Interests. The authors have no competing interests to declare that are relevant to the content of this article. The authors have not been using generative AI for writing this paper.

References

1. Aiello, M.: Spatial Reasoning: Theory and Practice. Ph.D. thesis, Institute of Logic, Language and Computation, University of Amsterdam (2002)
2. Aiello, M., Pratt-Hartmann, I., van Benthem, J. (eds.): Handbook of Spatial Logics. Springer (2007)
3. Andriaccio, Y., Ciancia, V., Latella, D., Massink, M.: Practical polyhedral model checking – a gentle introduction. In: Journeys Between Formal Methods and the Railway Industry. Essays Dedicated to Alessandro Fantechi on the Occasion of His 70th Birthday. Lecture Notes in Computer Science, vol. 16470. Springer (2026). https://doi.org/https://doi.org/10.1007/978-3-032-12484-5_8
4. Baier, C., Katoen, J.: Principles of model checking. MIT Press (2008)
5. Banci Buonamici, F., Belmonte, G., Ciancia, V., Latella, D., Massink, M.: Spatial logics and model checking for medical imaging. Int. J. Softw. Tools Technol. Transf. **22**(2), 195–217 (2020), https://doi.org/10.1007/s10009-019-00511-9
6. Belmonte, G., Broccia, G., Ciancia, V., Latella, D., Massink, M.: Feasibility of spatial model checking for nevus segmentation. In: Bliudze, S., Gnesi, S., Plat, N., Semini, L. (eds.) 9th IEEE/ACM International Conference on Formal Methods in Software Engineering, FormaliSE@ICSE 2021, Madrid, Spain, May 17-21, 2021. pp. 1–12. IEEE (2021), https://doi.org/10.1109/FormaliSE52586.2021.00007
7. Belmonte, G., Bussi, L., Ciancia, V., Latella, D., Massink, M.: Towards hybrid-AI in imaging using VoxLogicA. In: Margaria, T., Steffen, B. (eds.) Leveraging Applications of Formal Methods, Verification and Validation. Software Engineering Methodologies - 12th International Symposium, ISoLA 2024, Crete, Greece, October 27-31, 2024, Proceedings, Part IV. Lecture Notes in Computer Science, vol. 15222, pp. 205–221. Springer (2024). https://doi.org/10.1007/978-3-031-75387-9_13, https://doi.org/10.1007/978-3-031-75387-9_13

8. Belmonte, G., Ciancia, V., Latella, D., Massink, M.: Innovating medical image analysis via spatial logics. In: ter Beek, M.H., Fantechi, A., Semini, L. (eds.) From Software Engineering to Formal Methods and Tools, and Back - Essays Dedicated to Stefania Gnesi on the Occasion of Her 65th Birthday. Lecture Notes in Computer Science, vol. 11865, pp. 85–109. Springer (2019), https://doi.org/10.1007/978-3-030-30985-5_7
9. Belmonte, G., Ciancia, V., Latella, D., Massink, M.: VoxLogicA: A spatial model checker for declarative image analysis. In: Vojnar, T., Zhang, L. (eds.) Tools and Algorithms for the Construction and Analysis of Systems - 25th International Conference, TACAS 2019, Held as Part of the European Joint Conferences on Theory and Practice of Software, ETAPS 2019, Prague, Czech Republic, April 6-11, 2019, Proceedings, Part I. Lecture Notes in Computer Science, vol. 11427, pp. 281–298. Springer (2019), https://doi.org/10.1007/978-3-030-17462-0_16
10. Belmonte, G., Ciancia, V., Massink, M.: Symbolic and hybrid AI for brain tissue segmentation using spatial model checking. Artif. Intell. Medicine **167**, 103154 (2025). https://doi.org/10.1016/J.ARTMED.2025.103154, https://doi.org/10.1016/j.artmed.2025.103154
11. van Benthem, J., Bezhanishvili, G.: Modal logics of space. In: Aiello, M., Pratt-Hartmann, I., Benthem, J.v. (eds.) Handbook of Spatial Logics, pp. 217–298. Springer (2007), https://doi.org/10.1007/978-1-4020-5587-4_5
12. Bezhanishvili, N., Ciancia, V., Gabelaia, D., Grilletti, G., Latella, D., Massink, M.: Geometric Model Checking of Continuous Space. Log. Methods Comput. Sci. **18**(4), 7:1–7:38 (2022), https://lmcs.episciences.org/10348, DOI 10.46298/LMCS-18(4:7)2022. Published on line: Nov 22, 2022. ISSN: 1860-5974
13. Bezhanishvili, N., Bussi, L., Ciancia, V., Fernández-Duque, D., Gabelaia, D.: Logics of polyhedral reachability. In: Ciabattoni, A., Gabelaia, D., Sedlár, I. (eds.) Advances in Modal Logic, AiML 2024, Prague, Czech Republic, August 19-23, 2024. pp. 187–204. College Publications (2024)
14. Bezhanishvili, N., Bussi, L., Ciancia, V., Gabelaia, D., Jibladze, M., Latella, D., Massink, M., de Vink, E.P.: Weak simplicial bisimilarity and minimisation for polyhedral model checking. CoRR **abs/2411.11428** (2025). https://doi.org/10.48550/arXiv.2411.11428, https://doi.org/10.48550/arXiv.2411.11428, accepted for pubblication in Logical Methods in Computer Science
15. Bezhanishvili, N., Ciancia, V., Gabelaia, D., Jibladze, M., Latella, D., Massink, M., de Vink, E.P.: Weak simplicial bisimilarity for polyhedral models and SLCSη. In: Castiglioni, V., Francalanza, A. (eds.) Formal Techniques for Distributed Objects, Components, and Systems - 44th IFIP WG 6.1 International Conference, FORTE 2024, Held as Part of the 19th International Federated Conference on Distributed Computing Techniques, DisCoTec 2024, Groningen, The Netherlands, June 17-21, 2024, Proceedings. Lecture Notes in Computer Science, vol. 14678, pp. 20–38. Springer (2024). https://doi.org/10.1007/978-3-031-62645-6_2, https://doi.org/10.1007/978-3-031-62645-6_2
16. Bimbo, A.D., Vicario, E., Zingoni, D.: Symbolic description and visual querying of image sequences using spatio-temporal logic. IEEE Trans. Knowl. Data Eng. **7**(4), 609–622 (1995)
17. Broccia, G., Ciancia, V., Latella, D., Massink, M.: Towards a GUI for declarative medical image analysis: Cognitive and memory load issues. In: Stephanidis, C., Antona, M., Ntoa, S. (eds.) HCI International 2022 Posters - 24th International Conference on Human-Computer Interaction, HCII 2022, Virtual Event, June 26 -

July 1, 2022, Proceedings, Part II. Communications in Computer and Information Science, vol. 1581, pp. 103–111. Springer (2022). https://doi.org/10.1007/978-3-031-06388-6_14, https://doi.org/10.1007/978-3-031-06388-6_14
18. Bussi, L., Ciancia, V., Gadducci, F.: Towards a spatial model checker on GPU. In: Peters, K., Willemse, T.A.C. (eds.) Formal Techniques for Distributed Objects, Components, and Systems - 41st IFIP WG 6.1 International Conference, FORTE 2021, Held as Part of the 16th International Federated Conference on Distributed Computing Techniques, DisCoTec 2021, Valletta, Malta, June 14-18, 2021, Proceedings. Lecture Notes in Computer Science, vol. 12719, pp. 188–196. Springer (2021). https://doi.org/10.1007/978-3-030-78089-0_12, https://doi.org/10.1007/978-3-030-78089-0_12
19. Bussi, L., Ciancia, V., Gadducci, F.: A spatial logic with time and quantifiers. In: Gierasimczuk, N., Velázquez-Quesada, F.R. (eds.) Dynamic Logic. New Trends and Applications - 5th International Workshop, DaLí 2023, Tbilisi, Georgia, September 15-16, 2023, Revised Selected Papers. Lecture Notes in Computer Science, vol. 14401, pp. 1–19. Springer (2023). https://doi.org/10.1007/978-3-031-51777-8_1, https://doi.org/10.1007/978-3-031-51777-8_1
20. Bussi, L., Ciancia, V., Gadducci, F., Latella, D., Massink, M.: Towards model checking video streams using VoxLogicA on GPUs. In: Bowles, J., Broccia, G., Pellungrini, R. (eds.) From Data to Models and Back - 10th International Symposium, DataMod 2021, Virtual Event, December 6-7, 2021, Revised Selected Papers. Lecture Notes in Computer Science, vol. 13268, pp. 78–90. Springer (2021). https://doi.org/10.1007/978-3-031-16011-0_6, https://doi.org/10.1007/978-3-031-16011-0_6
21. Bussi, L., Ciancia, V., Gadducci, F., Latella, D., Massink, M.: On binding in the spatial logics for closure spaces. In: Margaria, T., Steffen, B. (eds.) Leveraging Applications of Formal Methods, Verification and Validation. Verification Principles - 11th International Symposium, ISoLA 2022, Rhodes, Greece, October 22-30, 2022, Proceedings, Part I. Lecture Notes in Computer Science, vol. 13701, pp. 479–497. Springer (2022). https://doi.org/10.1007/978-3-031-19849-6_27, https://doi.org/10.1007/978-3-031-19849-6_27
22. Caires, L., Cardelli, L.: A spatial logic for concurrency (part I). Information and Computation **186**(2), 194–235 (2003)
23. Cardelli, L., Gardner, P., Ghelli, G.: A spatial logic for querying graphs. In: Widmayer, P., Ruiz, F.T., Bueno, R.M., Hennessy, M., Eidenbenz, S.J., Conejo, R. (eds.) Automata, Languages and Programming, 29th International Colloquium, ICALP 2002, Malaga, Spain, July 8-13, 2002, Proceedings. Lecture Notes in Computer Science, vol. 2380, pp. 597–610. Springer (2002). https://doi.org/10.1007/3-540-45465-9_51, https://doi.org/10.1007/3-540-45465-9_51
24. Cardelli, L., Gordon, A.D.: Anytime, anywhere: Modal logics for mobile ambients. In: Proceedings of the 30th SIGPLAN-SIGACT Symposium on Principles of Programming Languages (POPL'00). pp. 365–377 (2000)
25. Čech, E.: Topological Spaces. In: Pták, V. (ed.) Topological Spaces, chap. III, pp. 233–394. Publishing House of the Czechoslovak Academy of Sciences/Interscience Publishers, John Wiley & Sons, Prague/London-New York-Sydney (1966), Revised edition by Zdeněk Frolíc and Miroslav Katětov. Scientific editor, Vlastimil Pták. Editor of the English translation, Charles O. Junge. MR0211373
26. Ciancia, V., Latella, D., Massink, M., de Vink, E.P.: Back-and-forth in space: On logics and bisimilarity in closure spaces. In: Jansen, N., Stoelinga, M., , van den Bos, P. (eds.) A Journey From Process Algebra via Timed Automata to Model Learning

- A Festschrift Dedicated to Frits Vaandrager on the Occasion of His 60th Birthday. Lecture Notes in Computer Science, vol. 13560, pp. 98–115. Springer (2022)
27. Ciancia, V., Belmonte, G., Latella, D., Massink, M.: A hands-on introduction to spatial model checking using VoxLogicA - - invited contribution. In: Laarman, A., Sokolova, A. (eds.) Model Checking Software - 27th International Symposium, SPIN 2021, Virtual Event, July 12, 2021, Proceedings. Lecture Notes in Computer Science, vol. 12864, pp. 22–41. Springer (2021). https://doi.org/10.1007/978-3-030-84629-9_2, https://doi.org/10.1007/978-3-030-84629-9_2
28. Ciancia, V., Gabelaia, D., Latella, D., Massink, M., de Vink, E.P.: On bisimilarity for polyhedral models and SLCS. In: Huisman, M., Ravara, A. (eds.) Formal Techniques for Distributed Objects, Components, and Systems - 43rd IFIP WG 6.1 International Conference, FORTE 2023, Held as Part of the 18th International Federated Conference on Distributed Computing Techniques, DisCoTec 2023, Lisbon, Portugal, June 19-23, 2023, Proceedings. Lecture Notes in Computer Science, vol. 13910, pp. 132–151. Springer (2023). https://doi.org/10.1007/978-3-031-35355-0_9, https://doi.org/10.1007/978-3-031-35355-0_9
29. Ciancia, V., Gilmore, S., Grilletti, G., Latella, D., Loreti, M., Massink, M.: Spatio-temporal model checking of vehicular movement in public transport systems. Int. J. Softw. Tools Technol. Transf. **20**(3), 289–311 (2018), https://doi.org/10.1007/s10009-018-0483-8
30. Ciancia, V., Grilletti, G., Latella, D., Loreti, M., Massink, M.: An experimental spatio-temporal model checker. In: Bianculli, D., Calinescu, R., Rumpe, B. (eds.) Software Engineering and Formal Methods - SEFM 2015 Collocated Workshops: ATSE, HOFM, MoKMaSD, and VERY*SCART, York, UK, September 7-8, 2015, Revised Selected Papers. Lecture Notes in Computer Science, vol. 9509, pp. 297–311. Springer (2015), https://doi.org/10.1007/978-3-662-49224-6_24
31. Ciancia, V., Groote, J., Latella, D., Massink, M., de Vink, E.: Minimisation of spatial models using branching bisimilarity. In: Chechik, M., Katoen, J.P., Leucker, M. (eds.) 25th International Symposium, FM 2023, Lübeck, March 6–10, 2023, Proceedings. Lecture Notes in Computer Science, vol. 14000, p. 263–281. Springer (2023). https://doi.org/10.1007/978-3-031-27481-7_16
32. Ciancia, V., Latella, D., Loreti, M., Massink, M.: Specifying and verifying properties of space. In: Díaz, J., Lanese, I., Sangiorgi, D. (eds.) Theoretical Computer Science - 8th IFIP TC 1/WG 2.2 International Conference, TCS 2014, Rome, Italy, September 1-3, 2014. Proceedings. Lecture Notes in Computer Science, vol. 8705, pp. 222–235. Springer (2014), https://doi.org/10.1007/978-3-662-44602-7_18
33. Ciancia, V., Latella, D., Loreti, M., Massink, M.: Model checking spatial logics for closure spaces. Log. Methods Comput. Sci. **12**(4) (2016), https://doi.org/10.2168/LMCS-12(4:2)2016
34. Ciancia, V., Latella, D., Massink, M.: Embedding RCC8D in the collective spatial logic CSLCS. In: Boreale, M., Corradini, F., Loreti, M., Pugliese, R. (eds.) Models, Languages, and Tools for Concurrent and Distributed Programming - Essays Dedicated to Rocco De Nicola on the Occasion of His 65th Birthday. Lecture Notes in Computer Science, vol. 11665, pp. 260–277. Springer (2019), https://doi.org/10.1007/978-3-030-21485-2_15
35. Ciancia, V., Latella, D., Massink, M., Paškauskas, R.: Exploring spatio-temporal properties of bike-sharing systems. In: 2015 IEEE International Conference on Self-Adaptive and Self-Organizing Systems Workshops, SASO Workshops 2015, Cambridge, MA, USA, September 21-25, 2015. pp. 74–79. IEEE Computer Society (2015), https://doi.org/10.1109/SASOW.2015.17

36. Ciancia, V., Latella, D., Massink, M., Paškauskas, R., Vandin, A.: A tool-chain for statistical spatio-temporal model checking of bike sharing systems. In: Margaria, T., Steffen, B. (eds.) Leveraging Applications of Formal Methods, Verification and Validation: Foundational Techniques - 7th International Symposium, ISoLA 2016, Imperial, Corfu, Greece, October 10-14, 2016, Proceedings, Part I. Lecture Notes in Computer Science, vol. 9952, pp. 657–673 (2016), https://doi.org/10.1007/978-3-319-47166-2_46
37. Ciancia, V., Latella, D., Massink, M., de Vink, E.P.: On bisimilarity for quasi-discrete closure spaces. Log. Methods Comput. Sci. **21**(3) (2025). https://doi.org/10.46298/LMCS-21(3:21)2025, https://doi.org/10.46298/lmcs-21(3:21)2025
38. De Nicola, R., Vaandrager, F.W.: Three logics for branching bisimulation. J. ACM **42**(2), 458–487 (1995), https://doi.org/10.1145/201019.201032
39. De Nicola, R., Ferrari, G.L., Pugliese, R.: Klaim: A kernel language for agents interaction and mobility. IEEE Trans. Software Eng. **24**(5), 315–330 (1998)
40. Gadducci, F., Lluch-Lafuente, A.: Graphical encoding of a spatial logic for the *pi* -calculus. In: Mossakowski, T., Montanari, U., Haveraaen, M. (eds.) Algebra and Coalgebra in Computer Science, Second International Conference, CALCO 2007, Bergen, Norway, August 20-24, 2007, Proceedings. Lecture Notes in Computer Science, vol. 4624, pp. 209–225. Springer (2007). https://doi.org/10.1007/978-3-540-73859-6_15, https://doi.org/10.1007/978-3-540-73859-6_15
41. Galton, A.: A generalized topological view of motion in discrete space. Theor. Comput. Sci. **305**((1-3)), 111–134 (2003), https://doi.org/10.1016/S0304-3975(02)00701-6
42. Groote, J.F., Vaandrager, F.W.: An efficient algorithm for branching bisimulation and stuttering equivalence. In: Paterson, M. (ed.) Automata, Languages and Programming, 17th International Colloquium, ICALP90, Warwick University, England, UK, July 16-20, 1990, Proceedings. Lecture Notes in Computer Science, vol. 443, pp. 626–638. Springer (1990), https://doi.org/10.1007/BFb0032063
43. Imbriani, M., Belmonte, G., Massink, M., Tofani, A., Ciancia, V.: A multi-resolution benchmark framework for spatial reasoning assessment in neural networks (2025), https://arxiv.org/abs/2508.12741
44. Jansen, D.N., Groote, J.F., Keiren, J.J.A., Wijs, A.: An $O(m\log n)$ algorithm for branching bisimilarity on labelled transition systems. In: Biere, A., Parker, D. (eds.) Tools and Algorithms for the Construction and Analysis of Systems - 26th International Conference, TACAS 2020, Held as Part of the European Joint Conferences on Theory and Practice of Software, ETAPS 2020, Dublin, Ireland, April 25-30, 2020, Proceedings, Part II. Lecture Notes in Computer Science, vol. 12079, pp. 3–20. Springer (2020). https://doi.org/10.1007/978-3-030-45237-7_1, https://doi.org/10.1007/978-3-030-45237-7_1
45. Marchetti, M.A., Codella, N.C., Dusza, S.W., Gutman, D.A., Helba, B., Kalloo, A., Mishra, N., Carrera, C., Celebi, M.E., DeFazio, J.L., Jaimes, N., Marghoob, A.A., Quigley, E., Scope, A., Yélamos, O., Halpern, A.C.: Results of the 2016 international skin imaging collaboration international symposium on biomedical imaging challenge: Comparison of the accuracy of computer algorithms to dermatologists for the diagnosis of melanoma from dermoscopic images. Journal of the American Academy of Dermatology **78**(2), 270–277.e1 (2018), https://doi.org/10.1016/j.jaad.2017.08.016
46. Massink, M., Paškauskas, R.: Model-based assessment of aspects of user-satisfaction in bicycle sharing systems. In: IEEE 18th International Conference on

Intelligent Transportation Systems, ITSC 2015, Gran Canaria, Spain, September 15-18, 2015. pp. 1363–1370. IEEE (2015), https://doi.org/10.1109/ITSC.2015.224
47. McCormick, M.M., Liu, X., Jomier, J., Marion, C., Ibanez, L.: Itk: enabling reproducible research and open science. Frontiers in Neuroinformatics **8**, 13 (2014). https://doi.org/10.3389/fninf.2014.00013
48. McKinsey, J., Tarski, A.: The algebra of topology. Annals of Mathematics **45**, 141–191 (1944). https://doi.org/10.2307/1969080
49. Menze, B. H. and others: The multimodal brain tumor image segmentation benchmark (BraTS). IEEE Transactions on Medical Imaging **34**(10), 1993–2024 (2015). https://doi.org/10.1109/TMI.2014.2377694
50. Nenzi, L., Bortolussi, L., Ciancia, V., Loreti, M., Massink, M.: Qualitative and quantitative monitoring of spatio-temporal properties with SSTL. Log. Methods Comput. Sci. **14**(4) (2018). https://doi.org/10.23638/LMCS-14(4:2)2018, https://doi.org/10.23638/LMCS-14(4:2)2018
51. Sebastio, S., Vandin, A.: Multivesta: statistical model checking for discrete event simulators. In: Horváth, A., Buchholz, P., Cortellessa, V., Muscariello, L., Squillante, M.S. (eds.) 7th International Conference on Performance Evaluation Methodologies and Tools, ValueTools '13, Torino, Italy, December 10-12, 2013. pp. 310–315. ICST/ACM (2013). https://doi.org/10.4108/ICST.VALUETOOLS.2013.254377, https://doi.org/10.4108/icst.valuetools.2013.254377
52. Smyth, M.B., Webster, J.: Discrete spatial models. In: Springer [2], pp. 713–798
53. Strippoli, A.: Voxlogica UI: Supporting declarative medical image analysis (2025), https://arxiv.org/abs/2504.13846

Software Engineering and AI

Revisiting the Role of Natural Language Code Comments in Code Translation

Monika Gupta[1], Ajay Meena[1], Anamitra Roy Choudhury[2], Vijay Arya[2], and Srikanta Bedathur[1]

[1] Indian Institute of Technology, New Delhi, India
[2] IBM Research - India, India

Abstract. The advent of large language models (LLMs) has ushered in a new era in automated code translation across programming languages. Since most code-specific LLMs are pretrained on well-commented code from large repositories like GitHub, it is reasonable to hypothesize that natural language code comments could aid in improving translation quality. Despite their potential relevance, comments are largely absent from existing code translation benchmarks, rendering their impact on translation quality inadequately characterized. In this paper, we present a large-scale empirical study evaluating the impact of comments on translation performance. Our analysis involves more than 80,000 translations, with and without comments, of 1100+ code samples from two distinct benchmarks covering pairwise translations between five different programming languages: C, C++, Go, Java, and Python. Our results provide strong evidence that code comments, particularly those that describe the overall purpose of the code rather than line-by-line functionality, significantly enhance translation accuracy. Based on these findings, we propose *COMMENTRA*, a code translation approach, and demonstrate that it can potentially *double* the performance of LLM-based code translation. To the best of our knowledge, our study is the first in terms of its comprehensiveness, scale, and language coverage on how to improve code translation accuracy using code comments.

Keywords: code comments, large language models, code translation, natural language comments

1 Introduction

Accurate and effective source code translation between programming languages (PLs) is a significant challenge for AI. Large language models (LLMs) such as CodeLlama [28], DeepSeekCoder [9], StarCoder [16], etc., are models pre-trained on a large set of code samples in multiple PLs and offer a potentially faster, less expensive, and more scalable way to automate code translation. The long-term aim of automated code translation is to handle repository-scale codebases of unbounded complexity; however, we are far from reaching that goal, as LLMs still struggle to consistently generate accurate and reliable translations, even for self-contained programs.

E. Albert and C. Pasareanu (Eds.): FASE 2026, LNCS 16504, pp. 21–42, 2026.
https://doi.org/10.1007/978-3-032-22774-4_2

Several active, ongoing research works (Section 2) focus on how to reduce translation bugs by providing relevant context that helps LLMs understand and execute the translation task better. Since LLMs are typically pre-trained using code and its associated pairwise comments [27], we suspect that LLMs may translate better when the original source code to be translated is augmented with corresponding natural language code descriptions or code comments. In this work, we first initiate a study of the role that natural language code comments play in LLM-based code translation. We address the following research questions:

- ***RQ1 - Usefulness of Code Comments:*** Do natural language code comments help LLMs improve their code translation performance?
- ***RQ2 - Intent of Code Comments:*** Comment intent refers to the underlying purpose, motivation, or goal a user or developer has when making a comment. Can we classify code comments based on their intent and comprehend the utility of different intent categories in code translation?
- ***RQ3 - Density, Language of Code Comments:*** Comment density is the percentage of comment lines relative to total lines of code. What role does the density of code comments play in code translation? Also, does the choice of comment language, English or others, affect translation accuracy?
- ***RQ4 - Location of Comments:*** Code comments are typically placed in specific locations to provide context and explanations for human readers, while being ignored by the compiler or interpreter. Natural language pseudocode can be placed at the beginning of the code; method specifications are usually placed at the method boundaries; and more fine-grained comments are positioned next to the line(s) of code with which they are associated. How does this placement affect translation performance?

To address these research questions, we collected 1100+ code samples in five different PLs, C, C++, Go, Java, Python, augmented them with model-generated comments and translated each commented and uncommented sample into other PLs, using several LLMs, obtaining more than $80K$ code translations. Our analysis indicates that while comments can enhance the code translation performance of LLMs, their indiscriminate usage can have a deleterious effect. We next propose a translation framework called **COMMENTRA**, which carefully introduces comments in programs to significantly improve the performance of LLM-based code translation. Experiments show that COMMENTRA offers an impressive gain in average translation performance across all PLs, benchmark datasets, and LLM models considered in our study. The attractiveness of COMMENTRA lies in its simplicity, low-cost implementation, and ease of integration with many recently proposed code translation frameworks, such as *InterTrans* [19], *LANTERN* [18], *UniTrans* [19], *UniTranslator* [14], etc. To the best of our knowledge, our work is the first comprehensive study of code comments in the LLM-based code translation process across a wide configuration.

2 Related Work

Code Translation Approaches. Rule-based, language-specific transpilers use explicitly defined linguistic and syntactic rules to convert source code from one

PL to another. While transpilers are reliable for known patterns, they struggle with complexity and generality. In contrast, LLMs are trained on data, produce more idiomatic code, but lack formal guaranties and can fail unpredictably. Examples of transpilers include Java2Python[3], Python2Java[4], C2Rust[5], C2Go[6], etc. Techniques such as lexical statistical machine translation [23], tree-based neural networks [3], deep learning, and unsupervised learning [15, 27] have also been explored for automatic code translation. LLM-based methods such as AlphaTrans [10], CoTran [12], InterTrans [19], UniTrans [33], UniTranslator [14], etc., have been proposed to improve the LLM's code translation accuracy. We compare these recent approaches with our work in the full paper version.

Use of Code Comments in Training Models. In earlier works, it was observed that keeping comments in the training dataset facilitates cross-language alignment and yields better results for some language pairs during unsupervised code translation [5,27]. Our work differs from these in that COMMENTRA does not use code comments to train models. In fact, the hypothesis that LLMs are pre-trained using code and its associated pairwise comments is the motivation behind this work.

Use of NL Specifications. Saha et al. [30] investigated the use of pseudocode, and Tang et al. [31] explored the usefulness of self-generated natural language explanations as an intermediate representation for code translation. Nitin et al. [24] generated multimodal specifications (invariants, tests, descriptions) and used them to augment the source code, thereby improving the translation performance of LLMs. Code comments differ from pseudocode and structured code specifications in their close, precise association with the corresponding line(s) of code. Additionally, while pseudocode and code specifications focus on explaining the basic code logic, code comments, in contrast, can depict various intents [21]. Our work differs from these as we present the first comprehensive study on the impact of code comments in the code translation process.

Code Comment Generation. Many models and approaches have been proposed [1,6–8,11] to generate natural language code summaries. A piece of code can be commented on with several intentions [22,34], such as its functionality, its usage, and its space/time complexity, etc.. Mu et al. [21] propose an intent-driven DOME code comment generation approach to produce a comment that is coherent with the given intent.

3 Experimental Setup

Figure 1 illustrates our experimental setup. We enrich uncommented code samples with LLM generated comments using a simple comment generation prompt that has no explicit mention of any specific comment intent, density, language, or comment location. Both commented and uncommented code samples are translated using a vanilla translation prompt to generate a large pool of translations.

[3] https://github.com/natural/java2python
[4] https://github.com/chrishumphreys/p2j
[5] https://github.com/immunant/c2rust
[6] https://github.com/gotranspile/cxgo

All prompts were used in their basic *vanilla* form (refer to Figure 1 for the exact prompts) to minimize potential bias due to the different ways in which various LLMs utilize more sophisticated prompts. A single A100 Nvidia GPU was used for all experiments.

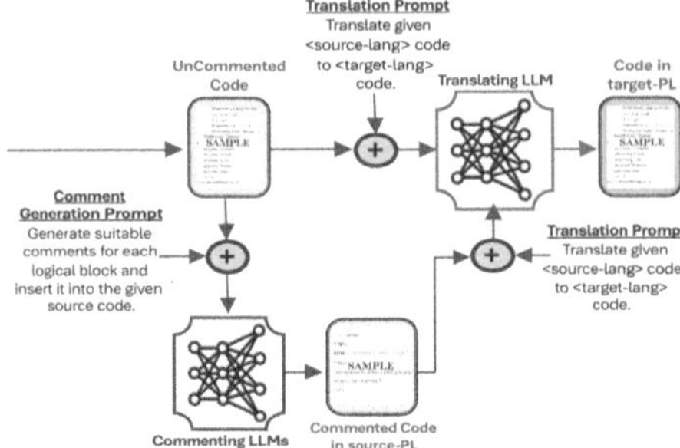

Fig. 1: Experimental Setup; The exact prompts used are also shown here.

Translating and Commenting LLMs. We used *Code Llama-13B-V1* [29], *DeepSeek-Coder-V2* [4], *GPT-4o-mini* [25], *Granite-8B-Code-Instruct* [20], and *StarCoder-1* [17] to translate all code samples. *DeepSeek-Coder-V2*, *GPT-4o-mini*, and *Mistral 7B* [13] were used as the Commenting Models. Henceforth, we refer to these models as *CodeLlama, DeepSeek, GPT, Granite, Mistral, and StarCoder*, accordingly. For all models, the token length was set to its maximum, and the greedy decoding algorithm, which selects only the top translation with the highest log probability, was used.

Dataset Statistics				
Code Set Source	Source PL	No. of Samples	Min-Max LOC in samples	Avg-TestCases per sample
AVATAR	Java	250	12 - 78	12
AVATAR	Python	250	1 - 64	12
CodeNet	C	200	7 - 318	1
CodeNet	C++	200	7 - 194	1
CodeNet	Go	200	7 - 393	1
Total Unique, Uncommented Code Samples : 1100				

Table 1: Benchmark Data Statistics

Datasets. We studied translations of code samples between five different PLs - C, C++, Go, Java, and Python - resulting in a total of 20 (i.e., 5 permute 2) unique *(source-PL, target-PL)* pairs. A total of 1100 unique code samples (see Table 1), along with their multiple test cases, from two standard, openly available, widely studied benchmark suites - AVATAR [2] and CodeNet [26] were used for the experiments. Since these code samples do not have any comments in them, we employed commenting models to generate comments. To rigorously assess the effectiveness of our proposed framework, COMMENTRA, we performed additional experiments on the CodeTransOcean benchmark [32], which is a multilingual reference for evaluating code translations in a variety of programming languages. These additional results are presented in the full paper version.

			Translating LLMs															
			StarCoder				CodeLlama				DeepSeek				GPT			
	SOURCE LANG.	TARGET LANG.	UnCom	(Gains over Uncommented) Mistral	DeepSeek	GPT	UnCom	(Gains over Uncommented) Mistral	DeepSeek	GPT	UnCom	(Gains over Uncommented) Mistral	DeepSeek	GPT	UnCom	(Gains over Uncommented) Mistral	DeepSeek	GPT
CodeNet Benchmark (200 Samples Each)	C	C++	0.76	-25.67%	2.0%	5.9%	0.89	-37.08%	-3.9%	1.1%	0.52	-8.96%	22.1%	45.2%	0.97	-30.93%	0.0%	-0.5%
		GO	0.21	-41.46%	-4.9%	-24.4%	0.52	-31.73%	-7.7%	-21.2%	0.64	-29.69%	2.3%	-3.1%	0.80	-30.19%	-1.9%	-6.3%
		JAVA	0.69	-8.70%	-3.6%	-10.1%	0.36	-11.27%	-22.5%	-63.4%	0.69	26.28%	29.9%	19.0%	0.96	0.52%	2.1%	1.6%
		PYTHON	0.36	-49.30%	-28.2%	-29.6%	0.04	-85.71%	28.6%	-57.1%	0.25	-24.49%	12.2%	14.9%	0.67	-28.36%	-2.2%	0.0%
	C++	C	0.22	69.77%	20.9%	9.3%	0.24	70.83%	0.0%	4.2%	0.23	163.04%	13.0%	0.0%	0.31	133.87%	-1.6%	-3.2%
		GO	0.18	-36.11%	-27.8%	-33.3%	0.45	-16.67%	-2.2%	-16.7%	0.64	-14.84%	-6.3%	-7.8%	0.84	-9.58%	-0.6%	0.6%
		JAVA	0.75	-12.67%	-7.3%	-14.0%	0.50	13.98%	13.0%	1.0%	0.88	5.71%	2.3%	2.3%	0.97	-1.04%	-2.6%	-0.5%
		PYTHON	0.31	-4.95%	3.3%	-9.8%	0.05	-90.00%	-30.0%	-40.0%	0.44	-26.14%	26.1%	34.1%	0.71	-17.02%	-4.3%	-5.7%
	GO	C	0.22	46.51%	-11.6%	-41.9%	0.24	41.67%	10.4%	-16.7%	0.10	435.00%	60.0%	70.0%	0.27	160.38%	1.9%	4.9%
		C++	0.40	-2.53%	-13.9%	-2.5%	0.69	-33.33%	-10.1%	-13.8%	0.56	-8.04%	8.0%	17.9%	0.91	-17.13%	1.7%	2.2%
		JAVA	0.84	-30.36%	-4.2%	-10.1%	0.78	-25.82%	3.2%	0.6%	0.57	33.07%	40.0%	43.4%	0.95	2.12%	0.5%	2.1%
		PYTHON	0.43	-42.35%	-11.8%	-21.2%	0.51	-65.35%	-24.8%	-40.6%	0.04	425.00%	262.3%	250.0%	0.73	-16.55%	-1.4%	-6.2%
AVATAR (250 Samples Each)	JAVA	C	0.27	-22.39%	0.0%	-3.0%	0.31	-23.98%	-7.2%	-24.0%	0.58	-20.68%	-8.9%	-8.3%	0.72	-27.22%	-0.6%	-7.8%
		C++	0.36	-28.57%	-72.5%	-36.3%	0.41	-20.37%	2.9%	-17.5%	0.63	-3.82%	7.6%	4.5%	0.82	-16.59%	1.0%	1.0%
		GO	0.02	49.58%	-33.3%	100.0%	0.19	-41.67%	-31.3%	-50.0%	0.48	-15.83%	-6.7%	-18.3%	0.72	-22.78%	-2.8%	-5.6%
		PYTHON	0.21	-53.85%	1.9%	25.0%	0.29	-26.03%	1.3%	-12.3%	0.55	-48.55%	-28.3%	19.6%	0.65	-30.67%	-3.1%	5.5%
	PYTHON	C	0.13	-21.88%	-28.1%	6.3%	0.15	-60.53%	-21.1%	-18.4%	0.11	-14.29%	-10.7%	3.6%	0.12	-25.81%	-12.9%	-3.2%
		C++	0.18	-15.22%	-21.8%	54.3%	0.28	-33.80%	7.0%	1.4%	0.40	-30.30%	25.3%	29.3%	0.58	-13.79%	4.1%	2.1%
		GO	0.09	-90.91%	-63.6%	-72.7%	0.18	-71.74%	-10.9%	-52.2%	0.23	8.62%	6.9%	53.4%	0.46	-11.21%	0.9%	12.9%
		JAVA	0.24	-57.38%	-1.6%	14.8%	0.21	-71.15%	11.5%	32.7%	0.52	-27.13%	-12.4%	73.6%	0.62	-12.99%	-3.9%	55.8%

Table 2: The impact of comments generated by various *commenting LLMs* over baseline translation performance (accuracy) of different *translating LLMs* across different pairwise language translations in benchmark datasets.

4 How Relevant are Code Comments?

4.1 RQ1 : Usefulness of Code Comments

To explore the usefulness of code comments, we injected all code samples with comments generated by three different commenting LLMs, resulting in 3300 commented code samples (refer to Section 3 for the various translation and comment generation prompts used in this experiment). The resultant collection of all uncommented and commented code samples was then translated into other target PLs using five different translating LLMs. For each 4-tuple set (*source-PL, target-PL, commenting-LLM, translating-LLM*), the percentage of successful translations was calculated as the ratio of the total number of successful translations achieved to the total number of translations attempted in the set. A translation is successful if the translated code compiles, passes runtime checks, and all existing test cases. For all our code samples, the corresponding input test cases were available as a formatted set of input values (see Listings 1.3, 1.10) as part of the source benchmark they were from, and therefore they could be used as-is for testing both the source program and the translated program. The higher the percentage of successful translations for an LLM, the better the translation performance of the LLM on the corresponding set. Due to space constraints, Table 2 presents these results[7] for a subset of translating LLMs. As an example of how to interpret the numbers in the table, consider the C to C++ translation numbers of StarCoder. The value 0.76 in *UnCom* column is the baseline; it indicates that the translation of 76% of the total number of code samples (200 in this case) was successful without any comments. With Mistral-comments, there was a 25.67% drop in StarCoder's translation performance; i.e., the number of successful translations was reduced to 113 out of 200. However, with DeepSeek-comments, the total number of successful translations increased by 2% from the baseline; that is, 155 of 200 samples were translated successfully. Similarly, with GPT-comments, the number of successful translations rose to 161 out of 200.

[7] Results for all translating LLMs are included in the full paper version.

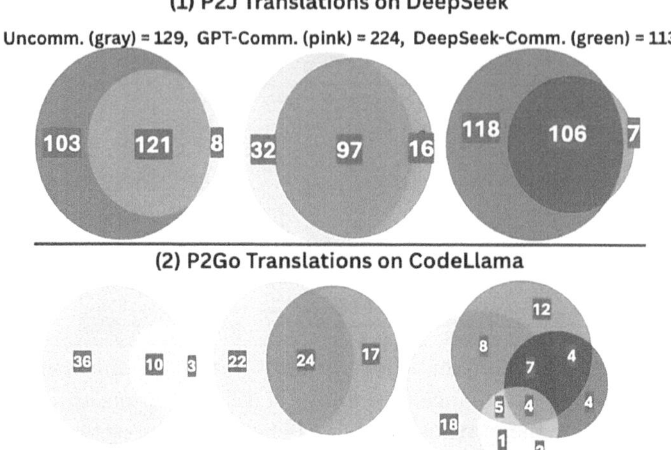

Uncomm. (gray) = 46, Mistral-Comm. (yellow) = 13, GPT-Comm. (pink) = 20, DeepSeek-Comm. (green) = 41

Fig. 2: Venn diagrams depicting increase and decrease in LLMs performance in the commented code samples. Left and center diagrams show the overlap between uncommented successful and successfully translated model-commented samples; the right diagrams show the overlap between the various successfully translated model-commented samples.

Green colored boxes in the table represent cases where the presence of code comments helped increase the translation performance of LLMs, while the yellow colored boxes indicate the contrary. Additionally, highlighted in dark green are the cases where, after adding code comments, the performance enhancement over the baseline was more than 50%. A nearly balanced distribution of green and yellow boxes is observed. With commented code, the gain in LLM translation performance ranged from -90% to +435% over the baseline uncommented code translation performance. This leads us to conclude that while model-generated code comments can help improve the translation performance of LLMs, they can also have a deleterious effect on the translations. This seems to be due to their injecting more noise or constraining the LLMs in translation logic. We discuss several examples in support of this conclusion in Section 4.2.

Understanding the increase in performance cases. Figure 2(1) presents Venn diagrams for an in-depth analysis of a representative case where the LLM showed an increase in performance in the commented sets, Python to Java (P2J) translations on DeepSeek. The total number of successful translations in the uncommented set (gray) was 129/250, compared to 224/250 in the GPT-commented (pink) and 113/250 in the DeepSeek-commented (green). The size of the gray bubble is smaller than the size of the pink bubble, indicating that the GPT-commented samples translated better than the uncommented ones; hence, there is an increase in performance in this case. Indeed, it is clear from the Venn diagrams that GPT-comments and DeepSeek-comments added value in at least 103/250 and 16/250 additional code samples, respectively, that were unsuccessful when there were no comments at all. These observations clearly

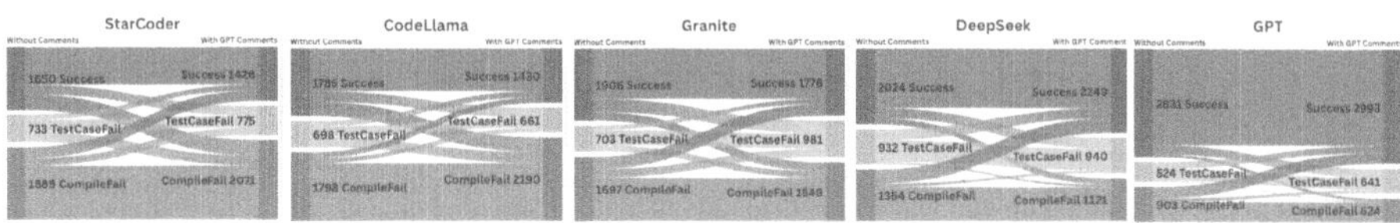

Fig. 3: Bird's eye view of how various translation models performed on commented and uncommented code.

highlight that code comments help to iron out technical flaws that may have occurred while translating uncommented code. Ideally, we would expect the uncommented sets (gray) to be completely contained within the commented sets (other colors). However, the fact that this is not the case indicates that comments can potentially deteriorate translations.

Understanding the decrease in performance cases. Figure 2(2) presents an in-depth analysis of another representative case - P2Go translations on CodeLlama, where the LLM shows a decrease in performance in the commented sets. The total number of successful translations in the uncommented set was 46/250 (gray), compared to 13/250 in the Mistral-commented (yellow), 20/250 in the GPT-commented (pink), and 41/250 in the DeepSeek-commented (green). Although gray bubbles are larger than colored bubbles, the overlap between them is not very large, indicating the usefulness of code comments in resolving some of the failed uncommented translations. As is clear from the diagram, GPT-comments and DeepSeek-comments added value in at least 8 and 17 additional code samples, respectively. These code samples were previously unsuccessful when there were no comments at all. These observations reaffirm that comments can have both a positive and a negative effect on the translation process.

Types of errors resolved / introduced by the presence of code comments. We compared the error-type distributions in GPT-commented translations and uncommented translations for all models (results in Figure 3). Across all unique *(source-PL, target-PL)* pairs, a total of 4,400 uncommented and 4,400 GPT-commented translations were attempted on each translation model in our study. Each of these translations was either a successful translation or contained an error, such as a testcase failure, compilation failure, or other errors like runtime failures or infinite loop errors, etc. As an example, with the StarCoder model, for uncommented translations, the error type distribution was (Total-Attempted:4400, Successful:1650, Testcase-Fail:733, Compile-Fail:1889, Other errors:128). With GPT-comments, a few samples from the original pool of successful translations began to either fail in testcases or compilation. In addition, a few samples from the original pool of testcase failures and compilation failures were transformed into successful translations. Clearly, for all models, across all language pairs, a substantial number of translations that originally (during the uncommented translation run) had compilation errors became successful with GPT-comments. On the contrary, compared to DeepSeek and GPT, in the StarCoder and CodeLlama models, a higher percentage of commented samples, which were originally successful when uncommented, began to fail with compilation errors, possibly hinting at the inability of these models to judiciously understand and use the additional context provided by the comments.

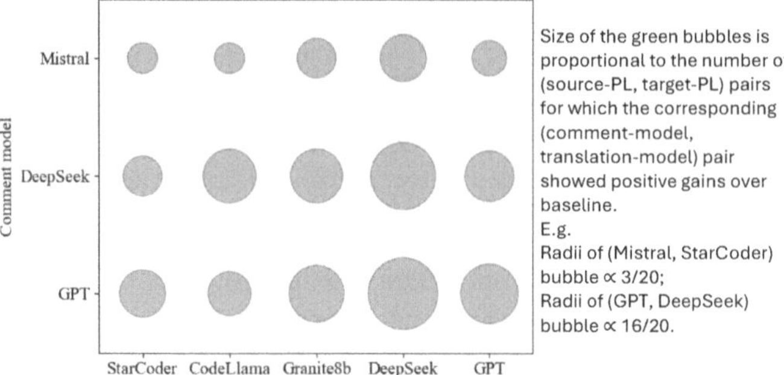

Fig. 4: Commenting Model Comparison. Size of the green bubbles $\propto$ no. of *(source-PL, target-PL)* pairs for which the corresponding *(comment-model, translation-model)* pair showed positive gains over the baseline.

Impact of commenting models on translation performance. For uncommented code, the translation performance of LLMs depends primarily on the chosen source and target PL. However, in the case of commented code, the specific NL words used in the code comments also influence the translating LLM. Since the performance of commenting models may itself be PL-specific, it is difficult to generalize and choose an overall best translating and commenting model. In our experiments, Mistral as a commenting model showed limited capabilities on many *(source-PL, target-PL)* translation pairs (e.g., Figure 2), although DeepSeek and GPT performed much better (e.g., for P2Go, P2J, P2C++, J2P translations). Figure 4 presents a high-level comparative analysis of the various commenting models by summarizing the results from Table 2, where we count the number of *(source-PL, target-PL)* pairs that benefited from adding comments. The smaller size of the bubbles in the row corresponding to the Mistral commenting model clearly highlights that DeepSeek and GPT proved to be better commenting models than Mistral for most *(source-PL, target-PL)* pairs.
Our key takeaways from this study are:

- Although well-written comments that describe the corresponding code are valuable in resolving several translation errors, they can sometimes contribute to noise, leading to translation errors.
- The added value of code comments varies across different source and target PLs and also across different translating and commenting LLMs.

4.2 Examples - Positive and Negative Impact of Code Comments

Example 1 : Code comments help resolve testcase failure bugs. Consider the given P2J translation on Granite, with GPT as the commenting LLM. The uncommented P2J translation compiled, but some test cases failed during execution. However, in the commented P2J translation, all test cases passed.

```
1 n = int ( input ( ) )
2 list = [ int ( x ) % 2 for x in input ( ).split ( ) ]
3 if sum ( list ) == 1 :
4     print ( list.index ( 1 ) + 1 )
5 else :
6     print ( list.index ( 0 ) + 1 )
```

Listing 1.1: Original Uncommented Python Source Code

The above Python program converts each input integer in the given list into either 0 or 1 based on whether it is odd or even, and stores them in an array. It then sums the array; if it equals 1, it prints the index of the entry that was "1"; otherwise, it prints the index of the first "0" entry. The translation to Java by Granite given below is erroneous in the for-loop in lines 12-17.

```
1 import java.util.Scanner;
2 public class Main {
3     public static void main(String[] args) {
4         Scanner scanner = new Scanner(System.in);
5         int n = scanner.nextInt();
6         int[] list = new int[n];
7         for (int i = 0; i < n; i++) {
8             list[i] = scanner.nextInt() % 2;
9         }
10        int index = 0;
11        for (int i = 0; i < n; i++) {
12            if (list[i] == 1) {
13                index = i;
14                break;
15            }
16        }
17        if (index == 0) {
18            for (int i = 0; i < n; i++) {
19                if (list[i] == 0) {
20                    index = i;
21                    break;
22                }
23            }
24        }
25        System.out.println(index + 1);
26    }
27 }
```

Listing 1.2: Output Java Language Translation

```
1 -- Input --
2 3
3 1 2 2
4 -- Expected Output --
5 1
6 -- Actual Output --
7 2
```

Listing 1.3: Failed Test Case

In the commented version of the Python program given below, GPT-comments, especially those in lines 7, 9, and 12, precisely describe the program logic.

```
1 # Read an integer input which represents the number of elements
2 n = int(input())
3 # Read a line of input, split it into individual elements, convert them to
     integers,
4 # and create a list that contains 1 for odd numbers and 0 for even numbers
5 list = [int(x) % 2 for x in input().split()]
6 # Check if there is exactly one odd number in the list
7 if sum(list) == 1:
8     # If there is one odd number, print its position (1-based index)
9     print(list.index(1) + 1)
10 else:
11    # else print the position of the first even number (1-based index)
12    print(list.index(0) + 1)
```

Listing 1.4: GPT-Commented Python Source Code

The translating LLM, Granite, is influenced by the GPT-comments and follows the program logic explained by the comments. Lines 11-16 seem to implement the comment in line 7 ; also, the if-else control from line 17 onward seems to result from the comments in lines 9 and 12 of Listing 1.4. As a result, the translation becomes *successful.* We tried the commented P2J translation after removing all code comments except those in lines 7, 9, and 12. The resultant Java output was also a successful translation, which further demonstrates the positive role played by the comments in these lines.

```
1 import java.util.Scanner;
2 public class Main {
3     public static void main(String[] args) {
4         Scanner scanner = new Scanner(System.in);
5         int n = scanner.nextInt();
6         int[] list = new int[n];
7         for (int i = 0; i < n; i++) {
8             list[i] = scanner.nextInt() % 2;
9         }
10        int count = 0;
11        for (int i = 0; i < n; i++) {
12            if (list[i] == 1) {
13                count++;
14            }
15        }
16        if (count == 1) {
17            for (int i = 0; i < n; i++) {
18                if (list[i] == 1) {
19                    System.out.println(i + 1);
20                    break;
21                }
22            }
23        } else {
24            for (int i = 0; i < n; i++) {
25                if (list[i] == 0) {
26                    System.out.println(i + 1);
27                    break;
28                }
29            }
30        }
31    }
32 }
```

Listing 1.5: Output Java Language Translation

Example 2 : Code comments negatively impact code translation. Consider the given J2Cpp Translation on CodeLlama with GPT as the commenting LLM. The uncommented J2Cpp translation was successful; however, in the commented J2Cpp translation, some test cases failed.

```
1 import java.io.BufferedWriter;
2 import java.io.IOException;
3 import java.io.OutputStreamWriter;
4 import java.util.Scanner;
5 public class Main {
6  public static void main(String[] args) throws IOException {
7   Scanner sc = new Scanner(System.in);
8   BufferedWriter bw = new BufferedWriter(new OutputStreamWriter(System.out
     ));
9   int H = sc.nextInt();
10  int W = sc.nextInt();
11  int A = sc.nextInt();
12  int B = sc.nextInt();
13  if (W < 2 * A || H < 2 * B) {
14   System.out.println(-1);
15   return;
16  }
17  for (int i = 0; i < H; i++) {
```

```
18        for (int j = 0; j < W; j++) {
19         if ((i < B && j < A) || (i >= B) && (j >= A))
20          bw.write("0");
21         else
22          bw.write("1");
23        }
24        bw.newLine();
25      }
26      bw.flush();
27    }
28  }
```

Listing 1.6: Original Uncommented Java Source Code

The above Java program inputs four integers: *H*, *W*, *A*, and *B*. It checks whether it is possible to construct the matrix; if not, it prints -1 and stops; otherwise, it directly prints the matrix row by row to the output. Its C++ translation (Listing 1.7) captures the intended logic and executes successfully.

```
 1 #include <iostream>
 2 #include <cstdio>
 3 #include <cstring>
 4 using namespace std;
 5 int main()
 6 {
 7     int H, W, A, B;
 8     cin >> H >> W >> A >> B;
 9     if (W < 2 * A || H < 2 * B)
10     {
11         cout << -1 << endl;
12         return 0;
13     }
14     for (int i = 0; i < H; i++)
15     {
16         for (int j = 0; j < W; j++)
17         {
18             if ((i < B && j < A) || (i >= B) && (j >= A))
19                 cout << "0";
20             else
21                 cout << "1";
22         }
23         cout << endl;
24     }
25     return 0;
26 }
```

Listing 1.7: Output C++ Language Translation

Consider the commented version (Listing 1.8) of the original Java code, and note the use of the word *grid* in the comments in lines 11, 12, 13, 16, 18, and 21.

```
 1 import java.io.BufferedWriter;
 2 import java.io.IOException;
 3 import java.io.OutputStreamWriter;
 4 import java.util.Scanner;
 5 public class Main {
 6     public static void main(String[] args) throws IOException {
 7         // Create a Scanner object for input and a BufferedWriter for
       output
 8         Scanner sc = new Scanner(System.in);
 9         BufferedWriter bw = new BufferedWriter(new OutputStreamWriter(
       System.out));
10         // Read the dimensions of the grid and the parameters A and B
11         int H = sc.nextInt(); // Height of the grid
12         int W = sc.nextInt(); // Width of the grid
13         int A = sc.nextInt(); // Parameter A
14         int B = sc.nextInt(); // Parameter B
15         // Check if the grid can accommodate the required number of 0s and
        1s
```

```
16         if (W < 2 * A || H < 2 * B) {
17             System.out.println(-1); // Print -1 if the grid is too small
18             return; // Exit the program
19         }
20         // Generate the grid based on the parameters A and B
21         for (int i = 0; i < H; i++) { // Iterate over each row
22             for (int j = 0; j < W; j++) { // Iterate over each column
23                 // Determine whether to write '0' or '1' based on the
       current position
24                 if ((i < B && j < A) || (i >= B && j >= A))
25                     bw.write("0"); // Write '0' for specified conditions
26                 else
27                     bw.write("1"); // Write '1' otherwise
28             }
29             bw.newLine(); // Move to the next line after finishing a row
30         }
31         // Flush the BufferedWriter to ensure all data is written out
32         bw.flush();
33     }
34 }
```

Listing 1.8: GPT-Commented Java Source Code

```
1 #include <iostream>
2 #include <cmath>
3 using namespace std;
4 int main() {
5     // Declare variables for input and output
6     int H, W, A, B;
7     char grid[100][100];
8     // Read the dimensions of the grid and the parameters A and B
9     cin >> H >> W >> A >> B;
10    // Check if the grid can accommodate the required number of 0s and 1s
11    if (W < 2 * A || H < 2 * B) {
12        cout << -1 << endl; // Print -1 if the grid is too small
13        return 0; // Exit the program
14    }
15    // Generate the grid based on the parameters A and B
16    for (int i = 0; i < H; i++) { // Iterate over each row
17        for (int j = 0; j < W; j++) { // Iterate over each column
18            // Determine whether to write '0' or '1' based on the current
      position
19            if ((i < B && j < A) || (i >= B && j >= A))
20                grid[i][j] = '0'; // Write '0' for specified conditions
21            else
22                grid[i][j] = '1'; // Write '1' otherwise
23        }
24    }
25    // Print the grid
26    for (int i = 0; i < H; i++) { // Iterate over each row
27        for (int j = 0; j < W; j++) { // Iterate over each column
28            cout << grid[i][j]; // Print the current character
29        }
30        cout << endl; // Move to the next line after finishing a row
31    }
32    return 0;
33 }
```

Listing 1.9: Output C++ Language Translation

```
1 -- Input --
2 1000 1000 0 0
3 -- Expected Output -- A matrix of 1000 columns and 1000 rows with each
     value 0/1
4 000000000000000000.....
5 000000000000000000.....
6 .......................
7 -- Actual Output -- Error due to inappropriate grid variable size
```

Listing 1.10: Failed Test Case

The use of the word *grid* in the comments in lines 11, 12, 13, 16, 18, and 21 of Listing 1.8 tricked the translating LLM into believing that *grid* is a declared variable in the program. The translating LLM now becomes biased and declares a variable *grid* (see Line 8, Listing 1.9) with some randomly fixed dimensions (100*100). It continues to use this *grid* variable to store the output matrix generated through the for loop in lines 17-25. It then prints the *grid* using the for loop in lines 27-32. As long as the output matrix dimensions are less than (100*100), the program works fine. As soon as it exceeds this limit, there is a memory fault, and the corresponding test case fails. An example is given in Listing 1.10. This example precisely demonstrates how translating LLMs are negatively impacted by the choice of words in code comments.

4.3 RQ2 : Impact of comment intent on translation performance

CJBench Code Sample Statistics	
Total commented Java programs	200
Avg. test cases per program	3
Min./Max./Avg. code lines per pgm.	35/257/88
Min./Max./Avg. author-comment lines per pgm.	13/120/44
Avg. author-comment words per line of code	2-3

Translating LLM	UnComm	Commenting LLM (Gains over uncommented)		
		Author	DeepSeek	GPT
StarCoder	0.18	21.99%	36.41%	50.73%
CodeLlama	0.292	4.45%	11.70%	12.71%
Granite	0.438	-3.90%	2.54%	3.34%
DeepSeek	0.576	5.75%	18.80%	19.13%
GPT	0.694	-1.73%	4.11%	5.92%

Table 3: CJBench Statistics and J2P Translation Results

Code comments can be model-generated, usually short and descriptive, or author-written, which can exhibit several intents, such as explaining the algorithm, the code, its complexity, usage, etc. To study the impact of comment intents on the translation performance of LLMs, we created a dataset : *CJBench* - **C**ommented **J**ava Programs **Bench**mark (Table 3) - a manually curated collection of 200 author-commented Java programs, sourced from (a) Java-Projects-Collection, a collection of various Java-Projects[8] and (b) *The Algorithms*, a large open-source algorithm library[9].

Are multi-line, multi-intent comments useful in code translation? Figure 5 presents an example of an elaborate multi-line, multi-intent comment extracted from a code sample in the CJBench dataset. It ***describes*** (highlighted in yellow) the objective of the associated method, ***cautions*** (highlighted in blue) that the method can change the order of elements in the list, and also the exceptions it can throw, and ***informs*** (highlighted in green) the list of I/O parameters. To understand how these multi-intent comments affect code translations, we performed Java to Python (J2P) translations of code samples in the CJBench dataset. For comparison with model-generated comments, which

[8] https://github.com/kishanrajput23/Java-Projects-Collections
[9] https://github.com/TheAlgorithms/Java/

```
/**
 * Selects the {@code n}-th smallest element of {@code list}, i.e., the element that would
 * be at index n if the list was sorted.
 * <p>
 * Calling this function might change the order of elements in {@code list}.
 *
 * @param list the list of elements
 * @param n    the index
 * @param <T>  the type of list elements
 * @return the n-th smallest element in the list
 * @throws IndexOutOfBoundsException if n is less than 0 or greater or equal to
 *                                   the number of elements in the list
 * @throws IllegalArgumentException  if the list is empty
 * @throws NullPointerException      if {@code list} is null
 */
public static <T extends Comparable<T>> T select(List<T> list, int n) {
    Objects.requireNonNull(list, "The list of elements must not be null.");

    if (list.isEmpty()) {
        throw new IllegalArgumentException("The list of elements must not be empty.");
```

Fig. 5: Example of one big multi-line (12 lines) comment with several intents

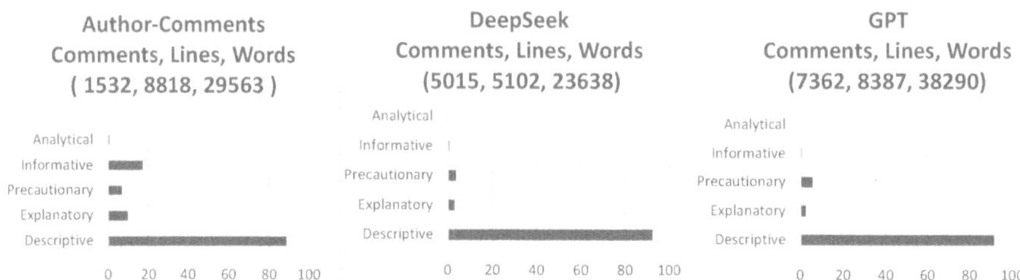

Fig. 6: Comparison of Intent Classes in Comments

are comparatively small and descriptive, we first removed the original author-comments, and then DeepSeek and GPT models were used to inject comments into the code samples. Table 3 presents the comparative translation performance on these three datasets. As expected and clearly seen from the low/negative gain numbers (in yellow), author-commented samples performed poorer than DeepSeek-commented or GPT-commented samples. To further establish the reason behind this comparatively poorer performance, we conducted an extensive intent-classification experiment.

Intent classification. All author and model generated comments in the CJBench code samples were extracted, and GPT was instructed to perform intent classification on the 50 largest comments. The resultant intent categories were:

- **Descriptive** - describe what the code does.
- **Explanatory** - explain the overall approach used.
- **Informative** - specify details about the I/O parameters.
- **Analytical** - mention the performance details.
- **Precautionary** - warn about potential risks/exceptions.

Subsequently, GPT was used to classify the remaining comments into one or more of these categories (see the full paper version for examples).

Which comment intent is most useful in code translation? From Figure 6, it can be calculated that the average number of words in an author-comment is $29563/1532 = 19$, while this value is around 5 for model-comments. In other words, each author-comment typically contains more words and lines than model-comments, as it touches on several aspects of the corresponding code (see Figure 5). Figure 6 proves this claim. While author-comments do have a Descriptive intent; however, unlike model-generated comments, there is also

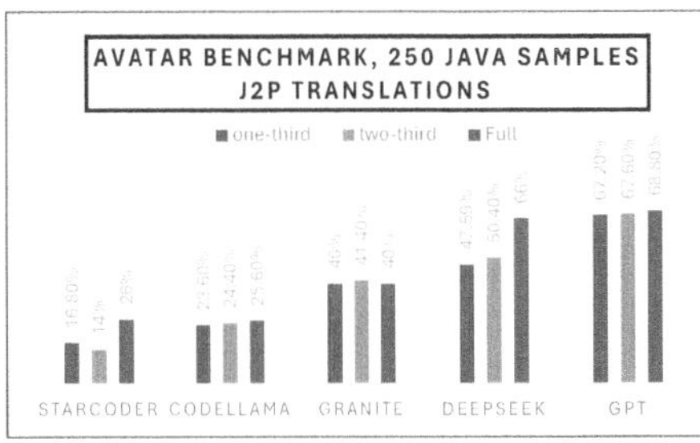

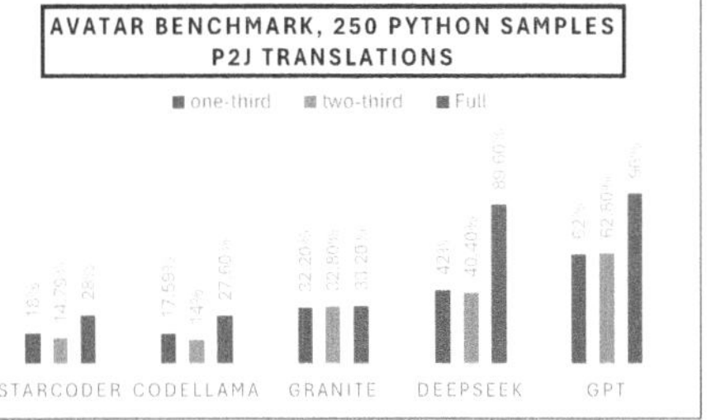

Fig. 7: Impact of Comment Density on Translation

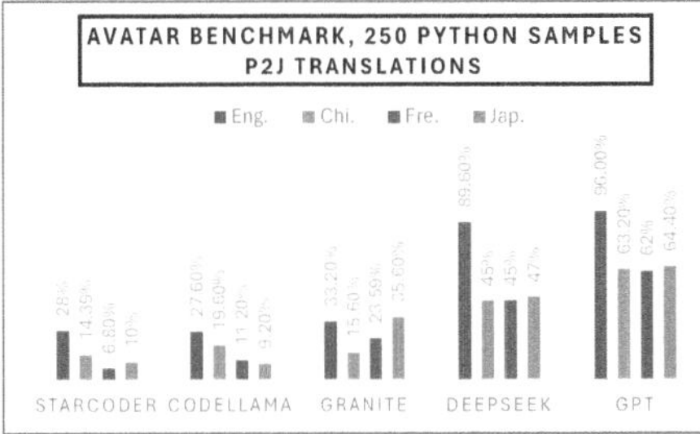

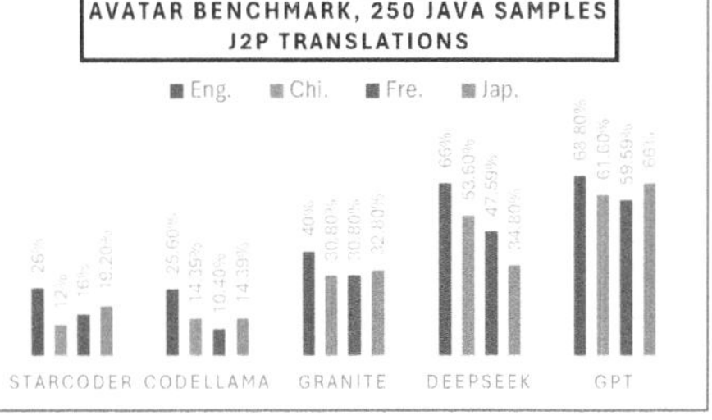

Fig. 8: Impact of Comment Language on Translation

a prominent presence of Explanatory, Precautionary, and Informative intents in them. Looking at the gain numbers in Table 3, we see that the author-comments result in nearly half the gain compared to the model-comments. The only reason behind this could be the presence of multiple other intents alongside the only necessary - Descriptive type - intent. Perhaps the close presence of other intents is creating noise that the translating LLM is unable to cancel out, resulting in comparatively poorer performance.

Key Takeaway : Short comments that *describe* what the code does are more useful to LLMs during code translation. Other comment types may add to noise.

4.4 RQ3 : Density and Language of Comments

Impact of Comment Density. We noted in the previous two studies that, although comments are helpful in code translation, they tend to add noise to the code being translated. In an attempt to shed light on how much code should be commented on without adding too much noise while still being useful for code translation, we conducted the following experiment. In 250 Java and 250 Python code samples from the AVATAR dataset, we instructed the commenting LLM - GPT, to restrict the inclusion of code comments to only the top one-third and two-thirds of the complex lines of code instead of the entire code. The commenting LLM was instructed to decide for itself which lines of code to comment. Usual J2P and P2J translations were then attempted on these differently commented samples using various translating LLMs, and the percentage of successful translations was recorded. The results are summarized in Figure 7. It is evident that limiting the density of comments did not prove beneficial. One could argue that this may be due to uncertainty about which sections of the code would be commented on when such restrictions are imposed. While this is

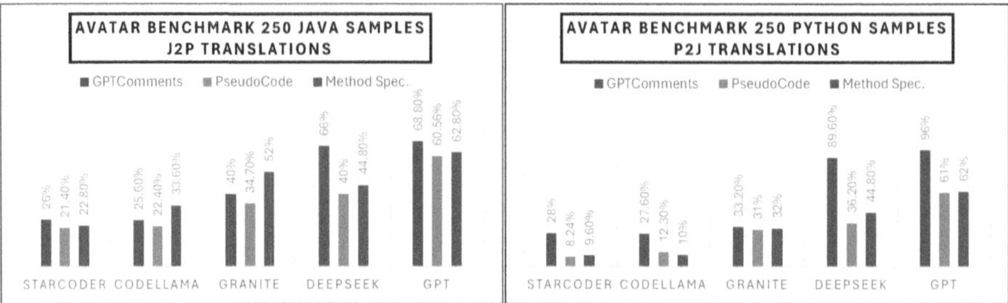

Fig. 9: Impact of Location on Translation : Code Comments vs. Method Specifications & Pseudo-code

valid, identifying which code blocks require comments remains a challenge until an error-to-code block mapping is obtained for the failed translation samples.

Key Takeaway : Arbitrary restrictions on comment density did not prove beneficial. More experiments may be needed to understand the role of selective commenting based on heuristics or error-localization–driven selection.

Is English as a commenting language better than other languages? To study whether the choice of natural language (English, Japanese, French, Chinese, etc.) for code comments impacts the code translation performance of LLMs, we conducted the following experiment. In 250 Java and 250 Python code samples from the AVATAR dataset, the English language comments generated by the GPT model were translated into 3 other natural languages: Japanese, French, and Chinese, using the GPT model itself. While generating comments natively in each of these 3 other natural languages using specialized multilingual code models was another option, for this experiment, we chose to translate English comments into these languages to avoid any potential bias in results comparison due to the introduction of new commenting models. J2P and P2J translations of these different language commented sets were then attempted using various translating LLMs. The results are presented in Figure 8. We observe that in almost all cases, English comments performed the best for both J2P and P2J translation tasks, the only exception being P2J translations on the Granite model, which show marginally better performance with Japanese comments.

4.5 RQ4 : Impact of Code Comments vs. Method Specifications & Pseudo-code

We now attempt to answer another important question about code comments: How does the placement of code specifications affect translation performance? We explore the impact of placing NL code specifications in 3 different forms at 3 different locations: (1) in the form of *pseudocode* , which will be appended to the source code in the translation prompt, (2) in the form of *method specifications*, placed at the beginning of each method within the source code, and (3) in the form of code comments, closely placed alongside lines-of-code. We used our commenting LLM, GPT, to generate pseudocode and method specifications (one for each method in the code sample) for a total of 500 (250 Java and 250 Python) AVATAR code samples. Pseudocodes were appended to the source code in the translation prompt, while method specifications were placed at the be-

Benchmark	SOURCE LANG.	TARGET LANG.	StarCoder UnCom	StarCoder (Gains over Uncommented) U+D	StarCoder U+G	StarCoder U+D+G	CodeLlama UnCom	CodeLlama (Gains over Uncommented) U+D	CodeLlama U+G	CodeLlama U+D+G	DeepSeek UnCom	DeepSeek (Gains over Uncommented) U+D	DeepSeek U+G	DeepSeek U+D+G	GPT UnCom	GPT (Gains over Uncommented) U+D	GPT U+G	GPT U+D+G
CodeNet Benchmark (200 Samples Each)	C	C++	0.76	11.18%	12.5%	16.4%	0.89	2.25%	4.5%	4.5%	0.52	40.38%	57.7%	67.3%	0.97	2.06%	1.0%	2.1%
		GO	0.21	48.78%	31.7%	68.3%	0.52	11.54%	10.6%	15.4%	0.64	15.63%	12.5%	19.5%	0.80	6.29%	7.5%	9.4%
		JAVA	0.69	10.87%	9.4%	15.9%	0.36	21.13%	4.2%	23.9%	0.69	37.23%	31.4%	40.9%	0.96	3.14%	3.1%	3.7%
		PYTHON	0.36	21.13%	19.7%	32.4%	0.04	85.71%	28.6%	100.0%	0.25	59.18%	59.2%	89.8%	0.67	4.48%	8.2%	9.7%
	C++	C	0.22	23.26%	16.3%	25.6%	0.24	12.50%	12.5%	14.6%	0.23	23.91%	17.4%	26.1%	0.31	0.00%	1.6%	1.6%
		GO	0.18	30.56%	33.3%	52.8%	0.45	20.00%	18.9%	25.6%	0.64	10.16%	9.4%	14.8%	0.84	7.19%	6.6%	9.0%
		JAVA	0.75	4.67%	6.7%	8.7%	0.50	28.00%	24.0%	40.0%	0.88	9.14%	9.1%	10.9%	0.97	1.55%	1.6%	1.6%
		PYTHON	0.31	37.70%	34.4%	55.7%	0.05	40.00%	50.0%	80.0%	0.44	44.32%	53.4%	61.4%	0.71	5.67%	4.3%	7.8%
	GO	C	0.22	20.93%	4.7%	23.3%	0.24	31.25%	10.4%	39.6%	0.10	95.00%	85.0%	130.0%	0.27	5.66%	209.4%	209.4%
		C++	0.40	11.39%	20.3%	25.3%	0.69	4.35%	8.0%	10.1%	0.56	30.36%	33.9%	46.4%	0.91	3.31%	3.9%	5.0%
		JAVA	0.84	7.14%	6.5%	10.1%	0.78	14.84%	15.5%	20.6%	0.57	50.43%	49.6%	62.6%	0.95	3.17%	3.7%	4.2%
		PYTHON	0.43	20.00%	11.8%	25.9%	0.51	16.63%	9.9%	20.8%	0.04	325.00%	312.5%	487.5%	0.73	8.28%	7.6%	13.8%
AVATAR (250 Samples Each)	JAVA	C	0.27	4.48%	9.7%	14.2%	0.31	16.02%	14.4%	28.3%	0.58	6.74%	9.2%	12.6%	0.72	10.28%	7.5%	13.2%
		C++	0.36	4.40%	15.4%	22.3%	0.41	9.95%	7.8%	19.4%	0.63	14.01%	10.8%	17.5%	0.82	3.66%	4.9%	8.9%
		GO	0.02	49.58%	66.7%	304.2%	0.19	11.46%	5.2%	28.1%	0.48	4.17%	2.1%	9.2%	0.72	8.89%	6.4%	11.1%
		PYTHON	0.21	55.77%	88.5%	128.8%	0.29	41.10%	56.2%	79.4%	0.55	15.94%	32.6%	40.6%	0.65	9.82%	35.0%	25.2%
	PYTHON	C	0.13	18.75%	37.5%	43.8%	0.15	23.68%	28.9%	36.8%	0.11	21.43%	28.6%	46.4%	0.12	12.90%	3.2%	12.9%
		C++	0.18	19.57%	89.1%	91.3%	0.28	30.99%	31.0%	45.1%	0.40	42.42%	48.5%	62.6%	0.58	12.41%	13.8%	20.0%
		GO	0.09	27.27%	22.7%	40.9%	0.18	36.96%	17.4%	45.7%	0.23	55.17%	79.3%	99.6%	0.46	0.86%	15.5%	22.4%
		JAVA	0.24	29.51%	85.2%	109.8%	0.21	32.21%	100.0%	121.2%	0.52	12.40%	79.8%	80.6%	0.62	8.28%	58.4%	58.4%
Avg. Gain over Baseline				**22.85%**	**31.1%**	**55.8%**		**24.53%**	**22.9%**	**40.0%**		**45.65%**	**51.1%**	**71.3%**		**5.90%**	**20.2%**	**22.5%**

Table 4: COMMENTRA - Gains in translation performance of various LLMs on different input samples. Dark green cells show the best performing configuration. Results are shown for a subset of translating LLMs. Results for all translating LLMs are in full paper version.

ginning of each method within the source code. J2P and P2J translation results of these code samples using various translating LLMs are presented in Figure 9. We observe that NL-specifications in the form of pseudocode, placed in the translation prompt, were definitely not as promising as method specifications or code comments, both of which were placed within the code itself. Apart from J2P translations on CodeLlama and Granite, for all other cases, the code comments approach yielded higher translation performance compared to the method specifications approach.

Key Takeaway : Code comments are more effective than method specifications or pseudocode in enhancing the translation performance of LLMs.

5 The COMMENTRA Approach

Based on the results and key takeaways from our study, we now propose a comment-based iterative translation approach - *COMMENTRA*. The central insight underpinning COMMENTRA is that, although comments can significantly improve the code translation capabilities of LLMs, their indiscriminate use may be counterproductive. Consequently, comments are incorporated only when initial translations without comments prove unsuccessful. This targeted approach delivers both time and cost efficiencies. By selectively introducing comments and reattempting failed translations, COMMENTRA achieves substantial improvements, resolving a wide range of test case failures as well as runtime and compilation errors. Figure 10 presents the setup of the proposed approach. The translation process works in iterations. In the initial iteration, translations of all uncommented code samples in source-PL are attempted. The output code samples in the target-PL are then tested for errors. All input samples for which the translation is erroneous move to the second iteration, wherein comments are first injected into the corresponding original source code files using a suitable commenting model, and then the translation is reattempted. Multiple iterations with different commenting models can be performed in a similar way, depending on the desired accuracy and the budget available for model invocations. As long

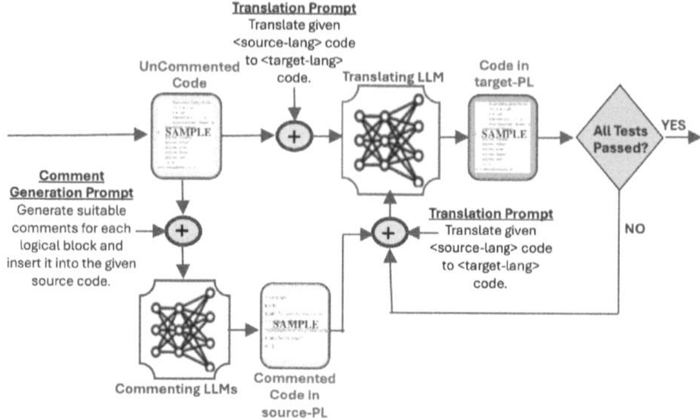

Fig. 10: COMMENTRA: Comment-Based Translation

as we follow the iterative approach suggested by COMMENTRA, performance consistently improves.

Table 4 shows the gains in translation performance achieved by the COMMENTRA approach with up to three iterations. For each translating LLM, the first iteration is the translation of uncommented code samples. The second iteration uses DeepSeek (labeled as **U+D** in the results table) or GPT (labeled as **U+G**) as the commenting model. The column labeled **U+D+G** shows the gains in translation performance after three iterations: iteration 1 of uncommented code samples, iteration 2 of DeepSeek-commented code samples[10], and iteration 3 of GPT-commented code samples[11]. As GPT is a paid model, a series of three iterations **U+D+G** may be performed in a cascade to reduce costs, wherein the maximum benefit is first derived from open source models such as DeepSeek, and then GPT is used only for the failed translation samples after iteration 2. The bold entries in the table correspond to the cases where the gain in translation performance is more than 50% after running through the two or three iterations of COMMENTRA. In our experiments, for all pairs of languages and LLMs that translated / commented, the average gain in translation performance achieved by one iteration of the commented code ranged between 6% and 51%. The same after two commented code iterations ranged from 23% to 71%.

To further validate COMMENTRA, we conducted additional experiments on the CodeTransOcean benchmark; detailed results are in the full paper version.

6 Threats to Validity

We conducted our study on standalone programs in 5 PLs. However, more research is needed to assess the impact of comments in the translation of other language pairs, as well as the impact of code comments on large-scale, real-world code repositories or complex codes. In the case of complex codes, measuring and comparing the quality of comments generated by LLMs will be important.

[10] DeepSeek is used to inject comments only in those uncommented code samples that failed to translate correctly in the first iteration.

[11] GPT is used to inject comments only in those uncommented code samples that failed to translate correctly even after the first and second iterations.

Our observations reveal that Mistral-generated comments did not result in a significant improvement in translation performance. Similarly, StarCoder and CodeLlama, as translation models, did not benefit much from the inclusion of code comments. However, it is important to interpret these numerical results with some reservations, as most of the models we examined are still evolving and improving in capability. Additionally, since the inclusion of comments contributes to a significant increase in contextual information, translating very large programs with comments can pose challenges due to LLM's token length constraints. One potential approach to mitigate this issue is to selectively add comments based on code complexity or error-localization analysis.

7 Conclusions

We explore the use of code comments as contextual information in the source code. Our experiments span multiple models and PLs, and we present a comprehensive study on the impact of code comments on code translation, considering multiple perspectives such as density, language, intent, and placement of comments. Our results demonstrate that while comments can enhance translation performance, they can also introduce noise and degrade translations. Building on all our insights, we propose COMMENTRA, an iterative translation approach to translating code with comments when the raw translation fails. Experimental results show that this simple-to-implement yet highly effective approach can substantially improve LLMs translation performance.

8 Acknowledgment

All authors acknowledge the support of the IBM AI Horizons Network at IIT Delhi for this work. Srikanta Bedathur acknowledges his DS Chair in AI professorship at IIT Delhi.

References

1. Ahmad, W.U., Chakraborty, S., Ray, B., Chang, K.W.: Summarize and generate to back-translate: Unsupervised translation of programming languages (2023), https://arxiv.org/abs/2205.11116
2. Ahmad, W.U., Tushar, M.G.R., Chakraborty, S., Chang, K.W.: Avatar: A parallel corpus for java-python program translation. arXiv preprint arXiv:2108.11590 (2021)
3. Chen, X., Liu, C., Song, D.: Tree-to-tree neural networks for program translation. Advances in neural information processing systems **31** (2018)
4. DeepSeek-AI, Zhu, Q., Guo, D., Shao, Z., Yang, D., Wang, P., Xu, R., Wu, Y., Li, Y., Gao, H., Ma, S., Zeng, W., Bi, X., Gu, Z., Xu, H., Dai, D., Dong, K., Zhang, L., Piao, Y., Gou, Z., Xie, Z., Hao, Z., Wang, B., Song, J., Chen, D., Xie, X., Guan, K., You, Y., Liu, A., Du, Q., Gao, W., Lu, X., Chen, Q., Wang, Y., Deng, C., Li, J., Zhao, C., Ruan, C., Luo, F., Liang, W.: Deepseek-coder-v2: Breaking the barrier of closed source models in code intelligence (2024), https://arxiv.org/abs/2406.11931

5. Du, Y., Ma, Y.F., Xie, Z., Li, M.: Beyond Lexical Consistency: Preserving Semantic Consistency for Program Translation . In: 2023 IEEE International Conference on Data Mining (ICDM). pp. 91–100. IEEE Computer Society, Los Alamitos, CA, USA (Dec 2023). https://doi.org/10.1109/ICDM58522.2023.00018, https://doi.ieeecomputersociety.org/10.1109/ICDM58522.2023.00018
6. Gao, S., Gao, C., He, Y., Zeng, J., Nie, L., Xia, X., Lyu, M.: Code structure–guided transformer for source code summarization. ACM Transactions on Software Engineering and Methodology **32**(1), 1–32 (Jan 2023). https://doi.org/10.1145/3522674, http://dx.doi.org/10.1145/3522674
7. Gao, Y., Lyu, C.: M2ts: Multi-scale multi-modal approach based on transformer for source code summarization (2022), https://arxiv.org/abs/2203.09707
8. Gong, Z., Gao, C., Wang, Y., Gu, W., Peng, Y., Xu, Z.: Source code summarization with structural relative position guided transformer (2022), https://arxiv.org/abs/2202.06521
9. Guo, D., Zhu, Q., Yang, D., Xie, Z., Dong, K., Zhang, W., Chen, G., Bi, X., Wu, Y., Li, Y.K., Luo, F., Xiong, Y., Liang, W.: Deepseek-coder: When the large language model meets programming – the rise of code intelligence (2024), https://arxiv.org/abs/2401.14196
10. Ibrahimzada, A.R., Ke, K., Pawagi, M., Abid, M.S., Pan, R., Sinha, S., Jabbarvand, R.: Alphatrans: A neuro-symbolic compositional approach for repository-level code translation and validation. Proceedings of the ACM on Software Engineering **2**(FSE), 2454–2476 (Jun 2025). https://doi.org/10.1145/3729379, http://dx.doi.org/10.1145/3729379
11. Iyer, S., Konstas, I., Cheung, A., Zettlemoyer, L.: Summarizing source code using a neural attention model. In: Erk, K., Smith, N.A. (eds.) Proceedings of the 54th Annual Meeting of the Association for Computational Linguistics (Volume 1: Long Papers). pp. 2073–2083. Association for Computational Linguistics, Berlin, Germany (Aug 2016). https://doi.org/10.18653/v1/P16-1195, https://aclanthology.org/P16-1195/
12. Jana, P., Jha, P., Ju, H., Kishore, G., Mahajan, A., Ganesh, V.: CoTran: An LLM-Based Code Translator Using Reinforcement Learning with Feedback from Compiler and Symbolic Execution. IOS Press (Oct 2024). https://doi.org/10.3233/faia240968, http://dx.doi.org/10.3233/FAIA240968
13. Jiang, A.Q., Sablayrolles, A., Mensch, A., Bamford, C., Chaplot, D.S., de las Casas, D., Bressand, F., Lengyel, G., Lample, G., Saulnier, L., Lavaud, L.R., Lachaux, M.A., Stock, P., Scao, T.L., Lavril, T., Wang, T., Lacroix, T., Sayed, W.E.: Mistral 7b (2023), https://arxiv.org/abs/2310.06825
14. Karanjai, R., Blackshear, S., Xu, L., Shi, W.: Collaboration is all you need: Llm assisted safe code translation (2025), https://arxiv.org/abs/2503.11237
15. Lachaux, M.A., Roziere, B., Szafraniec, M., Lample, G.: Dobf: A deobfuscation pre-training objective for programming languages. Advances in Neural Information Processing Systems **34**, 14967–14979 (2021)
16. Li, R., Allal, L.B., Zi, Y., Muennighoff, N., Kocetkov, D., Mou, C., Marone, M., Akiki, C., Li, J., Chim, J., et al.: Starcoder: may the source be with you! arXiv preprint arXiv:2305.06161 (2023)
17. Li, R., Allal, L.B., Zi, Y., Muennighoff, N., Kocetkov, D., Mou, C., Marone, M., Akiki, C., Li, J., Chim, J., et al.: Starcoder: may the source be with you! arXiv preprint arXiv:2305.06161 (2023)
18. Luo, W., Keung, J.W., Yang, B., Klein, J., Bissyande, T.F., Tian, H., Le, B.: Unlocking llm repair capabilities in low-resource programming lan-

guages through cross-language translation and multi-agent refinement (2025), https://arxiv.org/abs/2503.22512
19. Macedo, M., Tian, Y., Nie, P., Cogo, F.R., Adams, B.: Intertrans: Leveraging transitive intermediate translations to enhance llm-based code translation (2024), https://arxiv.org/abs/2411.01063
20. Mishra, M., Stallone, M., Zhang, G., Shen, Y., Prasad, A., Soria, A.M., Merler, M., Selvam, P., Surendran, S., Singh, S., Sethi, M., Dang, X.H., Li, P., Wu, K.L., Zawad, S., Coleman, A., White, M., Lewis, M., Pavuluri, R., Koyfman, Y., Lublinsky, B., de Bayser, M., Abdelaziz, I., Basu, K., Agarwal, M., Zhou, Y., Johnson, C., Goyal, A., Patel, H., Shah, Y., Zerfos, P., Ludwig, H., Munawar, A., Crouse, M., Kapanipathi, P., Salaria, S., Calio, B., Wen, S., Seelam, S., Belgodere, B., Fonseca, C., Singhee, A., Desai, N., Cox, D.D., Puri, R., Panda, R.: Granite code models: A family of open foundation models for code intelligence (2024), https://arxiv.org/abs/2405.04324
21. Mu, F., Chen, X., Shi, L., Wang, S., Wang, Q.: Developer-intent driven code comment generation (2023), https://arxiv.org/abs/2302.07055
22. Mu, F., Chen, X., Shi, L., Wang, S., Wang, Q.: Developer-intent driven code comment generation (2023), https://arxiv.org/abs/2302.07055
23. Nguyen, A.T., Nguyen, T.T., Nguyen, T.N.: Lexical statistical machine translation for language migration. In: Proceedings of the 2013 9th Joint Meeting on Foundations of Software Engineering. pp. 651–654 (2013)
24. Nitin, V., Krishna, R., Ray, B.: Spectra: Enhancing the code translation ability of language models by generating multi-modal specifications (2024), https://arxiv.org/abs/2405.18574
25. OpenAI: GPT-4o mini. Available from the OpenAI API at https://openai.com/index/gpt-4o-mini-advancing-cost-efficient-intelligence/ (2024), https://openai.com/index/gpt-4o-mini-advancing-cost-efficient-intelligence/, version used: gpt-4o-mini-2024-07-18. Accessed March 1, 2026.
26. Puri, R., Kung, D.S., Janssen, G., Zhang, W., Domeniconi, G., Zolotov, V., Dolby, J., Chen, J., Choudhury, M., Decker, L., et al.: Codenet: A large-scale ai for code dataset for learning a diversity of coding tasks. In: Thirty-fifth Conference on Neural Information Processing Systems Datasets and Benchmarks Track (Round 2) (2021)
27. Roziere, B., Lachaux, M.A., Chanussot, L., Lample, G.: Unsupervised translation of programming languages. Advances in Neural Information Processing Systems **33**, 20601–20611 (2020)
28. Rozière, B., Gehring, J., Gloeckle, F., Sootla, S., Gat, I., Tan, X.E., Adi, Y., Liu, J., Sauvestre, R., Remez, T., Rapin, J., Kozhevnikov, A., Evtimov, I., Bitton, J., Bhatt, M., Ferrer, C.C., Grattafiori, A., Xiong, W., Défossez, A., Copet, J., Azhar, F., Touvron, H., Martin, L., Usunier, N., Scialom, T., Synnaeve, G.: Code llama: Open foundation models for code (2024), https://arxiv.org/abs/2308.12950
29. Rozière, B., Gehring, J., Gloeckle, F., Sootla, S., Gat, I., Tan, X.E., Adi, Y., Liu, J., Sauvestre, R., Remez, T., Rapin, J., Kozhevnikov, A., Evtimov, I., Bitton, J., Bhatt, M., Ferrer, C.C., Grattafiori, A., Xiong, W., Défossez, A., Copet, J., Azhar, F., Touvron, H., Martin, L., Usunier, N., Scialom, T., Synnaeve, G.: Code llama: Open foundation models for code (2024), https://arxiv.org/abs/2308.12950
30. Saha, S.K., Rabbi, F., Wang, S., Yang, J.: Specification-driven code translation powered by large language models: How far are we? (2024), https://arxiv.org/abs/2412.04590

31. Tang, Z., Agarwal, M., Shypula, A., Wang, B., Wijaya, D., Chen, J., Kim, Y.: Explain-then-translate: an analysis on improving program translation with self-generated explanations. In: Bouamor, H., Pino, J., Bali, K. (eds.) Findings of the Association for Computational Linguistics: EMNLP 2023. pp. 1741–1788. Association for Computational Linguistics, Singapore (Dec 2023). https://doi.org/10.18653/v1/2023.findings-emnlp.119, https://aclanthology.org/2023.findings-emnlp.119/
32. Yan, W., Tian, Y., Li, Y., Chen, Q., Wang, W.: Codetransocean: A comprehensive multilingual benchmark for code translation (2023), https://arxiv.org/abs/2310.04951
33. Yang, Z., Liu, F., Yu, Z., Keung, J.W., Li, J., Liu, S., Hong, Y., Ma, X., Jin, Z., Li, G.: Exploring and unleashing the power of large language models in automated code translation (2024), https://arxiv.org/abs/2404.14646
34. Zhai, J., Xu, X., Shi, Y., Tao, G., Pan, M., Ma, S., Xu, L., Zhang, W., Tan, L., Zhang, X.: Cpc: Automatically classifying and propagating natural language comments via program analysis. In: 2020 IEEE/ACM 42nd International Conference on Software Engineering (ICSE). pp. 1359–1371 (Oct 2020)

From Words to Code: Do NLP Prompting Strategies Generalize to Code Generation?

Erin Woo[1]*, Sangyeop Yeo[2], Hyungkook Jun[2], Sangcheol Kim[2], Seung-won Hwang[3], and Yu-Seung Ma[2]

[1] Korea National University of Science and Technology, Daejeon 34113, South Korea
[2] Electronics and Telecommunications Research Institute, Daejeon 34129, South Korea
[3] Seoul National University, Seoul 08826, South Korea
{yrwoo,sangyeop,hkjun,sheart,ysma}@etri.re.kr
seungwonh@snu.ac.kr

Abstract. Prompt engineering plays an important role in optimizing the performance of Large Language Models (LLMs). Although various prompting techniques have achieved substantial gains in natural language processing (NLP), their transferability to code generation remains underexplored. This paper presents an empirical study that examines the effects of NLP-inspired prompting methods on code generation using five LLMs and two established benchmarks, HumanEval and LiveCodeBench. We find that instruction-based prompting produces surprisingly limited or inconsistent improvements in programming contexts, while reasoning-based prompting delivers stronger and more stable performance. Our analysis identified two forms of reasoning-based prompting—procedural and goal-oriented—each addressing different aspects of reasoning and both effective for code generation. Building on these findings, we explore prompt designs that more fully leverage the reasoning capabilities of advanced LLMs, achieving measurable improvements in code generation accuracy. These results emphasize the continuing importance of prompt design in advancing AI-assisted programming.

Keywords: Large Language Model · Code Generation · Prompt Engineering.

1 Introduction

Large Language Models (LLMs) have demonstrated remarkable capabilities across a wide range of natural language processing (NLP) tasks, and their use has expanded rapidly into software engineering tasks, including code generation, testing, and summarization [15, 36, 19, 26]. These advances have stimulated growing interest in employing LLMs as automated programming assistants, or even as agents capable of performing software development tasks autonomously.

* A project page is available at https://github.com/eyrwoo/FromWords2Code

E. Albert and C. Pasareanu (Eds.): FASE 2026, LNCS 16504, pp. 43–63, 2026.
https://doi.org/10.1007/978-3-032-22774-4_3

A critical factor influencing the performance of LLMs is **prompting**—the design of input instructions that guide the model's reasoning and output. In NLP, various prompting strategies [4, 30, 29, 27, 28] such as few-shot prompting, chain-of-thought prompting, and self-consistency have shown significant effects in improving task performance and reliability. Naturally, researchers have adapted these prompting paradigms to programming-related tasks, hoping to obtain similar benefits in software engineering domains [9, 20, 22].

However, it remains unclear whether prompting strategies that are effective in natural language contexts also yield comparable improvements in programming contexts. Programming languages differ fundamentally from natural languages in their formal syntax, compositional semantics, and execution-based evaluation criteria. Therefore, a prompting strategy that enhances reasoning coherence in NLP tasks may not necessarily improve—or might even hinder—the structural and functional quality of generated code. For instance, while minor ambiguities in natural language may be tolerable, similar ambiguities in source code can result in syntax or runtime errors [6, 21]. These differences raise our research question for AI-assisted software development: **Do prompting techniques designed primarily for NLP generalize effectively to programming tasks?**

To address this question, we conduct an empirical study on NLP-inspired prompting methods for code generation. We evaluate 22 prompting techniques across five LLMs—LLaMA3.1 8B Instruct, LLaMA3.1 70B Instruct, Qwen2.5 Coder 32B Instruct, Deepseek-R1-Distill-LLaMA-70B, and GPT-4o [10, 17, 12, 2]—using two established benchmarks, HumanEval [7] and LiveCodeBench [18].

The contributions of this paper are below:

- We systematically evaluate existing NLP-inspired prompting techniques on code generation tasks using five LLMs and two benchmarks.
- We show that instruction-based prompting yields limited or inconsistent improvements in code generation, whereas reasoning-based prompting achieves more stable and reliable performance across models and benchmarks.
- We design prompts that enable reasoning-specialized LLMs to integrate both procedural and goal-oriented forms of reasoning, leveraging their complementary strengths for more effective code generation.

The rest of this paper is organized as follows: Section 2 reviews related work, Section 3 describes our methodology, Section 4 presents results and analysis, and Section 5 concludes with implications and future directions.

2 Related Works

A variety of prompting strategies have been developed in natural language processing to improve the reasoning capability of large language models without additional fine-tuning. Few-shot prompting [4] provides minimal in-context examples for task adaptation. Chain-of-Thought (CoT) prompting [30] encourages step-by-step thinking, and Tree-of-Thought [33] extends it by structuring reasoning into hierarchical steps. ReAct [34] and Chain-of-Knowledge [24] integrate external knowledge retrieval to ground reasoning in a factual context. Role-play prompting [31] guides models through specific reasoning personas, while self-consistency [29] enhances reliability by aggregating multiple reasoning paths. Beyond these, various other prompting approaches [15, 36] have been introduced to strengthen model reasoning and decision-making.

Motivated by the success of these prompting techniques in NLP, researchers have attempted to adapt them for programming tasks to achieve similar improvements in reasoning and reliability. Huang et al. [16] proposed CodeCoT, which encourages models to think step by step for code generation by extending the chain of thought paradigm, while Yang et al. [32] suggested a framework that automatically generates high-quality reasoning traces to improve the reliability of CoT-based code generation. In addition, some studies have approached code generation by emphasizing explicit planning and requirement analysis. Self-Planning [20] encourages models to formulate task plans before producing code. AceCoder [23] and ArchCode [13] guide models to analyze and translate problem requirements into code generation steps, ensuring alignment between specifications and implementation. SEK [11] focuses on extracting and emphasizing key functional elements from requirements, enabling models to attend to the most critical aspects during code generation.

While these studies indicate that certain NLP prompting principles show potential applicability to programming, the transition from natural language to code remains nontrivial. To this end, we systematically evaluate a range of NLP-inspired prompting strategies to examine whether their effectiveness transfers to programming contexts. This investigation is further motivated by our preliminary observations that prompting methods often regarded as effective—such as few-shot prompting—do not consistently yield improvements in code generation.

3 Methodology

This section describes how we adapt existing NLP-inspired prompting techniques for code generation and evaluated their effectiveness. We first introduce the models used in our experiments, followed by the benchmarks and performance metrics, and finally outline the prompts employed in the study.

3.1 Models

We used five LLMs with different sizes, architectures, and specializations to reflect the diversity of current LLMs.

- **LLaMA3.1 (8B, 70B) Instruct:** Two models at small and medium scales, representing general-purpose instruction-tuned LLMs.
- **Qwen2.5 Coder 32B Instruct:** A code-specialized model optimized for multilingual programming tasks, trained with extended code datasets.
- **GPT-4o (2024-11-20):** A large-scale multimodal model with advanced architecture and strong overall performance across text and code tasks.
- **DeepSeek-R1-Distill-LLaMA-70B:** A reasoning-focused model distilled from a larger expert reasoning model, DeepSeek-R1.

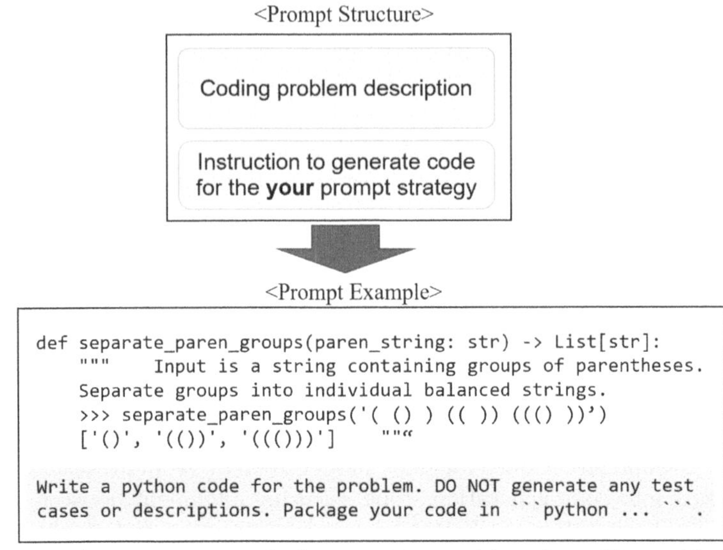

Fig. 1 A prompt example for a coding problem from HumanEval.

3.2 Datasets and Evaluation Metric

We use two widely recognized benchmarks for code generation:

- **HumanEval** [7]: A set of 164 Python coding tasks where each task provides a code snippet, a docstring description, and test cases.
- **LiveCodeBench** [18]: A larger and more diverse benchmark featuring tasks from various programming challenge sources. Our set contains 400 problems (cutoff May 2023–March 2024) with text descriptions and test cases.

To quantify performance, we measure the functional correctness of generated solutions using the $pass@k$ metric [7]. The $pass@k$ metric calculates how often at least one of the model's top-k generated solutions successfully passes all unit tests. We focus mainly on $pass@1$ as a representative measure of the accuracy of the model.

3.3 Experimental NLP Prompts

Code generation prompts typically consist of instructions placed before or after the problem description. As shown in Fig. 1, the HumanEval prompt includes a code snippet beginning with `def` and a gray instruction block reading "Write a Python code...". This example represents the widely used basic prompting.

For our experiments, prompt templates were drawn from the publicly available ATLAS benchmark [5], which was originally designed for evaluating prompting strategies in NLP tasks. ATLAS encompasses diverse prompting strategies, including affirmative directives (e.g., "do"), chain of thought, and interactive prompts. By leveraging this well-organized collection, we ensured objectivity, transparency, and reproducibility across experiments. The original intent and linguistic structure of the prompts were preserved wherever possible, with minor adaptations to fit the code generation context.

Table 1 presents the instructions utilized in our experiments. We categorized the prompts into two main groups: *instruction-based prompting* and *reasoning-based prompting*. The reasoning-based prompting refers to cases where the LLM autonomously extracts additional information and uses it to generate code. Among the 26 referenced instructions, 20 were employed, maintaining the original numbering for clarity in the Table 1. Four instructions were excluded for the reasons below. Since code generation using LLMs is typically evaluated without user intervention, we adjusted prompts that required user interaction by enabling the LLM to handle the interaction autonomously. Prompts that could not be automated or that were incompatible with code generation tasks were excluded from the experiments: prompts #15, #22, #24, and #26. The evaluation compared the performance of the Basic Prompt with the proposed prompts. The Basic Prompt already incorporates some elements of the 26 principled instructions, such as removing polite expressions like "please" (specifically, prompt #1), which were unnecessary and excluded. Prompt #23, which involves generating code across multiple files, was also excluded due to the single-file structure of the evaluation datasets. Appendix A provides examples of the problem descriptions with the Basic Prompt applied to HumanEval and LiveCodeBench tasks for reference.

4 Results and Discussion

4.1 Initial Evaluation on LLaMA3.1 70B Instruct and HumanEval

We began by conducting a preliminary evaluation using the LLaMA3.1 70B Instruct model on the HumanEval benchmark, applying all prompts listed in Table 1 to this single model–dataset combination due to the high computational costs involved. To assess both deterministic and diverse output scenarios, experiments were performed with Greedy decoding (temperature = 0) and Nucleus sampling (temperature = 0.8) [14]. The baseline Basic Prompt achieved *pass*@1 scores of 79.04% (Nucleus) and 78.04% (Greedy).

Fig. 2 summarizes the results for the 21 prompts detailed in Table 1. The color gradient represents changes in *pass*@1 performance relative to the Basic Prompt, where red denotes improvement and blue indicates a decrease in performance.

Reasoning-based prompts showed clear advantages, improving performance by up to 8.55 percentage points with prompt #21 ("Write the list of what information you should consider to solve this problem."). This suggests that reasoning-based prompting helps models clarify requirements and structure intermediate reasoning steps, thereby providing richer contextual grounding for code generation. In contrast, instruction-based prompting yielded only modest or inconsistent gains—typically within 1–2 percentage points—adding overhead

Table 1 An overview of the prompts. The prompt numbers are the same as the principles listed in ATLAS [5], with the Basic Prompt.

Category	# Prompts	Description
Basic Prompt		A basic instruction such as "Write a Python code ...".
Instruction -based prompting	2	Integrate the intended audience in the prompt, e.g., the audience is a software developer.
	4	Employ affirmative directives such as "do", while steering clear of negative language like "don't".
	5	When you need clarity or a deeper understanding of a coding problem, utilize the following prompts: "Write the code and then explain the code."
	6	Add "I will give you a reward if you can solve the problem."
	7	Implement example-driven prompting (Use few-shot prompting).
	8	When formatting your prompt, start with "### Description", followed by "### Instruction". Subsequently, present your content. Use one or more line breaks to separate instructions, examples, questions, context, and input data.
	9	Incorporate the following phrases: "Your task is ..." and "You MUST ...".
	10	Incorporate the following phrases: "You will be penalized."
	11	Use the phrase "Write a code given in a natural, human-like manner" in your prompts.
	12	Use leading words like writing "Let's think step by step."
	13	Add to your prompt the following phrase: "Ensure that your answer is unbiased and avoids relying on stereotypes."
	16	Assign a role, "Professional Programmer", to the large language models.
	17	Use delimiter such as " ".
	18	Repeat a specific word or phrase multiple times within a prompt, such as "coding" or "code".
	20	Use output primers, which involve concluding your prompt with the beginning of the desired output. Utilize output primers by ending your prompt with the start of the anticipated response: such as "Answer: "
Reasoning -based prompting	3	Break down complex tasks into a sequence of simpler prompts in an interactive conversation.
	14	Allow the model to elicit precise details and requirements from you by asking you questions until it has enough information to provide the needed output (for example, "From now on, I would like you to ask me questions to ...").
	19	After instructing to generate a chain of thought (CoT), provide the self-CoT as an additional context.
	21	To write an information/resource or any type of text that should be detailed: "Write the list of what information you should consider to solve this problem."
	25	After instructing to generate the clear requirements that the model must follow in order to solve the problem, in the form of the keywords, regulations, hint, or instructions, provide the self-requirements as an additional context.

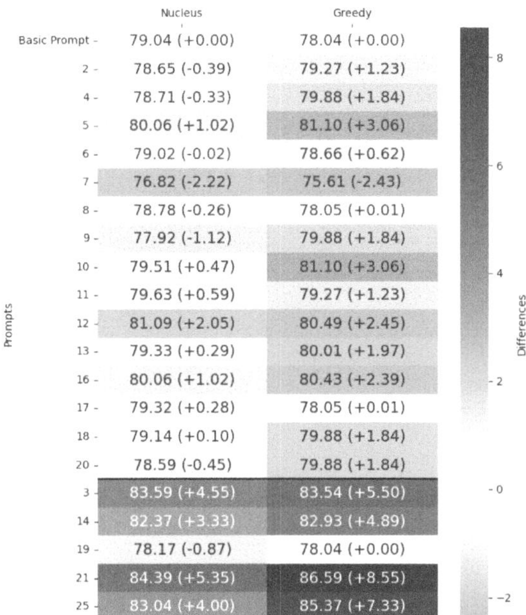

Fig. 2 Results of the initial experiment using HumanEval on LLaMA3.1 70B Instruct model.

without substantial benefit. Given these modest returns, simpler formulations such as the Basic Prompt may offer a more practical and efficient choice, particularly when token or computational costs are limited.

Across the 21 prompts, most instruction-based variants underperformed relative to the Basic Prompt. Explicit constraints, such as penalizing or conditional phrasing, often degraded results. As shown in Fig. 3, prompt #6 ("I will give you a reward if you can solve the problem.") generated erroneous code, whereas the Basic Prompt correctly solved the same problem, suggesting that excessive instruction can distract models from the actual code generation process.

Prompts #7 and #19 are particularly noteworthy: both are well-known techniques in NLP but failed to transfer effectively to code generation. Prompt #7 (few-shot) showed significant decline, while prompt #19 (chain of thought) offered no measurable gain and occasionally produced code that did not satisfy the requirements. As illustrated in Fig. 4, prompt #19 produced incorrect logic, whereas prompt #25, which explicitly guided the model to reason about and apply requirements, generated the correct output. This suggests that encouraging the model to clarify its reasoning goals and requirements—rather than merely following step-by-step procedures—helps align its reasoning process with programming semantics.

Overall, these initial observations underscore the challenges of transferring prompting strategies from NLP to code generation tasks. The results provide

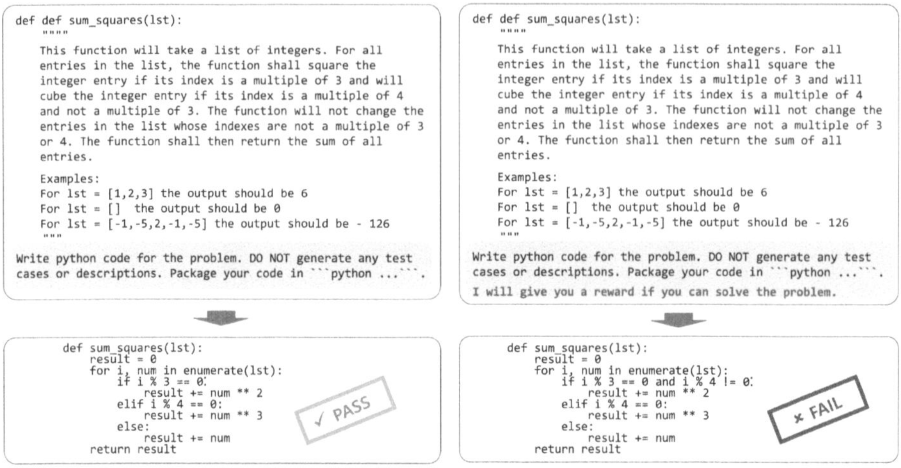

```
def def sum_squares(lst):
    """
    This function will take a list of integers. For all
    entries in the list, the function shall square the
    integer entry if its index is a multiple of 3 and will
    cube the integer entry if its index is a multiple of 4
    and not a multiple of 3. The function will not change the
    entries in the list whose indexes are not a multiple of 3
    or 4. The function shall then return the sum of all
    entries.
    Examples:
    For lst = [1,2,3] the output should be 6
    For lst = [] the output should be 0
    For lst = [-1,-5,2,-1,-5] the output should be - 126
    """
Write python code for the problem. DO NOT generate any test
cases or descriptions. Package your code in ```python ...```.
```

```
def sum_squares(lst):
    result = 0
    for i, num in enumerate(lst):
        if i % 3 == 0:
            result += num ** 2
        elif i % 4 == 0:
            result += num ** 3
        else:
            result += num
    return result
```

✓ PASS

(a) Correct answer with Basic Prompt.

```
def def sum_squares(lst):
    """
    This function will take a list of integers. For all
    entries in the list, the function shall square the
    integer entry if its index is a multiple of 3 and will
    cube the integer entry if its index is a multiple of 4
    and not a multiple of 3. The function will not change the
    entries in the list whose indexes are not a multiple of 3
    or 4. The function shall then return the sum of all
    entries.
    Examples:
    For lst = [1,2,3] the output should be 6
    For lst = [] the output should be 0
    For lst = [-1,-5,2,-1,-5] the output should be - 126
    """
Write python code for the problem. DO NOT generate any test
cases or descriptions. Package your code in ```python ...```.
I will give you a reward if you can solve the problem.
```

```
def sum_squares(lst):
    result = 0
    for i, num in enumerate(lst):
        if i % 3 == 0 and i % 4 != 0:
            result += num ** 2
        elif i % 4 == 0:
            result += num ** 3
        else:
            result += num
    return result
```

× FAIL

(b) Bad answer with Prompt #6.

Fig. 3 Comparison of Basic Prompt and instruction-based prompts on HumanEval. The LLaMA3.1 70B Instruct model generated correct code with the Basic Prompt (a), whereas Prompt #6 (b) produced an incorrect implementation (highlighted line).

preliminary evidence that NLP-inspired prompting techniques do not generalize effectively to code generation, highlighting the need for broader evaluation across diverse models. Accordingly, we expand our analysis to include models of varying sizes, architectures, and levels of specialization. To ensure consistency, we use the HumanEval benchmark to systematically assess whether the observed trends persist across this extended set of models.

4.2 Instruction-based Prompting vs. Reasoning-based Prompting

This subsection extends our experiment across four LLMs and two benchmarks: HumanEval and LiveCodeBench. The results are averaged over three runs. We reduced the scope to 11 prompts, selected from an initial pool of 21, prioritizing those most relevant to code generation tasks to balance evaluation depth with computational cost. The selection ensured balanced representation across both instruction- and reasoning-based categories to maintain fair comparison.

HumanEval Results Fig. 5 presents the performance outcomes of various prompting strategies evaluated across four models on the HumanEval benchmark. While certain prompts (e.g., #6, #10, #12) resulted in modest improvements for models such as LLaMA3.1 8B Instruct, the overall gains from prompt engineering were relatively limited for high-performing models like Qwen2.5

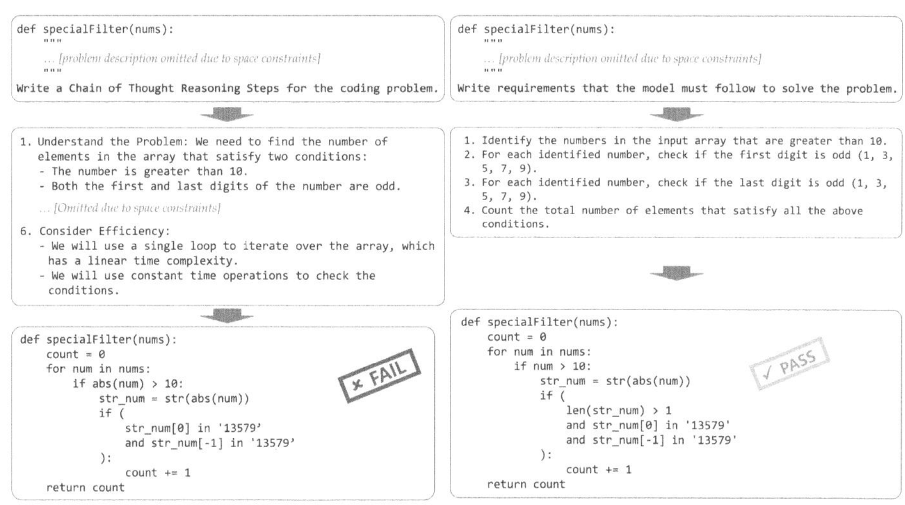

(a) Bad answer with Prompt #19. (b) Correct answer with Prompt #25.

Fig. 4 Comparison between Prompt #19 and Prompt #25 from HumanEval (reasoning-based prompting).

Coder and GPT-4o. These models already achieved baseline accuracies exceeding 90% with the Basic Prompt, leaving limited room for further improvement through more sophisticated prompts.

Interestingly, smaller models such as LLaMA3.1 8B tended to benefit more noticeably than larger ones from explicit or instruction-based prompts, suggesting that direct guidance may be advantageous for models with constrained reasoning capabilities. In contrast, prompts incorporating procedural or goal-oriented reasoning (e.g., #21 and #25) exhibited comparatively stronger performance with larger models like LLaMA3.1 70B.

The limited variability observed in prompting effectiveness across the benchmark likely stems from the simplicity and self-contained nature of HumanEval tasks. Consequently, the following section presents experiments on LiveCodeBench —a more complex and demanding benchmark—to more comprehensively evaluate the potential benefits of advanced prompt engineering.

LiveCodeBench Results LiveCodeBench includes coding competition problems that are more complex and realistic than those in HumanEval. Fig. 6 summarizes the experimental results, showing that reasoning-based prompts generally outperformed the Basic Prompt across all evaluated models. In contrast, instruction-based prompts exhibited higher variability and less robust performance. For instance, prompts such as #8 and #12 produced slight improvements for LLaMA models but showed notable declines (up to −7.15%) with GPT-4o, indicating limited generalizability in code generation tasks.

Prompts	Llama3.1 8B		Llama3.1 70B		Qwen2.5 Coder		GPT-4o	
	Nucleus	Greedy	Nucleus	Greedy	Nucleus	Greedy	Nucleus	Greedy
Basic Prompt	67.43 (+0.00)	67.07 (+0.00)	79.04 (+0.00)	78.04 (+0.00)	90.91 (+0.00)	91.46 (+0.00)	91.09 (+0.00)	85.98 (+0.00)
6	70.18 (+2.75)	70.12 (+3.05)	79.02 (-0.02)	78.66 (+0.62)	90.48 (-0.43)	91.46 (+0.00)	90.73 (-0.36)	84.15 (-1.83)
7	67.43 (+0.00)	65.24 (-1.83)	76.82 (-2.22)	75.61 (-2.43)	90.18 (-0.73)	91.46 (+0.00)	90.67 (-0.42)	85.98 (+0.00)
8	66.76 (-0.67)	65.85 (-1.22)	78.78 (-0.26)	78.05 (+0.01)	91.03 (+0.12)	93.29 (+1.83)	91.21 (+0.12)	85.37 (-0.61)
10	71.89 (+4.46)	71.95 (+4.88)	79.51 (+0.47)	81.10 (+3.06)	90.54 (-0.37)	91.46 (+0.00)	90.36 (-0.73)	89.02 (+3.04)
12	69.93 (+2.50)	69.51 (+2.44)	81.09 (+2.05)	80.49 (+2.45)	88.29 (-2.62)	89.64 (-1.82)	89.45 (-1.64)	86.59 (+0.61)
16	66.64 (-0.79)	68.29 (+1.22)	80.06 (+1.02)	80.43 (+2.39)	89.93 (-0.98)	91.46 (+0.00)	89.57 (-1.52)	84.76 (-1.22)
3	68.17 (+0.74)	67.68 (+0.61)	83.59 (+4.55)	83.54 (+5.50)	90.24 (-0.67)	90.24 (-1.22)	91.89 (+0.80)	84.15 (-1.83)
19	67.86 (+0.43)	67.07 (+0.00)	78.17 (-0.87)	78.04 (+0.00)	87.25 (-3.66)	87.19 (-4.27)	90.73 (-0.36)	86.59 (+0.61)
21	68.78 (+1.35)	72.56 (+5.49)	84.39 (+5.35)	86.59 (+8.55)	90.79 (-0.12)	90.85 (-0.61)	91.70 (+0.61)	87.20 (+1.22)
25	67.49 (+0.06)	66.53 (-0.54)	83.04 (+4.00)	85.37 (+7.33)	89.51 (-1.40)	91.46 (+0.00)	90.79 (-0.30)	84.76 (-1.22)

Fig. 5 Results on HumanEval. The heatmap represented *pass*@1(%), with the values in parentheses indicating the changes relative to the Basic Prompt (red = improvement, blue = decline).

Reasoning-based prompts, on the other hand, yielded more consistent gains, with some achieving up to a 7 percentage point improvement (e.g., Prompts #3, #21, and #25). These results indicate that leveraging supplementary information—such as requirements generated by the LLM itself through reasoning—is an effective approach for generating accurate code.

The inherent complexity of coding problems often demands systematic reasoning, structured task decomposition, and precise contextual nuances. Consequently, instruction-based prompts, which typically involve superficial modifications such as rephrasing, role assignment, or reward framing, may not effectively guide the model through these challenges. In contrast, reasoning-based prompts provide richer contextual grounding and procedural cues, making them better suited for navigating the intricacies of coding tasks.

Analysis on Difficulty Level The LiveCodeBench benchmark dataset is categorized into three difficulty levels: Easy, Medium, and Hard. This section analyzes the performance of four models across each difficulty level, as summarized in Table 2. Cases where a prompt achieved higher performance than the Basic Prompt are highlighted in bold. The top-3 prompts within each difficulty level (i.e., the three highest-performing prompts among the eleven evaluated for that level) are underlined for each model.

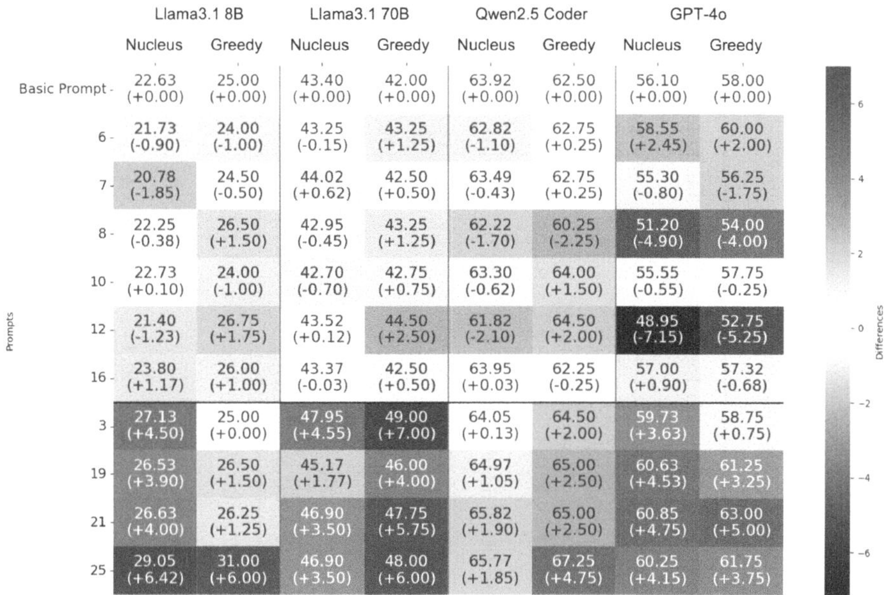

Fig. 6 Results of LiveCodeBench Overall. The heatmap represented $pass@1(\%)$, with the values in parentheses indicating the changes relative to the Basic Prompt (red = improvement, blue = decline).

Reasoning-based prompting showed stable and substantial improvements in the Easy and Medium categories across all models. The fact that most of the top-3 results belong to reasoning-based prompts suggests that such strategies are more effective than instruction-based methods even in realistic and diverse programming tasks, as represented by LiveCodeBench. For Hard category problems, inconsistent results likely stemmed from their unfamiliarity and difficulty for the model, requiring deeper reasoning beyond the scope of prompt engineering alone, suggesting the need for additional advancements or resources.

Taken together, results from the HumanEval and LiveCodeBench benchmarks reaffirm that reasoning-based prompting enhances model performance across both simple and complex programming tasks. This demonstrates that the benefits of prompt engineering stem not from surface-level instruction tuning, but from encouraging structured reasoning processes that better reflect programming semantics.

4.3 Integrating Procedural and Goal-Oriented Reasoning for Code Generation in Reasoning LLMs

Recent LLMs incorporate explicit reasoning mechanisms in their training and architecture. Models such as DeepSeek-R1 [12], Llama-3.1-Nemotron-Ultra-253B-v1 [3], Gemini 2.5 [8], and GPT-o1 [25] are designed to generate intermediate

Table 2 The results of LiveCodeBench by difficulty for each model with Nucleus sampling. Bold indicates *pass*@1(%) values higher than Basic Prompting, and the top-3 results per difficulty are underlined.

Category	# Prompts	LLaMA3.1 8B Instruct			LLaMA3.1 70B Instruct			Qwen2.5 Coder 32B Instruct			GPT-4o		
		Easy	Medium	Hard	Easy	Medium	Hard	Easy	Medium	Hard	Easy	Medium	Hard
	Basic Prompt	48.31	10.24	5.22	76.90	31.25	13.22	89.44	60.24	30.56	79.65	53.75	23.33
Instruction -based prompting	6	44.37	**11.07**	**5.89**	76.54	30.77	**13.99**	**89.51**	60.06	25.89	**84.37**	**54.29**	**25.78**
	7	42.11	**10.65**	**6.00**	**77.04**	**31.94**	**14.55**	**90.00**	60.06	28.11	74.01	**56.37**	**23.78**
	8	46.27	**10.95**	**5.44**	75.56	31.13	**13.55**	88.38	58.57	27.78	72.82	49.11	21.00
	10	47.68	**11.01**	5.22	76.33	31.07	11.33	**90.00**	**60.36**	26.67	79.01	**53.99**	21.44
	12	44.37	**10.42**	**5.67**	76.83	**31.54**	**13.33**	**89.65**	58.21	24.67	70.00	48.51	16.56
	16	**49.01**	**12.02**	**6.00**	76.05	31.13	**14.66**	**90.21**	**60.89**	28.22	**79.72**	**55.65**	**23.67**
Reasoning -based prompting	3	**51.55**	**17.02**	**7.44**	**81.33**	**36.66**	**16.33**	**90.07**	60.18	30.22	**84.72**	**57.98**	**23.56**
	19	**49.93**	**16.43**	**8.44**	**78.23**	**33.75**	**14.33**	**92.32**	**61.85**	27.67	**87.32**	**60.06**	19.56
	21	**50.21**	**15.83**	**9.56**	**80.14**	**35.29**	**16.11**	**91.48**	**63.10**	30.44	**88.38**	**58.81**	21.22
	25	**55.49**	**17.79**	**8.33**	**80.56**	**34.28**	**17.33**	**91.12**	**63.39**	29.66	**87.25**	**57.97**	21.77

Table 3 Results of recent LLMs evaluated on the LiveCodeBench benchmark leaderboard, including model size specifications and *pass*@1 scores, based on the same cutoff dataset, May 2023–March 2024.

Model	**Size**	*Pass*@1
DeepSeek-R1-preview	671B	86.2
Llama-3.1-Nemotron-Ultra-253B-v1	253B	84.0
Gemini 2.5 Pro	undisclosed (200–300B)*	94.2
GPT-o1-2024-12-17	undisclosed (200B)*	90.1

* Estimates, not officially confirmed.

reasoning steps before producing final outputs. These reasoning-focused models have achieved high functional accuracy in programming benchmarks, as shown in Table 3 based on the LiveCodeBench leaderboard [1].

Reasoning-oriented prompts often take the form of either procedural, step-by-step reasoning (*how*) or goal-oriented reasoning that foregrounds objectives and constraints (*what*) without prescribing procedures [35]. In our earlier experiments (Sections 4.1 to 4.2), the most effective prompts—#3, #14, #19, #21, and #25 (Table 1)—spanned both categories: prompt #19 induced step-by-step procedures, whereas prompts #3, #14, #21, and #25 emphasized sub-goals and objectives. These results show that both reasoning styles can support effective code generation, each emphasizing different aspects of reasoning.

We next investigated how modern reasoning-specialized LLMs employ these two forms of reasoning during code generation. Specifically, we examined whether such models inherently integrate both procedural and goal-oriented reasoning, or whether they tend to rely predominantly on one form. Examining this distinction would help reveal how current reasoning mechanisms contribute to structured problem solving in programming tasks.

To explore this question, we analyzed samples from the training dataset of Llama-3.1-Nemotron-Ultra-253B-v1 [3]. We initially expected that both procedural and goal-oriented reasoning would be reflected in the data. However, as illustrated by an example in Fig. 7, the dataset primarily emphasizes sequential reasoning, guiding the model to produce detailed step-by-step inferences. Given the nature of this training data, it is not surprising that the model's reasoning behavior is largely procedural, with little evidence of reasoning about goals or requirements—an element that our earlier experiments identified as beneficial for code generation.

Motivated by this observation, we examined whether explicitly prompting reasoning-focused models to articulate goals could complement their procedural reasoning and thereby improve code generation performance. To test this idea, we conducted an experiment using the DeepSeek-R1-Distill-LLaMA-70B model on the LiveCodeBench benchmark. Specifically, we modified only the initial in-

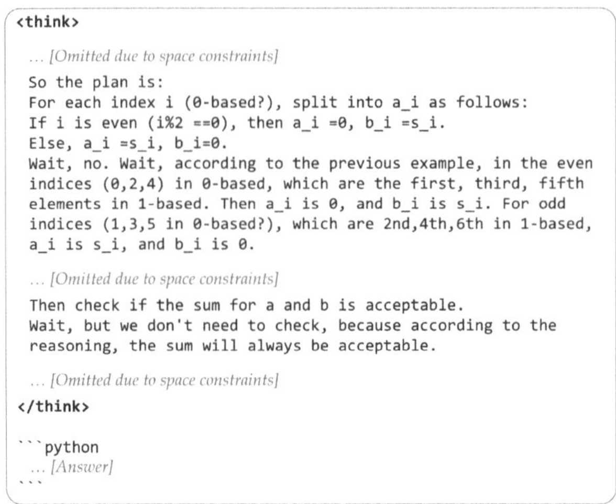

Fig. 7 A training sample from the Llama-3.1-Nemotron-Ultra-253B-v1 dataset [3], containing procedural reasoning with actions generated sequentially in response to defined conditions.

Table 4 *Pass*@1 results(%) on the Deepseek-R1-Distill-LLaMA-70B model for HumanEval and LiveCodeBench. LiveCodeBench results were the overall performance (cutoff May 2023–March 2024).

Prompt	**HumanEval**	**LiveCodeBench**
Basic Prompt	92.68	81.75
Tailored Prompt	**93.90**	**83.00**

struction from "Write a Python code for the problem." (basic prompt) to "First, define the objectives to solve the problem, and then write the Python code based on them." (tailored prompt).

This tailored prompt resulted in measurable performance improvements, as summarized in Table 4, improving *pass*@1 accuracy from 92.68% to 93.90% on HumanEval and from 81.75% to 83.00% on LiveCodeBench.

This result indicates that explicitly instructing reasoning-focused models to articulate problem goals further improves their performance. Consequently, they highlight the importance of developing prompting strategies tailored explicitly for programming tasks, combining procedural reasoning with clearly defined objectives to fully leverage the advanced reasoning capabilities of modern LLMs.

5 Limitations

This study provided an empirical examination of NLP-inspired prompting strategies for code generation, but several limitations should be acknowledged.

First, our experiments involved five LLMs and two widely used benchmarks, HumanEval and LiveCodeBench. Although this setup did not cover all programming domains, it combined models of different scales with both standard and large-scale benchmarks, providing a meaningful basis for comparative evaluation. Nonetheless, future studies on more diverse programming tasks and alternative benchmarks would help validate the generality of these observations, and extending goal-oriented prompting beyond DeepSeek to other LLMs would further test whether the effects generalize across models.

Second, our evaluation relied primarily on the *pass*@1 metric, which indicated whether generated code passed functional tests. While this metric captured functional correctness effectively, it did not reflect other important aspects such as readability, maintainability, runtime efficiency, or code style.

Third, we examined a curated set of prompting methods from the ATLAS benchmark. This selection offered diverse coverage but remained finite; consequently, newer techniques—such as multi-turn self-refinement or reflection-based prompting—were not explored in our setup.

Finally, the prompting methods evaluated in this study did not incorporate execution feedback, human feedback, or iterative error correction (e.g., running intermediate code and refining it). We excluded such feedback to maintain objectivity, reproducibility, and full automation of the experiments, as human involvement could introduce subjectivity and variability across runs.

6 Conclusion

This study investigated how prompting strategies originally developed for natural language processing transfer to code generation tasks. Through systematic experiments with five LLMs and two widely used benchmarks, we observed that instruction-based prompting provides only limited or inconsistent benefits in programming contexts, whereas reasoning-based prompting consistently leads to stronger and more stable performance. These findings highlight that prompt effectiveness depends strongly on the alignment between reasoning behavior and the structure of the target task.

Our analysis further revealed that both procedural reasoning—emphasizing step-by-step problem solving—and goal-oriented reasoning—focusing on clarifying problem objectives—contribute to successful code generation. However, current reasoning-focused LLMs exhibit a tendency to rely predominantly on procedural reasoning while underutilizing goal-oriented reasoning. To address this imbalance, we designed prompts that explicitly encourage models to define problem goals before generating code, while maintaining procedural reasoning during synthesis. This approach resulted in measurable gains in code generation accuracy, demonstrating that balanced reasoning can lead to more coherent and functionally correct code outputs. These results suggest that even reasoning-capable models require careful prompt design to fully exploit their reasoning potential. Thoughtful prompt engineering thus remains a critical factor in advancing the reliability and effectiveness of AI-assisted programming.

Acknowledgements This work was supported by Institute of Information & communications Technology Planning & Evaluation (IITP) grant funded by the Korea government(MSIT) (No.2022-0-00995, Automated reliable source code generation from natural language descriptions)

References

1. LiveCodeBench Leaderboard (2025), https://livecodebench.github.io/leaderboard.html, accessed: 2025-04-24
2. Achiam, J., Adler, S., Agarwal, S., Ahmad, L., Akkaya, I., Aleman, F.L., Almeida, D., Altenschmidt, J., Altman, S., Anadkat, S., et al.: Gpt-4 technical report. arXiv preprint arXiv:2303.08774 (2023)
3. Bercovich, A., Levy, I., Golan, I., Dabbah, M., El-Yaniv, R., Puny, O., Galil, I., Moshe, Z., Ronen, T., Nabwani, N., et al.: Llama-nemotron: Efficient reasoning models. arXiv preprint arXiv:2505.00949 (2025)
4. Brown, T.B., Mann, B., Ryder, N., Subbiah, M., Kaplan, J., Dhariwal, P., Neelakantan, A., Shyam, P., Sastry, G., Askell, A., Agarwal, S., Herbert-Voss, A., Krueger, G., Henighan, T., Child, R., Ramesh, A., Ziegler, D.M., Wu, J., Winter, C., Hesse, C., Chen, M., Sigler, E., Litwin, M., Gray, S., Chess, B., Clark, J., Berner, C., McCandlish, S., Radford, A., Sutskever, I., Amodei, D.: Language models are few-shot learners. In: Advances in Neural Information Processing Systems (NeurIPS) 2020 (2020)
5. Bsharat, S.M., Myrzakhan, A., Shen, Z.: Principled instructions are all you need for questioning llama-1/2, gpt-3.5/4. arXiv preprint arXiv:2312.16171 (2023), code available at https://github.com/VILA-Lab/ATLAS
6. Casalnuovo, C., Sagae, K., Devanbu, P.: Studying the difference between natural and programming language corpora. Empirical Software Engineering **24**(4), 1823–1868 (2019)
7. Chen, M., Tworek, J., Jun, H., Yuan, Q., Pinto, H.P.D.O., Kaplan, J., Edwards, H., Burda, Y., Joseph, N., Brockman, G., et al.: Evaluating large language models trained on code. arXiv preprint arXiv:2107.03374 (2021)
8. DeepMind, G.: Gemini 2.5: Our most intelligent ai model. Tech. rep. (2025), https://blog.google/technology/google-deepmind/gemini-model-thinking-updates-march-2025/
9. Ding, H., Fan, Z., Guehring, I., Gupta, G., Ha, W., Huan, J., Liu, L., Omidvar-Tehrani, B., Wang, S., Zhou, H.: Reasoning and planning with large language models in code development. In: Proceedings of the 30th ACM SIGKDD Conference on Knowledge Discovery and Data Mining. p. 6480–6490. KDD '24, Association for Computing Machinery, New York, NY, USA (2024). https://doi.org/10.1145/3637528.3671452, https://doi.org/10.1145/3637528.3671452
10. Dubey, A., Jauhri, A., Pandey, A., Kadian, A., Al-Dahle, A., Letman, A., Mathur, A., Schelten, A., Yang, A., Fan, A., et al.: The llama 3 herd of models. arXiv preprint arXiv:2407.21783 (2024)

11. Fan, L., Chen, M., Liu, Z.: SEK: Self-explained keywords empower large language models for code generation. In: Che, W., Nabende, J., Shutova, E., Pilehvar, M.T. (eds.) Findings of the Association for Computational Linguistics: ACL 2025. pp. 6249–6278. Association for Computational Linguistics, Vienna, Austria (Jul 2025). https://doi.org/10.18653/v1/2025.findings-acl.324, https://aclanthology.org/2025.findings-acl.324/
12. Guo, D., Yang, D., Zhang, H., Song, J., Zhang, R., Xu, R., Zhu, Q., Ma, S., Wang, P., Bi, X., et al.: Deepseek-r1: Incentivizing reasoning capability in llms via reinforcement learning. arXiv preprint arXiv:2501.12948 (2025)
13. Han, H., Kim, J., Yoo, J., Lee, Y., Hwang, S.w.: Archcode: Incorporating software requirements in code generation with large language models. In: Proceedings of the 62nd Annual Meeting of the Association for Computational Linguistics (Volume 1: Long Papers). pp. 13520–13552 (2024)
14. Holtzman, A., Buys, J., Du, L., Forbes, M., Choi, Y.: The curious case of neural text degeneration. arXiv preprint arXiv:1904.09751 (2019)
15. Hou, X., Zhao, Y., Liu, Y., Yang, Z., Wang, K., Li, L., Luo, X., Lo, D., Grundy, J., Wang, H.: Large language models for software engineering: A systematic literature review **33**(8) (2024)
16. Huang, D., Bu, Q., Qing, Y., Cui, H.: Codecot: Tackling code syntax errors in cot reasoning for code generation. arXiv preprint arXiv:2308.08784 (2023)
17. Hui, B., Yang, J., Cui, Z., Yang, J., Liu, D., Zhang, L., Liu, T., Zhang, J., Yu, B., Lu, K., et al.: Qwen2.5-coder technical report. arXiv preprint arXiv:2409.12186 (2024)
18. Jain, N., Han, K., Gu, A., Li, W.D., Yan, F., Zhang, T., Wang, S., Solar-Lezama, A., Sen, K., Stoica, I.: Livecodebench: Holistic and contamination free evaluation of large language models for code. arXiv preprint arXiv:2403.07974 (2024)
19. Jha, S.K., Jha, S., Ewetz, R., Velasquez, A.: Co-synthesis of code and formal models using large language models and functors. In: MILCOM 2024 - 2024 IEEE Military Communications Conference (MILCOM). pp. 215–220 (2024). https://doi.org/10.1109/MILCOM61039.2024.10773930
20. Jiang, X., Dong, Y., Wang, L., Fang, Z., Shang, Q., Li, G., Jin, Z., Jiao, W.: Self-planning code generation with large language models. ACM Transactions on Software Engineering and Methodology **33**(7) (Sep 2024). https://doi.org/10.1145/3672456, https://doi.org/10.1145/3672456
21. Kong, A., Zhao, S., Chen, H., Li, Q., Qin, Y., Sun, R., Zhou, X., Wang, E., Dong, X.: Better zero-shot reasoning with role-play prompting. arXiv preprint arXiv:2308.07702 (2023)
22. Li, J., Li, G., Li, Y., Jin, Z.: Structured chain-of-thought prompting for code generation. ACM Transactions on Software Engineering and Methodology **34**(2) (Jan 2025). https://doi.org/10.1145/3690635, https://doi.org/10.1145/3690635
23. Li, J., Zhao, Y., Li, Y., Li, G., Jin, Z.: Acecoder: An effective prompting technique specialized in code generation. ACM Trans. Softw. Eng. Methodol. **33**(8) (Nov 2024). https://doi.org/10.1145/3675395, https://doi.org/10.1145/3675395
24. Li, X., Zhao, R., Chia, Y.K., Ding, B., Joty, S., Poria, S., Bing, L.: Chain-of-knowledge: Grounding large language models via dynamic knowledge adapting over heterogeneous sources. arXiv preprint arXiv:2305.13269 (2023)
25. OpenAI: Openai o1 system card. Tech. rep., OpenAI (2024), https://openai.com/index/openai-o1-system-card/
26. Peng, Q., Zhang, C., Mangal, R., Pasareanu, C., Jia, L.: Random Perturbation Attack on LLMs for Code Generation . In: 2025 IEEE/ACM

4th International Conference on AI Engineering – Software Engineering for AI (CAIN). pp. 285–287. IEEE Computer Society, Los Alamitos, CA, USA (Apr 2025). https://doi.org/10.1109/CAIN66642.2025.00052, https://doi.ieeecomputersociety.org/10.1109/CAIN66642.2025.00052
27. Qiao, S., Ou, Y., Zhang, N., Chen, X., Yao, Y., Deng, S., Tan, C., Huang, F., Chen, H.: Reasoning with language model prompting: A survey. In: Rogers, A., Boyd-Graber, J., Okazaki, N. (eds.) Proceedings of the 61st Annual Meeting of the Association for Computational Linguistics (Volume 1: Long Papers). pp. 5368–5393. Association for Computational Linguistics, Toronto, Canada (Jul 2023). https://doi.org/10.18653/v1/2023.acl-long.294, https://aclanthology.org/2023.acl-long.294/
28. Sahoo, P., Singh, A.K., Saha, S., Jain, V., Mondal, S., Chadha, A.: A systematic survey of prompt engineering in large language models: Techniques and applications (2025), https://arxiv.org/abs/2402.07927
29. Wang, X., Wei, J., Schuurmans, D., Le, Q.V., Chi, E.H., Narang, S., Chowdhery, A., Zhou, D.: Self-consistency improves chain of thought reasoning in language models. In: The Eleventh International Conference on Learning Representations (2023), https://openreview.net/forum?id=1PL1NIMMrw
30. Wei, J., Wang, X., Schuurmans, D., Bosma, M., Xia, F., Chi, E., Le, Q.V., Zhou, D., et al.: Chain-of-thought prompting elicits reasoning in large language models. Advances in neural information processing systems **35**, 24824–24837 (2022)
31. Xu, B., Yang, A., Lin, J., Wang, Q., Zhou, C., Zhang, Y., Mao, Z.: Expertprompting: Instructing large language models to be distinguished experts. arXiv preprint arXiv:2305.14688 (2023)
32. Yang, G., Zhou, Y., Chen, X., Zhang, X., Zhuo, T.Y., Chen, T.: Chain-of-thought in neural code generation: From and for lightweight language models. IEEE Transactions on Software Engineering (2024)
33. Yao, S., Yu, D., Zhao, J., Shafran, I., Griffiths, T., Cao, Y., Narasimhan, K.: Tree of thoughts: Deliberate problem solving with large language models. Advances in Neural Information Processing Systems **36** (2024)
34. Yao, S., Zhao, J., Yu, D., Du, N., Shafran, I., Narasimhan, K., Cao, Y.: React: Synergizing reasoning and acting in language models. In: International Conference on Learning Representations (ICLR) (2023)
35. Yeo, S., Hwang, S.W., Ma, Y.S.: Chain of Grounded Objectives: Concise goal-oriented prompting for code generation. In: 39th European Conference on Object-Oriented Programming (ECOOP 2025). pp. 35–1. Schloss Dagstuhl–Leibniz-Zentrum für Informatik (2025)
36. Zheng, Z., Ning, K., Zhong, Q., Chen, J., Chen, W., Guo, L., Wang, W., Wang, Y.: Towards an understanding of large language models in software engineering tasks. Empirical Software Engineering **30**(2) (Dec 2024). https://doi.org/10.1007/s10664-024-10602-0, https://doi.org/10.1007/s10664-024-10602-0

A Examples of Prompts

LiveCodeBench prompt was standardized with function declarations extracted directly from the ground-truth code for consistency. Examples of problem descriptions on HumanEval and LiveCodeBench are provided in Table 5.

Table 5 Examples of Problem Descriptions on HumanEval and LiveCodeBench

HumanEval Prompt

```
def separate_paren_groups(paren_string: str) -> List[str]:
    """
    Input is a string containing groups of parentheses.
    Separate groups into individual balanced strings.
    >>> separate_paren_groups('( ) (( )) (( )( ))')
    ['()', '(())', '(()())']
    """

Write a Python code for the problem.
DO NOT generate any test cases or descriptions.
Package your code in ```python ... ```.
```

LiveCodeBench Prompt

```
You are given a string s consisting only of uppercase English
 letters. You can apply some operations to this string where,
 in one operation, you can remove any occurrence of one of
 the substrings "AB" or "CD" from s. Return the minimum
 possible length of the resulting string that you can obtain.
Note that the string concatenates after removing the
 substring and could produce new "AB" or "CD" substrings.

Example 1:
Input: s = "ABFCACDB"
Output: 2
Explanation: We can do the following operations:
- Remove the substring "ABFCACDB", so s = "FCACDB".
- Remove the substring "FCACDB", so s = "FCAB".
- Remove the substring "FCAB", so s = "FC".
So the resulting length of the string is 2.
It can be shown that it is the minimum length thatwe can
 obtain.

Example 2:
Input: s = "ACBBD"
Output: 5
Explanation: We cannot do any operations on the string so the
            length remains the same.

Constraints:
1 <= s.length <= 100
s consists only of uppercase English letters.

class Solution:
    def minLength(self, s: str) -> int:\n

Write a Python code for the problem.
DO NOT generate any test cases or descriptions.
Package your code in ```python ... ```.
```

LusGen: Leveraging LLMs for Safety-Critical Lustre Design and Requirements Traceability

Yili Jiang[1*], Zhuoran Yan[1**], Ning Ge[1,2,3***], Yuan Wang[1], Jiahao Weng[1], and Chunming Hu[1,3]

[1] Beihang University, Beijing, China
[2] Zhongguancun Laboratory, Beijing, China
[3] State Key Laboratory of Complex & Critical Software Environment, Beijing, China
{jiangyili,nathony,gening,ayuan,wengjiahao,hucm}@buaa.edu.cn

Abstract. Safety-critical systems require precise software modeling and requirements traceability, with Lustre widely used for formal design. Large language models (LLMs) struggle with Lustre's syntax and semantics. We propose LusGen, the first LLM-based Lustre generation approach that integrates domain knowledge via prompt engineering and retrieval-augmented generation, combined with syntax checking and semantic verification feedback for iterative refinement. LusGen also enables fine-grained requirements-to-design traceability compliant with DO-178C. We conduct an empirical study revealing hallucination patterns in Lustre generation to guide our approach. Evaluations on four datasets show that LusGen improves syntax correctness to 98%, semantic correctness to 94%, and achieves over 88% accuracy in traceability, demonstrating practical industrial applicability. We also construct a benchmark dataset to advance future research.

Keywords: LLMs · Lustre · Formal Verification · Safety-Critical System · Prompt Engineering.

1 Introduction

Safety-critical systems [15], such as medical devices, flight control, and nuclear facilities, require high-assurance software. To meet rigorous certification standards, model-driven engineering (MDE) is increasingly adopted [2,24,6,18,28,8]. DO-178C [26] provides comprehensive guidance for quality assurance across the avionic software lifecycle, emphasizing objectives such as requirements traceability and verification [7]. Domain-specific safety standards exist in other fields: ISO 26262 [23] defines ASIL levels for automotive systems, while IEC 60880 [16] governs the development of software used in nuclear safety systems, focusing on determinism and rigorous verification. These standards share the common goal

* Equal contribution.
** Equal contribution.
*** Corresponding author.

E. Albert and C. Pasareanu (Eds.): FASE 2026, LNCS 16504, pp. 64–85, 2026.
https://doi.org/10.1007/978-3-032-22774-4_4

of ensuring software reliability through structured, traceable, and verifiable development processes. To this end, safety-critical systems often use SCADE [4], Simulink [14], or Lustre[4] [12] for software design, verify correctness through simulation or formal methods, and generate code automatically using certified tools.

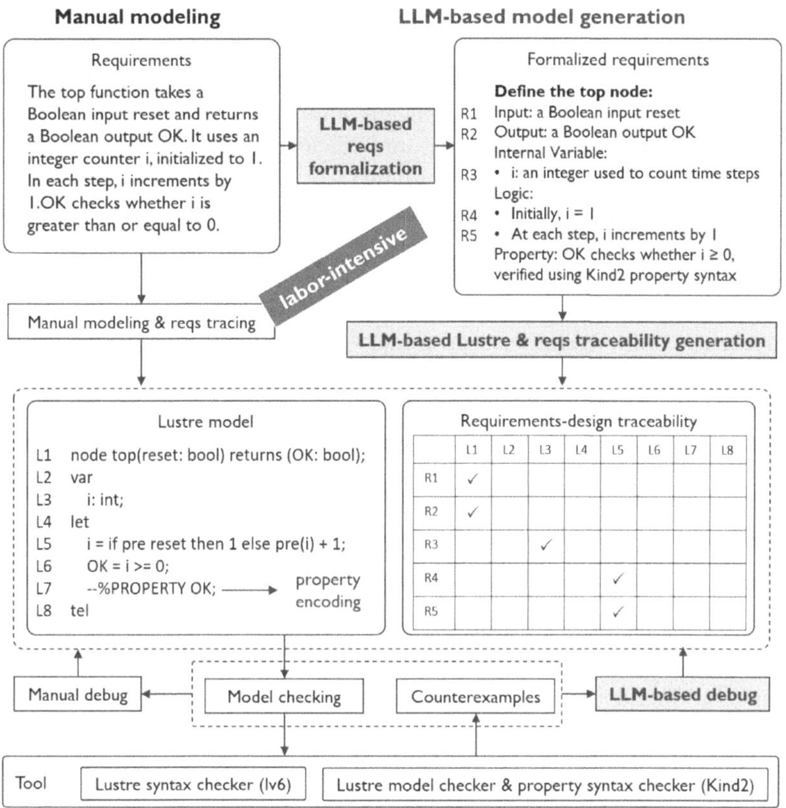

Fig. 1. Problem Statement

Constructing detailed design models for safety-critical systems often requires substantial manual effort due to intricate logic and timing constraints. Although graphical modeling tools such as Simulink provide intuitive visual representations, they may introduce additional overhead when modeling detailed logic for systems with numerous signals and constraints. Moreover, manual model construction is prone to inconsistencies and specification errors, which can further

[4] Lustre forms the formal language core underlying SCADE and is excellent for formal analysis and academic research.

increase verification and debugging efforts. As shown in Figure 1, manual modeling is time-consuming and error-prone, especially for complex systems. Using the airborne wind speed system (8 requirements, 159 lines of Lustre model) as an example, manual Lustre modeling takes approximately 39.8 minutes, whereas Simulink graphical modeling requires 92.6 minutes, more than doubling the effort. These measured times explicitly cover only the manual modeling phase, excluding subsequent formal verification or review processes. Requirement-design traceability is typically limited to the function level, as linking to Lustre code lines is highly labor-intensive. Moreover, debugging design bugs requires manual interpretation of verification feedback, adding significant cost. These issues highlight the need for an intelligent approach to design modeling, accurate requirements-design traceability, and efficient debugging, aimed at reducing manual effort and enhancing design quality.

Large language models (LLMs) have shown strong performance in generating code for general-purpose languages (e.g., Python, Java), improving development efficiency [31,22,25]. However, their performance drops significantly on domain-specific languages (DSLs) like Lustre due to limited training data, distinctive syntax and semantics, and a lack of embedded domain knowledge [10]. Existing techniques like syntax prompting [17], knowledge injection [11], and fine-tuning [13] have shown promise in other DSLs but remain rarely applied to Lustre. To date, there are no dedicated studies on LLM-based Lustre generation, leaving automated modeling largely unexplored. Moreover, requirement traceability and bug fixing remain unaddressed challenges.

To address these challenges, we propose LusGen, a novel approach for generating high-quality Lustre designs and fine-grained requirement-to-design traceability matrices using LLMs guided by domain-specific knowledge. A key difficulty lies in LLMs' limited understanding of Lustre syntax, verification property specification, and traceability principles. To overcome this, we conduct an empirical study on the Lustre model and traceability generation, revealing how domain knowledge can effectively guide LLM outputs. Based on these insights, LusGen integrates three components: requirements formalization, Lustre and property generation, and traceability generation, all powered by LLMs. Crucially, LusGen incorporates syntax and semantic checkers based on formal verification to provide feedback and iteratively refine the generated results. We constructed four datasets and defined evaluation metrics. Results show that LusGen improves Lustre generation, raising syntax correctness to 98% and semantic correctness to 94% compared to the SOTA approach. For requirements traceability generation, LusGen achieves over 88% accuracy, reaching a level suitable for industrial application. We conduct experiments using two representative LLMs, demonstrating that LusGen exhibits strong generalizability across different LLMs.

The contribution of this paper can be summarized as follows:

- We present the first systematic taxonomy of hallucinations in LLM-based Lustre generation, covering Lustre, property specification, and requirements traceability tasks. This study not only reveals the key failure patterns of

LLMs in formal modeling but also establishes a foundational understanding to guide future improvements in LLM-driven Lustre design.
- We propose **LusGen**, the first LLM-based approach for Lustre generation. LusGen takes free-form natural language requirements as input and performs automated requirements formalization, domain knowledge infusion via prompt engineering and RAG, and iterative refinement through model checking feedback. This comprehensive approach significantly improves the correctness of the generated Lustre model. In addition, LusGen supports fine-grained requirements-to-design traceability aligned with safety-critical standards such as DO-178C, advancing the practical applicability of LLMs in certified software development.
- We create the first benchmark dataset for Lustre generation and fine-grained requirements traceability, enabling standardized, reproducible evaluation to advance research and ensure fair comparisons.

2 Preliminaries and Related Work

2.1 Preliminaries

Lustre language. Safety-critical systems, such as those in avionics, automotive control, and railway signaling, are typically embedded systems that require precise timing and deterministic behavior. In industrial practice, these systems often rely on C code for efficiency and hardware-level control. However, as an imperative language, C lacks explicit timing semantics, making it error-prone, hard to verify, and difficult to maintain—especially under real-time constraints. Lustre, a synchronous dataflow language, addresses these issues by providing precise timing semantics, deterministic execution. In Lustre, system behavior is specified using nodes, which are modular computational units that define input/output streams and their synchronous dataflow relations. It supports formal verification, making it well-suited for specifying and analyzing safety-critical system behaviors. In model-based development workflows, Lustre is widely used to model and verify critical control functions before generating certified C code for deployment. C code automatically generated from Lustre preserves these formal properties, facilitating better structure, traceability, and compliance with safety standards such as DO-178C or IEC 61508 [1]. Compared to hand-written C, Lustre offers a more reliable and verifiable foundation for embedded software development. Despite its advantages, constructing Lustre models remains a highly manual and expertise-intensive task, requiring engineers to carefully encode timing logic and data dependencies. Due to the significant differences between Lustre and general-purpose programming languages, LLMs trained mainly on mainstream code corpora often perform poorly when generating correct Lustre models. This highlights both the practical importance and the technical challenges of automated Lustre model generation.

Lustre model checkers. lv6 is a Lustre compiler and static analysis tool supporting parsing, syntax checking, type checking, contract checking, and intermediate representation generation. Kind2 is an SMT-based automatic model checker for safety properties of finite-state or infinite-state synchronous reactive systems expressed in Lustre language. It takes as input Lustre models annotated with properties to be proven invariant and outputs for each property either a confirmation or a counterexample, i.e., a sequence of inputs that falsifies the property. Kind2 verifies that the property P is invariant for the system S using a combination of different induction-based model checking engines: K-induction [5], IC3 [3] and various invariant generation methods [29].

2.2 Related work

Lustre generation. DSL generation with LLMs remains challenging. Recent studies enhance performance by integrating domain knowledge and verification feedback. Zhong et al. [32] introduced a RAG-based method in EDA, building retrieval corpora from design artifacts to enrich prompts and iteratively correct Verilog code using error logs and expert knowledge. Wang et al. [30] conducted an empirical study on SysML behavior generation using LLMs by introducing the feedback of syntax checking and semantic checking. Sevenhuijsen et al.[27] proposed VeCoGen, which generates safety-critical DSLs from natural language and ACSL specs, using Frama-C feedback for iterative refinement. Liu et al. [21] developed FDC, which extracts requirements and constraints from documents, reformulates them into model-friendly prompts, and guides LLMs to generate safety-critical C code with embedded safety rules. To our knowledge, no prior work has addressed LLM-based generation for the Lustre language.

Requirements traceability. Early requirements traceability studies relied on static analysis and heuristics. Ghabi et al.[9] analyzed method call chains using structural patterns to infer requirement-code traces. More recently, learning-based methods address the semantic gap between natural language and code. Lin et al.[19] proposed T-BERT, leveraging transfer learning with BERT variants and online negative sampling to improve trace prediction, outperforming traditional IR and RNN methods. Unlike prior work focused on general-purpose code or coarse-grained links, our approach targets fine-grained traceability between formalized requirements and domain-specific models, integrating LLM-based tracing directly into the model generation pipeline.

3 Approach

Figure 2 presents an overview of LusGen. The core idea is to extract domain knowledge on requirement specification, Lustre modeling, property specification, and requirements traceability from empirical studies, and systematically incorporate this knowledge to guide LLMs in learning and applying it effectively. This domain knowledge is embedded through prompt engineering, RAG, and feedback-guided learning to enhance the reliability of LLM outputs. LusGen consists of four key steps: (1) extract and structure domain knowledge from empirical studies; (2) formalize unrestricted natural language requirements using LLMs; (3) generate Luster models and verification properties with LLM assistance, verify them using model checkers, and automatically debug based on the checking feedback; (4) generate a requirements-design traceability matrix using LLMs.

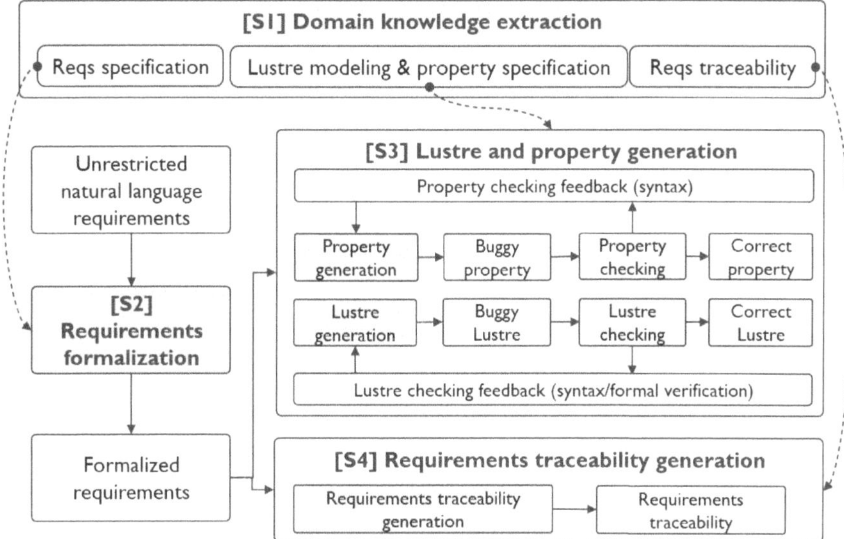

Fig. 2. LusGen Overview

3.1 Domain Knowledge Extraction

We construct a benchmark dataset based on the kind2 collection by annotating 96 Luster nodes, comprising 1,333 lines of Luster code and 98 properties. Using natural language requirements as input, we prompt a large language model (Qwen2.5-Coder-32B-Instruct) to generate corresponding Lustre models, properties, and requirements traceability matrices. We then manually analyze the generated outputs to identify hallucinations, where the model produces incorrect, inconsistent, or unsupported content concerning the given requirements. Following an existing hallucination taxonomy in code generation[20], we categorize the observed hallucinations into three major types: Lustre code errors, property errors, and traceability errors. As illustrated in Figure 3, we identify 204 Lustre code errors, 69 property errors, and 213 traceability errors among a total of 932 traceability links. This taxonomy of hallucination types provides insights that directly inform the design of LusGen.

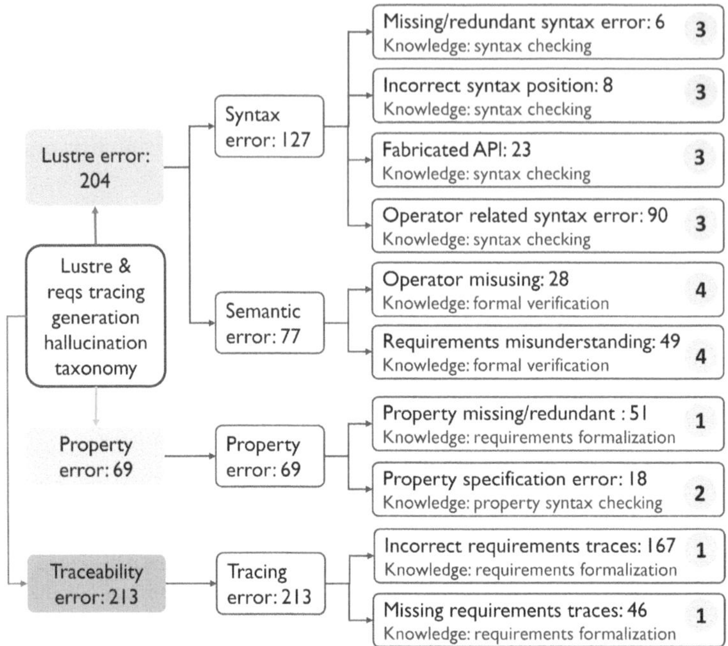

Fig. 3. Hallucination Taxonomy of Lustre & Traceability Generation.

Lustre modeling knowledge. LLM-based Lustre generation exhibits two primary types of hallucinations: syntactic errors and semantic errors. Syntactic issues include missing or redundant elements (6), incorrect syntax positions (8), fabricated APIs (23), and operator-related syntax errors (90). Semantic issues involve operator misuse (28) and requirements misunderstanding (49). These findings highlight the challenges LLMs face in generating syntactically and semantically correct Lustre code, emphasizing the need for a repair framework guided by syntax checking and formal verification feedback.

Property specification knowledge. LLM-based property generation exhibits two primary types of hallucinations: missing or redundant properties (51) and property specification errors (18). These issues reflect the LLMs' difficulty in accurately interpreting requirement specifications and generating correct property expressions. This underscores the need for a repair approach grounded in requirements formalization and property syntax checking.

Requirements traceability knowledge. LLM-based requirements traceability generation exhibits two primary types of hallucinations: incorrect requirement traces (167) and missing traces (46). These results highlight the limitations of LLMs in ensuring the correctness and completeness of requirement-to-model traceability. This underscores the need for a requirements formalization-driven approach to improve traceability accuracy and reliability.

3.2 LLM-based Requirements Formalization

During Lustre model generation, LLMs often hallucinate property errors and tracing errors due to misinterpreting requirements. To address this, we introduce a three-stage requirement formalization process: from unrestricted natural language requirements to structured XML, and then to formalized specifications. We first use a few-shot prompt to extract key elements into a structured XML format. Then, we convert XML into formalized requirements with six components, as shown in Figure 4: node name, inputs, outputs, variable declarations, logic, and properties. These formalized requirements guide the LLM in generating semantically complete Lustre models.

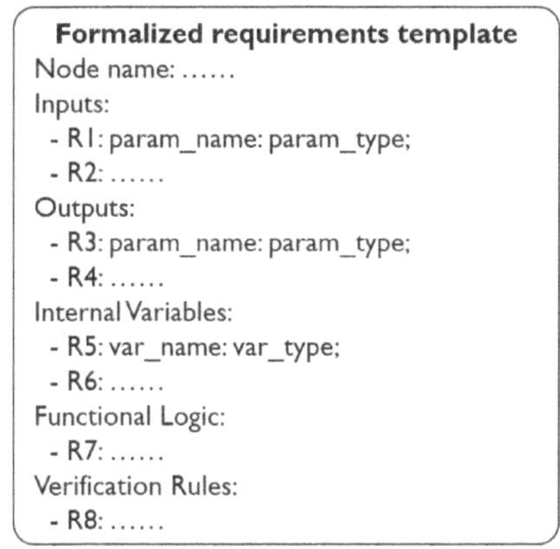

Fig. 4. Formalized Requirements Template

3.3 LLM-based Lustre and Property Generation

Figure 5 illustrates the workflow of Lustre generation, which consists of two main stages. First, verification properties are generated with the aid of syntax-checking feedback. Then, Lustre model is produced by guiding the LLM using both Lustre syntax rules and feedback from the Kind2 model checker to ensure syntactic and semantic correctness.

Property Generation Properties encode formal behavioral expectations and are essential for verifying Lustre models. As shown in Figure 6, we design a feedback-driven prompt that assigns the LLM an expert role, provides domain knowledge about property specification, and uses formalized requirements with a one-shot example to guide property generation. We then apply Kind2 for syntax

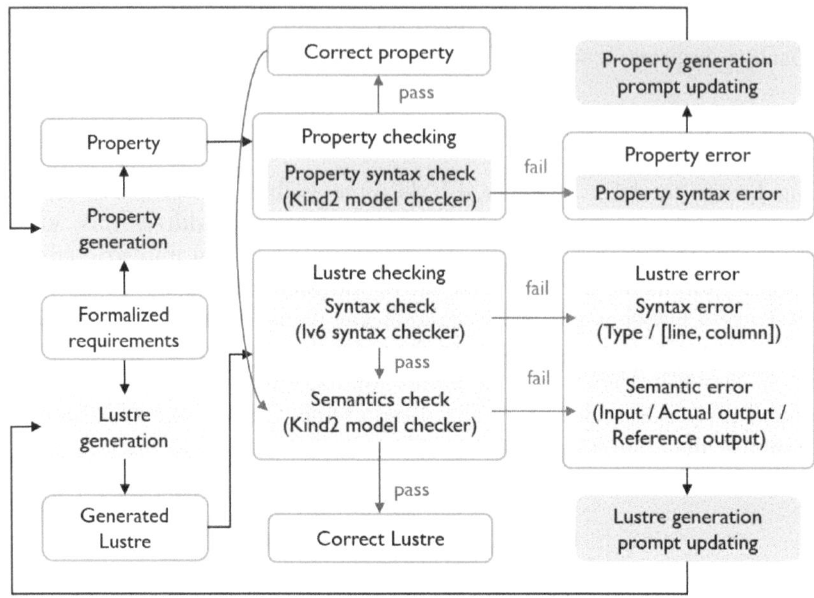

Fig. 5. LLM-based Lustre and Property Generation

checking and iteratively refine the prompt using its feedback. This approach improves reliability and reduces hallucinations by combining explicit instruction, domain grounding, and tool-assisted repair.

Role Definition	You are an expert in the Lustre language and proficient in using Kind2 model checker and expressing properties.
Domain Knowledge	Please strictly refer to the following knowledge context to generate properties: {context}
Task Instruction	Generate property based on the following information: (detailed instructions)
Initial Input (Req)	Formalized task requirements: {req}
Iterative Input (property & feedback)	The following property failed syntax check: {property} syntax feedback + Fix guidance: {Kind2 property syntax report}
One-shot Example	For the requirement (req example), the generated example is (Lustre and property example).

Fig. 6. Prompt Template of Property Generation

Lustre Generation. Algorithm 1 presents an iterative process for Lustre generation using LLMs with syntax and semantic feedback. It takes formalized requirements and leverages RAG to provide task-specific domain knowledge. The LLM generates a candidate model, which is first checked by the lv6 tool for syntax correctness. If errors are found, feedback is extracted and used to update the prompt. Once the syntax is correct, the Kind2 verifier checks the semantic validity of the model. Any verification failures are similarly used to refine the prompt. This loop continues until a valid Lustre model is produced or the maximum number of iterations is reached. We set distinct limits for the iterative repair process based on repair types: $\theta = 2$ steps for syntactic repair and $\theta = 5$ steps for semantic repair, balancing effectiveness and efficiency. In practice, most errors are resolved within five iterations, while further steps yield diminishing returns. Figure 7 shows the prompt structure for Lustre generation.

Algorithm 1 LLM-based Lustre Generation with Feedback

Require: Formalized requirements R, Domain database D
Ensure: Verified Lustre program P
1: Initialize vector database V
2: Initialize LLM with RAG capability
3: Initialize domain knowledge context $K \leftarrow \text{RAGRetrieve}(R, V)$
4: Initialize prompt $p \leftarrow$ `BuildPrompt`(R, K)
5: **for** $i = 1$ to θ **do**
6: $P \leftarrow$ `LLMGenerateLus`(p)
7: *// Step 1: Lustre syntax checking using lv6*
8: $sRes \leftarrow$ `SyntaxCheck`(P)
9: **if** SynErr(sRes) == True **then**
10: $f_s \leftarrow$ `ExtractSyntaxFeedback`$(sRes)$
11: $K \leftarrow$ `RAGRetrieve`$(R + f_s, V)$
12: $p \leftarrow$ `UpdatePrompt`(R, K, f_s)
13: **continue**
14: **end if**
15: *// Step 2: Lustre semantic verification using Kind2*
16: $vRes \leftarrow$ `SemanticCheck`(P)
17: **if** $vRes$ indicates failure **then**
18: $f_v \leftarrow$ `ExtractSemanticFeedback`$(vRes)$
19: $K \leftarrow$ `RAGRetrieve`$(R + f_v, V)$
20: $p \leftarrow$ `UpdatePrompt`(R, K, f_v)
21: **continue**
22: **end if**
23: **return** P *// Correct Lustre*
24: **end for**
25: **return** Failure (Max iterations reached)

3.4 LLM-based Requirements Traceability Generation

We employ LLMs to automate fine-grained requirement-to-design traceability, aligning with safety-critical standards like DO-178C. To enhance accuracy, we assign unique IDs to each requirement and line of Lustre model—essential for correct mapping, as unstructured inputs often lead to trace errors. As shown in Figure 8, our domain-specific prompt includes five components: (1) Role assignment as a senior software engineer; (2) DO-178C-based domain knowledge (e.g., completeness, bidirectionality); (3) Clear task definition; (4) Structured input with requirements and Lustre model; and (5) A one-shot example. Generated trace matrices are manually reviewed for completeness and correctness.

Role Definition	You are an expert in the Lustre language and proficient in using the Kind2 formal verification tool.
Domain Knowledge	Please strictly refer to the following knowledge context to generate Lustre code: {context}
Task Instruction	Generate Lustre model based on the following information: (detailed instructions)
Initial Input (Req)	Formalized task requirements: {req}
Iterative Input (Lustre & feedback)	The following model failed verification: {Lustre} Verification tool feedback + Fix guidance: {lv6 or kind2 reports}
One-shot Example	For the requirement (req example), the generated example is (lustre example)

Fig. 7. Prompt Template of Lustre Generation

This traceability template is embedded in our generation pipeline, enabling automatic trace generation immediately after the Lustre model is produced, guided by domain-specific prompts.

Role Definition	You are now a senior software engineer specializing in safety-critical syst ems.Your mission is to (detailed mission) Any inaccuracies in traceability may lead to catastrophic failures, so rigor and precision are paramount.
Domain Knowledge	According to DO-178C, traceability between requirements and detailed design (including Lustre model) must adhere to: 1. Completeness: (detailed info) 2. Bidirectional Traceability: (detailed info)
Task Instructions	Your Task: For the input requirements and Lustre, genrate traceability between requirements and Lustre line, ensuring compliance with DO-178C.
Input (Req & Lustre)	The requirements and model to generate traceability are as follows: - Requirements: {req} - Lustre {Lustre model}
One-shot example	Example: Airborne Wind Speed System Node - Input requirements: (req example) - Input Lustre code: (Lustre example) - Traceability output: (tracing example)

Fig. 8. Prompt Template of Requirements Traceability Generation

4 Evaluation Design

4.1 Research Questions (RQs)

RQ1 (property generation): To what extent does LusGen enhance the accuracy of LLM-generated properties in Lustre models?
RQ2 (iteration efficiency): How does the number of iterative refinement cycles influence the efficiency and convergence point for achieving high-quality Lustre models in LusGen?
RQ3 (Lustre generation): To what extent can LusGen mitigate syntactic and semantic hallucinations in Lustre models generated by LLMs?
RQ4 (Requirements traceability generation): How effective can LusGen generate correct requirements traceability matrix?

4.2 Dataset

To assess the effectiveness and generalizability of LusGen, we construct a comprehensive benchmark consisting of four sub-datasets, as shown in Table 1. The benchmark includes 63 Lustre nodes from three sources: the Kind2 dataset (D1 and D2), VeCoGen [27] (D3), and an industry-provided cockpit wind speed display system (WSDS) (D4). The Kind2 dataset is split into two subsets: D1 (24 cases without formal properties) and D2 (26 cases with 53 formal properties). D3 includes 5 cases and 10 properties, while D4 contains 8 cases and 14 properties. The benchmark dataset is available online.[5]

Table 1. Dataset Statistics

Sets	Source	# Lustre Node	# Properties
D1	Lustre examples	24	0
D2	Kind2 dataset	26	53
D3	VeCoGen Dataset	5	10
D4	WSDS	8	14
Sum	/	63	77

4.3 Baselines

The core component of LusGen is Lustre model generation. We compare LusGen with VeCoGen [27], an LLM-based safety-critical C code generator guided by formal verification, enabling a fair comparison within a verification-driven generation framework.

4.4 Evaluation Metrics

We designed the evaluation metrics for three RQs in Table 2.

[5] The dataset is available at https://github.com/jiangyili446/LusGen-Benchmark.git.

Table 2. Evaluation Metrics

RQ	Metric	Formula	Explanation
RQ1	Property correctness (P-corr@1)	P-corr@1 $= \frac{N_c^P}{N_a^P}$	N_c^P denotes the number of generated correct properties, and N_a^P is the total number of generated properties.
RQ2	Syntax correctness (Syn@1)	Syn@1 $= \frac{N_g^L}{N_a^L}$	N_g^L denotes the number of generated Lustre models that pass syntax checking, and N_a^L denotes the total number of generated Lustre models.
RQ3	Semantic correctness (Sem@1)	Sem@1 $= \frac{N_s^P}{N_a^P}$	N_g^P denotes the number of properties for which the generated Lustre models are verified as correct. N_a^P denotes the total number of properties.
RQ4	Traceability accuracy (T-acc)	T-acc $= \frac{2 \cdot P \cdot R}{P + R}$	Precision P $= \frac{TP}{TP + FP}$, recall R $= \frac{TP}{TP + FN}$, where TP denotes correctly traced requirements in the generated matrices, FP denotes incorrectly traced requirements, and FN denotes missing requirement traces. The F1 score (T-acc) measures the accuracy of the generated traceability matrix against the ground truth.

4.5 Evaluation Process Design

Process. Figure 9 depicts the evaluation process. For RQ1, we set up three groups: M_O^P with original unrestricted requirements, M_F^P with formalized requirements, and LusGen combining formalized requirements with Kind2-based property syntax checking, evaluated using P-corr@1. For RQ2, we investigate the optimal number of iterative repairs by applying the LusGen method with a varying number of iterations (0 to 9). We then assess the quality convergence point of the generated Lustre models using syntax and semantic checkers. For RQ3's syntax correctness, three groups are considered: M^L without RAG and syntax checking, VeCoGen removing only RAG, and LusGen as the full method; similarly for semantic correctness, where M^L excludes RAG and semantic checking and VeCoGen excludes RAG, with Syn@1 and Sem@1 as metrics. For RQ4, we generate traceability matrices from formalized requirements and Luster models using LusGen, manually annotate results, and evaluate them with T-acc.

Tool setting. Table 3 summarizes the tool settings used in our experiments. Syntax and semantic checking are fully automated through formal tools integrated within a scripted evaluation pipeline. For each generation strategy and dataset, the pipeline sequentially performs model generation, verification, and metric computation. We use four representative LLMs, including two open-source models (Qwen2.5-Coder-32B-Instruct and DeepSeek-Chat) and two closed-source models (GPT-4o and Gemini-2.5-Flash).

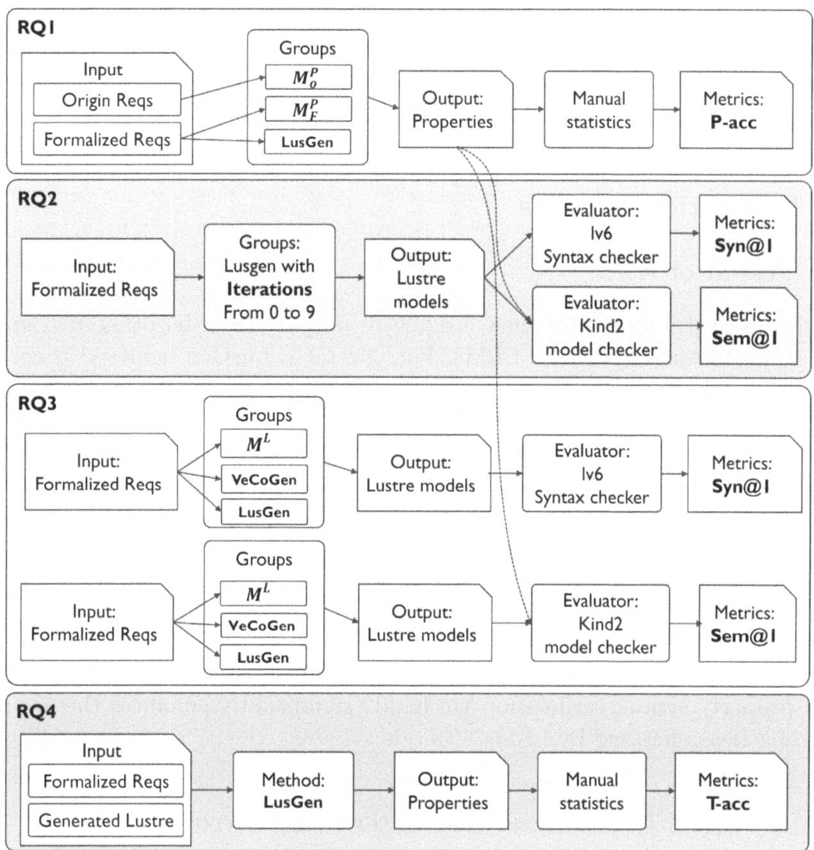

Fig. 9. Evaluation Process Design

Table 3. Tool Setting in the Evaluation

Module	Tool	Usage
LLM	1. Qwen2.5-Coder-32B-Instruct 2. GPT-4o 3. Deepseek-chat 4. Gemini2.5-flash	Lustre, property and requiremens traceability generation
RAG	Dashscope text-embedding-v3	Vector encoder for reqs and domain knowledge
Lustre Checker	lv6 v6.107.1 Kind2 v1.4	Lustre syntax checker Lustre model verifier & Property syntax checker

Participants. Our study involved a total of four participants: two graduate students (a doctoral student and a master's student) and two domain experts. The graduate students possessed expertise in formal methods and the Lustre language. The evaluation was structured as follows: RQ1 (Property Correctness) and RQ4 (Traceability Correctness) were manually assessed by the two graduate students, and their results were subsequently reviewed and validated by the two domain experts. RQ2 (Lustre Syntax Correctness) and RQ3 (Lustre Semantic Correctness) were evaluated automatically using formal verification and syntax checking tools.

5 Evaluation Results

5.1 Result of RQ1

As shown in Table 4, LusGen consistently outperforms the other two groups across all datasets and both LLMs. For Qwen2.5, LusGen achieved a correctness rate of 74.4%, significantly higher than 29.3% for M_O^P and 39.0% for M_F^P. Similarly, for GPT-4o, LusGen reached 69.5%, outperforming 47.6% for M_O^P and 56.1% for M_F^P. The integration of requirement formalization M_F^P provides a substantial initial gain, notably for Deepseek, raising its rate from a baseline of 13.4% to 68.2%. With the full LusGen pipeline, Deepseek reaches 70.7%. For Gemini, the rate improves from 28.0% (M_O^P) and 59.7% (M_F^P) to 63.4%. The improvements are particularly pronounced on datasets D2 and D3, where LusGen more than doubles the correctness compared to the baseline groups. On D4, all groups performed better overall, but LusGen still leads or matches the highest accuracy. These results demonstrate that integrating requirement formalization with property syntax verification via Kind2 significantly enhances the accuracy of properties generated by LLMs.

Table 4. Results of RQ1 (Property Correctness)

Dataset	Qwen2.5			GPT-4o			Deepseek-chat			Gemini2.5-flash		
	M_O^P	M_F^P	LusGen	M_O^P	M_F^P	LusGen	M_O^P	M_F^P	LusGen	M_O^P	M_F^P	LusGen
D2	17/58	22/58	41/58	25/58	26/58	36/58	8/58	36/58	36/58	19/58	34/58	37/58
D3	2/10	2/10	8/10	0/10	7/10	7/10	0/10	8/10	9/10	0/10	3/10	6/10
D4	5/14	8/14	12/14	14/14	13/14	14/14	3/14	12/14	13/14	4/14	12/14	9/14
Sum	29.3%	39.0%	74.4%	47.6%	56.1%	69.5%	13.4%	68.2%	70.7%	28.0%	59.7%	63.4%

5.2 Result of RQ2

To effectively address RQ2 regarding the optimal trade-off between repair cycles and model quality, we conducted a study to analyze the convergence behavior of LusGen. We tracked the improvement in both syntactic and semantic compliance across nine iterative cycles, employing two distinct LLMs (Deepseek and Qwen) and performing two repetitions for robust validation, as shown in Figure 10. The results indicate a clear difference in the convergence speed between the two refinement stages. For syntactic quality (Figure 10, left), the rate of models successfully passing the Lustre syntax checker demonstrated remarkably fast convergence, consistently reaching its maximum quality point after only two iterations. This rapid stabilization highlights the high efficiency of the syntax-checking feedback loop in eliminating structural hallucinations. However, achieving convergence for semantic correctness required a deeper refinement process. The number of passed Lustre properties (Figure 10, right) showed continued, stable improvement until the system reached its best-performing quality plateau at five iterations. Beyond this point, further iterations yielded marginal or negligible gains. Consequently, the study identifies the optimal convergence setting for LusGen, balancing efficiency and quality, as requiring two iterations for initial syntactic correction followed by five iterations dedicated to semantic and formal property verification.

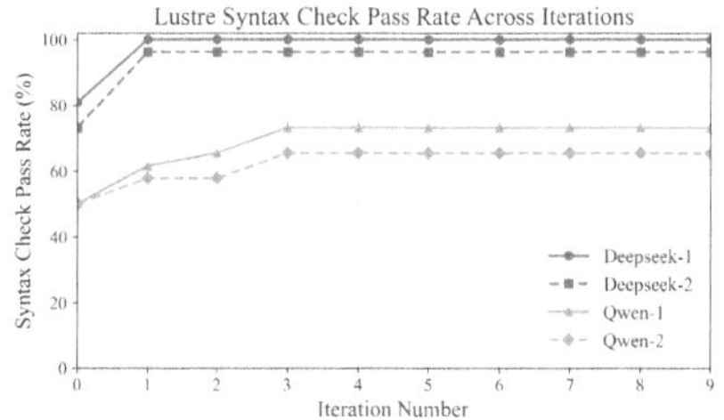

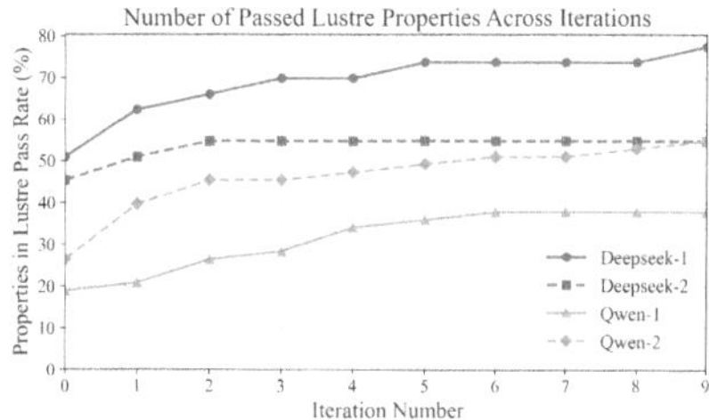

Fig. 10. Results of Lustre Syntactic and Semantic Analysis Across Iterations

5.3 Result of RQ3

For evaluating Lustre syntax correctness, we compared three groups: M^L, which excludes both RAG and syntax checking; VeCoGen, which excludes RAG and requirements formalization; and LusGen, which incorporates the full pipeline. The evaluation metric is the syntax correctness rate, as shown in Table 5. Across all datasets and both LLMs, LusGen consistently achieves the highest syntax correctness rates. Specifically, for Deepseek-chat, LusGen increases the syntax correctness rate from 84.1% (VeCoGen) to 93.7%. The most compelling result is achieved by Gemini2.5-flash, where LusGen elevates the correctness rate from 93.7% (VeCoGen) to an impressive 98.4%. The gains are especially notable on datasets D2 and D3, where LusGen reaches near-perfect correctness, demonstrating the effectiveness of integrating both RAG and syntax checking. These results validate that LusGen's combined approach substantially reduces syntactic errors in Lustre models generated by LLMs.

To confirm that the observed performance gains were not coincidental, we performed six independent runs for each LLM and method configuration. The detailed results are summarized in Table 6. The consistently low variance for LusGen (e.g., 1.029% for Gemini2.5-flash) across all models, coupled with its highest mean syntax correctness rate, confirms the robustness and repeatability of its Lustre models' generation capabilities.

Table 5. Results of RQ3 (Lustre Syntax Correctness)

Dataset	Qwen2.5			GPT-4o			Deepseek-chat			Gemini2.5-flash		
	M^L	VeCoGen	LusGen	M^L	VeCoGen	LusGen	M^L	VeCoGen	LusGen	M^L	VeCoGen	LusGen
D1	7/24	18/24	21/24	17/24	17/24	23/24	7/24	23/24	23/24	19/24	23/24	23/24
D2	3/26	19/26	21/26	11/26	24/26	25/26	18/26	21/26	25/26	16/26	23/26	26/26
D3	1/5	1/5	5/5	1/5	5/5	5/5	1/5	3/5	5/5	3/5	5/5	5/5
D4	5/8	7/8	8/8	2/8	8/8	6/8	3/8	6/8	6/8	5/8	8/8	8/8
Sum	25.4%	71.4%	87.3%	49.2%	85.7%	93.7%	46.0%	84.1%	93.7%	68.3%	93.7%	98.4%

Table 6. Replicate Experiments of RQ3 (Lustre Syntax Correctness)

Times	Qwen2.5			GPT-4o			Deepseek-chat			Gemini2.5-flash		
	M^L	VeCoGen	LusGen	M^L	VeCoGen	LusGen	M^L	VeCoGen	LusGen	M^L	VeCoGen	LusGen
1	25.4%	71.4%	87.3%	49.2%	85.7%	93.7%	46.0%	84.1%	93.7%	68.3%	93.7%	98.4%
2	23.1%	53.8%	76.3%	43.6%	74.4%	92.1%	59.0%	84.6%	84.2%	60.6%	88.9%	92.3%
3	25.6%	56.4%	71.1%	51.3%	78.9%	76.9%	56.4%	84.2%	84.6%	64.1%	86.8%	94.9%
4	23.1%	51.3%	65.8%	46.2%	81.6%	84.6%	59.0%	71.1%	87.2%	64.1%	89.2%	91.9%
5	30.8%	50.0%	66.7%	46.2%	86.8%	82.1%	53.8%	81.6%	84.6%	53.8%	89.5%	94.9%
6	20.5%	48.7%	65.8%	46.2%	84.2%	87.2%	48.7%	76.3%	87.2%	51.3%	87.2%	92.1%
Mean	**24.7%**	**55.3%**	**72.2%**	**47.1%**	**81.9%**	**86.1%**	**53.8%**	**80.3%**	**86.9%**	**60.4%**	**89.2%**	**94.1%**
Variance	**1.426%**	**3.416%**	**3.460%**	**1.109%**	**1.914%**	**2.568%**	**2.214%**	**2.246%**	**1.461%**	**2.683%**	**1.001%**	**1.029%**

For evaluation on Lustre semantic correctness, we evaluated three groups: M^L, which excludes both RAG and semantic checking; VeCoGen, which excludes only RAG; and LusGen, the full approach integrating both retrieval-augmented generation and semantic verification. The metric used is Sem@1, representing the proportion of properties verified as correct. As shown in Table 7, LusGen demonstrates a massive and consistent improvement in semantic correctness across all models, especially when compared to the naive baseline M^L. For Qwen2.5, the semantic correctness rate rises dramatically from 1.4% in M^L and 42.9% in VeCoGen to a final rate of 57.1% with LusGen. Similarly, GPT-4o sees an increase from 1.4% (M^L) and 42.9% (VeCoGen) to 62.9%. The effectiveness of LusGen is most pronounced in the strong-performing models. For Deepseek-chat, LusGen boosts the rate from 40.3% (VeCoGen) to 64.9%. The best overall performance is achieved by Gemini2.5-flash, where LusGen elevates the semantic correctness from an already strong 79.2% (VeCoGen) to an exceptional 93.5%. These results demonstrate that LusGen's combined strategy effectively enhances the semantic validity of Lustre models generated by LLMs.

To ensure the reliability of the semantic correctness results, we conducted six independent experimental runs, as detailed in Table 8. The consistently low variance for LusGen across all models (e.g., 2.98% for Deepseek-chat and 4.88%

for Gemini2.5-flash) indicates that the formal verification feedback mechanism is highly robust and repeatable, demonstrating its stability in achieving high-quality Lustre models.

Table 7. Results of RQ3 (Lustre Semantic Correctness)

Dataset	Qwen2.5			GPT-4o			Deepseek-chat			Gemini2.5-flash		
	M^L	VeCoGen	LusGen	M^L	VeCoGen	LusGen	M^L	VeCoGen	LusGen	M^L	VeCoGen	LusGen
D2	1/53	25/53	24/53	1/53	22/53	33/53	7/53	21/53	37/53	4/53	42/53	50/53
D3	0/10	6/10	9/10	0/10	6/10	6/10	2/10	6/10	8/10	0/10	7/10	8/10
D4	0/14	2/14	11/14	0/14	5/14	8/14	3/14	4/14	5/14	8/14	12/14	14/14
Sum	1.4%	42.9%	57.1%	1.4%	42.9%	62.9%	15.6%	40.3%	64.9%	15.6%	79.2%	93.5%

Table 8. Replicate Experiments of RQ3 (Lustre Semantic Correctness)

Times	Qwen2.5			GPT-4o			Deepseek-chat			Gemini2.5-flash		
	M^L	VeCoGen	LusGen	M^L	VeCoGen	LusGen	M^L	VeCoGen	LusGen	M^L	VeCoGen	LusGen
1	1.4%	42.9%	57.1%	1.4%	42.9%	62.9%	15.6%	40.3%	64.9%	15.6%	79.2%	93.5%
2	0.0%	29.9%	46.8%	0.0%	36.4%	62.3%	15.6%	75.3%	85.7%	7.8%	71.4%	100.0%
3	0.0%	27.3%	42.9%	3.9%	59.7%	54.5%	14.3%	76.6%	80.5%	10.4%	85.7%	100.0%
4	0.0%	20.8%	36.4%	7.8%	57.1%	70.1%	15.6%	70.1%	79.2%	16.9%	68.8%	94.8%
5	0.0%	29.9%	31.2%	15.6%	54.5%	64.9%	18.2%	79.2%	83.1%	23.4%	94.8%	70.1%
6	0.0%	26.0%	37.7%	5.2%	64.9%	76.6%	2.6%	71.4%	76.6%	19.5%	62.3%	100.0%
Mean	**0.2%**	**29.4%**	**42.0%**	**5.6%**	**52.6%**	**65.2%**	**13.6%**	**68.8%**	**78.3%**	**15.6%**	**77.1%**	**93.9%**
Variance	**0.217%**	**3.018%**	**3.738%**	**2.284%**	**4.417%**	**3.065%**	**2.269%**	**5.869%**	**2.979%**	**2.347%**	**4.867%**	**4.879%**

5.4 Results of RQ4

RQ4 investigates the effectiveness of LusGen in generating correct requirements traceability matrices. We evaluate precision, recall, and their harmonic mean (F1 score, denoted as T-acc) to measure accuracy against the ground truth. As summarized in Table 9, LusGen achieves high traceability accuracy (T-acc) across all four LLMs, with scores ranging from 85.1% to 88.4%. GPT-4o demonstrates the highest overall accuracy at 88.4%, securing the most True Positives (TP=482) and the fewest False Negatives (FN=31), indicating superior Recall (fewer missed links). Deepseek-chat also performs exceptionally well with a T-acc of 88.0%, notably achieving the lowest total False Negatives (FN=10), suggesting high Recall capabilities, despite having a lower True Positive count (TP=286). Gemini2.5-flash achieves a strong T-acc of 86.5% (TP=327, FN=14), while Qwen2.5 has an overall T-acc of 85.1% (TP=437, FN=73). The results demonstrate that LusGen can effectively generate traceability matrices with high precision and recall, confirming its capability to accurately link requirements and generated Lustre models.

Table 9. Results of RQ4 (Traceability Correctness)

Dataset	Qwen2.5				GPT-4o				Deepseek-chat				Gemini2.5-flash			
	TP	FP	FN	T-acc	TP	FP	FN	T-acc	TP	FP	FN	T-acc	TP	FP	FN	T-acc
D2	262	48	53	83.8%	310	51	22	89.5%	163	35	5	89.1%	141	31	4	89.0%
D2	35	9	6	82.3%	42	12	2	81.5%	38	5	2	79.0%	66	8	4	76.3%
D3	140	23	14	88.3%	130	33	7	81.1%	85	28	3	82.1%	120	49	6	79.0%
Sum	437	80	73	85.1%	482	96	31	88.4%	286	68	10	88.0%	327	88	14	86.5%

6 Threats to Validity

Internal validity. The evaluation of property and traceability correctness involves manual annotation by two students with formal methods expertise. Although care was taken to ensure consistency, subjective bias may still exist. To mitigate the potential impact, both annotators were trained with consistent guidelines and example cases. A portion of the data was annotated by both individuals to measure inter-annotator agreement and ensure consistency. **External validity.** While the benchmark covers multiple datasets, it remains limited in scope and may not fully represent all safety-critical domains. Moreover, the evaluation is conducted on four representative LLMs, and generalizability to other LLMs or tasks remains to be further validated. Although LusGen is designed for the Lustre language, several of its core components, including the prompt engineering strategy, retrieval-augmented generation (RAG) mechanism, and the iterative feedback loop, are language-agnostic. By replacing the Lustre-specific grammar and semantic checkers with corresponding analyzers for another DSL, the same framework could be adapted to support automated model generation in other formal languages. **Construct validity.** The use of @1 metrics in RQ2 and RQ3 ignores the potential of multiple candidate generations. As future work, we plan to explore LLM output reranking.

7 Conclusion

This paper proposes LusGen, a novel approach for generating Lustre models and fine-grained requirements traceability from unrestricted inputs. It introduces the first taxonomy of hallucinations in LLM-based Lustre generation and establishes a benchmark dataset to support research and fair comparison. LusGen significantly improves model correctness and aligns traceability with safety-critical standards like DO-178C, enhancing the practical use of LLMs in certified software development.

Acknowledgment

This work was supported by the National Key Research and Development Program of China (Grant No. 2022YFB4501901).

References

1. Bell, R.: Introduction to iec 61508. In: Acm international conference proceeding series. vol. 162, pp. 3–12 (2006)
2. Burmester, S., Giese, H., Hirsch, M., Schilling, D., Tichy, M.: The fujaba real-time tool suite: model-driven development of safety-critical, real-time systems. In: Proceedings of the 27th international conference on Software engineering. pp. 670–671 (2005)
3. Cimatti, A., Griggio, A.: Software model checking via ic3. In: International Conference on Computer Aided Verification. pp. 277–293. Springer (2012)
4. Colaço, J.L., Pagano, B., Pouzet, M.: Scade 6: A formal language for embedded critical software development. In: 2017 International Symposium on Theoretical Aspects of Software Engineering (TASE). pp. 1–11. IEEE (2017)
5. Donaldson, A.F., Haller, L., Kroening, D., Rümmer, P.: Software verification using k-induction. In: International Static Analysis Symposium. pp. 351–368. Springer (2011)
6. Ge, N., Dieumegard, A., Jenn, E., Voisin, L.: Correct-by-construction specification to verified code. Journal of Software: Evolution and Process **30**(10), e1959 (2018)
7. Ge, N., Jenn, E., Breton, N., Fonteneau, Y.: Integrated formal verification of safety-critical software. International Journal on Software Tools for Technology Transfer **20**(4), 423–440 (2018)
8. Geng, R., Weng, J., Ge, N., Li, J., Hu, C.: Drem: Efficiently generating domain-specific requirements modeling tool. In: Proceedings of the 33rd ACM International Conference on the Foundations of Software Engineering. pp. 1025–1029 (2025)
9. Ghabi, A., Egyed, A.: Code patterns for automatically validating requirements-to-code traces. In: Proceedings of the 27th IEEE/ACM International Conference on Automated Software Engineering. pp. 200–209 (2012)
10. Gu, X., Chen, M., Lin, Y., Hu, Y., Zhang, H., Wan, C., Wei, Z., Xu, Y., Wang, J.: On the effectiveness of large language models in domain-specific code generation. ACM Transactions on Software Engineering and Methodology **34**(3), 1–22 (2025)
11. Gu, X., Chen, M., Lin, Y., Hu, Y., Zhang, H., Wan, C., Wei, Z., Xu, Y., Wang, J.: On the effectiveness of large language models in domain-specific code generation. ACM Transactions on Software Engineering and Methodology **34**(3), 1–22 (2025)
12. Halbwachs, N., Caspi, P., Raymond, P., Pilaud, D.: The synchronous data flow programming language lustre. Proceedings of the IEEE **79**(9), 1305–1320 (2002)
13. Joel, S., Wu, J.J., Fard, F.H.: A survey on llm-based code generation for low-resource and domain-specific programming languages. arXiv preprint arXiv:2410.03981 (2024)
14. Karris, S.T.: Introduction to Simulink with engineering applications. Orchard Publications (2006)
15. Knight, J.C.: Safety critical systems: challenges and directions. In: Proceedings of the 24th international conference on software engineering. pp. 547–550 (2002)
16. Lahtinen, J., Johansson, M., Ranta, J., Harju, H., Nevalainen, R.: Comparison between iec 60880 and iec 61508 for certification purposes in the nuclear domain. In: International Conference on Computer Safety, Reliability, and Security. pp. 55–67. Springer (2010)
17. Lamas, V., R. Luaces, M., Garcia-Gonzalez, D.: Dsl-xpert: Llm-driven generic dsl code generation. In: Proceedings of the ACM/IEEE 27th International Conference on Model Driven Engineering Languages and Systems. pp. 16–20 (2024)

18. Lamrani, I., Banerjee, A., Gupta, S.K.: Toward operational safety verification via hybrid automata mining using i/o traces of ai-enabled cps. In: SafeAI@ AAAI. pp. 186–194 (2020)
19. Lin, J., Liu, Y., Zeng, Q., Jiang, M., Cleland-Huang, J.: Traceability transformed: Generating more accurate links with pre-trained bert models. In: 2021 IEEE/ACM 43rd International Conference on Software Engineering (ICSE). pp. 324–335. IEEE (2021)
20. Liu, F., Liu, Y., Shi, L., Huang, H., Wang, R., Yang, Z., Zhang, L., Li, Z., Ma, Y.: Exploring and evaluating hallucinations in llm-powered code generation. arXiv preprint arXiv:2404.00971 (2024)
21. Liu, M., Wang, J., Lin, T., Ma, Q., Fang, Z., Wu, Y.: An empirical study of the code generation of safety-critical software using llms. Applied Sciences **14**(3), 1046 (2024)
22. Lu, S., Guo, D., Ren, S., Huang, J., Svyatkovskiy, A., Blanco, A., Clement, C., Drain, D., Jiang, D., Tang, D., et al.: Codexglue: A machine learning benchmark dataset for code understanding and generation. arXiv preprint arXiv:2102.04664 (2021)
23. Palin, R., Ward, D., Habli, I., Rivett, R.: Iso 26262 safety cases: Compliance and assurance. In: 6th IET International Conference on System Safety 2011. p. B12. IET (2011)
24. Ramaswamy, A., Monsuez, B., Tapus, A.: Modeling non-functional properties for human-machine systems. In: 2014 AAAI Spring Symposia, Stanford University, Palo Alto, California, USA, March 24-26, 2014. AAAI Press (2014)
25. Roziere, B., Gehring, J., Gloeckle, F., Sootla, S., Gat, I., Tan, X.E., Adi, Y., Liu, J., Sauvestre, R., Remez, T., et al.: Code llama: Open foundation models for code. arXiv preprint arXiv:2308.12950 (2023)
26. RTCA: DO-178C, Software Considerations in Airborne Systems and Equipment Certification (2011)
27. Sevenhuijsen, M., Etemadi, K., Nyberg, M.: Vecogen: Automating generation of formally verified c code with large language models. arXiv preprint arXiv:2411.19275 (2024)
28. Street, C., Warsame, Y., Mansouri, M., Klauck, M., Henkel, C., Lampacrescia, M., Palmas, M., Lange, R., Ghiorzi, E., Tacchella, A., et al.: Towards a verifiable toolchain for robotics. In: Proceedings of the AAAI Symposium Series. vol. 4, pp. 398–403 (2024)
29. Tiwari, A., Rueß, H., Saïdi, H., Shankar, N.: A technique for invariant generation. In: International Conference on Tools and Algorithms for the Construction and Analysis of Systems. pp. 113–127. Springer (2001)
30. Wang, Y., Ge, N., Liu, J., Cao, Z., Chen, Z., Hu, C.: Generating sysml behavior models via large language models: an empirical study. In: Proceedings of the 16th International Conference on Internetware. pp. 366–377 (2025)
31. Wang, Y., Wang, W., Joty, S., Hoi, S.C.: Codet5: Identifier-aware unified pre-trained encoder-decoder models for code understanding and generation. arXiv preprint arXiv:2109.00859 (2021)
32. Zhong, R., Du, X., Kai, S., Tang, Z., Xu, S., Zhen, H.L., Hao, J., Xu, Q., Yuan, M., Yan, J.: Llm4eda: Emerging progress in large language models for electronic design automation. arXiv preprint arXiv:2401.12224 (2023)

BY NC ND

Quantifying Privacy Risks in Synthetic Data: A Study on Black-Box Membership Inference

Giacomo Fantino[1], Marco Rondina[1], Antonio Vetrò[1], and Juan Carlos De Martin[1]

Politecnico di Torino, Torino, Italy {giacomo.fantino, marco.rondina, antonio.vetro, juancarlos.demartin}@polito.it

Abstract. The use of synthetic data has grown steadily in recent years, particularly to support AI research and data sharing. However, synthetic data remains vulnerable to privacy risks such as membership inference attacks (MIAs), where an attacker identifies whether a data record was in the original dataset, whose recent variants increasingly exploit overfitting in generative models to boost their accuracy. Privacy metrics have been proposed to assess the protection offered by synthetic datasets and the risk of information leakage. However, their ability to reflect actual risks of MIAs remains unexplored. This study empirically evaluates the trade-offs between utility and privacy in the generation of synthetic tabular data leveraging a variety of black-box MIAs, providing a novel assessment of privacy risks. Using state-of-the-art generative models, we repeatedly generated synthetic datasets, assessed their utility, measured vulnerability to black-box MIAs, and evaluated privacy using commonly used privacy metrics. Our analysis reveals that CTGAN and CTAB-GAN+ can mitigate the risks of membership disclosure without significantly compromising the utility of the data, while the other generators showed weaker privacy-utility trade-offs. However, the analysis of the privacy metrics suggests that their reliance on proximity to training data limits their ability to fully measure an attacker's exploitation capabilities. The results observed in this study highlight the potential applicability of the aforementioned generative models to privacy-sensitive domains, demonstrating their ability to balance utility and privacy even under the challenge of diverse black-box MIAs. Our analysis of privacy metrics provides empirical evidence on the real-world privacy risks of synthetic tabular data and call for developing new, empirically validated privacy metrics.

Keywords: Synthetic Data · Membership Inference Attacks · Privacy.

1 Introduction

Providing access to code and data from AI/ML research studies and industrial applications is a step forward in addressing the reproducibility crisis [15], while also enhancing the transparency and reliability of AI system development in

E. Albert and C. Pasareanu (Eds.): FASE 2026, LNCS 16504, pp. 86–106, 2026.
https://doi.org/10.1007/978-3-032-22774-4_5

industrial applications [27]. However, although transparency, accountability and reproducibility are fundamental aspects to achieve, compromising the privacy of individuals is not acceptable: if personal data is used, it cannot be shared, and even if no personal data is included in the training processes, it is still possible to uniquely identify individuals [23].

Synthetic data offers a promising means to address this trade-off: by creating a new anonymized dataset that has the same general statistical characteristics of the original data, it is possible to train a new model and obtain results that are consistent with the use of the original data [12]. Many generators have emerged, most recently based on architectures such as Generative Adversarial Networks (GAN) [14] and Variational Autoencoders (VAE) [22]. However, these approaches are undermined by a number of attacks: using the generated synthetic data and integrating it with additional information, an attacker can infer part of the original data, including sensitive attributes.

Among these attacks, Membership Inference Attacks (MIAs) have emerged as one of the most effective techniques, aiming to determine whether a particular data record was part of the training dataset of the target model [20]. The ability to infer such information is a serious threat to the privacy and fairness of an individual, as it may disproportionately expose vulnerable groups or amplify biases in decision-making. Exposure of sensitive information about an individual's health could be inferred through such attacks [18]. Bias amplification could occur in the employment sector, where sensitive details about a person's socioeconomic or ethical background could lead to potential biases in the hiring process [35]. Therefore, synthetic data generation that is trained on personal data or other types of sensitive information needs to be made robust against privacy attacks. This paper focuses on the MIA attack due to the growing research on this topic in the last years [31] and its impact on fairness and privacy.

Existing work has evaluated synthetic data with respect to membership inference attacks [21, 24, 45]; however, with the advent of new attacks [19, 3], a comprehensive evaluation of the privacy robustness of synthetic data generators for tabular data and privacy metrics remains absent. In this paper, we perform an evaluation of the robustness of synthetic data generators for tabular data against recently proposed MIAs, and analyze the extent to which commonly used privacy metrics reflect the actual success of these attacks.

The main contribution of this study is as follows:

1. We use empirical analysis to assess the risk of using synthetic data to share data containing sensitive information or personal data under multiple black-box membership inference attacks.
2. We evaluate the extent to which commonly used privacy metrics accurately reflect actual membership inference attack success.

To achieve these goals, we evaluated four state-of-the-art synthetic tabular data generators on datasets containing personal information, measuring their resilience to MIAs and analyzing how three privacy metrics correlate with attack success.

The rest of the article is structured as follows. Section 2 provides an overview of synthetic data generation techniques (Sect. 2.1), attacks on synthetic data (Sect. 2.2), and privacy metrics (Sect. 2.3). Section 3 presents the related work. Section 4 introduces our research questions and the privacy metrics used for evaluation. Section 5 describes our methodology in detail. In Section 6, we analyze the results and address our research questions. In Section 7, we discuss the limitations of our approach. Finally, Section 8 presents our conclusions and suggests directions for future research.

2 Background

2.1 Synthetic data generation

Synthetic data is obtained through models that reproduce the statistical properties of real data [12]. While this study focuses on tabular data, similar approaches have also been applied to other modalities such as images and audio [11]. Typical motivations for generating synthetic data include the removal of personal or sensitive information [12], data augmentation in data-scarce contexts [28], and fairness enhancement in machine learning applications [4].

Synthetic data generation methods can be broadly categorized by their underlying mechanisms [12]. Three main classes can be distinguished: Probability-based, where synthetic data is generated by estimating and sampling from a data distribution; Randomized, which involves generating samples through perturbation or interpolation; and Network-based, which encompasses generative methods that utilize neural network architectures.

Simple interpolation-based techniques such as Mixup represent baseline strategies. Mixup generates synthetic samples by linearly combining pairs of real instances using a mixing parameter λ drawn from a beta distribution. While effective for data augmentation, such methods provide limited control over privacy preservation or distributional fidelity.

More sophisticated network-based methods have recently gained prominence, particularly those based on Generative Adversarial Networks (GANs) [5]. GANs comprise two models trained in opposition: a generator and a discriminator. During the learning phase, the generator learns to mimic the training data distribution, while the discriminator attempts to distinguish real from synthetic samples. Through this adversarial process, the generator is optimized to produce synthetic data that are increasingly indistinguishable from real data.

Another prominent family of generative models are Variational Autoencoders (VAEs) [22], which learn probabilistic latent representations of the input data. A VAE consists of an encoder that maps data to a latent space and a decoder that reconstructs new samples by sampling from this latent representation.

These architectures were initially designed for continuous domains such as image and audio synthesis [11, 36]. When applied to tabular data, however, their performance may degrade due to the presence of categorical variables and complex feature dependencies [41]. To address these challenges, specialized models have been proposed.

CTGAN is a state-of-the-art GAN-based generator for tabular data [41]. It employs a preprocessing stage based on a Variational Gaussian Mixture Model (VGM) to normalize continuous variables and applies one-hot encoding to categorical columns. A conditional vector guides the generator toward learning minority categories in unbalanced features.

TVAE, proposed by the same authors, adopts the same preprocessing pipeline but replaces the GAN architecture with a VAE, enabling probabilistic sampling while maintaining compatibility with tabular structures [41].

CTAB-GAN+ extends CTGAN with domain-specific improvements [44]. Continuous features are min–max scaled for better VGM compatibility, long-tailed distributions are log-transformed to prevent unrealistic values, and mixed-column strategies handle highly unbalanced or sparse features. These refinements yield more stable and realistic tabular data generation, particularly in datasets containing heterogeneous variable types.

2.2 Attacks

With the growing adoption of generative AI across domains, adversarial methods have emerged to extract sensitive information from trained models [25]. Among these, the Membership Inference Attacks (MIAs) are one of the most studied, as they directly target the confidentiality of training data. In this type of attack, an adversary aims to determine whether a specific data sample was part of a model's training data [37].

Existing surveys classify MIAs according to the type of target model and the nature of the data [31]. Early work focused on discriminative models [37], while subsequent work extended MIAs to generative models such as GANs [17]. This evolution led to increasingly sophisticated attack strategies designed to enhance attack performance [19, 6, 3].

MIAs can be broadly divided into two families: black box and white box settings. In the white-box scenario, the attacker can inspect model parameters or architectures, whereas in the black-box case, only the synthetic data is observable. While both settings are relevant and capture different threat models, this study focuses on the black-box scenario, which naturally arises in many realistic data-sharing and publishing use cases where only synthetic datasets are released and the underlying generative model remains inaccessible.

Formally, the MIA can be expressed as a function $A(x|G)$, estimating the probability that sample x belongs to the training set underlying the synthetic dataset G [6]. Assuming that the synthetic dataset closely resembles the distribution of the real data, this probability can be derived from the learned density, denoted as $P_G(x)$. The resulting formulation, where membership is inferred from the synthetic data distribution, is known as a distribution-based MIA.

In practice, this remains challenging because estimating the distribution may require many samples, which the attacker may not have. To address this, distance-based MIA infers membership by assuming that real samples close to synthetic records are more likely to originate from the training data [6]. Let

$d(x, x')$, denote a distance function between x and its nearest synthetic neighbor $x' \in G$, then:

$$A(x|G) = \min_{x' \in G} d(x, x') \tag{1}$$

The Monte Carlo-based MIA improves upon distance-based MIAs by considering multiple synthetic samples instead of just one [19]. Its key insight is that an overfitted generator tends to repeatedly produce samples near real training instances. Only distances below a threshold ϵ are considered, ensuring that outliers are excluded from the analysis.

A more recent variant, DOMIAS (Detecting Overfitting for Membership Inference Attacks against Synthetic Data) [3] assumes limited access to a subset of training data, denoted as R. The key idea is to compare the likelihood of a sample x under the synthetic data distribution G and the known training subset R. This is done by computing the ratio:

$$A(x|G) = \frac{p_G(x)}{p_R(x)} \tag{2}$$

A high ratio suggests that the synthetic data generator has overfitted to x, making it more likely that x was part of the training set.

Another line of work, shadow modeling, involves the attacker training a surrogate generator locally using the released synthetic data [17]. This surrogate allows the use of white-box inference methods: high discriminator confidence in the shadow model indicates a stronger likelihood of membership.

2.3 Privacy metrics

Synthetic data privacy metrics provide quantitative proxies to assess how effectively synthetic datasets balance privacy and utility. They aim to capture potential privacy leakage risks, especially under adversarial settings such as membership and attribute inference attacks [39]. We focus on three widely adopted metrics—Distance to Closest Record (DCR) [29], Nearest Neighbor Distance Ratio (NNDR) [26], and Privacy loss [42]—chosen for their prevalence in both academic and industrial practice [32, 43, 42]. Newly proposed metrics are outside the present scope and reserved for future work.

The DCR measures the Euclidean distance between each synthetic sample and its nearest neighbor in the original training data. A high concentration of synthetic samples with DCR values close to zero suggests potential information leakage, as these samples closely resemble individual training records. On the other hand, NNDR evaluates the ratio between the distances of a synthetic sample to its closest and second-closest real neighbors. A NNDR value close to zero indicates that the nearest neighbor is significantly closer than the second, implying that the synthetic sample may inadvertently reveal details about a specific training instance. In contrast, when the NNDR value is close to 1 both distances are similar, thus the sample likely resides in a densely populated region of the feature space, thereby mitigating identifiability risks [26]. To prevent any feature from dominating the computed distances, all variables are normalized prior to measurement for both metrics.

A direct comparison between the synthetic and training sets alone fails to capture the broader distributional context in which samples are embedded. To address this limitation, metrics such as DCR and NNDR are computed using not only the training data but also a holdout set: a dataset drawn from the same distribution as the training data but excluded from the training process [33]. By comparing synthetic samples to both the training and holdout sets, one can assess whether proximity to the training data is exceptional or expected given the overall data distribution. If synthetic samples are similarly close to both sets, it suggests that they preserve general statistical properties without overfitting to specific training records. This adjustment makes DCR and NNDR more robust indicators of potential overfitting.

While these two metrics have been widely adopted, studies have highlighted their limitations, noting the lack of strong theoretical grounding and the challenges they face in capturing privacy risks for outliers or minority groups [13]. As they remain the most commonly used indicators in both academic and industrial settings, evaluating these limitations empirically is therefore crucial to understand how well such metrics reflect actual privacy risks.

The Privacy Loss metric quantifies how much a generative model exposes information about its training data [42]. It measures the difference in an attacker's ability to distinguish between samples that were part of the training set and those that were not. If the attacker cannot make this distinction, both accuracies are approximately 0.5, resulting in zero privacy loss. Conversely, if the model is overfitted, the accuracy on training samples will be considerably higher, leading to a high privacy loss. In our study, this attacker is instantiated through the Nearest Neighbor Adversarial Accuracy (NNAA) framework [42].

3 Related Work

Early research on applying MIAs to synthetic tabular data focused primarily on distance-based approaches [21, 24, 45]. These studies reported high attack success rates but also revealed the difficulty of achieving an optimal privacy–utility balance when using GAN-based or other generators. Parallel work explored shadow modeling techniques, where a local model is trained to replicate the target's behavior. While early attempts on synthetic image data achieved limited performance without auxiliary information [17], later studies using model predictions improved inference accuracy [37, 30]. Further evaluations combining distance-based and shadow-based attacks confirmed that naive MIAs were weak, but shadow modeling substantially increased inference success, particularly when no explicit defenses were applied [38]. These findings underscore the need for a unified empirical framework capable of evaluating multiple MIA families under consistent conditions.

Building on these findings, we quantitatively assess whether the use of synthetic data generators for sharing tabular data poses a risk to privacy. While prior studies have largely focused on distance-based MIAs or shadow modeling, our work expands this scope by incorporating newer black-box MIA attacks, aiming to provide a more comprehensive evaluation of privacy vulnerabilities. Our analysis takes into account a variety of synthetic data generators, three datasets, all containing personal data, and the aforementioned black-box MIA attacks.

Due to the high computational cost of training multiple shadow models and given that this attack has been extensively studied in the literature, we did not include shadow modeling in our main analysis. Its resource intensity makes it impractical in many real-world scenarios; however, we consider it a valuable direction for future work. Instead, we focus on the most representative black-box MIAs and complement our attack-based evaluation with a detailed assessment of widely adopted privacy metrics, analyzing their reliability in reflecting actual privacy robustness.

4 Research Questions and Metrics

The Research Questions that drive the study are:

- RQ1: How do different synthetic tabular data generators perform in terms of utility and resistance to a variety of black-box membership inference attacks: distribution-based MIA, distance-based MIA, Monte Carlo-based MIA, and DOMIAS?
- RQ2: Are the selected privacy metrics, Distance to Closest Record (DCR), Nearest Neighbors Distance Ratio (NNDR) and Privacy loss, reliable for evaluating synthetic data quality when faced with a variety of black-box MIAs?

To address RQ1, we evaluate two complementary aspects: utility and privacy.

Utility of a synthetic dataset can be evaluated using both statistical properties of the data, i.e. measuring the difference between the trained and synthetic data, and machine learning, which measures the difference in performance between training a model with the original data and the synthetic data [18]. Since it has been shown a weak correlation between statistical utility metrics and an overall absence of utility measurement [8], we focus on the machine learning utility: we measure the difference in accuracy, F1-score and AUC-ROC when training an XGBoost classifier [7] on synthetic data. A minimal drop in performance implies better synthetic data. This approach provides a consistent and reproducible basis for comparing generators using measurable downstream performance. In addition, we assess the coverage of the synthetic data by comparing, for each training record, its distance to the nearest synthetic sample and to the nearest holdout sample. This helps reveal whether the generator misses parts of the real distribution or places synthetic records too close to training data (a sign of overfitting) [33].

For privacy evaluation, we will use the black-box MIAs discussed in Section 2.2. Each attack was executed on balanced subsets consisting of 20% of training samples (expected to be classified as members of the training set) and an equal number of test samples (expected to be classified as non-members). The attack success was measured using the AUC-ROC score, where values near 0.5 indicate resistance (equivalent to random guessing) and values approaching 1.0 indicate a privacy risk [10].

While RQ1 measures empirical robustness, RQ2 examines whether existing privacy metrics can reliably predict this robustness. To this end, we compute DCR and NNDR for both training and holdout data, and Privacy Loss for the synthetic data, expecting a positive correlation between the metrics' values and the AUC-ROC of the attacks

Given a synthetic dataset S and the original dataset R, DCR is computed for all synthetic samples as the distance to the closest sample in R:

$$min_{r \in R} d(s, r) \tag{3}$$

On the other hand NNDR considers the ratio for all synthetic samples of the closest and the second-closest samples in R:

$$\frac{d(s, NN_1(R))}{d(s, NN_2(R))} \tag{4}$$

For measuring Privacy Loss, we adopt Nearest Neighbor Adversarial Accuracy (NNAA) to assess an attacker's performance on distinguishing real data from synthetic counterparts [42]. Real samples that remain distant from synthetic data are treated as true positives, while synthetic samples that remain distant from real data are considered true negatives. NNAA is computed as the balanced accuracy between the true positive rate and the false negative rate; an NNAA value of 0.5 corresponds to random guessing. Privacy Loss is then measured as the discrepancy in attacker performance between training and holdout samples: if NNAA is close to 0.5 on both sets, the resulting difference is near zero, indicating minimal membership leakage, while larger gaps indicate increased leakage due to overfitting.

5 Methodology

This section details the three main phases of our methodology: data pre-processing and splitting (Section 5.1), synthetic data generation (Section 5.2) and attack execution (Section 5.3). Figure 1 provides an overview of the experimental workflow, designed to address both RQ1 (utility and resistance of synthetic data generators to black-box MIAs) and RQ2 (reliability of privacy metrics). First, the datasets were preprocessed and split into training and test sets. The training set was used to generate synthetic data, while the test set served as an independent evaluation set. Finally, the synthetic data was evaluated using MIAs, privacy metrics, and utility measures to answer the research questions. Defensive

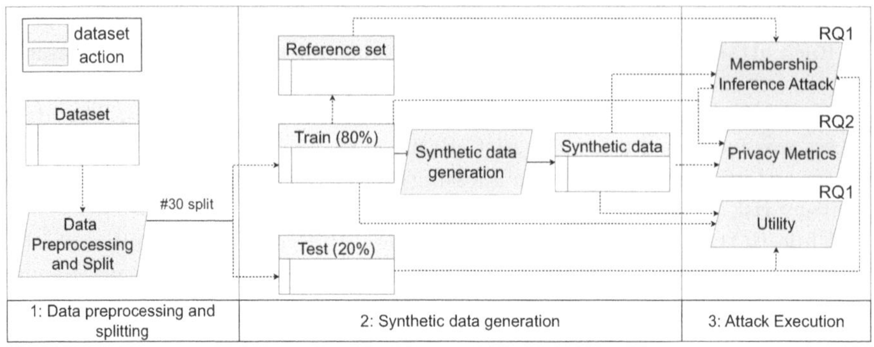

Fig. 1. Overview of the proposed methodology, divided into three main phases: data preprocessing and splitting, synthetic data generation, and attack execution.

mechanisms such as Differential Privacy (DP) were intentionally excluded. Preliminary exploratory tests using conservative privacy budgets for GAN-based generators indicated a reduction in attack performance, approaching random guessing, but at the cost of a substantial degradation in data utility. As differential privacy entails an explicit privacy–utility trade-off that depends critically on the choice of parameters, and a systematic evaluation of this trade-off falls outside the scope of this work, we focus on the inherent privacy–utility properties of existing generators without DP. The integration of DP-based defenses is therefore left for future work.

5.1 Data Preprocessing and Splitting Strategy

We used the Adult [2], COMPAS [34], and Southern German Credit (hereafter referred to as Credit) [1] datasets, which are widely adopted benchmarks in fairness research [9] and exhibit complementary structural characteristics, varying in sample size, feature dimensionality, and balance between categorical and numerical attributes (Table 1). Each dataset underwent preprocessing to ensure consistency and privacy compliance: duplicates and missing values were removed, and features typically excluded in standard machine learning pipelines, including identifiers that could link a record to an individual, were dropped. To enhance statistical robustness and reproducibility, we generated 30 independent train–test splits for each dataset, thereby mitigating the variability introduced by random partitioning. For each split, 80% of the data was used to train the generative models, while the remaining 20% served as a holdout set for evaluating both synthetic data utility and resistance to MIAs. To ensure comparability and simulate realistic data-sharing scenarios, the synthetic dataset generated in each run contained the same number of samples as the corresponding training set.

Dataset	#Samples	#Columns	#Categorical
Adult	26,904	13	12
COMPAS	2,294	9	9
Credit	1,000	21	21

Table 1. Dataset statistics after preprocessing

5.2 Synthetic Data Generation

We employed the four synthesizers introduced in Section 2.1: Mixup, TVAE, CTGAN, and CTAB-GAN+, using off-the-shelf implementations from publicly available libraries and repositories. Since TVAE and GAN-based generators require model training, we tuned hyperparameters—such as number of epochs, batch size, and discriminator steps for GANs—to ensure convergence and maximize fidelity of the generated samples. The tuning process prioritized data-utility metrics, reflecting common practice where generative models are optimized for downstream performance rather than explicit privacy preservation.

5.3 Attack Execution

The membership inference attacks were executed across all dataset splits to mitigate bias arising from random partitioning, as certain training subsets may inherently be more vulnerable to inference. Each attack received the synthetic dataset, a subset of the training set and the test set: the attack should infer membership with maximal accuracy. All attacks were re-implemented by the authors, closely following the threat models and parameter choices described in the respective original papers. Prior to execution, data were preprocessed to ensure comparability across attacks: Min–Max scaling was applied for distance-based MIAs to prevent feature dominance, Standard scaling for density-based attacks to stabilize density estimation, and PCA to remove low-variance features. The AUC-ROC metric was computed across splits to assess attack effectiveness. Although it may not capture all aspects of attack performance, it remains the most widely used metric in the literature for assessing MIA success, allowing direct comparison with previous work.

For the DOMIAS attack, a subset of the training data was used as a reference set. This reference set represents a portion of the leaked training data that the attacker can access to infer information about the overall training distribution. To ensure a realistic evaluation, this reference set was completely disjoint from the subset of training data used for assessing the attack, preventing trivial membership identification. We initially set the reference set to 10% of the training data and later examined the impact of increasing its size.

Complementary to the attack analysis, the utility and privacy metrics were computed for each split to quantify the trade-off between data utility and MIAs resistance. For the privacy metrics, we reused the test sets as holdout sets to account for the data distribution. After computing the distances, following the methodology of Platzer and Reutter [33], for each synthetic sample we determined whether the closer sample was in the training or holdout set. We then calculated the ratio of samples closer to the training data: as the value gets closer to 1 the probability of information leakage increases.

Since the Monte Carlo–based MIA requires a value for the threshold parameter ϵ, we have used the median heuristic proposed by Hilprecht et al. [19]: it computes ϵ as the median of the minimum distances between the samples in the training and test sets and the synthetic samples, ensuring stable and reproducible attack behavior across splits.

Finally, Kernel Density Estimation (KDE) was used to approximate the distribution of both synthetic and real data. A grid search over multiple splits identified an exponential kernel with a bandwidth of 0.05 as optimal for modeling the distribution. The same configuration was used for DOMIAS, following prior evidence that it provides robust estimation under limited sample sizes.

6 Results and Discussion

In this section, we present the results addressing the research questions defined in Section 4. Specifically, in Section 6.1 we examine the outcomes of MIAs to assess the resilience of different synthetic data generators, considering both their privacy protection and the utility of the data produced. Subsequently, Section 6.2 investigates the relationship between the computed privacy metrics and the corresponding AUC-ROC values of the attacks, to determine whether such metrics can reliably predict a generator's resistance to black-box MIAs. All code and datasets are available for reproducibility.[1]

6.1 Utility and Resistance against black-box MIAs (RQ1)

This subsection addresses RQ1 by jointly analyzing the utility of the synthetic data and its resistance to black-box MIAs. We compare the AUC-ROC values of different attacks across generators and datasets, summarizing the distributions over 30 iterations of synthetic data generation.

Figure 2 shows the AUC-ROC distribution for each attack, with respect to the datasets and the generators. Mixup consistently yields the highest AUC-ROC values across attacks and datasets, reaching 0.8 on the Credit dataset, indicating strong vulnerability to MIAs likely due to its interpolation-based generation strategy. In contrast, TVAE, CTGAN, and CTAB-GAN+ exhibit near-optimal resistance, with AUC-ROC values below 0.6 across all attacks and datasets. Since an AUC-ROC of 0.5 corresponds to random guessing, values around 0.8 reflect strong separability between members and non-members, whereas values only moderately above 0.5 indicate a limited attacker advantage [10]. DOMIAS and Monte Carlo achieve only marginal gains against these generators, further confirming their robustness even against recent and more sophisticated MIAs.

[1] Source codes and data are available at: https://github.com/giacomofantino/Synthetic-Data-Privacy

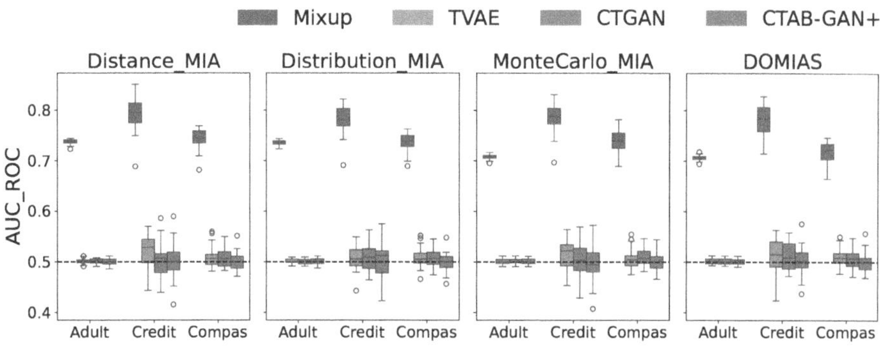

Fig. 2. AUC-ROC scores for each Membership Inference Attack across different datasets and synthetic data generators.

These findings are broadly consistent with prior observations on distance-based MIAs for tabular data [21, 45], reinforcing their validity across different settings. A direct comparison with [24] is less straightforward due to methodological differences (e.g., their use of a fixed synthetic sample size independent of the real dataset), but the overall trend of low attack performance against GAN-based generators is comparable. Our work extends these studies by systematically evaluating a wider range of black-box MIAs, including more recent attacks such as DOMIAS and Monte Carlo. Crucially, we show that generators previously regarded as strong (TVAE, CTGAN, CTAB-GAN+) retain their robustness even under these novel attacks. Finally, the consistently low AUC-ROC values across generators validate our decision to exclude differential privacy: given the already strong resilience of these models, adding DP would likely degrade utility without offering meaningful privacy gains.

Attack performance also varies with dataset characteristics. Mixup remains highly vulnerable across all datasets, though its AUC-ROC values are slightly lower for COMPAS and Adult than for Credit. CTGAN, CTAB-GAN+, and TVAE maintain low AUC-ROC values overall, but Credit and COMPAS display greater variance, consistent with prior findings that smaller training datasets increase susceptibility to information leakage.

The utility evaluation, shown in Figure 3, reveals distinct trade-offs across generators. Mixup consistently achieves the smallest differences in all three metrics, with values clustered just below zero, suggesting that classifiers trained on Mixup-generated data closely replicate the performance obtained on real data. However, this high utility comes at the cost of substantial privacy risk, as confirmed by the attack results. GAN-based generators show mild performance degradation, particularly on the Credit dataset, where CTGAN and CTAB-GAN+ display noticeable declines in AUC-ROC. Conversely, CTGAN performs well on COMPAS, achieving high utility with positive metric differences, while CTAB-GAN+ tends to underperform on this dataset. TVAE represents an intermediate case, showing moderate differences across metrics and datasets.

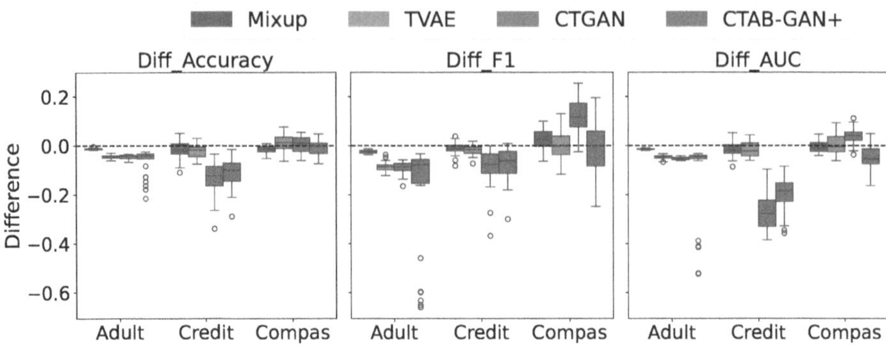

Fig. 3. Differences in utility metrics (Accuracy, F1-score, and AUC) across datasets and synthetic data generators.

Dataset complexity also affects utility stability. The Credit dataset exhibits the largest utility discrepancies across generators, indicating that its heterogeneous feature space challenges synthetic data generation. In contrast, the Adult dataset yields more consistent utility results, with smaller performance gaps, suggesting its structure is more conducive to accurate synthetic reproduction.

As outlined in Section 5.1, the DOMIAS attack was initially provided with 10% of the training data as a reference set. We then tested larger subsets to verify whether additional reference samples improved attack success. Consistent with the original findings [3], Figure 4 shows no significant improvement beyond 10%, apart from a minor increase in attack performance for Mixup on the COMPAS dataset.

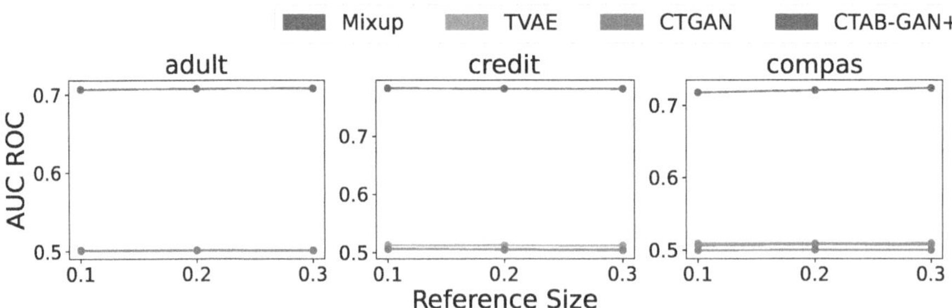

Fig. 4. DOMIAS performance as a function of the percentage of training data available, evaluated across different datasets and synthetic data generators.

To further analyze generator behavior, we examined the spatial relationship between real and synthetic samples by comparing, for each training record, the difference in distance to its closest synthetic sample versus its closest test sample.

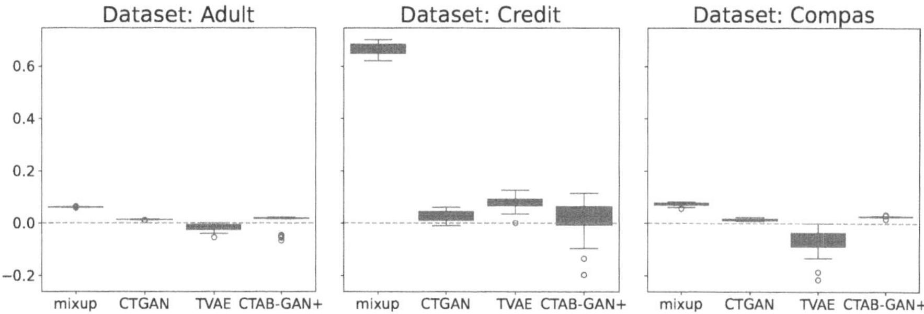

Fig. 5. Difference in distance to closest record between synthetic and test samples for each training data sample across datasets and synthetic data generators.

As shown in Figure 5, for the Credit dataset, Mixup produces synthetic samples that lie extremely close to the training data, confirming excessive proximity and potential leakage. In contrast, for COMPAS and partially for Adult, TVAE generates samples that remain consistently distant from the training distribution, indicating only partial coverage of the data space and a loss of information. This behavior reflects a known limitation of VAEs on tabular data: their tendency toward over-pruning (posterior collapse) [40]. The regularization term in the ELBO loss can dominate training, forcing the latent distribution to approximate a fixed prior (typically a unit Gaussian) and reducing dependence on the input data [16]. Consequently, TVAE maintains reasonable predictive utility but omits underrepresented data regions, reducing the fidelity and completeness of the generated samples.

Overall, CTGAN and CTAB-GAN+ achieve the best balance between utility and privacy, making them suitable for privacy-sensitive scenarios where minor utility degradation is acceptable. Mixup provides high utility but poor privacy protection, while TVAE, despite competitive performance, fails to fully reconstruct the training data distribution in COMPAS. Among the attacks, Monte Carlo and DOMIAS, though recently proposed, did not outperform traditional distance-based MIAs. In most cases, the distance-based attack remained the most effective, suggesting that direct overfitting exploitation continues to be the dominant threat to tabular synthetic data privacy.

CTGAN and CTAB-GAN+ emerge as promising candidates for applications requiring both acceptable predictive utility and protection against diverse black-box MIAs. They demonstrate a balanced trade-off between utility and privacy, offering practical solutions for generating synthetic data that can be shared without compromising the confidentiality of personal information

6.2 Reliability of Privacy Metrics Under Black-Box MIAs (RQ2)

To answer RQ2, we assess whether the selected privacy metrics (DCR, NNDR, and Privacy Loss) correlate with the success of black-box MIAs, thereby evaluating their validity as indicators of privacy risk. We hypothesize that higher metric values should correspond to stronger MIA performance. Since each dataset split produces one value per metric and multiple AUC-ROC scores—one for each attack—we compute the average AUC-ROC across all attacks. This aggregation provides a holistic view of the relationship between privacy metrics and attack effectiveness, avoiding overemphasis on any single attack variant.

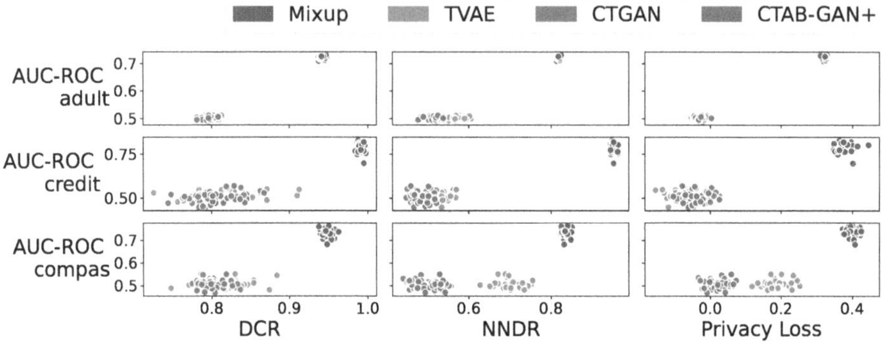

Fig. 6. Comparison of privacy metric values and MIA AUC-ROC scores across different datasets.

Figure 6 plots the metric values against the averaged AUC-ROC scores for all datasets. A general positive trend emerges: higher DCR, NNDR, and Privacy Loss values tend to coincide with stronger MIA performance, suggesting that these metrics partially capture underlying vulnerability patterns.

However, TVAE exhibits anomalous behavior on the COMPAS dataset, yielding comparatively high NNDR and Privacy Loss values while maintaining low AUC-ROC scores. This suggests that proximity-based metrics may not reliably quantify privacy risk under conditions such as latent-space underfitting, since they capture only geometric closeness without considering how an attacker could exploit this proximity to infer membership. In fact, the underfitting phenomenon discussed in Section 6.1—posterior collapse—led TVAE to generate synthetic samples that covered only a subset of the original feature space. This restricted coverage likely triggered proximity-based metrics to signal higher risk, even though it did not translate into stronger attack performance as reflected by AUC-ROC. By contrast, Mixup consistently records higher privacy metric values, aligned with its poor resistance to MIAs, whereas CTGAN and CTAB-GAN+ display lower metric outputs and reduced attack success. This alignment supports the expected relationship between metric magnitude and empirical vulnerability

Dataset-specific trends also emerge. In both the COMPAS and Credit datasets, the privacy metrics exhibit a wide spread of values across the metric axis, yet the corresponding AUC-ROC scores remain relatively stable, suggesting a reduced effectiveness in detecting privacy leakage. This pattern suggests that in datasets with fewer samples, proximity-based metrics may fluctuate more due to local density variations, without reflecting a proportional change in actual attack success.

Overall, the findings demonstrate that while DCR, NNDR, and Privacy Loss capture broad vulnerability trends, they fail to fully characterize leakage in models with uneven data coverage or latent-space collapse. Complementing these metrics with distributional or adversarially informed measures would improve the reliability and comprehensiveness of privacy validation frameworks for synthetic data.

The analysis indicates that DCR, NNDR, and Privacy Loss provide a partial but incomplete picture of privacy robustness under black-box MIAs. While these metrics capture general vulnerability trends, their limitations—exemplified by the anomalous behavior of TVAE—highlight that proximity-based measures alone cannot fully represent the multifaceted nature of privacy leakage. This finding suggests the need for more comprehensive, empirically validated metrics that account for model architecture, data coverage, and attack strategy diversity.

7 Threats to validity

In this section we discuss the potential threats to validity that may influence the interpretation, reliability, or generalizability of our findings.

Internal validity: A potential threat lies in uncontrolled factors that might influence the outcomes, such as the choice of datasets or random initialization of models. To overcome this, we employed multiple, diverse datasets and repeated experiments across 30 random train/test splits to reduce bias. To ensure consistency and replicability of results, we have made the codebase fully replicable, allowing others to verify the experimental setup and results [1]. This reduces the likelihood of errors or biases affecting the results.

External validity: Although the datasets are diverse in structure and domain, they all represent socio-economic decision-making datasets and may not fully capture the variability of real-world applications. In addition, our study focuses on three widely-used deep tabular data generators, and the observed trends may not directly transfer to other synthesis approaches. Similarly, while the considered attacks and privacy metrics represent the current state of the art, they might not encompass all possible adversarial strategies or future privacy assessment techniques. Consequently, the generalizability of the results to unseen domains or emerging attack paradigms may be limited.

Construct validity: Our evaluation primarily relies on AUC-ROC, chosen for its widespread use in MIA literature and comparability with prior work, though it may not capture nuances such as class imbalance. Utility is evaluated using a single downstream model (XGBoost), reflecting a task-specific notion of utility; therefore, the observed privacy–utility trade-offs may differ for other downstream models. Conversely, privacy is assessed using record-level metrics and

MIAs, which do not explicitly account for domain-specific harm from disclosure. For RQ2, we average AUC-ROC across attacks to obtain an attack-agnostic view, potentially obscuring differences among attack types. Finally, we do not consider group-level disclosure risks, which may persist even when record-level membership inference is limited.

Conclusion Validity: The statistical significance of the observed differences among attacks and generators could be influenced by the limited number of experimental runs. To mitigate random variance and strengthen the robustness of conclusions, we conducted multiple independent repetitions and reported aggregate statistics across all runs.

8 Conclusion

This work establishes an empirical framework for quantifying privacy risks in synthetic tabular data, providing a systematic comparison of black-box membership inference attacks and privacy metrics, grounded in fairness-related tabular benchmarks and deep tabular generators, to better understand the privacy robustness of generative models and how effectively privacy metrics capture privacy leakage.

Among the evaluated generators, CTAB-GAN+ and CTGAN demonstrated the best balance between privacy and utility, achieving low AUC-ROC values across diverse MIAs while maintaining predictive performance. Conversely, Mixup exhibits the highest susceptibility to MIAs, making it unsuitable for privacy-sensitive applications, while TVAE offers strong resistance to MIA at the cost of loss of information.

Our evaluation of the privacy metrics, DCR, NNDR, and Privacy Loss, reveals that while they correlate with attack effectiveness, their reliance on proximity-based assumptions limits their sensitivity to distributional coverage. Anomalies such as TVAE's inflated privacy scores emphasize that current metrics do not fully capture attacker capabilities or structural gaps in the generated data. These findings underscore the need for improved measures that integrate both data coverage and exploitability perspectives. Finally, our study challenges the assumed superiority of newer MIAs, such as Monte Carlo-based attacks and DOMIAS, which failed to outperform traditional distance-based attacks in our experiment. Future work should focus on defining privacy metrics that incorporate data coverage and attacker modeling, extending this framework to other data modalities and attack families, and analyzing the conditions under which newer attacks may generalize more effectively.

Ultimately, this study contributes to the empirical validation of privacy properties in generative models—an essential step toward trustworthy and testable AI systems within the broader context of software engineering research.

Acknowledgments. This study was carried out within the FAIR - Future Artificial Intelligence Research and received funding from the European Union Next-GenerationEU

(PIANO NAZIONALE DI RIPRESA E RESILIENZA (PNRR) – MISSIONE 4 COMPONENTE 2, INVESTIMENTO 1.3 – D.D. 1555 11/10/2022, PE00000013). This publication is part of the project PNRR-NGEU which has received funding from the MUR – DM 630/2024. This manuscript reflects only the authors' views and opinions, neither the European Union nor the European Commission can be considered responsible for them.

Disclosure of Interests. The authors have no competing interests to declare that are relevant to the content of this article.

References

1. South German Credit. UCI Machine Learning Repository (2020), DOI: https://doi.org/10.24432/C5QG88
2. Becker, B., Kohavi, R.: Adult. UCI Machine Learning Repository (1996), DOI: https://doi.org/10.24432/C5XW20
3. van Breugel, B., Hao, S., Zhaozhi, Q., van der Schaar, M.: Membership inference attacks against synthetic data through overfitting detection (2023), https://arxiv.org/abs/2302.12580
4. van Breugel, B., Kyono, T., Berrevoets, J., van der Schaar, M.: Decaf: Generating fair synthetic data using causally-aware generative networks (2021), https://arxiv.org/abs/2110.12884
5. Chakraborty, T., S, U.R.K., Naik, S.M., Panja, M., Manvitha, B.: Ten years of generative adversarial nets (gans): A survey of the state-of-the-art (2023), https://arxiv.org/abs/2308.16316
6. Chen, D., Yu, N., Zhang, Y., Fritz, M.: Gan-leaks: A taxonomy of membership inference attacks against generative models. In: Proceedings of the 2020 ACM SIGSAC Conference on Computer and Communications Security. pp. 343–362. ACM, Virtual Event, USA (Oct 2020). https://doi.org/10.1145/3372297.3417238, https://dl.acm.org/doi/10.1145/3372297.3417238
7. Chen, T., Guestrin, C.: Xgboost: A scalable tree boosting system. In: Proceedings of the 22nd ACM SIGKDD International Conference on Knowledge Discovery and Data Mining. p. 785–794. Association for Computing Machinery, New York, NY, USA (2016). https://doi.org/10.1145/2939672.2939785, https://doi.org/10.1145/2939672.2939785
8. Dankar, F.K., Ibrahim, M.K., Ismail, L.: A multi-dimensional evaluation of synthetic data generators. IEEE Access **10**, 11147–11158 (2022). https://doi.org/10.1109/ACCESS.2022.3144765, https://ieeexplore.ieee.org/document/9686689/
9. Fabris, A., Messina, S., Silvello, G., Susto, G.A.: Algorithmic fairness datasets: The story so far. Data Mining and Knowledge Discovery **36**, 2074–2152 (2022). https://doi.org/10.1007/s10618-022-00854-z, https://doi.org/10.1007/s10618-022-00854-z
10. Fawcett, T.: An introduction to ROC analysis. Pattern Recognition Letters **27**(8), 861–874 (2006). https://doi.org/10.1016/j.patrec.2005.10.010, https://www.sciencedirect.com/science/article/pii/S016786550500303X
11. Figueira, A., Vaz, B.: Survey on synthetic data generation, evaluation methods and gans. Mathematics **10**(15), 2733 (2022). https://doi.org/10.3390/math10152733, https://www.mdpi.com/2227-7390/10/15/2733

12. Fonseca, J., Bacao, F.: Tabular and latent space synthetic data generation: A literature review. Journal of Big Data **10**(1), 115 (Jul 2023). https://doi.org/10.1186/s40537-023-00792-7, https://journalofbigdata.springeropen.com/articles/10.1186/s40537-023-00792-7
13. Ganev, G.: Synthetic data, similarity-based privacy metrics, and regulatory (non-)compliance (2024), https://arxiv.org/abs/2407.16929
14. Goodfellow, I.J., Pouget-Abadie, J., Mirza, M., Xu, B., Warde-Farley, D., Ozair, S., Courville, A., Bengio, Y.: Generative adversarial nets. In: Proceedings of the 28th International Conference on Neural Information Processing Systems - Volume 2. p. 2672–2680. NIPS'14, MIT Press, Cambridge, MA, USA (2014)
15. Gundersen, O.E., Gil, Y., Aha, D.W.: On reproducible ai: Towards reproducible research, open science, and digital scholarship in ai publications. AI Magazine **39**(3), 56–68 (Sep 2018). https://doi.org/10.1609/aimag.v39i3.2816, https://onlinelibrary.wiley.com/doi/10.1609/aimag.v39i3.2816
16. Guo, C., Zhou, J., Chen, H., Ying, N., Zhang, J., Zhou, D.: Variational autoencoder with optimizing gaussian mixture model priors. IEEE Access **8**, 43992–44005 (2020). https://doi.org/10.1109/ACCESS.2020.2977671
17. Hayes, J., Melis, L., Danezis, G., Cristofaro, E.D.: Logan: Membership inference attacks against generative models (2018), https://arxiv.org/abs/1705.07663
18. Hernandez, M., Epelde, G., Alberdi, A., Cilla, R., Rankin, D.: Synthetic data generation for tabular health records: A systematic review. Neurocomputing **493**, 28–45 (2022). https://doi.org/10.1016/j.neucom.2022.04.053, https://linkinghub.elsevier.com/retrieve/pii/S0925231222004349
19. Hilprecht, B., Härterich, M., Bernau, D.: Reconstruction and membership inference attacks against generative models (2019), https://arxiv.org/abs/1906.03006
20. Hu, H., Salcic, Z., Sun, L., Dobbie, G., Yu, P.S., Zhang, X.: Membership inference attacks on machine learning: A survey. ACM Computing Surveys **54**(11s), 1–37 (Jan 2022). https://doi.org/10.1145/3523273, https://dl.acm.org/doi/10.1145/3523273
21. Hyeong, J., Kim, J., Park, N., Jajodia, S.: An empirical study on the membership inference attack against tabular data synthesis models. In: Proceedings of the 31st ACM International Conference on Information & Knowledge Management. pp. 4064–4068. ACM, A (Oct 2022)
22. Kingma, D.P., Welling, M.: Auto-encoding variational bayes (2013), https://arxiv.org/abs/1312.6114
23. Latanya, S.: Simple demographics often identify people uniquely (2000)
24. Liu, Q., Khalil, M., Jovanovic, J., Shakya, R.: Scaling while privacy preserving: A comprehensive synthetic tabular data generation and evaluation in learning analytics. In: Proceedings of the 14th Learning Analytics and Knowledge Conference. pp. 620–631. ACM, Kyoto, Japan (Mar 2024). https://doi.org/10.1145/3636555.3636921, https://dl.acm.org/doi/10.1145/3636555.3636921
25. Liu, Y., Huang, J., Li, Y., Wang, D., Xiao, B.: Generative ai model privacy: A survey. Artificial Intelligence Review **58**(1), 33 (Dec 2024). https://doi.org/10.1007/s10462-024-11024-6, https://link.springer.com/10.1007/s10462-024-11024-6
26. Lowe, D.G.: Distinctive image features from scale-invariant keypoints. International Journal of Computer Vision **60**, 91–110 (2004). https://doi.org/10.1023/B:VISI.0000029664.99615.94, https://doi.org/10.1023/B:VISI.0000029664.99615.94

27. Lu, Y., Shen, M., Wang, H., Wang, X., van Rechem, C., Fu, T., Wei, W.: Machine learning for synthetic data generation: A review (2024), https://arxiv.org/abs/2302.04062
28. Mariani, G., Scheidegger, F., Istrate, R., Bekas, C., Malossi, C.: Bagan: Data augmentation with balancing gan (2018), https://arxiv.org/abs/1803.09655
29. Mateo-Sanz, J.M., Sebé, F., Domingo-Ferrer, J.: Outlier protection in continuous microdata masking. In: Privacy in Statistical Databases. pp. 201–215. Springer Berlin Heidelberg, Berlin, Heidelberg (2004)
30. Niu, B., Sun, J., Chen, Y., Zhang, L., Cao, J., Geng, K., Li, F.: Evaluating the impact of adversarial factors on membership inference attacks. In: 2023 IEEE Smart World Congress (SWC). pp. 1–8. IEEE (2023). https://doi.org/10.1109/SWC57546.2023.10448806, https://ieeexplore.ieee.org/document/10448806/
31. Niu, J., Liu, P., Zhu, X., Shen, K., Wang, Y., Chi, H., Shen, Y., Jiang, X., Ma, J., Zhang, Y.: A survey on membership inference attacks and defenses in machine learning. Journal of Information and Intelligence **2**(5), 404–454 (Sep 2024). https://doi.org/10.1016/j.jiixd.2024.02.001, https://linkinghub.elsevier.com/retrieve/pii/S2949715924000064
32. Park, N., Mohammadi, M., Gorde, K., Jajodia, S., Park, H., Kim, Y.: Data synthesis based on generative adversarial networks. Proceedings of the VLDB Endowment **11**(10), 1071–1083 (2018). https://doi.org/10.14778/3231751.3231757, https://dl.acm.org/doi/10.14778/3231751.3231757
33. Platzer, M., Reutterer, T.: Holdout-based empirical assessment of mixed-type synthetic data. Frontiers in Big Data **4** (2021). https://doi.org/10.3389/fdata.2021.679939
34. ProPublica: Compas analysis (2016), https://github.com/propublica/compas-analysis
35. Raghavan, M., Barocas, S., Kleinberg, J., Levy, K.: Mitigating bias in algorithmic hiring: evaluating claims and practices. In: Proceedings of the 2020 Conference on Fairness, Accountability, and Transparency. p. 469–481. FAT* '20, Association for Computing Machinery, New York, NY, USA (2020). https://doi.org/10.1145/3351095.3372828, https://doi.org/10.1145/3351095.3372828
36. Razavi, A., van den Oord, A., Vinyals, O.: Generating diverse high-fidelity images with vq-vae-2. In: Wallach, H., Larochelle, H., Beygelzimer, A., d'Alché-Buc, F., Fox, E., Garnett, R. (eds.) Advances in Neural Information Processing Systems. vol. 32. Curran Associates, Inc. (2019)
37. Shokri, R., Stronati, M., Song, C., Shmatikov, V.: Membership inference attacks against machine learning models. In: 2017 IEEE Symposium on Security and Privacy (SP). pp. 3–18. IEEE (2017). https://doi.org/10.1109/SP.2017.41
38. Stadler, T., Oprisanu, B., Troncoso, C.: Synthetic data – anonymisation groundhog day. In: 31st USENIX Security Symposium (USENIX Security 22). pp. 1451–1468. USENIX Association (2022), https://www.usenix.org/conference/usenixsecurity22/presentation/stadler
39. Steier, A., Ramaswamy, L., Manoel, A., Haushalter, A.: Synthetic data privacy metrics (2025), https://arxiv.org/abs/2501.03941
40. Tazwar, S.M., Knobbout, M., Quesada, E.H., Popa, M.: Tab-vae: A novel VAE for generating synthetic tabular data. In: Proceedings of the 13th International Conference on Pattern Recognition Applications and Method. SCITEPRESS, Maastricht, The Netherlands (2024)

41. Xu, L., Skoularidou, M., Cuesta-Infante, A., Veeramachaneni, K.: Modeling tabular data using conditional GAN, pp. 659–669. Curran Associates Inc., Red Hook, NY, USA (2019)
42. Yale, A., Dash, S., Dutta, R., Guyon, I., Pavao, A., Bennett, K.: Generation and evaluation of privacy preserving synthetic health data. Neurocomputing **416** (04 2020). https://doi.org/10.1016/j.neucom.2019.12.136
43. Zhao, Z., Kunar, A., Birke, R., Chen, L.Y.: CTAB-GAN: Effective table data synthesizing. In: Balasubramanian, V.N., Tsang, I. (eds.) Proceedings of The 13th Asian Conference on Machine Learning. Proceedings of Machine Learning Research, vol. 157, pp. 97–112. PMLR (Nov 2021)
44. Zhao, Z., Kunar, A., Birke, R., Van Der Scheer, H., Chen, L.Y.: CTAB-GAN+: Enhancing tabular data synthesis **6**, 1296508. https://doi.org/10.3389/fdata.2023.1296508, https://www.frontiersin.org/articles/10.3389/fdata.2023.1296508/full
45. Zhu, C., Tang, J., Brouwer, H., Pérez, J.F., van Dijk, M., Chen, L.Y.: Quantifying and mitigating privacy risks for tabular generative models (2024), https://arxiv.org/abs/2403.07842

Formally Correct Search for Interpretable DNFs

Imane Bousdira[1], Martin Cooper[2], and Aurélie Hurault[1]

[1] IRIT, Toulouse INP, France
[2] IRIT, University of Toulouse, France
{imane.bousdira, cooper, aurelie.hurault}@irit.fr

Abstract. Interpretable models are a key aspect of explainable machine learning. A model can be considered to be interpretable if for each decision there is an explanation involving only k features, for some small constant k. For boolean functions κ this means that both κ and its complement $\overline{\kappa}$ are expressible as k-DNFs. Nested k-DNFs are one such family of interpretable models. We show how to find such models and provide software, based on a formally-verified SAT encoding, to do so. We report experiments indicating that nested DNFs are an interpretable alternative to random forests while retaining the same accuracy.

Keywords: Machine learning · Interpretable models

1 Introduction

Extensive deployment of Machine Learning (ML) must go hand-in-hand with explainable AI, in order to provide explanations to human users of decisions taken by ML models. Interpretable models are particularly user-friendly since they provide a guarantee of human comprehensibility of all decisions taken by the model.

Traditionally, decision trees (DTs) have been advocated as the interpretable alternative to black-box models. In recent work, it was pointed out that DTs are not the only family of interpretable models and a novel alternative (called nested DNFs) was proposed [11]. Whereas the learning and explaining of DTs have been well-studied [20,3,13], this is not the case for other interpretable models. The present paper helps to fill this gap by showing how SAT and MaxSAT solvers can be used to learn alternative interpretable models. Indeed, we provide software with formal guarantees for the investigation and construction of nested DNFs.

In recent years, a new domain of research has emerged concerning applying formal reasoning to explaining decisions of classifiers [16,38,26] with some works focusing on desirable properties of explanations [1,2] and others on the computational complexity of producing one or more explanations [7,6,12]. This is in contrast with popular and widely-used techniques, such as LIME [33], SHAP [24] and Anchors [34], which unfortunately do not provide any formal guarantees of correctness of explanations [25,27,23]. The formal reasoning approach is usually

E. Albert and C. Pasareanu (Eds.): FASE 2026, LNCS 16504, pp. 107–125, 2026.
https://doi.org/10.1007/978-3-032-22774-4_6

based on the notion of prime implicant or abductive explanation [37]. A binary boolean classifier κ is defined by its prime implicants and, for an instance x such that $\kappa(x) = 1$, any prime implicant consistent with x can be considered as an abductive explanation of the decision $\kappa(x) = 1$. This leads to the following definition of abductive explanation (also known as prime-impicant explanation or sufficient reason). We consider a classifier $\kappa : \{0,1\}^N \rightarrow \{0,1\}$ and an instance $x = (x_1, \ldots, x_N)$ composed of N boolean features.

Definition 1. *A* weak abductive explanation *(weak AXp) of the decision $\kappa(x) = c$ is a set $A \subseteq \{1, \ldots, N\}$ of features such that*

$$\forall y \in \{0,1\}^N \left(\left(\bigwedge_{i \in A} (x_i = y_i) \right) \longrightarrow \kappa(y) = c \right).$$

An abductive explanation *(AXp) is a subset-minimal weak AXp.*

Observe that the AXp's of a positive decision $\kappa(x) = 1$ are the prime implicants of κ consistent with x, whereas the AXp's of a negative decision $\kappa(x') = 0$ are the prime implicants of $\overline{\kappa}$ consistent with x'.

We now give a formal definition of interpretability, based on the size of explanations. This definition is parameterized by k, a small integer.

Definition 2. *A classifier κ is k-AXp interpretable if every decision $\kappa(x) = c$ has an AXp of size at most k.*

As an example, consider DTs of maximum depth k. They are k-AXp interpretable since each decision corresponds to a path of length $l \leq k$ and the set of l features tested along the path is a weak AXp. If a boolean function κ is given in the form of a k-DNF, then its positive decisions each have a weak AXp of size at most k corresponding to a term which evaluates to true. However, for such a k-DNF to be k-AXp interpretable, its complement $\overline{\kappa}$ must also be expressible as a k-DNF so that negative decisions also have AXp's of size at most k.

2 Nested k-DNFs and nested (k, k')-DNFs

In this section we revisit the notion of nested k-DNFs defined in [11]. This is a class of k-DNFs whose complement is also a k-DNF thus guaranteeing k-AXp interpretability. As a running example, consider the following 3-DNF with 9 terms:

$$\kappa_1 = abc + def + ghi + abd + deg + agh + abg + ade + dgh \quad (1)$$

Remarkably, its complement also simplifies (after eliminating subsumed terms) to a 3-DNF:

$$\begin{aligned} \overline{\kappa_1} = \; & \overline{a}\,\overline{d}\,\overline{i} + \overline{a}\,\overline{d}\,\overline{g} + \overline{a}\,\overline{e}\,\overline{g} + \overline{b}\,\overline{d}\,\overline{g} + \overline{b}\,\overline{e}\,\overline{g} + \overline{c}\,\overline{d}\,\overline{g} \\ & + \overline{a}\,\overline{f}\,\overline{g} + + \overline{a}\,\overline{d}\,\overline{h} + \overline{a}\,\overline{e}\,\overline{h} + \overline{b}\,\overline{d}\,\overline{h} + \overline{b}\,\overline{e}\,\overline{h} \end{aligned}$$

This is a consequence of the fact that κ_1 is a nested 3-DNF (which we will define and explain in this section).

Consider k^2 literals $\ell_{i,j}$ $(1 \leq i, j \leq k)$. We can view $\{\ell_{i,j}\}$ as a $k \times k$ matrix:

$$\mathcal{L} = \begin{pmatrix} \ell_{1,1}\ \ell_{1,2} \ldots \ell_{1,k} \\ \vdots \\ \ell_{k,1}\ \ell_{k,2} \ldots \ell_{k,k} \end{pmatrix}$$

Using this matrix as a base, we can generate a large number of k-DNFs κ, composed of an arbitrary number n of terms, such that $\overline{\kappa}$ is also expressible as a k-DNF. For each $p = 1, \ldots, n$, let r_{pi} $(i = 1, \ldots, k)$ be k integers between 0 and k such that $\sum_{i=1}^{k} r_{pi} \leq k$. Then define κ as follows:

$$\kappa(x) = \bigvee_{p=1}^{n} \bigwedge_{i=1}^{k} \bigwedge_{j=1}^{r_{pi}} \ell_{i,j}$$

It is easy to see that the condition that $\sum_{i=1}^{k} r_{pi} \leq k$ for each $i = 1, \ldots, k$ ensures that κ is a k-DNF. Such a DNF is known as a *nested* k-DNF. For each $p = 1, \ldots, n$, the pth term of κ is the conjunction of the r_{pi} leftmost elements in row i of the matrix $\mathcal{L}$ (for $i = 1, \ldots, k$). It is this specific structure (the nested nature of the possible sets of literals from each row) that guarantees that the complement of κ is also a k-DNF [11].

We now generalize the notion of a nested k-DNF to a k-DNF whose complement is a k'-DNF, where k, k' are arbitrary and possible distinct positive integers, by considering $k' \times k$ matrices $\mathcal{L}$.

Definition 3. *A* nested (k, k')-DNF *is a k-DNF κ such that there exists a $k' \times k$ matrix of literals $\mathcal{L} = \{\ell_{i,j}\}$ and a set of integers $r_{pi} \in \{0, \ldots, k\}$ $(1 \leq p \leq n$, $1 \leq i \leq k')$ such that*

$$\kappa(x) = \bigvee_{p=1}^{n} \bigwedge_{i=1}^{k'} \bigwedge_{j=1}^{r_{pi}} \ell_{i,j}$$

In Definition 3, κ is a k-DNF, but note that we allow the possibility that $\sum_{i=1}^{k'} r_{pi}$ is greater than k: this can occur if there are repeated literals in the pth term.

Proposition 1. *The complement $\overline{\kappa}$ of a nested (k, k')-DNF is expressible as a k'-DNF.*

Proof. Clearly we have

$$\overline{\kappa}(x) = \bigwedge_{p=1}^{n} \bigvee_{i=1}^{k'} \bigvee_{j=1}^{r_{pi}} \overline{\ell_{i,j}} \tag{2}$$

We can expand this into a DNF: each term is obtained by selecting one literal from each of the n clauses in equation 2. An arbitrary term in the resulting DNF will necessarily have the following form:

$$t = \bigwedge_{i=1}^{k'} \bigwedge_{j \in S_i} \overline{\ell_{i,j}}$$

where the S_i ($i = 1, \ldots, k'$) are subsets of $\{1, \ldots, k\}$ such that $\sum_{i=1}^{k'} |S_i| = n$. Let NE denote the set of $i \in \{1, \ldots, k'\}$ such that $S_i \neq \emptyset$. For each $i \in NE$, let $m(i)$ denote the minimum value in S_i. By construction of the terms of κ as the conjunction of the leftmost elements in rows of $\mathcal{L}$, if a clause in equation 2 contains $\overline{\ell_{i,j}}$, where $j > m(i)$, then it also contains $\overline{\ell_{i,m(i)}}$. It follows that the DNF necessarily contains another term

$$t' = \bigwedge_{i \in NE} \overline{\ell_{i,m(i)}}$$

obtained by selecting $\ell_{i,m(i)}$ instead of $\ell_{i,j}$ for all $j > m(i)$ and for all $i \in NE$. It is easy to see that t is subsumed by t' (since $m(i) \in S_i$). By elimination of all strictly subsumed terms, it follows that $\overline{\kappa}$ is equivalent to a DNF composed of terms of the form $\wedge_{i \in NE} \overline{\ell_{i,m(i)}}$, and hence $\overline{\kappa}$ can be expressed as a k'-DNF (since $NE \subseteq \{1, \ldots, k'\}$).

Returning to our running example, observe that the 3-DNF κ_1 of equation 1, is a nested (3,3)-DNF (i.e. nested 3-DNF) derived from the square matrix

$$\mathcal{L} = \begin{pmatrix} \ell_{1,1} & \ell_{1,2} & \ell_{1,3} \\ \ell_{2,1} & \ell_{2,2} & \ell_{2,3} \\ \ell_{3,1} & \ell_{3,2} & \ell_{3,3} \end{pmatrix} = \begin{pmatrix} a & b & c \\ d & e & f \\ g & h & i \end{pmatrix}$$

For κ_1, the number of terms $n = 9$ and, for example, $(r_{11}, r_{12}, r_{13}) = (3, 0, 0)$, meaning that the first term abc is the conjunction of the three literals in the first row of $\mathcal{L}$, whereas $(r_{91}, r_{92}, r_{93}) = (0, 1, 2)$, meaning that the ninth (and last) term dgh is the conjunction of the first literal in the second row and the first two literals in the third row of $\mathcal{L}$.

3 Verifying that a k-DNF is a nested (k, k')-DNF

We study the problem of determining whether a k-DNF given as input is a nested (k, k')-DNF. We propose a SAT encoding.

3.1 The SAT encoding

The encoding we propose is based on the definition of a nested (k, k')-DNF, with constraints that ensure the terms align with Definition 3. Specifically, we start with an initial list of terms of size at most k, and the SAT encoding is employed to infer a $k' \times k$ matrix, if it exists, from which all the terms can be generated. The resulting SAT instance is satisfiable iff such a matrix exists (i.e. the terms

Variable	Description
$X_{i,j,l}$	True if the literal $\ell_{i,j}$ is l
$R_{p,i,j}$	True if the literal $\ell_{i,j}$ is used in the term p
$T_{p,i,j,l}$	True if the literal $\ell_{i,j}$ is l and used in the term p

Table 1. Variables used in the SAT encoding.

form a nested (k, k')-DNF). Table 1 summarizes the variables introduced for the encoding.

The constraints are formulated by the following set of clauses where m and n represent the number of literals and the number of terms, respectively.

- **Each element of the matrix has at least one literal**
  For each $i \in [0, k'-1]$ and $j \in [0, k-1]$, we add the clauses:

$$\bigvee_{l=0}^{m-1} X_{i,j,l} \tag{3}$$

- **Each element of the matrix has at most one literal**
  For each $i \in [0, k'-1]$ and $j \in [0, k-1]$ and each two distinct literals a and b where $(0 \leq a, b \leq m-1)$, we add the clauses:

$$\neg X_{i,j,a} \vee \neg X_{i,j,b} \tag{4}$$

- **Nested : If a term contains $\ell_{i,j+1}$, then it also contains $\ell_{i,j}$**
  For each $i \in [0, k'-1]$, $j \in [0, k-2]$ and $p \in [0, n-1]$, we add the clauses:

$$\neg R_{p,i,j+1} \vee R_{p,i,j} \tag{5}$$

- **$T_{p,i,j,l}$ is true iff $X_{i,j,l}$ is true and $R_{p,i,j}$ is true**
  For each $i \in [0, k'-1]$, $j \in [0, k-1]$, $l \in [0, m-1]$ and $p \in [0, n-1]$, we add the clauses:

$$\begin{gathered} \neg T_{p,i,j,l} \vee X_{i,j,l} \\ \neg T_{p,i,j,l} \vee R_{p,i,j} \\ \neg X_{i,j,l} \vee \neg R_{p,i,j} \vee T_{p,i,j,l} \end{gathered} \tag{6}$$

- **Identification of the literals that are present or absent in a term**
  For each $l \in [0, m-1]$ and $p \in [0, n-1]$, we add the following clauses (where $literals(p)$ is the set of literals in the term p of the input):

$$\begin{gathered} \text{If } l \in literals(p) \;:\; \bigvee_{i=0}^{k'-1} \bigvee_{j=0}^{k-1} T_{p,i,j,l} \\ \text{Otherwise, for each } i \in [0, k'-1] \text{ and } j \in [0, k-1] \;:\; \neg T_{p,i,j,l} \end{gathered} \tag{7}$$

3.2 Mechanized proof of correction

The SAT encoding is proven to be sound and complete using Why3 [10][3]. In other words, the encoding will return SAT if and only if the input k-DNF, represented by a list of terms, is a nested (k, k')-DNF.

Why3 Why3 is a platform based on the WhyML language, which combines imperative and functional aspects. It facilitates the specification and proof of programs by providing tools for specifying logical specifications (preconditions, postconditions, loop invariants, etc.) in first-order logic. It offers subgoal decomposition tactics and facilitates proof by connecting to various SMT solvers (automatic provers) as well as proof assistants such as Coq / Rocq (interactive provers). Why3 offers several libraries with lemmas and theorems that can be reused to facilitate the writing of proofs.

Why3 formalization The sources, including the Why3 formalization and the experiments, are available online : see page 16.

The SAT encoding relies on a k-DNF defined over a set of literals. To model this problem in Why3, we define a type `problem` using a record that includes a k-DNF `d`, a set `features` of features, the integer `k`, the number `n` of terms in the DNF, the number `m` of literals, and a bijection between the literals and integers (`num_to_literal`). It is notable that various constraints link these elements within the record (for instance, `m` is twice the cardinality of `features`). These constraints are defined in a predicate called `problem_valid`.

A witness proving that a k-DNF, with `n` terms, is a nested (k,k')-DNF is a pair consisting of a $k' \times k$ matrix of literals `lm` and a $n \times k'$ matrix `rpi` of integers representing the r_{pi} (of Definition 3). The type `nested_witness` represents such a witness using a record. To simplify manipulation in Why3, matrices have been encoded as sequences of sequences. A validity predicate (`nested_witness_valid (k':int) (input:problem) (nw:nested_witness)`) indicates that `lm` is a matrix of size $k' \times k$, `rpi` is a matrix of size $n \times k'$, all literals in `lm` are defined from the features of `features`, and all elements of `rpi` are positives. Finally, a predicate (`is_nested_witness (k':int) (input:problem) (nw:nested_witness)`) defines that the DNF (`input.d`) is a nested (k, k')-DNF, thanks to the witness `nw`. For `nw` to be a valid witness, each element of the matrix `rpi` must be less than `k`, and each term of the DNF `d` must be exactly defined by `lm` and `rpi` following Definition 3.

```
predicate is_nested_witness
        (k':int) (input:problem) (nw:nested_witness) =
    nested_witness_valid k' input nw
  ∧ (* All elements of the rpi matrix are at most k  *)
    (forall p: int. forall i:int.
    0 ≤ p < input.d.length → 0 ≤ i < k'
```

[3] https://www.why3.org

```
    → nw.rpi[p][i] ≤ input.k)
    (* Each term of the DNF d is exactly defined by lm and rpi *)
  ∧ (forall p: int. (0 ≤ p < input.d.length)
    → forall l:literal. (mem l input.d[p] ↔ exists i,j:int.
    0 ≤ i < k' ∧ 0 ≤j < nw.rpi[p][i] ∧ l = nw.lm[i][j]))
```

A k-DNF represented as an element of type problem is a nested (k, k')-DNF if there exists a witness that validates the predicate is_nested_witness.

```
predicate is_nested_k_kp_dnf (k':int) (pb:problem) =
   problem_valid pb
∧ exists nw:nested_witness. is_nested_witness k' pb nw
```

Similarly, the SAT encoding is described by a type sat_witness representing the variables of the encoding (see Table 1) : x a three-dimensional sequence, r a three-dimensional sequence and t a four-dimensional sequence. A predicate (sat_witness_valid (k':int) (input:problem) (nw:nested_witness)) signifies that x possesses a dimension of $k' \times k \times m$, whereas r has a dimension of $n \times k' \times k$ and t has a dimension of $n \times k' \times k \times m$. All clauses of the SAT encoding are described by predicates. For instance, the clauses described in (3) modelize that each element of the matrix has at least one literal. For the disjunctions to be true, at least one element must be true. So the clauses are represented as follows:

```
(* Each element of the matrix lm has at least one literal *)
predicate atLeastOneElement
          (k':int) (input:problem) (sw:sat_witness) =
  forall i,j : int. 0 ≤ i < k' → 0 ≤ j < input.k
  → (exists l:int. 0 ≤ l < input.m ∧ sw.x[i][j][l])
```

The clauses described in (4) are translated more directly as follows:

```
(* Each element of the matrix lm has at most one literal *)
predicate atMostOneElement
          (k':int) (input:problem) (sw:sat_witness) =
  forall i,j,a,b : int.
    0 ≤ i < k' → 0 ≤ j < input.k → 0 ≤ a < input.m
    → 0 ≤ b < input.m → a ≠ b
    → (¬ sw.x[i][j][a]) ∨ (¬ sw.x[i][j][b])
```

The same work is done for all clauses described in the section 3.1. Finally, a predicate (is_sat_witness (k':int) (input:problem) (sw : sat_witness)) defines that the sw witness is a solution of the SAT encoding of the original problem (input) as the conjunction of the six predicates derived from the SAT encoding.

```
predicate is_sat_witness
          (k':int) (input:problem) (sw:sat_witness) =
    sat_witness_valid k' input sw
  ∧ atLeastOneElement k' input sw
```

```
 ∧ atMostOneElement k' input sw
 ∧ nested k' input sw
 ∧ linkTXR k' input sw
 ∧ buildTMem k' input sw
 ∧ buildTNotMem k' input sw
```

The SAT encoding based on a k-DNF is satisfiable if there exists a witness that validates the predicate `is_sat_witness`.

```
predicate is_satisfiable (k':int) (pb:problem) =
    problem_valid pb
 ∧ exists sw:sat_witness. is_sat_witness k' pb sw
```

Indeed, if the initial problem is satisfiable, each of the clauses, and therefore each of the six predicates, will be satisfied.

Soundness The encoding is sound if when the SAT problem returns a solution, then the DNF is a nested (k, k')-DNF. This is expressed in Why3 as the following goal:

```
goal soundness : forall k':int. forall pb:problem.
  is_satisfiable k' pb → is_nested_k_kp_dnf k' pb
```

Since both parts of the implication are defined by the existence of a witness, the proof is based on the exhibition of a `nested_witness` from a `sat_witness`. A function `build_nested_witness` that creates a `nested_witness` from an integer `k'`, an input problem and a `sat_witness` is defined axiomatically. Two axioms define the size constraints of the `lm` and `rpi` matrices. One axiom defines the construction of the `lm` matrix. The combination of the `atLeastOneElement` and `atMostOneElement` ensures that, for all `i,j` there exists a unique integer `l`, such that `x[i][j][l]` is true. `lm[i][j]` is the literal associated with `l` via `num_to_literal`.

```
axiom buildLM :
 forall k':int. forall input:problem. forall sw:sat_witness.
   let nw = build_nested_witness k' input sw in
   forall i,j : int.  0 ≤ i < k' → 0 ≤ j < input.k
   → (exists l:int. 0 ≤ l < input.m ∧ sw.x[i][j][l]
       ∧ nw.lm[i][j] = (input.num_to_literal l))
```

A fourth axiom defines the construction of the `rpi` matrix from the `r` matrix. For all `p,i`, `rpi[p][i]` is the number of `j` such that `r[p][i][j]` is true. So `rpi[p][i]` $= \sum_{j=0}^{k-1}$ `(if r[p][i][j] then 1 else 0)`. The conditional is defined in a function `srpij` and the sum is the one defined in the module `Sum` of the integers (predefined in Why3).

```
use int.Sum as SI

function srpij (sw:sat_witness) : int → int → int → int=
```

```
  fun p → fun i → fun j → if sw.r[p][i][j] then 1 else 0

axiom buildRPI :
 forall k':int. forall input:problem. forall sw:sat_witness.
    let nw = build_nested_witness k' input sw in
    forall p,i: int. 0 ≤ p < input.n → 0 ≤ i < k'
    → nw.rpi[p][i] = SI.sum (srpij sw p i) 0 input.k
```

The proof of soundness therefore consists of proving that the witness constructed by the function `build_nested_witness` is indeed a nested witness.

```
lemma build_nested_witness_is_nested_witness :
  forall k':int. forall pb:problem. forall sw:sat_witness.
  problem_valid pb
  → is_sat_witness k' pb sw
  → is_nested_witness k' pb (build_nested_witness k' pb sw)
```

Unsurprisingly, the fact that all literals of the leftmost part (defined by `rpi`) of the matrix `lm` are in the term of the DNF `d` required the most lemmas. This proof is based on a lemma that is proven on the SAT encoding, namely that if the predicate associated with clauses (5) is true, then all lines of `rpi[p][i]` consist of 1 followed by 0. Thus, if `j < rpi[p][i]`, then `r[p][i][j]` is true, by definition of `rpi`. The existence of an `l` such that `x[i][j][l]` is true (clauses 3), leads to the existence of a `t[p][i][j][l]` and so to a literal of the DNF.

Completeness The encoding is complete if when the DNF is a nested (k, k')-DNF then the SAT problem returns a solution. This is expressed in Why3 as the following goal:

```
goal completness : forall k':int. forall pb:problem.
  is_nested_k_kp_dnf k' pb → is_satisfiable k' pb
```

Similarly to soundness, the proof is based on the exhibition of a `sat_witness` from a `nested_witness`. A function `build_satisfiable_witness` that creates a `sat_witness` from an integer `k'`, an input problem and a `nested_witness` is defined axiomatically. One axiom defines the size constraints of the `x`, `r` and `t` matrices. One axiom defines the construction of the `x` matrix from the `lm` matrix, i.e. `x[i][j][l]` is true iff `lm[i][j]` contains the literal associated to `l` (remember that a conversion literal to integer is needed).

```
axiom buildX :
 forall k':int. forall input:problem. forall nw:nested_witness.
    let sw = build_satisfiable_witness k' input nw in
    forall i,j,l : int.
    0 ≤ i < k' → 0 ≤ j < input.k → 0 ≤ l < input.m
    → sw.x[i][j][l]↔ nw.lm[i][j] = input.num_to_literal l
```

One axiom defines the construction of the `r` matrix from the `rpi` matrix, i.e. `r[p][i][j]` is true iff `j < rpi[p][i]`.

```
axiom buildR :
 forall k':int. forall input:problem. forall nw:nested_witness.
   let sw = build_satisfiable_witness k' input nw in
   forall i,j,p : int.
   0 ≤ i < k' → 0 ≤ j < input.k →  0 ≤ p < input.n
   → sw.r[p][i][j] ↔ j < nw.rpi[p][i]
```

One axiom defines the construction of the `t` matrix from the `x` and `r` matrices, i.e. `t[p][i][j][l]` is true iff `x[i][j][l] ∧ r[p][i][j]`.

```
axiom buildT :
 forall k':int. forall input:problem. forall nw:nested_witness.
   let sw = build_satisfiable_witness k' input nw in
   forall i,j,p,l:int.
     0 ≤ i < k' → 0 ≤ j < input.k
     → 0 ≤ p < input.n → 0 ≤ l < input.m
     → sw.t[p][i][j][l] ↔ sw.x[i][j][l] ∧ sw.r[p][i][j]
```

The proof of completeness therefore consists of proving that the witness constructed by the function `build_satisfiable_witness` is indeed a sat witness. The completeness is then ensured by the following lemma :

```
lemma build_satisfiable_witness_is_sat_witness :
  forall k':int. forall pb:problem. forall nw:nested_witness.
  problem_valid pb
  → is_nested_witness k' pb nw
  → is_sat_witness k' pb (build_satisfiable_witness k' pb nw)
```

The proof is almost entirely done automatically by SMT solvers. The two lemmas that required manual proof were those that required manipulation of the bijection between literals and integers.

Proof effort All lemmas and goals are proven using Why3 (version 1.8.1) coupled with Z3[4] (version 4.15.2) [29], Alt-Ergo[5] (version 2.6.2), CVC5[6] (version 1.1.2) and Coq / Rocq[7] (version 8.20.1) [8]. The proof of the two goals requires 43 lemmas, of which 25 are proven automatically using SMT solvers, while 18 are proven manually with Coq / Rocq.

4 Learning nested (k, k')-DNFs

From a practical standpoint, it is interesting to construct a nested (k, k')-DNF starting with a given dataset. Therefore, we propose a MaxSAT encoding grounded on the previous SAT encoding, with the aim of satisfying the established constraints while maximizing accuracy.

[4] https://github.com/Z3Prover/z3
[5] https://alt-ergo.ocamlpro.com/
[6] https://cvc5.github.io/
[7] https://rocq-prover.org/

4.1 The MaxSAT encoding

In the previous section, the starting point was a k-DNF composed of a list of terms, with the task being to verify whether it is a nested (k, k')-DNF by identifying a generating matrix for all terms. We now study an approach that takes as input a dataset alongside candidate terms of size at most k, from which a subset of terms will be retained forming a nested (k, k')-DNF with the intention of maximizing accuracy. Hence, the goal is to select terms that maximize the coverage of target class examples in the dataset, while minimizing the coverage of the examples labelled by the other class. Therefore, in addition to the variables presented in Table 1, we introduce the two variables defined in Table 2.

Variable	Description
M_p	True if the term p is taken in the DNF
E_i	True if the example e_i is covered by the DNF

Table 2. Variables used in the MaxSAT encoding.

The MaxSAT encoding we propose consists of hard clauses that must be satisfied while aiming to maximize the satisfaction of soft clauses. As hard clauses, clauses (3), (4), (5) and (6) remains unchanged, whereas the literal $\neg M_p$ is added to clauses (7), indicating the condition that the corresponding term is taken in the final DNF. Moreover, in order to determine which terms cover the dataset examples, we add, for each example e_i, the following clauses, which come from $E_i \leftrightarrow \bigvee_{p \in P_i} M_p$, where P_i denotes the set of terms that cover e_i. In other words, if the example e_i is covered by the DNF, then at least one of the terms that covers it (i.e., one of the terms of P_i) is taken in the DNF. Furthermore, if a term $p \in P_i$ is taken in the DNF, then the example e_i is covered by the DNF. Finally, if P_i is empty, no term covers the example e_i, so it cannot be covered by the DNF.

$$\begin{gathered}\text{If } P_i \text{ is not empty :}\\ \neg E_i \vee \bigvee_{p \in P_i} M_p\\ \text{for each } p \in P_i \text{ , } \neg M_p \vee E_i\\ \text{Otherwise : } \neg E_i\end{gathered} \tag{8}$$

As soft clauses, given that the goal is to maximize accuracy, the clauses are defined as follows, for each example e_i in the dataset, with $\mathcal{E}_c$ referring to the set of examples of the target class c intended to be represented by the DNF.

$$\begin{gathered}\text{If } e_i \in \mathcal{E}_c \text{ : } E_i\\ \text{Otherwise : } \neg E_i\end{gathered} \tag{9}$$

The output of the MaxSAT is a nested (k, k')-DNF The proof that the SAT solver output generates a nested (k, k')-DNF is based on the creation of witnesses from the variables X, R, and T of the encoding. To show that the MaxSAT encoding also generates a nested (k, k')-DNF, it suffices to look at the clauses that manipulate these variables and that have been modified, namely clauses (7). The addition of $\neg M_p$ is logically equivalent to $M_p \rightarrow$ the SAT formula (7).

Let CT be the set of candidate terms used as input to the MaxSAT solver. When MaxSAT returns an answer, this set can be partitioned as follows: $CT = \{p \in CT | M_p\} \cup \{p \in CT | \neg M_p\}$ that is, the terms taken in the DNF and the terms not taken in the DNF. Let $n = |\{p \in CT | M_p\}|$ and $f : \{p \in CT | M_p\} \rightarrow \{0, .., n-1\}$ be a bijection that defines a reindexing of the terms included in the DNF such that the new indices $q < n$. The clauses in the SAT encoding, when these terms are given as inputs, are satisfied by X, R' and T' such that:

- R' is a $n \times k' \times k$ matrix such that $R'[q][i][j] = R[f^{-1}(q)][i][j]$
- T' is a $n \times k' \times k \times m$ matrix such that $T'[q][i][j][l] = T[f^{-1}(q)][i][j][l]$

Indeed, for all $q < n$, $M_{f^{-1}(q)}$ is true, so each clause (7) in the SAT encoding is satisfied since it is the right-hand side of an implication whose left-hand side is true. The DNF constructed from X, R' and T' is a nested (k, k')-DNF (Proof 3.2). This same DNF is obtained from X, R and T. Therefore, the DNF extracted from the MaxSAT answer is a nested (k, k')-DNF.

4.2 Description of the Experiments

In order to guarantee k-AXp interpretability (see Definition 2) of learned models, we investigated the construction of a nested (k, k)-DNF from a dataset.

The number of possible terms for a maximum term size k and a given number of literals m is $\sum_{i=1}^{k} \binom{m}{i}$, which includes all combinations of literals with cardinality up to k. Even when the search space is restricted to consistent terms (i.e. those that do not contain both a literal and its negation) and further filtering to retain only the terms that cover more examples of the target class (than of the other class), the number of candidate terms remains large, causing a notable increase in the overall number of clauses in the MaxSAT encoding. In order to address this, we suggest beginning by considering decision trees paths as potential terms. Specifically, we construct a random forest (i.e. a collection of DTs) and take the paths that lead to the target class as terms (see Figure 1).

We used the Random Forest Classifier with default parameters from the sklearn package in Python to generate the trees. A random forest with $10 \times k$ trees of maximum depth k is considered for every value of k. We report the accuracy of the RFs and the accuracy of the nested (k, k)-DNFs found by the MaxSAT solver, where the paths of the trees of depth from 2 to k are the candidate terms taken into consideration. We used the incomplete MaxSAT solver NuWLS-c-IBR from the MaxSAT Evaluation 2024[8] with a timeout. Note that

[8] https://maxsat-evaluations.github.io/2024/descriptions.html

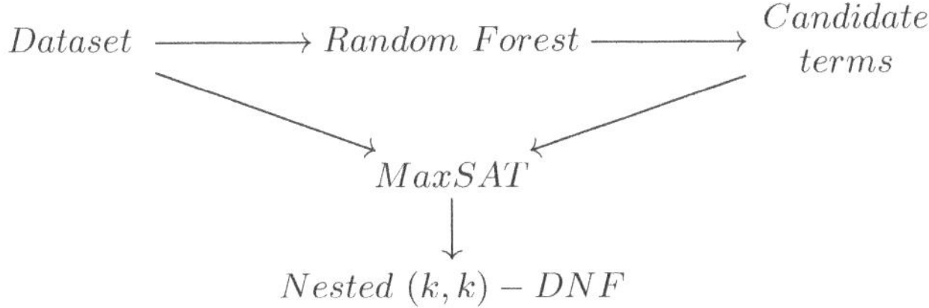

Fig. 1. General Architecture of the software

we searched for the nested (k,k)-DNFs for both classes, since the expressibility of a function as a nested (k,k)-DNF is not generally preserved under complementation (the complement of a nested (k,k)-DNF is guaranteed to be a k-DNF but not necessarily a nested (k,k)-DNF).

4.3 Datasets

We selected a collection of datasets from the UCI Repository[9] that contain categorical features in order to avoid the possibility of having a large number of literals, which would be the case if continuous features were used. All datasets consist of two classes, except for Balance Scale and Car Evaluation, which originally had 3 and 4 classes, respectively. To convert them to binary classification, the majority class was retained as one class, while the remaining classes were merged into a single second class. Additionally, label encoding was applied to convert some features into numeric values. An overview of these datasets is given in Table 3, with the last column indicating the average number of distinct values per feature. For each dataset, 80% of the examples was used for training while the rest was used for testing, except for the Monks and SPECT Heart datasets, where the train and test sets are provided separately.

Dataset	# Examples	# Features	Avg. Cardinality
Balance Scale	625	4	5.0
Car Evaluation	1728	6	3.5
Chess kr vs. kp	3196	36	2.0
Monks-1	432	6	2.8
Monks-2	432	6	2.8
Monks-3	432	6	2.8
SPECT Heart	267	22	2.0
Tic-Tac-Toe	958	9	3.0

Table 3. Characteristics of the datasets used in the experiments.

[9] https://archive.ics.uci.edu/datasets

4.4 Results

Our experimental results, presented in Table 4, indicate that the MaxSAT solver effectively finds nested (k, k)-DNFs with high accuracy, outperforming random forests (which do not have a guarantee of k-AXp interpretability) in certain datasets. For instance, in the Monks datasets, which consist of three artificial domains with specific structures, the nested (k, k)-DNFs formulas accurately represents the data. Note that the 5% noise in the Monks-3 training set causes overfitting as k increases beyond 3, although the nested $(3, 3)$-DNF model achieves 100% test accuracy. However, due to the restriction of only being able to contain up to k^2 distinct literals, the datasets used were relatively small to medium in size, particularly in terms of the number of features. In such cases, when the number of literals is not large, as in boolean domains, nested (k, k)-DNFs demonstrated good performance due to their ability to express a great variety of dependencies between literals. In contrast, the increasing number of candidate terms to be considered can become significant as the number of literals increases, especially when combined with a large value of k, which may cause the nested (k, k)-DNFs to underperform. More specifically, this results in an excessive increase in the number of clauses in the MaxSAT, making it difficult to find a model. Mitigating this issue demands reducing the number of clauses, though doing so requires considering fewer candidate terms, which may limit the DNF's ability to accurately represent the dataset.

From another viewpoint, the approach used in the experiments can be seen as extracting the knowledge from the trees into a smaller model, a nested (k, k)-DNF, thereby enhancing the model's interpretability. Notably, we observed that the nested (k, k)-DNFs for $k = 7$ do not exceed 20 terms in size. With regard to runtime, the solver successfully finds a model within a 2 minute timeout across all cases, except for a single representation of one class of the Chess dataset for $k = 7$, which requires increasing the timeout. Hence, we extended the timeout to 3 minutes for all datasets for $k = 7$, providing the solver more time to potentially find better models due to the larger size of the formulas.

5 State of the art

In [18], the authors provide an overview of recent progress in reasoning and constraint-based approaches to learning interpretable machine learning models, and discuss their advantages and limitations. They mainly consider as interpretable: decision trees, decision sets and decision lists. Depth-k decisions trees are known to be k-AXp interpretable and have been compared experimentally with nested k-DNFs [11]. However, unlike nested k-DNFs and depth-k decision trees, decision sets and decision lists do not provide guarantees on the size of explanations of default decisions, and hence cannot be considered k-AXp interpretable.

Definition 3 provides a generalisation of nested k-DNFs to nested (k, k')-DNFs. In the context of learning interpretable models, as in our experiments, it makes sense to choose $k = k'$, but there are potential applications in which

Dataset	RF (k=2)	DNF$_1$ (k=2)	DNF$_0$ (k=2)	RF (k=3)	DNF$_1$ (k=3)	DNF$_0$ (k=3)	RF (k=4)	DNF$_1$ (k=4)	DNF$_0$ (k=4)
Balance Scale	**85.60**	72.80	72.00	**93.60**	83.20	83.20	**93.60**	87.20	82.40
Car Evaluation	78.61	**87.86**	**87.86**	**95.38**	94.51	94.51	98.27	**98.55**	96.24
Chess kr vs. kp	**90.00**	80.78	84.38	**93.12**	**93.12**	**93.12**	93.12	**94.38**	94.22
Monks-1	**75.46**	75.00	75.00	86.11	83.33	**91.67**	89.81	91.67	**100.0**
Monks-2	**67.13**	60.19	61.81	68.29	64.12	**71.76**	70.14	67.36	**70.83**
Monks-3	96.99	**97.22**	**97.22**	97.22	94.44	**100.0**	97.22	95.37	**99.07**
SPECT Heart	70.05	68.45	**71.12**	73.26	73.26	**73.80**	**73.80**	63.10	57.75
Tic-Tac-Toe	65.62	67.71	**68.75**	72.92	75.00	**80.73**	79.69	**84.38**	82.29

Dataset	RF (k=5)	DNF$_1$ (k=5)	DNF$_0$ (k=5)	RF (k=6)	DNF$_1$ (k=6)	DNF$_0$ (k=6)	RF (k=7)	DNF$_1$ (k=7)	DNF$_0$ (k=7)
Balance Scale	**89.60**	83.20	84.80	**92.80**	80.00	86.40	**91.20**	77.60	75.20
Car Evaluation	97.98	98.27	**98.84**	**98.84**	**98.84**	98.27	**99.13**	**99.13**	**99.13**
Chess kr vs. kp	93.12	**94.53**	93.44	93.12	**95.47**	94.06	93.12	93.59	**94.22**
Monks-1	89.35	**100.0**	**100.0**	90.51	**100.0**	**100.0**	91.67	**100.0**	**100.0**
Monks-2	72.92	70.37	**75.00**	77.78	**90.05**	77.55	80.09	**83.80**	65.05
Monks-3	**97.45**	95.14	94.44	**97.22**	88.89	91.90	**95.60**	93.06	90.74
SPECT Heart	**74.33**	69.52	62.57	**74.33**	71.12	66.31	**75.94**	67.38	59.89
Tic-Tac-Toe	85.42	**90.10**	85.42	86.46	74.48	**86.98**	88.02	**92.19**	69.27

Test accuracy (%)

Table 4. Test accuracy of depth-k Random Forests and Nested (k, k)-DNFs. Columns RF, DNF$_1$ and DNF$_0$ denote Random Forest, DNF representation of class 1 and DNF representation of class 0, respectively.

$k \neq k'$. For example, if a given model κ is determined to be a nested (k, k')-DNF, where $k' < k$, then we may prefer to present its complement $\overline{\kappa}$ (which is a k'-DNF) to the user. A minor difference between nested k-DNFs and nested (k, k)-DNFs is that the latter imposes only that the number of *distinct* literals taken from the matrix $\mathcal{L}$ to build a term be at most k.

The use of (Max)SAT encodings for model learning has been explored in a variety of studies. Notably, several works have proposed SAT-based approaches for generating decision trees [9,30,21,4], as well as methods based on MaxSAT [15]. In [35], they combine the scalability of heuristic methods with the strength of encoding-based exact methods. A parallel can be drawn with our method: we use heuristics to identify candidate terms using a Random Forest, followed by MaxSAT which provides guarantees on the generated model. A (Max)SAT formulation has also been used in learning oblique decision trees (i.e. trees with linear combinations of features at each node) [5]. Furthermore, a (Max)SAT encoding has been introduced for training other models, namely decision sets and decision lists, as shown in [19,40,17]. For instance, [40] construct decision sets and decision lists that achieve complete accuracy on the training data while being minimal in size, leveraging modern SAT-solving techniques to do so. Lastly, a novel MaxSAT encoding for learning Binary Decision Diagrams has been proposed in [36]. Clearly, models of different types impose structural requirements that must be met. In our work as well, we construct DNF formulas that satisfy a specific structural property. We go further by formally proving that this property is correctly enforced by the (Max)SAT encoding.

DNF formulas offer a simple and intuitive representation of boolean functions. Since their introduction, learning these models has been extensively studied [39,31,22,14]. Moreover, DNF simplification has been addressed in prior works, including the classical techniques introduced in [32,28]. Unlike studies that focus only on maximizing accuracy, our approach prioritizes maintaining the desired structure (i.e. nested DNF), even if it comes at the cost of some performance degradation. Doing so enables a gain in interpretability, given the guarantee that the size of the terms in the complement are bounded by a fixed constant.

6 Conclusion

Confidence in decisions taken by a machine-learning model requires explanations which are comprehensible by humans. We have investigated a recently-discovered class of interpretable models called nested DNFs. In order to ensure formal correctness of our experimental investigation of nested DNFs, we formally verified an encoding of the problem of deciding whether a DNF is expresssible as a nested DNF. This allowed us to use produce reliable software for learning a nested DNF from a dataset.

The subsequent experimental comparison of the learnt nested DNFs with random forests allowed us to confirm the viability of learning interpretable models whose accuracy is comparable with models which do not have a guarantee of interpretability. One avenue of possible future research is to develop heuristics for larger datasets and models. Another is the search for other interpretable models such as hybrid models combining decision trees and nested DNFs.

Data availability

The sources, including the Why3 formalization and the experiments, are available through DOI https://doi.org/10.5281/zenodo.18330397. Any modifications made after the publication of the paper will be visible at https://github.com/hurault/FASE26.

Acknowledgement

This work was funded by the French National Research Agency project ForML ANR-23-CE25-0009.

References

1. Amgoud, L., Ben-Naim, J.: Axiomatic foundations of explainability. In: Raedt, L.D. (ed.) IJCAI. pp. 636–642. ijcai.org (2022). https://doi.org/10.24963/ijcai.2022/90
2. Amgoud, L., Cooper, M.C., Debbaoui, S.: Axiomatic characterisations of sample-based explainers. In: ECAI. Frontiers in Artificial Intelligence and Applications, vol. 392, pp. 770–777. IOS Press (2024). https://doi.org/10.3233/FAIA240561
3. Audemard, G., Lagniez, J., Marquis, P., Szczepanski, N.: Deriving provably correct explanations for decision trees: The impact of domain theories. In: IJCAI. pp. 3688–3696. ijcai.org (2024), https://www.ijcai.org/proceedings/2024/408
4. Avellaneda, F.: Efficient inference of optimal decision trees. In: AAAI. pp. 3195–3202. AAAI Press (2020). https://doi.org/10.1609/AAAI.V34I04.5717
5. Avellaneda, F.: Learning optimal oblique decision trees with (max)sat. In: IJCAI 2025. pp. 2558–2565. ijcai.org (2025). https://doi.org/10.24963/IJCAI.2025/285
6. Barceló, P., Monet, M., Pérez, J., Subercaseaux, B.: Model interpretability through the lens of computational complexity. In: Larochelle, H., Ranzato, M., Hadsell, R., Balcan, M., Lin, H. (eds.) NeurIPS (2020), https://proceedings.neurips.cc/paper/2020/hash/b1adda14824f50ef24ff1c05bb66faf3-Abstract.html
7. Bassan, S., Amir, G., Katz, G.: Local vs. global interpretability: A computational complexity perspective. In: ICML. Proceedings of Machine Learning Research, vol. 235, pp. 3133–3167 (2024), https://openreview.net/forum?id=veEjiN2w9F
8. Bertot, Y., Castéran, P.: Interactive Theorem Proving and Program Development - Coq'Art: The Calculus of Inductive Constructions. Texts in Theoretical Computer Science. An EATCS Series, Springer (2004). https://doi.org/10.1007/978-3-662-07964-5
9. Bessiere, C., Hebrard, E., O'Sullivan, B.: Minimising decision tree size as combinatorial optimisation. In: Gent, I.P. (ed.) CP 2009. LNCS, vol. 5732, pp. 173–187. Springer (2009). https://doi.org/10.1007/978-3-642-04244-7_16
10. Bobot, F., Filliâtre, J.C., Marché, C., Paskevich, A.: Why3: Shepherd your herd of provers. In: Boogie 2011: First International Workshop on Intermediate Verification Languages. pp. 53–64 (2011)
11. Cooper, M.C., Bousdira, I., Carbonnel, C.: Interpretable DNFs. In: IJCAI. pp. 4985–4993 (2025). https://doi.org/10.24963/IJCAI.2025/555
12. Cooper, M.C., Marques-Silva, J.: Tractability of explaining classifier decisions. Artif. Intell. **316** (2023). https://doi.org/10.1016/J.ARTINT.2022.103841
13. Demirovic, E., Hebrard, E., Jean, L.: Blossom: an anytime algorithm for computing optimal decision trees. In: Krause, A., Brunskill, E., Cho, K., Engelhardt, B., Sabato, S., Scarlett, J. (eds.) ICML. vol. 202, pp. 7533–7562. PMLR (2023)
14. Feldman, V.: Hardness of approximate two-level logic minimization and PAC learning with membership queries. J. Comput. Syst. Sci. **75**(1), 13–26 (2009). https://doi.org/10.1016/J.JCSS.2008.07.007
15. Hu, H., Siala, M., Hebrard, E., Huguet, M.: Learning optimal decision trees with MaxSAT and its integration in AdaBoost. In: Bessiere, C. (ed.) IJCAI. pp. 1170–1176 (2020). https://doi.org/10.24963/IJCAI.2020/163
16. Hurault, A., Marques-Silva, J.: Certified logic-based explainable AI - the case of monotonic classifiers. In: Prevosto, V., Seceleanu, C. (eds.) Tests and Proofs - 17th International Conference, TAP 2023. LNCS, vol. 14066, pp. 51–67. Springer (2023). https://doi.org/10.1007/978-3-031-38828-6_4
17. Ignatiev, A., Lam, E., Stuckey, P.J., Marques-Silva, J.: A scalable two stage approach to computing optimal decision sets. In: AAAI. pp. 3806–3814. AAAI Press (2021). https://doi.org/10.1609/AAAI.V35I5.16498

18. Ignatiev, A., Marques-Silva, J., Narodytska, N., Stuckey, P.J.: Reasoning-based learning of interpretable ML models. In: Zhou, Z. (ed.) IJCAI. pp. 4458–4465. ijcai.org (2021). https://doi.org/10.24963/IJCAI.2021/608
19. Ignatiev, A., Pereira, F., Narodytska, N., Marques-Silva, J.: A sat-based approach to learn explainable decision sets. In: Galmiche, D., Schulz, S., Sebastiani, R. (eds.) IJCAR 2018. LNCS, vol. 10900, pp. 627–645. Springer (2018). https://doi.org/10.1007/978-3-319-94205-6_41
20. Izza, Y., Ignatiev, A., Marques-Silva, J.: On tackling explanation redundancy in decision trees. J. Artif. Intell. Res. **75**, 261–321 (2022)
21. Janota, M., Morgado, A.: SAT-based encodings for optimal decision trees with explicit paths. In: Pulina, L., Seidl, M. (eds.) SAT 2020. LNCS, vol. 12178, pp. 501–518. Springer (2020). https://doi.org/10.1007/978-3-030-51825-7_35
22. Klivans, A.R., Servedio, R.A.: Learning DNF in time $2^{\tilde{O}(n^{1/3})}$. J. Comput. Syst. Sci. **68**(2), 303–318 (2004). https://doi.org/10.1016/J.JCSS.2003.07.007
23. Létoffé, O., Huang, X., Marques-Silva, J.: Towards trustable SHAP scores. In: Walsh, T., Shah, J., Kolter, Z. (eds.) AAAI-25. pp. 18198–18208. AAAI Press (2025). https://doi.org/10.1609/AAAI.V39I17.34002
24. Lundberg, S.M., Lee, S.I.: A unified approach to interpreting model predictions. Curran Associates, Inc. (2017), http://papers.nips.cc/paper/7062-a-unified-approach-to-interpreting-model-predictions.pdf
25. Marques-Silva, J.: Disproving XAI myths with formal methods - initial results. In: Aït-Ameur, Y., Khendek, F., Méry, D. (eds.) ICECCS 2023. pp. 12–21. IEEE (2023). https://doi.org/10.1109/ICECCS59891.2023.00012
26. Marques-Silva, J.: Logic-based explainability: Past, present & future. CoRR **abs/2406.11873** (2024), https://doi.org/10.48550/arXiv.2406.11873
27. Marques-Silva, J., Huang, X.: Explainability is *Not* a game. Commun. ACM **67**(7), 66–75 (2024). https://doi.org/10.1145/3635301
28. McCluskey, E.J.: Minimization of boolean functions. The Bell System Technical Journal **35**(6), 1417–1444 (1956). https://doi.org/10.1002/j.1538-7305.1956.tb03835.x
29. de Moura, L., Bjørner, N.: Z3: An efficient SMT solver. In: Ramakrishnan, C.R., Rehof, J. (eds.) Tools and Algorithms for the Construction and Analysis of Systems. pp. 337–340. Springer (2008)
30. Narodytska, N., Ignatiev, A., Pereira, F., Marques-Silva, J.: Learning optimal decision trees with SAT. In: Lang, J. (ed.) IJCAI 2018. pp. 1362–1368. ijcai.org (2018). https://doi.org/10.24963/IJCAI.2018/189
31. Pitt, L., Valiant, L.G.: Computational limitations on learning from examples. J. ACM **35**(4), 965–984 (1988). https://doi.org/10.1145/48014.63140
32. Quine, W.V.: The problem of simplifying truth functions. The American Mathematical Monthly **59**(8), 521–531 (1952), http://www.jstor.org/stable/2308219
33. Ribeiro, M.T., Singh, S., Guestrin, C.: "Why should I trust you?": Explaining the predictions of any classifier. In: Proceedings of the 22nd ACM SIGKDD International Conference on Knowledge Discovery and Data Mining. pp. 1135–1144 (2016)
34. Ribeiro, M.T., Singh, S., Guestrin, C.: Anchors: High-precision model-agnostic explanations. In: McIlraith, S.A., Weinberger, K.Q. (eds.) AAAI. pp. 1527–1535. AAAI Press (2018). https://doi.org/10.1609/AAAI.V32I1.11491
35. Schidler, A., Szeider, S.: SAT-based decision tree learning for large data sets. J. Artif. Intell. Res. **80**, 875–918 (2024). https://doi.org/10.1613/JAIR.1.15956

36. Shati, P., Cohen, E., McIlraith, S.A.: Sat-based learning of compact binary decision diagrams for classification. In: Yap, R.H.C. (ed.) CP 2023. LIPIcs, vol. 280, pp. 33:1–33:19. Schloss Dagstuhl - Leibniz-Zentrum für Informatik (2023). https://doi.org/10.4230/LIPICS.CP.2023.33
37. Shih, A., Choi, A., Darwiche, A.: A symbolic approach to explaining bayesian network classifiers. In: IJCAI. pp. 5103–5111 (2018)
38. Törnblom, J., Nadjm-Tehrani, S.: Formal verification of input-output mappings of tree ensembles. Sci. Comput. Program. **194**, 102450 (2020). https://doi.org/10.1016/J.SCICO.2020.102450
39. Valiant, L.G.: A theory of the learnable. Communications of the ACM **27**, 1134–1142 (1984)
40. Yu, J., Ignatiev, A., Stuckey, P.J., Bodic, P.L.: Learning optimal decision sets and lists with SAT. J. Artif. Intell. Res. **72**, 1251–1279 (2021). https://doi.org/10.1613/JAIR.1.12719

DivKC: A Divide-and-Conquer Approach to Knowledge Compilation

Olivier Zeyen[1], Karim Tit[1], Maxime Cordy[1], and Gilles Perrouin[2]

[1] Interdisciplinary Centre for Security, Reliability and Trust, University of Luxembourg, Luxembourg
[2] PReCISE/NaDI, University of Namur, Belgium

Abstract. Knowledge compilation (KC) transforms Boolean formulae into alternative representations that allow for more efficient reasoning. However, KC still fails to scale on some Boolean formulae, including some representing the variability of large configurable systems (e.g., OS kernels, automotive product lines, etc.), for which these analyses are paramount. We hypothesise that a divide-and-conquer strategy to knowledge compilation may push its scalability further. Concretely, our DivKC algorithms decompose a large Boolean formula into two smaller ones, which we can easily compile into the d-DNNF form. When evaluated on a diversified benchmark of 4,656 formulae, DivKC compiles 114 formulae out of the 672 formulae that were previously out of reach for the D4 state-of-the-art d-DNNF compiler. We then show how to leverage DivKC decompositions to build an approximate model counter and a uniform random sampler.

1 Introduction

Knowledge compilation (KC) is the task of transforming Boolean formulae into alternative representations that allow for more efficient reasoning [7]. Boolean formulae are typically expressed in conjunctive normal form (CNF), which facilitates specific operations such as conditioning and conjunction. However, fundamental tasks such as model counting (#SAT) and uniform random sampling (URS) remain computationally intractable for large CNF instances. URS plays an important role in software product line (SPL) analysis, where it is used for tasks such as software testing, statistical inference, and optimal configuration search [18]. Knowledge compilation can help overcome the intractability of URS and #SAT by transforming CNF formulae into representations that are more amenable to #SAT [28] and URS [23].

One such language is the deterministic decomposable negation normal form (d-DNNF) [6], which is known to scale well in practice [27]. Efficient compilers for the d-DNNF language exist — most prominently D4 [14] — thereby enabling efficient solving of #SAT and URS. Despite these significant advances, formulae with large and intricate solution spaces remain out of reach for existing compilers [27]. Approximate algorithms exist for #SAT like ApproxMC 7 [21]. However, approximate model counting does not generate the reusable data

E. Albert and C. Pasareanu (Eds.): FASE 2026, LNCS 16504, pp. 126–146, 2026.
https://doi.org/10.1007/978-3-032-22774-4_7

structures that KC offers. Therefore, an approximate algorithm can be unsuitable if multiple calls to a model counter are necessary (e.g., feature cardinality computation [28]) or for problems that necessitate solving other reasoning tasks.

In order to enhance the effectiveness of KC, we propose DivKC, a divide-and-conquer approach for d-DNNF compilation. The key principle of our method is to decompose an input formula F to produce two smaller formulae that can be compiled independently and at a lower computational cost than F. This decomposition brings many advantages, including its application to #SAT and URS and the production (by construction) of sound lower and upper bounds for the model count of F. We combine these advantages into an effective statistical method to estimate $|R_F|$, the number of models of F. This method relies on computing approximate lower and upper bounds for $|R_F|$, which are shown to be tighter than the two bounds obtained during the decomposition. As for URS, we can similarly simplify the resolution of this problem by successfully sampling from the two decomposed formulae.

To assess the benefits of our approach, we conduct extensive experiments on four datasets totalling 4,656 formulae. By using our method, we manage to compile to d-DNNF 114 formulae out of the 672 formulae that were previously out of reach for D4 [14]. We thereby demonstrate that DivKC can enhance the compilation ability of the state-of-the-art d-DNNF compiler. Moreover, we show that our statistical method to compute upper and lower bounds of $|R_F|$ achieves 85% coverage of the true model count, while producing intervals that are significantly smaller than the theoretical bounds (about 9.5 billion times smaller for the median case). Finally, we show that our random sampler based on DivKC is the first heuristic-based random sampler to validate at least one test of the test suite proposed by Zeyen et al. [34]. All of the programs and experimental results are available on our companion GitHub [32].

2 Related Work

Model counting is the problem of counting the number of solutions to a formula. Model counting can be done either by specialised algorithms like sharpSAT [29] or GANAK [22], or by using knowledge compilers. Knowledge compilation can generate a reusable data structure that accelerates computations, as shown by Sundermann et al. [28]. Approximate model counters have been proposed to overcome the lack of scalability of exact model counting. A notable approximate model counter is ApproxMC 7 [21], which provides theoretical guarantees on the quality of the model counts and is generally considered to be the state-of-the-art in approximate model counting. Other approximate model counters are ApproxCount [31], which offers no guarantees, and SampleCount [11], which returns a lower bound to the true model count with high confidence. However, approximate model counting has the disadvantage of not generating a reusable data structure. Therefore, an approximate model counter is unlikely to be suitable if multiple calls to a model counter are necessary.

Uniform random sampling is a problem related to model counting, as model counting can be used to sample uniformly at random from a formula, *e.g.*, SPUR [1] and Smarch [19]. A uniform random sampler is a procedure that, given a formula F, will return a solution to F at random. There exist heuristic-based samplers like STS [9], and Quicksampler [8] or true uniform random samplers like SPUR [1]. A notable uniform random sampler is KUS [23], which uses D4 [14] to compile a formula to d-DNNF and then uses the compiled form to sample solutions of F.

Sundermann et al. [28] showed that knowledge compilation can be instrumental in practice but also exposed its limitations [27]. Many knowledge compilers exist, such as C2D [5], D4 [14], and DSharp [17]. While all of them scale to many large formulae, some remain out of reach for any of these compilers.

DMC [15] is a distributed model counter based on D4 [14]. DMC distributes the workload similarly to work stealing. Worker nodes try to solve the problem and notify the master node when they are idle. If a worker node is idle, the master suggests help to busy worker nodes. A worker node can either accept the help and delegate some work or reject the help.

Given the many uses of knowledge compilation and the limitations of current approaches, we propose an algorithm which allows us to push the limits of current knowledge compilers by splitting the input formula into smaller, more manageable parts before using the state-of-the-art D4 [14] compiler. Importantly, our work differs from DMC because we do not use variable assignments to split the input formula. Consequently, we only use two calls to D4 [14] to obtain our final d-DNNF.

3 Preliminaries

A Boolean formula F is defined over a set of Boolean variables $Var(F)$ and evaluates to either true or false. A literal is either a variable x or its negation $\neg x$. The notation $Var(x)$ (or $Var(\neg x)$) refers to the variable associated with the literal x (or $\neg x$, respectively).

A formula F is in negation normal form (NNF) if the negation only appears in front of variables. A clause is a disjunction of literals and can be represented as a set of literals. F is in conjunctive normal form (CNF) if F is written as a conjunction of clauses ($F = \bigwedge_{C_i} \bigvee_{l \in C_i} l$). A CNF formula can be represented as a set of clauses.

An assignment a to the variables $Var(F)$ is a set of literals such that $\forall x \in a : (\neg x \notin a)$. An assignment a is a partial assignment if $\exists x \in Var(F) : (x \notin a \wedge \neg x \notin a)$. An assignment a is a complete assignment if $\forall x \in Var(F) : (x \in a \vee \neg x \in a)$. A model m of F ($m \models F$) is a complete assignment such that F evaluates to true under m. We define R_F as the set of models m of F such that $m \in R_F$ if and only if $m \models F$. We define $|R_F|$ as the number of models of F. A partial assignment a is sufficient if for a CNF formula F we have $\forall c \in F : (c \cap a \neq \emptyset)$, i.e., any complete assignment b with $a \subseteq b$ is a model of F ($b \models F$). Two assignments a, b are orthogonal if they disagree on at least one literal, i.e., $\exists x \in a : (\neg x \in b)$. A set of partial assignments is orthogonal if and only if every pair of assignments is orthogonal. We denote by $F|_a$ the conditioning of F with a (i.e., the propagation of the literals of a in F).

F is in deterministic decomposable NNF (d-DNNF) if every conjunction is *decomposable* and every disjunction is *deterministic*. A conjunction $\bigwedge A_i$ is *decomposable* if $\forall i \neq j : (Var(A_i) \cap Var(A_j) = \emptyset)$. A disjunction $\bigvee O_i$ is *deterministic* if $\forall i \neq j : (R_{O_i \wedge O_j} = \emptyset)$.

Variable forgetting is defined as $Forget(F, v) = (F[v \leftarrow false]) \vee (F[v \leftarrow true])$, with $F[v \leftarrow c]$ the formula obtained by substituting variable v by c in F [30, 13]. Projecting F on a set of variables $P \subseteq Var(F)$ (denoted by $Project(F, P)$) is equivalent to forgetting every variable in $Var(F) \setminus P$. By definition, we have $R_{Project(F,P)} = \{m \cap L \mid m \in R_F\}$ with $L = \{x, \neg x \mid x \in P\}$. We define a function $Split(F)$ that returns a set of variables $P \subseteq Var(F)$.

Definition 1. *Model Counting (# SAT) is the problem of computing the size of R_F.*

Definition 2. *Uniform random sampling (URS) is the problem of sampling a model from R_F such that every model $m \in R_F$ has probability $\frac{1}{|R_F|}$ of being sampled.*

4 DivKC

Our approach is based on the idea that splitting a formula F into smaller parts facilitates its compilation into a target language. More specifically, Zeyen et al. [33] show a strong correlation between the time and memory needed to compile a formula to d-DNNF and the number of variables and clauses in the formula. Our approach explicitly utilises this correlation by decomposing an input formula into subformulae with fewer variables and/or fewer clauses. A key strength of our approach, and one that distinguishes it from previous work, is that it does not rely on Shannon decomposition, which keeps the number of decompositions both predictable and small.

4.1 Overview of the Decomposition Algorithm

Algorithm 1 *Compile*(F)

Require: F is a satisfiable Boolean formula in CNF
1: $P \leftarrow Split(F)$
2: $G_P \leftarrow Project(F, P)$
3: $G_U \leftarrow \{c \in F \mid Var(c) \not\subseteq P\}$
4: **return** $ddnnf(G_P), ddnnf(G_U)$

A high-level description of our approach is shown in Algorithm 1. To compile a formula F into d-DNNF, we begin by applying a function *Split*(F), which returns a set of variables $P \subseteq \mathit{Var}(F)$ that will be used for projection (we present the algorithm to appropriately determine this subset P in Section 4.2). We then compute the projection of F onto P, yielding G_P. To do so, we use a resolution-based algorithm, which has been shown to be effective in [25, 13]. We compute G_U as the CNF resulting from the subset of clauses of F that have at least one variable not in P. Finally, we compile G_P and G_U in d-DNNF form using an off-the-shelf CNF to d-DNNF compiler. The main rationale behind our decomposition is that we isolate reasoning over the clauses strictly containing variables in P (via the compilation of G_P), whereas the other clauses are represented in G_U. The decomposition of F into G_P and G_U can later be exploited to design effective d-DNNF-based reasoning methods; We show how to exploit G_P and G_U for #SAT and URS in Sections 4.3 and 4.4, respectively. Before going into the details of these specific reasoning procedures, we demonstrate the structural and semantic properties of this decomposition.

Theorem 1. *Let* $\Gamma = \bigvee_{y \in R_{G_P}} ((G_U|_y) \wedge y)$ *and* $R_\Gamma = \bigcup_{y \in R_{G_P}} R_{(G_U|_y) \wedge y}$. *If* F *is satisfiable, then* $R_F = R_\Gamma$.

Proof. We sequentially prove $R_F \subseteq R_\Gamma$ and $R_\Gamma \subseteq R_F$.

$R_F \subseteq R_\Gamma$: Let $m \in R_F$. We know that $m \in R_{G_U}$ because $G_U \subseteq F$. By definition of *Project*(F, P) we know that $\exists y \in R_{G_P} : (y \subseteq m)$. Moreover, since R_Γ contains the models of $(G_U|_y) \wedge y$, we have that $m \in R_\Gamma$ and $R_F \subseteq R_\Gamma$.

$R_\Gamma \subseteq R_F$: Let $m \in R_\Gamma$. By definition of Γ we have $m \in R_{G_U}$. Let $G'_U = F \setminus G_U = \{c \in F \mid \mathit{Var}(c) \subseteq P\}$. Hence, $R_F = R_{G_U} \cap R_{G'_U}$. By definition of *Project*(F, P), we have $G'_U \subseteq G_P$. In other words, for any complete assignment a to the variables in $\mathit{Var}(F)$ we have $(\exists y \in R_{G_P} : y \subseteq a) \Rightarrow (a \in R_{G'_U})$. Since $m \in R_\Gamma$, there exists a $y \in R_{G_P}$ such that $m \models (G_U|_y) \wedge y$. Therefore, we have $m \in R_{G'_U}$ and $R_\Gamma \subseteq R_F$.

We conclude that $R_F = R_\Gamma$.

Theorem 2. *If* G_U *is in d-DNNF form then* $\Gamma = \bigvee_{y \in R_{G_P}} ((G_U|_y) \wedge y)$ *is in d-DNNF form.*

Proof. If $(G_U|_y) \wedge y$ is obtained by conditioning G_U on the literals in y, i.e., propagating the unit literals from y in G_U, then $(G_U|_y) \wedge y$ is a d-DNNF since conditioning a d-DNNF creates a new d-DNNF [7].

Let $a, b \in R_{G_P}$ such that $a \neq b$ then $\bigwedge_{l \in a} l \wedge \bigwedge_{l \in b} l$ is unsatisfiable because a and b are two distinct models of G_P. By definition, there exists at least one literal on which a and b disagree. Otherwise, the models would not be distinct.

Therefore, the main disjunction of Γ is deterministic, and Γ is indeed in d-DNNF form.

4.2 Choosing the Projection Set P

We decided to use hypergraph partitioning to choose a good projection set P. Other methods exist [2], but hypergraph partitioning offers a good balance between simplicity and efficiency [14]. While hypergraph partitioning is known to be NP-hard [16], similarly to SAT-solving, efficient solvers do exist [4]. Our approach is described in Algorithm 2.

To take advantage of hypergraph partitioning tools, we have to formulate our problem as a hypergraph partitioning problem. We construct the variable incidence graph (VIG) as follows. Each node n_v of the VIG is associated with a variable $v \in Var(F)$. Each clause of F (in CNF) is a hyperedge, i.e., for each clause $c \in F$ we construct a hyperedge that contains every node n_v such that $v \in Var(c)$.

We continue by running a hypergraph partitioning tool on the VIG of the formula F. The partitioning tool returns a function that associates each node n_v with a partition p. Partitioning tools try to create balanced partitions by cutting the smallest possible number of hyperedges. In our case, this means that the tool will partition the set of variables $Var(F)$ into subsets of roughly the same size. Moreover, the hypergraph partitioner will try to minimise the number of clauses expressed by using variables of different subsets. In other words, most clauses will be expressed within a single subset of the partition.

With our partition p computed, we can continue by computing our projection set P. We start by building a formula $\Delta = \{c \in F \mid \exists x, y \in c : (p(Var(x)) \neq p(Var(y)))\}$. The formula Δ contains every clause that connects at least two subsets of $Var(F)$ as defined by the partition p. We return $P = Var(\Delta)$.

Notice that G_U can be partitioned into subsets of clauses such that every subset has zero variables in common. In other words, G_U is built in such a way that a d-DNNF compiler can create a conjunction node early in the compilation process. An alternative is to form a partition $G_{U_1} \cup ... \cup G_{U_n} = G_U$ such that $\forall i, j : (i \neq j \Rightarrow (Var(G_{U_i}) \cap Var(G_{U_j}) = \emptyset))$. A consequence of this is that every component G_{U_i} can be compiled independently and, thus, in parallel.

Algorithm 2 *Split*(F)

Require: F is a Boolean formula in CNF
1: $vig \leftarrow \{Var(c) \mid c \in F\}$
2: $p \leftarrow hypergraph\_partitioner(vig)$
3: {p is a partition function, $p(var)$ tells us to which partition variable var belongs.}
4: $P \leftarrow \emptyset$
5: **for all** $c \in F$ **do**
6:     **if** $\exists x, y \in c : (p(Var(x)) \neq p(Var(y)))$ **then**
7:         $P \leftarrow P \cup \{Var(l) \mid l \in c\}$
8:     **end if**
9: **end for**
10: {P contains the variables of every clause that connects multiple partitions.}
11: **return** P

4.3 Application to Model Counting

Direct Method Based on the G_P, G_U Decomposition. Our decomposition of F into G_P and G_U provides an immediate approach to model counting. We illustrate this approach in Figure 1. We consider $F = (a \vee b) \wedge (c \vee d) \wedge (a \vee c)$. Selecting $P = \{a, c\}$ yields $G_P = a \vee c$ and $G_U = (a \vee b) \wedge (c \vee d)$. By compiling G_P to a d-DNNF, we find $R_{G_P} = \{a \wedge c, a \wedge \neg c, \neg a \wedge c\}$. The resulting d-DNNF (according to Theorem 2) is shown graphically in Figure 1. By computing the sum of $|R_{(G_U|_y) \wedge y}|$ for every $y \in R_{G_P}$ we find the model count of F as indicated by Theorems 1 and 2.

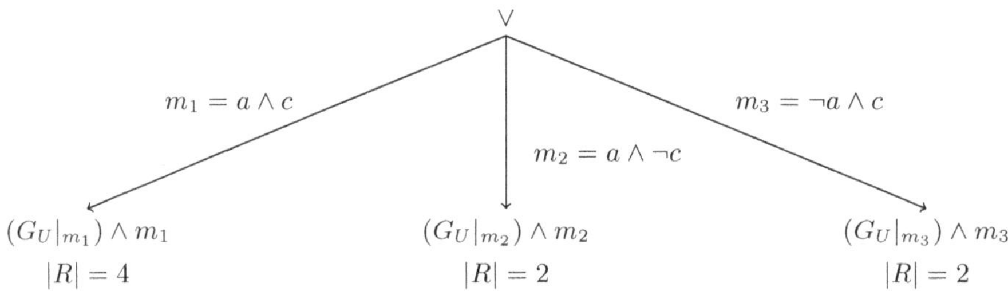

Fig. 1: The d-DNNF that we obtain by using Algorithm 1 to compile $F = (a \vee b) \wedge (c \vee d) \wedge (a \vee c)$ with $P = \{a, c\}$.

The issue with this direct approach is that $|R_{G_P}|$ is often huge, therefore prohibiting an exhaustive enumeration. To alleviate this, we use an optimisation shown by Lagniez and Lonca [12], which reduces the number of computations by enumerating orthogonal sufficient partial assignments of G_P instead of models of G_P. The number of orthogonal sufficient partial assignments of G_P is likely much smaller than the number of models $|R_{G_P}|$. Let a be such a sufficient partial assignment. Then a satisfies every clause in $G'_U = \{c \in F \mid \mathit{Var}(c) \subseteq P\}$. The remaining variables are unconstrained, and every model of $a \wedge G_U$ is a model of F (cf. Theorem 1). In other words, if we have a partial assignment a such that $|a| < |\mathit{Var}(G_P)|$ and G_P is satisfied by a (i.e., the variables not in a are unconstrained and G_P will evaluate to true under every assignment m such that $a \subseteq m$), then every model of $(G_U|_a) \wedge a$ is a model of F. Fortunately, d-DNNF compilation naturally produces orthogonal sufficient partial assignments. These can be extracted by considering the paths that originate at the root of the directed acyclic graph representing the d-DNNF of G_P. Each path corresponds to a sufficient partial assignment over the variables of G_P. These assignments are necessarily orthogonal due to the structural properties of d-DNNFs — specifically, the determinism condition ensures that no model y can be a superset of more than one path in the d-DNNF [12].

G_P and G_U as Lower and Upper Bounds for F. In case enumerating R_{G_P} and applying the direct method remains intractable due to large $|R_{G_P}|$, we demonstrate that our compilation process naturally generates lower and upper bounds to $|R_F|$.

Lemma 1. *G_P and G_U are such that* $|R_{G_P}| \leq |R_F| \leq |R_{G_U}|$

Proof. By construction, we have $\forall x \in R_{G_P} : \exists y \in R_F : (x \subseteq y)$ and $R_F \subseteq R_{G_U}$, therefore, $|R_{G_P}| \leq |R_F| \leq |R_{G_U}|$.

This implies that G_P and G_U can immediately be used to compute a sound interval for $|R_F|$. In practice, however, this interval can be too large (as confirmed in our experiments). This is why we next propose a statistical computation of tighter bounds.

Approximate Model Counting with Lower and Upper Bounds. Algorithm 3 shows how we approximately count the number of models of F given G_P and G_U. According to Theorem 1 and Theorem 2 we find that $|R_F| = \sum_{a \in R_{G_P}} |R_{(G_U|_a) \wedge a}|$. Instead of computing $|R_{(G_U|_a) \wedge a}|$ for every model a of G_P, we can estimate $\frac{|R_F|}{|R_{G_P}|}$, i.e., the average number of models that each model of G_P contributes to the total number of models. Suppose we have the multiset $A = \{|R_{(G_U|_a) \wedge a}| \mid a \in R_{G_P}\}$. If we sample uniformly at random from A then we have a random variable Y with expected value $\mathbb{E}[Y] = \sum_{Y_i \in A} Y_i \frac{1}{|R_{G_P}|} = \frac{|R_F|}{|R_{G_P}|}$. By linearity of expectation, we have $\mathbb{E}[|R_{G_P}| \times Y] = |R_F|$. Therefore, our algorithm, which approximates this expectation through sampling (see Algorithm 3), provides a consistent unbiased estimator of $|R_F|$ as a consequence of the law of large numbers.

Moreover, we use the central limit theorem [3] to construct asymptotic confidence intervals with confidence level $\alpha \in (0, 1)$, i.e., empirical intervals which will, in the limit $N \to \infty$, contain the true value of $|R_F|$ with probability at least $1 - \alpha$.

4.4 Application to Uniform Random Sampling

Directly sampling a model from F by sampling a model a from G_P and then returning a model from $(G_U|_a) \wedge a$ is unfortunately not uniform as we rarely have $\forall x, y \in R_{G_P} : (|R_{(G_U|_x) \wedge x}| = |R_{(G_U|_y) \wedge y}|)$. To this end, we propose to sample $S \subseteq R_{G_P}$ with $|S| = k$. We then sample uniformly from $R_T = \bigcup_{a \in S} R_{(G_U|_a) \wedge a}$ as demonstrated in Algorithm 4. When F is given in d-DNNF form, the procedure *random_model*(F) admits an efficient implementation based on the method of Sharma et al. [23]. In particular, they show that sampling from a d-DNNF is highly efficient.

Ideally, we would want our sampling algorithm to have a uniform probability of returning a model $m \in R_F$ (i.e., $P(m) = \frac{1}{|R_F|}$). While our algorithm does not allow for such guarantees (at least not most of the time with reasonable values for k), we can show that the value for $P(m)$ is bounded.

Algorithm 3 *AppMC*(G_P, G_U, α, N)

1: $v \leftarrow$ *empty array*
2: **for all** $1 \leq i \leq N$ **do**
3: $\quad a \leftarrow$ *random_model*(G_P)
4: $\quad Y_i \leftarrow |R_{(G_U|_a) \wedge a}| \times |R_{G_P}|$
5: $\quad v \leftarrow v \cup \{Y_i\}$
6: **end for**
7: $\overline{Y} \leftarrow$ *average*(v)
8: $S^2 \leftarrow \frac{\sum_{Y_i \in v}(Y_i - \overline{Y})^2}{N-1}$
9: $\sigma \leftarrow \frac{\sqrt{S^2}}{\sqrt{N}}$
10: $Y_l \leftarrow \overline{Y} - z_{\frac{\alpha}{2}}\sigma$
11: $Y_h \leftarrow \overline{Y} + z_{\frac{\alpha}{2}}\sigma$
12: **return** $\overline{Y}$, Y_l, Y_h

Lemma 2. *The probability $P(m)$ that Algorithm 4 returns model m is bounded as follows: $P_H \frac{\binom{|R_{G_P}|-1}{k-1}}{\binom{|R_{G_P}|}{k}} \leq P(m) \leq P_L \frac{\binom{|R_{G_P}|-1}{k-1}}{\binom{|R_{G_P}|}{k}}$, with $P_H = \frac{1}{\sum_{h \in H_k} h}$, $P_L = \frac{1}{\sum_{l \in L_k} l}$, and L_k (resp. H_k) the multiset containing the k smallest (resp. largest) values of $A = \{|R_{(G_U|_a) \wedge a}| \mid a \in G_P\}$.*

Proof. Suppose we have the multiset $A = \{|R_{(G_U|_a) \wedge a}| \mid a \in G_P\}$. Let L_k and H_k be the multisets containing the k smallest and k largest numbers of A, respectively. Notice that for any subset $S \subseteq R_{G_P}$, the sum of the respective model counts (i.e., $\sum_{a \in S} |R_{(G_U|_a) \wedge a}|$) is bounded by the sum of the elements in L_k and H_k: $\sum_{l \in L_k} l \leq \sum_{a \in S} |R_{(G_U|_a) \wedge a}| \leq \sum_{h \in H_k} h$. Therefore, if S is fixed, the probability of returning a model $m \in S$ is bounded as well: $P_H \leq P(m \mid S) \leq P_L$, with $P_H = \frac{1}{\sum_{h \in H_k} h}$ and $P_L = \frac{1}{\sum_{l \in L_k} l}$. We know that there are a total of $\binom{|R_{G_P}|}{k}$ different subsets of R_{G_P} of size k and that for $\binom{|R_{G_P}|-1}{k-1}$ of those ways, the model m is part of the selected subset of models (as a consequence of Theorem 2). Thus, the probability $P(m)$ is bounded as follows: $P_H \frac{\binom{|R_{G_P}|-1}{k-1}}{\binom{|R_{G_P}|}{k}} \leq P(m) \leq P_L \frac{\binom{|R_{G_P}|-1}{k-1}}{\binom{|R_{G_P}|}{k}}$.

We would like to add that if $k = |R_{G_P}|$, we have $P_H^{-1} = P_L^{-1} = |R_F|$ and thus our algorithm converges towards uniform random sampling with the limit $k \rightarrow |R_{G_P}|$.

5 Experimental Evaluation

5.1 Experimental Setup

We report on experiments assessing the benefits of DivKC. First, we demonstrate the ability of Algorithm 1 to compile into the d-DNNF form for challenging

Algorithm 4 *K-Sampler*(G_P, G_U, k, N)

1: $R \leftarrow$ *empty array*
2: **for all** $1 \leq i \leq N$ **do**
3: $\quad S \leftarrow$ *subset of size k from* R_{G_P}
4: $\quad L \leftarrow$ *empty array*
5: $\quad lmc \leftarrow 0$
6: $\quad$**for all** $a \in S$ **do**
7: $\quad\quad s_i \leftarrow |R_{(G_U|_a) \wedge a}|$
8: $\quad\quad L \leftarrow L \cup \{(a, s_i)\}$
9: $\quad\quad lmc \leftarrow lmc + s_i$
10: $\quad$**end for**
11: $\quad id \leftarrow random\_number(1 \leq r \leq lmc)$
12: $\quad$**for all** $(a, s_i) \in L$ **do**
13: $\quad\quad$**if** $id \leq s_i$ **then**
14: $\quad\quad\quad R \leftarrow R \cup \{random\_model((G_U|_a) \wedge a)\}$
15: $\quad\quad\quad$break current loop
16: $\quad\quad$**else**
17: $\quad\quad\quad id \leftarrow id - s_i$
18: $\quad\quad$**end if**
19: $\quad$**end for**
20: **end for**
21: **return** R

formulae that D4 [14] was not able to compile. Thereby, we demonstrate that DivKC can complement D4 and enhance its knowledge compilation capability, making it compile formulae it could not without DivKC.

Second, we want to show the benefits of DivKC in an application to #SAT. We aim to demonstrate the quality of the confidence intervals produced by Algorithm 3 in terms of coverage and precision. For coverage, we measure the percentage of formulae for which the true model count lies within the interval (i.e., how often we have $|R_F| \in [Y_l; Y_h]$). For precision, we compare the interval with that of the lower and upper bounds produced by Lemma 1 (which guarantees 100% coverage by construction). We measure the percentage of formulae for which the confidence interval is included in the interval formed by Lemma 1's lower and upper bounds, and in these cases, we measure the relative size of the two intervals.

Third, we evaluate the ability of DivKC to generate uniform random samples for various formulae. For this, we generate samples using Algorithm 4 and execute the uniformity test suite proposed by Zeyen et al. [34].

Datasets. To test the compilation and model counting abilities of DivKC, we collected multiple datasets from Lagniez and Marquis [14], Soos [24], Sundermann et al. [26], and Plazar et al. [20]. For the sake of fine-grained traceability, we keep these datasets separated in our result tables. Detailed tables are provided in our companion GitHub repository [32]. Table 1 presents the characteristics of the formulae included in these datasets. Each line represents a specific dataset.

The line marked as global groups the datasets into one. Each subsequent line represents a different dataset.

The Lagniez and Marquis [14] dataset is a diverse dataset containing 1979 formulae. The dataset contains diverse problems ranging from Bayesian networks to digital circuits and configuration. This dataset also contains handmade and random formulae.

The Soos [24] dataset contains 1896 formulae from various sources, including the Model Counting Competitions.

The Sundermann et al. [26] dataset consists of 278 formulae, most of which come from the configurable software domain. The dataset contains multiple versions and variants of each formula. To avoid having too many similar formulae, we restricted our experiments to the most recent version and variant of each formula.

The Plazar et al. [20] dataset contains 503 formulae consisting of a feature model benchmark as well as other formulae collected from [8].

Dataset	$\#F_{total}$	$\min(\|Var(F)\|)$	$\max(\|Var(F)\|)$	$\min(\|F\|)$	$\max(\|F\|)$
Global	4656	0	8286433	0	7689680
↪ Lagniez [14]	1979	5	229100	10	399794
↪ Soos [24]	1896	2	8286433	1	7689680
↪ Plazar [20]	503	14	486193	31	2598178
↪ Sundermann [26]	278	0	31012	0	350120

Table 1: Dataset summary. The first column indicates the dataset, and the #F column indicates how many formulae the dataset contains. The following columns indicate the minimum and maximum number of variables (resp. clauses) in the dataset.

To test the uniformity of our approach, we used the same dataset as used by Zeyen et al. [34] to allow for a direct comparison with their results. Using the same dataset allows us to use the results in [34] as a baseline and use our results to construct a direct comparison between the samplers tested by Zeyen et al. [34] and our proposed sampler.

Infrastructure. The experiments were computed on an HPC containing 354 nodes, each of which has 256 GB of RAM and 2 AMD Epyc ROME 7H12 CPUs running at 2.6 GHz.

Computation Budget. We set the following computational budget for the evaluated approaches. Compiling a formula with D4 [14] is limited to 64GB of memory and five hours of computation for each formula. Algorithm 1 is limited to 30 minutes for the splitting procedure, two hours for the computation of the projection G_P (both within 64GB of memory), and one hour and 16GB of memory to compile each component (G_P and G_U) by using D4 [14]. Therefore,

Algorithm 1 is given a total of three hours and 30 minutes, considering that compiling G_P and G_U can be done in parallel. Our approximate model counting procedure (Algorithm 3) is limited to one and a half hours of computation and 64GB of memory. Therefore, our approach to approximate model counting is limited to five hours of computation (including the compilation phase), which is the same limit given to D4 [14].

5.2 Experimental Results

Dataset	$\#F_{total}$	#D4 ∧ ¬DivKC	#¬D4	#DivKC ∧ ¬D4
Global	4656	643	672	**114**
↪ Lagniez [14]	1979	256	214	**54**
↪ Soos [24]	1896	311	394	**54**
↪ Plazar [20]	503	58	61	**6**
↪ Sundermann [26]	278	18	3	0

Table 2: Experimental results regarding the scalability of Algorithm 1. Column $\#F_{total}$ indicates the total number of formulae in each dataset. The next column shows the number of formulae compiled only by D4 [14] but not by Algorithm 1. Column #¬D4 shows the number of formulae not compiled by D4. The last column indicates the number of formulae that were only compiled by Algorithm 1, but not by D4.

Knowledge Compilation. We compare DivKC with D4 to evaluate the compilation capabilities of our approach. The results for our compilation algorithm are shown in Table 2. The $\#F_{total}$ column indicates the total number of formulae in each dataset. The main columns for our evaluation are #¬D4 and #DivKC ∧ ¬D4. The former shows how many formulae could not be compiled with D4 within our computational budget (64GB of memory and five hours), while the latter shows how many of these were successfully compiled by our approach.

Our main result shows that, among the 672 formulae that D4 failed to compile initially within our computational budget and given our current hardware, 114 can be successfully compiled using our DivKC approach, with D4 serving as the backbone d-DNNF compiler.

Approximate Model Counting. To evaluate Algorithm 3, we start by measuring the coverage (Table 3) and precision (Table 4) of the intervals constructed by our approach (with parameters $\alpha = 0.01$ and $N = 10{,}000$). Coverage reflects how often the returned bounds contain the true model count, thereby indicating the accuracy of Algorithm 3. We constrained the computational budget to 64GB of memory and a maximum runtime of 1.5 hours per execution of Algorithm 3.

Dataset	#F	$Y_l \leq \lvert R_F \rvert$	$Y_h \geq \lvert R_F \rvert$	Coverage	$\lvert R_{G_P} \rvert \leq \lvert R_F \rvert \leq \lvert R_{G_U} \rvert$
Global	3341	0.988	0.869	0.857	1.000
↪ Lagniez [14]	1509	0.993	0.914	0.907	1.000
↪ Soos [24]	1191	0.981	0.915	0.896	1.000
↪ Plazar [20]	384	0.987	0.815	0.802	1.000
↪ Sundermann [26]	257	0.996	0.475	0.471	1.000

Table 3: Experimental results for Algorithm 3. Column #F indicates with how many formulae the statistics have been computed. The 'Coverage' column indicates how often $|R_F|$ is within the confidence interval $[Y_l; Y_h]$ and thus measures the accuracy of our method.

In Table 3, the column #F shows for how many formulae we managed to compute both the exact model count with D4 [14] (within the same computational budget as mentioned above) and our approximate model counter. The following columns indicate how often the returned lower bound was smaller than the true model count ($Y_l \leq |R_F|$), and how often the returned upper bound was larger than the true model count ($Y_h \geq |R_F|$). The 'Coverage' column indicates how often $|R_F|$ is within the confidence interval $[Y_l; Y_h]$ and thus measures the accuracy of our method. The last column serves as a sanity check for the bounds obtained by using Lemma 1. We observe that the bounds obtained by using Lemma 1 are as expected.

We begin our evaluation of Algorithm 3 by discussing its coverage performance. For 98% of all formulae, our approach correctly calculates a lower bound to the total number of models. However, the upper bound is only correct in 86% of the cases, showing that our approach tends to underestimate the model count of the formula. Similarly, our approach correctly computes a lower bound in 100% of the cases for the feature model subset of the Plazar et al. [20] dataset (as can be seen on our companion GitHub [32]) and in 99% of the cases for the Sundermann et al. [26] dataset. However, the upper bound is only correct in 47% of the cases. The Sundermann et al. [26] dataset mostly contains feature models of software systems. Coverage is lower than expected for the Sundermann et al. [26] dataset because our approach converges only asymptotically under the central limit theorem [3] and law of large numbers, and limiting computations to 10,000 samples per formula can prevent full convergence. Therefore, we deduce that our approach underestimates the number of models of a feature model. Over all datasets, both the upper and lower bounds are correct in 85% of the cases, and the lower bounds have an experimental reliability of 98%, showing the accuracy of our approximate method.

To evaluate the precision of Algorithm 3, we compare its computed bounds with those obtained using Lemma 1. Table 4 relates the upper and lower bounds computed by Algorithm 3 with the bounds obtained by using Lemma 1. As above, the #F column indicates the number of formulae on which the following statistics have been computed. The third column indicates how often the lower bound computed by Algorithm 3 is greater than the lower bound obtained

Dataset	#F	$Y_l \geq \lvert R_{G_P}\rvert$	$Y_h \leq \lvert R_{G_U}\rvert$	Both	$median(r_c)$	$max(r_c)$
Global	3341	0.834	0.869	0.752	9.58e-9	1.0
↪ Lagniez [14]	1509	0.868	0.913	0.801	7.53e-9	1.0
↪ Soos [24]	1191	0.940	0.915	0.863	2.55e-7	0.085
↪ Plazar [20]	384	0.763	0.815	0.656	6.61e-14	0.0137
↪ Sundermann [26]	257	0.249	0.471	0.089	1.6e-13	0.126

Table 4: Experimental results comparing the bounds obtained with Algorithm 3 and with Lemma 1. Column #F indicates with how many formulae the statistics have been computed. The 'Both' column indicates how often we have $Y_l \geq |R_{G_P}| \wedge Y_l \leq |R_F|$ and $Y_h \leq |R_{G_U}| \wedge Y_h \geq |R_F|$. The last two columns represent the observed median and maximum values of the ratio $r_c = \frac{min(Y_h,|R_{G_U}|)-max(Y_l,|R_{G_P}|)}{|R_{G_U}|-|R_{G_P}|}$, which was calculated exclusively if $Y_l \leq |R_F| \leq Y_h$. The number of formulae on which the last two columns are computed can easily be obtained by multiplying the #F column with the 'Coverage' column in Table 3.

through Lemma 1 and smaller than the true model count ($Y_l \geq |R_{G_P}| \wedge Y_l \leq |R_F|$). The fourth column indicates a similar result but for the upper bound ($Y_h \leq |R_{G_U}| \wedge Y_h \geq |R_F|$). In other words, these two columns show how often Algorithm 3 gives us bounds that are better than or equal to those provided by Lemma 1. The 'Both' column indicates how often the bounds returned by Algorithm 3 were both correct and better than the bounds obtained with Lemma 1. The last two columns indicate the median and maximum value for the ratio $r_c = \frac{min(Y_h,|R_{G_U}|)-max(Y_l,|R_{G_P}|)}{|R_{G_U}|-|R_{G_P}|}$, which was calculated exclusively for the bounds that meet the predicate $Y_l \leq |R_F| \leq Y_h$ (the number obtained by multiplying the #F column in this table with the 'Coverage' column in Table 3). The r_c ratio quantifies the difference between the bounds obtained by using Lemma 1 and the bounds obtained by using Algorithm 3. To compute r_c we use $min(Y_h, |R_{G_U}|)$ and $max(Y_l, |R_{G_P}|)$ because detecting that the bounds returned by Algorithm 3 are worse than the bounds obtained with Lemma 1 is easy, and therefore, a user can easily use the better bounds.

We observe that in general, Algorithm 3 provides tighter bounds than Lemma 1 in 75% of the cases. As previously noted, the results vary depending on the dataset. As an example, Algorithm 3 performs poorly on the Sundermann et al. [26] dataset and on the feature model subset of the Plazar et al. [20] dataset. On the other hand, Algorithm 3 performs well on the Bayesian network subset of the Lagniez and Marquis [14] dataset, as we observe a success rate of 86%. Moreover, we find that the bounds returned by Algorithm 3 are overall much tighter than the bounds obtained by using Lemma 1 as the global median value for $r_c = 9.5 \times 10^{-9}$.

To complete our evaluation of Algorithm 3, we compare it against ApproxMC 7 [21] because it is generally considered to be the state-of-the-art in approximate model counting. Moreover, ApproxMC has strong theoretical guarantees.

Dataset	#F	$l \leq Y_{\text{ApproxMC}} \leq h$	$l \leq Y \leq h$
Global	2782	0.977	0.881
↪ Lagniez [14]	1386	1.000	0.882
↪ Soos [24]	1180	0.970	0.873
↪ Plazar [20]	203	0.862	0.921
↪ Sundermann [26]	13	1.000	0.846

Table 5: Experimental results comparing the accuracy of Algorithm 3 with ApproxMC 7. Column #F indicates with how many formulae the statistics have been computed. Column $l \leq Y_{\text{ApproxMC}} \leq h$ (resp. $l \leq Y \leq h$) indicates how often the model count returned by ApproxMC 7 (resp. Algorithm 3) is within the indicated bounds, with $l = \frac{|R_F|}{1.2}$ and $h = 1.2 \times |R_F|$.

Dataset	#F	#DivKC	$log_{10}(min)$	$mean$	$median$	$log_{10}(max)$
Global	2888	2265	-3.2	124.5	4.8	5.3
↪ Lagniez [14]	1436	1179	-2.9	80.5	5.5	4.4
↪ Soos [24]	1235	953	-3.0	29.6	4.5	4.4
↪ Plazar [20]	204	122	-3.2	2.7	1.7	1.5
↪ Sundermann [26]	13	11	-0.6	15904.5	29.6	5.3

Table 6: Experimental results comparing the runtime of Algorithm 3 with ApproxMC 7 for 20 runs. Column #F indicates the number of formulae over which the statistics were computed, and column #DivKC shows how often DivKC was faster than ApproxMC 7. The remaining columns report how much faster DivKC was, based on the logarithm of the minimum, the mean, the median, and the logarithm of the maximum of the ratio: ApproxMC 7 execution time divided by DivKC execution time.

The results of this comparison are presented in Tables 5 and 6, which highlight differences in accuracy and runtime performance.

Table 5 presents the accuracy results. Column #F reports the number of formulae for which the statistics were computed from the results produced by ApproxMC 7 and Algorithm 3. Thus, #F indicates the number of formulae on which we successfully ran ApproxMC 7, Algorithm 3, and D4. Column $l \leq Y_{\text{ApproxMC}} \leq h$ (resp. $l \leq Y \leq h$) reports how often the model count returned by ApproxMC 7 (resp. Algorithm 3) falls within the specified bounds, with $l = \frac{|R_F|}{1.2}$ and $h = 1.2 \times |R_F|$.

The bounds we use follow the definition of a probably approximately correct (PAC) counter from [21], where a probabilistic algorithm, given parameters δ and ε, returns an estimate Y such that $P(l \leq Y \leq h) \geq 1 - \delta$, with $l = \frac{|R_F|}{1+\varepsilon}$ and $h = (1 + \varepsilon)|R_F|$. In our experiments, we set $\varepsilon = 0.2$ and $\delta = 0.1$ as input parameters to ApproxMC. The value of ε matches the value used by Pote et al. [21], while $\delta = 0.1$ is a standard choice in statistical settings. Additionally, we modified Algorithm 3 to use at most 10,000 samples, and to terminate early if $(Y_l \geq \frac{Y}{1.1}) \wedge (Y_h \leq 1.1Y)$.

Overall, ApproxMC demonstrates better accuracy, returning estimates within bounds in approximately 98% of cases, compared to 88% for Algorithm 3. While this indicates a performance gap, 88% still reflects a reasonably high level of accuracy, especially considering the added benefit of the reusable data structure produced by DivKC. This may make DivKC particularly appealing in scenarios where repeated queries are expected. Therefore, ApproxMC may not always be the most practical choice despite its higher accuracy.

Table 6 compares the runtimes of ApproxMC and Algorithm 3. To compare both algorithms, we simulate 20 runs of both approaches per formula (to limit the computational budget). For ApproxMC, we performed 4 actual runs per formula and multiplied the total runtime by 5. For Algorithm 3, we ran the compilation phase once and then executed the algorithm 4 times per formula; the total runtime of Algorithm 3 was also multiplied by 5 to simulate 20 runs. The reported execution time for Algorithm 3 includes one call to DivKC and 20 simulated runs of Algorithm 3. ApproxMC had a computational budget of five hours and 64GB of memory per run.

Column #F indicates the number of formulae over which the statistics were computed, and column #DivKC shows how often DivKC was faster than ApproxMC. Thus, #F indicates the number of formulae on which we successfully ran ApproxMC 7 and Algorithm 3. The remaining columns report how much faster DivKC was, based on the logarithm of the minimum, the mean, the median, and the logarithm of the maximum of the ratio: ApproxMC execution time divided by DivKC execution time.

We observe that DivKC was faster than ApproxMC in approximately 78% of the cases. The speedup was substantial — on average, 124.5 times faster, with a median speedup of 4.8. In the most extreme case, DivKC was up to $197,602.8$ times faster.

Therefore, while Algorithm 3 may not be as reliable as ApproxMC in terms of accuracy, it offers significant performance advantages. Moreover, the reusable data structure generated by DivKC can make it particularly useful in scenarios where repeated model counting is required.

Approximate Uniform Random Sampling. We used the test suite and dataset proposed by Zeyen et al. [34] to test our heuristic-based sampler presented in Algorithm 4. Algorithm 4 is run with $k = 50$ and with batch sizes of $N = 1000$, similarly to the experimental setup in [34]. We used the same dataset (which the authors called the Ω dataset) to facilitate the comparison with their results. The authors proposed five tests, of which we used only four, as the last test faces scalability issues according to the authors' original experiments. The simplest test is the modbit test. Table 7 shows a reproduction of the results in [34]. The table contains the results for heuristic-based samplers. The results for UniGen3 are provided as a baseline because UniGen3 comes with strong theoretical guarantees of uniformity (at the cost of performance [20]) and is therefore out of scope. We extended the table with our results for Algorithm 4. With our sampler, we obtained a Harmonic mean p-value of 0.13 for the modbit

Sampler	Modbit (q = 8)		VF		Birthday		SFpC	
	#F	p-value	#F	p-value	#F	p-value	#F	p-value
K-Sampler	178	**0.129**	176	0.000	140	0.005	77	0.000
QuickSampler	188	0.000	186	0.000	139	0.000	77	0.000
STS	193	0.000	191	0.000	138	0.000	81	0.000
CMSGen	144	0.000	143	0.000	93	0.000	71	0.000
UniGen3	192	**0.234**	183	**0.083**	130	**0.274**	76	**0.253**

Table 7: Experimental results for the Ω dataset introduced in [34] and extended with our results for Algorithm 4. For each test (and for each formula), each sampler was called multiple times to generate samples of size 1000. The bold p-values are all greater than our significance level $\alpha = 0.01$. #F indicates the number of formulae on which the test was successfully performed (i.e., without timeouts or out-of-memory errors).

test with $q = 8$, which indicates that our sampler passed the modbit ($q = 8$) test. Our sampler also passed the modbit test with $q = 2$ and $q = 4$.

Our sampler is already an improvement, as none of the heuristic-based samplers (i.e., samplers with no guarantees of uniformity) tested in [34] passed a single test on the dataset. For the VF, SFpC, and Birthday tests, we obtained a harmonic mean p-value of 0. Given that the harmonic mean p-value is below the usual threshold value ($\alpha = 0.01$), we conclude that Algorithm 4 fails the VF, SFpC, and Birthday tests. However, the Birthday test also indicates the number of observed repetitions, i.e., the number of times the sampler under test returned the same model. This is interesting information as it indicates whether a sampler often returns the same model or if it seldom returns the same model. Frequent repetition may indicate poor exploration of the model space, which can be problematic. The Birthday test is also the only test proposed by [34] which allows for a finer quantitative analysis.

In our experiments, we set the expected number of duplicates for the birthday test to 10, exactly like in [34]. By doing so, we obtain results that are comparable with the results in [34]. Table 8 shows a reproduction of the results in [34]. We extended the table with our results for Algorithm 4.

Discussing the quantitative details of the failed tests, we still observe that our approach brings improvements over the other heuristic-based URS approaches as it generates much fewer repeats than QuickSampler [8] and CMSGen [10]. Moreover, we find that our results are competitive with other URS approaches as the average number of observed repeats is only off by 10% when comparing with UniGen3, a uniform random sampler which offers theoretical guarantees of uniformity.

Overall, our heuristic-based sampler **passes more tests than any other** heuristic-based sampler that is tested by Zeyen et al. [34].

Sampler	Uniformity		Observed number of repetitions			
	#F	p-value	min	max	average	median
K-Sampler	140	0.005	3	26	10.75	10
QuickSampler	139	0.000	0	29858	480.01	4
STS	138	0.000	0	27	5.20	4
CMSGen	93	0.000	5	12846	991.37	33
UniGen3	130	**0.274**	3	18	9.78	10

Table 8: Extended experimental results for the birthday test with the Ω dataset introduced in [34] and extended with our results for Algorithm 4. The bold p-values are all greater than our significance level $\alpha = 0.01$. #F indicates the number of formulae on which the test was successfully performed (i.e., without timeouts or out-of-memory errors).

6 Conclusion

In this paper, we developed DivKC, a divide-and-conquer method to split a formula into components that can then be compiled independently to d-DNNF. By using Theorems 1 and 2, we obtain a d-DNNF that is equivalent to the original formula. Our experiments demonstrated that DivKC compiles 114 formulae that were previously out of reach for the state-of-the-art D4 [14] compiler. We also explored two other applications of DivKC. First, we designed an approximate model counter that comes with statistical guarantees. While this new model counter accurately estimates 85% of the formulae, it struggles with formulae coming from feature models. Second, we exploited DivKC to build a heuristic-based uniform random sampler.

This heuristic-based sampler is the first heuristic-based sampler to validate at least one test of the test suite proposed in [34]. This paves the way to the design of novel quasi-uniform samplers, which are of interest for many practical applications, knowing that truly uniform samplers do not scale well [20]. For future work, we plan to explore alternative split heuristics to improve the efficiency and generality of our approach. Another promising direction is to investigate further how the upper bound used in our method could be exploited.

Acknowledgements

This research was funded in whole, or in part, by the Luxembourg National Research Fund (FNR). Gilles Perrouin is a FNRS Research Associate.

Maxime Cordy and Olivier Zeyen are supported by FNR Luxembourg (grants C23/IS/18177547/VARIANCE and AFR Grant 17047437).

References

[1] D. Achlioptas, Zayd Hammoudeh, and P. Theodoropoulos. "Fast Sampling of Perfectly Uniform Satisfying Assignments". In: *SAT*. 2018 (cit. on p. 3).

[2] Carlos Ansótegui, Jesús Giráldez-Cru, and Jordi Levy. "The Community Structure of SAT Formulas". In: *International Conference on Theory and Applications of Satisfiability Testing.* 2012 (cit. on p. 5).
[3] Robert B Ash and Catherine A Doléans-Dade. *Probability and measure theory.* Academic press, 2000 (cit. on pp. 8, 13).
[4] Ümit V Çatalyürek and Cevdet Aykanat. *PaToH (Partitioning Tool for Hypergraphs).* 2011 (cit. on p. 6).
[5] Adnan Darwiche et al. "New advances in compiling CNF to decomposable negation normal form". In: *Proc. of ECAI.* Citeseer. 2004, pp. 328–332 (cit. on p. 3).
[6] Adnan Darwiche. "On the tractable counting of theory models and its application to belief revision and truth maintenance". In: *arXiv preprint cs/0003044* (2000) (cit. on p. 1).
[7] Adnan Darwiche and Pierre Marquis. "A Knowledge Compilation Map". In: *J. Artif. Intell. Res.* 17 (2002), pp. 229–264 (cit. on pp. 1, 5).
[8] Rafael Dutra et al. "Efficient sampling of SAT solutions for testing". In: *Proceedings of the 40th International Conference on Software Engineering, ICSE 2018, Gothenburg, Sweden, May 27 - June 03, 2018.* 2018, pp. 549–559. DOI: 10.1145/3180155.3180248. URL: http://doi.acm.org/10.1145/3180155.3180248 (cit. on pp. 3, 11, 17).
[9] Stefano Ermon, Carla Gomes, and Bart Selman. "Uniform Solution Sampling Using a Constraint Solver as an Oracle". In: *Proceedings of the Twenty-Eighth Conference on Uncertainty in Artificial Intelligence.* UAI'12. Catalina Island, CA: AUAI Press, 2012, pp. 255–264. ISBN: 9780974903989 (cit. on p. 3).
[10] Priyanka Golia et al. "Designing Samplers is Easy: The Boon of Testers". In: *2021 Formal Methods in Computer Aided Design (FMCAD)* (2021), pp. 222–230 (cit. on p. 17).
[11] Carla P Gomes et al. "From Sampling to Model Counting." In: *IJCAI.* Vol. 2007. 2007, pp. 2293–2299 (cit. on p. 2).
[12] Jean-Marie Lagniez and Emmanuel Lonca. "Leveraging decision-DNNF compilation for enumerating disjoint partial models". In: *21st International Conference on Principles of Knowledge Representation and Reasoning (KR 2024).* 2024 (cit. on p. 7).
[13] Jean-Marie Lagniez, Emmanuel Lonca, and Pierre Marquis. "Improving Model Counting by Leveraging Definability". In: *International Joint Conference on Artificial Intelligence.* 2016. URL: https://api.semanticscholar.org/CorpusID:6303269 (cit. on pp. 4, 5).
[14] Jean-Marie Lagniez and Pierre Marquis. "An Improved Decision-DNNF Compiler". In: *IJCAI.* 2017 (cit. on pp. 1–3, 6, 10–15, 18).
[15] Jean-Marie Lagniez, Pierre Marquis, and Nicolas Szczepanski. "DMC: a distributed model counter". In: *27th International Joint Conference on Artificial Intelligence (IJCAI'18).* 2018, pp. 1331–1338 (cit. on p. 3).
[16] Thomas Lengauer. *Combinatorial algorithms for integrated circuit layout.* Springer Science & Business Media, 2012 (cit. on p. 6).

[17] Christian Muise et al. “D sharp: fast d-DNNF compilation with sharpSAT”. In: *Advances in Artificial Intelligence: 25th Canadian Conference on Artificial Intelligence, Canadian AI 2012, Toronto, ON, Canada, May 28-30, 2012. Proceedings 25*. Springer. 2012, pp. 356–361 (cit. on p. 3).

[18] Jeho Oh et al. “Finding near-optimal configurations in product lines by random sampling”. In: *Proceedings of the 2017 11th Joint Meeting on Foundations of Software Engineering, ESEC/FSE 2017, Paderborn, Germany, September 4-8, 2017*. Ed. by Eric Bodden et al. ACM, 2017, pp. 61–71. DOI: 10.1145/3106237.3106273. URL: https://doi.org/10.1145/3106237.3106273 (cit. on p. 1).

[19] Jeho Oh et al. *Scalable Uniform Sampling for Real-World Software Product Lines*. Tech. rep. TR-20-01. 2020 (cit. on p. 3).

[20] Quentin Plazar et al. “Uniform Sampling of SAT Solutions for Configurable Systems: Are We There Yet?” In: *12th IEEE Conference on Software Testing, Validation and Verification, ICST 2019, Xi'an, China, April 22-27, 2019*. 2019, pp. 240–251 (cit. on pp. 10–16, 18).

[21] Yash Pote, Kuldeep S Meel, and Jiong Yang. “Towards Real-Time Approximate Counting”. In: *Proceedings of the AAAI Conference on Artificial Intelligence*. Vol. 39. 11. 2025, pp. 11318–11326 (cit. on pp. 1, 2, 14, 15).

[22] Shubham Sharma et al. “GANAK: A Scalable Probabilistic Exact Model Counter.” In: *IJCAI*. Vol. 19. 2019. 2019, pp. 1169–1176 (cit. on p. 2).

[23] Shubham Sharma et al. “Knowledge Compilation meets Uniform Sampling”. In: *Proceedings of International Conference on Logic for Programming Artificial Intelligence and Reasoning (LPAR)*. Nov. 2018 (cit. on pp. 1, 3, 8).

[24] Mate Soos. *Benchmarks used for Approximate Model Counting*. Zenodo, Jan. 2024. DOI: 10.5281/zenodo.10449477. URL: https://doi.org/10.5281/zenodo.10449477 (cit. on pp. 10–15).

[25] Mate Soos and Kuldeep S Meel. “Arjun: An Efficient Independent Support Computation Technique and its Applications to Counting and Sampling”. In: *arXiv preprint arXiv:2110.09026* (2021) (cit. on p. 5).

[26] Chico Sundermann et al. “Collecting Feature Models from the Literature: A Comprehensive Dataset for Benchmarking”. In: *Proceedings of the 28th ACM International Systems and Software Product Line Conference*. New York, NY, USA: ACM, Sept. 2024, pp. 54–65 (cit. on pp. 10–15).

[27] Chico Sundermann et al. “Evaluating state-of-the-art # SAT solvers on industrial configuration spaces”. In: *Empirical Software Engineering* 28 (2023) (cit. on pp. 1, 3).

[28] Chico Sundermann et al. “Reusing d-DNNFs for Efficient Feature-Model Counting”. In: *ACM Transactions on Software Engineering and Methodology* 33.8 (2024), pp. 1–32 (cit. on pp. 1–3).

[29] Marc Thurley. “sharpSAT – Counting Models with Advanced Component Caching and Implicit BCP”. In: *Theory and Applications of Satisfiability Testing - SAT 2006*. Ed. by Armin Biere and Carla P. Gomes. Berlin,

Heidelberg: Springer Berlin Heidelberg, 2006, pp. 424–429. ISBN: 978-3-540-37207-3 (cit. on p. 2).
[30] Yisong Wang. "On Forgetting in Tractable Propositional Fragments". In: *ArXiv* abs/1502.02799 (2015). URL: https://api.semanticscholar.org/CorpusID:6588613 (cit. on p. 4).
[31] Wei Wei and Bart Selman. "A new approach to model counting". In: *Theory and Applications of Satisfiability Testing: 8th International Conference, SAT 2005, St Andrews, UK, June 19-23, 2005. Proceedings 8.* Springer. 2005, pp. 324–339 (cit. on p. 2).
[32] Olivier Zeyen. *DivKC: A Divide-and-Conquer Approach to Knowledge Compilation.* https://github.com/serval-uni-lu/divkc. Zenodo archive: https://doi.org/10.5281/zenodo.18097437. 2025 (cit. on pp. 2, 10, 13).
[33] Olivier Zeyen et al. "Preprocessing is What You Need: Understanding and Predicting the Complexity of SAT-based Uniform Random Sampling". In: *Proceedings of the 2024 IEEE/ACM 12th International Conference on Formal Methods in Software Engineering (FormaliSE).* 2024, pp. 23–32 (cit. on p. 4).
[34] Zeyen, Olivier and Cordy, Maxime and Gubri, Martin and Perouin, Gilles and Acher, Mathieu: Testing Uniform Random Samplers: Methods, Datasets and Protocols. ACM Transactions on Software Engineering and Methodology. ACM New York, NY (2025). https://dl.acm. org/ doi/ abs/ 10.1145/3797477 (cit. on pp. 2, 10, 11, 16–18).

Advanced Software Development

QEMI: A Quantum Software Stacks Testing Framework via Equivalence Modulo Inputs

Junjie Luo[1], Shangzhou Xia[2],
Fuyuan Zhang[3]*, and Jianjun Zhao[4]

[1] Kyushu University, Japan luo.junjie.609@s.kyushu-u.ac.jp
[2] Kyushu University, Japan xia.shangzhou.218@s.kyushu-u.ac.jp
[3] Zhejiang University, China fuyuanzhang@zju.edu.cn
[4] Kyushu University, Japan zhao@ait.kyushu-u.ac.jp

Abstract. As quantum algorithms and hardware continue to evolve, ensuring the correctness of the quantum software stack (QSS) has become increasingly important. However, testing QSSes remains challenging due to the oracle problem, i.e., the lack of a reliable ground truth for expected program behavior. Existing metamorphic testing approaches often rely on equivalent circuit transformations, backend modifications, or parameter tuning to address this issue. In this work, inspired by Equivalence Modulo Inputs (EMI), we propose Quantum EMI (QEMI), a new testing approach for QSSes. Our key contributions include: (1) a random quantum program generator that produces code with dead code based on quantum control-flow structures, and (2) an adaptation of the EMI technique from classical compiler testing to generate variants by removing dead code. By comparing the behavior of these variants, we can detect potential bugs in QSS implementations. We applied QEMI to Qiskit, Q#, and Cirq, and successfully identified 11 crash bugs and 1 behavioral inconsistency. QEMI expands the limited set of testing techniques available for quantum software stacks by going beyond structural transformations and incorporating semantics-preserving ones into quantum program analysis.

Keywords: Quantum computing · Metamorphic testing · Software testing · Equivalent program variants

1 Introduction

Quantum computing promises advantages on specific problem classes [7,19]. Superposition and entanglement, as key qubit properties, enable algorithmic speedups but also make it hard for classical languages to faithfully represent and manipulate quantum states.

Quantum software stacks (QSSes) address this gap by providing the tools to construct, compile, and execute quantum programs on simulators or hardware.

* Fuyuan Zhang is with the State Key Laboratory of Blockchain and Data Security, Zhejiang University, Hangzhou, China.

E. Albert and C. Pasareanu (Eds.): FASE 2026, LNCS 16504, pp. 149–169, 2026.
https://doi.org/10.1007/978-3-032-22774-4_8

They offer high-level abstractions for expressing quantum logic while handling backend-specific details. A typical QSS comprises a domain-specific interface for building circuits, utilities for circuit transformation/optimization, and runtime/backends for execution. Representative systems include *Qiskit* (IBM) [12], *Q#* (Microsoft) [23], and *Cirq* (Google) [4], each with its own language syntax, runtime semantics, and toolchain.

Unlike classical software systems, quantum software often integrates both quantum and classical components. For instance, a quantum algorithm may include classical control logic (*e.g.*, conditionals or loops around quantum operations) or quantum control logic (*e.g.*, using qubits as control conditions). This hybrid nature, combined with the probabilistic behavior of quantum programs, presents unique challenges for the design and verification of quantum software systems. As these stacks continue to evolve, ensuring their correctness and reliability has become an important concern in the development of practical quantum software.

Testing plays a crucial role in validating the correctness of quantum software stacks (QSSes). QSS testing faces two major challenges. As mentioned in [18], QSS testing now faces two challenges: the lack of quantum programs for testing and the oracle problem. Existing approaches often leverage random quantum program generators in combination with techniques such as differential and metamorphic testing. These strategies have proven effective at identifying real-world bugs in QSSes. For instance, *QuteFuzz* [11], which applies differential testing on randomly generated programs, uncovered 17 bugs across multiple versions of Qiskit, Cirq, and Pytket [21]. Other tools such as *QDiff* [24] and *MorphQ* [18] also demonstrate strong effectiveness, detecting 4 and 13 crash bugs, respectively.

However, existing methods still have room for improvement. Current random program generators largely emphasize composing quantum gate operations while paying limited attention to broader QSS APIs (e.g., the predefined circuits in *qiskit.circuit.library*), which risks overlooking API-specific bugs during testing. In addition, many existing techniques prioritize circuit-level or transformation-based equivalence, placing less emphasis on language-level semantic equivalence between quantum programs. To address these gaps, this paper revisits *Equivalence Modulo Inputs* (EMI) [14]—a technique that generates program variants which are semantically equivalent with respect to a given input set by modifying code that does not affect behavior for that input—so as to enable differential detection of implementation bugs. Applying EMI to quantum software stacks, however, poses unique challenges: due to superposition-induced probabilistic outputs, even with deterministic quantum inputs, the program behavior can be non-deterministic, making input-irrelevant code hard to identify. Moreover, some QSSes execute quantum and classical code separately, limiting the use of classical variables to locate dead code within quantum control structures.

In our approach, we propose **QEMI**[5], a framework that adapts EMI to quantum software stacks. QEMI targets quantum-specific control-flow structures and

[5] We provide access to QEMI artifacts at `https://github.com/Xzore19/QEMI`

generates semantically equivalent variants by removing dead code inside quantum conditional statements. Unlike classical EMI, where dynamic execution can reveal dead code, the probabilistic nature of quantum outputs makes such a strategy impractical. Instead, QEMI analyzes quantum control statements and, by preparing specific quantum states in advance, ensures that designated code blocks do not affect program outputs. Based on this insight, QEMI defines a set of dead-code patterns and constructs the corresponding quantum states during program generation. We focus on dead-code insertion, and richer equivalence-preserving rewrites inside these regions are left as future work. Using this static approach, QEMI uncovered 12 bugs across three widely used QSSes (Qiskit, Q#, and Cirq). To improve efficiency, QEMI further incorporates an early-stop strategy that terminates once a predefined statistical-confidence threshold is met for distinguishing output distributions, thereby reducing the number of final measurements per execution and yielding at least a 53.83% speedup in our experiments.

The main contributions of this work include:

- Developing a quantum random program generator capable of producing programs with both classical and quantum control flow, designed for testing with the latest APIs.
- Integrating a static pattern-based EMI approach for quantum programs into the random program generator.
- Designing an early stopping strategy for detecting consistency between measurement distributions during quantum program comparison.
- Implementing the framework on popular QSSes, including Qiskit, Q#, and Cirq, and uncovering 12 unique real-world bugs, including both distributional and crash-related errors.

The rest of the paper is organized as follows. Section 2 provides background information relevant to our work. Section 3 describes the design of QEMI. Section 4 presents our experimental setup and results. Threats to validity are discussed in Section 5. We review related work in Section 6, and conclude the paper in Section 7.

2 Background

2.1 Quantum Computing

Quantum computing provides a fundamentally new approach to information processing by leveraging quantum mechanical phenomena, including superposition, entanglement, and interference. Unlike classical computation, which is based on deterministic operations over binary bits, quantum computation is built upon quantum circuits operating on qubits.

Qubits and Quantum Gates. The basic unit of quantum information is the *qubit*. A qubit can exist in a superposition of classical states 0 and 1, and its state is generally expressed as:

$$|\psi\rangle = \alpha\,|0\rangle + \beta\,|1\rangle\,,$$

where α and β are complex numbers that satisfy the normalization condition $|\alpha|^2 + |\beta|^2 = 1$. To manipulate qubit states, quantum gates are applied. These gates are unitary matrices that transform the state of one or more qubits in a reversible manner. Common quantum gates include Pauli-X, Hadamard, and phase gates for single-qubit operations, as well as multi-qubit gates like CNOT, Toffoli, and SWAP. By composing these gates, one can construct quantum circuits capable of encoding complex quantum algorithms.

Quantum Circuits and Measurement. A quantum program is typically implemented as a circuit that applies a sequence of quantum gates to an initial state. If the system starts in state $|\psi_0\rangle$ and performs operations $U_1, U_2, \ldots, U_k$, then the final state is as follows:

$$|\psi_f\rangle = U_k U_{k-1} \ldots U_1 |\psi_0\rangle .$$

After the circuit is executed, a measurement projects the final quantum state onto a classical bitstring. Because measurement outcomes are probabilistic, a quantum program is usually executed multiple times to estimate the output distribution. These repeated executions are called *shots* (one shot produces one bitstring sample). The statistical nature of measurement plays a crucial role in many quantum algorithms, where desired results appear with high probability only after repeated trials.

2.2 Equivalence Modulo Inputs

Equivalence Modulo Inputs (EMI) is a relaxed notion of semantic equivalence, originally formalized by Le et al. [14]. Let $\mathcal{L}$ be a deterministic programming language with semantics $[\![\cdot]\!]$.

Two programs $P, Q \in \mathcal{L}$ are said to be *EMI-equivalent* with respect to an input set $I \subseteq \text{dom}(P) \cap \text{dom}(Q)$ if and only if:

$$\forall i \in I.\ [\![P]\!](i) = [\![Q]\!](i)$$

This relation is denoted by $[\![P]\!] =_I [\![Q]\!]$, indicating that P and Q exhibit identical behavior for all inputs in I, even if they differ syntactically or produce different outputs on other inputs.

Given a program P and an input set $I \subseteq \text{dom}(P)$, the set of all programs Q that are EMI-equivalent to P with respect to I constitutes the **EMI variants** of P:

$$\{Q \in \mathcal{L} \mid [\![P]\!] =_I [\![Q]\!]\}$$

When $I = \{\texttt{void}\}$, meaning the programs do not take inputs, EMI reduces to classical semantic equivalence. In this case:

$$[\![P]\!] = [\![Q]\!] \quad \Rightarrow \quad [\![P]\!] =_I [\![Q]\!]$$

If a compiler produces different outputs for P and Q under a fixed execution configuration, this indicates a potential semantic bug. EMI leverages this principle by constructing program variants that are guaranteed to behave identically under the same configuration. This enables compiler testing without the need for a reference implementation or ground truth, while preserving the semantic validity of test programs.

2.3 Control Flow in Quantum Programs

Since control flow in quantum programs differs in certain ways from that in classical programs, this section provides a detailed overview of control flow constructs in quantum programming.

Quantum Conditions To clearly explain the control flow in quantum programs, we begin by introducing the concept of a quantum condition. In classical programs, a condition typically refers to a Boolean expression whose evaluation determines whether a certain block of code is executed or repeated. This expression involves only classical variables, and thus its expressive power is limited in the context of quantum programs. Unlike classical conditions that rely exclusively on classical variables, quantum conditions refer to control constructs that depend on quantum states (Figure 1a) or on qubit measurement outcomes (Figure 1b), including direct use of such outcomes as control inputs. It allows quantum programs to express more sophisticated control flow structures.

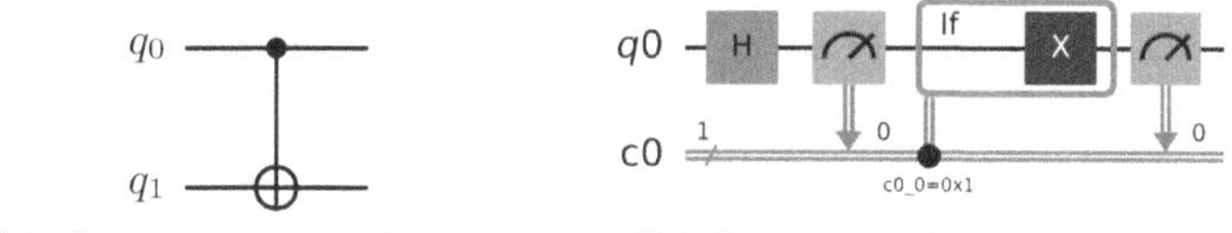

(a) Quantum control gate. (b) Quantum dynamic circuit.

Fig. 1: Two types of quantum conditions.

Quantum Control Flow. For this work, any control flow that involves quantum operations in either the condition or in the controlled operation is considered a quantum control flow. QEMI focuses on quantum-target control flows. Based on this focus, we identify several common control flow structures in quantum programs that serve as the basis for subsequent random program generation and the design of dead code patterns.

Conditional Branching Structure. Quantum programs mainly include three forms of conditional branching structures.

The first is to use a classical condition to control quantum operations, where the overall structure closely resembles conditional code constructs in classical programs. When the classical condition evaluates to false, certain regions of the program become dead code. For example, using the *if_else* statement implements the logic:

```
1    if (a == 1) { Op(tgt) }
```

where a is a classical variable and *Op(tgt)* is a quantum operation, and when $a \neq 1$, the *Op(tgt)* will not execute.

The second is an extension of the classical *if-else* statement to the quantum setting, where quantum variables are used as a condition. In this case, when the quantum variable does not match a specific quantum state, which is represented as an int value, the code within the true branch will not be executed. For example, in Q#, the function *ApplyIfEqualL(Op, c, ctrl, tgt)* [2] implements the logic:

```
1       if (c == ctrl) { Op(tgt) }
```

where the operation *Op* is applied to the target quantum register *tgt* if the quantum register *ctrl* equals the specific quantum state c, which is represented as a classical value *c*. Since *ctrl* could be in superposition states, the control flow governed by such statements will only satisfy the non-execution property of certain code blocks for a very limited subset of quantum states.

The third is a quantum-native control structure that is integrated into quantum operations as a fundamental concept of quantum computing. Certain quantum operations can be directly controlled by specific qubit states. For example, the controlled-NOT gate (CX) is typically represented by $CX\,|ctrl, tgt\rangle = |ctrl, tgt \oplus ctrl\rangle$. From a semantic point of view, the CX gate can also be interpreted as a form of conditional branching: when the control qubit *ctrl* is in the state *1*, apply the X gate to the target qubit *tgt*:

```
1       if (ctrl == 1) { X(tgt) }
```

Loop Structure. Loop-related constructs in quantum programs are similar to those in classical programs and mainly include iteration and conditional loops. Some commonly used loop constructs include:

- **Iterations**, such as: *for i in 1..n { Operation }*
- **Condition-controlled loops**, including:
  - *while condition { Operation }*
  - *repeat { Operation } until condition fixup { Operation }*

The *condition* in these statements can be implemented using either classical variables or quantum states and measurement results. The fundamental logic of quantum conditions is essentially the same as that in conditional branching structures. While a quantum condition can be logically represented as a classical statement, during execution, the inherent probabilistic nature of quantum measurements leads the *condition* to evaluate to *True* or *False* in a probabilistic manner.

3 Methodology

Figure 2 presents an overview of QEMI, a framework for testing QSSes based on EMI. QEMI consists of three main steps. First, a random program generator constructs a seed program by randomly selecting classical or quantum control

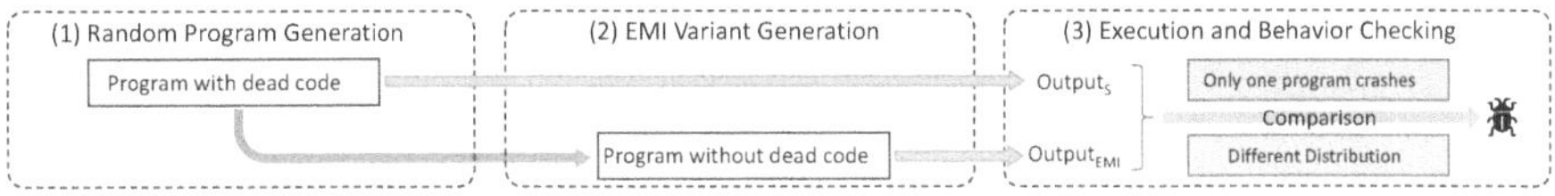

Fig. 2: The workflow of QEMI.

structures, basic quantum gates, and API calls (Section 3.2). During generation, dead code is inserted based on predefined patterns (Section 3.1). Second, a static analysis pass removes the inserted dead code, yielding an EMI variant that is semantically equivalent to the original program (Section 3.2). Finally, QEMI executes both the original and variant, checking for behavioral discrepancies such as crashes or divergences in the output distributions to identify potential bugs in QSS (Section 3.3).

3.1 Dead Code Pattern Design

Due to the presence of control flow structures, dead code may exist in quantum programs. However, analyzing the presence of dead code in randomly generated quantum programs presents unique challenges. In classical software testing, dead code is typically identified by static reachability analysis or dynamic execution profiling. However, both approaches are difficult to apply in the context of quantum programs.

First, reachability analysis remains underdeveloped at the level of high-level quantum programming languages. While progress has been made in reachability analysis at the circuit level (*e.g.*, for quantum Markov chains [3]), there remains a lack of practical tools capable of analyzing control flow in high-level quantum programming languages. Developing such tools represents an important direction for future work.

Second, classical dead-code identification based on deterministic inputs (e.g., dynamic coverage tools like Python's *coverage*) is incompatible with quantum control flow. Such tools execute a program on fixed inputs and mark lines as executed or not; in classical EMI, this reveals input-irrelevant code for generating semantically equivalent variants. In quantum programs, however, behavior remains probabilistic even from a well-defined initial state. For example, $|\phi\rangle = 0.8\,|0\rangle + 0.6\,|1\rangle$ collapses to $|1\rangle$ with probability 0.64 and to $|0\rangle$ with 0.36, so a path that seems dead in one run may be taken in another. Hence, a single execution trace cannot reliably classify dead code and may yield false positives when comparing "equivalent" program variants. This limitation is compounded by the structure of many frameworks (e.g., Qiskit), where quantum and classical code are constructed and handled separately. Therefore, classical methods based on deterministic inputs cannot effectively identify dead code regions within quantum-specific control-flow structures.

To address these limitations, we adopt a static strategy: instead of dynamically running programs and identifying dead code regions via coverage analysis, we generate corresponding dead-code patterns based on different types of quantum control statements. These patterns ensure that the dead code regions remain

```
1 qc.measure(qreg, condition)
2 with qc.if_test(condition,
  ↪ 0) as else_0:
3     # DEADCODE START
4     qc.x(0)
5     # DEADCODE END
6 with else_0:
7     qc.h(0)
```

(a) if_test_dead

```
1 qc.measure(qreg, condition)
2 with qc.while_loop(
  ↪ condition, 0):
3     # DEADCODE START
4     qc.x(0)
5     # DEADCODE END
```

(b) while_dead

```
1 qc.measure(qreg, condition)
2 with qc.switch(condition)
  ↪ as case:
3     with case(0):
4         # DEADCODE START
5         qc.x(0)
6         # DEADCODE END
7     with case(1):
8         qc.h(0)
```

(c) *switch_dead*

```
1 with qc.for_loop(range(0))
  ↪ as i:
2     # DEADCODE START
3     qc.x(0)
4     # DEADCODE END
```

(d) for_zero

```
1 with qc.for_loop(range(5))
  ↪ as i:
2     qc.h(1)
3     qc.continue_loop()
4     # DEADCODE START
5     qc.x(0)
6     # DEADCODE END
```

(e) for_continue

```
1 with qc.for_loop(range(5))
  ↪ as i:
2     qc.h(1)
3     qc.break_loop()
4     # DEADCODE START
5     qc.x(0)
6     # DEADCODE END
```

(f) for_break

Fig. 3: Some examples for dead code patterns in Qiskit. For *if_test_dead*, *while_dead*, and *switch_dead*, we first prepare $|1\rangle$ in *qreg*. After measurement, the *condition* equals 1 deterministically.

unexecuted under any input set, thereby preserving semantic equivalence among program variants. Furthermore, by replacing dead code regions with alternative quantum operations, we can efficiently expand the number of program variants. In QEMI, we nest multiple dead code patterns to generate more complex control flow structures.

Figure 3 presents several dead code patterns in Qiskit. The dead code patterns that we designed are mainly divided into two categories:

- **Input-dependent:** These patterns ensure that the dead code region remains unexecuted only when a specific quantum state is provided as input. For example, in Figure 3a, if the quantum state does not match the target state $|1\rangle$, the measurement output (line 1) may yield 0, potentially triggering the execution of the dead code region. To handle these, we introduce an additional quantum register *qreg* to prepare the desired target quantum state $|1\rangle$.
- **Input-independent:** These patterns guarantee that the dead code region is never executed under any input. For example, in Figure 3e, the semantics of *qc.continue_loop* ensure that the code following is never executed.

These patterns are deliberately constructed to ensure that the enclosed dead code is never executed under any condition, while preserving the syntactic and semantic structure of valid quantum control flows. Note that not all QSSes support every dead code pattern listed above; in practice, applicable patterns are selected based on the capabilities of each QSS.

3.2 Program Generation

We next describe how QEMI generates EMI variants by applying dead code patterns and how this mechanism is incorporated into the random program generation process.

Quantum EMI Variants generation Based on defined dead-code patterns, QEMI instantiates each pattern with concrete operations, such as quantum subcircuits, nested control-flow constructs, or nested dead code, to form a complete dead-code block. These operations are typically encapsulated into a callable function, which is then invoked at the designated dead code location. The inserted region is explicitly marked as semantically unreachable to ensure that it does not affect the program behavior. While Qiskit allows users to construct reusable control logic through Python functions, Q# exposes quantum control structures as built-in operations. These control-flow APIs encapsulate conditional logic at the language level, providing a modular, structured way to express complex control behavior. To demonstrate this feature, we provide a Q# example. Figure 4 presents an example of a Q# code segment generated from a dead code pattern and its corresponding EMI variant. In this case, the operation *ApplyControlledOnInt(7, DeadBlock, ctrl, q)* is semantically equivalent to the conditional construct:

```
1       if (ctrl == 7) { DeadBlock(q) }
```

Since *ctrl* is initialized to *0*, the condition *ctrl == 7* always evaluates false, which means that *deadBlock (q)* is never executed. As a result, *ApplyControlledOnInt(7, DeadBlock, ctrl, q)* does not affect the behavior of the program. During code generation, this region is marked as dead (e.g., lines 7 and 9 in Figure 4a), and can be removed directly to generate an EMI variant (Figure 4b).

```
1  operation DeadBlock(q : Qubit[]) : Unit is
   ↪ Adj + Ctl {
2      Rzz(5.86706, q[1], q[2]);
3  }
4
5  operation ApplyRandomBlock1(q : Qubit[]) :
   ↪ Unit {
6      use ctrl = Qubit[3];
7      // --- DEADCODE START ---
8      ApplyControlledOnInt(7, DeadBlock, ctrl
   ↪ , q);
9      // --- DEADCODE END ---
10 }
```

(a) DCB in the original program.

```
1  operation DeadBlock(q : Qubit[]) : Unit is
   ↪ Adj + Ctl {
2      Rzz(5.86706, q[1], q[2]);
3  }
4
5  operation ApplyRandomBlock1(q : Qubit[]) :
   ↪ Unit {
6      use ctrl = Qubit[3];
7
8
9
10
11 }
```

(b) DCB in QEMI variant.

Fig. 4: An example for the dead code block(DCB) generation.

Random Quantum Program generation The quantum programs generated by QEMI mainly consist of the following four components:

- **Basic Prologue Part:** To ensure that the quantum program runs correctly, the generator loads the required quantum libraries, the basic program configurations, and the chosen random seed into the program module.

- **Quantum Operation Part:** Based on the configuration settings, we initialize the required quantum and classical registers. For each quantum operation, the generator randomly selects from basic quantum gates, quantum API calls, and composite gates constructed from subcircuits, with the corresponding random parameters.
- **Dead Code Part:** Within the selected dead code patterns, the generator randomly inserts quantum operations. Due to the inherent uncertainty of quantum measurement outcomes, some dead code patterns (such as *if_test*, *while_loop*, *ApplyIfEqual*, etc.) only exhibit strictly non-executable behavior under specific quantum states. For these patterns, we allocate additional quantum registers to prepare the desired quantum state, ensuring that the condition in the quantum control flow deterministically evaluates to either *True* or *False*. Given the transformable nature of dead code, the generator also outputs this module and marks the non-executable regions.
- **Optimization Pass Part (Optional):** Since some quantum platforms include built-in program optimization processes, we randomly apply optimization passes to the generated programs to ensure a more thorough testing of QSSes.

Based on the configuration settings, we construct the corresponding executor and parameter information for each generated quantum program.

3.3 Execution and Behavior Checking

The *Hellinger distance* [8] is a widely used metric to quantify the similarity between two discrete probability distributions. Given two distributions $P = (p_1, p_2, \ldots, p_n)$ and $Q = (q_1, q_2, \ldots, q_n)$ over the same finite domain, the Hellinger distance is defined as:

$$H(P, Q) = \frac{1}{\sqrt{2}} \sqrt{\sum_{i=1}^{n} \left(\sqrt{p_i} - \sqrt{q_i}\right)^2} \tag{1}$$

The value of $H(P, Q)$ lies in the range $[0, 1]$, where $H(P, Q) = 0$ if and only if $P = Q$, and $H(P, Q) = 1$ when P and Q have a disjoint distribution. In our context, P and Q typically represent the normalized output distributions of the two quantum circuits being compared. We prefer the Hellinger distance over other divergences such as the Kolmogorov-Smirnov (K-S) test [13], [22] or cross-entropy [6], [20], as it remains well defined on zero-probability events and aligns naturally with quantum fidelity measures [16]. Although we recommend using the Hellinger distance as the primary evaluation metric, our method also supports alternative options such as the K-S test and cross-entropy, allowing users to choose according to their specific needs. In addition, users can extend QEMI by designing and integrating custom metrics into the framework.

Early Termination for Distribution Divergence Detection While we can assess the similarity between two distributions using the Hellinger distance to determine whether two quantum programs exhibit equivalent behavior, in practice, there is a trade-off between the confidence of the Hellinger estimate and the measurement cost. Existing research [5] shows that, for a Hellinger threshold δ, determining whether two distributions are identical versus δ-far in Hellinger distance with 2/3 confidence requires at least

$$S_{\text{std}} = S(\delta, N) = \min\left\{\frac{N^{2/3}}{\delta^{8/3}}, \frac{N^{3/4}}{\delta^2}\right\}, \tag{2}$$

where $N = 2^n$ is the size of the output space for a quantum program that acts on n qubits. For example, setting $\delta = 0.1$ and $n = 8$ results in a sample requirement of approximately 6,400 measurements.

However, in practical test scenarios, a confidence level of 2/3 results in a relatively high error rate, potentially incurring additional cost due to the need for manual verification of samples flagged as inconsistent [18]. To raise the confidence level to a target of $1 - \eta$, it is necessary to apply confidence amplification [1] by repeating the measurement process multiple times and aggregating the results. While confidence amplification boosts the reliability of the Hellinger estimate by repeating independent comparisons, it also leads to a proportional increase in the total number of measurements. Using too few measurements reduces the confidence of the estimated distance, while excessive measurements incur significant overhead. To reduce measurement cost without compromising statistical confidence, we aim to design an adaptive stopping strategy that terminates the comparison once sufficient evidence of equivalence has been observed.

For programs generated by QEMI, we have a useful prior: the two quantum programs produced by QEMI are expected to yield identical output distributions, which implies that $H(P, Q) = 0$. This implies that as the number of measurements increases, the Hellinger distance between the two resulting distributions should asymptotically converge to zero.

Moreover, due to the inherent indeterminacy of quantum behavior, the output space size 2^n specified by a circuit only represents an upper bound. Causes that reduce the effective output space include entanglement between qubits, the use of phase gates that do not affect measurement probabilities, and, more directly, the absence of randomness-inducing operations on certain qubits. As a result, the actual set of outcomes that appear with non-negligible probability may be much smaller.

Based on the above reasoning, we design an early-stopping strategy for QEMI when using the Hellinger distance to compare output distributions. For each randomly generated quantum program and its corresponding EMI variant, we repeatedly performed measurements with a limited number of shots in each round. Specifically, the number of shots per round is defined as

$$S_{\text{round}(\delta,N)} = S(\delta, N^{1/2}). \tag{3}$$

This design leverages the two priors mentioned above. First, by using a smaller number of shots per round, we can observe the convergence of $H(P, Q)$ to below the threshold δ quickly, assuming that the programs are indeed equivalent.

Second, the choice of using $N^{1/2}$ as the effective output space size reflects our assumption that the true support of the output distribution is much smaller than the full $N = 2^n$ space. By iteratively executing rounds with this reduced shot count, we aim to minimize the total number of measurements required to confidently determine whether $H(P, Q) < \delta$.

After each measurement round, we compute the Hellinger distance between the two distributions. If the distance is smaller than δ, we perform one additional measurement round using the same number of shots S_{round}. If the Hellinger distance remains below δ for two consecutive rounds, we terminate the process and conclude that there is no significant difference between the distributions.

However, if the total number of measurements reaches the maximum allowed shot budget S_{max} without observing two consecutive rounds with Hellinger distance below δ, we consider the distributions to be different. Here S_{max} is a user-defined threshold: a larger value corresponds to a higher confidence level. In practice, we empirically set

$$S_{\text{max}} = 2 \cdot S_{\text{std}}, \tag{4}$$

which demonstrates its effectiveness in practice.

3.4 Algorithm

Algorithm 1 describes how QEMI composes the three main steps. The first step of the entire process is to select the appropriate compiler configuration set (line 3), program generator (line 4), and quantum program executor (line 5) for the specified quantum programming platform. Based on the Hellinger threshold δ and the number of qubits n, QEMI calculates the required maximum and minimum number of measurements s and r. In the main loop of the algorithm, QEMI randomly selects a conditional statement or a nested structure of multiple conditional statements from the dead code patterns N_p supported by the specified quantum programming language (line 9). Based on N_p, QEMI generates a complete quantum program P that contains the corresponding dead code segments D_c (line 10). For a given program P, by modifying or transforming D_c, QEMI can obtain a new quantum program P' that preserves the same semantics as P (line 11). For all executable configurations, both programs P and P' are executed (line 13). Based on the results of the two programs, we perform different actions:

1) For simultaneous crashes with different errors or a single crash, QEMI will save these programs and label them as *crash* (line 15).

2) For a no-crash situation, QEMI will utilize the Hellinger-based early stop strategy (lines 17-25). In this process, we iteratively add additional measurement times to the target program pair (P, P'). Each new set of results (R, R') is merged with the previous ones (line 23) and checked against violations of the $Hellinger()$ (line 19). If the total number of measurements exceeds the maximum times s, the early-stop process will terminate, and a final probability distribution result will be used to determine whether QSS exists a bug. If $Hellinger()$ rejects

the hypothesis of identical distributions, QEMI will save these programs and label them as *wrong* (line 26).

3) In all other cases, QEMI will not take any action. After reaching the maximum number of executions, QEMI will output all identified potential buggy program pairs.

Algorithm 1 : Quantum EMI

Input: $i \leftarrow$ Quantum Language Platform; $n \leftarrow$ Number of qubits; $\delta \leftarrow$ Hellinger threshold
Output: $B \leftarrow$ set of buggy programs
1: $N \leftarrow 2^n$
2: $B \leftarrow \emptyset$
3: $config \leftarrow ConfigChoice(i)$
4: $G \leftarrow ProgramGenerator(i)$
5: $E \leftarrow Executor(i)$
6: $s \leftarrow S(\delta, N)$
7: $r \leftarrow S(\delta, N^{1/2})$
8: **for** $j \leftarrow 0$ to $MaxIter$ **do**
9: $N_p \leftarrow DeadCodePattern(i)$
10: $P,\ D_c \leftarrow G.generate(N_p)$
11: $P' \leftarrow Remove(P, D_c)$
12: **for** $\sigma \in config$ **do**
13: $R,\ R' \leftarrow E.execute(P,\ P',\ r,\ \sigma)$
14: **if** $Error(R) \neq Error(R')$ **then**
15: $B \leftarrow B\ \cup\ \{(P,\ P',\ 'crash')\}$
16: **else if** $Error(R) = Error(R') = None$ **then**
17: $m_r \leftarrow r$
18: **while** $m_r < s$ **do**
19: **if** $Hellinger(Output(R,\ R'))$ **then**
20: $Break$
21: **end if**
22: $m_r \leftarrow m_r + r$
23: $R,\ R' \leftarrow Merge(E.execute(P,\ P',\ r,\ \sigma))$
24: **end while**
25: **if** $\neg Hellinger(Output(R,\ R'))$ **then**
26: $B \leftarrow B\ \cup\ \{(P,\ P',\ 'wrong')\}$
27: **end if**
28: **end if**
29: **end for**
30: **end for**
31: **return** B

4 Experimental Evaluation

Our experiments focus on the following research questions (**RQ**s):

- **RQ1:** What kinds of real-world bugs did QEMI uncover?
- **RQ2:** How does QEMI compare with the baseline methods on bug detection?
- **RQ3:** How much does QEMI's early termination measurement strategy improve efficiency?

4.1 Testing Setup

Hardware and QSSes Version We conducted our experiments on a workstation running Ubuntu 20.04, equipped with an Intel Core i9-10940X processor (14 cores, 28 threads) and 208 GB of RAM. We conduct our tests on the latest version of each QSS, including Qiskit (versions 2.0.0 to 2.1.0), Cirq (versions 1.6.0.dev20250702012506), and Q# (version 1.17).

Table 1: Real-world bugs found by QEMI.

ID	Report	Platform	Status	Crash Message	Bug Reason
1	#14254 #14338 #14385	Qiskit	Fixed	Unable to translate the operations in the circuit: [*if_else*, *clifford*] to backend's basis: {h, mcphase, ...}.	Failing to decompose a Clifford operator within a control-flow block.
2*	#14521	Qiskit	Fixed	No viable alternative at input "_".	The *ForLoopOp* does not support dynamic range.
3	#14407	Qiskit	Fixed	Invalid param type *complex* for gate *initialize_dg*.	Instruction *Initialize* is not invertible.
4	#14635 #14409	Qiskit	Fixed	*inverse()* not implemented for *for_loop*.	*for_loop* does not have inverse methods.
5	#14645	Qiskit	Fixed	*Clifford* object has no attribute *is_parameterized*.	Cliffords do not have *is_parameterized* methods.
6	#14319	Qiskit	Confirmed	Program enters an infinite loop after *RemoveFinalMeasurements* optimization.	–
7	#14646 #14647	Qiskit	Confirmed	Called *Option::unwrap()* on a *None* value.	Failing to revalidate analysis before *ConsolidateBlocks* after intermediate transformation.
8	#14522	Qiskit	Reported	Declarations of type int are not supported.	–
9	#2534	Q#	Fixed	The generated program and its EMI variant results are in different distributions.	A bug in the gate queueing optimization of the underlying simulator.
10	#7473	Cirq	Fixed	Coefficient is not unitary.	The identity gate is not preserving the qubit order as expected.
11	#7472	Cirq	Confirmed	Measurement key *c* missing when testing classical control.	Incorrectly skips commutativity checks on disjoint qubits, missing classical control constraints.
12	#7474	Cirq	Confirmed	Measurement key *c* missing when testing classical control.	Failing to reverse the operation order within moments during circuit reversal.

Metric for Behavior Checking In our experiments, we use a Hellinger distance threshold of $\delta = 0.1$ to determine whether two output distributions differ.

4.2 RQ1: Bug Summary

Table 1 summarizes the real-world bugs that QEMI found in three mainstream quantum software stacks—Qiskit, Cirq, and Q#—by running each stack for 24 hours independently on its latest release. In total, we identified 12 bugs: 11 crash-inducing issues and 1 output-distribution discrepancy. Reports with the same or similar root cause were grouped under a single entry; one entry (marked with a star) is a duplicated issue that was independently rediscovered. For each entry, we list the platform, the report ID, status (Reported/Confirmed/Fixed), crash message, and a brief root-cause summary. As of submission, 7/12 have been fixed, 4 have been confirmed by upstream developers, and 1 is pending confirmation. The bugs span low-level failures (e.g., crashes in circuit transformation/optimization) and higher-level issues (e.g., semantic mismatches or incorrect output distributions). We next analyze their causes, focusing on quantum control flow and how dead code exposes these faults.

QEMI identified *four* bugs (IDs 1, 2, 4, and 7) directly tied to quantum control flow, triggered either by optimizations applied to control structures or by transformations across quantum languages—highlighting that code transformation remains challenging for current QSSes in the presence of quantum control.

The remaining bugs are not directly caused by control flow, yet EMI was still crucial to reveal them. Dead code in the original program contributed in two ways. First, the faulty code itself lay inside the dead region; removing it in

EMI variants made only the original crash (e.g., Qiskit #14338, Cirq #7472). Second, the dead region contained a control structure; some passes do not support control, so the original program silently skipped an optimization while the EMI variant proceeded along the unsupported path and crashed (e.g., Qiskit #14254, #14407).

Answer to RQ1: QEMI identified 12 unique bugs in the latest versions of QSSes, including 1 duplicate. Among them, 11 have been confirmed or fixed by the official developers of the respective QSSes.

4.3 RQ2: Baselines Comparison

We compare QEMI with three baseline methods: QDiff, MorphQ, and QuteFuzz, which are automated techniques for testing QSSes. All experiments are conducted on the Qiskit platform, targeting versions 2.0.0 to 2.1.0. To ensure a fair comparison under consistent experimental conditions, we independently ran the complete workflow for each baseline method for 24 hours, covering program generation, execution, and checking for behavioral consistency.

Table 2: Coverage after 24 hours of execution on each method.

QEMI	QDiff	MorphQ	QuteFuzz
14.80%	6.24%	9.58%	14.18%

Code Coverage Table 2 presents the code coverage achieved by QEMI and three baseline methods. Among the four approaches, QEMI achieves the highest code coverage. This is likely because, unlike QDiff and MorphQ, which generate test programs using only basic gates, QEMI combines optimization passes and control flow structures during the test generation process. In this respect, QuteFuzz adopts a similar strategy by incorporating both optimization passes and control flow. However, QEMI has a slight advantage over QuteFuzz because it additionally invokes API functionalities from the QSS during generation, further contributing to its higher coverage.

Bug-exposing capability In our experiments, among the three baselines, only QuteFuzz triggered a bug, which corresponds to the known Qiskit issue #13165. Under the same experimental settings, we did not observe any bugs triggered by QDiff or MorphQ. This suggests that QEMI is complementary to existing approaches and can trigger failure modes that are difficult to expose without EMI-style dead-code construction.

We conjecture that QEMI missed this issue due to its evaluation strategy. QEMI executes the original program and its EMI variant independently and reports a bug only when their observed behaviors diverge. If both executions crash in the same manner, QEMI treats them as behaviorally consistent and thus does not flag the failure. Consequently, crash bugs that manifest identically in both the original and EMI-augmented executions can be missed by this strategy.

Answer to RQ2: Compared to prior work, QEMI can detect bugs that are difficult for existing approaches to expose. Although it performs fewer tests within the same time, the programs generated by QEMI achieve higher code coverage.

4.4 RQ3: Effectiveness of the Early Stop Strategy

We assess the effectiveness of QEMI's early stopping by measuring its impact on checking efficiency and on the accuracy of distributional consistency validation. We quantitatively evaluate 2,000 Q# programs with 6 and 8 qubits generated by QEMI, using a Hellinger threshold of $\delta = 0.1$. Each program is measured up to $S_{\max}$ shots while tracking whether its Hellinger distance ever exceeds the threshold to detect potential false negatives (i.e., classifying discrepant pairs as equivalent). Across all cases where early stopping was triggered, the Hellinger distance never exceeded the threshold even when measurements continued to $S_{\max}$, indicating a low false-negative rate in practice. We also record the shot count at which each program terminates.

Table 3: Distribution of Early Stop Shots ($\delta = 0.1$)

(a) Qubit number $n = 6$

multiple ($\times S_{\text{round}}$)	2	3	4	S_{std}	5	6	7	8	9	$S_{\max}$
shots	952	1428	1904	2263	2380	2856	3332	3808	4284	4526
count	1806	80	47	–	53	13	1	0	0	–

(b) Qubit number $n = 8$

multiple ($\times S_{\text{round}}$)	2	3	4	5	6	7	S_{std} (8)	9	10	11	12	13	14	15	$S_{\max}$ (16)
shots	1600	2400	3200	4000	4800	5600	6400	7200	8000	8800	9600	10400	11200	12000	12800
count	1832	78	44	10	6	5	0	5	14	6	0	0	0	0	0

The detailed distributions are shown in Table 3. Each column reports the number of programs that terminated after performing a specific number of measurements, which is always a multiple of the round size S_{round}. The first row labels each column with its corresponding multiple of S_{round} to clarify its relation to the standard and maximum budgets. The column marked S_{std} corresponds to the number of measurements required to achieve a 2/3 confidence level based on theoretical bounds. We use S_{std} as the baseline for the number of measurements needed to verify distributional consistency between program outputs. Accordingly, we quantify the speedup enabled by the early stopping strategy by computing the ratio between the total number of measurements actually performed and the baseline total, as follows:

$$\text{Speedup Ratio} = 1 - \frac{\sum_{i=1}^{T} S_i^{\text{early}}}{T \cdot S_{\text{std}}} \tag{5}$$

where S_i^{early} denotes the number of shots required for the i-th program under the early stopping strategy, and T is the total number of programs. Using this formula, we observe a speedup of **53.83%** for $n = 6$ and **72.21%** for $n = 8$.

The columns to the right of the S_{std} divider represent programs for which early stopping was not triggered within the standard budget. These programs continued sampling beyond S_{std} but terminated before reaching the maximum limit S_{max}. Notably, all of these programs would be incorrectly classified as inequivalent under a fixed-budget strategy based solely on S_{std} measurements, despite their distributions ultimately satisfying the Hellinger threshold. In contrast, QEMI's early stopping strategy correctly identified these programs as equivalent. This highlights the advantage of QEMI's adaptive strategy in avoiding such false positives.

Answer to RQ3: QEMI's early stopping strategy demonstrates significant acceleration in practical testing scenarios. It effectively reduces measurement cost while also mitigating false positives, thereby improving the overall efficiency and reliability of QSS testing.

5 Threats to Validity

Our implementation currently supports three major QSSes: Q#, Qiskit, and Cirq. However, other frameworks such as Pytket also support quantum circuits with control flow. Extending QEMI to additional QSSes would require implementing corresponding quantum random program generators and constructing appropriate dead-code templates for the target platforms. Nonetheless, the core idea of testing QSSes by generating semantically equivalent quantum programs via EMI remains generalizable.

The early stopping strategy that we employ to accelerate the validation of behavioral consistency is primarily based on empirical observations rather than formal theoretical guarantees. Although no false positives or false negatives have been observed in our experiments so far, this outcome is not theoretically guaranteed. Nevertheless, our strategy enables testing more program instances within the same time budget, which we consider a worthwhile trade-off.

Finally, our evaluation is currently limited to simulations due to classical hardware limitations. All experiments are conducted on simulators, restricting us to circuits with up to 8 qubits. While we have not yet performed large-scale evaluations on real quantum hardware, we believe our approach is inherently applicable to real-device scenarios, as it relies solely on observable measurement distributions and does not depend on backend-specific simulation properties. Nevertheless, the presence of hardware noise and device-specific behavior may introduce new challenges, which we leave for future investigation.

6 Related Work

Our methodology is closely connected to prior research in classical compiler testing as well as the testing of quantum software stacks. In this section, we review relevant and representative studies organized into two subsections. Section 6.1 discusses classical compiler testing, and Section 6.2 focuses on testing methodologies for quantum software stacks.

6.1 Classical Compiler Testing.

Classical compiler testing has been extensively studied in the programming languages and systems community. *Csmith* [25] is a widely used random program generator based on differential testing that detects crashing or miscompilation bugs by generating random C programs and comparing their behavior across compilers. *Yarpgen* [10], developed at Intel, further improves random generation by statically tracking constraints to avoid undefined behavior and by steering toward optimization-relevant patterns. *Orion* [14] was the first framework to apply Equivalence Modulo Inputs (EMI) to C compilers, and subsequent tools such as *CLsmith* [15] extended similar ideas to other languages. These approaches have been highly effective for exposing compiler bugs in the classical setting. However, quantum programs bring domain-specific challenges—superposition, entanglement, and measurement-induced randomness—and operate on qubits rather than classical bits, making a direct transfer of classical techniques to quantum software stacks non-trivial.

6.2 Quantum Software Stacks Testing.

Several studies have focused on testing QSSes. *QDiff* [24] detects inconsistencies by applying semantics-preserving transformations, such as equivalent gate replacements and optimization level changes, to a small set of hand-written quantum programs and checks whether their behaviors remain consistent. *MorphQ* [18] adopts a metamorphic testing approach by applying a broader range of transformations to randomly generated quantum programs. Then it verifies whether the transformed variants exhibit the same behavior as the original program. Neither QDiff nor MorphQ addresses testing of quantum control flow, and our approach does not overlap with their transformation techniques, making them complementary to our method. Among existing tools, *QuteFuzz* [11] is the only one that explicitly targets quantum control flow. It generates random quantum programs with control constructs and examines behavioral consistency under varying optimization levels or injected passes. However, QuteFuzz does not incorporate EMI techniques, which are central to our design. Moreover, QuteFuzz and MorphQ do not incorporate certain built-in circuit structures—such as QFT [17]—that are directly available in QSS APIs when generating random programs. In contrast, our approach addresses this limitation by explicitly supporting such predefined modules. *Upbeat* [9] focuses specifically on the Q# platform. Instead of testing for semantic equivalence, it extracts constraints from the use of Q# APIs and checks whether the compiler respects these constraints, thereby detecting potential boundary bugs. While effective in exposing API-level violations, Upbeat does not target the behavioral consistency of compiled quantum programs or address quantum control-flow structures.

7 Conclusion

We presented QEMI, the first framework that adapts the classical Equivalence Modulo Inputs (EMI) approach to quantum software testing. QEMI automatically generates quantum programs with dead code and corresponding EMI variants with that code removed; by executing both and checking for behavioral inconsistencies, it reveals defects in quantum software platforms. In our evaluation, QEMI uncovered 12 unique bugs across three major QSSes (Qiskit, Q#, Cirq), 11 of which have been confirmed or fixed. Beyond detection, an adaptive early-stopping strategy reduces measurement cost while preserving equivalence-checking accuracy and avoiding false positives that arise under fixed-budget testing, improving the robustness and scalability of QSS testing.

For future work, pattern-based insertion of dead code can be replaced with analyses that detect it automatically, either statically (via control and data-flow reasoning across quantum–classical boundaries) or dynamically when feasible, improving scalability and enabling reuse by QSS optimizers. Beyond simple dead-code removal, richer semantics-preserving transformations within the identified regions could be applied; such mutations are expected to increase the likelihood of surfacing subtle defects while maintaining equivalence for the target inputs.

Acknowledgments. This work was supported in part by the JST SPRING Grant No. JPMJSP2136, and JSPS KAKENHI grants Grant No. JP23K28062, No. JP24K02920, and No. JP24K14908.

References

1. Canonne, C.L.: A Survey on Distribution Testing: Your Data is Big. But is it Blue? No. 9 in Graduate Surveys, Theory of Computing Library (2020). https://doi.org/10.4086/toc.gs.2020.009, http://www.theoryofcomputing.org/library.html
2. Corporation, M.: Q# api reference (2025), https://learn.microsoft.com/en-us/qsharp/api/, accessed: 2025-07-04
3. Dai, A., Ying, M.: Qreach: A reachability analysis tool for quantum markov chains. In: Computer Aided Verification: 36th International Conference, CAV 2024, Montreal, QC, Canada, July 24–27, 2024, Proceedings, Part III. p. 520–532. Springer-Verlag, Berlin, Heidelberg (2024). https://doi.org/10.1007/978-3-031-65633-0_23, https://doi.org/10.1007/978-3-031-65633-0_23
4. Developers, C.: Cirq. Zenodo (Apr 2025). https://doi.org/10.5281/ZENODO.4062499, https://zenodo.org/doi/10.5281/zenodo.4062499
5. Diakonikolas, I., Kane, D.M.: A new approach for testing properties of discrete distributions. CoRR **abs/1601.05557** (2016), http://arxiv.org/abs/1601.05557

6. Good, I.J.: Some terminology and notation in information theory (1956), https://api.semanticscholar.org/CorpusID:121348458
7. Grover, L.K.: A fast quantum mechanical algorithm for database search (1996), https://arxiv.org/abs/quant-ph/9605043
8. Hellinger, E.: Neue begründung der theorie quadratischer formen von unendlichvielen veränderlichen. Journal für die reine und angewandte Mathematik **136**, 210–271 (1909), http://eudml.org/doc/149313
9. Hu, T., Ye, G., Tang, Z., Tan, S.H., Wang, H., Li, M., Wang, Z.: Upbeat: Test input checks of q# quantum libraries. In: Proceedings of the 33rd ACM SIGSOFT International Symposium on Software Testing and Analysis. p. 186–198. ISSTA 2024, Association for Computing Machinery, New York, NY, USA (2024). https://doi.org/10.1145/3650212.3652120, https://doi.org/10.1145/3650212.3652120
10. Intel Corporation: Yarpgen: Yet another random program generator. https://github.com/intel/yarpgen (2018), accessed: 2025-06-30
11. Iwumbwe, I., Liu, B.Z., Wickerson, J.: QuteFuzz: Fuzzing quantum compilers using randomly generated circuits with control flow and subcircuits. In: PLanQC '25: Programming Languages for Quantum Computing Workshop, co-located with POPL 2025. ACM SIGPLAN (2025)
12. Javadi-Abhari, A., Treinish, M., Krsulich, K., Wood, C.J., Lishman, J., Gacon, J., Martiel, S., Nation, P.D., Bishop, L.S., Cross, A.W., Johnson, B.R., Gambetta, J.M.: Quantum computing with qiskit (2024), https://arxiv.org/abs/2405.08810
13. Kolmogorov, A.N.: Sulla determinazione empirica di una legge di distribuzione. Giornale dell'Istituto Italiano degli Attuari **4**(1), 83–91 (1933)
14. Le, V., Afshari, M., Su, Z.: Compiler validation via equivalence modulo inputs. SIGPLAN Not. **49**(6), 216–226 (Jun 2014). https://doi.org/10.1145/2666356.2594334, https://doi.org/10.1145/2666356.2594334
15. Lidbury, C., Lascu, A., Chong, N., Donaldson, A.F.: Many-core compiler fuzzing. SIGPLAN Not. **50**(6), 65–76 (Jun 2015). https://doi.org/10.1145/2813885.2737986, https://doi.org/10.1145/2813885.2737986
16. Luo, S., Zhang, Q.: Informational distance on quantum-state space. Phys. Rev. A **69**, 032106 (Mar 2004). https://doi.org/10.1103/PhysRevA.69.032106, https://link.aps.org/doi/10.1103/PhysRevA.69.032106
17. Nielsen, M.A., Chuang, I.L.: Quantum Computation and Quantum Information: 10th Anniversary Edition. Cambridge University Press (2010)
18. Paltenghi, M., Pradel, M.: Morphq: Metamorphic testing of the qiskit quantum computing platform. In: Proceedings of the 45th International Conference on Software Engineering. p. 2413–2424. ICSE '23, IEEE Press (2023). https://doi.org/10.1109/ICSE48619.2023.00202, https://doi.org/10.1109/ICSE48619.2023.00202
19. Shor, P.W.: Polynomial-time algorithms for prime factorization and discrete logarithms on a quantum computer. SIAM Journal on Computing **26**(5), 1484–1509 (Oct 1997). https://doi.org/10.1137/s0097539795293172, http://dx.doi.org/10.1137/S0097539795293172
20. Shore, J., Johnson, R.: Axiomatic derivation of the principle of maximum entropy and the principle of minimum cross-entropy. IEEE Transactions on Information Theory **26**(1), 26–37 (1980). https://doi.org/10.1109/TIT.1980.1056144
21. Sivarajah, S., Dilkes, S., Cowtan, A., Simmons, W., Edgington, A., Duncan, R.: t|ket⟩: a retargetable compiler for nisq devices. Quantum Science and Technology **6**(1), 014003 (nov 2020). https://doi.org/10.1088/2058-9565/ab8e92, https://dx.doi.org/10.1088/2058-9565/ab8e92

22. Smirnov, N.V.: On the estimation of the discrepancy between empirical curves of distributions for two independent samples. Moscow University Mathematics Bulletin **2**, 3–26 (1939)
23. Svore, K., Geller, A., Troyer, M., Azariah, J., Granade, C., Heim, B., Kliuchnikov, V., Mykhailova, M., Paz, A., Roetteler, M.: Q#: Enabling Scalable Quantum Computing and Development with a High-level DSL. In: Proceedings of the Real World Domain Specific Languages Workshop 2018. RWDSL2018, ACM (Feb 2018). https://doi.org/10.1145/3183895.3183901, http://dx.doi.org/10.1145/3183895.3183901
24. Wang, J., Zhang, Q., Xu, G.H., Kim, M.: Qdiff: differential testing of quantum software stacks. In: Proceedings of the 36th IEEE/ACM International Conference on Automated Software Engineering. p. 692–704. ASE '21, IEEE Press (2022). https://doi.org/10.1109/ASE51524.2021.9678792, https://doi.org/10.1109/ASE51524.2021.9678792
25. Yang, X., Chen, Y., Eide, E., Regehr, J.: Finding and understanding bugs in c compilers. In: Proceedings of the 32nd ACM SIGPLAN Conference on Programming Language Design and Implementation. p. 283–294. PLDI '11, Association for Computing Machinery, New York, NY, USA (2011). https://doi.org/10.1145/1993498.1993532, https://doi.org/10.1145/1993498.1993532

Towards Decentralised Dynamic Reconfiguration of Software Systems

Mina Yavari and Damian Arellanes

School of Computing and Communications, Lancaster University, United Kingdom

Abstract. As software systems become more complex, researchers are looking for novel approaches to manage changes at scale without human intervention. As a result, on the one hand, dynamically reconfigurable software systems are designed to automatically adjust to environmental perturbations to help systems stay reliable even in uncertain situations. On the other hand, decentralised software systems are promising because they make it easier to manage large complex systems and they fit well in emergent paradigms like the Internet of Things. Most existing reconfiguration approaches rely on a central control to perform runtime changes, leading to well-known issues in terms of robustness and performance bottlenecks. In this paper, we introduce the notion of a Software Architecture Generator which enables the dynamic selection of concrete software architectures at runtime. Adaptive selection is performed in a decentralised manner using a hierarchical control structure that relies on protocols for starting reconfiguration as well as updating and aggregating weights without any exogenous, intrusive, centralised entity (e.g., a feedback control loop). Instead, software architectures themselves are equipped with multiple control entities which collectively find the optimal software architecture configuration that best adapts to the current operation environment.

Keywords: Dynamic Reconfiguration . Decentralised Software systems . Software Architectures .

1 Introduction

Modern software is becoming more complex and is used in constantly changing environments. This has led to research in autonomic, self-adaptive and self-organising software systems [1, 2], focusing on making software reconfigurable and improving its ability to adjust to changing conditions at runtime.

In general, there are two main classifications in software systems to dynamic reconfiguration [3]. In the first one, the system configuration is modified based on an external control. This is known as exogenous (centralised) reconfiguration. Exogenous reconfiguration relies on an external coordinator, which introduces potential reliability issues. If the coordinator fails, it can lead to system failures, delays or incorrect adaptations. These issues are addressed by endogenous (decentralised) reconfiguration in which system components adjust their own

E. Albert and C. Pasareanu (Eds.): FASE 2026, LNCS 16504, pp. 170–179, 2026.
https://doi.org/10.1007/978-3-032-22774-4_9

configuration to meet changing requirements and collaborate to adapt the system. Over the years, decentralised software systems have become more and more popular. Their design helps large and complex systems to run when subsystems are distributed in different locations. They are also fundamental to modern technologies like the Internet of Things (IoT), Edge computing and Cyber-Physical systems [4]. In this paper, decentralised reconfiguration is about the absence of a single global controller responsible for orchestrating architectural reconfigurations. Instead, decision-making is collectively performed by a hierarchy of controllers that communicate directly (not necessarily in a distributed fashion).

This paper proposes a framework for dynamic selection through what we call a Software Architecture Generator (SAG). A SAG defines a formal structure that hierarchically organises alternative software architectures and their components. Based on monitored environmental data (such as latency and memory), optimal architectural instances are selected using a decentralised hierarchical process comprising three reconfiguration protocols for initiation, updating and aggregation. The contribution of this work is providing a formal and decentralised planning framework for architectural reconfiguration that avoids centralised decision-making by distributing architectural selection across cooperating controllers operating on local information. Separating reconfiguration into three protocols provides a structured basis for architectural decision-making. This positions the work as a formally grounded alternative to existing centralised or loosely decentralised reconfiguration approaches.

The remainder of the paper is structured as follows. Section 2 reviews related work. Section 3 introduces a running example. Section 4 details our decentralised reconfiguration approach. Section 5 describes a validation and Section 6 presents the concluding remarks and future work.

2 Related Work

A weighted decision graph to guide model transformations for service level adaptation in an online shopping system is introduced in [5]. Authors in [6] present the concept of emergent software, where architectures are assembled at runtime using online, unsupervised learning. Its demonstration framework [7] contrasts manual and automated reconfiguration, but still operates within a centralised runtime system. In comparison, our work focuses specifically on the planning phase of reconfiguration and introduces a new formal mechanism for selecting software architectures. We propose an approach in which decision-making is done across components, without relying on machine learning or a central coordinator.

Decentralised dynamic reconfiguration focuses on enabling software systems to adapt their structure without relying on a central controller. A decentralised mechanism for adapting service-based applications in the cloud using distributed coordination strategies is presented in [8]. Moreover, an agent-based approach where components collaborate to monitor the system, manage resources and apply reconfigurations is proposed in [9]. Authors in [10] introduce a set of design patterns for managing multiple interacting MAPE-K loops, supporting decentralised control in large-scale systems. Finally, component-based architecture using aspect-oriented programming and custom languages to support modular and decentralised reconfiguration is introduced in [11]. Compared to these, our approach emphasises formal decentralised planning.

Formal approaches to dynamic reconfiguration have employed rewriting rules [12, 13], logic-based reasoning [14] and algebraic techniques to describe evolving architectures. While these approaches offer structural clarity and correctness guarantees, they often assume a global system view or a centralised controller. Our work maintains formal rigour but is designed for decentralised execution, particularly supporting more scalable and distributed deployment scenarios.

3 Running example

Large-scale component-based systems can be designed using microservices, where each microservice performs a specific task. A common architectural pattern for these systems is the Single-Head-Single-Tail (SHST) pattern [15]. To explain how DRSS works in a real SHST situation, we use an example inspired by Amazon's order processing where services such as handling the request, checking inventory, processing payment, shipping, tracking delivery and sending notifications are involved. These services are represented as components V_1 (head) through V_{11} (tail) and their structure is simplified through a SAG that shows joint sets of alternative components. As shown in Figure 1(a), the flow of the order starts with V_1 receiving the request, then proceeds through inventory checks by one of V_2, V_3 or V_4, payment processing at V_5, shipping via V_6 or V_7, delivery tracking with V_8, V_9 or V_{10} and finally order confirmation through the notification service V_{11}. Some stages have multiple alternatives and DRSS dynamically selects among them to optimise system performance.

In Figure 1(a), each dotted box, called joint set, offers multiple implementations of the same functionality but with different non-functional requirements (NFRs). Inside each blue box, there is a vector showing latency and memory usage values. These values, expressed as vector components, are weights assigned to each NFR. Although the number of NFRs can be any number greater than zero, we consider only two here. Note that some components (V_1, V_5, V_{11}) are fixed with a vector of $(1, 1)$ since there are no alternatives to compare with and choose from.

The key idea is that the system's architecture changes dynamically in response to environmental conditions like memory, availability or traffic load. For example, during peak traffic, the system might select lighter components such as V_3, V_7 and V_{10} to conserve memory and handle many requests simultaneously.

4 Decentralised Reconfiguration

In this section, we present key concepts that are essential for the rest of the paper. For the sake of it, we treat software components as vectors which are organised in the form of joint sets within a SAG via the function μ (see Definitions 1 and 2). In Definition 2, there is only one component in V that has no joint set assigned to it (called bottom) and a single joint set in $\mathcal{J}$ that does not have any corresponding component (called head). The bottom represents the starting point of reconfiguration. Figure 1(d) illustrates the process of defining a SAG in three steps. First, components are defined; second, a set of joint sets is defined to group alternative components and, third, a mapping function μ assigns each component in V to the corresponding joint set, forming the structure of a SAG for dynamic architectural control. An id function Ω is defined for joint sets.

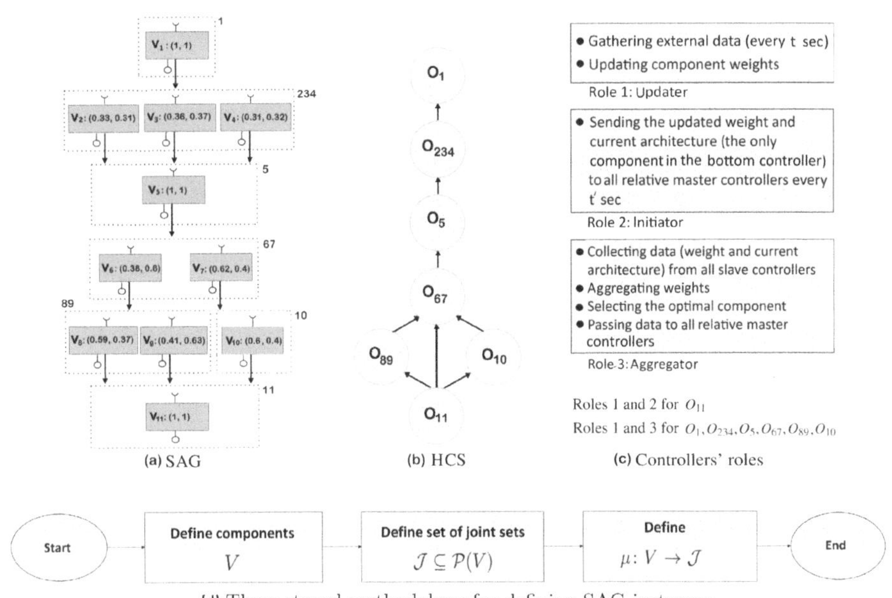

(a) SAG (b) HCS (c) Controllers' roles

(d) Three-staged methodology for defining SAG instances

Fig. 1. SAG vs HCS and controllers' roles

Definition 1 (Component). *A component is a vector of real numbers, where each element denotes the preference of some non-functional requirement.*

Definition 2 (Software Architecture Generator (SAG)). *A SAG is a quintuple $(V, \mathcal{J}, \mu, \Omega, n)$ where:*

- *V is a non-empty finite set $\{V_i\}_{i \in \mathbb{Z}^+}$ of n-dimensional components, equipped with the order relation $<$ given by $v_i < v_j \iff i \leq j$ for all $v_i, v_j \in V$,*
- *$\mathcal{J} \subseteq \mathcal{P}(V)$ is a set where $\mathcal{P}$ denotes power set and for each $\gamma \in \mathcal{J}$, called a joint set, we have $\sum_{k=\min I}^{\max I} k = \frac{(\max I + \min I)(\max I - \min I + 1)}{2} = \sum_{k \in I} k$ where $I = \{i \in \mathbb{Z}^+ | v_i \in \gamma\}$,*

- $\mu: V \to \mathcal{J}$ *is a non-surjective total function where* $\exists!\ v \in V$ *with* $\mu(v) = \emptyset$, $\exists!\ \gamma \in \mathcal{J}$ *with* $\gamma \notin \mu(V)$ *and, if* R *is the relation given by* μ, $\forall(v,\gamma) \in R$, $\nexists(v',\gamma') \in R, v \in \gamma'$ *and*
- $\Omega: \mathcal{J} \to \mathbb{Z}^+$ *is an id function for joint sets given by* $\Omega(\gamma) = i \times 10^{|\gamma|-1} + (i+1) \times 10^{|\gamma|-2} + \cdots + (i+|\gamma|-1)) \times 10^0$ *where* $\gamma \in \mathcal{J}$ *with* $i = \min\{i \in \mathbb{Z}^+ | v_i \in \gamma\}$.

After constructing a SAG, a Hierarchical Control Structure (HCS) is formed (e.g., Figure 1(b)). A HCS is a master-slave relationship that identifies how joint set ids are connected to each other via a master function m and a slave function s. The main purpose of a HCS is to deal with joint set ids since, programmatically, it is more efficient to compute identifiers than joint sets themselves. Nevertheless, ω maps from identifiers to joint sets. After creating the master-slave relationship, one component from each joint set is selected to use as the initial state. A state function assigns a selected component to each joint set identifier.

Definition 3 (Hierarchical Control Structure (HCS)). *A HCS is an 8-tuple* $(V, \mathcal{J}, \mu, G, m, s, \delta, \omega)$ *where:*

- V *is a set of components,*
- $\mathcal{J} \subseteq \mathcal{P}(V)$ *is a set where* $\mathcal{P}$ *denotes power set and for each* $\gamma \in \mathcal{J}$, *called a joint set, we have* $\sum_{k=\min I}^{\max I} k = \frac{(\max I + \min I)(\max I - \min I + 1)}{2} = \sum_{k \in I} k$ *where* $I = \{i \in \mathbb{Z}^+ | v_i \in \gamma\}$,
- $\mu: V \to \mathcal{J}$ *is a non-surjective total function where* $\exists!\ v \in V$ *with* $\mu(v) = \emptyset$ *and* $\exists!\ \gamma \in J$ *with* $\gamma \notin \mu(V)$,
- $G \subset \mathbb{Z}^+$ *is a set of joint set identifiers,*
- $m: G \to \mathcal{P}(G)$ *is a master function that assigns a set of master ids to each master id, such that there exists exactly one* $i \in G$ *satisfying* $m(i) = \emptyset$,
- $s: G \to \mathcal{P}(G)$ *is a slave function that assigns a set of slave ids to each id, such that there exists exactly one* $i \in G$ *satisfying* $s(i) = \emptyset$,
- $\delta: G \to V$ *is a state function and*
- $\omega: G \to \mathcal{J}$ *maps each joint set id to its corresponding joint set.*

For each joint set id, a controller is defined, which is a construct that contains data about a specific joint set (see Definition 4). Controllers in the HCS contain information about the list of components in its corresponding joint set, which controllers act as its masters, which as its slaves and a mapping between its components and their related joint sets. It also stores a weight for each component. Controllers in a HCS can be deployed on a single or multiple (distributed) machines. HCS partitioning/deployment is out of the scope of this paper.

Definition 4. *A controller* o *is a 8-tuple* $(G, M, S, V, \mu, n, i, \sigma)$ *where:*

- $G \subset \mathbb{Z}^+$ *is a set of joint set identifiers,*
- $M \subset G$ *is a finite set of joint set ids that identify master ids,*
- $S \subset G$ *is a finite set of joint set ids that identify slave ids,*
- V *is a finite set of components,*
- $\mu: V \to G$ *is a non-surjective total function where* $\exists!\ v \in V$ *with* $\mu(v) = \emptyset$ *and* $\exists!\ \gamma \in J$ *with* $\gamma \notin \mu(V)$,

- *$n \in \mathbb{N}$ is the fixed dimension of all the components in V,*
- *$i \in \mathbb{Z}^+$ is the id of the controller o and*
- *$\sigma: V \to \mathbb{R}$ is a state function that assigns a real-valued number to each component.*

Algorithm 1 handles deployment requests in a host machine by receiving controller instances, creating shared memory (for each controller) and starting three protocols: (i) initiating reconfiguration (i.e., Algorithm 5), (ii) "start-update-thread" (i.e., Algorithm 2) to gather external data and update component weights and (iii) "startAggregationThread" (i.e., Algorithm 3) to collect data from slave controllers, select the optimal component and pass data to the relatives masters. Algorithm 4 defines the behaviour for choosing an optimal component. Algorithm 2 is designed to update the component's state (weight) by using environmental data every t seconds. After collecting the new states, it updates the shared memory for the threads of a controller. There is no shared memory to exchange data among controllers.

Algorithm 1: Manager (Input: Controller: $O = (G, M, S, V_o, \mu_o, n, i_o, \sigma)$)

while 1
    $O :=$ receiveController()
    sharedMem := new-shared-memory($G, M, S, V_o, \mu_o, n, i_o, \sigma$)
    startUpdateThread(sharedMem, 2)
    startAggregationThread(sharedMem)
    if sharedMem(S) $= \emptyset$ **then** startInitiatorThread(sharedMem, 10)

For a controller with no slaves, the manager assigns the protocol "startInitiatorThread" (i.e., Algorithm 5) which finds the optimal component at the bottom of the HCS and sends this updated information to all master controllers. To make the protocols easier to understand, we assign three distinct roles to each controller, as illustrated in Figure 1(c): Role 1 corresponds to the start-update-thread protocol, Role 2 to the startInitiatorThread protocol and Role 3 to the startAggregationThread protocol. Role 1 gathers external environmental data (every t seconds) and updates the weights of its associated components. Role 2 operates only on the bottom controller and is responsible for sending the updated weights and current architecture (i.e., the single component of the bottom controller) to all relevant master controllers at fixed intervals (every t' seconds). Role 3 collects weights and current optimal architectures from all relative slave controllers, aggregates these weights, selects the optimal component and passes the result to the relevant masters.

Algorithm 3 allows a master controller to collect data from its slaves. When it receives data from all them, it computes compound weights for each component and then chooses the one with the minimum value by Algorithm 4. The chosen component is then appended to the previously selected components to update the optimal architecture. After that, the master controller sends the new optimal architecture and the new compound weight to its relative masters.

Algorithm 2: startUpdateThread (Input: sharedMem, t)

```
while 1
    sleep(t); e := getVectorFromExtEnv()
    lock sharedMem
        state' := ∅
        for v ∈ sharedMem(V_o)
            state' := state' ∪ {(v, v.e)}
        update_hared_memory(sharedMem, σ, state')
    release sharedMem
```

Algorithm 3: startAggregationThread (Input: sharedMem)

```
count_slaves := 0; slaveArchWeight := ∅
while 1
    (slaveId, slaveArch, slaveWeight) := receive_from_slave()
    count_slaves := count_slaves + 1
    slaveArchWeight := slaveArchWeight ∪ {(slaveId, slaveArch, slaveWeight)}
    lock sharedMem
    if count_slaves = sharedMem(S).size()
        (arch, weight) := chooseOptimalComponent(sharedMem, slaveArchWeight)
        for master in sharedMem(M)
            send(sharedMem(i_o), arch, weight)
        count_slaves := 0; slaveArchWeight := ∅
    release sharedMem
```

5 Validation

To make the whole process clear, let us consider the running example of Amazon's order processing. In Role 1, every t seconds, component weights are updated (e.g., with environmental weights $(0.54, 0.67)$, V_{11} updates to $0.54 \times 1 + 0.67 \times 1 = 1.21$). In Role 2, the initiator sends the updated weights and architecture (V_{11}) to its masters (O_{89} and O_{10}). In Role 3, each master aggregates the received weights with its own component's weights to select the optimal one. For example, O_{89} compares V_8 ($0.54 \times 0.59 + 0.67 \times 0.37 \approx 0.57$) and V_9 ($0.54 \times 0.41 + 0.67 \times 0.63 \approx 0.64$) and selects V_8, forming the partial architecture $V_{11} \rightarrow V_8$ with weight $1.21 + 0.57 = 1.78$. If the current environmental weights for latency and memory are $(0.5, 0.61)$, the weights of V_{10} is $0.5 \times 0.6 + 0.61 \times 0.4 \approx 0.54$ and O_{10} chooses V_{10} with compound weight $1.21 + 0.54 = 1.75$ which is sent to O_{67}. The calculations of O_{89} and O_{10} are performed simultaneously, with no dependency between them. Note that each aggregator uses the most recent environmental weights available when the calculation is done. This process continues until the top-level controller O_1 receives the data and makes the final selection. For instance, assuming O_{67} and O_{234} respectively choose V_6 and V_3, the optimal configuration determined by O_1 is: $V_1 \rightarrow V_3 \rightarrow V_5 \rightarrow V_6 \rightarrow V_8 \rightarrow V_{11}$. This final configuration represents the optimal configuration under current environmental conditions.

To validate the proposed approach, we implemented it and made its source code available at https://github.com/mstrn0682394262/Dynamic-Reconfiguration.

Algorithm 4: chooseOptimalComponent (Input: sharedMem, slaveArchWeight)

```
optimalWeight := ∞; optimalCompArch := []
lock sharedMem
  for v_j in sharedMem(V_o)
   aggWeight := π_1(slaveArchWeight(sharedMem(μ_o)(v_j))) + sharedMem(σ)(v_j)
   if aggWeight ≤ optimalWeight
     optimalWeight := aggWeight
     optimalCompArch := π_0(slaveArchWeight(sharedMem(μ_o)(v_j))) ++ [j]
release sharedMem
return (optimalCompArch, optimalWeight)
```

Algorithm 5: startInitiatorThread (Input: sharedMem, t)

```
while 1
  sleep(t)
  lock sharedMem
    optimalArch := ∅, optimalWeight := ∞
    for v_j ∈ sharedMem(V_o)
      if sharedMem(σ)(v_j) ≤ optimalWeight
        optimalWeight := sharedMem(σ)(v_j)
        optimalArch := [j]
    for master in sharedMem(M)
      send(sharedMem(i_o), optimalArch, optimalWeight)
  release sharedMem
```

6 Conclusion

This paper introduced the notions of SAG and HCS as well as three main protocols to realise decentralised reconfiguration of software architectures. Our approach groups software components into joint sets and manages them using a hierarchical control structure, allowing a system to adjust itself at runtime without the need of a central controller. To support runtime adaptation, the system triggers reconfiguration every t seconds via a well-defined protocol. The other two protocols are used to update component weights using environmental data and combine information from corresponding slaves, respectively. Once information is received, the component with the minimum compound weight is chosen and then appended to the currently selected software architecture. The new architecture information is then sent to all the corresponding masters for further decision making. This process is repeated until reaching the top-level component. To validate that our proposed method enables the dynamic selection of software architectures at runtime, we implemented and published it. This method is especially helpful for changable environments like cloud computing and the IoT, where systems need to be flexible and work without constant human control. In the future, we plan to evaluate the efficiency of our approach by analysing its execution time empirically. We also plan to validate its applicability in a real-world scenario.

References

1. De Sanctis, M., Bucchiarone, A., Marconi, A.: Dynamic Adaptation of Service-Based Applications: A Design for Adaptation Approach. Journal of Internet Services and Applications 11(1) (2020). https://doi.org/10.1186/s13174-020-00123-6
2. Arellanes, D.: Self-Organizing Software Models for the Internet of Things: Complex Software Structures That Emerge Without a Central Controller. In: IEEE Systems, Man, and Cybernetics Magazine, vol. 7, no. 3, pp. 4–9. IEEE (2021). https://doi.org/10.1109/MSMC.2021.3062822
3. Weyns, D., Haesevoets, R., Van Eylen, B., Helleboogh, A., Holvoet, T., Joosen, W.: Endogenous versus Exogenous Self-Management. In: Proceedings of the 2008 International Workshop on Software Engineering for Adaptive and Self-Managing Systems, pp. 41–48. ACM, Leipzig, Germany (2008). https://doi.org/10.1145/1370018.1370027
4. Kratzke, N., Quint, P.-C.: Understanding Cloud-Native Applications after 10 Years of Cloud Computing – A Systematic Mapping Study. Journal of Systems and Software 126, 1–16 (2017). https://doi.org/10.1016/j.jss.2017.01.001
5. Chen, B., Peng, X., Yu, Y., Nuseibeh, B., Zhao, W.: Self-Adaptation through Incremental Generative Model Transformations at Runtime. In: Proceedings of the 36th International Conference on Software Engineering, pp. 676–687. ACM, Hyderabad, India (2014). https://doi.org/10.1145/2568225.2568310
6. Rodrigues Filho, R., Porter, B.: Defining Emergent Software Using Continuous Self-Assembly, Perception and Learning. ACM Transactions on Autonomous and Adaptive Systems 12(3), 1–25 (2017). https://doi.org/10.1145/3092691
7. Rodrigues Filho, R., Porter, B.: Demonstrating a Runtime Machine-Centric Emergent Software Architecture Framework. In: Proceedings of the 2016 IEEE International Conference on Autonomic Computing (ICAC), pp. 239–240. IEEE, Würzburg, Germany (2016). https://doi.org/10.1109/ICAC.2016.35
8. Nallur, V., Bahsoon, R.: A Decentralised Self-Adaptation Mechanism for Service-Based Applications in the Cloud. In: Proceedings of the IEEE (2012)
9. Saadi, A., Oussalah, M., Henni, A., Bennouar, D.: Handling the Dynamic Reconfiguration of Software Architectures Using Intelligent Agents. In: Proceedings (2015)
10. Weyns, D., Schmerl, B., Grassi, V., Malek, S., Mirandola, R., Prehofer, C., Wuttke, J. andersson, J., Giese, H., Göscha, K.: On Patterns for Decentralised Control in Self-Adaptive Systems. In: Proceedings (2013)
11. Baresi, L., Guinea, S., Tamburrelli, G.: Towards Decentralized Self-Adaptive Component-Based Systems. In: Proceedings of the 2008 International Workshop on Software Engineering for Adaptive and Self-Managing Systems, pp. 57–64. ACM, Leipzig, Germany (2008) https://doi.org/https://doi.org/10.1145/1370018.1370029
12. Arellanes, D.: Composition Machines: Programming Self-Organising Software Models for the Emergence of Sequential Program Spaces. In: Chin, W.-N., Xu, Z. (eds.) TASE 2024, LNCS, vol. 14777, pp. 19–37. Springer, Cham (2024). https://doi.org/10.1007/978-3-031-64626-3_2
13. Fernández, M., Mackie, I.: Hierarchical Higher-Order Port Graphs: A Rewriting-Based Modeling Language. ACM (2024)
14. Bozga, M., Bueri, L., Iosif, R.: Decision Problems in a Logic for Reasoning About Reconfigurable Distributed Systems. In: IJCAR 2022, LNCS, vol. 13385, pp. 659–677. Springer, Cham (2022). https://doi.org/10.1007/978-3-031-10769-6_40
15. Xue, Gang, Shuiguang Deng, Di Liu and Zeming Yan. 2021. 'Reaching Consensus in Decentralized Coordination of Distributed Microservices'. Computer Networks 187 (March): 107786. https://doi.org/10.1016/j.comnet.2020.107786.

Analyses as First-Class Citizens in Model-Driven Development

Tianhai Liu[1], Shmuel Tyszberowicz[2], and Bernhard Beckert[1]

[1] Karlsruhe Institute of Technology (KIT), Karlsruhe, Germany
tianhai.liu@kit.edu, bernhard.beckert@kit.edu
[2] Afeka Academic College of Engineering, Tel Aviv, Israel
tyshbe@afeka.ac.il

Abstract. Analyses are central to the engineering of cyber-physical systems: they support design decisions, ensure safety, and provide evidence for certification. Yet re-executing analyses as models evolve is costly, and it is often unclear which prior results remain valid after a change. Existing formalisations in model-driven development (MDD) address models and their consistency, but leave the analyses themselves and their interdependencies underexplored. This limitation prevents systematic reuse of analysis results and inhibits techniques such as analysis slicing or incremental reanalysis, both of which require precise reasoning about analyses and their dependencies. We formalise analyses as first-class citizens alongside models. We define a formal model that characterises inputs, outputs, preconditions, properties, and trigger conditions, and we capture interdependencies through an analysis dependency graph. We further present an incremental recertification procedure that computes an analysis slice, identifying those analyses that must be re-executed to preserve global certification goals after model changes. We prove a core analysis theorem, establishing the soundness and completeness of this procedure. We enable analysis-aware consistency management across heterogeneous models. Two illustrative examples, in software development and ISO 26262-compliant automotive safety assurance, demonstrate the applicability of the approach and show analytically that selective re-execution can substantially reduce reanalysis effort. This paper contributes to the foundational theory of MDD by establishing a formal semantic framework for analyses and their interdependencies, laying the groundwork for future tool support and empirical validation.

Keywords: Model-Driven Development · Analysis Formalisation · Incremental Recertification · Consistency Management · Cyber-Physical Systems · Virtual Single Underlying Model (V-SUM)

1 Introduction

Throughout the development lifecycle of cyber-physical systems (CPS), analyses of design models must be efficiently re-applied as these models evolve. Analyses

E. Albert and C. Pasareanu (Eds.): FASE 2026, LNCS 16504, pp. 180–201, 2026.
https://doi.org/10.1007/978-3-032-22774-4_10

serve multiple purposes: they support design decisions by comparing alternatives and demonstrating properties such as safety (e.g., through explicitly defined safety cases). They also enable comprehensive assessments across multiple models, such as those required for vehicle homologation [3], which certifies that the vehicle meets all legal criteria. However, conducting such analyses, especially when spanning multiple heterogeneous models, still requires considerable manual effort. This makes them costly and time-consuming, hindering iterative design cycles and slowing certification processes. Industrial surveys indicate that functional-safety activities account for roughly 42% of the total development cycle on average [22], while toolchain qualification alone can introduce measurable additional effort [23]. Practitioner estimates indicate that compliance costs can increase by up to an order of magnitude between low and high Automotive Safety Integrity Levels (ASILs) [20], underscoring the economic impact of certification and recertification efforts. Systematic reasoning about analyses and their reuse is therefore essential for the efficient development and certification of CPS.

The trend toward over-the-air (OTA) software updates further amplifies this need. Although OTA promises faster deployment, each safety-relevant update remains subject to formal rehomologation. For example, UNECE Regulation No. 156 integrates software OTA update management into the type-approval process [25], and TÜV SÜD confirms that OTA delivered updates require full homologation procedures. As of 2024, the global market for homologation and digital compliance exceeds USD 1.4 billion and is growing at over 13% annually [28]. In parallel, OTA-based recall management is projected to save automakers USD 1.5 billion by 2028 [27], underscoring substantial baseline regulatory costs. Hence, digitalised update mechanisms add new verification, traceability, and approval loops, rather than removing the certification effort.

To address this burden and the resulting need for efficient, reusable safety analyses, we advocate a formalisation of analyses as first-class citizens in model-driven development (MDD). This formalisation provides the theoretical foundation for analysis slicing [4] and incremental recertification, and it enables integration of analyses into the Virtual Single Underlying Model (V-SUM) framework [13] for analysis-aware consistency management. Without it, analyses remain external to the model management process, making it difficult to reason about their validity or to combine them systematically with consistency mechanisms.

The contributions of this paper are threefold: (i) we elevate analyses as first-class entities in model-driven development, focusing on their semantic interfaces, correctness conditions, and interdependencies, rather than on their internal execution semantics, thereby enabling formal reasoning about their correctness, modularity, and reuse; (ii) we introduce the analysis dependency graph (ADG)

[3] Homologation is a regulatory approval process that certifies a vehicle, system, or component complies with all legal, safety, environmental, and technical requirements of a target market before it can be sold or operated.

[4] Analysis slicing identifies the subset of analyses whose results may be affected by a modification to the analysed model.

to represent inter-analysis dependencies and support incremental recertification through analysis slicing and selective re-execution, ensuring that only semantically affected analyses are re-executed after model changes; (iii) we extend the V-SUM framework with analysis models for analysis-aware consistency management, bridging the gap between syntactic consistency maintenance and semantic assurance. Together, these contributions lay the theoretical foundation for scalable and certifiable reanalysis across heterogeneous models as illustrated through examples. This paper focuses on the theoretical foundations required to treat analyses as first-class entities in model-driven development. Our goal is to establish precise definitions, correctness criteria, and compositional reasoning principles that can later support tool implementation. Accordingly, we do not present an empirical evaluation at this stage.

1.1 Preliminaries

Model-driven development (MDD). MDD tackles system complexity by providing abstractions that capture different aspects of a system. Each model corresponds to a stakeholder concern (e.g., structure, behaviour, deployment, quality). This modularity introduces inter-model dependencies, whose maintenance is essential for correctness. Thus, managing consistency as models evolve is a central challenge.

Single Underlying Model (SUM). The *Single Underlying Model (SUM)* approach [2] represents a complete, redundancy-free system description from which all views are projections, eliminating inconsistencies by construction. Ideally, SUM relies on a single metamodel with unified semantics, but in practice, this is infeasible because engineering domains use diverse tools and standards, many of which are legacy or externally mandated. Thus, maintaining a monolithic SUM is impractical in industrial settings.

V-SUM. V-SUM [13] integrates heterogeneous models through explicit mappings and consistency relations rather than a single metamodel. A V-SUM consists of (i) models from different metamodels, (ii) consistency specifications defining inter-model relations, and (iii) rules that propagate modifications where needed. This enables models to behave as if derived from one representation while preserving modularity and tool diversity, making V-SUM suitable for real-world system development.

Consistency in SUM and V-SUM. In MDD, consistency is a relation ensuring that models can jointly describe a realisable system: Consistency $\subseteq M_1 \times M_2 \times \cdots \times M_n$, where each M_i denotes the set of valid models of metamodel i. A tuple $\langle m_1, \ldots, m_n \rangle$ is consistent if it belongs to this relation. Vitruvius [13] defines consistency rules between metamodel elements: each rule specifies how model elements correspond across domains (e.g., matching components by identifier). Models are consistent if all such correspondences hold.

V-SUM focuses on syntactic consistency (structural alignment), which does not ensure semantic validity. For example, after updating engine parameters, alignment may persist even as safety analyses become invalid. To capture both aspects, Pascual et al. [21] define a general consistency relation CR, where models are consistent if (i) structural features align and (ii) their semantics are compatible (e.g., co-satisfiable behaviour). This motivates extending V-SUM with analyses as first-class citizens, enabling reasoning about both consistency and the validity or reuse of analysis results.

Observables. Following Färber et al. [7], observables denote measurable system properties constrained by multiple models (e.g., axle distance, vehicle weight, braking force). Formally, for an observable o with value space V_o, each model m_i induces $V_o(m_i) \subseteq V_o$; models are observationally consistent with respect to o iff $\bigcap_i V_o(m_i) \neq \emptyset$. For example, overlapping weight intervals $[1000, 1200]$ and $[1100, 2000]$ imply consistency, while disjoint ones do not. Observables thus provide semantic anchors across heterogeneous models, supporting verification of terminological and quantitative consistency within a unified framework.

1.2 Motivation

As discussed in the introduction, a central challenge in CPS engineering is to determine which prior analysis results remain valid after model changes and which must be recomputed. While MDD provides effective mechanisms for maintaining syntactic or semantic consistency among heterogeneous models, these mechanisms do not address the *semantic validity of analyses* that depend on them.

Safety analyses exemplify this challenge particularly well. The main automotive safety standard, ISO 26262 [31], requires assessing the ASIL of developed functions, along with specifying the corresponding safety requirements and countermeasures. To achieve this, the standard mandates the application of diverse analysis methods, including inductive analyses (e.g., Failure Mode and Effects Analysis, FMEA), deductive analyses (e.g., Fault Tree Analysis, FTA), and qualitative analyses (e.g., Dependent Failure Analysis, DFA) [11]. In practice, however, the prevailing conservative approach is to re-analyse all models after every change, a process that not only slows down agile development but also complicates software updates once the system is in operation.

What is needed instead are precise mechanisms to assess the validity of previous analyses, i.e., identifying when results can be safely reused and when reanalysis is required. Because each analysis is typically modularised into distinct components (as specified, for example, in ISO 26262), it becomes essential to determine which specific parts must be re-executed following a change, as also mandated by UNECE Regulation No. 157 on software updates. Achieving such selective reanalysis requires reasoning beyond the level of individual models. Given a model delta across heterogeneous CPS models, one must accurately identify the analyses affected by the change and re-execute only those necessary to restore overall system consistency.

SUM [2] was introduced as a unified, redundancy-free representation of a system. Later work developed the V-SUM as a more practical alternative that integrates multiple heterogeneous models without requiring a monolithic metamodel. Yet, the notion of consistency in V-SUM is essentially syntactic: rule-based preservation mechanisms ensure that models remain structurally aligned, but this alone does not guarantee that the system's semantics remain valid. For instance, after a change in engine weight, the engine model and braking system model remain syntactically consistent; however, the stopping distance analysis may no longer be valid. Ensuring these semantic properties requires specific analyses to check aspects such as safety, timing, and resource constraints, which V-SUM itself does not yet support.

This gap motivates a formalisation of analyses that: (i) enables slicing and incremental change analysis for efficient reanalysis after model changes, and (ii) integrates analyses into the V-SUM framework as first-class elements. Such a formalisation provides a foundation for systematic reasoning about analyses, their reuse, and their integration with model consistency mechanisms, supporting scalable development and certification of CPS.

2 Formalisation of analyses

In this paper, we deliberately abstract from the process by which an analysis is performed and instead formalise analyses solely by their semantic input–output relation. This abstraction covers both fully automated analyses (e.g., static analysis, model checking) and human-guided or semi-formal analyses (e.g., FMEA, design reviews), provided that their outcomes are captured as explicit, stable artefacts. Consequently, any nondeterminism, iteration, or subjectivity occurring during the execution of an analysis is assumed to be resolved before formalisation. The resulting artefact is therefore deterministically interpretable. The formalisation, therefore, applies to the analysis results that are consumed and reused, rather than to the internal decision-making process that produced them.

2.1 Analysis

In our setting, the notion of a model is generalised to encompass all artefacts relevant to system analysis, including programs, specifications, documentation, and intermediate analysis results. The granularity at which an artefact is regarded as a model is determined by the specific objectives and abstraction level of the analysis in question.

An analysis takes models as input, computes over them, and outputs a model describing their properties or relations (e.g., inferred attributes, verification results, diagnostics) without changing the inputs. For instance,

- *Code compliance checking.* Given a source-code model m_{code} and coding rules model m_{rule} as input, a MISRA-C++ compliance analysis produces an output model m_{report} indicating whether coding rules are complied with or violated.
- *Fault Tree Analysis (FTA).* Starting from a system architecture model m_{arch} and a derivation specification model m_{spec} prescribed by ISO 26262, the analysis derives a fault tree m_{fta} that captures the minimal cut sets of component failures leading to system-level hazards.
- *Consistency checking between models.* Given two coupled models, such as a braking-system state machine m_{state} and a physical brake-dynamics model m_{physical}, a consistency analysis determines whether both admit a common behaviour and its output model $m_{\text{consistency}}$ records the result.

Definition 1 (Analysis—abstract view). *Let $\mathcal{M}$ denote the universe of all models, and let $M \subseteq \mathcal{M}$ be a non-empty set of models relevant to a particular context. An analysis is a (possibly partial) function $h : M \rightarrow M$, that, given a model $m_{\text{in}} \in M$, which may itself comprise multiple interrelated submodels, produces a derived model $m_{\text{out}} \in M$ expressing properties or relations of m_{in}.*

Each analysis $h : M \rightarrow M$ derives artefacts that express properties or relations of its inputs without modifying them. This abstract definition is intentionally general, yet it is too coarse to capture the concrete aspects needed for real-case reasoning; conversely, an overly specific formulation would sacrifice generality. Therefore, to balance abstraction with practical applicability, we refine the definition to make the operational elements of analyses, such as inputs, assumptions, objectives, and outputs, explicit.

We emphasise that h abstracts from the operational execution of the analysis and captures only the semantic relation between input artefacts and the resulting analysis artefact.

Definition 2 (Analysis—balanced view). *Let $h : M \rightarrow M$ be an analysis defined in Definition 1. To bridge the abstract and operational perspectives, the analysis is refined into a collection of semantically distinct, structurally composed components:*

$$f : I \otimes C \otimes P \;\rightarrow\; \mathit{Validity} \otimes \mathit{Evidence},$$

where $\otimes$ denotes structural composition, and:
- *$I \subset M$ denotes the set of input models subject to analysis;*
- *$C \subset M$ represents the set of preconditions under which the analysis is valid;*
- *$P \subset M$ defines the set of properties the analysis aims to verify over the inputs.*
- *$\mathit{Validity} = \{true, false\}$ indicates whether the input models satisfy the properties;*
- *Evidence denotes evidential artefacts, such as traces, proofs, counterexamples, or metrics, that substantiate the analysis result Validity.*

The semantics of Definition 2 is captured by the relation, for $i \in I, c \in C, p \in P$, $i \models p \iff f(i, c, p) = \langle b \in \mathit{Validity}, e \in \mathit{Evidence} \rangle$. This clause expresses that, under the precondition model c, the input model i satisfies the property model p according to the analysis f, yielding a set e of evidential artefacts that justify the validity judgement b. For example, when $f(i, c, p) = \langle \mathsf{false}, e \rangle$, the analysis identifies evidence of violation or inconsistency with respect to p. Restricting the output to this structure $\{\mathit{Validity}, \mathit{Evidence}\}$ enables a clean and uniform formalisation, abstracting away from tool-specific or resource-dependent details.[5]

[5] Although in practice *validity* may also take the value *unknown* at the process level (e.g., due to undecidability, imprecision, or resource limitations), we restrict it here to boolean values. This simplification is justified because our focus lies on the semantic relation between models and properties, rather than on the meta-level aspects of incomplete or resource-bounded reasoning.

Example 1 (Code compliance checking). Let $f_{\mathsf{MISRA}}: I \times C \times P \to \mathit{Validity} \times \mathit{Evidence}$ check a program against MISRA rules, where $I = \{m_{\mathsf{code}}, m_{\mathsf{rule}}\}$, $C = \{\mathsf{compilable}(m_{\mathsf{code}})\}$, and $P = \forall r \in m_{\mathsf{rule}}: r(m_{\mathsf{code}})$. For $i \in I$, $c \in C$, and $p \in P$,

$$f_{\mathsf{MISRA}}(i, c, p) = \begin{cases} \langle \mathsf{true}, \{\text{"All rules satisfied"}\} \rangle & \text{if } i \models p, \\ \langle \mathsf{false}, \{\text{"violated rules and source locations"}\} \rangle & \text{otherwise.} \end{cases}$$

Definition 3 (Analysis correctness). *Let $f : I \otimes C \otimes P \to \mathit{Validity} \otimes \mathit{Evidence}$ be an analysis as defined in Definition 2. We define a projection $\mathit{valid} : \mathit{Validity} \otimes \mathit{Evidence} \to \mathbb{B}$ which returns* true *iff the first component is* true*. We say that f is correct with respect to $(I, C, P, \models)$ iff*

$$\forall i \in I, c \in C, p \in P : i \models c \ \wedge \ f(i, c, p) \Rightarrow \big(\mathit{valid}(f(i, c, p)) \ \Leftrightarrow \ i \models p\big), \tag{1}$$

where $i \models c$ denotes that the input model i satisfies the analysis precondition c, and $i \models p$ denotes that the property p holds for i.

The concrete definition of $\models$ depends on the modelling formalism and analysis domain (e.g., logical satisfaction), but is assumed to be well defined for each analysis. Definition (3) expresses that, under admissible conditions, the validity produced by f coincides precisely with the semantic truth of the property. Specifically:

- The analysis is **sound** if $\mathit{valid}(f(i, c, p))$ implies $i \models p$, ensuring the absence of *false positives*; and
- The analysis is **complete** if $i \models p$ implies $\mathit{valid}(f(i, c, p))$, ensuring the absence of *false negatives*.

2.2 Modularity of analyses

Complex systems are typically evaluated against multiple interrelated goals. A global system objective, such as functional safety, performance, or reliability, can often be decomposed into a hierarchy of local goals, each achieved through specialised analyses of different models or artefacts. This modular perspective enables distributed verification across heterogeneous disciplines (e.g., software, electronic, and mechanical), while maintaining a coherent assurance argument at the system level.

Local goal achievement. A local goal g associated with an analysis f_g is formalised by a property p_g over the analysis inputs. We say that g is achieved by f_g (written $f_g \models g$) when f_g satisfies the correctness criterion of Definition (1).

Global goal achievement. A global goal G aggregates local goals $\{g_1, \ldots, g_n\}$, each of which is addressed by a distinct analysis f_{g_i} operating on models that may stem from heterogeneous disciplines. We say that G is achieved if all local goals are achieved and their conjunction entails the satisfaction of G:

$$\bigwedge_{i=1}^{n} (f_{g_i} \models g_i) \implies f_G \models G. \tag{2}$$

This expresses that the collective satisfaction of local properties is sufficient to entail the overarching system objective. Such a structure reflects the *modularity of analyses*, where individual analyses can be composed into a global one.

Example 2 (Automotive Braking System). Consider a global goal G_{safety} for an automotive braking system: "The braking system must reliably stop the vehicle within a safe distance." This goal can be decomposed into three local goals, each defined over heterogeneous models from distinct engineering principles:
g_{sw} : "Control algorithm computes appropriate brake pressure."
g_{el} : "Sensor readings are accurate within specified tolerances."
g_{me} : "Actuator delivers the commanded brake force within bounds."
Each local goal g_i is verified by a dedicated analysis on its corresponding model, which yields an output tuple $O = \langle \mathit{Validity}, \mathit{Evidence} \rangle$ as in Definition 2:
$f_{g_{sw}}$ performs control verification and timing analysis on the software model;
$f_{g_{el}}$ performs sensor calibration and fault detection analysis on the electronic model;
$f_{g_{me}}$ performs actuation and stress analysis on the mechanical model.
A higher-level analysis f_G takes the outputs of the local analyses as input, $f_G : (O_{\text{sw}}, O_{\text{el}}, O_{\text{me}}) \rightarrow \mathit{Validity} \times \mathit{Evidence}$, and encodes its goal G_{safety} as the property $p_{G_{\text{safety}}} = \mathit{valid}(O_{\text{sw}}) \wedge \mathit{valid}(O_{\text{el}}) \wedge \mathit{valid}(O_{\text{me}})$, where *valid* projects the validity component from each O_i, reflecting the compositional structure of the decomposition. If each local analysis achieves its goal ($f_{g_i} \models g_i$ for all i), then all validity components satisfy $\mathit{valid}(O_i) = \mathsf{true}$, the property $p_{G_{\text{safety}}}$ holds, and consequently the global goal is achieved, i.e., $f_{G_{\text{safety}}} \models G_{\text{safety}}$.

This compositional perspective exposes the *modularity of analyses*. Local analyses operate over domain-specific models, while higher-level aggregating analyses combine their verdicts with evidence. It aligns with industrial safety processes. In ISO 26262, for example, functional safety requires structured analyses such as FMEA and FTA [29, 30] on hierarchical heterogeneous models. Each analysis verifies a local property, while their integrated outcomes provide collective evidence for the overall system-level safety.

2.3 Model consistency through analyses

To reason uniformly about the consistency of heterogeneous models, we consider metamodels such as UML, CAD, and Simulink, each with its own set of conforming models. Consistency across these models can be established through analyses that evaluate whether their combined configurations satisfy a shared global goal. The following definition formalises this notion of model consistency via analyses, relating local analysis outcomes to the global consistency relation.

Definition 4 (Model consistency via analyses). *Let $MM_1, \ldots, MM_n$ be heterogeneous metamodels (e.g., UML, CAD, Simulink). For each $i \in \{1, \ldots, n\}$, let M_i denote the set of well-formed models conforming to MM_i, and let each $m_i \in M_i$ be an instance of MM_i. Consistency among models is defined by a relation $CR \subseteq M_1 \times \cdots \times M_n$, whose elements are tuples of models that can be* *jointly realised [21]. Let $F = \{f_{g_1}, \ldots, f_{g_n}\}$ be the set of analyses, where each f_{g_i} (cf. Definition 2) is associated with a local goal g_i. Let G denote the global consistency goal. A tuple $m = \langle m_1, \ldots, m_n \rangle$ is consistent for G regarding F, written $Consistent_G(m, G, F)$, iff*

$$Consistent_G(m, G, F) \iff m \in CR_G \iff \Big(\bigwedge_{i=1}^{n} valid(f_{g_i}(m)) \wedge (\bigwedge_{i=1}^{n} g_i) \Rightarrow G \Big).$$

Analyses thus act as decision procedures for determining whether a given tuple of models belongs to CR_G. The global analysis f_G is composed of individual analyses to decide the global consistency of models.

Intuitively, local analyses establish their respective goals g_i and contribute evidence fragments toward achieving the global objective G. When all local goals are satisfied and collectively entail G, the models are considered consistent, i.e., they belong to the consistency relation CR_G.

From the perspective of model consistency based on observables, each analysis f_{g_i} inspects a model through its observables, which represent the model behaviour or property. Let $Obs(m_i)$ denote the set of observables associated with model m_i, such as state variables, physical quantities, or constraints. Formally, analyses can thus be viewed as evaluating predicates over these observables: $f_{g_i}(m) = f_{g_i}(Obs(m_1), \ldots, Obs(m_n))$. Consistency relations are accordingly defined over observables: $CR_G = \big\{ \langle m_1, \ldots, m_n \rangle \big| (Obs(m_1), \ldots, Obs(m_n)) \in R_G \big\}$, where R_G is a relation expressing cross-model compatibility of observables regarding the goal G. Analyses therefore realise the decision procedure by reasoning over observables, establishing whether models exhibit mutually compatible behaviour at their shared interfaces. When all observable-level relations hold, the corresponding models are consistent under the global relation CR_G.

Recall the automotive braking system example from Section 2.2, where the global goal G is achieved by satisfying its decomposed local goals g_i. In this case, the corresponding analyses ensure not only the correctness of individual models but also their cross-domain consistency by comparing their observables. Each model exposes a set of observable quantities, such as the brake pressure computed by the software control model, the mechanical force generated by the actuator, and the vehicle deceleration measured by sensors. Analyses evaluate these observables against their cross-model relations (e.g., compatibility of pressure, force and sensed deceleration) to ensure that behaviour predicted in one model is consistent with that manifested in another. When all observable-level relations are satisfied, the collective evidence establishes that the models jointly fulfil the global consistency relation CR_G.

2.4 Analysis dependency graph

Since analyses seldom operate in isolation, their results often depend on preceding analyses and may vary with changes to the associated domain models. To reason uniformly and compositionally about these interdependencies, we introduce the *Analysis Dependency Graph (ADG)* (Fig. 1), which provides the

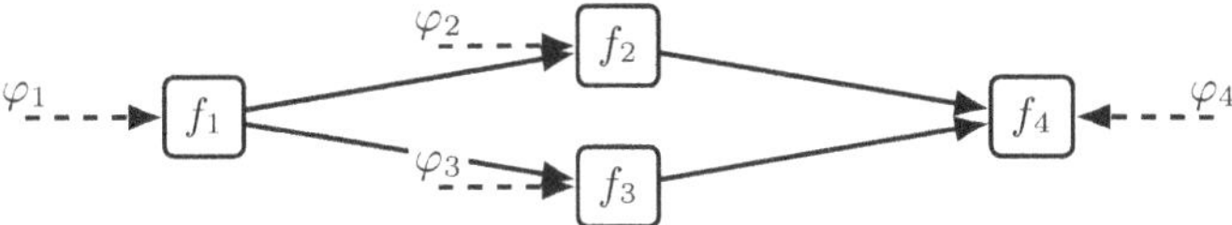

Fig. 1: Structure of the analysis dependency graph. Each edge $e_{i,j}$ indicating that analysis f_j follows f_i based on a predefined schedule or data dependencies. Each analysis f_i has a trigger φ_i that dictates whether f_i must run.

structural backbone for incremental execution and recertification. A concrete ADG example is shown in Fig. 2.

Definition 5 (Analysis dependency graph). *An analysis dependency graph (ADG) is a labelled directed graph* $A = (V, E, \Phi)$, where:

- V is a finite set of nodes, each representing an instantiated analysis f_i (cf. Definition 2) associated with a local goal g_i;
- $E \subseteq V \times V$ is a finite set of directed edges, where an edge $e_{i,j} = (v_i, v_j)$ indicates that the execution of f_j depends on the successful completion of f_i;
- Φ is a finite set of trigger functions, where each $\varphi_i \in \Phi : \Delta \to \mathbb{B}$ determines whether a model change Δ in the models associated with f_i requires the re-execution of f_i.

An edge $e_{i,j} = (v_i, v_j)$ captures an *activation dependency* between analyses f_i and f_j. It expresses that f_j is enabled after f_i has successfully achieved its goal g_i. Such dependencies can be (i) *structural relations*, such as a predefined analysis workflow (e.g., test before release, FMEA before FTA); or (ii) *semantic relations*, where f_j uses the outputs of f_i as its input regarding *use-define* relation. An edge does not necessarily mean that data is directly passed from f_i to f_j; it only indicates that the execution of f_j relies on the successful completion of f_i. If a path exists from v_i to v_j, a change affecting f_i may eventually trigger the re-execution of f_j, depending on the evaluation of the re-execution conditions associated with the analyses leading to f_j.

Definition 6 (Trigger function and trigger condition). *Let O denote the set of observables with value space V_O, and each model m induces a valuation $\nu_m : O \to V_O$. Given two model states m, m', the model delta is defined as: $\Delta_O(m, m') = \{(o, v, v') \mid o \in O,\ v = \nu_m(o),\ v' = \nu_{m'}(o),\ v \neq v'\}$. A trigger function $\varphi_i : \Delta_O \to \mathbb{B}$ is defined as $\varphi_i(\Delta_O) = \exists (o, v, v') \in \Delta_O : \psi_i(o, v, v')$, where $\psi_i : O \times V_O \times V_O \to \mathbb{B}$ is the trigger condition of f_i.*

Intuitively, the *trigger function* φ_i evaluates to true whenever the trigger condition ψ_i holds for at least one changed observable in the model transition from m to m'. The trigger function operates at the orchestration layer and Δ denotes domain-specific model changes. For example, for an observable weight (e.g., engine mass in an automotive system model), a threshold-based trigger can be defined as $\varphi(\Delta_{\mathsf{weight}}) = |\Delta_{\mathsf{weight}}| \geq 10$. By default, the trigger evaluates

Algorithm 1: Incremental recertification with analysis slicing

```
1  Subroutine AnalysisSlicing(A = (V, E, Φ), Δ)
2  |  Seed ← InitialAffected(A, Φ, Δ)
3  |  if Seed = ∅ then
4  |  |  return ∅
5  |  return ComputeImpactSlice (A, Seed)
6  Subroutine IncrementalRecertification(A = (V, E, Φ), Δ)
7  |  ℰ_Δ ← ∅
8  |  O ← ∅
9  |  V_Δ ← AnalysisSlicing(A, Δ)
10 |  ℰ_Δ ← ℰ_Δ ∪ V_Δ
11 |  V_Δ ← TopologicalOrder(V_Δ)
12 |  while V_Δ ≠ ∅ do
13 |  |  v_i ← Dequeue(V_Δ)
   |  |  // φ_i(Δ) is defined by users
14 |  |  if φ_i(Δ) = true then
15 |  |  |  o_i ← ExecuteAnalysis(v_i)
16 |  |  |  O ← O ∪ {o_i}
17 |  |  |  if IsInvalid (o_i) then
18 |  |  |  |  Δ' ← ModelRepair(v_i, o_i)
19 |  |  |  |  V'_Δ ← AnalysisSlicing(A, Δ')
20 |  |  |  |  V_Δ ← V_Δ ∪ V'_Δ
21 |  |  |  |  ℰ_Δ ← ℰ_Δ ∪ V_Δ
22 |  |  |  |  V_Δ ← TopologicalOrder(V_Δ)
23 |  |  |  else
   |  |  |  |  // No model repair needed. Continue
24 |  |  else
   |  |  |  // No rerun needed for v_i
25 |  return (ℰ_Δ, O)
26 return IncrementalRecertification(A = (V, E, Φ), Δ)
```

to false when $\Delta = \emptyset$ and true otherwise. Users (typically methodologists) may override this default to define domain-specific re-execution conditions.

The semantic dependency of an edge $e_{i,j}$ can be expressed by a trigger function associated with f_j, denoted as $\varphi_j(\Delta(f_i))$, indicating that a change in the output of f_i may trigger the re-execution of f_j. In contrast, a pure syntactic dependency is represented by a trigger that evaluates to true, meaning that f_j is activated immediately once f_i has completed, irrespective of semantic changes in its output. Therefore, an analysis f_i re-executes when its trigger function requests re-execution, i.e., $\varphi_i(\Delta)$ = true. Otherwise, f_i remains idle unless explicitly requested, for example, during audits or user-initiated runs.

3 Analysis Management

3.1 Incremental recertification via analysis slicing

We employ *analysis slicing* to determine which analyses must be re-executed during incremental recertification. As shown in Algorithm 1, the subroutine AnalysisSlicing computes the set of analyses potentially affected by a model change. Given a model delta Δ, it first determines the initial set of impacted analyses, i.e., the *seed set*. This subroutine evaluates the trigger functions $\varphi_i(\Delta)$ defined for each analysis node in the ADG; analyses whose trigger functions return true constitute the initial re-execution set. If the seed set is empty, no recertification is required. Otherwise, it derives the *analysis impact slice*, i.e., the closure of all analyses reachable through the dependency edges of the ADG starting from the seed nodes. This slice represents an induced subgraph of the ADG that contains every analysis potentially affected by the given model change.

Formally, with respect to the *use-define* relations among models (particularly their observables), the analysis slicing step captures two kinds of dependencies: (i) *forward dependencies*, where an analysis f_j consumes an output model produced by another analysis f_i; and (ii) *backward dependencies*, where an analysis f_k produces an input model required by f_i. By recursively applying these dependency relations, we obtain a complete and self-contained set of interdependent analyses. Analyses outside the slice remain unaffected and can safely reuse their previous results.

The second subroutine, INCREMENTALRECERTIFICATION, orchestrates the analysis slicing and model repair process. It begins by invoking ANALYSISSLICING to compute the analysis impact slice V_Δ. The analyses in the slice are examined in topological order to ensure dependency-consistent execution. If an analysis' trigger function $\varphi_i(\Delta)$ evaluates to `true` the analysis is re-executed. The corresponding analysis result o_i is collected in the output set O.

If the analysis result violates its local goal g_i, the model repair process is started to generate corrective model deltas Δ' to regain this goal. Because the repair may affect models not directly connected to the failing analysis, the slicing procedure is re-applied with Δ', thereby extending and updating the impact slice. The expanded slice is merged with the current one, re-ordered topologically, and the loop continues until all analyses in the updated slice have been successfully validated. This iterative process ensures that every repair-triggered modification is fully propagated and reanalysed until global consistency is re-established.

Conceptually, Algorithm 1 incrementally restores certification evidence by localising reanalysis and model repair to the necessary subset of analyses.

Termination and determinism.[6] The algorithm *terminates* under the following *operational* assumptions. First, all user-defined components are well-behaved: (i) every trigger function terminates when evaluated and yields a deterministic Boolean result; (ii) each analysis execution terminates and produces a deterministic outcome; and (iii) each model repair process terminates, produces a finite set of model deltas, and is *progress-seeking*, that is, every successive repair strictly decreases the number of invalid analyses. Finally, (iv) model repairs do not alter the ADG structure: its vertex and edge sets remain fixed throughout the execution. These conditions are not mandatory for using the framework; rather, they are sufficient conditions under which our proof establishes termination. If one or more assumptions are violated, termination is not guaranteed (the procedure may still terminate in practice, but this is outside the proven conditions).

Theorem 1 (Core analyses). *Let $A = (V, E, \Phi)$ be the analysis dependency graph as defined in Definition 5, and let $F = \{f_1, f_2, \ldots, f_n\}$ denote the finite*

[6] The semantic assumptions on analyses (Section 2) concern result correctness and reuse, whereas the assumptions stated here are purely operational and serve only to guarantee termination of the algorithm.

set of analyses represented in A. Assume that executing all analyses in F entails the global goal G, formally, $F \models G$. The incremental recertification procedure, given the graph A and a model Δ, computes a subset $F_{\mathsf{core}} \subseteq F$ referred to as the core analyses. The following equivalence holds:

$$\forall G \,.\, (F \models G) \iff (F_{\mathsf{core}} \models G).$$

Reasoning. For $f_i \in F_{\mathsf{core}}$, all its predecessors either lie in F_{core} (re-executed in the same topological order) or outside it $f_i \notin F_{\mathsf{core}}$. In the latter case, none of its inputs is (transitively) affected by Δ, and thus re-executing f_i would yield its cached output; hence, omitting f_i is observationally inert (soundness). Any analysis whose output could change and propagate (via analysis dependencies) to the global goal must lie on a dependency path from a seed node; the closure of analyses computed by the analysis slicing includes all such nodes (completeness). Therefore, proving equivalence.

Note that if the analyses F do not initially satisfy the global goal G, the incremental recertification procedure invokes model repair operations to restore consistency during its execution. Each model repair produces a new model delta Δ' aimed at achieving the corresponding local analysis goal. The algorithm then recomputes the cumulative model update as the union of all such deltas, to which the same reasoning applies.

If model repair functions are deterministic and progress-seeking, the procedure is guaranteed to terminate at a fixed point equivalent to the outcome of a full re-execution with the same repairs applied. At this fixed point, no further repairs are required, and the global goal G is satisfied by F and F_{core}, thereby preserving equivalence with the complete reanalysis, as specified in Theorem 1.

3.2 Integration with V-SUM

V-SUM provides a formal foundation for maintaining consistency across heterogeneous domain models. To integrate analyses into this framework, we extend the notion of a V-SUM instance to explicitly include analysis models and their relations to domain models. This extension enables consistency management to encompass not only model synchronisation but also the semantic dependencies between models and analyses. Formally, the extended V-SUM is defined as:

$$\text{V-SUM}^+ = \langle M, F, CR, CR^+ \rangle,$$

where M is the set of *domain models*, each conforming to its own metamodel; F is the set of *analysis models*, represented as ADG instances (Section 2.4); $CR \subseteq M \times M$ denotes the conventional *domain-to-domain consistency relations* as formalised in the Vitruvius approach [13]; and $CR^+ \subseteq M \times F$ denotes the *domain-to-analysis relations*, capturing which analyses consume or produce which models. Each relation $r \in CR^+$ is associated with a *consistency condition* that ensures the analysis is well-defined, valid, and synchronised with the model(s) it references.

A V-SUM$^+$ instance is *consistent* if and only if all pairs $(m_i, m_j) \in CR$ and $(m_i, a_k) \in CR^+$ satisfy their respective consistency conditions. Syntactic and semantic consistency are handled within a unified framework, V-SUM$^+$. Syntactic consistency is preserved by V-SUM$^+$'s built-in consistency specifications and preservation rules. These preservation rules, originally defined for domain-to-domain relations, are now generalised to cover domain-to-analysis relations. The extended rules ensure that changes in a domain model trigger appropriate structural updates of the affected analyses. Hence, structural consistency is preserved holistically across both the domain and analysis layers. Semantic consistency is maintained through the incremental recertification procedure presented in Algorithm 1 and formally characterised in Definition 4. Terminology and observable relations across models and analyses are assumed to be aligned, ensuring that deltas propagate coherently through both domain and analysis layers. This extension makes the semantic coupling between models and analyses explicitly represented within the V-SUM$^+$ framework. Consequently, consistency preservation holds for both CR and CR^+, enabling unified reasoning about model evolution and the selective re-execution of analyses within a formally well-defined foundation. Furthermore, the set of analyses can be regarded as a coherent model in its own right, subject to the same model-management operations (e.g., versioning, consistency checking, and delta propagation) as any other model within V-SUM$^+$.

4 Illustrative examples

To demonstrate the proposed formalisation and quantify the efficiency of incremental reanalysis, we present two complementary examples: (i) software development analyses, illustrating efficiency in reanalysis reduction; and (ii) ISO 26262 safety analyses, illustrating assurance preservation across dependent models. Both examples demonstrate how explicit dependencies enable targeted reanalysis while preserving correctness, and how the proposed formalisation supports specifying and reasoning about analysis dependencies and trigger functions in realistic, certification-relevant contexts.

4.1 Software development analyses

We now consider the models and analyses that represent essential, though not exhaustive, elements of a software-development workflow that includes testing and code review before release. The models are: (i) a *program* model m_{prog} representing the implementation; (ii) a *test* model m_{test} describing the structure and contents of the test suite; (iii) a *guideline* model m_{guid} capturing coding guidelines or policies (e.g., MISRA C++, AUTOSAR C++ 14); and (iv) a *coverage* model m_{cov} defining the coverage criteria for safety-critical code. They are linked through explicit structural consistency relations, such as traceability links between test cases and source methods. These links align their observables by mapping synonymous items to canonical identifiers and resolving naming inconsistencies.

We use a finite set of analyses: (i) f_{stat}: *Static code analysis.* Checks that all program artefacts are syntactically and semantically well-formed. (ii) f_{test}:

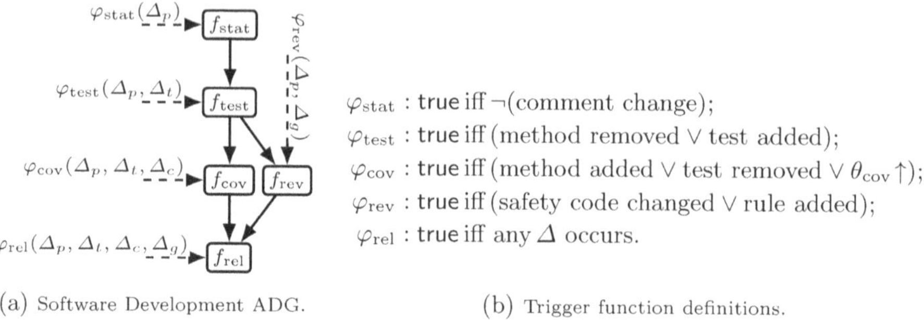

(a) Software Development ADG. (b) Trigger function definitions.

Fig. 2: Software development analyses ADG and their trigger functions.

Unit test result analysis. Evaluates the outcomes of executing the test suite on the implementation. (iii) f_{cov}: *Coverage analysis.* Checks whether the achieved coverage meets the threshold θ_{cov}. (iv) f_{rev}: *Code review analysis.* Manually assesses the architectural integrity, safety, and maintainability that cannot be fully verified automatically regarding guidelines. (v) f_{rel}: *Release checking.* Integrates previous results to ensure the system is ready for release.

Figure 2a depicts the ADG for this example. Solid directed edges express that unit testing depends on static checks; coverage and review depend on unit results, and the release decision combines both coverage and review outcomes. External dashed arrows correspond to trigger functions whose definitions are specified in Fig. 2b. They determine whether a change (Δ) in the underlying models, i.e., program (Δ_p), test (Δ_t), coverage (Δ_c), or guideline (Δ_g) should activate a reanalysis. Each φ_i evaluates domain-specific deltas and returns true only when the change is semantically relevant. For example, adding new non-safety methods activates static and coverage analysis but not unit tests and code review, while updates related to guidelines or safety trigger the review. The release check is re-invoked whenever any upstream artefact changes, ensuring that only consistent and verified results are considered for release.

Conceptual correctness sketch. A change "non-safety method added" makes $\{\varphi_{\text{stat}}, \varphi_{\text{cov}}\}$ true; thus the seed is $\{f_{\text{stat}}, f_{\text{cov}}\}$ and the slice is its forward and backward closure $\{f_{\text{stat}}, f_{\text{cov}}, f_{\text{rel}}\}$ regarding use-define relations. Others are unreachable and reuse cached results. Similarly, a "rule added" change seeds $\{f_{\text{rev}}\}$ and slices to $\{f_{\text{rev}}, f_{\text{rel}}\}$. Hence, by definition, slicing is the reachability closure for *use-define* relations from triggered nodes, and the procedure isolates exactly the affected analyses (sound and complete for this ADG).

Table 1 summarises the re-executed and saved analyses for a representative set of model changes. Across all typical change scenarios defined by the trigger functions, instead of rerunning all five analyses (as a baseline) after every change, our approach substantially reduces the number of analyses that need to be re-executed. In the most favourable cases, such as comment-only modifications or decreases in the coverage threshold, only the release analysis f_{rel} is triggered, resulting in an 80% reduction in effort. In more involved cases, such as changing safety-critical code, three analyses (f_{stat}, f_{rev}, and f_{rel}) are rerun, corresponding to a 40% reduction. Averaged across all considered change types, the approach saves 2.9 of 5 analyses, achieving an overall reduction of $\approx 58\%$ in the number of re-executed analyses compared to the baseline, which re-executes every analysis after any change.

4.2 ISO 26262 safety analyses

Consider a typical ISO 26262 automotive safety workflow. A HARA identifies the hazard *unintended acceleration at highway speed*, initially rated ASIL B. From this, a technical safety requirement is derived: *the throttle actuator must return to idle within* 100 *ms upon fault detection*, and a verification plan defines a requirements-based test to confirm this behaviour in at least 95% of trials.

If the hazard is later reclassified as ASIL C, the change invalidates downstream analyses: traceability must be rechecked since linked requirements now require ASIL C compliance, and the verification plan must adopt stricter validation methods such as extended fault injection or higher coverage. To capture these dependencies, three artefacts are modelled: (i) the HARA model m_{hara}, identifying hazards and ASIL levels; (ii) the Safety Requirements model m_{req}, refining and tracing derived requirements; and (iii) the Verification Plan model m_{ver}, defining verification and validation activities.

The corresponding analyses are: f_{hara} for hazard classification, f_{req} for traceability and risk alignment, and f_{ver} for coverage verification. Their dependencies are hierarchical: f_{ver} depends on f_{req}, which depends on f_{hara}. This ensures that downstream assurance remains valid only if upstream artefacts are sound.

As shown in Fig. 3a, changes in the HARA model (e.g., new hazards or ASIL updates) trigger f_{hara} and cascade through f_{req} to f_{ver}, maintaining consistency across artefacts. Modifications limited to the verification artefacts affect only f_{ver}; new or updated requirements trigger f_{req} and its dependents. Formally modelling these dependencies allows computing the reanalysis set needed to restore assurance soundness while avoiding redundant recomputation.

According to Table 1, six of nine possible analyses are re-executed, saving about 33% of total effort while preserving the integrity of the safety argument. Compared with the software-development case, which achieves about 60% savings through greater analysis reuse, the ISO 26262 workflow gains less due to its stricter dependency structure.

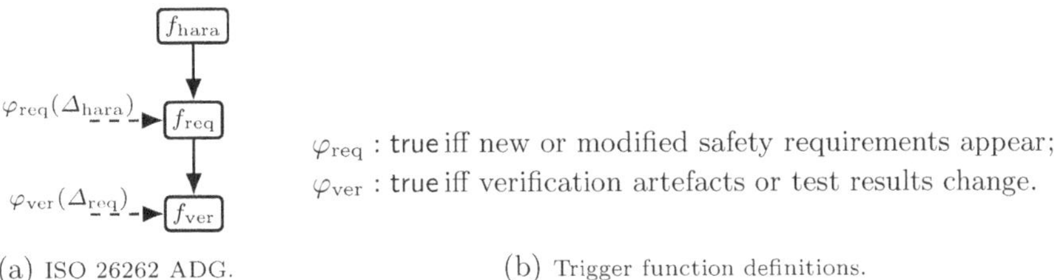

(a) ISO 26262 ADG. (b) Trigger function definitions.

Fig. 3: ISO 26262 safety analyses and their trigger conditions.

Table 1: Analyses saved per model change.

Model Change (Δ)	Re-executed	Saved
Software-development example		
Comment-only change in code	f_{rel}	4
Decrease of coverage threshold ($\theta_{cov} \downarrow$)	f_{rel}	4
Method added	$f_{stat}, f_{cov}, f_{rel}$	2
Method removed	$f_{stat}, f_{test}, f_{rel}$	2
Test added	f_{test}, f_{rel}	3
Test removed	f_{cov}, f_{rel}	3
Safety-critical code changed	$f_{stat}, f_{rev}, f_{rel}$	2
Guideline rule added	f_{rev}, f_{rel}	3
Increase of coverage threshold ($\theta_{cov} \uparrow$)	f_{cov}, f_{rel}	3
Sum		**26/45**
Average (9 changes)		**2.9/change (58%)**
ISO 26262 safety-assurance example		
Hazard or ASIL added	$f_{hara}, f_{req}, f_{ver}$	0
New or modified safety requirement	f_{req}, f_{ver}	1
Verification artefacts changed	f_{ver}	2
Sum		**3/9**
Average (3 changes)		**1.0/change (33%)**

These scenarios show that the approach reduces unnecessary reanalyses while preserving correctness. It treats automated and manual analyses uniformly, recognising both as integral to the assurance process and to informed release decisions. In doing so, the formalisation achieves a practical balance between efficiency and assurance, enabling selective re-execution without compromising certification validity.

5 Related work

Prior research has addressed various aspects related to the representation, composition, and incremental execution of analyses. Our work builds on these foundations and adapts established ideas to the setting of MDD, especially V-SUM, with a particular focus on heterogeneous models, certification artefacts, and analysis-aware consistency management.

Program analysis. Compiler frameworks such as LLVM [14] and SOOT [26] provide architectures for composing analyses and executing them incrementally within a single program representation. Szabó et al. [24] develop formal foundations for incremental program analysis, supporting the maintenance of recursive lattice-value aggregation in Datalog [1]. In contrast, our work focuses on selective re-execution across heterogeneous analyses within an MDD setting.

Analyses in software product lines. Murphy et al. [17, 19, 18] study analysis-based assurance for software product lines (SPLs) by lifting analyses, assurance arguments, and analysis workflows from individual products to variability-aware artefacts. In these works, analyses are given explicit semantics and are reused across products through feature-based configuration and variability-aware regression mechanisms.

Existing SPL approaches reason about validity and reanalysis mainly in terms of configuration changes and SPL evolution. We instead reason over explicit model deltas at the level of semantic observables and use these deltas to trigger re-execution through an explicit analysis dependency graph. Moreover, SPL analyses are usually formal and automated and serve as evidence in assurance-case templates. In contrast, our formalisation abstracts uniformly over automated, semi-formal, and manual analyses, enabling dependency- and delta-based selective re-execution of heterogeneous analyses without relying on product-line variability models.

Rule-based impact analysis. Early research on change impact focused on detecting artefacts affected by a modification. Lehnert et al. [15] proposed a rule-based mechanism that propagates changes across heterogeneous software artefacts within the Eclipse Modelling Framework. Their method computes a minimal set of impacted elements using dependency and change-type rules, thereby reducing the need for conservative recomputation. Goknil et al. [10] extended this idea to requirements–architecture traceability, using first-order logic to infer propagation paths. Both approaches, however, reason at the level of artefacts and trace links. In contrast, our work treats analyses themselves as explicit elements whose validity and reuse can be reasoned about formally. This enables selective re-execution based not only on structural dependencies, but also on semantic correctness conditions and global certification goals.

Formalisation and incremental evaluation of analyses. Hinkel et al. [12] formalised implicit incremental model analyses using category-theoretic functors, achieving efficient recomputation of query results. Their contribution is complementary to ours. They optimise the execution of a single analysis, while we determine which analyses must be re-executed after a change. At the modelling level, languages such as OCL and EVL [16] provide declarative validation rules, and frameworks such as EMF-IncQuery and VIATRA [4] maintain query consistency under model updates. Our formalisation generalises these ideas by abstracting analyses, preconditions, and properties in a uniform semantic framework, enabling sound and complete selective re-execution. SysML treats analyses as explicit model elements, whereas our work focuses on formal reasoning about their reuse and re-execution under change.

Contract-based and compositional verification. The notion of expressing analyses through explicit assumptions and guarantees aligns with contract-based design frameworks such as AGREE and OCRA [8, 5, 6] and with the general contract theory of Benveniste et al. [3]. Unlike those approaches, which focus on component-level reasoning, we apply contracts to the orchestration of heterogeneous analyses, enabling incremental recertification across domains.

Consistency management and the V-SUM framework. The Single Underlying Model (SUM) [2] and its practical realisation, the Virtual SUM (V-SUM) [13], provide the foundation for integrating heterogeneous models through explicit consistency relations. Pascual et al. [21] extended these notions with formal semantics for syntactic and semantic consistency. Our contribution complements this line by incorporating analyses as first-class entities within V-SUM, bridging syntactic consistency management and semantic assurance. Giese et al. [9] use Triple Graph Grammars to maintain consistency between model pairs via bidirectional, incremental synchronisation. In contrast, our work focuses on selectively re-execution analyses that consume and produce models.

Prior work has focused on artefact-level impact analysis or on optimising individual analyses. The novelty of our approach lies in integrating analysis-level dependency reasoning, trigger-based incremental recertification, and the soundness-preserving reuse of analysis results within the unified model-driven V-SUM framework.

6 Conclusion

We introduced a formalisation of analyses as first-class citizens within model-driven development, complementing traditional notions of model and consistency management. By characterising analyses through their inputs, outputs, preconditions, properties, and trigger conditions, we established a foundation for reasoning about their correctness, soundness, and reuse.

We further proposed the Analysis Dependency Graph (ADG) as a unifying abstraction to capture inter-analysis dependencies and to guide incremental recertification. The formal semantics of analyses and their trigger functions enable selective re-execution after model changes, ensuring that only semantically affected analyses are repeated. Together, these contributions enable the extension of the Virtual Single Underlying Model (V-SUM) framework toward analysis-aware consistency reasoning, bridging the gap between syntactic consistency maintenance and semantic assurance. This work establishes the theoretical foundation for analysis formalisation and incremental recertification, which we will use to build practical tools.

Several directions remain for further investigation: (i) We plan to automate trigger derivation using change-type taxonomies and data-driven learning over historical deltas, and to investigate the reuse of prior validity results under concurrent or overlapping triggers. (ii) The model-repair process is treated abstractly as a deterministic, progress-seeking step that may introduce new deltas and re-invoke slicing. In practice, repair operations in MDD are often heuristic and nondeterministic. A rigorous formalisation of model repair semantics, including measurable notions of progress and confluence, would strengthen termination guarantees of the incremental procedure. (iii) This work does not include an empirical evaluation. Reported efficiency gains, for example, a 58% reduction in re-executed analyses, are derived analytically from dependency-graph structure rather than from tool-based measurements. As future work, we will develop a prototype within the Vitruvius/V-SUM toolchain to enable empirical validation on industrial-scale systems.

Acknowledgments. This work was funded by the German Research Foundation (DFG) – SFB 1608 – 501798263.

References

1. Abiteboul, S., Hull, R., Vianu, V.: Foundations of Databases. Addison-Wesley (1995)
2. Atkinson, C., Stoll, D., Bostan, P.: Orthographic software modeling: A practical approach to view-based development. In: Maciaszek, L.A., González-Pérez, C., Jablonski, S. (eds.) ENASE. vol. 69, pp. 206–219 (2009). https://doi.org/10.1007/978-3-642-14819-4_15
3. Benveniste, A., Caillaud, B., Ferrari, A., Mangeruca, L., Passerone, R., Sofronis, C.: Contracts for system design. Foundations and Trends in Electronic Design Automation **12**(2-3), 124–400 (2018). https://doi.org/10.1561/1000000053
4. Bergmann, G., Dávid, I., Hegedüs, Á., Horváth, Á., Ráth, I., Ujhelyi, Z., Varró, D.: VIATRA 3: A reactive model transformation platform. In: Kolovos, D., Wimmer, M. (eds.) ICMT. LNCS, vol. 9152, pp. 101–110. Springer (2015). https://doi.org/10.1007/978-3-319-21155-8_8
5. Cimatti, A., Tonetta, S.: Contracts for system design. In: SEFM. LNCS, vol. 9276, pp. 186–203. Springer (2015). https://doi.org/10.1007/978-3-319-22969-0_14
6. Cimatti, A., Tonetta, S., Sokoly, D.: Contract-based design for system requirements and architecture. In: FM. LNCS, vol. 9109, pp. 99–115. Springer (2015). https://doi.org/10.1007/978-3-319-19249-9_7
7. Färber, H., Pascual, R., Stübinger, T., Ulbrich, M.: Observable semantics for characterising consistency between heterogeneous models. In: Bianculli, D., Gómez-Martínez, E. (eds.) SEFM. pp. 110–128. Springer (2025)
8. Gacek, A., Backes, J., Cofer, D., Slind, K., Whalen, M.: Agree: Assume guarantee reasoning environment. In: NFM. LNCS, vol. 8430, pp. 402–409. Springer (2014). https://doi.org/10.1007/978-3-319-06200-6_32
9. Giese, H., Wagner, R.: Incremental model synchronization with triple graph grammars. In: Nierstrasz, O., Whittle, J., Harel, D., Reggio, G. (eds.) Model Driven Engineering Languages and Systems. pp. 543–557. Springer Berlin Heidelberg, Berlin, Heidelberg (2006)
10. Goknil, A., Kurtev, I., van den Berg, K.: A rule-based change impact analysis approach in software architecture for requirements changes. CoRR **abs/1608.02757** (2016)
11. Hillenbrand, M.: Funktionale Sicherheit nach ISO 26262 in der Konzeptphase der Entwicklung von Elektrik/Elektronik Architekturen von Fahrzeugen. Ph.D. thesis, Karlsruhe Institute of Technology, Karlsruhe, Germany (2012)
12. Hinkel, G., Heinrich, R., Reussner, R.: An extensible approach to implicit incremental model analyses. Software and Systems Modeling **18**(5), 3151–3187 (2019). https://doi.org/10.1007/s10270-019-00719-y
13. Klare, H., Kramer, M.E., Langhammer, M., Werle, D., Burger, E., Reussner, R.H.: Enabling consistency in view-based system development - the vitruvius approach. J. Syst. Softw. **171**, 110815 (2021). https://doi.org/10.1016/J.JSS.2020.110815
14. Lattner, C., Adve, V.: LLVM: A compilation framework for lifelong program analysis & transformation. In: Proceedings of the International Symposium on Code Generation and Optimization (CGO). pp. 75–86. IEEE (2004)
15. Lehnert, S., Farooq, Q., Riebisch, M.: Rule-based impact analysis for heterogeneous software artifacts. In: Cleve, A., Ricca, F., Cerioli, M. (eds.) CSMR. pp. 209–218. IEEE Computer Society (2013). https://doi.org/10.1109/CSMR.2013.30
16. Madani, S., Kolovos, D.S., Paige, R.F.: Parallel model validation with Epsilon. In: Pierantonio, A., Trujillo, S. (eds.) ECMFA. LNCS, vol. 10890, pp. 115–131. Springer (2018). https://doi.org/10.1007/978-3-319-92997-2_8

17. Murphy, L., Di Sandro, A., Shahin, R., Chechik, M.: Reusing your favourite analysis framework to handle workflows of product line models. In: Proceedings of the 27th ACM International Systems and Software Product Line Conference - Volume A. p. 117–128. SPLC '23, Association for Computing Machinery, New York, NY, USA (2023). https://doi.org/10.1145/3579027.3608983, https://doi.org/10.1145/3579027.3608983
18. Murphy, L., Viger, T., Sandro, A.D., Babikian, A.A., Chechik, M.: Assurance case development for evolving software product lines: A formal approach (2025), https://arxiv.org/abs/2511.03026
19. Murphy, L., Viger, T., Sandro, A.D., Chechik, M.: Placidus: Engineering product lines of rigorous assurance cases. In: Kosmatov, N., Kovács, L. (eds.) Integrated Formal Methods. pp. 87–108. Springer Nature Switzerland, Cham (2025)
20. NewEagle: How ISO 26262 updates affect you. https://neweagle.net/blog/how-iso-26262-2018-update-affects-you/ (2018), accessed 12 October 2025.
21. Pascual, R., Beckert, B., Ulbrich, M., Kirsten, M., Pfeifer, W.: Formal foundations of consistency in model-driven development. In: Margaria, T., Steffen, B. (eds.) ISoLA. LNCS, vol. 15221, pp. 178–200. Springer (2024). https://doi.org/10.1007/978-3-031-75380-0_11
22. Siemens Verification Academy: Functional safety for ISO 26262. https://verificationacademy.com/solutions/functional-safety/fusa-for-iso-26262/ (2025), accessed 12 October 2025.
23. Slotosch, O., Wildmoser, M., Philipps, J., Jeschull, R., Zalman, R.: ISO 26262 - tool chain analysis reduces tool qualification costs. In: Automotive - Safety & Security 2012, pp. 27–38. Gesellschaft für Informatik e.V. (2012)
24. Szabó, T., Bergmann, G., Erdweg, S., Voelter, M.: Incrementalizing lattice-based program analyses in datalog. Proc. ACM Program. Lang. **2**(OOPSLA) (Oct 2018). https://doi.org/10.1145/3276509, https://doi.org/10.1145/3276509
25. UNECE: UN regulation No. 156: Software update and software update management system. https://unece.org/transport/documents/2021/03/standards/un-regulation-no-156-software-update-and-software-update (2021), accessed 12 October 2025.
26. Vallée-Rai, R., Co, P., Gagnon, E., Hendren, L., Lam, P., Sundaresan, V.: Soot: A java bytecode optimization framework. In: Proceedings of the Conference of the Centre for Advanced Studies on Collaborative Research (CASCON). pp. 125–135. IBM (1999)
27. ABI Research: By 2028, automakers will save US$1.5 billion using over-the-air updates to fix recalled cars. https://www.abiresearch.com/press/by-2028-automakers-will-save-us15-billion-using-over-the-air-updates-to-fix-recalled-cars/ (2023), accessed 12 October 2025.
28. DataIntelo Research Team, Automotive digital homologation platform market report 2024–2032. https://dataintelo.com/report/automotive-digital-homologation-platform-market (2024), accessed 12 October 2025.
29. ISO 26262-9:2018 Road vehicles — Functional safety — Part 9: Automotive Safety Integrity Level (ASIL)-oriented and safety-oriented analyses. International Standard (2018)
30. ISO 26262-4:2018 Road vehicles — Functional safety — Part 4: Product development at the system level. International Standard (2018)
31. ISO 26262:2018 Road vehicles — Functional safety. International Standard (2018), second edition, Parts 1–12

Don't go MAD with Anomalies! Design-time Microservice Anomaly Detection in Migration to Microservices

Valentim Romão, Rafael Soares,
Luís Rodrigues, and Vasco Manquinho

INESC-ID, Instituto Superior Técnico - Universidade de Lisboa, Portugal
{valentim.romao, joao.rafael.pinto.soares, ler,
vasco.manquinho}@tecnico.ulisboa.pt

Abstract. The advent of microservices has led multiple companies to migrate their monolithic systems to this new architecture. When decomposing a monolith, a functionality previously implemented as a transaction may need to be implemented as a set of independent sub-transactions, possibly executed by multiple microservices, paving the way for anomalies to emerge. The ability to assess, at design time, the anomalies that different decompositions may generate is key to guide the programmers in finding the most appropriate decomposition that matches their goals. This paper introduces *MAD*, the first framework for automatically detecting anomalies that are introduced by a given decomposition of a monolith into microservices. *MAD* operates by encoding the executions of the original functionalities as an SMT formula and then using a solver to find satisfiable assignments that capture the anomalous interleavings made possible by that specific decomposition. We have applied *MAD* to different benchmarks and show that it can identify precisely the causes of potential anomalous behavior.

Keywords: Anomaly Detection · Microservices · Satisfiability Modulo Theories.

1 Introduction

Microservices have emerged as a promising architecture for implementing large-scale applications. When using microservices, applications are designed as a set of loosely coupled components that may be easily developed and maintained by independent teams [31,21]. The adoption of this architectural style has led many companies, including large companies such as Amazon, Netflix, and Uber, to migrate applications that have been previously implemented as monoliths to microservices [19,5,27,20,10,37,15].

Unfortunately, migrating an application to the microservice architecture is not a trivial task [25,16]. Functionalities that have been designed in the monolith to execute as a single ACID transaction may be required to execute as a sequence of independent transactions after the migration, each implemented by

E. Albert and C. Pasareanu (Eds.): FASE 2026, LNCS 16504, pp. 202–222, 2026.
https://doi.org/10.1007/978-3-032-22774-4_11

a different microservice. This breaks the isolation among functionalities that are executed concurrently, leading to anomalous application behavior. Handling anomalous behavior is costly as it often requires the implementation of additional code, such as compensating actions [17], to correct the undesired effects of the loss of isolation and atomicity. Dealing with anomalies typically dominates the migration cost [32] and, in some cases, these costs outweigh the advantages of microservices, forcing developers to revert the application to a monolith [34].

The importance of estimating the complexity associated with a monolith decomposition has been recognized in the literature [4], motivating several works on how to aggregate the domain entities when migrating from a monolith to microservices [29,9,24,22]. However, none captures concrete anomalous behaviors that may result from concurrent executions of functionalities. They also fail to give hints regarding the type of anomalies that can occur, a key information to estimate the cost of compensating actions [26,36].

Testing tools, such as *MonkeyDB* [8] and *Cobra* [35], can detect anomalies by using a black box approach. However, there is no guarantee that all possible interleavings are tested and some anomalies may pass unnoticed. Moreover, they require a target decomposition to be implemented before being tested. In opposition, we aim to detect problematic decompositions at design time, avoiding implementing decompositions that generate many anomalies.

Early validation work for transactional systems, such as [13,23], assume a single database and a set of transactions that can be executed in any order. More recent works such as *ANODE* [28] and *CLOTHO* [30] consider distributed storage but assume that all storage nodes replicate all entities, which is not the case in microservice decompositions.

This paper proposes the *Microservices Anomaly Detector* (*MAD*), a new framework to identify anomalies that result from the decomposition of a monolith into microservices considering bounded executions of the system. *MAD* takes a monolithic application, a target decomposition, and the application's SQL schema to automatically generate the set of independent transactions that execute the same functionality in the microservices. Then, *MAD* encodes the interleavings of these transactions that correspond to non-serializable executions of the original functionalities as a *Satisfiability Module Theories* (SMT) formula. The SMT formula's solution provides the interleavings that may generate anomalous behaviors. Hence, *MAD* is the first system that precisely detects the anomalies that will result from the decomposition of monoliths into microservices.

Because *MAD* exhaustively searches the space of all transaction interleavings, the time it takes to analyze a decomposition may be large. To circumvent this limitation, *MAD* implements a novel divide-and-conquer approach to parallelize the search. This makes *MAD* suitable to be applied to non-trivial code bases.

In summary, the contributions of this paper are as follows: (1) we formulate the problem of finding anomalies in a microservice decomposition of a monolith as an SMT problem, (2) we propose a strategy to parallelize the task of finding the satisfiable assignments that capture anomalies, (3) we provide the developer

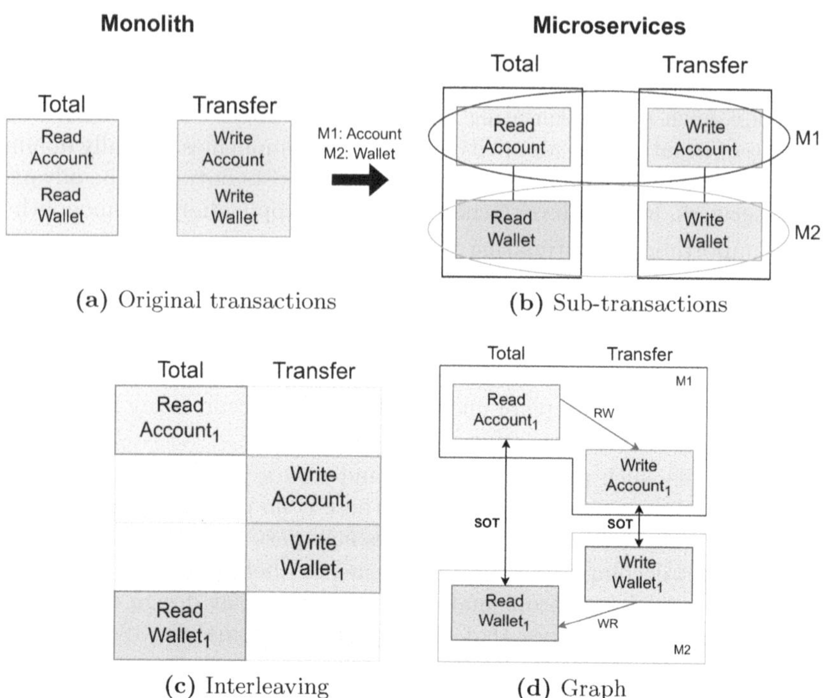

(a) Original transactions (b) Sub-transactions

(c) Interleaving (d) Graph

Fig. 1. Example of how two functionalities (a) can be divided when migrating from monolith to microservices (b) and of an interleaving (c) that leads to an anomaly (d).

with the classification of the type of anomaly and the entities and functionalities involved and, (4) we present an experimental evaluation of the resulting system with 7 different benchmarks.

2 Motivation Example

Figure 1 illustrates an example of how a given microservices decomposition originates a previously non-existing interleaving. In this scenario, there are two entities (`Account` and `Wallet`), two transactions (Total and Transfer), and a decomposition where `Account` is managed by microservice M_1 and `Wallet` is managed by microservice M_2. Total gets the total amount of a client's money (its account balance plus its wallet balance). Transfer withdraws an amount of funds from the client's account balance and deposits it in their wallet. Considering that a client's balance can only be transferred from their account to their wallet, it is expected that the total amount of funds of a client always remains the same.

Since entities `Account` and `Wallet` are in different microservices, Total and Transfer would be split into sub-transactions, each of which executes in a different

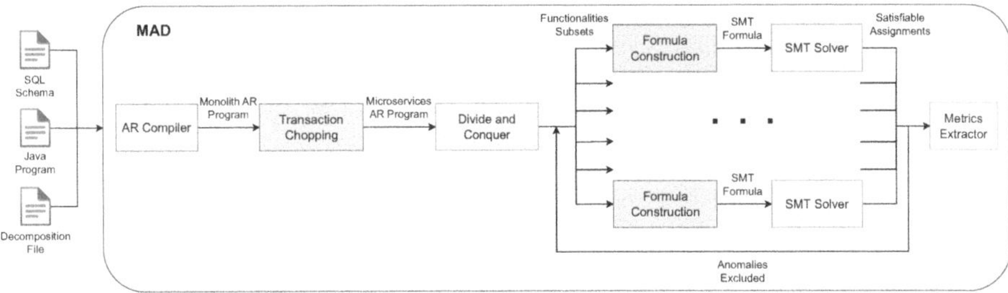

Fig. 2. *MAD*'s pipeline.

```
CREATE TABLE Account (
  clientId INT,
  balance INT,
  PRIMARY KEY (clientId)
);

CREATE TABLE Wallet (
  clientId INT,
  balance INT,
  PRIMARY KEY (clientId)
);
```

Listing 1.1. Example of *MAD*'s input SQL schema file.

microservice. This can lead to anomalies that were not possible in the monolithic version, as illustrated in Figure 1(c). In this example, the execution of Transfer interleaves with the execution of Total. Total sees an older version of a client's account ($\texttt{Account}_1$), implying that Total is executed before Transfer. However, Total sees the new version of the client's wallet ($\texttt{Wallet}_1$), whose balance was already updated by Transfer, implying that Total is executed after Transfer. There is no serial order of the two functionalities that may lead to this execution. From this execution, one could incorrectly observe that the total funds of the client have changed, something impossible in this scenario.

3 Microservices Anomaly Detector

This section describes the *Microservices Anomaly Detector* (*MAD*), a framework to automatically detect anomalies that would result from implementing a given microservices decomposition of a monolithic application.

3.1 Overview

MAD is modular and its execution performs multiple steps in sequence. Figure 2 presents *MAD*'s pipeline. Next, we provide a description of each step.

```
public class exampleScenario {
  private Connection connect = null;
  private int _ISOLATION = Connection.TRANSACTION_READ_COMMITTED;
  private int id;
  Properties p;

  public exampleScenario(int id) {
    this.id = id;
    p = new Properties();
    p.setProperty("id", String.valueOf(this.id));
    Object o;
    try {
      o = Class.forName("MyDriver").newInstance();
      DriverManager.registerDriver((Driver) o);
      Driver driver = DriverManager.getDriver("jdbc:mydriver://");
      connect = driver.connect("", p);
    } catch (InstantiationException | IllegalAccessException |
        ClassNotFoundException | SQLException e) {
      e.printStackTrace();
    }
  }

  public void Total(int clientId) throws SQLException {
    PreparedStatement stmt1 = connect.prepareStatement("SELECT␣balance␣FROM␣Account"+"␣WHERE␣clientId␣=␣?");
    stmt1.setInt(1, clientId);
    ResultSet rs = stmt1.executeQuery();
    rs.next();
    int account_balance = rs.getInt("balance");

    PreparedStatement stmt2 = connect.prepareStatement("SELECT␣balance␣FROM␣Wallet"+"␣WHERE␣clientId␣=␣?");
    stmt2.setInt(1, clientId);
    ResultSet rs2 = stmt2.executeQuery();
    rs2.next();
    int wallet_balance = rs2.getInt("balance");

    int total_money = account_balance + wallet_balance;
  }

  public void Transfer(int clientId, int accountBalance, int walletBalance, int amount) throws SQLException {
    PreparedStatement stmt1 = connect.prepareStatement("UPDATE␣Account␣SET␣balance␣=␣?"+"␣WHERE␣clientId␣=␣?");
    stmt1.setInt(1, accountBalance - amount);
    stmt1.setInt(2, clientId);
    stmt1.executeUpdate();

    PreparedStatement stmt2 = connect.prepareStatement("UPDATE␣Wallet␣SET␣balance␣=␣?"+"␣WHERE␣clientId␣=␣?");
    stmt2.setInt(1, walletBalance + amount);
    stmt2.setInt(2, clientId);
    stmt2.executeUpdate();
  }
}
```

Listing 1.2. Example of *MAD*'s input Java file.

Input: MAD takes as input a monolithic implementation of an application (including its SQL schema and source code) and a high-level description of how the monolith is decomposed into multiple microservices. Currently, the source code must be a *Java program* written using the JDBC syntax (i.e., that uses SQL queries to access the entities, which are maintained by the application in a database). As an illustration, the input files for the scenario from Figure 1 are depicted in Listings 1.1, 1.2 and 1.3. Although the current prototype only supports Java, the framework has been designed such that it can be extended to support additional programming languages. The decomposition of the monolith is expressed as the clustering of the domain entities into aggregates [29] (entities grouped in the same cluster are assumed to be managed by the same microservice) and is represented by a JSON file (*Decomposition File*). The JSON file used in the example scenario is depicted in Listing 1.3. Using this input, *MAD*

```
{
  "M1": ["Account"],
  "M2": ["Wallet"]
}
```

Listing 1.3. JSON file with a microservices decomposition.

executes the pipeline presented in Figure 2, which is composed of the following sequence of steps:

Step 1 (AR Compiler): The source code is compiled to an *abstract representation* (AR) that captures how the functionalities access the domain entities. In the AR, each functionality is represented as a sequence of read and write operations on domain entities (*Monolith AR Program*). The AR compiler is the only component that needs to be changed to support other programming languages.

Step 2 (Transaction Chopping): From the AR of the functionalities, an AR of the microservice decomposition is automatically generated (*Microservices AR Program*) by chopping the functionalities code into multiple sub-sequences. Each sub-sequence accesses domain entities from a single aggregate, capturing a sub-transaction to be executed at a single microservice. In the microservice decomposition, sub-sequences that are part of the same parent functionality are executed as a sequence of independent transactions.

Step 3 (Divide and Conquer): Often, the AR program is too complex to be represented in a single encoding that can be effectively analyzed. Employing a divide and conquer strategy, *MAD* generates subsets of the functionalities (*Functionalities Subsets*). Each subset represents a possible combination of concurrent functionality executions. These can be analyzed independently and in parallel, allowing the whole problem to terminate in a reasonable time.

Step 4 (Formula Construction): Based on the Microservices AR, for each subset of functionalities, *MAD* generates an SMT formula encoding the possible functionalities' interleavings. The satisfiable assignments of these formulas are the possible interleavings that can lead to anomalies in the decomposition.

Step 5 (SMT Solver): MAD uses Z3 [11] to solve the SMT formulas. Satisfiable assignments correspond to cyclic graphs, with the vertices being operations and the edges the relations between operations, representing unserializable executions of functionalities [2]. These cycles have their length bounded by a system parameter denoted the *Maximum Cycle Length* (MCL), defined as the maximum number of edges to be considered when looking for satisfiable assignments.

Step 6 (Metrics Extractor): After all satisfiable assignments are found, *MAD* processes the anomalies found and extracts metrics to report to the user. These metrics include the total number of anomalies, dividing them in *core anomalies* (cyclic graphs with the minimum cycle length required to represent an anomaly) and their *extensions* (cyclic graphs that are supersets of the *core anomalies* graphs), the anomalies types, and the entities, functionalities, and sub-transactions involved.

3.2 Supported Syntax

In the current version of *MAD*, the source code needs to be a program written in Java using the JDBC syntax. If needed, it is possible to extend the *AR Compiler* to support additional programming languages. Furthermore, the current version is not able to parse joins or implicit updates. This is not a fundamental limitation, because these operations can be represented through combinations of reads and writes, which are supported by the *AR Compiler* and are enough to cover all benchmarks used in the evaluation. To define a join, one can divide the query with the join operation into two or more queries, each accessing only one table. Similarly, to represent an implicit update, one can divide it into a read, to retrieve the current value, followed by a write with the update expression. These transformations could be implemented by leveraging the current *AR Compiler* or by adding a pre-processing step to automatically decompose the operations. However, this exercise falls outside the scope of this work.

3.3 Abstract Representation

MAD builds a *Monolith AR Program* from the Java source code. The AR facilitates the extraction of information, such as transactions, types of parameters, and execution order. *MAD* receives as input the Java source code of the monolith and compiles it to an abstract representation (AR), originating the *Monolith AR Program*. The AR facilitates the extraction of information, including the transactions, types of parameters, and execution order. Figure 3 presents the structure of the monolith AR.

To represent the SQL schema, *MAD* uses two elements, *Table* and *Column*. *Table* is represented by a *name* and a list of *Columns*. *Column* is represented by a *name*, and a *type* (int, real, string, Boolean).

The application implementation is represented by a set of *Original Transactions*. Each *Original Transaction* captures the code of a functionality in the monolith and has a *name*, a list of *Statements*, a list of *Expressions*, and a list of *Parameters*. Each *Statement* is represented by a *name*, an SQL *query* (select, update, insert or delete), and a *path condition*, which is an expression that associates the execution of the statement with a condition in the program if it occurs inside a conditional block. The *Expressions* can be of four types: *Unary Operation*; *Binary Operation*; *Value*; and *Variable*. The *Unary* and *Binary Operations* have one *operation* and the *Expression(s)* to which the *operation* is applied, respectively. The *Value* expressions represent the static values of the Java program using a *type* and a *value*. At last, the *variable* expressions represent the variables used in the Java program using the variable *name*. These variables include the ones used for the instructions, to store the read rows, and to hold the values of columns read from the database. To conclude, the *Parameters* are a specific type of *Value* expression, which are represented additionally by their *name*.

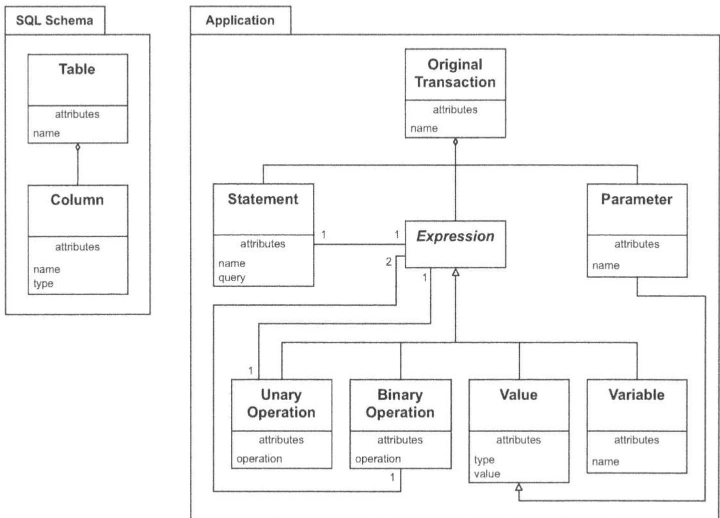

Fig. 3. Monolith AR structure.

3.4 Microservices Decomposition AR

From the Monolith AR Program and the JSON Decomposition File, *MAD* proceeds to create the *Microservices AR Program.* This step consists of applying a transaction chopping algorithm to the original functionalities of the monolith to transform each of them in a sequence of sub-transactions. The *sub-transactions* are represented in the AR by the following attributes: *name*; list of SQL *operations*; their *original transaction name*; and their *microservice name.*

The transaction chopping algorithm works as follows. For each original transaction, *MAD* iterates over the original sequence of operations and splits them into sub-transactions, according to their accessed entities. As an example, consider the scenario from Figure 1. By applying the chopping algorithm, from the original transactions depicted in Figure 1(a), we obtain a representation of the microservices version depicted in Figure 1(b). Each sub-transaction only accesses one microservice and is executed as an independent transaction.

3.5 Divide and Conquer

The *Divide and Conquer* strategy generates all the combinations of functionalities (original transactions) of size smaller than the system parameter *Maximum Cycle Length* (MCL). Note that, since an anomalous interleaving requires that at least two operations belong to the same instance of a functionality, at most $MCL - 1$ functionalities can be involved in a cycle without exceeding the MCL.

Let n be the number of functionalities. The number of generated combinations is given by $\sum_{x=1}^{MCL-1} {}_nC_x$. *MAD* starts by creating one thread for each combination of size 1 (i.e., involving a single functionality). Each thread explores the possible interleavings between the operations of each functionality. When all these threads finish their analysis, the process is repeated for size 2 combinations, already excluding the anomalies involving only size 1 combinations. This process continues until all combinations of size $MCL - 1$ are analyzed.

Our approach has resemblances to the well-known Cube-and-Conquer algorithm [18], except that *MAD* splits the search space explicitly by taking advantage of domain knowledge. Hence, our approach is closer to a classic divide-and-conquer algorithm. Note that each thread analyzes a different combination of functionalities. Moreover, constraints are added such that solutions with $k - 1$ functionalities are excluded when solving a formula involving k functionalities.

3.6 SMT Encoding

MAD encodes the Microservices AR program into an SMT formula such that any satisfiable assignment corresponds to an anomaly. We first provide a high-level view of the SMT formulas and the information required to be represented in it, and later present the detailed representation.

Observe that *MAD* needs to consider all possible executions of functionalities, transactions and interleavings where each execution is represented as a graph of operations. Hence, *MAD* implicitly searches over all possible graphs that can be built using the available system components. *MAD* does not explicitly build these graphs, but rather leverages SMT to encode the search space in order to check if it is possible to build a graph corresponding to an anomaly. Therefore, each satisfiable assignment to the SMT formula will correspond to a particular execution with an anomaly. Otherwise, if the SMT formula is unsatisfiable, then no anomaly can be produced for all possible executions of the system's functionalities.

We base our anomaly detection on Adya et al. definition of anomaly [2]. An execution is represented as a graph, where vertices correspond to operations belonging to transactions and edges represent data dependencies between operations. An anomaly is present if the graph is cyclic and contains at least two dependency edges and at least two operations belonging to the same transaction, also represented as an edge. As such, we must encode the transactions' operations and the data dependencies that different operations may present.

Two operations might belong to different transactions, executing in different microservices, but belong to the same functionality. Operations in the same functionality must also execute in isolation to provide equivalent execution to the monolith, and interleavings may generate anomalies. Hence, we encode information regarding the functionality and microservice associated with each operation.

First, we represent the basic elements of the system (operations, sub-transactions, original transactions, and microservices). Second, the associations between the basic elements (e.g., to which sub-transaction does a given operation belongs). Third, the consistency guarantees offered by the environment where the microservices execute. Fourth, the possible types of relations between operations. Lastly, the format of the cycles *MAD* wants the SMT solver to find.

Table 1. Key functions used in formulas.

Function	Description
otime(O)	returns the instant of time when operation O executes
oname(O)	returns the operation name ($OName$) of operation O
tname(T)	returns the sub-transaction name ($TName$) of sub-transaction T
fname(F)	returns the original transaction name ($FName$) of original transaction F
mname(O)	returns the microservice's name ($MName$) where operation O is executed
parent(O)	returns the instance of sub-transaction (T) where operation O belongs
origtx(O)	returns the instance of original transaction (F) where operation O belongs

Table 2. Key predicates used in formulas.

Predicate	Description
is_update(O)	true if operation O is an update operation (update, insert, delete)
ST(O, O)	true if both operation's instances (O, O) belong to the same instance of sub-transaction (ST)
SOT(O, O)	true if both operation's instances (O, O) belong to the same instance of original transaction (SOT)
WR(O, O)	true if there is a write followed by a read dependency (WR) between operation's instances (O, O)
RW(O, O)	true if there is a read followed by a write dependency (RW) between operation's instances (O, O)
WW(O, O)	true if there is a write followed by a write dependency (WW) between operation's instances (O, O)
vis(O, O)	true if the visibility effects of the first instance are visible to the second instance of operation's instances (O, O)
ar(O, O)	true if the first instance is executed before the second instance of the operation's instances (O, O)
D(O, O)	true if there is any dependency relation between operation's instances (O, O) (WR, RW, or WW)
X(O, O)	true if there is any relation between operation's instances (O, O) (ST, SOT, WR, RW, or WW)

Representation of the Basic Elements To represent instances of the operations, sub-transactions, and original transactions, MAD uses three sorts, O, T, and F, respectively. Based on the AR, MAD defines a unique name for each operation, sub-transaction, original transaction, and microservice. These unique identifiers are declared using the following sorts: $ONames$ for operations; $TNames$ for sub-transactions; $FNames$ for original transactions; and $MNames$ for microservices. Associated with the basic elements, there are functions and predicates used in the formulas, listed in Table 1 and Table 2.

Formula Components Let $FNames = \{Txn_1, \ldots, Txn_f\}$ denote the name set of f original transactions and let $TNames = \{Txn_{1,1}, \ldots, Txn_{f,t}\}$ denote the name set of sub-transactions, where $Txn_{i,j}$ refers to the jth sub-transaction in original transaction Txn_i. Moreover, let $ONames = \{Op_1, \ldots, Op_k\}$ and $MNames = \{M_1, \ldots, M_m\}$ denote the name set of k update operations and m microservices, respectively. For any two operations Op_i and Op_j from the same transaction where Op_i occurs before Op_j, then we have $j > i$. Finally, let $F(Op_i)$, $T(Op_i)$ and $M(Op_i)$ denote the names of the original transaction, sub-transaction and microservice of execution for operation Op_i. Note that all these name sets and name associations are defined through a simple analysis of the program. Afterwards, these are used to encode the relations between the system's components as follows (see Figure 4):

System Component's Constraints:

$$\forall o_1, o_2 \in O : WR(o_1, o_2) \Rightarrow vis(o_1, o_2) \tag{1}$$
$$\forall o_1, o_2 \in O : WW(o_1, o_2) \Rightarrow ar(o_1, o_2) \tag{2}$$
$$\forall o_1, o_2 \in O : RW(o_1, o_2) \Rightarrow \neg vis(o_2, o_1) \tag{3}$$
$$\forall o_1 \in O : is\_update(o_1) \Leftrightarrow (oname(o_1) = Op_1 \vee \ldots \vee oname(o_1) = Op_k) \tag{4}$$
$$\forall o_1 \in O,\ Op_j \in ONames : (oname(o_1) = Op_j) \Rightarrow ((tname(parent(o_1)) = T(Op_j)) \tag{5}$$
$$\forall o_1 \in O,\ Op_j \in ONames : (oname(o_1) = Op_j) \Rightarrow ((fname(origtx(o_1)) = F(Op_j)) \tag{6}$$
$$\forall o_1 \in O,\ Op_j \in ONames : (oname(o_1) = Op_j) \Rightarrow (mname(o_1) = M(Op_j)) \tag{7}$$
$$\forall o_1, o_2 \in O : ar(o_1, o_2) \Rightarrow (otime(o_1) < otime(o_2)) \tag{8}$$
$$\begin{aligned}&\forall o_1, o_2 \in O,\ Op_i, Op_j \in ONames,\ j > i,\ F(Op_i) = F(Op_j) :\\ &\qquad ((parent(o_1) = parent(o_2)) \vee (origtx(o_1) = origtx(o_2)) \wedge (oname(o_1) = Op_i) \wedge\\ &\qquad (oname(o_2) = Op_j)) \Rightarrow (otime(o_1) < otime(o_2))\end{aligned} \tag{9}$$
$$\forall o_1, o_2 \in O : D(o_1, o_2) \Rightarrow (\neg(ST(o_1, o_2) \vee SOT(o_1, o_2)) \wedge (WW(o_1, o_2) \vee WR(o_1, o_2) \vee RW(o_1, o_2))) \tag{10}$$
$$\forall o_1, o_2 \in O : X(o_1, o_2) \Rightarrow (ST(o_1, o_2) \vee SOT(o_1, o_2) \vee D(o_1, o_2)) \tag{11}$$

Consistency Models Constraints:

$$\forall o_1, o_2, o_3 \in O : (ST(o_1, o_2) \wedge vis(o_1, o_3) \wedge (mname(o_1) = mname(o_3))) \Rightarrow vis(o_2, o_3) \tag{12}$$
$$\forall o_1, o_2, o_3 \in O : (ST(o_1, o_2) \wedge vis(o_3, o_1) \wedge (mname(o_1) = mname(o_3))) \Rightarrow vis(o_3, o_2) \tag{13}$$
$$\forall o_1, o_2 \in O : (ar(o_1, o_2) \wedge (mname(o_1) = mname(o_2))) \Rightarrow vis(o_1, o_2) \tag{14}$$

Edge Type Constraints:

$$\forall o_1, o_2 \in O : (parent(o_1) = parent(o_2)) \Leftrightarrow ST(o_1, o_2) \tag{15}$$
$$\forall o_1, o_2 \in O : ((origtx(o_1) = origtx(o_2)) \wedge (parent(o_1) \neq parent(o_2))) \Leftrightarrow SOT(o_1, o_2) \tag{16}$$

Cycle Length Constraints:

$$\begin{aligned}&\exists o_1, o_2, \ldots o_k \in O : Distinct(o_1, o_2, \ldots, o_k) \wedge (ST(o_1, o_2) \vee SOT(o_1, o_2)) \wedge D(o_2, o_3) \wedge \ldots\\ &\qquad \wedge X(o_i, o_{i+1}) \wedge \ldots \wedge D(o_k, o_1)\end{aligned} \tag{17}$$

Fig. 4. ***MAD***'s models constraints

- **C1:** Every two instances of operations related by an *WR* edge have the effects of the first instance visible to the second instance (Equation 1).
- **C2:** Every two instances of operations related by an *WW* edge have the first instance happening before the second instance (Equation 2).
- **C3:** Every two instances of operations related by an *RW* edge have the effects of the second instance not visible to the first instance (Equation 3).
- **C4:** Every instance of an update operation must have an *OName* from the set of update operations names, and vice-versa (Equation 4).
- **C5-C7:** Every instance operation with a given *OName* needs to belong to an instance of sub-transaction (specific *TName*), original transaction (specific *FName*) and microservice (specific *MName*) as specified in Equations 5, 6 and 7.
- **C8:** Every two instances of operations with an *ar* relation between them follow an execution order where the first instance occurs before the second (Equation 8).
- **C9:** Every two instances of operations that belong to the same original transaction instance need to follow a sequential execution order according to their order in the Java program (Equation 9).

- **C10:** Every two instances of operations that have a dependency relation between them (D) do not have an ST or SOT relation and do have an WW, WR or RW relation (Equation 10).
- **C11:** Every two instances of operations that have any relation between them (X) do have an ST, SOT, WW, WR or RW relation (Equation 11).

Consistency Models To make an analysis faithful to the environment where the microservice systems will execute, operations of the same sub-transaction respect Serializability. Also, all sub-transactions that execute at a given microservice respect Serializability (even if they belong to different functionalities). Serializability is encoded into the SMT formula by the combination of three constraints: *Read Committed*, *Repeatable Read*, and *Linearizability* [6,1], which are presented in Figure 4.

- **C12 (Read Committed):** for every three instances of operations (o_1, o_2, o_3), if o_1 and o_2 belong to the same instance of sub-transaction, the effects of o_1 are visible to o_3, and o_1 and o_3 belong to the same microservice, then the effects of o_2 are also visible to o_3 (Equation 12).
- **C13: (Repeatable Read):** for every three instances of operations (o_1, o_2, o_3), if o_1 and o_2 belong to the same instance of sub-transaction, the effects of o_3 are visible to o_1, and o_1 and o_3 belong to the same microservice, then the effects of o_3 are also visible to o_2 (Equation 13).
- **C14 (Linearizability):** for every two instances of operations (o_1, o_2), if o_1 happens before o_2, and o_1 and o_2 belong to the same microservice, then the effects of o_1 are visible to o_2 (Equation 14).

Types of Edges To encode the ST and SOT edges, *MAD* expresses the following two properties, respectively:

- **C15:** Every two instances of operations that belong to the same instance of sub-transaction are related via an ST edge, and vice-versa (Equation 15).
- **C16:** Every two instances of operations that belong to the same instance of original transaction and do not belong to the same instance of sub-transaction are related via an SOT edge, and vice-versa (Equation 16).

For the dependency edges (RW, WR, WW), constraints are defined for each pair of sub-transactions to establish whether or not it is possible to have a dependency between instances of operations of those sub-transactions. If two operations o_1 and o_2 access different tables, no dependency can ever occur. Otherwise, if either o_1 or o_2 executes an update operation, then a constraint is added to verify if it is possible to have a row where the operations conflict.

Cycles Assertions A cyclic anomalous graph is a cycle with at least one *ST* or *SOT* edge and at least two dependency edges (*RW*, *WR*, *WW*). This is captured in Equation 17 where k denotes the size of the cycle.

Recalling the example anomaly presented in Figure 1(c). *MAD* detects that anomaly by finding the cyclic graph that can be seen in Figure 1(d). The cycle contains two *SOT* edges and two dependency edges (*RW* and *WR*), and represents the interleaving of the original transactions Total and Transfer.

3.7 Metrics Extractor

MAD includes a Metrics Extractor component, which gathers information regarding the possible anomalies that the microservices application may face when the given decomposition is used. The information collected includes the total number of anomalies, the number of anomalies per type and, finally, the entities, functionalities, and sub-transactions involved in each anomaly. These indicators allow the programmer to have a better understanding of the potential anomalies and the amount of effort required to prevent each of them. Furthermore, these metrics capture the types of anomalous behaviors to be expected and the combinations that originate these anomalies.

All metrics are generated based on the analysis of the satisfiable assignments of the SMT formula. Each satisfiable assignment corresponds to an anomaly, and its type is classified as defined in Adya et al [2]. Moreover, *MAD* also groups the anomalies by sets of entities, functionalities, and sub-transactions. Furthermore, *MAD* categorizes the anomalies as either *core anomalies* or *extensions*. A *core anomaly* is one whose execution cycle has the minimum size required to express its categorized anomaly. *Extensions* are anomalies whose execution cycle includes a *core anomaly* with additional operations that do not affect the categorized anomaly. This distinction is important since if a developer fixes the source of the *core anomalies*, it will also remove its related *extensions*.

4 Evaluation

MAD [1] aims at identifying the anomalies that can emerge when migrating a monolith to microservices following a given decomposition. Note that *MAD* is the first tool that automatically identifies anomalies when migrating an application from a monolithic to a microservices architecture. Hence, the experimental evaluation is mainly targeted at analyzing *MAD*'s performance, since we are unable to perform a direct comparison with other tools. Our experimental evaluation focuses on the following key research questions:

- **RQ1:** Can *MAD* find differences between decompositions?
- **RQ2:** How long does it take to execute *MAD*?

[1] *MAD*'s code, benchmarks, and results presented in this paper are publicly available at https://doi.org/10.5281/zenodo.18302601.

- **RQ3:** Can *MAD* classify the anomalies to help identify access patterns that cause the errors?
- **RQ4:** How effective is the *Divide and Conquer* strategy?

4.1 Experimental Setup

We use seven applications found on GitHub as benchmarks for the experimental evaluation. Our process to set the benchmarks consists of three steps: 1) gathering monolithic applications from GitHub; 2) adapting them to the syntax processed by *MAD* ; 3) generating two microservices decompositions of each application with the help of a migration tool [29] that supports programmers on the task of grouping the entities by the microservices.

The applications we have used in the evaluation are the following:

- **TPC-C**[2] is defined in the OLTP-Bench [12] project and simulates the behavior of a delivery and warehouse management system;
- **FindSportMates**[3] (findmates) is an application used as a benchmark in other microservices works [38,33] and simulates a platform where users can manage and find events to connect with other users;
- **jpabook**[4] simulates a shop where members can order items and track the delivery process;
- **JPetStore**[5] (jpetstore) is an application highly used by previous microservices works [38,14,9,22,39] and simulates an online pet store where each user has an account and can browse through a catalog of pets to choose which pets they want to order;
- **spring-petclinic**[6] (petclinic) is an application used as a benchmark by a previous microservices work [14] and simulates the operation of a pet clinic;
- **myweb**[7] is an application that simulates the behavior of the web allowing users to have roles and manage resources;
- **spring-mvc-react**[8] (react) is a platform where users can post questions and answers with tags associated with them. Besides that, the system also allows users to upvote or downvote publications, which influences the users' popularity.

We have selected these benchmarks because they cover a wide range of domain areas and have implementations that address real-world scenarios and, yet, they are simple enough to be processed by the *MAD* prototype in a reasonable time. For each benchmark, we analyze three decompositions. First, the *mono*

[2] https://github.com/oltpbenchmark/oltpbench/tree/master/src/com/oltpbenchmark/benchmarks/tpcc
[3] https://github.com/chihweil5/FindSportMates
[4] https://github.com/holyeye/jpabook/tree/master/ch12-springdata-shop
[5] https://github.com/mybatis/jpetstore-6
[6] https://github.com/spring-projects/spring-petclinic
[7] https://github.com/Jdoing/myweb
[8] https://github.com/noveogroup-amorgunov/spring-mvc-react

Table 3. Application Profiles.

			microservices			transactions		
Benchmark	**#E**	**#F**	**mono**	**"best"**	**full**	**mono**	**"best"**	**full**
TPC-C	9	5	1	9	9	5	6	22
findmates	2	9	1	2	2	9	13	13
jpabook	5	10	1	2	5	10	15	21
jpetstore	13	11	1	3	13	11	17	48
petclinic	6	12	1	2	6	12	14	27
myweb	5	20	1	2	5	20	22	32
react	5	23	1	2	5	23	28	39

(E=entities; F=functionalities)

decomposition, which represents the monolithic version of the benchmark. For this decomposition, the number of sub-transactions equals the number of functionalities. Second, the *"best"* decomposition, which is the one with the highest *Silhouette Score* (a metric used to assess how well the clustering of the entities is done) calculated by the migration tool [29]. At last, in the *full* decomposition, each entity is managed by a different microservice. Table 3 provides an overview of application complexity, such as the number of entities and functionalities, and the resulting decomposition sizes.

In this context, we use *MAD* considering four as the maximum cycle length. The process to choose this value consisted of starting with value three since it is the minimum number of edges required to detect a cycle with an anomaly, and incrementing it to ensure that all core anomaly types could be detected (requires length four [7,30]), while still assuring that *MAD* was able to analyze the benchmarks within a timeout limit of 4 hours (14400 seconds).

The evaluation was performed in a virtual machine with 32 virtual CPU cores running on two Intel(R) Xeon(R) Gold 5320 CPUs at 2.2GHz and 128GB of DDR4 RAM with Intel Optane Memory configured in App Mode. The virtual machine uses Ubuntu 18.04.4 LTS, Java 8, and version 4.12.3 of Z3 with the default configuration.

4.2 RQ1: Can *MAD* find differences between decompositions?

Table 4 presents the results obtained when applying *MAD* to our benchmarks. Results show that *MAD* allows the programmers to assess how problematic each decomposition will be, therefore enabling them to make a more informed decision when migrating to microservices. For instance, in *jpabook*, *jpetstore*, and *react*, even their *"best"* decompositions have anomalies. This occurs because the *"best"* decompositions for these cases require the functionalities to be chopped into multiple sub-transactions, opening the door for more interleaving between the functionalities. Note also that all microservices decompositions, except *jpetstore best* and *myweb full*, have a fairly higher number of anomalies when compared with the number of *core anomalies*. Thus, a fair portion of the anomalies found

Table 4. Anomalies detected.

	MAD								
	core anomalies			total anomalies			execution time (s)		
Benchmark	**mono**	**"best"**	**full**	**mono**	**"best"**	**full**	**mono**	**"best"**	**full**
TPC-C	0	0	28	0	0	98	10	9	306
findmates	0	0	0	0	0	0	23	31	31
jpabook	0	22	25	0	70	79	48	136	222
jpetstore	0	40	85	0	52	188	454	7,239	10,249
petclinic	0	0	0	0	0	0	93	89	128
myweb	0	0	7	0	0	7	309	358	514
react	0	13	18	0	45	58	545	996	1,517

(E=entities; F=functionalities)

(between 54 and 72 percent) are simply *extensions* of smaller number of core anomalies and, therefore, can be eliminated if the core anomalies are eliminated. The *findmates* and *petclinic* benchmarks have no anomalies in any of their decompositions because their operations are mostly reads and the functionalities tend to be short. This, respectively, leads to fewer conflicts between accesses and fewer interleavings between functionalities.

4.3 RQ2: What is *MAD*'s execution time?

The last column of Table 4 shows the time required to execute MAD on each decomposition. As can be observed, although *MAD* can analyze these cases, *MAD* often requires non-negligible time to perform the analysis. *MAD* does not require long executions for simple applications, nor when the decompositions do not use many sub-transactions. However, for complex applications with a high number of functionalities and/or sub-transactions, *MAD* needs to analyze a large number of combinations of transactions, therefore taking more time to finish its execution. Nevertheless, since this is done at design-time, programmers can use *MAD* to try several decompositions to microservices before implementation.

4.4 RQ3: Can *MAD* Classify Anomalies?

Table 5 shows the number of anomalies found for each decomposition by type of anomaly. We are only considering the analysis of the sub-transactions metrics for one decomposition, but this can be done for all decompositions. Note that we omit the results for the *findmates* and *petclinic* benchmarks since they have no anomalies in any decomposition. Also, the *Write Skews* are counted together with the *Lost Updates* because the write skew pattern also corresponds to one of the lost update patterns. The only way to distinguish between them would be to also consider the rows accessed. If the same row was being accessed, then it would be a *Lost Update*. Otherwise, it would be a *Write Skew*. However, the current patterns used in our approach only consider the graph cycle edges and

Table 5. *MAD* anomalies found per type.

Benchmark	#DR "best" / full	#DW "best" / full	#LU/WS "best" / full	#LU/ "best" / full	#NRR "best" / full	#PR "best" / full	#RS "best" / full	#Ext "best" / full	#Total "best" / full
TPC-C	/	/ 13	/	/ 3	/	/	/ 12	/ 70	/ 98
jpabook	/	/	3 / 3	10 / 11	/	/	9 / 11	48 / 54	70 / 79
jpetstore	/	4 / 7	/	12 / 14	/ 2	/	24 / 62	12 / 103	52 / 188
myweb	/	/	/	/ 3	/	/	/ 4	/	/ 7
react	/	/	/	/	1 / 2	1 / 4	11 / 11	32 / 40	45 / 58

(DR=dirty read, DW=dirty write; LU=lost update; WS=write skew, NRR=non-repeatable read; PR=phantom read; RS=read skew, Ext=extensions)

Table 6. *TPC-C full core anomalies* entities.

Entities	#Anomalies	Anomalies Types
[oorder, order_line]	5	[DW, RS]
[customer, district]	4	[DW]
[customer, warehouse]	4	[DW]
[new_order, order_line]	4	[LU/WS, RS]
[new_order, oorder]	3	[LU/WS, RS]
[customer, new_order]	2	[LU/WS, RS]
[customer, oorder]	1	[DW]
[customer, order_line]	1	[DW]
[district, order_line]	1	[RS]
[district, stock]	1	[DW]
[district, warehouse]	1	[DW]
[order_line, stock]	1	[RS]

(DW=dirty write; LU=lost update; WS=write skew, RS=read skew

operation types, and do not include information regarding the accessed rows which are required to make this distinction.

Finally, *MAD* also analyses the satisfiable assignments provided by the SMT solver and provides the programmer access to which entities and functionalities are associated with the anomalies found. For example, Table 6 presents the *core anomalies* found in the *TPC-C full* decomposition. Developers may leverage this information to guide their decomposition design, identifying the most costly entity decouplings. For instance, notice that the combination of entities *[oorder, order_line]* are heavily coupled, as decomposing these entities into different microservices generates five new anomalies. Merging these entities into the same microservice could significantly reduce anomaly mitigation costs when migrating the application. Furthermore, Table 7 presents the combinations of sub-transactions that originate the *core anomalies* in the decomposition. This information highlights the key sections in the application that require more care when migrating the application, allowing developers to be better informed during the decomposition process on what anomalies they will face and what kind of techniques will be required to mitigate the effects of said anomalies.

4.5 RQ4: How effective is the Divide and Conquer strategy?

The results in Table 8 show that the divide and conquer strategy can significantly shorten the analysis time. Gains are more significant for complex cases since each SMT formula is much smaller, and it mitigates the time and space complexities by not considering all the original transactions simultaneously. As a result, all

Table 7. *TPC-C full core anomalies* sub-transactions.

Functionalities	Sub-transactions	#Anomalies	Anomalies Types
[payment]	[payment_0, payment_2]	4	[DW]
[payment]	[payment_1, payment_2]	4	[DW]
[delivery]	[delivery_0, delivery_1]	2	[LU/WS, RS]
[delivery]	[delivery_0, delivery_2]	2	[LU/WS, RS]
[delivery]	[delivery_0, delivery_3]	2	[LU/WS, RS]
[orderStatus, newOrder]	[orderStatus_1, orderStatus_2, newOrder_3, newOrder_7]	2	[RS]
[delivery, newOrder]	[delivery_0, delivery_2, newOrder_4, newOrder_7]	2	[RS]
[delivery, newOrder]	[delivery_1, delivery_2, newOrder_3, newOrder_7]	2	[RS]
[payment]	[payment_0, payment_1]	1	[DW]
[newOrder]	[newOrder_2, newOrder_6]	1	[DW]
[delivery]	[delivery_1, delivery_2]	1	[DW]
[delivery]	[delivery_1, delivery_3]	1	[DW]
[delivery]	[delivery_2, delivery_3]	1	[DW]
[newOrder, stockLevel]	[stockLevel_0, stockLevel_1, newOrder_2, newOrder_7]	1	[RS]
[newOrder, stockLevel]	[stockLevel_1, stockLevel_2, newOrder_6, newOrder_7]	1	[RS]
[delivery, newOrder]	[delivery_0, delivery_1, newOrder_3, newOrder_4]	1	[RS]

(DW=dirty write; LU=lost update; WS=write skew, RS=read skew

Table 8. Divide and conquer performance (s).

Benchmark	Without			Sequential			Parallel		
	mono	"best"	full	mono	"best"	full	mono	"best"	full
TPC-C	7	7	1,715	18	20	339	10	9	306
findmates	4	5	5	20	24	24	23	31	31
jpabook	7	4,263	5,342	37	220	286	48	136	222
jpetstore	38	(timeout)	(timeout)	850	7,670	10,435	454	7,239	10,249
petclinic	10	11	13	67	68	92	93	89	128
myweb	11	11	213	218	227	353	309	358	514
react	153	(timeout)	(timeout)	406	982	1,209	545	996	1,517

analysis can be performed within the time limit (4 hours = 14,400 seconds). Without this strategy, *MAD* exceeds the timeout when analyzing decompositions *"best"* and *full* of the *jpetstore* and *react* benchmarks. However, for simple cases, *MAD*'s performance tends to be worse with the divide and conquer strategy. This occurs because the strategy originates an overhead to *MAD*'s analysis by requiring unnecessary iterations over combinations with no anomalies. We also note that the strategy is not fully parallelizable, since the threads of bigger size combinations need to wait for all the threads of smaller size combinations to finish in order to start. Therefore, the analysis time for a given combination size is bounded by the analysis time of the slowest thread that is analyzing a combination of that size.

5 Conclusions and Future Work

This paper has presented *MAD*, the first framework that automatically detects anomalies that result from the migration of a monolith application to a microservices architecture. *MAD* avoids the under/overestimation limitations of previous works and can classify the anomalies according to the access patterns that cause them, thus helping the programmer by identifying scenarios that result in anomalies. Experimental results from applying *MAD* to different decompositions of benchmarks inspired by applications on GitHub show that *MAD* can offer insights on the complexity of a decomposition that are more precise than the metrics extracted by related work. We plan to extend the framework in several ways. For instance, we will add support for associations between entities in different microservices, such as JPA relationships, foreign keys, and semantic invariants that the system must respect.

Acknowledgments. This work was supported by national funds through Fundação para a Ciência e a Tecnologia, I.P. (FCT) under projects UID/50021/2025 (DOI: doi.org/10.54499/UID/50021/2025), UID/PRR/50021/2025 (DOI: doi.org/10.54499/-UID/PRR/50021/2025), PTDC/CCI-COM/2156/2021 (DOI: doi.org/10.54499/PTDC/-CCI-COM/2156/2021), 2023.14280.PEX (DOI: doi.org/10.54499/2023.14280.PEX), and LISBOA2030-FEDER-00771200 (DOI: doi.org/10.54499/2023.18452.ICDT).

Disclosure of Interests. The authors have no competing interests to declare that are relevant to the content of this article.

References

1. Jepsen consistency models. https://jepsen.io/consistency. Accessed: 24/12/2022.
2. Atul Adya, Barbara Liskov, and Patrick O'Neil. Generalized isolation level definitions. In *ICDE*, San Diego (CA), USA, February 2000.
3. Deepthi Akkoorath, Alejandro Tomsic, Manuel Bravo, Zhongmiao Li, Tyler Crain, Annette Bieniusa, Nuno Preguiça, and Marc Shapiro. Cure: Strong semantics meets high availability and low latency. In *ICDCS*, pages 405–414, Nara, Japan, June 2016.
4. João Almeida and António Silva. Monolith migration complexity tuning through the application of microservices patterns. In *ECSA*, L'Aquila, Italy, September 2020.
5. Nuha Alshuqayran, Nour Ali, and Roger Evans. A systematic mapping study in microservice architecture. In *SOCA*, Macau, China, 2016.
6. Peter Bailis, Aaron Davidson, Alan Fekete, Ali Ghodsi, Joseph Hellerstein, and Ion Stoica. Highly available transactions: Virtues and limitations. In *VLDB*, volume 7, page 181–192, Trento, Italy, November 2013.
7. Hal Berenson, Phil Bernstein, Jim Gray, Jim Melton, Elizabeth O'Neil, and Patrick O'Neil. A critique of ANSI SQL isolation levels. In *SIGMOD*, page 1–10, San Jose (CA), USA, May 1995.
8. Ranadeep Biswas, Diptanshu Kakwani, Jyothi Vedurada, Constantin Enea, and Akash Lal. MonkeyDB: Effectively testing correctness under weak isolation levels. In *OOPSLA*, Chicago (IL), USA, October 2021.
9. Miguel Brito, Jácome Cunha, and João Saraiva. Identification of microservices from monolithic applications through topic modelling. In *SAC*, page 1409–1418, Virtual Event, Republic of Korea, March 2021.
10. Phil Calçado. Building products at SoundCloud — Part I: Dealing with the monolith. https://developers.soundcloud.com/blog/building-products-at-soundcloud-part-1-dealing-with-the-monolith. Accessed: 14/12/2023.
11. Leonardo De Moura and Nikolaj Bjørner. Z3: An efficient SMT solver. In *TACAS*, TACAS'08, Budapest, Hungary, April 2008.

12. Djellel Difallah, Andrew Pavlo, Carlo Curino, and Philippe Cudre-Mauroux. OLTP-Bench: An extensible testbed for benchmarking relational databases. In *VLDB*, page 277–288, Trento, Italy, December 2013.
13. Alan Fekete, Dimitrios Liarokapis, Elizabeth O'Neil, Patrick O'Neil, and Dennis Shasha. Making snapshot isolation serializable. *ACM Trans. Database Syst.*, 30(2):492–528, jun 2005.
14. Gianluca Filippone, Nadeem Qaisar Mehmood, Marco Autili, Fabrizio Rossi, and Massimo Tivoli. From monolithic to microservice architecture: an automated approach based on graph clustering and combinatorial optimization. In *ICSA*, pages 47–57, L'Aquila, Italy, 2023.
15. Jonas Fritzsch, Justus Bogner, Stefan Wagner, and Alfred Zimmermann. Microservices migration in industry: Intentions, strategies, and challenges. In *ICSME*, pages 481–490, Cleveland (OH), USA, 2019.
16. Yu Gan and Christina Delimitrou. The architectural implications of cloud microservices. *IEEE Computer Architecture Letters*, PP:1–1, 05 2018.
17. Hector Garcia-Molina and Kenneth Salem. Sagas. In *SIGMOD*, page 249–259, San Francisco (CA), USA, December 1987.
18. Marijn Heule, Oliver Kullmann, Siert Wieringa, and Armin Biere. Cube and conquer: Guiding CDCL SAT solvers by lookaheads. In *HVC*, Haifa, Israel, 2011. Springer.
19. Jeremy Hillpot. 4 microservices examples: Amazon, Netflix, Uber, and Etsy. https://blog.dreamfactory.com/microservices-examples/. Accessed: 12/12/2023.
20. Steven Ihde and Karan Parikh. From a monolith to microservices + REST: the evolution of LinkedIn's service architecture. https://www.infoq.com/presentations/linkedin-microservices-urn/. Accessed: 14/12/2023.
21. Pooyan Jamshidi, Claus Pahl, Nabor Mendonça, James Lewis, and Stefan Tilkov. Microservices: The journey so far and challenges ahead. *IEEE Software*, 35:24–35, 05 2018.
22. Wuxia Jin, Ting Liu, Qinghua Zheng, Di Cui, and Yuanfang Cai. Functionality-oriented microservice extraction based on execution trace clustering. In *ICWS*, pages 211–218, San Francisco (CA), USA, 2018.
23. Sudhir Jorwekar, Alan Fekete, Krithi Ramamritham, and S. Sudarshan. Automating the detection of snapshot isolation anomalies. In *Proceedings of the 33rd International Conference on Very Large Data Bases*, page 1263–1274, Vienna, Austria, 2007. VLDB Endowment.
24. Anup Kalia, Jin Xiao, Rahul Krishna, Saurabh Sinha, Maja Vukovic, and Debasish Banerjee. Mono2micro: A practical and effective tool for decomposing monolithic java applications to microservices. In *ESEC/FSE*, page 1214–1224, Athens, Greece, August 2021.
25. Miika Kalske, Niko Mäkitalo, and Tommi Mikkonen. Challenges when moving from monolith to microservice architecture. In *ICWE*, pages 32–47, Rome, Italy, 02 2017.
26. Tim Kraska, Martin Hentschel, Gustavo Alonso, and Donald Kossmann. Consistency rationing in the cloud: Pay only when it matters. *Proc. VLDB Endow.*, 2(1):253–264, August 2009.
27. Tony Mauro. Adopting microservices at Netflix: Lessons for architectural design. https://www.nginx.com/blog/microservices-at-netflix-architectural-best-practices/. Accessed: 14/12/2023.
28. Kartik Nagar and Suresh Jagannathan. Automated detection of serializability violations under weak consistency. In *CONCUR*, Beijing, China, September 2018.

29. Luís Nunes, Nuno Santos, and António Silva. From a monolith to a microservices architecture: An approach based on transactional contexts. In *ECSA*, page 37–52, Paris, France, September 2019. Springer-Verlag.
30. Kia Rahmani, Kartik Nagar, Benjamin Delaware, and Suresh Jagannathan. Clotho: Directed test generation for weakly consistent database systems. In *OOPSLA*, Athens, Greece, October 2019.
31. Chris Richardson. *Microservices Patterns: With examples in Java*. November 2018.
32. Nuno Santos and António Silva. A complexity metric for microservices architecture migration. In *ICSA*, Salvador, Brazil, March 2020.
33. Anfel Selmadji, Abdelhak-Djamel Seriai, Hinde Lilia Bouziane, Rahina Oumarou Mahamane, Pascal Zaragoza, and Christophe Dony. From monolithic architecture style to microservice one based on a semi-automatic approach. In *ICSA*, pages 157–168, Salvador, Brazil, 2020.
34. Ruoyu Su, Xiaozhou Li, and Davide Taibi. Back to the future: From microservice to monolith. In *Microservices*, 2023.
35. Cheng Tan, Changgeng Zhao, Shuai Mu, and Michael Walfish. Cobra: Making transactional key-value stores verifiably serializable. In *OSDI*, Virtual Event, November 2020.
36. Douglas Terry, Vijayan Prabhakaran, Ramakrishna Kotla, Mahesh Balakrishnan, Marcos Aguilera, and Hussam Abu-Libdeh. Consistency-based service level agreements for cloud storage. In *SOSP '13*, November 2013.
37. Johannes Thones. Microservices. *IEEE Software*, 32(1):116, January 2015.
38. Pascal Zaragoza, Abdelhak-Djamel Seriai, Abderrahmane Seriai, Anas Shatnawi, and Mustapha Derras. Leveraging the layered architecture for microservice recovery. In *ICSA*, pages 135–145, Honolulu (HI), USA, 2022.
39. Yukun Zhang, Bo Liu, Liyun Dai, Kang Chen, and Xuelian Cao. Automated microservice identification in legacy systems with functional and non-functional metrics. In *ICSA*, pages 135–145, Salvador, Brazil, 2020.

EasyRpl

A web-based tool for modelling and analysis of cross-organisational workflows

Muhammad Rizwan Ali[1], Violet Ka I Pun[1], and Guillermo Román-Díez[2]

[1] Western Norway University of Applied Sciences, Bergen, Norway
[2] Universidad Politécnica de Madrid, Spain
{mral,violet.ka.i.pun}@hvl.no
guillermo.roman@upm.es

Abstract. Cross-organisational workflows involve multiple concurrent, collaborative workflows across different departments or organisations, needing effective coordination due to their interdependent nature and shared resource requirements. The complexity of designing and managing these workflows stems from the need for comprehensive domain knowledge and a unified understanding of task dependencies and resource allocation. This paper introduces EasyRpl, a web-based tool suite designed to manage cross-organisational workflows. EasyRpl consists of a simulator for visualising the impact of workflow changes, a peak resource analysis for identifying potential resource bottlenecks, and a time analysis for estimating execution time. These tools assist planners with detailed insights to optimise workflow efficiency and minimise disruptions, enhancing the management of complex, interdependent workflows.

Keywords: Cross-organisational workflow management · simulation · time analysis · peak resource analysis

1 Introduction

A cross-organisational workflow involves concurrent, collaborative workflows operating across different departments or multiple organisations. These workflows are interdependent, with tasks in one workflow often relying on the completion of tasks in other collaborative workflows. Additionally, they may share resources for task execution, necessitating effective coordination and synchronisation. For example, in a supply chain management workflow, different entities such as suppliers, manufacturers, distributors, and retailers each have their own workflows. Efficient coordination of these entities based on task dependencies and shared resources is required to ensure the timely and efficient delivery of products.

Designing cross-organisational workflows is inherently complex. It requires a comprehensive understanding of multiple specific domains and an overarching view of the dependencies on shared resources and task completion across the concurrent collaborative workflows, which makes the management and optimisation of these workflows challenging and error-prone. Minor local changes can be propagated unpredictably through the system, potentially disrupting the

E. Albert and C. Pasareanu (Eds.): FASE 2026, LNCS 16504, pp. 223–233, 2026.
https://doi.org/10.1007/978-3-032-22774-4_12

entire workflow network. This can lead to substantial financial loss or, in the context of critical supply chain, significant delays and customer dissatisfaction. In particular, in sectors such as healthcare, minor mistakes can result in fatalities, highlighting the critical need for meticulous workflow management. Our earlier work [10] introduced $\mathcal{R}$PL, a resource-sensitive formal modelling language designed to model cross-organisational workflows with shared resources. $\mathcal{R}$PL employs an actor-based concurrency model [1], incorporating notions of time advancement, task completion deadlines, and explicit task dependencies. A static cost analysis has been proposed to approximate the worst-case execution time (WCET) of workflows modelled in $\mathcal{R}$PL [9]. The analysis is implemented as part of the proof of concept tool $\mathcal{R}$PLTool [11], which also includes functionalities for modelling and simulation. However, $\mathcal{R}$PLTool has certain limitations: its static cost analysis module only translates an $\mathcal{R}$PL program into a set of cost equations, without providing the upper bound on the execution time as a solution. Solving these equations requires feeding them into a constraint solver, thus adding another layer of complexity, particularly for non-technical users. Furthermore, the simulator of $\mathcal{R}$PLTool only provides results in the form of raw data, which can be challenging to interpret when a high number of simulations are performed.

This paper presents EASY$\mathcal{R}$PL, a tool suite with a web-based interface, designed to assist in cross-organisational workflows management. EASY$\mathcal{R}$PL comprises three tools: *simulator*, *peak resource analysis* and *time analysis*. The *simulator* allows planners to see the potential impacts of changes in resource availability, efficiency (e.g., the experience of a human resource or the power of a machine), and the number of concurrent cases on metrics, such as deadline violations, execution time, and financial costs within collaborative workflows. Compared to $\mathcal{R}$PLTool, the simulation module in EASY$\mathcal{R}$PL uses graphical representation to present detailed simulation information, making it easier for users to visualise and understand the results. The *time analysis* in EASY$\mathcal{R}$PL, compared to [9], specifies the time to be consumed as a parametrised expression, and is coupled with PUBS [4], an off-the-shelf solver, so that the analysis returns an upper bound on the execution time in closed-form instead of a set of equations. Besides, EASY$\mathcal{R}$PL includes an additional *peak resource analysis* returning the maximum amount of resources that could be allocated at the same time in a cross-organisational workflow defined in $\mathcal{R}$PL, utilising the *peak* resource analysis presented in [6]. This helps identify potential resource bottlenecks and optimising resource allocation.

The paper is organised as follows: Sec. 2 introduces the architecture of EASY-$\mathcal{R}$PL and the characteristics of $\mathcal{R}$PL. Sec. 3 presents the web-interface of EASY-$\mathcal{R}$PL as well as the three accompanying tools. Sec. 4 concludes with the related work and future work. We refer the readers to the extended version of the paper [12] for further details of the tool suite.

2 Background

EASY$\mathcal{R}$PL is a web-based tool suite designed for workflow modelling and analysis, and its architecture is shown in Fig. 1. Through its web-interface, it takes as inputs a workflow modelled in $\mathcal{R}$PL, a map of shared resources along with tool-specific parameter configurations. Based on the selected analysis, users can execute one of the three tools, namely, Simulator, Peak Resource Analysis, and Time Analysis by first translating the input $\mathcal{R}$PL program in a tool-specific ABS [24] format prior to conducting the corresponding simulation or analysis. The execution results will subsequently be visualised on EASY$\mathcal{R}$PL's web-interface. In the remaining section we briefly describe the formal modelling language $\mathcal{R}$PL [9], illustrating with a simple example how workflows can be coupled through task dependencies and shared resources.

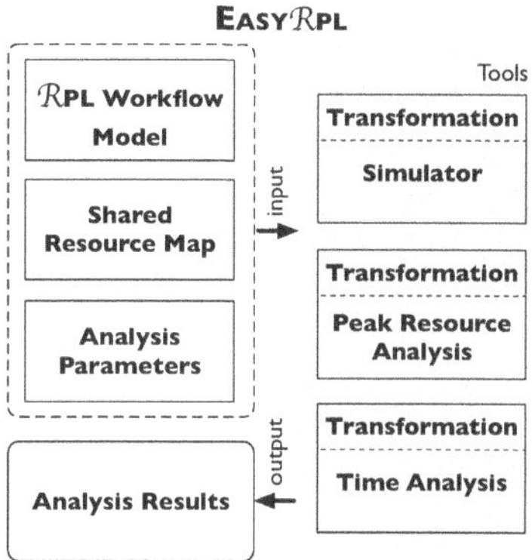

Fig. 1: EASY$\mathcal{R}$PL architecture

Resource Sensitive Workflow Modelling Language $\mathcal{R}$PL. The primary input of EASY$\mathcal{R}$PL is a workflow modelled in $\mathcal{R}$PL, which is a formal modelling language, inspired by ABS [24], designed for cross-organisational workflows. $\mathcal{R}$PL couples multiple workflows through shared resources and task dependencies and supports explicit notions of time advancement and task completion deadlines. An $\mathcal{R}$PL program consists of several components: first, the declaration of a module name, followed by interface and class declarations, and finally, a main block. Tasks in workflows are modelled as methods in a class in $\mathcal{R}$PL and are executed through method invocations, which can be either synchronous or asynchronous. The former type blocks the caller objects until the called methods return, whereas the latter is non-blocking, enabling both callers and callees to run in parallel. Each asynchronous method invocation is associated with a future, wherein the invoked method stores the return value upon completion. Every task may have a completion deadline, denoted by the notion **dl**, and can only be invoked if the tasks it depends on are completed, captured by an **after** clause containing the futures associated with the depending tasks. Time advancement in $\mathcal{R}$PL models is captured by **cost** statements.

Resources can be acquired and returned with statements **hold** and **release**. Resources shared across collaborative workflows are represented using a map that binds each resource r to a pair (b, Q), where b is a Boolean value indicating the availability, and Q is a set describing the qualities. These qualities include the category, efficiency, and financial usage cost of a resource r per time unit. For example, $[\ldots, \mathtt{r}_1 \mapsto (\mathit{true}, \{\mathtt{Doctor}, 25, 500, 1\}), \mathtt{r}_2 \mapsto (\mathit{false}, \{\mathtt{Nurse}, 7, 100, 1\}), \ldots]$ is a resource map where r_1 is a doctor with twenty five years of experience who costs 500 and is currently free, while r_2 is a nurse with seven years of experience who costs 100 and is currently busy. Note that the quality set Q each of the resource type can be extended with additional features. The rest of the language is rather standard, and we refer the readers to [9] for the full syntax and semantics.

Fig. 2 shows a simple example of patient-diagnosis workflow in a clinic that we use to illustrate the syntax of $\mathcal{R}$PL handling resource management and time advancement, namely, **hold**, **release** and **cost**. To diagnose a patient p in the example, a nurse is first acquired on Line 6 (L6), who takes a sample of the patient, which takes 5 time units (L7), and sents it to the lab for examination through an asynchronous method call on L8, expecting to receive the test report within 30 time unit. Note that the first parameter of the method refers to the identifier of the callee. While the sample is being examined, a doctor is acquired (L9) to perform diagnosis on the patient, which takes 10 time units (L10), together with the nurse. Based on the diagnosis and the test report from the lab, a prescription is issued. Note that $f?$ in the **after** clause on L11 ensures that the prescription can only be written after receiving the test report. Finally, both the nurse and doctor are released (L12). Another example illustrating other features of $\mathcal{R}$PL is shown in the extended version of the paper [12].

```
1  class Clinic {
2    Lab lab = new Lab;
3    Unit diagnose(Patient p) {
4      Unit x,y; Fut⟨Unit⟩ f;
5      Pair⟨List⟨Int⟩,Int⟩ r1, r2;
6      r1=hold({{Nurse,...}});
7      cost(5); // take sample
8      f=!test(lab,p) after dl 30;
9      r2=hold({{Doctor,...}});
10     cost(10); // perform diagnosis
11     x=prescribe(this) after f? dl null;
12     release(r1); release(r2);
13     return x;
14   }
15 }
```

Fig. 2: Patient-diagnosis workflow

3 EASY$\mathcal{R}$PL

EASY$\mathcal{R}$PL[3], is developed using the open-source toolkit EASYINTERFACE [18], which simplifies the process of building web-based GUIs. Fig. 3 shows the web-interface of EASY$\mathcal{R}$PL, which are divided into two parts: the top corresponds to the inputs to the tool suite while the bottom is a console for visualising the analysis results. The top part consists mainly of three modules, a code editor in the middle for editing $\mathcal{R}$PL code, an outline module shows the different classes and methods, and a File Manager on the left for file navigations. A toolbar on top of these three modules allows users to select the tool to be executed and specify the corresponding settings. As it is shown in the Tool Menu, EASY$\mathcal{R}$PL includes three tools to evaluate and analyse an $\mathcal{R}$PL model: a *simulator* that runs the model to detect potential violated deadlines and costs; a *peak analysis* that statically analyses the model and obtained the upper-bound on the resources allocated simultaneously; and a *time analysis* that infers the WCET of a workflow. We provide in the rest of the section the details of these three tools.

3.1 Simulator

The simulator in EASY$\mathcal{R}$PL, built on top of the ABS compiler, takes as input an $\mathcal{R}$PL program that is transformed into an ABS format, a map of shared resources, and the simulation parameters, including resource availability and efficiency as well as the number of concurrent instances and simulation iterations.

Resource availability and efficiency are key parameters, as in real-world conditions, resources often do not meet ideal availability or performance levels due

[3] https://costa.ls.fi.upm.es/rpltools/easyrpl/clients/web/

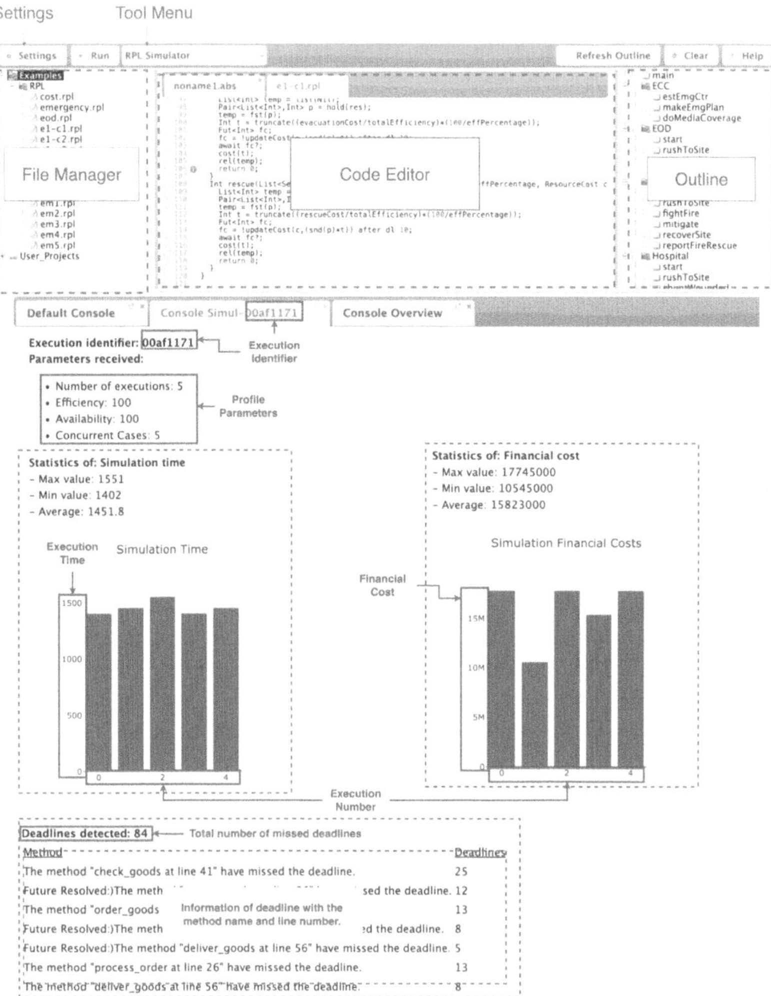

Fig. 3: Web-interface of EASY$\mathcal{R}$PL.

to factors such as maintenance or personnel inefficiency. Concurrent instances allow users to define how many instances of a workflow can run simultaneously. This helps in determining the limits of the current resource pool under different stress levels and demand scenarios, providing insights into system performance and behaviour under such conditions. Lastly, adjusting the number of simulation iterations allows the users to determine how many times the simulation runs to ensure consistent performance across trials.

The console at the bottom of Fig. 3 contains the output produced by the simulation of the code in the code editor. We can see that EASY$\mathcal{R}$PL shows the parameters used for the simulation, the execution time and the financial cost obtained for the different simulations and the missed deadlines with their corresponding source code lines.

3.2 Peak Resource Analysis

As described earlier, cross-organisational workflows have a set of shared resources which are acquired for performing some specific tasks and, when the tasks are finished, these resources are released to be used in other tasks. In this context, one of the most relevant information that an organisation needs to know is the maximum amount of resources of each type that could be required at the same time. To model this behaviour, as it was described in Sec. 2, $\mathcal{R}$PL includes two statements to acquire/free resources: **hold** and **release**.

Traditional cost analysis techniques [4,21,3,5] are defined to obtain an upper-bound on the amount of cumulative resources, i.e., resources that are never released. On the contrary, the resource analysis defined in [6] is able to obtain a *peak* upper-bound in the form of a cost expression, which over-approximates the maximum amount of resources that could be allocated simultaneously along the execution of an ABS [24] program. This peak analysis combines the *may-happen-in-parallel* analysis [7], which infers the sets of resource allocations that could occur simultaneously, and the resource analysis [3] of ABS programs, which obtains the resources allocated by each set of allocation sites.

In EASY$\mathcal{R}$PL, we apply this peak resource analysis to a cross-organisational workflow modelled in $\mathcal{R}$PL to obtain the peak upper-bound on the amount of resources that could be allocated at the same time. To do so, thanks to the similarities of the concurrency model, we use a specific transformation to produce an ABS program that preserves the concurrent properties relevant to the resource analysis: (1) we keep the classes, object creations and method invocations as they are in the $\mathcal{R}$PL program; (2) we keep the **await** statements to preserve the concurrent behaviour; (3) we transform the **hold** and **release** $\mathcal{R}$PL statements into ABS **acquire** and **release** statements to keep the type and cost of the resource allocated. The application of the peak cost analysis on the ABS program produces a list of upper-bound expressions (UBs) where each UB corresponds to the resources acquired by each set of **hold** statements that might be in use simultaneously. The peak cost of the entry method being analyzed is the maximum of all these UBs, which are of the form:

$$UB(p_1, p_2, \ldots, p_n)[l_1, l_2, \ldots, l_m] : \sum \#n_i * c(res(qua_i, res_i)) * k_i + \ldots ,$$

which sums the cost allocated simultaneously at different **hold** statements. For each **hold** statement, we have: $p_1, p_2, \ldots, p_n$, which are the parameters of the entry method; $l_1, l_2, \ldots, l_m$ corresponds to the line numbers in the $\mathcal{R}$PL of the **hold** statement; $\#n_i$ is the number of times the **hold** is executed; qua_i and res_i correspond, respectively, to the quality and type of resource defined in the **hold** statement; and, k_i which is the amount of resources allocated by the **hold** statement. Note that $c(\_)$ and $res(\_)$ are constructors used to keep in the UBs the quality and the type of resource allocated in the **hold** statement.

Remark that, the EASY$\mathcal{R}$PL interface also provides the **hold** statements whose resources might be allocated simultaneously. This information is indicated in EASY$\mathcal{R}$PL by having an arrow on the left of the corresponding line of code and, by clicking on the arrow, the interface highlights the **hold** statements that might occur simultaneously with the one of the selected line (see [12] for further details).

3.3 Time Analysis

In addition to the definition and allocation of the available resources, $\mathcal{R}$PL also allows the users to specify the amount of time needed to perform specific parts of a cross-organisational workflow using the statement **cost**(t), and with which time advances for t time units in the $\mathcal{R}$PL workflow model.

The work presented in [9] extends the time analysis proposed in [25] to analyse workflows modelled in $\mathcal{R}$PL. The idea is based on the use of synchronisation sets containing objects whose executions might be related to create a set of cost equations, which captures the execution time of the model. The solution to this set of cost equations represents an upper bound on the time taken for executing the model. The main difference between the analyses presented in [25] and [9] is in the input language and the features included: the one in [25] is a basic language intended to serve as a compiler target and includes neither conditional statements nor while loops. On the contrary, $\mathcal{R}$PL in the latter is a full modelling language which is intended to allow the users to define cross-organisational workflows. Another main difference between the time analysis of [25] and the analysis of [9] is in the generation and the resolution of the cost equations. While the latter expresses the WCET in the form of a set of cost equations without coupling to any constraint solvers, the former has been coupled with PUBS [4], an off-the-shelf equation solver, which includes a size analysis and a maximisation process, solving the cost equations and obtaining a closed-form upper-bound expressed in terms of the input parameters.

To calculate a closed-form upper bound of an $\mathcal{R}$PL model with EasyRPL, we first generate the corresponding ABS programs on which we apply the time analysis defined in [25]. To handle conditional statements in $\mathcal{R}$PL models, EasyRPL produces as many ABS programs as the number of potential execution paths the $\mathcal{R}$PL program could have. As a result, the WCET of the $\mathcal{R}$PL model is the maximum of the WCET of the produced ABS programs. The transformation for the time analysis is similar to the one in Sec. 3.2: it preserves the concurrent features of the program by keeping object creations, method invocations and synchronisations, but it transforms the $\mathcal{R}$PL **cost** statements into **wait** statements in the ABS program, on which we apply the PUBS solver, returning a closed-form upper-bound of the execution time of the $\mathcal{R}$PL model expressed in terms of the input parameters of the program or in terms of the maximum value taken by the actor fields in case the upper-bound depends on them.

Note that, the time analysis in both [25] and [9] cannot handle loops, and the loops used in $\mathcal{R}$PL models is for iterating simulation and does not involve any **cost** statement; thus, they are removed during the translation from $\mathcal{R}$PL to ABS for time analysis, whose correctness is not affected by such removal.

4 Related Work and Conclusions

This paper introduced EasyRPL, a tool suite with a web-based interface that assists workflow planners in simulating workflow changes, analysing resource usage, and estimating execution times. The simulator enables users to inspect the potential impacts of changes in resource availability, efficiency and concurrency level, which are presented graphically, on key performance metrics. The peak resource analysis tool helps identify potential resource bottlenecks, ensuring optimal resource allocation and preventing inefficiencies. The time analysis tool provides closed-form upper-bound time estimates, contributing to more precise planning and execution of workflows.

Related Work. Simulation-based tools and techniques have gained attention for their ability to assess resource policies, evaluate performance, and address real-world system issues [2,26]. UPPAAL [15] is being employed for modelling, simulating, and verifying workflows represented in timed automata. SWEET [19] has the capability to generate models using UPPAAL syntax [28], whose constructs are designed to be very small and simple [13]. In contrast, EASY$\mathcal{R}$PL allows the simulation of workflows modelled in $\mathcal{R}$PL, facilitating the integration of cross-organisational workflows involving shared resources and task dependencies.

Most research on cost analysis of sequential imperative programs has primarily focused on resource usage in terms of memory consumption with garbage collection [8,23]. Furthermore, resource analysis through the use of **malloc** and **free** instructions (analogous to our **hold** and **release** statements), has been extensively studied for sequential programs [16,17]. In [22], such analyses have been extended to parallel settings but do not deal with concurrency. The static analysis method introduced in [20] aimed at determining the peak cost of live virtual machines in a concurrent programming language that uses explicit **acquire** and **release** operations for virtual machines. Their technique primarily focuses on calculating the count of virtual machines, assigning one virtual machine per **acquire** instruction. In contrast, the approach we used in EASY$\mathcal{R}$PL extends beyond this by handling multiple types of resources concurrently.

Various tools have been developed to estimate the execution time of systems, e.g., Chronos [27] is a static WCET analysis tool specialised for embedded systems, modelling features like branch prediction, instruction cache, and out-of-order execution; and OTAWA [14] provides a framework for static analysis of machine code and WCET calculation. However, these existing tools are criticised for lacking advanced control flow mechanisms necessary for workflow modelling. In contrast, EASY$\mathcal{R}$PL supports a more expressive language enabling modelling of workflows with task dependencies, synchronisation, and shared resources.

Future Work. A natural extension would be an additional interface allowing users to graphically design workflows that can be translated to $\mathcal{R}$PL models. We also plan to validate the tool suite through real-world case studies in different industries to investigate its applicability in practice. In addition, we intend to assess the performance of the three tools, in particular their scalability, efficiency and accuracy, by comparing with other workflow modelling tools.

Acknowledgements. This work is part of the CROFLOW project: Enabling Highly Automated Cross-Organisational Workflow Planning, funded by the Research Council of Norway (grant no. 326249), and is partially funded by the Spanish MCIU, AEI and FEDER (EU) projects PID2021-122830OA-C44 and PID2024-157044OB-C33 and by the Comunidad de Madrid grant TEC-2024/COM-235 (DESAFíO-CM).

References

1. Agha, G.: Actors: a model of concurrent computation in distributed systems. MIT Press (1986). https://doi.org/10.7551/mitpress/1086.001.0001
2. Ahuja, H.N., Nandakumar, V.: Simulation model to forecast project completion time. Journal of construction engineering and management **111**(4), 325–342 (1985). https://doi.org/10.1061/(ASCE)0733-9364(1985)111:4(325)
3. Albert, E., Arenas, P., Correas, J., Genaim, S., Gómez-Zamalloa, M., Puebla, G., Román-Díez, G.: Object-Sensitive Cost Analysis for Concurrent Objects. Software Testing, Verification and Reliability **25**(3), 218–271 (2015). https://doi.org/10.1002/stvr.1569
4. Albert, E., Arenas, P., Genaim, S., Puebla, G.: Closed-Form Upper Bounds in Static Cost Analysis. Journal of Automated Reasoning **46**(2), 161–203 (2011). https://doi.org/10.1007/s10817-010-9174-1
5. Albert, E., Correas, J., Johnsen, E.B., Román-Díez, G.: Parallel Cost Analysis of Distributed Systems. In: Blazy, S., Jensen, T. (eds.) Proceedings of the 22nd International Static Analysis Symposium (SAS). LNCS, vol. 9291, pp. 275–292. Springer (2015). https://doi.org/10.1007/978-3-662-48288-9_16
6. Albert, E., Correas, J., Román-Díez, G.: Peak Resource Analysis of Concurrent Distributed Systems. Journal of Systems and Software **149**, 35 – 62 (2019). https://doi.org/10.1016/j.jss.2018.11.018
7. Albert, E., Flores-Montoya, A., Genaim, S., Martin-Martin, E.: May-Happen-in-Parallel Analysis for Actor-based Concurrency. ACM Transactions on Computational Logic **17**(2), 11:1–11:39 (2016). https://doi.org/10.1145/2824255
8. Albert, E., Genaim, S., Gómez-Zamalloa, M.: Heap space analysis for garbage collected languages. Science of Computer Programming **78**(9), 1427–1448 (2013). https://doi.org/https://doi.org/10.1016/j.scico.2012.10.008
9. Ali, M.R., Lamo, Y., Pun, V.K.I: Cost analysis for a resource sensitive workflow modelling language. Science of Computer Programming **225**, 102896 (2023). https://doi.org/10.1016/j.scico.2022.102896
10. Ali, M.R., Pun, V.K.I: Cost analysis for an actor-based workflow modelling language. In: Campos, S., Minea, M. (eds.) Proceedings of the 24th Brazilian Symposium on Formal Methods (SBMF). LNCS, vol. 13130, pp. 104–121. Springer (2021). https://doi.org/10.1007/978-3-030-92137-8_7
11. Ali, M.R., Pun, V.K.I: A static analyser for resource sensitive workflow models. In: David, C., Sun, M. (eds.) Proceedings of 17th International Symposium on Theoretical Aspects of Software Engineering (TASE). LNCS, vol. 13931, pp. 305–312. Springer (2023). https://doi.org/10.1007/978-3-031-35257-7_18
12. Ali, M.R., Pun, V.K.I, Román-Díez, G.: EasyRpl: A web-based tool for modelling and analysis of cross-organisational workflows. CoRR **abs/2502.20972** (2025). https://doi.org/10.48550/ARXIV.2502.20972
13. Andreas Gustavsson and Andreas Ermedahl and Björn Lisper and Paul Pettersson: Towards WCET analysis of multicore architectures using UPPAAL. In: Björn Lisper (ed.) Proceedings of the 10th International Workshop on Worst-Case Execution Time Analysis (WCET). OASIcs, vol. 15, pp. 101–112. Schloss Dagstuhl–Leibniz-Zentrum fuer Informatik (2010). https://doi.org/10.4230/OASIcs.WCET.2010.101
14. Ballabriga, C., Cassé, H., Rochange, C., Sainrat, P.: OTAWA: An Open Toolbox for Adaptive WCET Analysis. In: Min, S.L., Pettit, R., Puschner, P., Ungerer, T. (eds.) Proceedings of the 8th IFIP WG 10.2 International Workshop on Software

Technologies for Embedded and Ubiquitous Systems (SEUS). LNCS, vol. 6399, pp. 35–46. Springer (2010). https://doi.org/10.1007/978-3-642-16256-5_6

15. Behrmann, G., David, A., Larsen, K.G., Håkansson, J., Pettersson, P., Yi, W., Hendriks, M.: UPPAAL 4.0. In: Proccedings of the 3rd International Conference on the Quantitative Evaluation of Systems (QEST). pp. 125–126. IEEE Computer Society (2006). https://doi.org/10.1109/QEST.2006.59
16. Carbonneaux, Q., Hoffmann, J., Shao, Z.: Compositional certified resource bounds. In: Grove, D., Blackburn, S.M. (eds.) Proceedings of the 36th ACM SIGPLAN Conference on Programming Language Design and Implementation (PLDI). pp. 467–478. ACM (2015). https://doi.org/10.1145/2737924.2737955
17. Cook, B., Gupta, A., Magill, S., Rybalchenko, A., Simsa, J., Singh, S., Vafeiadis, V.: Finding heap-bounds for hardware synthesis. In: Proceedings of 9th International Conference on Formal Methods in Computer-Aided Design (FMCAD). pp. 205–212. IEEE (2009). https://doi.org/10.1109/FMCAD.2009.5351120
18. Doménech, J., Genaim, S., Johnsen, E.B., Schlatte, R.: EasyInterface: A toolkit for rapid development of GUIs for research prototype tools. In: Huisman, M., Rubin, J. (eds.) Proceedings of the 20th International Conference on Fundamental Approaches to Software Engineering (FASE). pp. 379–383. LNCS, Springer (2017). https://doi.org/10.1007/978-3-662-54494-5_22
19. Ermedahl, A.: A Modular Tool Architecture for Worst-Case Execution Time Analysis. Ph.D. thesis, Uppsala University, Sweden (2003), https://nbn-resolving.org/urn:nbn:se:uu:diva-3502
20. Garcia, A., Laneve, C., Lienhardt, M.: Static analysis of cloud elasticity. Science of Computer Programming **147**, 27–53 (2017). https://doi.org/https://doi.org/10.1016/j.scico.2017.03.008
21. Giachino, E., Johnsen, E.B., Laneve, C., Pun, V.K.I: Time complexity of concurrent programs – A technique based on behavioural types. In: Braga, C., Ölveczky, P.C. (eds.) Proceedings of the 12th International Conference on Formal Aspects of Component Software (FACS). LNCS, vol. 9539, pp. 199–216. Springer (2015). https://doi.org/10.1007/978-3-319-28934-2_11
22. Hoffmann, J., Shao, Z.: Automatic Static Cost Analysis for Parallel Programs. In: Vitek, J. (ed.) Proceedings of the 24th European Symposium on Programming (ESOP). LNCS, vol. 9032, pp. 132–157. Springer (2015). https://doi.org/10.1007/978-3-662-46669-8_6
23. Hofmann, M., Rodriguez, D.: Automatic type inference for amortised heap-space analysis. In: Felleisen, M., Gardner, P. (eds.) Proceedings of the 22nd European Symposium on Programming, (ESOP). LNCS, vol. 7792, pp. 593–613. Springer (2013). https://doi.org/10.1007/978-3-642-37036-6_32
24. Johnsen, E.B., Hähnle, R., Schäfer, J., Schlatte, R., Steffen, M.: ABS: A Core Language for Abstract Behavioral Specification. In: Aichernig, B.K., de Boer, F.S., Bonsangue, M.M. (eds.) Proceedings of the 9th International Symposium on Formal Methods for Components and Objects (FMCO). LNCS, vol. 6957, pp. 142–164. Springer (2012). https://doi.org/10.1007/978-3-642-25271-6_8
25. Laneve, C., Lienhardt, M., Pun, K.I, Román-Díez, G.: Time analysis of actor programs. Journal of Logical and Algebraic Methods in Programming **105**, 1 – 27 (2019). https://doi.org/10.1016/j.jlamp.2019.02.007
26. Li, J., González, M., Zhu, Y.: A hybrid simulation optimization method for production planning of dedicated remanufacturing. International Journal of Production Economics **117**(2), 286–301 (2009). https://doi.org/10.1016/j.ijpe.2008.11.005

27. Li, X., Liang, Y., Mitra, T., Roychoudhury, A.: Chronos: A timing analyzer for embedded software. Science of Computer Programming **69**(1), 56–67 (2007). https://doi.org/10.1016/j.scico.2007.01.014
28. Sundmark, D.: Structural System-Level Testing of Embedded Real-Time Systems. Ph.D. thesis, Mälardalen University, Sweden (2008), https://urn.kb.se/resolve?urn=urn:nbn:se:mdh:diva-488

ForumSeeker: Fusion Retrieval of Online Technical Forums for Effective Troubleshooting

Youyang Kim[1], Yaoping Ruan[2⋆], Young-Kyoon Suh[1], Liqiang Wang[3], and Byungchul Tak[1⋆]

[1] Kyungpook National University, Daegu, Republic of Korea
{youyangkim, yksuh, bctak}@knu.ac.kr
[2] PARC LLC, Independent researcher
ruanyaoping@gmail.com
[3] University of Central Florida, Orlando, FL, USA
Liqiang.Wang@ucf.edu

Abstract. Large language models (LLMs) have been actively applied in system troubleshooting, yet their effectiveness and accuracy are limited by the complexity of system domains. Online technical forums, rich with expert-contributed troubleshooting insights, are valuable resources for practitioners. However, finding the most relevant information for a given issue often requires considerable manual effort. We attribute this challenge to the multi-modality of forum posts, which contain a diverse mix of data artifacts, including code snippets, log messages, console outputs, commands, and descriptions. Traditional retrieval methods, which focus on a subset of these data types or treat the entire content as natural language, often fail to be effective. To address these challenges, we propose a comprehensive framework, *ForumSeeker*. The core concept is to incorporate the complete stack from the failure site and independently process heterogeneous data artifacts within forum posts, calculating relevance scores between different pairs of artifacts, then aggregating the results of individual pairs to achieve superior performance. Our evaluation demonstrates that *ForumSeeker* significantly outperforms five baselines, achieving at least 44.7% improvements in search ranking quality over the best competitor. Moreover, *ForumSeeker* successfully ranks ground-truth relevant forum posts within the top 10 results in 96.1% of cases.

1 Introduction

While generative AI using large language models (LLMs) excels at handling general questions and producing coherent responses, their reliability in providing correct answers remains a critical concern, especially in high-stakes domains like software troubleshooting. Modern software systems are increasingly complex to better handle time-consuming tasks. Technical forums such as Stack Overflow [1], Quora [2], Microsoft Community [3], and Apple Support Community [4] have become popular resources for technical staff. These forums offer a vast repository

⋆ Corresponding authors

E. Albert and C. Pasareanu (Eds.): FASE 2026, LNCS 16504, pp. 234–255, 2026.
https://doi.org/10.1007/978-3-032-22774-4_13

of knowledge and experience, allowing users to publish, discuss, and retrieve solutions to domain-specific issues.

However, retrieving the most relevant post remains a major NLP challenge, as practitioners heavily rely on search engines with significant limitations. First of all, it is quite arbitrary to compose the search query. Most queries focus on problem descriptions without runtime stack information, such as code snippets, command lines, etc. Second, both keyword-based search and semantic search using language models [5–7] yield fairly poor results. This inefficiency highlights the need for more robust NLP-driven retrieval methods that better leverage structured and unstructured technical context. Advances in dense retrieval, cross-encoder re-ranking, and LLM-augmented search could significantly improve precision, reducing manual effort in troubleshooting workflows.

To address these concerns, we propose a comprehensive troubleshooting approach, ForumSeeker, that retrieves relevant forum posts with significantly improved matching accuracy. The results can be used as a reference for troubleshooting or as a context for retrieval augmented generation (RAG) [8, 9] using LLMs. To this end, we first analyze the data characteristics of online forums and use multiple natural language processing (NLP) algorithms to retrieve the most relevant posts from them. At its core, our technique pairs each post with individual data artifact granularity with those from the failure system and evaluates the relevance by utilizing the most suitable language model for each artifact pair. Our scheme is an overarching approach of separating data artifacts in online forums, computing and aggregating relevance scores *across pairs of the artifacts* for better accuracy. Specific artifacts include code snippets, log messages, console output, command line with arguments, and failure description texts. We compose an ensemble approach with multiple language models, including CodeBERT[10], GraphCodeBERT[11], BM25[12], CodeT5+[13], and Sentence-BERT[14] by computing the individual relevance score between each data artifact collected from the failed system and forum articles, then aggregating using the weighted geometric mean. To the best of our knowledge, this is the *most comprehensive and general approach* to leveraging the multi-modality of the online forum as a reference for system troubleshooting.

We evaluated our ForumSeeker framework on several popular distributed applications (OpenStack [15], Spark [16], Elasticsearch [17], MongoDB [18], and Kafka [19]) on failures drawn from online forum cases we inspected. We meticulously reproduced 77 failure cases in total in our environment. The evaluation metrics are the Mean Reciprocal Rank (MRR) and the SuccessRate@k (R@k). The experimental results demonstrated that ForumSeeker showed significantly better performance in finding the relevant troubleshooting forum posts compared to 5 other baselines, including Google search, Text-embedding (Stella-en), GPT-4o, BM25, and an ensemble of 4 models (BM25, Sentence-BERT, CodeBERT, and CodeT5+). Overall, the MRR of ForumSeeker was 44.7% better than the best competitor. Furthermore, ForumSeeker ranked the ground-truth Stack Overflow documents within the top-10 of the returned list in 96.1% of the times, whereas the runner-up competitor obtained 72.7%. Our contributions are:

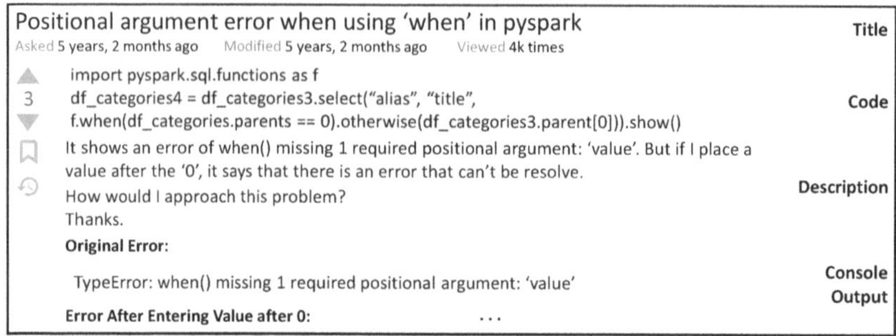

Fig. 1: Stack Overflow question with various data artifacts

- We propose a hierarchical relevance scoring framework that aggregates signals across heterogeneous technical artifacts (code, logs, console output, descriptions, commands) using an ensemble of domain-tuned language models and weighted geometric mean aggregation. Our approach outperforms public off-the-shelf retrievers by adapting to the linguistic patterns of troubleshooting discourse, achieving a 44.7% improvement in MRR.
- We introduce a structure-preserving chunking method that respects forum data topology, enabling joint encoding of runtime artifacts, a key gap in existing NLP pipelines. This is critical for tasks like semantic search and retrieval-augmented generation in technical domains.
- We release the first dataset with aligned failure descriptions, code snippets, logs, and console outputs to support research in technical QA and multi-modal retrieval. Alongside, we provide fine-tuned language models that address domain shift, supporting reproducibility in industrial NLP applications.

2 Background and Motivation

This section describes the characteristics of artifacts from online forums and why a straightforward search fails to retrieve the posts relevant to the user input.

2.1 Characteristics of Data in Online Forums

Taking Stack Overflow as an example, online technical forums contain a title, a question section, and zero or multiple follow-up posts, with some trying to provide an answer and some having further clarification questions. Within the multiple follow-up posts, one might be marked as an "accepted" answer by the question owner. The title and question sections usually describe the problem and, most likely, the operating environment where the problem was encountered. Given the nature of the technical forums, question sections may contain code snippets, commands, console outputs, log messages, configuration declaratives, etc., besides descriptive texts in human language.

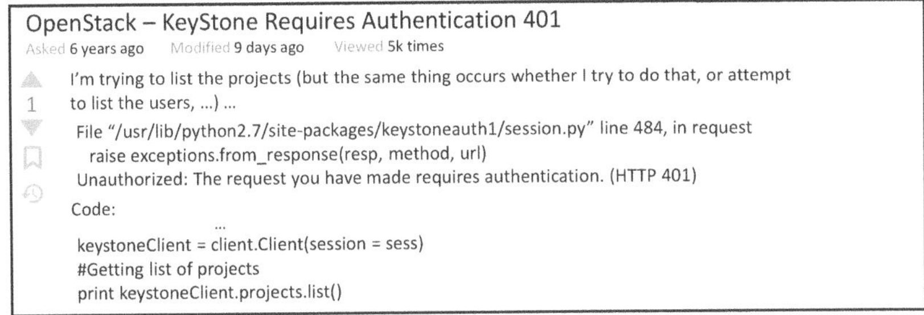

(a) Stack Overflow search results using the system output "The request you have made requires authentication." The URL of the Stack Overflow question is as follows: `https://stackoverflow.com/questions/46907661`

I cannot create a domain in openstack
Asked 6 years, 4 months ago Modified 6 years, 4 months ago Viewed 335 times

0

I am trying to create a domain in openstack. I tried this code

openstack domain create –description "Default Domain" default

...

The error is "the request you have made requires authentication. (HTTP 401)"

(b) Another Stack Overflow search result obtained using the same system output as (a). `https://stackoverflow.com/questions/44924242`

Fig. 2: Examples of two different posts obtained using the same system output message as input search text

When using forum knowledge for troubleshooting, the process generally involves two steps:

- *Identification of online posts most relevant to the problem encountered.* This step searches for sentences or keywords in error logs or human-generated descriptions.
- *Reviewing relevant posts and finding the best matching one.* This includes manually inspecting the information in the posts and trying solutions suggested by follow-up posts.

There are prior works trying to improve the quality of online forums [20, 21]. However, our primary focus in this work is to find the most relevant posts. Ideally, the successful first step returns a set of highly relevant posts whose size is small enough for human processing. From this point, it is relatively low-cost for the user to inspect them and identify the root cause or solutions of the problem among them. In general, we believe this step incurs much less effort than the efforts required to search for the most relevant posts in the first step. Figure 1 showcases the data artifacts in forum posts. Besides the title and description of the problem, forum users may upload various data items, such as code snippets, commands, log messages, and console output. Similarly, those data types (i.e., artifacts) are also available on the failed systems under investigation. Details of each data artifact are in technical report [22].

2.2 Why Straightforward Approaches Fail?

We provide two reasons why straightforward approaches fail.

- *Relevant posts may not always contain searchable descriptive text.* When a user searches for a failure description, the user hopes to find similar descriptive text, but the relevant post may have this information manifested in codes or commands. As shown in Figure 1, the codes in the post reveal a new data frame with conditions; however, the description part lacks sufficient information about what the codes do. In this case, simply comparing words in the user's descriptions with those in the posts may not give high similarity scores. It is necessary to compare the text and the code snippets, rather than relying solely on the user's descriptions, to better capture the relevant information.
- *Interpretation of log messages or console output needs to be context-dependent.* Posts with different problems may contain the same log messages or console output. For example, in Figure 2a, `"Unauthorized: The request you have made requires authentication."` appears when a user tries to list the project in `OpenStack`. But it also appears under a different operation as in Figure 2b. In this case, to correctly identify the relevant posts, it is necessary to leverage additional data, including code and commands, in the retrieval process.

A major challenge in retrieving relevant posts is that relying solely on the user's description is insufficient. Effective search requires utilizing multiple types of data and comparing information across these different artifacts, rather than depending only on textual descriptions. Moreover, existing methods typically rely on logs or descriptive text alone, which is often inadequate. To accurately identify relevant posts, retrieval techniques must incorporate contextual information, such as code snippets and commands, which convey essential details not always present in natural language descriptions or logs.

3 Design of ForumSeeker

3.1 ForumSeeker Workflow Overview

The core idea of this work is to utilize all the artifacts available in each post and tune the best-performing model for each artifact. To meet this design goal, we divide the workflow into three main steps: (i) dissecting forum posts into data artifacts (ii) calculating the relevance score of each artifact pair and (iii) aggregating the individual scores from all those pairs.

A close examination of the data artifacts reveals that they fall into three categories: (1) programming language type such as code snippet (`cod`), (2) (semi) natural language types such as log (`log`), console output (`cns`), and description (`des` and `tnd`), and (3) short phrase or token type such as commands (`cmd`).

Based on the characteristics of the artifact, we adopt five popular models: CodeBERT [10] or GraphCodeBERT [11] or CodeT5+ [13] for programming language type since all these models are trained with code, Sentence-BERT [14] for natural language types, and BM25 [12] for short phrases. The selection is primarily based

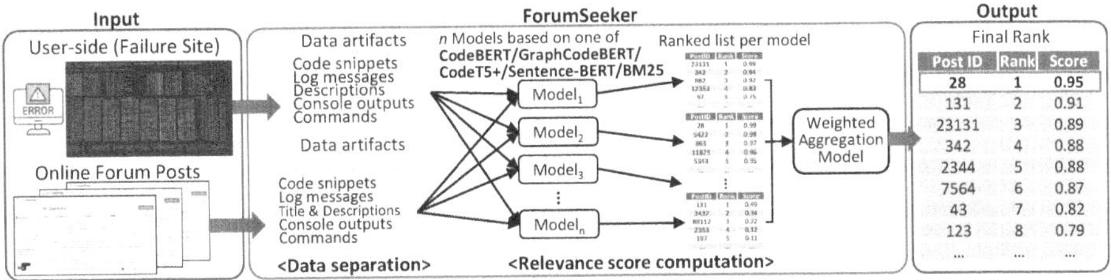

Fig. 3: Overall workflow of ForumSeeker. Online forum data are preprocessed into different data artifacts. Data artifacts of the failure sites are directly collected separately. CodeBERT, GraphCodeBERT, CodeT5+, Sentence-BERT, and BM25 are assigned to each artifact pair based on their data type. The final relevance score is computed using a weighted aggregation model from the individual relevance scores.

on the performance score of each model and is fairly intuitive. Figure 3 shows the overall workflow and pipelines. To enable the comparison of *heterogeneous* data artifact pairs, we introduce n models with the most suitable one for each data artifact pair, depicted at the center of Figure 3. The complete list of models and pairs is shown in Figure 4. For example, `m3` indicates the computation using CodeBERT for code from the user side and natural language in a forum post (`cod:tnd`).

We discover that not all pairs contribute to the matching results; thus, they are excluded from the computation. For example, the `cod` and `cmd` pair (m_5, m_{21}) and `log` and `cns` (m_9, m_{17}) rarely coexist; thus, they do not generate meaningful relevance scores. Intuitively, many operations are achieved by either commands or codes, but not both, and log messages usually contain console outputs. Only about 4.14% of posts in Stack Overflow contain both `cod` and `cmd`. We also found that only 4.91% of posts contained both `cmd` and `cns`, and 2.88% of posts contained both `cmd` and `log`. The scarcity of such data pairs also implies that the relationship between them is weak in the real world, and thus, models for them are likely unnecessary.

For `cod`, since CodeBert, GraphCodeBERT, and CodeT5+ are all relevant, we perform additional accuracy analysis using the Mean Reciprocal Rank (MRR) metric by applying each model to `cod:tnd`(m_3), `cod:log`(m_2), `cod:cns`(m_4), `des:cod`(m_{11}), `log:cod`(m_6), and `cns:cod` (m_{16}). It turns out that GraphCodeBERT generally performs better than CodeT5+ and CodeBERT at `cod:log`, `log:cod`, `cod:cns`, `cns:cod`. Presumably, this is due to the recognition of data flow structure in GraphCodeBERT, which resonates with the flow of code executions.

3.2 Data Artifacts Separation

Online forums do not provide interfaces to directly extract different types of data artifacts from posts. To address this, we designed a set of heuristics to automatically identify and extract such artifacts. Among five data artifact types, four types (code, command, log message, and console output) were all located

Data artifacts in forum posts (question part)

User-side data artifacts	Code snippet (cod)	Logs (log)	Description (tnd)	Console output (cns)	Command string (cmd)
Code snippet (cod)	cod:cod m_1 CodeT5+	cod:log m_2 GraphCodeBERT	cod:tnd m_3 CodeBERT	cod:cns m_4 GraphCodeBERT	cod:cmd m_5 X
Logs (log)	log:cod m_6 GraphCodeBERT	log:log m_7 Sentence-BERT	log:tnd m_8 Sentence-BERT	log:cns m_9 X	log:cmd m_{10} X
Description (des)	des:cod m_{11} CodeT5+	des:log m_{12} Sentence-BERT	des:tnd m_{13} Sentence-BERT	des:cns m_{14} Sentence-BERT	des:cmd m_{15} BM25
Console output (cns)	cns:cod m_{16} GraphCodeBERT	cns:log m_{17} X	cns:tnd m_{18} Sentence-BERT	cns:cns m_{19} Sentence-BERT	cns:cmd m_{20} X
Command string (cmd)	cmd:cod m_{21} X	cmd:log m_{22} X	cmd:tnd m_{23} BM25	cmd:cns m_{24} X	cmd:cmd m_{25} BM25

Fig. 4: Data artifact pairs and associated models (m_i) to compute the relevance scores. CodeBERT and GraphCodeBERT models are fine-tuned.

Table 1: Examples of each data artifact type

Data Type	Example
Code	spark = SparkSession.builder.master(*).appName(*)getOrCreate()
Log	[WARNING] nova.scheduler.utils [req-*] [instance: *] Setting instance to ERROR state.
Console output	Exception in thread * : Unable to make field private transient.
Command	Openstack image create * –file *
Description	I tried to retrieve a project list using the Keystone client. However, authentication failed.

within the same tag, such as the *<code>* tag in Stack Overflow. We came up with a set of regular expressions per data artifact type. The code was recognized by patterns such as assignments (e.g., 'a=b'), attribute access (e.g., 'a.b'), and common keywords (e.g., 'import', 'print', 'for', 'while', 'if', 'else', 'return', etc). To recognize logs, we looked for the lines that included timestamps and log levels such as 'ERROR', 'WARNING', 'DEBUG', and 'INFO'. Console output was classified based on keywords. Error messages in console output typically contain words like "Traceback (most recent call last)," "exception in thread," "exception," and "errno=," and we classified messages containing these words as console output. For command identification, we collected the shell commands of applications from the documentation and used them in the regex matching. Specifically, `OpenStack` commands follow the format "openstack [command] [options]", while `MongoDB` commands takes the form "db.[collection].[method].()". Examples of the classified data types are shown in Table 1.

3.3 Relevance Score Computation

Comparison of Natural and Programming Languages. To compare natural language (NL) and programming language (PL), we adopt the transformer-based code-pretrained model. The transformer-based code-pretrained model has two types of architectures, known as 'cross-encoder' and 'bi-encoder.' The cross-encoder, such as `CodeBERT` [10], encodes the pair of NL and PL and computes the relevance between NL-PL. The `GraphCodeBERT[11]` and `CodeT5+-embedding` [13] are bi-encoders that encode NL and PL separately and compute the similarity between the two embeddings. Fine-tuning of these models are described in Section 4.1

Relevance score of cross-encoder. In a given user-side data artifact u_i and forum-side k^{th} post's data artifact $v_{j,k}$, we assume there are X number of artifact type i in u_i and Y number of artifact type j in $v_{j,k}$. For example, three separate code blocks can be in the kth post, $v_{cod,k}$, which gives $Y = 3$. We denote the xth and y^{th} artifacts in u and v as $u_{i,x}$ and $v_{j,k,y}$, respectively, and $1 \leq x \leq X$ and $1 \leq y \leq Y$. For cross-encoder, we concatenate the code and other data artifacts. Then, the concatenated artifact is tokenized into `[CLS]` $u^1_{i,x}$ $u^2_{i,x}$, $\cdots$ $u^N_{i,x}$ `[SEP]` $v^1_{j,k,y}$ $v^2_{j,k,y}$, $\cdots$, $v^M_{j,k,y}$ `[SEP]`, where N and M are the token counts of $u_{i,x}$ and $v_{j,k,y}$, respectively. This sequence of input tokens is passed to `CodeBERT` to compute the contextualized representation of each token. We feed the representation of `[CLS]` token into a binary classification layer followed by a softmax function. To measure the semantic relevance between two given artifacts $u_{i,x}$ and $v_{j,k,y}$ (e.g., code, $u_{cod,1}$ and the natural language description, $v_{tnd,k,2}$), we use the predicted probability of the classifier as the relevance score computed as follows:

$$s_{h,k} = \sum_{x=1}^{X} \max \{prob_{i,j,x,y,k} | 1 \leq y \leq Y\} \tag{1}$$

where h is the model index, and $prob_{i,j,x,y,k}$ denotes the relevance probability (i.e., the probability of the positive class). This is obtained by feeding the `[CLS]` token representation of the input pair ($u_{i,x}$ and $v_{j,k,y}$) into a binary classifier followed by a softmax function.

Relevance score of bi-encoder. We assume the same calculation method as in `CodeBERT`. In `GraphCodeBERT` and `CodeT5+-embedding`, the embedding (denoted as `[VEC]`) of two data artifacts is separately generated, and the inner product is computed to obtain the relevance score, $s_{h,k}$.

$$s_{h,k} = \sum_{x=1}^{X} \max \{([VEC]_{i,x} \cdot [VEC]_{j,k,y}) | 1 \leq y \leq Y\} \tag{2}$$

where h is model index, $[VEC]_{i,x}$ and $[VEC]_{j,k,y}$ are embedding representations of xth user-side data of artifact type i and y^{th} forum-side data of artifact type j in k^{th} forum post, respectively.

Comparison between Natural Language. We adopt `Sentence-BERT` to compute the relevance between two natural languages. We first preprocess the input data to be as sentence-like as possible to comply with the expected model input. Then, we compute the cosine similarity between a user-side data artifact (u_i) and every question part data artifact ($v_{j,k}$). There exist other models than `Sentence-BERT` that can be used, such as `nomic-ai/nomic-embed-textv1` [23], but their focus is on extending the number of input tokens. For our purpose, 512 tokens (300,400 words) of `Sentence-BERT` is sufficient for preprocessed-text comparison.

Table 2: Weight w_i assignments ($1.0 \leq w_i \leq 10.0$)

Model	Artifact Pair	Weight
m_1	cod:cod	3.23
m_2	cod:log	2.00
m_3	cod:tnd	4.27
m_4	cod:cns	2.00
m_6	log:cod	1.93
m_7	log:log	8.24
m_8	log:tnd	1.92
m_{11}	des:cod	2.87
m_{12}	des:log	2.12

Model	Artifact Pair	Weight
m_{13}	des:tnd	2.41
m_{14}	des:cns	1.69
m_{15}	des:cmd	1.86
m_{16}	cns:cod	1.15
m_{18}	cns:tnd	1.94
m_{19}	cns:cns	8.21
m_{23}	cmd:tnd	2.14
m_{25}	cmd:cmd	2.60

Relevance score computation. The relevance of each sentence pair is calculated using cosine similarity, and the relevance score of the post is the maximum similarity among the sentence pairs. Assume that there are X sentences from the user failure case (e.g., u_{cns}) and Y sentences from the kth post (e.g., $v_{tnd,k}$). First, for each sentence in X, we compute the cosine similarity against all Y sentences and select the highest one. Then, the relevance score between the user failure case and the kth post is the sum of all X cosine similarities. This process is repeated for all K from the forum. That is:

$$s_{h,k} = \sum_{x=1}^{X} \max \{\cos (\boldsymbol{u_{i,x}}, \boldsymbol{v_{j,k,y}}) | 1 \leq y \leq Y\} \tag{3}$$

where h is a model index, $\boldsymbol{u_{i,x}}$ and $\boldsymbol{v_{j,k,y}}$ are the vectors of xth sentence of failure case and y^{th} sentence in the kth forum post respectively. The length of `Sentence-BERT` vector is set to 384.

Comparison between Tokens or Short Phrases. We adopt the `BM25` for comparing two tokens or short phrases. `BM25` is a bag-of-words retrieval function that estimates the relevance of documents to a given query input. This function works well in scenarios that can be ranked using keywords. Applications such as `OpenStack` and `Mongodb` have a large set of commands (`cmd`) to operate various tasks. Unlike the codes, system commands are primarily used in a fixed form and for specific tasks and functions. We use the return value for a specific input query as the relevance score.

3.4 Aggregating Relevance Using Weighted Geometric Mean

As defined earlier, let v_k be one of the documents (e.g., `Stack Overflow` post) in the set Q. Each model m_h generates a relevance score $s_{h,k}$ for all v_k. Here, we explain how we obtain one unified score per v_k from its relevance score set.

We use the *weighted geometric mean* of ranks from 17 models for v_k. Let n be the number of data artifact types on the user-side, and w_i be the weight assigned to m_i, generating its relevance score $s_{i,k}$. We use the $rank()$ function that returns an integer that indicates the rank of v from the given entire sequence of values. Let $\mathcal{V}$ be an array of numbers of which v is a member. Then, the $rank()$ function is defined as $rank(v, \mathcal{V}) = index(v, sort(\mathcal{V}))$. That is, it returns the position (rank) in the sorted list of numbers. Let $S_i(Q)$ be the list of entire relevance scores from m_i. In some cases, posts with only a few artifact types may output higher scores than posts with many artifact types. We give preference to the posts with more information by penalizing the ones with missing artifact types by applying the weight sum ratio. Incorporating this, the unified relevance score p_k for v_k is defined as this:

$$p_k = \left(\prod_{i=1}^{|m|} rank(s_{i,k}, S_i(Q))^{w_i} \right)^{\frac{1}{\sum_{i=1}^{|m|} w_i}} \times \frac{\sum_{i=1}^{|n|} w_i}{\sum_{i=1}^{|m|} w_i} \tag{4}$$

Let P denote the list of entire p_k values. Then, the final rank of v_k is determined as $FR_k = rank(p_k, P)$.

Using weighted geometric mean reflects our intention to reward high m_i scores more through multiplication rather than adding the arithmetic means. The more high-scored models there are, the more amplified the p_k will be. The existence of low-scored models would negatively impact p_k through multiplication, especially when there are multiple of them. Another essential factor to consider is that, for v_k, not all relevance scores $s_{i,k}$ from m_i are always available because forum posts differ in what kind of data artifact they contain. Thus, we take the average of a product by the jth root, where j is the sum of weights.

Weight determination. We utilized *gradient descent* [24] technique to determine the weight w_i of each artifact pair. To avoid overfitting, we applied 7-fold cross-validation on 77 failure cases we reproduced. Then, we determined the best weights that resulted in the highest MRR value on the *testing set* in each fold. These seven sets of weights from the testing runs are averaged per model to generate the final weights. On average, a single run of the gradient descent algorithm took about 35 seconds. We ran the algorithm 100,000 times and chose the weights that resulted in the highest MRR value. We set the range of weights from 1.0 to 10.0. Table 2 exhibits the obtained weights.

4 Evaluation

We evaluate ForumSeeker on these aspects:

- Accuracy of finding correct online forum document(§4.2): Due to the lack of a curated dataset, we reproduce a total of 77 problem cases from 5 popular applications and evaluate how well the ground truth is ranked on an individual case basis.
- Comparison with other techniques (§4.3): We compared ForumSeeker against five baseline techniques. Compared techniques showed mixed results of high variance and very low ranks. ForumSeeker produced 44.74% better search quality compared with the best competitor.

Code:
```
import openstack
os_connect = openstack.connect(auth_url=AUTH_URL,project_name=PROJECT_NAME,
             username=USERNAME, password=PASSWORD, region_name=REGION_NAME,
             user_domain_name=USER_DOMAIN_NAME, app_version='1.0')
for project in os_connect.list_projects() :
   print("Project list :", project['name'])
```

Console output:
```
keystoneauth1.exceptions.http.Unauthorized: The request you have made
requires authentication. (HTTP 401) (Request-ID: req-X)
```

Failure description:
I tried to retrieve a list of projects using the Keystone client.
However, based on the output, it appears that the authentication failed.
The error message indicates that the request made by the code requires authentication, and a 401 Unauthorized response was returned by the Keystone server.

Fig. 5: Data artifacts of a reproduced OpenStack case. The URL of the Stack Overflow question is as follows: `https://stackoverflow.com/questions/46907661`

- Contribution of each artifact pair to the overall accuracy (§4.4): We measure the contribution of each artifact pair to understand which pair was the most influential.

4.1 Experimental Design

Data Collection and Preprocessing. We use the Stack Overflow data dump from the Stack Exchange Archive [4] as our dataset. It contains 23,272,950 posts in total. There were 3,451, 172,209, 100,640, 57,523, and 30,896 posts for OpenStack, MongoDB, Spark, Elasticsearch, and Kafka, respectively. The dataset for each application is filtered using the corresponding name tag. Each post in the dataset is processed into artifacts based on the heuristics we defined at Section 3.2. Each classified data artifact went through preprocessing. They were preprocessed differently based on the data type. First, all data artifacts were converted to lowercase. Then, for codes, whitespace and strings within quotes were removed. For logs or console outputs, variables such as timestamps, dates, hyperlinks, file paths, and IP addresses were removed. For title and descriptions, stopwords were removed using NLTK [5]. User-side data artifacts were identically preprocessed.

Target Applications and Reproducing Failure Cases. We evaluated ForumSeeker on five popular open-source applications: OpenStack, MongoDB, Spark, Elasticsearch, and Kafka. In choosing target applications, we selected highly popular ones representative of four different categories: document-based NoSQL, big data platform, distributed event processor, and search engine type. We used the number of posted questions as a measure of popularity. Although OpenStack was not as popular as others, we included it due to its unmatched diversity of components and high architectural complexity.

[4] `https://archive.org/details/stackexchange`
[5] `https://www.nltk.org/api/nltk.corpus.html`

To select the troubleshooting cases for each application, we followed these steps. First, we searched with "`[application name] error` or `failure`" search terms in the Stack Overflow search interface. Second, we attempted to reproduce the cases one by one from the top of the list (i.e., from high relevance to low) on our HW. Finally, we selected the reproducible one and added it to our cases. We designated the Stack Overflow post that we referenced for reproducing as the ground truth relevant post for failure cases. We needed to reproduce the cases in our environment to collect the user-side data for each case. Also, verifying all the failure cases ourselves ensured the validity of the technique we developed and tested. To obtain all the data artifacts of failure cases, we installed the same version of the software as mentioned in the forum and then reproduced each failure case by performing the same operations. Priorities were given to the posts with at least one command or code snippet. For resolutions, we also followed the steps given in the posts to perform further verification. In short, we collected and successfully reproduced 24, 22, 18, 8, and 5 cases (a total of 77 cases) from OpenStack, MongoDB, Spark, Elasticsearch, and Kafka, respectively. These 77 selected cases are listed in Table 4. Figure 5 shows sample data artifacts from one of the reproduced OpenStack cases (Case O10 in Table 4). The entire dataset of each reproduced case is to be made available to the research community.

Fine-tuning Pre-trained Code Models. We describe how we fine-tuned the code-pretrained models, `CodeBERT` and `GraphCodeBERT`, for our data search task. We constructed the dataset by pairing code and natural language data, such as descriptions, log, and console output, collected from the posts, as shown in Figure 6. The negative dataset was created by randomly pairing code and natural language text from two different (unrelated) posts. Both positive and negative data items were prepared to be in equal proportion (Table 3) in the training, validation, and testing datasets.

- Fine-tuning `CodeBERT` (cross-encoder): For the cross-encoder, we concatenated the code and other data artifacts and fed them as input to the cross-encoder. We fine-tuned the model using a binary classification loss function, with a softmax layer connected. In the fine-tuning step, we set the learning rate at 1e-5, the batch size to 256, the max sequence length to 512, and the epoch to 10. We utilized the Adam optimizer to update the parameters. The model that performed the best was selected for evaluation and inference. We trained the model with implementation in the released repository [6].
- Fine-tuning `GraphCodeBERT` (bi-encoder): We trained the model to maximize the similarity between embeddings of code and positive data items. The embedding of each data artifact was generated separately by the model. In the fine-tuning step, we used the learning rate 1e-5, the batch size of 256, and the max sequence length of code and other data artifacts (log, console output) as 256 and 128, respectively. We used the Adam optimizer to update model parameters. The model is trained with implementation in the released repository [7].

[6] https://github.com/microsoft/CodeBERT

[7] https://github.com/microsoft/CodeBERT/tree/master/GraphCodeBERT

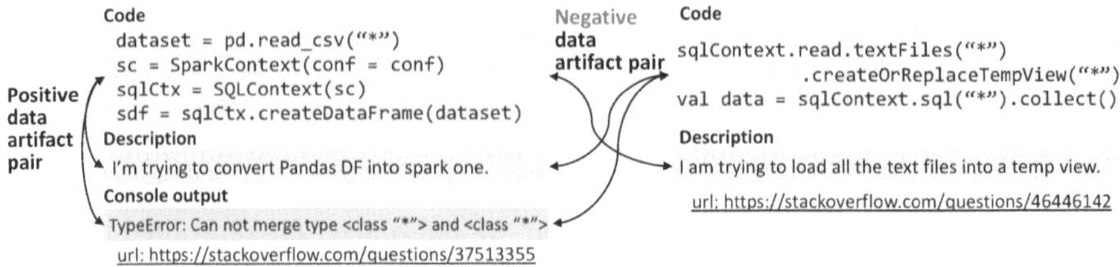

Fig. 6: Construction of fine-tuning dataset from Stack Overflow posts

Table 3: Dataset used for fine-tuning code-pretrained model

	Size of dataset								
	Training			Validation			Testing		
	cod:tnd	cod:log	cod:cns	cod:tnd	cod:log	cod:cns	cod:tnd	cod:log	cod:cns
Positive	187,433	37,196	40,040	46,858	9,299	10,009	24,982	12,031	19,216
Negative	187,433	37,196	39,961	46,858	9,299	9,990	25,018	12,032	19,217
Total	374,866	74,392	80,001	93,716	18,598	19,999	50,000	24,063	38,433

Experimental Settings. The following library versions and models were used to implement each baseline and ForumSeeker.

- BM25: rank-bm25 v.0.2.2.
- Sentence-BERT: all-MiniLM-L6-v2 v.2.2.2.
- CodeBERT: codebert-base
- GraphCodeBERT: graphcodebert-base
- CodeT5+: Salesforce/codet5p-110m-embedding
- Fine-tuning CodeBERT and GraphCodeBERT: Pytorch v.1.13.1 and HuggingFace Library v.4.26.1. We used RobertaForSequenceClassification and RobertaModel classes in HuggingFace.

Our evaluation was performed on an NVIDIA Quadro RTX 6000 server running on CUDA 11.2 and cudnn 8.2.1, and an NVIDIA DGX-2 server equipped with 4 Tesla v100 GPUs.

Comparison Methods. We compare the performance of ForumSeeker with several popular approaches as baselines: BM25, embedding-based semantic search (Text-Embedding), an ensemble of models, Google search, and GPT-4o. For these baselines, the input forum data was given as a single text body instead of being broken down into data artifact types. Details of each comparison method are provided in the technical report [22].

Performance Measure. We measure the ranking quality of ForumSeeker and baseline techniques using two widely adopted metrics in the information retrieval field: MRR (Mean Reciprocal Rank) and the SuccessRate@k metric [25]. MRR is expressed as:

$$MRR = \frac{1}{|C|} \sum_{c=1}^{|C|} \frac{1}{Rank_c} \tag{5}$$

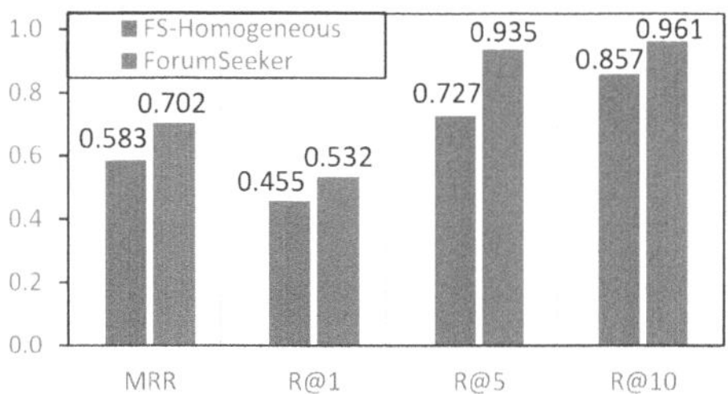

Fig. 7: Accuracy comparison between ForumSeeker and FS-Homogeneous. The latter refers to the relevant question search using only the homogeneous data artifact models.

where C is the number of reproduced cases. The maximum value of MRR is 1, and the higher the better. Since MRR is concerned with the rank of a single best item in the list, this metric indicates the quality of each retrieval approach.

The SuccessRate@k (also denoted as $R@k$) metric measures the average proportion of ground truth questions ranked within the top k. If the target entry is ranked within the top k, $\delta(Rank_c)$ returns 1, otherwise 0. It is defined as follows:

$$R@k = \frac{1}{|C|} \sum_{c=1}^{C} \delta(Rank_c \leq k), k \in \{1, 5, 10\} \tag{6}$$

4.2 Accuracy of ForumSeeker

Overall Accuracy of ForumSeeker. Table 4 shows how well ForumSeeker ranked the relevant forum post (i.e., the ground-truth Stack Overflow post) from the given failure case data. The 'Forum GT ID' column is the ID of the ground-truth relevant question in Stack Overflow of each case. The 'FS Rank' column is the ranking of ground-truth Stack Overflow posts reported by ForumSeeker. The 'User-side Data artifacts' column indicates the types of data artifacts in the data artifacts collected from the user-side. Results show that ForumSeeker was able to rank the ground-truth Stack Overflow document within the top range consistently. It failed to obtain single-digit ranks in only 3 cases. The main reasons are: first of all, a single model works better than ForumSeeker when relevant posts are short or share common words with failure cases. In this case, baselines such as BM25, Ensemble, or Google search rank the relevant post high. Since ForumSeeker is a combination of multiple models, one underperforming model can adversely affect the result. Secondly, the text in the relevant post (`tnd`) did not properly describe the failure case (i.e., lack of information). One of the models in ForumSeeker compares the user-side `cod` and the forum-side `tnd` to determine the similarity. For `cod:tnd` to work, the text description in the post should describe what the code does. But, we found that the `tnd` in some posts merely stated an error, as in `'Getting error in system'` with no information on what it does. In such cases, `cod:tnd` resulted in a low similarity score and even canceled out the gains from other models.

Table 4: Full evaluation results of ForumSeeker.

App	Case No.	Forum GT ID	Type of case	User-side Data artifacts					FS Rank	
				cod	cmd	log	cns	des		
Open-stack	O1	63650069	Launch Server (Case1)	o	x	o	x	o	1	out of 3451
	O2	68236671	Launch Server (Case2)	o	x	x	o	o	3	
	O3	50136230	List Services	o	x	x	o	o	3	
	O4	71998698	List Compute Services	x	o	o	x	o	1	
	O5	43091643	Create Image	x	o	o	x	o	2	
	O6	47698116	List Network Services	x	o	o	x	o	1	
	O7	61286693	Create Network	x	o	o	x	o	1	
	O8	72544674	Create Cloud	x	o	x	o	o	1	
	O9	41928122	List Servers (Case1)	x	o	x	o	o	1	
	O10	46907661	List Projects	o	x	x	o	o	1	
	O11	50418750	Create Keypair	x	o	x	o	o	1	
	O12	15978149	Add Custom Filter	o	x	x	o	o	1	
	O13	32114520	Request Token	x	o	x	o	o	1	
	O14	72025462	Pull Image with Ansible	x	o	x	o	o	1	
	O15	63749573	List Servers (Case2)	o	x	x	o	o	2	
	O16	23994688	Launch Server (Case3)	x	o	x	o	o	2	
	O17	69665323	Launch Server (Case4)	o	x	x	o	o	1	
	O18	63766864	Attach Volume to Server	x	o	o	x	o	1	
	O19	56430521	Issuing command	x	o	x	o	o	1	
	O20	51558107	Launch Server (Case5)	o	x	x	o	o	3	
	O21	45466370	Restart Compute Service	x	o	o	x	o	2	
	O22	72349021	Launch Server (Case6)	x	o	o	x	o	1	
	O23	21090545	Launch Server (Case7)	o	x	x	o	o	1	
	O24	32724282	Launch Server (Case8)	o	x	x	o	o	2	
Mong-odb	M1	46523321	Connect MongoDB (Case1)	o	x	x	o	o	1	out of 172209
	M2	70673818	Connect MongoDB (Case2)	x	o	x	o	o	2	
	M3	17545311	Search with id Entries	o	x	x	o	o	1	
	M4	58150528	Mongoimport with Atlas	x	o	o	x	o	1	
	M5	28640281	Restore Collection	x	o	x	o	o	1	
	M6	50173080	Connect MongoDB from Node.js	o	x	x	o	o	1	
	M7	19228474	Mongodump from remote server	x	o	o	x	o	4	
	M8	26585433	Start & Connect MongoDB	x	o	x	o	o	3	
	M9	19065615	Delete Document with Query	o	x	x	o	o	2	
	M10	18931668	Load & Restore Data	x	o	o	x	o	3	
	M11	31993168	Create Backup with MongoDump	x	o	x	o	o	1	
	M12	28981718	Collection with insert method	o	x	x	o	o	1	
	M13	37705231	Insert Data into Collection	o	x	x	o	o	1	
	M14	10242149	Retrieve Sorted Data	o	x	x	o	o	2	
	M15	65914156	Insert Data with Pymongo	o	x	x	o	o	4	
	M16	47884387	Sort & Get Record	o	x	x	o	o	1	
	M17	58414909	Access Large Document	o	x	x	o	o	1	
	M18	61095888	Update Collection	o	x	x	o	o	5	
	M19	48665104	Connect MongoDB (Case3)	o	x	x	o	o	2	
	M20	62150647	Fetch Data with Pymongo	o	x	x	o	o	4	
	M21	71132796	Configure Mongdb Replicaset	o	x	x	o	o	3	
	M22	71742822	Retrieve a distinct list of value	o	x	x	o	o	2	
Spark	S1	42757888	KMeans with Python	o	x	x	o	o	1	out of 100640
	S2	47000648	Connect Mongodb from spark	o	x	o	x	o	3	
	S3	31684842	Calling Java/Scala Function	o	x	x	o	o	1	
	S4	52420831	Create DataFrame with Condition	o	x	x	o	o	1	
	S5	33151861	Use Multiple Conditions	o	x	x	o	o	1	
	S6	44199328	Pyspark Mongodb Connector	o	x	x	o	o	2	
	S7	68561363	Check Dataframe with Condition	o	x	x	o	o	5	
	S8	72881355	Create Spark Session	o	x	x	o	o	1	
	S9	47682927	Create User Defined Function	o	x	x	o	o	4	
	S10	72565834	Read & Write Table	o	x	x	o	o	1	
	S11	65627330	Create RDD & Apply Map	o	x	x	o	o	2	
	S12	31464727	Delete & Recreate Context	o	x	x	o	o	2	
	S13	39419712	Create DataFrame	o	x	o	x	o	2	
	S14	46710934	Run Classification	o	x	x	o	o	1	
	S15	33369989	Run Mllib	o	x	o	x	o	1	
	S16	53161939	Initializing Spark Context	o	x	x	o	o	1	
	S17	59816635	Delete or Create Spark Context	o	x	x	o	o	46	
	S18	73234414	Run Spark in Cluster Mode	o	x	o	x	o	58	
Elastic-search	E1	70990983	Add Range Filter to Search Query	o	x	x	o	o	1	out of 57523
	E2	29735483	Send Req with Apache HttpClient	o	x	x	o	o	1	
	E3	51852960	Re-Index	o	x	x	o	o	1	
	E4	22770391	Create Index & Mapping	o	x	x	o	o	1	
	E5	45462126	Create Transport Client & Search	o	x	x	o	o	40	
	E6	35322292	Index a New Document	o	x	x	o	o	2	
	E7	56677645	Read Document with Index	o	x	x	o	o	1	
	E8	69801258	Take a Snapshot of Index	o	x	x	o	o	2	
Kafka	K1	21020347	Send Large Msg	o	x	x	o	o	2	out of 30896
	K2	28146409	Create Kafka Cluster & Send Msg	o	x	x	o	o	1	
	K3	23491596	Consume Msg with Zookeeper	o	x	x	o	o	6	
	K4	23770057	Create Producer	o	x	x	o	o	2	
	K5	39351046	Connect Kafka with Kafka-Python	o	x	x	o	o	8	

Table 5: The ranking comparison of baselines and ForumSeeker in terms of MRR and Successrate@K. The 'improvement' column shows how much better ForumSeeker is against the corresponding baseline technique.

	MRR		R@1		R@5		R@10	
	Value	Improvement	Value	Improvement	Value	Improvement	Value	Improvement
BM25	0.275	155.27%	0.208	155.77%	0.312	199.68%	0.416	131.01%
Text-Embedding	0.200	251%	0.130	309.23%	0.299	212.71%	0.390	146.41%
Ensemble	0.485	44.74%	0.403	32.01%	0.571	63.75%	0.662	45.17%
Google Search	0.454	54.63%	0.325	63.69%	0.662	41.24%	0.727	32.19%
GPT-4o	0.372	88.71%	0.325	63.69%	0.416	124.76%	0.494	94.53%
ForumSeeker	**0.702**		**0.532**		**0.935**		**0.961**	

Criticality of Heterogeneous Comparison of Data Artifacts. One of our key findings in ForumSeeker is that it is critical to compare the similarities across various heterogeneous data artifacts to obtain high accuracy. To support our findings and verify the magnitude of its effectiveness, we measured the MRR and R@k of two cases: *i)* using only the models that compare the same artifact types (called FS-Homogeneous), and *ii)* using all models that include heterogeneous comparisons. Figure 7 depicts the MRR and R@k of two cases. The result shows that the inclusion of heterogeneous models in ForumSeeker boosts the MRR by 20.4% (from the MRR of .583 to .702). The R@k results also show that the contribution of heterogeneous models to the overall accuracy is significant. Based on R@5, ForumSeeker achieved 93.5%, indicating that it identified the relevant post within the top-5 for 94% of cases, while FS-Homogeneous achieved it for only 73% of cases.

4.3 Comparison with Other Techniques

We present the comparison results of several baseline techniques against our ForumSeeker. The key focus of comparisons with baselines is to observe how well these techniques perform when the user-side data and forum data are *used as a whole* as opposed to being *disassembled* into artifact types, the approach taken by our ForumSeeker.

Results Overview. Table 5 shows the overall results of five baselines and ForumSeeker in terms of MRR and Successrate@k (in short, R@k) to demonstrate the accuracy of the techniques. Regarding MRR, ForumSeeker obtained the highest mark, outperforming 'Ensemble' with 0.485, the best competitor, by a margin of 44.74%. ForumSeeker outperformed all competitors in R@1, R@5 and R@10 metrics as well. ForumSeeker achieved 0.961 R@10 value, while the highest value was 0.727 from Google search. None of the competitors was able to reach above .9 R@k scores. We point out that R@k metrics are concerned with the status of ranks only within the top k. While we observed the cases in which ForumSeeker found the ground truth beyond k was still not far from the top k rank, other techniques often returned an unacceptably low rank (i.e.,high-rank

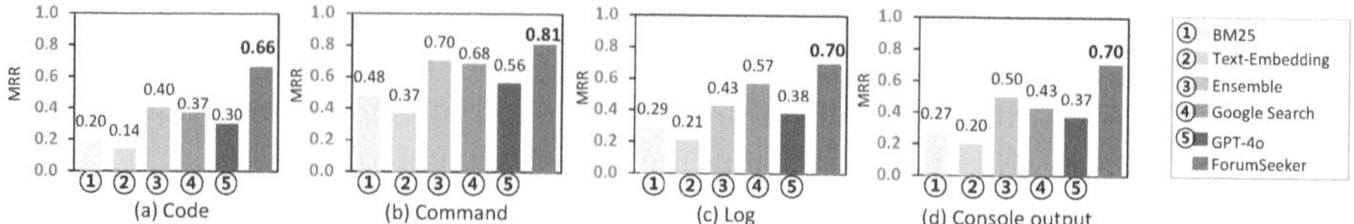

Fig. 8: Ranking quality comparison of 5 baselines and ForumSeeker based on user-side data artifact

value). Thus, the magnitude of low performers is not well reflected in the R@k metric, and the ranking quality presented here for the competitors is somewhat overestimated.

Significance of Code Artifact. We present the MRR computed by filtering the 77 failure cases based on the existence of each data artifact type in the user-side data. We intend to observe whether there is any correlation between accuracy and the artifact types for the baselines and ForumSeeker. Figure 8 shows the comparison of MRR of the baselines and ForumSeeker for four data artifact types. For example, Figure 8(a) is the MRR of only the cases in Table 4 that has the '`cod`' column marked as '`o`'. Note that since all posts have `des`, MRR comparison for `des` is irrelevant.

We observe a few interesting points. If user-side data includes code, ForumSeeker shows significantly better MRR than the other baseline techniques. ForumSeeker achieved the highest MRR of 0.66, surpassing the best competitor, Ensemble's MRR of 0.40 as shown in Figure 8(a). When the user-side data includes code, ForumSeeker improves the accuracy by at least 65% from baselines. In other cases, ForumSeeker improves the accuracy compared with the best competitor by 15.71%, 22.81%, and 40% when user-side includes the command, log, and console output, respectively. This implies that when user-side data has code, keyword comparison, or comparison among the same data types (i.e., homogeneous comparison) is insufficient to find relevant posts correctly. Comparing code with other types of data in forum posts, such as description (`tnd`), is vital. This, in turn, highlights the importance of dissecting data artifacts and treating them separately in the *heterogeneous search*, the key component of ForumSeeker.

On the other hand, if user-side data includes commands, ForumSeeker shows only a small MRR improvement over the baselines. In these cases, the user-side and forum-side data commonly share the same keywords, such as exact command names or component names. Such direct information at the word level helps all the baselines perform better than three other cases, as can be seen from the high MRRs in Figure 8(b). In summary, the effectiveness of ForumSeeker's approach varies by the data artifact types. The accuracy gain of ForumSeeker is the largest when codes are involved, requiring code semantics comparisons using our *heterogeneous* search approach. The accuracy gain is not as large for the data artifacts whose similarities can be computed at the word level.

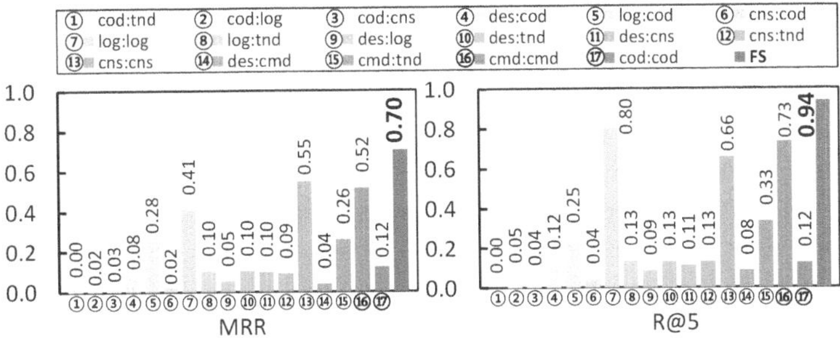

Fig. 9: Ranking quality breakdown by data artifact pairs. FS stands for ForumSeeker. (R@1,10 omitted.)

4.4 Dissecting Accuracy by Data Artifacts (Ablation Study)

We investigated individual models' contributions to accuracy to understand which data type pairs were the most crucial. Figure 9 presents the result. The `cns:cns` model produced the highest MRR of 0.55, followed by `cmd:cmd`. This indicates that it is important to utilize the console output(`cns`) in the search for the most relevant online forum documents whenever available. However, when we looked at the ranking output produced by only using homogeneous data pair models such as the `cns:cns` or `cmd:cmd`, we found that the rank variance was high. This observation supports ForumSeeker's approach of using multiple data types and comparing heterogeneous data type models together complementarily to achieve high search performance. Furthermore, even if a data artifact pair may show low MRR when used alone, they are indispensable to ForumSeeker since their synergy is needed to produce high overall search accuracy.

5 Related Work

Recommending Relevant Information in Online Forum. Prior work on information retrieval in online forums has addressed various tasks such as question recommendation, API or code snippet retrieval, topic clustering, and answer summarization. Several techniques aim to retrieve relevant content based on user queries. For example, Que2Code [26] recommends code snippets from Stack Overflow using Euclidean distance of query and question embeddings. Similarly, [27] and GitterAns [28] focus on finding relevant Stack Overflow and Discord posts in response to user questions. These approaches typically rely on natural language queries, in contrast to ForumSeeker, which takes a set of system-generated data artifacts as input. Ponzanelli et al. [29] and Rahman et al. [30] integrate online forums into development environments by computing relevance between programming problems and Stack Overflow discussions. While their methods are effective in retrieving queries helpful content, they generally assume that the input is a human-authored question, whereas ForumSeeker is designed to work with data artifacts derived from system behavior.

System Troubleshooting. System troubleshooting has long been a popular research topic, but many challenges remain. Researchers have attempted to tackle this problem in various ways, including historical experience [31], by building an anomaly propagation graph [32], employing time-series key performance indicators [33], and exploiting functional connectivity inference [34]. Other attempts have involved analyzing the time-series metrics of sensors in the system [35], network fingerprint [36], and system calls [37]. Most of the analyses focus on localizing the root cause of the problem by finding the component or service causing the issue or identifying the problem-induced component or system call. But there is a drawback, such that they can *not* find the root cause of the problem. Pan et al. [38] proposed a host metrics analysis toolkit for investigating the causality of host failure operations in large-scale data centers. Although their toolkit helped system admins to better understand the failure mechanism inside the host, it did not concern retrieving online forum data for such analysis. Recently, with the accumulation of crowd-sourced content, much attention has been paid to automatically utilizing forum data, including discussion forums and community QA platforms [39] for system troubleshooting. Most existing research has focused on understanding user intents in the forums [40] and coding aspects [41]. Although we share the goal of troubleshooting system problems based on online forum posts, we differ in applying posts to more operation-oriented problems.

6 Conclusion

We present ForumSeeker, a novel NLP-driven retrieval framework for technical forum search that advances failure diagnosis through structured artifact-aware analysis. The key principles of our technique are to decompose forum posts into semantically coherent artifact types, apply specialized models to evaluate cross-artifact relationships, and use a fusion retrieval mechanism that aggregates relevance signals across heterogeneous data pairs, addressing a key gap in the multi-modal technical QA area. Performing beyond simple log search or keyword search, our technique was able to leverage more relevant information between disparate data types in the posts, improving the accuracy of matching significantly. To evaluate ForumSeeker, we built a reproducible benchmark with 77 real-world failure cases, demonstrating a 70.2% search accuracy and a 44.7% improvement over state-of-the-art retrievers.

Data Availability Statement. Our tool and data artifacts are publicly available at the following URL: `https://doi.org/10.6084/m9.figshare.31017706`.

Acknowledgment

This work was supported by the National Research Foundation of Korea (NRF) grants funded by the Korean government (RS-2021-NR060080, RS-2025-16067408) and by the BK21 FOUR project funded by the Ministry of Education, School of CSE at Kyungpook National University, Korea (4120240214871).

References

1. Stack Overflow. Webpage. https://stackoverflow.com/, 2026.
2. Quora, Inc. Homepage. https://quora.com/, 2026.
3. Microsoft. Support Community. https://answers.microsoft.com/, 2026.
4. Apple. Support Community. https://discussions.apple.com/, 2026.
5. Antonio L Alfeo, Mario GCA Cimino, and Gigliola Vaglini. Technological troubleshooting based on sentence embedding with deep transformers. *Journal of Intelligent Manufacturing*, 32(6):1699–1710, 2021.
6. Anup Anand Deshmukh and Udhav Sethi. Ir-bert: leveraging bert for semantic search in background linking for news articles. *arXiv preprint arXiv:2007.12603*, 2020.
7. Nicole Peinelt, Dong Nguyen, and Maria Liakata. tbert: Topic models and bert joining forces for semantic similarity detection. In *Proceedings of the 58th annual meeting of the Association for Computational Linguistics (ACL 2020)*, pages 7047–7055, 2020.
8. Alireza Salemi and Hamed Zamani. Evaluating retrieval quality in retrieval-augmented generation. In *Proceedings of the 47th International ACM SIGIR Conference on Research and Development in Information Retrieval (SIGIR 2024)*, page 2395–2400. ACM, 2024.
9. Shamane Siriwardhana, Rivindu Weerasekera, Elliott Wen, Tharindu Kaluarachchi, Rajib Rana, and Suranga Nanayakkara. Improving the Domain Adaptation of Retrieval Augmented Generation (RAG) Models for Open Domain Question Answering. *Transactions of the Association for Computational Linguistics*, 11:1–17, 01 2023.
10. Zhangyin Feng, Daya Guo, Duyu Tang, Nan Duan, Xiaocheng Feng, Ming Gong, Linjun Shou, Bing Qin, Ting Liu, Daxin Jiang, and Ming Zhou. CodeBERT: A pre-trained model for programming and natural languages. In *Findings of the Association for Computational Linguistics: EMNLP 2020 (Findings of EMNLP 2020)*, pages 1536–1547. Association for Computational Linguistics, November 2020.
11. Daya Guo, Shuo Ren, Shuai Lu, Zhangyin Feng, Duyu Tang, Shujie Liu, Long Zhou, Nan Duan, Alexey Svyatkovskiy, Shengyu Fu, Michele Tufano, Shao Kun Deng, Colin B. Clement, Dawn Drain, Neel Sundaresan, Jian Yin, Daxin Jiang, and Ming Zhou. GraphCodeBERT: Pre-training Code Representations with Data Flow. In *9th International Conference on Learning Representations, (ICLR 2021)*, 2021.
12. Stephen E Robertson, Steve Walker, Susan Jones, Micheline M Hancock-Beaulieu, Mike Gatford, et al. Okapi at trec-3. *Nist Special Publication Sp*, 109:109, 1995.
13. Yue Wang, Hung Le, Akhilesh Deepak Gotmare, Nghi D.Q. Bui, Junnan Li, and Steven C. H. Hoi. Codet5+: Open code large language models for code understanding and generation. *arXiv preprint arXiv:2305.07922*, 2023.
14. Nils Reimers and Iryna Gurevych. Sentence-BERT: Sentence embeddings using Siamese BERT-networks. In *Proceedings of the 2019 Conference on Empirical Methods in Natural Language Processing and the 9th International Joint Conference on Natural Language Processing (EMNLP-IJCNLP 2019)*, pages 3982–3992. Association for Computational Linguistics, November 2019.
15. OpenInfra Foundation. OpenStack Webpage. https://openstack.org/, 2026.
16. The Apache Software Foundation. Apache Spark. https://spark.apache.org/.
17. Elasticsearch B.V. Elasticsearch. https://www.elastic.co/kr/elasticsearch/.
18. MongoDB Inc. Mongodb. https://www.mongodb.com/.
19. The Apache Software Foundation. Apache Kafka. https://kafka.apache.org/.

20. Stefanie Beyer, Christian Macho, Martin Pinzger, and Massimiliano Di Penta. Automatically classifying posts into question categories on stack overflow. In *Proceedings of the 26th Conference on Program Comprehension (ICPC 2018)*, page 211–221. ACM, 2018.
21. Gao Cong, Long Wang, Chin-Yew Lin, Young-In Song, and Yueheng Sun. Finding question-answer pairs from online forums. In *Proceedings of the 31st Annual International ACM SIGIR Conference on Research and Development in Information Retrieval (SIGIR 2008)*, page 467–474. ACM, 2008.
22. Kyungpook National University, CSE Technical Report. https://drive.google.com/file/d/1iw1NA4z3d2bhV9N2dtcSQAcG80o9O8Xf/view, January 2026.
23. Zach Nussbaum, John X. Morris, Brandon Duderstadt, and Andriy Mulyar. Nomic embed: Training a reproducible long context text embedder. *arXiv preprint arXiv:2402.01613*, 2024.
24. James A. Anderson. *An Introduction to Neural Networks.* The MIT Press, 03 1995.
25. Xiaodong Gu, Hongyu Zhang, and Sunghun Kim. Deep code search. In *Proceedings International Conference on Software Engineering (ICSE 2018)*, pages 933–944, 2018.
26. Zhipeng Gao, Xin Xia, David Lo, John Grundy, Xindong Zhang, and Zhenchang Xing. I know what you are searching for: Code snippet recommendation from stack overflow posts. *ACM Trans. Softw. Eng. Methodol.*, 32(3), April 2023.
27. Alexander Lill, André N. Meyer, and Thomas Fritz. On the Helpfulness of Answering Developer Questions on Discord with Similar Conversations and Posts from the Past. In *Proceedings of the IEEE/ACM 46th International Conference on Software Engineering (ICSE 2024)*, pages 1–13, 2024.
28. Ricardo Romero, Esteban Parra, and Sonia Haiduc. Experiences building an answer bot for gitter. In *Proceedings of the IEEE/ACM 42nd International Conference on Software Engineering Workshops (ICSEW 2020)*, page 66–70. ACM, 2020.
29. Luca Ponzanelli, Gabriele Bavota, Massimiliano Di Penta, Rocco Oliveto, and Michele Lanza. Mining stackoverflow to turn the ide into a self-confident programming prompter. In *Proceedings of the 11th working conference on Mining Software Repositories (MSR 2014)*, pages 102–111, 2014.
30. Mohammad Masudur Rahman, Shamima Yeasmin, and Chanchal K Roy. Towards a context-aware ide-based meta search engine for recommendation about programming errors and exceptions. In *2014 Software Evolution Week-IEEE Conference on Software Maintenance, Reengineering, and Reverse Engineering (CSMR-WCRE 2014)*, pages 194–203. IEEE, 2014.
31. Cristina Melchiors and Liane Margarida Rockenbach Tarouco. Troubleshooting Network Faults Using Past Experience. In *IEEE/IFIP Network Operations and Management Symposium (NOMS 2000) 'The Networked Planet: Management Beyond 2000' (Cat. No. 00CB37074)*, pages 549–562. IEEE, 2000.
32. Jieyu Lin, Qi Zhang, Hadi Bannazadeh, and Alberto Leon-Garcia. Automated anomaly detection and root cause analysis in virtualized cloud infrastructures. In *IEEE/IFIP Network Operations and Management Symposium (NOMS 2016)*, pages 550–556. IEEE, 2016.
33. Chia-Cheng Yen, Wenting Sun, Hakimeh Purmehdi, Won Park, Kunal Rajan Deshmukh, Nishank Thakrar, Omar Nassef, and Adam Jacobs. Graph neural network based root cause analysis using multivariate time-series kpis for wireless networks. In *IEEE/IFIP Network Operations and Management Symposium (NOMS 2022)*, pages 1–7. IEEE, 2022.

34. Giles Winchester, George Parisis, and Luc Berthouze. Exploiting functional connectivity inference for efficient root cause analysis. In *IEEE/IFIP Network Operations and Management Symposium (NOMS 2022)*, pages 1–5. IEEE, 2022.
35. Myunghwan Kim, Roshan Sumbaly, and Sam Shah. Root cause detection in a service-oriented architecture. *ACM SIGMETRICS Performance Evaluation Review*, 41(1):93–104, 2013.
36. Jörg Thalheim, Antonio Rodrigues, Istemi Ekin Akkus, Pramod Bhatotia, Ruichuan Chen, Bimal Viswanath, Lei Jiao, and Christof Fetzer. Sieve: Actionable insights from monitored metrics in distributed systems. In *Proceedings of the 18th ACM/IFIP/USENIX Middleware Conference (Middleware 2017)*, pages 14–27, 2017.
37. Zhilei Ren, Changlin Liu, Xusheng Xiao, He Jiang, and Tao Xie. Root cause localization for unreproducible builds via causality analysis over system call tracing. In *2019 34th IEEE/ACM International Conference on Automated Software Engineering (ASE 2019)*, pages 527–538. IEEE, 2019.
38. Yicheng Pan, Yang Zhang, Tingzhu Bi, Linlin Han, Yu Zhang, Meng Ma, Xiangzhuang Shen, Xinrui Jiang, Feng Wang, Xian Liu, et al. HEAL: Performance Troubleshooting Deep inside Data Center Hosts. *Proceedings of the ACM on Measurement and Analysis of Computing Systems*, 7(3):1–24, 2023.
39. Ahmad Abdellatif, Diego Costa, Khaled Badran, Rabe Abdalkareem, and Emad Shihab. Challenges in chatbot development: A study of stack overflow posts. In *Proceedings of the 17th International Conference on Mining Software Repositories (MSR 2020)*, pages 174–185, 2020.
40. Kaibo Cao, Chunyang Chen, Sebastian Baltes, Christoph Treude, and Xiang Chen. Automated query reformulation for efficient search based on query logs from stack overflow. In *IEEE/ACM 43rd International Conference on Software Engineering (ICSE 2021)*, pages 1273–1285. IEEE, 2021.
41. Sebastian Baltes, Lorik Dumani, Christoph Treude, and Stephan Diehl. Sotorrent: Reconstructing and analyzing the evolution of stack overflow posts. In *Proceedings of the 15th international conference on mining software repositories (MSR 2018)*, pages 319–330, 2018.

Autonomous Systems and Applications

Failure Modes and Effects Analysis: An Experience from the E-Bike Domain

Andrea Bombarda§1, Federico Conti§1, Marcello Minervini[1], Aurora Zanenga[1], and Claudio Menghi[1,2]

[1] University of Bergamo, Bergamo, Italy
f.conti12@studenti.unibg.it
{andrea.bombarda,marcello.minervini,aurora.zanenga, claudio.menghi}@.unibg.it
[2] McMaster University, Hamilton, Canada

Abstract. Software failures can have catastrophic and costly consequences. Failure Mode and Effects Analysis (FMEA) is a standard technique used within Cyber-Physical Systems (CPS) to identify software failures and assess their consequences. Simulation-driven approaches have recently been shown to be effective in supporting FMEA. This paper presents our experience with using FMEA to analyze the safety of a CPS from the e-Bike domain. We used Simulink Fault Analyzer, an industrial tool that supports engineers with FMEA. We identified 13 realistic faults, modeled them, and analyzed their effects. We sought expert feedback to analyze the appropriateness of our models and the effectiveness of the faults in detecting safety breaches. Our results reveal that for the faults we identified, our models were accurate or contained minor imprecision that we subsequently corrected. They also confirm that FMEA helps engineers improve their models. Specifically, the output provided by the simulation-driven support for 38.4% (5 out of 13) of the faults did not match the engineers' expectations, helping them discover unexpected effects of the faults. We discuss our results and ten lessons learned.

Keywords: E-Bikes, Simulink® Fault Analyzer™, Safety Analysis

1 Introduction

Failure Mode and Effects Analysis (FMEA) is widely used in Cyber-Physical Systems (CPS) development to analyze software safety [52,67,47]. For example, it has been used in NASA programs [49,46] such as Apollo and Skylab, and it is used by Ford [21]. FMEA requires identifying potential failure modes (Failure Mode - FM) and analyzing their causes and effects (Effects Analysis - EA).

Safety assurance and safety analysis are increasingly becoming essential in software engineering [11,56,69]. To support software safety analysis from the early stages of the software development process, researchers have developed approaches that embed safety analysis within system modeling [28,33,24,51,31,6]. For example, Simulation-driven FMEA [54] is an automated software engineering solution that checks the effects of the faults defined in an FMEA table by

E. Albert and C. Pasareanu (Eds.): FASE 2026, LNCS 16504, pp. 259–282, 2026.
https://doi.org/10.1007/978-3-032-22774-4_14

performing simulations of models enriched with faults. The results of these simulations enable engineers to analyze the effects of the faults and, depending on their criticality, develop strategies that mitigate them. Simulation-driven FMEA provided encouraging results on a pivotal study that represented a flight control system of an unmanned ultralight helicopter [54]; it is currently integrated within the Simulink® Fault Analyzer™ [39]. The Simulink® Fault Analyzer™ is a tool for the safety management of software systems developed in Simulink®; it enables the connection of faults, hazards, and mitigation logic.

Safety analysis experts need empirical evidence regarding the benefits and limitations of the different techniques to decide whether to incorporate them into their working pipeline. Simulation-driven FMEA [54] and the Simulink® Fault Analyzer™ have been recently introduced within Simulink® (R2023b). To assess the industrial applicability of Simulation-driven FMEA, it is paramount to empirically evaluate its effectiveness and provide practitioners with guidelines and lessons learned [3], as widely recognized by the research and industrial software engineering communities [3,15,30,50,57,42,17,43,66]. This need is of primary importance for Simulink® [7,60,8,9], as Simulink projects and models are typically industrial and usually not shared or available due to corporate policies [5,14].

To mitigate this need, this paper reports on industrial applicability and the usefulness of Simulation-driven FMEA on a study subject from the e-Bikes domain. Specifically, our study subject is a Simulink® model related to the software controller of an e-Bike. It is developed in the context of a project which aims at improving "green" mobility solutions, including e-Bikes, and involving two large companies operating in the automotive and mobility sectors. E-Bikes are vehicles that support riders with power from an electric motor. Our case study is relevant because (a) the e-Bike software is often designed in Simulink® [62]; (b) e-Bikes have a considerable market size (27.15 USD billion in 2022, expected to grow to USD 82.84 billion by 2030 [25]); (c) they are software-intensive systems [64], as the software controls the electrical motor of the e-Bike and regulates its speed and possibly the regenerative power; (d) they are safety-critical systems which must comply with safety regulations and requirements [58,59]; and (e) our results and lessons learned are based on the interaction with an expert (the third author of this paper) who is designing the software for the controller of an e-Bike within the context of an EU-funded project that involves several industrial partners who specialize in the e-Bike domain as well as on discussions with Simulink® engineers. Our findings are useful for software engineers who work as Simulink® engineers, use the Simulink® Fault Analyzer™, or work as safety analysts.

To evaluate the industrial applicability of Simulation-driven FMEA, we considered 13 realistic faults; we (a) modeled them within the Simulink® model using the Simulink® Fault Analyzer™ and (b) analyzed their effects. This is a significant number of software faults considering the application domain. Designing these faults required a holistic view of the system, including its motor and battery. Acquiring this knowledge is time-consuming. It required us to interact with domain experts and thoroughly study the application domain to acquire the knowledge to operate in this field. We retrospectively estimate this effort as six months of work for the entire team.

To assess the industrial applicability and the benefits of Simulation-driven FMEA in our case study, we interviewed our expert to ensure that the models of our faults reflected their intended behavior. Our results reveal that all faults were modeled correctly (53.8%) or with minor imprecisions (46.2%) that were fixed. Our discussion with Simulink® experts enabled us to fix the models for these faults. We interviewed the expert to understand the expected consequences of the faults and compare them with those provided by Simulation-driven FMEA. For over 38% of the faults, the output provided by the simulation-driven support for FMEA provided by the Simulink® Fault Analyzer™ did not match the engineer's expectation, thereby leading to the field engineers discovering unexpected effects of the faults. To provide a thorough interpretation of our results, we discussed them with Simulink® engineers, where we presented the objective of the work, our results, and collected their informal feedback and interpretation of the results. These discussions led to the formalization of ten lessons learned — i.e., five Simulink® specific (useful for Simulink® engineers and users of the Simulink® Fault Analyzer™) and five Simulink® agnostic (useful for safety analysts).

This paper is organized as follows. Section 2 introduces our study subject. Section 3 summarizes Simulation-driven FMEA. Section 4 presents our empirical evaluation. Section 5 discusses our results and presents lessons learned. Section 6 presents related work. Section 7 concludes our work.

2 The E-Bike Study Subject

Figure 1 presents our study subject: The Simulink® model of an e-Bike. This model is developed within the context of a project that involves two large companies operating in the automotive and mobility sectors. Its development time is approximately 100 hours of work by a single electronic engineer. The controlled system consists of several components.

The *Environment* models external forces (e.g., the friction and aerodynamic drag). It models external loads, mimicking the actual resistance an e-Bike would encounter during operation and that would influence motor performance. Its input is the speed of the e-Bike (*Measured speed*). Its output is a signal that simulates the effects of friction and aerodynamic torque (R).

The *Brushless Direct Current Motor (BLDC)* converts electrical energy into rotational motion and torque. Its inputs are the currents (a, b, c) applied to the three phases of the BLDC and the neutral point (n). Its outputs are the mechanical rotation of the rotor of the motor (R) and motor case (C).

The *Sensor* monitors the torque of the e-Bike, and the speed and the sector of its rotor. Its input is the torque of the rotor (R). Its outputs are the active sector (*Sector*) of the BLDC motor and the e-Bike speed (*Measured speed*).

The *Battery* stores and retrieves electrical energy. It receives the current that recharges the battery (- *Batt*) as input. It outputs a current from the energy stored within the battery (+ *Batt*) to feed the motor.

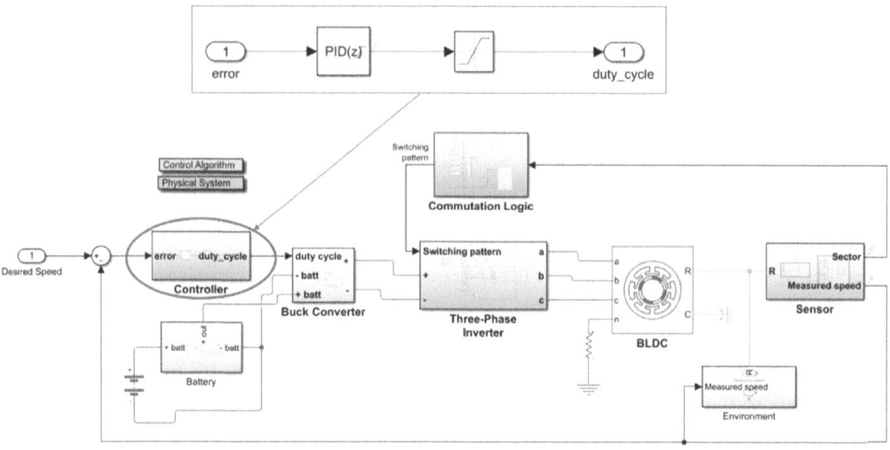

Fig. 1: Simulink® model for the e-Bike.

The *Three-Phase Inverter* converts the direct current into alternating current. It receives two inputs (*-Batt* and *+Batt*) from the buck converter. It acts on the motor, depending on the direct current (DC) signal (*Switching pattern*) received from the software controller (*Controller*). It outputs the currents applied to the three phases of the BLDC (a, b, c).

The *Commutation Logic* determines the voltage to be supplied by the three-phase inverter that is used to regulate the stator winding currents and to create a rotating magnetic field of the rotor of the BLDC motor. Its input is the active sector of the BLDC (*Sector*). Its outputs are the control signals sent to the electronic switches of the three-phase inverter (*Switching pattern*).

The *Buck Converter* converts a higher input voltage to a lower output voltage based on the duty cycle value. Its inputs are the duty cycle (*duty_cycle*) and the voltage from the battery (- *Batt*, + *Batt*). Its output is the voltage to be fed into the Three-Phase Inverter (-, +).

The *(Software) Controller* regulates the BLDC motor to ensure that the measured speed (the model's output) matches the desired speed selected by the user (the model's input). Its input is the error difference (*Error*) between the desired and the measured speed. Its output is the duty cycle (*duty_cycle*).

Engineers *did not* analyze the *safety* of their system design. This work aims to analyze how Simulation-driven FMEA and the tool support provided by Simulink® Fault Analyzer™ can enable engineers to design a safer system.

3 Simulation-driven FMEA

Simulink® Fault Analyzer™ enables engineers to perform FMEA safety analysis by providing support for (a) defining potential failure modes (FM) by modeling faults (Section 3.1) and (b) analyzing their effect (EA) by simulating their consequences (Section 3.2).

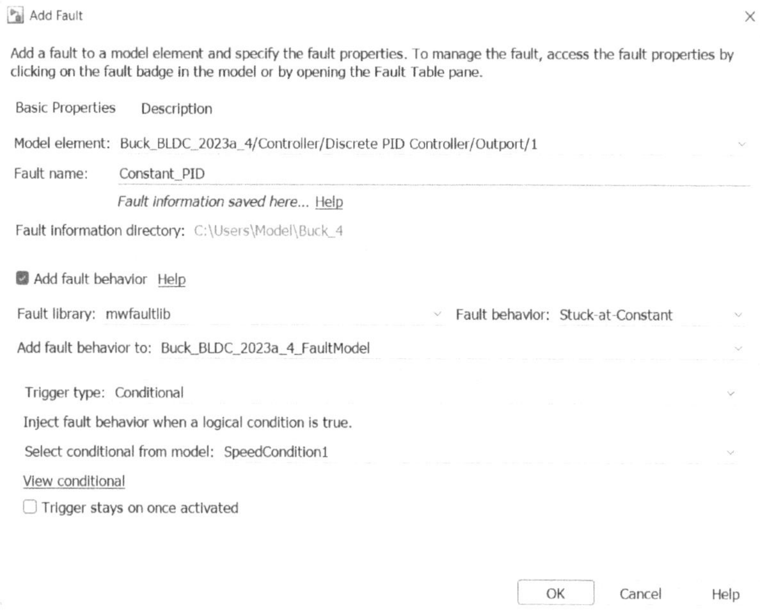

Add Fault

Add a fault to a model element and specify the fault properties. To manage the fault, access the fault properties by clicking on the fault badge in the model or by opening the Fault Table pane.

Basic Properties Description

Model element: Buck_BLDC_2023a_4/Controller/Discrete PID Controller/Outport/1

Fault name: Constant_PID

Fault information saved here... Help

Fault information directory: C:\Users\Model\Buck_4

Add fault behavior Help

Fault library: mwfaultlib Fault behavior: Stuck-at-Constant

Add fault behavior to: Buck_BLDC_2023a_4_FaultModel

Trigger type: Conditional

Inject fault behavior when a logical condition is true.

Select conditional from model: SpeedCondition1

View conditional

Trigger stays on once activated

OK Cancel Help

Fig. 2: Adding new faults with the Simulink® Fault Analyzer™.

3.1 Support for Failure Mode - FM

Simulink® Fault Analyzer™ enables engineers to extend the design model with faults. For example, Figure 1 presents three faults that are inserted on the *Sector*, *Measured speed*, and *PID(z)* signals. Simulink® Fault Analyzer™ graphically identifies faults with a lightning symbol on the signal on which the fault is applied (or on a component, for the Simscape™ [37] toolbox).

To insert a fault, engineers should select a signal (or component) and use the graphical interface presented in Figure 2. The interface displays the model element related to the fault ("*Model element*") and enables engineers to set the fault name ("*Fault name*") as well as to define its behavior ("*Add fault behavior*"). Simulink® Fault Analyzer™ maintains the fault logic encapsulated in specific blocks to keep it separated from the model logic and prevent the fault logic from inadvertently becoming part of the model. To define the fault behaviors, engineers can reuse existing faults from a predefined library ("*Fault library*"). Table 1 presents the list of faults provided by the Simulink® Fault Analyzer™ and a short description. For example, for the "*Constant_PID*" from Figure 2, the engineer selected the "*Stuck-at-Constant*" fault behavior from the library *mwfaultlib*, thereby forcing the signal to assume a constant value. Graphically, the fault is modeled as in Figure 3: The fault input is discarded, and the constant value 1 is always given as output.

Furthermore, faults can be activated via triggers. Table 2 presents the triggers provided by the Simulink® Fault Analyzer™ and a short description. For

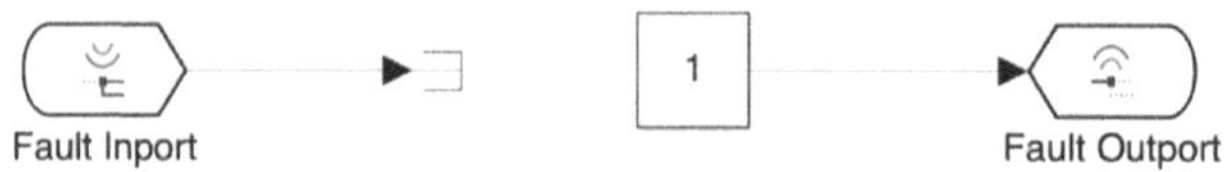

Fig. 3: Graphical representation of the "*Constant_PID*" fault.

Table 1: Fault behavior

Fault behavior	Description
Add Noise	Adds random noise to the signal.
Negate Value	Negates the value of a signal.
Absolute Value	Transforms the signal into its absolute value.
Stuck-at-Ground	Sets the signal to the ground.
Gain	Adds a gain to the signal.
Offset-by-1	Adds an offset to the input signal.
Unit Delay	Delays the signal by a single time unit.
Stuck-at-Constant	Sets the signal to a constant value.

example, for the "*Sector_fault*", the engineer selected the "*Conditional*" trigger, and specifies a condition ("*SpeedCondition1*") that forces the fault to be activated when the speed becomes greater than 50 *rpm*.

3.2 Support for Effect Analysis - EA

Simulation-driven FMEA supports EA by providing engineers the possibility of simulating the model with the faults injected to analyze their effects.

The Simulink® Fault Analyzer™ provides Fault Tables that enable engineers to activate different faults. For example, Figure 4 presents (a portion of) the Faults Table for our e-Bike model. The engineers activated the fault "*Constant_PID*" and disabled all the other faults.

Then, simulating the model within Simulink® enables the analysis of the fault effect. For example, Figure 5 depicts the desired speed (yellow line), the speed of a simulation where the fault is not enabled (blue line), and the speed of the current simulation (pink line). The simulation reveals that when the condition on the speed ("*SpeedCondition1*") is triggered — i.e., when the motor speed exceeds 50 *rpm* — the speed of the e-Bike suddenly stops following the desired speed. It then increases until 300 *rpm*, decreases until 20 *rpm*, and begins oscillating. This result enables engineers to understand the consequences of the fault. Specifically, forcing the gain of the PID to a constant value results in a significant increase in the speed of the e-Bike that exceeds the maximum speed of $25 km/h$ (i.e., 170 *rpm* wheel speed, considering a 28-inch wheel), which is mandated by most European countries [58,59].

Information regarding the effects of the faults helps engineers improve their models. For example, engineers can decide to mitigate the fault "*Constant_PID*"

Table 2: Trigger types

Trigger type	Description
Conditional	Activates a fault when a specific condition, on any of the signals or measures available in the model, is satisfied.
Timed	Activates a fault after the specified simulation time.
Manual	Activates a fault manually during the simulation by clicking on a button.

Fig. 4: A portion of the Fault Table for our e-Bike.

by applying appropriate strategies (e.g., adding another PID that takes control when problems occur or adding saturation mechanisms).

4 Evaluation

To assess the usefulness of Simulation-driven FMEA, we consider the following research questions (RQ):

- **RQ1**: How helpful is the support from the Simulink® Fault Analyzer™ in *modeling* the faults?
- **RQ2**: How helpful is the Simulation-driven FMEA for *safety* analysis?

We present our benchmark (Section 4.1) and answer RQ1 (Section 4.2) and RQ2 (Section 4.3).

4.1 Benchmark Design

To answer our research questions, two of the authors analyzed the e-Bike study subject and identified 15 faults. Table 3 provides the identifier ("ID") and a textual description ("Description") for each of these faults. Our faults involve both the cyber (*Controller*) and the physical (*Sensor*) parts of the CPS specified in the lower and upper parts of Table 3, and are applied both to Simulink® and Simscape™ components. For example, fault F1 refers to the breakage of the speed sensor, while fault F12 refers to the software controller and involves some noise on the output of the PID.

To ensure that our evaluation is based on realistic faults, we interacted with our expert to assess the criticality, plausibility, and frequency of each fault. We considered realistic faults that are either plausible, frequent, or critical.

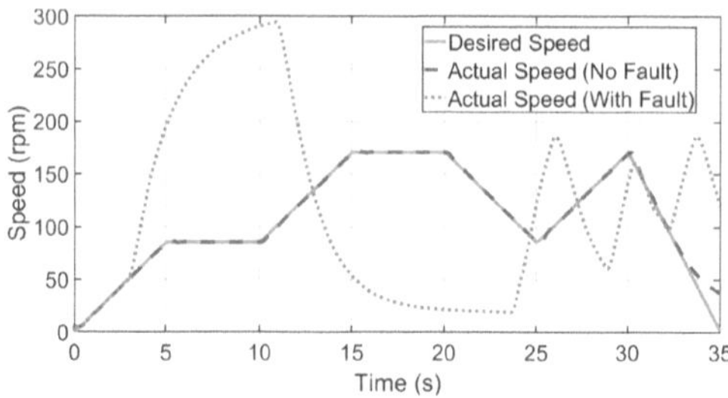

Fig. 5: The desired speed and the speed of the e-Bike when the fault is activated and deactivated.

We conducted a structured interview with the designer of the e-Bike controller to identify realistic faults. The designer had to assign a score between one and five for plausibility, frequency, and criticality; Moreover, the designer was required to justify their decision. The lowest bound (0) represents lower plausibility, frequency, or criticality, and the highest bound (5) corresponds to highly plausible, frequent, or critical faults. Table 3 reports the score provided by the expert for the plausibility (Plaus.), frequency (Freq.), and criticality (Critc.) of each fault. We considered a fault plausible, frequent, and critical if the score assigned by the expert is greater than or equal to 3.

The majority of our faults are plausible (66%), critical (74%), and not frequent (74%). Note that we expected the majority of faults to be infrequent, as undesirable behavior is not expected to be common.

We excluded faults F3 and F8 (identified with a blue background in Table 3). These faults involve an amplification error in the speed or sector sensors. We considered them to be non-realistic as they are not plausible, critical, and frequent, i.e., they had both plausibility, frequency, and criticality values lower than 3. Therefore, our benchmark consists of the remaining 13 realistic faults that are used to answer our RQs.

4.2 RQ1: Support of Simulink Fault Analyzer

To assess how the Simulink® Fault Analyzer™ helps in modeling faults, we proceeded as follows.

• *Step 1.* We considered each of the 13 faults and modeled them. The goal of this step is to assess whether we could model all the faults of our benchmark using the Simulink® Fault Analyzer™ (see Section 3.1). However, our models can potentially be inaccurate and not adequately reflect the expected fault behavior. Indeed, we considered a fault to be *accurate* when the model we provided matched the real behavior of the fault. To mitigate this problem, we performed an additional step.

• *Step 2.* We interviewed our expert to determine whether the models of our faults were appropriate. For inaccurate models, we tried to fix them.

Table 3: Plausibility, frequency, and criticality of the faults from our benchmark

ID	Description	Plaus.	Freq.	Critic.
F1	Breakage of the speed sensor [65]	4	4	5
F2	Noisy speed sensor [48]	4	2	1
F3	Amplification error in the speed sensor	1	1	1
F4	Delayed speed sensor [13]	1	1	3
F5	Speed sensor with constant value	4	4	5
F6	Breakage of the sector sensor	4	4	5
F7	Noisy sector sensor	4	2	1
F8	Amplification error in the sector sensor	1	1	1
F9	Delayed sector sensor [13]	1	1	3
F10	Sector sensor with constant value	4	4	5
F11	PID controller design error	3	2	5
F12	Noise on the output of the PID	4	2	4
F13	Amplification of the output of the PID	4	2	3
F14	Inverted PID output	1	1	5
F15	Constant output of the PID	3	2	5

Results. Table 4 presents the models of the faults from *Step 1* (Table 3). Note that, for many faults, multiple models (determined by several trigger types) were produced. Table 4 provides the identifier of the modeled fault ("ID"), the modeled behavior ("Fault behavior"), and the selected trigger type ("Trigger type"). For certain faults, we could not decide whether a "Timed" or a "Conditional" trigger was more appropriate because we did not discuss the triggers when we identified our faults with our expert. Therefore, we proposed alternative trigger options for discussion with our expert. For example, for fault F1, we considered the behavior "Stuck-at-Ground" and two triggers: Timed and Conditional.

The feedback from the domain expert (*Step 2*) confirmed that 53.8% (7 out of 13) of the models selected for the faults were accurate. These models are those with white background in Table 4. For the faults that had multiple trigger options (F1, F2, F4, F5, F6, F7, F9, and F10), the expert confirmed that "Conditional" was the appropriate trigger. Indeed, expert confirmed that faults do not typically emerge after a fixed time interval; rather, they occur when certain conditions arise, and those conditions cannot be defined a priori in purely time-based terms.

Further, the expert confirmed that 46.2% (6 out of 13) of our faults were correctly modeled, except for minor inaccuracies, e.g., a non fully correct condition or timing in the trigger. These models are those with a blue background color in Table 4. Examples of inaccuracies include incomplete conditions in conditional triggers and incorrect constant values (e.g., in F10 and F15). The minor inaccuracies have been fixed.

To summarize, Simulink® Fault Analyzer™ enables us to model all the 13 faults of our benchmark. In this process, we did not identify any major limitations in the support provided by this tool. Nevertheless, we learned a few lessons (see Section 5) that may help further improve this tool.

Table 4: Identifier (ID), fault behavior, and trigger type for our faults.

ID	Fault behavior	Trigger type
F1	Stuck-at-Ground	Timed & Conditional
F2	Add Noise	Timed & Conditional
F4	Unit Delay	Timed & Conditional
F5	Stuck-at-Constant	Timed & Conditional
F6	Stuck-at-Ground	Timed & Conditional
F7	Add Noise	Timed & Conditional
F9	Unit Delay	Timed & Conditional
F10	Stuck-at-Constant	Timed & Conditional
F11	Stuck-at-Ground	Conditional
F12	Add Noise	Conditional
F13	Gain	Conditional
F14	Negate Value	Conditional
F15	Stuck-at-Constant	Conditional

RQ1: Tool support

Simulink® Fault Analyzer™ successfully helped us design the models for the 13 faults of our benchmark.

4.3 RQ2: Usefulness of FMEA for Safety Analysis

To assess the usefulness of FMEA for safety analysis, we proceeded as follows.
• *Step 1.* We collected feedback from the expert regarding the expected effects of the faults by conducting a structured interview. During the interview, we asked what the expected system behavior was when each of the faults from Section 4.2 was activated and recorded their answer.
• *Step 2.* We used the support for EA provided by Simulation-driven FMEA (Section 3.2) to analyze the effect of the fault.
• *Step 3.* We compared the expected effect from the expert and the experimental effect from Simulation-driven FMEA.

Results. For each fault model presented in Table 4, Table 5 describes the expected effect from the expert (*Step 1*). Table 6 reports faults for which the experimental results did not match the expectations of the engineer (*Step 2* and *Step 3*). The portion of the effect that did not match the expectation is highlighted in italic. The expectation of the engineer is confirmed in 61.6% (8 out of 13) of the faults. For the remaining 38.4% (5 out of 13) of the faults, the simulation revealed effects that deviated from the engineer's expectation.

We observed that the differences identified during our experiments deviated from experts' expectations for two reasons. In certain cases (i.e., F7), the expected outcomes did not align with the actual results obtained during simulation. Indeed, for fault F7, while the expert expected "*extremely high currents until the motor stops spinning,*" the simulation stopped with an error message caused by the sector signal having a value of "0", which falls outside the accepted range of 1 to 6. This error is due to a bug in the modeling of the three-phase

Table 5: Expected effect from the expert

ID	Expected Effect
F1	The PID will have a high duty cycle. Additionally, at least one of the three current phases (and the battery currents) will show high values.
F2	The duty cycle will reach its maximum value.
F4	The PID will take more time to regulate the speed.
F5	The PID will increase the duty cycle, leading to an actual speed higher than the desired one.
F6	The system will stop because it is unable to encode the value, which lies between 1 and 6.
F7	The system will show extremely high currents, and the motor will stop spinning.
F9	The system will stop.
F10	The system will show very high phase currents until the motor slows down and eventually stops, then remains stationary.
F11	The duty cycle will fall to zero, and the motor will slow down until it stops.
F12	Phase currents will significantly oscillate.
F13	The PID will saturate, and the system will try to accelerate even if unnecessary.
F14	The system will slow down until it stops.
F15	The system will accelerate the motor regardless of speed, until electrical equilibrium is reached or until the fault disappears.

inverter. The engineer did not consider the case in which the component could receive invalid values, which could happen because of noise or external factors in real environments. Thus, the three-phase inverter does not correctly handle invalid sector values, causing the simulation to stop prematurely instead of exhibiting the expected system behavior in the presence of the fault. Ideally, the system should perform an emergency stop and slowly decelerate till the motor completely stops. In other instances (i.e., F10, F12, F13, and F15), while the outcomes partially matched the expectations, additional effects were observed during the experiments, or minor inaccuracies emerged. For example, for fault F13, the expert expected the PID to force the system to accelerate, even if this was unnecessary. The simulation revealed that the PID output had significant oscillations when the fault occurred, which was not expected. Therefore, this analysis demonstrates the effectiveness of the Simulation-driven FMEA supported by Simulink® Fault Analyzer™.

RQ2: Usefulness

FMEA was useful for analyzing the safety of our e-Bike. It enabled the engineers to uncover fault side-effects that had previously been overlooked. In addition, it helped identify unexpected effects.

5 Discussion and Lessons Learned

We present the lessons learned (Section 5.1), discuss them (Section 5.2), and summarize threats to the validity of our findings and experiments (Section 5.3).

Table 6: Experimental effect from Simulation-driven FMEA

ID	Experimental Effect
F7	*The simulation stops with an error message since the value "0" for the sector signal is not included within the accepted range [1-6].*
F10	The system shows very high phase currents. When the fault is triggered, the measured speed shows marked oscillations around zero, if the initial speed is low, or it decreases slowly, showing evident oscillations. *When the fault is deactivated, the PID maximizes the duty cycle to restore the speed as desired from the desired speed input. This process is very aggressive, especially if compared to the scenario in which the fault is not triggered, where smoother control actions are performed.*
F12	*Constant, but slight,* oscillations in the phase currents.
F13	*The PID shows evident oscillations when the fault occurs,* then restores standard behavior. *There is no relationship between the initial value of the PID and the experimental outcome.*
F15	The system accelerates the motor as much as possible, with duty cycle 1, then drops to 0 when the fault deactivates. *This causes an alternation of very high and very low measured speeds, and also of very high and very low phase currents, both when the fault alternates between active and inactive.*

5.1 Lessons learned

We held joint meetings with MathWorks experts to describe and analyze our results and outline the lessons learned from this study. The feedback from MathWorks experts was pivotal to confirm a proper usage of the Simulink® Fault Analyzer™, its modeling capabilities, and the Simulation-driven FMEA support. In the following account, we outline our lessons learned by classifying them into two categories: Simulink® Specific and Simulink® Agnostic.

Simulink®-specific. These lessons are related to the usage of the Simulink® environment. They are useful for SW engineers working as Simulink® engineers and for users of the Simulink® Fault Analyzer™.

- *Lesson 1 (Triggers).* Simulink® Fault Analyzer™ offers several types of triggers, including manually activated, activated at a specific time instant (timed), or activated when a specific condition is true (conditional). For our e-Bike example, we had to model an event-based trigger. For example, the trigger for fault F1 (Stuck-at-ground) applies when the sensor breaks. This problem is likely to occur when the desired speed undergoes a sudden change — for example, in the case of a sudden acceleration or braking. Therefore, the fault should apply to the measured speed when the sensor suddenly breaks and remains broken till the end of the simulation. By default, conditional triggers activate the faults each time a specific system condition is true and stop the fault injection as soon as it becomes false. To force the fault to remain active until the end of the simulation, the flag "Trigger stays on once activated" must be activated. We initially overlooked this flag and defined the logic to detect the sudden change and to maintain the condition of the trigger to true until the end of the simulation within the

Simulink® model (partially defeating the benefits of using the Simulink® Fault Analyzer™). The meeting with the Simulink® experts evidenced the presence of the flag. We modified the model of the fault to appropriately utilize the features provided by the Simulink® Fault Analyzer™.

- *Lesson 2 (Target of the fault application).* For Simulink® models, faults are typically applied to physical signals, except for the Simscape™ portion of the models [36]. For Simscape™, faults are applied to components rather than to signals. We believe that extending Simscape™ by providing the opportunity to add faults to signals can benefit practical applications. For example, fault F2 requires adding noise to the speed sensor. This fault may occur when electromagnetic noise is present on the controller board's cables. However, to directly apply the fault to an electrical (Simscape™) signal, it is necessary to drive a Simscape™ component (e.g., a variable resistor [41]) that changes the resistance depending on the value of a Simulink® signal that is affected by the fault.
- *Lesson 3 (Single fault activation on a specific signal).* The Simulink® Fault Analyzer™ enables the activation of multiple faults (related to different signals) within a single simulation using the multiple simulations panel [38]. However, activating both F1 and F2 requires simultaneously activating two faults on the same signal. This situation either requires (a) inserting the two faults at the source and the destination of the connection, respectively, or (b) creating an additional fault behavior that mimics the scenario in which both faults are activated. Note that while the second solution also applies to situations in which more than two faults need to be activated, the first solution only applies to the case of two faults. Extending the Simulink® Fault Analyzer™ by providing the activation of multiple faults on the same signal will avoid the creation of additional fault behavior.
- *Lesson 4 (Activation of a fault on multiple signals).* In certain cases, we had to simultaneously apply the same fault to multiple signals. For example, fault F7 requires considering noise on the sector sensor caused by electromagnetic interference. In this case, the same noise should be applied to more than one signal, i.e., all cables in the same area of the controller's board. To represent this situation, we modified the model by adding a Simulink® block that generated a constant signal with value "0", adding the noise fault to this signal, and summing the value of this signal to all signals subjected to electromagnetic interference. In this manner, when the fault is activated, the noise is applied to all the signals subjected to electromagnetic interference. Extending the Simulink® Fault Analyzer™ by providing the opportunity to apply the same fault to multiple signals would avoid modifying the model under analysis.
- *Lesson 5 (Accelerator Execution Mode).* Unlike the normal execution mode, the accelerator mode uses Just-in-Time (JIT) acceleration to generate an execution engine in memory instead of generating C code or MEX files [40]. This mode increases performance and reduces the simulation time. This mode is useful to support quick prototyping. The Simulink® Fault Analyzer™ does not currently support the accelerator mode. In our scenario, the accelerator mode would have enabled us to save approximately 30 seconds for each simulation.

Simulink®- agnostic. These lessons are not Simulink-specific. They are valuable for safety analysts, regardless of the safety framework they use.

• *Lesson 6 (Fault modeling — Section 4.2).* Explicitly modeling faults enabled us to discuss and reason with our e-Bike expert regarding the possible causes for the system's malfunctions. Our e-Bike expert confirmed that this practice helped with reasoning regarding the causes of possible safety breaches. These faults were not explicitly identified, discussed, and documented earlier. It also enabled the analysis of conditions (modeled by triggers) that activate these faults. This enabled the strengthening of the reasoning regarding situations and conditions that are more critical for the e-Bike software and its safety, and thus, more likely leading to faults. It encouraged deeper reflection, which led to the identification of faults that were not considered earlier. For example, the engineer identified additional faults, such as those related to the battery degradation or those involving the inverter, that they had never considered in their design. These faults are added by the engineer pipeline to continuously assess the safety of the e-Bike. To summarize, explicitly modeling faults can benefit CPS applications as they support a more rigorous safety analysis.

• *Lesson 7 (Fault simulation — Section 4.3).* Engineers typically assess the safety of their system by manually defining inputs and visually inspecting the models' outputs. This is a common practice in industrial environments, particularly when preliminary and high-level models of the system (such as the one we considered) are evaluated. However, this practice may lead engineers to overlook certain possible issues and the effects of these faults. Having a framework that enables the automatic analysis of CPS failure, such as the Simulink® Fault Analyzer™, mitigates this problem. The engineer who developed the model utilized in this study acknowledged that the proposed Simulation-driven FMEA approach was significantly beneficial for reasoning about plausible faults and their effects. Using this framework enables the identification of discrepancies between the expected and observed effects for certain faults (Section 4.3). For example, Figure 5 depicts the measured speed of the e-Bike when fault F15 occurs, thereby highlighting the maximum speed reached (in orange) and the regions where significant deceleration is observed (in purple). First, it can be noted that when F15 is active, the e-Bike reaches a maximum speed of approximately 40 km/h, which is above the maximum legal speed limit (25 km/h) [20] for an e-Bike. This limit is exceeded when the fault is active. Moreover, the sections highlighted in purple in Figure 6 exhibit a deceleration of approximately 2 m/s^2 — i.e., about 0.20 g — which is within the same order of magnitude as the deceleration of a commercial aircraft during a normal landing typically between 1.54 m/s^2 and 3.09m/s^2 and approximately one-fifth of the deceleration experienced during an emergency stop (rejected take-off), which can reach 5.14 m/s^2 [61]. However, the critical issue is that such braking is neither expected nor commanded by the user, which poses safety and stability risks for both the vehicle and the rider. To summarize, fault simulation support benefits CPS designers in performing a more systematic and rigorous analysis of the effects of faults.

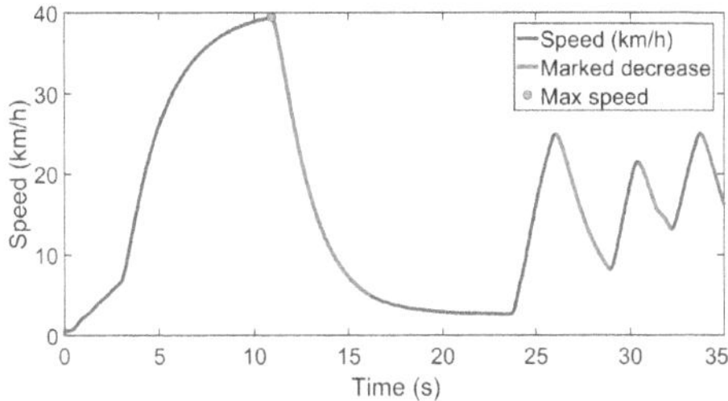

Fig. 6: The measured speed of the e-Bike when fault F15 is activated.

• *Lesson 8 (Development of mitigations).* Our expert not only modeled and analyzed the effects of faults but also initiated reasoning regarding possible mitigations. During our informal discussions preceding the structured interviews, the expert provided possible mitigations that could have been activated when specific faults occurred. For example, for fault F2 (noisy speed sensor), adding a backup sensor is a possible mitigation. The control logic switches the active sensor when it detects that the noise on the monitored speed exceeds a certain threshold. Figure 7 depicts the system behavior when this mitigation is activated. Figure 7a presents the desired speed and the monitored speed by the original (and faulty) sensor, while Figure 7b illustrates the measured speed when the mitigation is applied. Figure 7c depicts the activation status of the mitigation strategy: When mitigation is *On*, the backup sensor is used; when it is *Off*, the speed is read from the original sensor. The mitigation enables the system to switch between the two sensors when the fault is activated. This strategy enables the e-Bike to maintain the desired speed, mitigating the fault effect.

• *Lesson 9 (Mindset instauration).* Nowadays, developing safer and more secure systems is becoming pivotal, particularly considering that new CPS are ubiquitous, more connected, and perform more critical activities. Therefore, it is necessary to instantiate a proper engineering mindset based on rigorous and systematic safety reasoning. While this is a well established mindset in the research community, we found that it may be overlooked by industries. The results of this study confirm that a proper interaction among software engineers, system experts, academics, and industries developing tools for safety reasoning can help create this mindset by sharing knowledge, experiences, and solutions.

• *Lesson 10 (Software engineering for e-Bikes).* Bikes are traditionally not controlled and regulated by software. Therefore, e-Bike design typically considers both electrical aspects (e.g., the performance of the e-Bike) and physical aspects related to traditional bikes (e.g., material selection and aerodynamics). This traditional view is also reflected in recent analyses of e-Bike safety studies (e.g., [12]) that mostly consider the behavior of the rider, maximum speed of the electrical motors, etc. However, as software becomes a central part of these vehicles, safety analysis cannot be limited to hardware. It must also consider software-related aspects that may lead the vehicle to violate the safety standards and behave improperly. The results of this study reveal that as e-Bikes

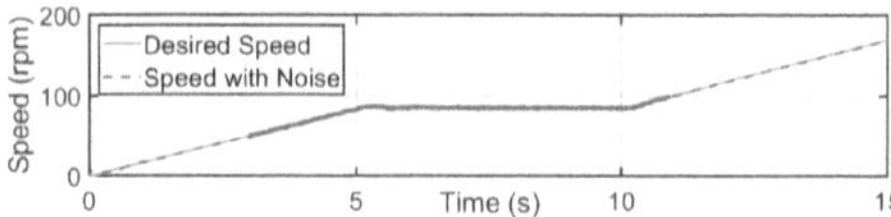

(a) The desired speed and measured speed of the e-Bike without mitigation.

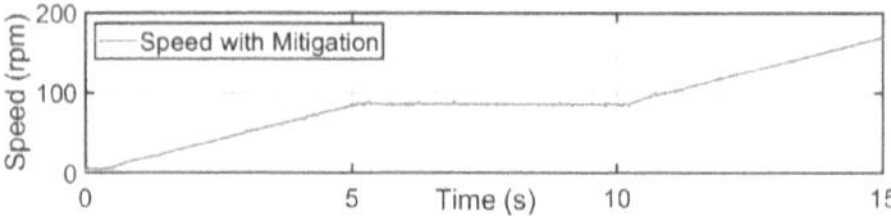

(b) The measured speed of the e-Bike with mitigation.

(c) Mitigation activation status.

Fig. 7: Mitigation of fault F2. Two sensors are used to measure the speed, and the backup sensor is activated when the noise exceeds the threshold.

are becoming software systems, software engineering techniques are needed to support rigorous development as well as the safety analysis of these systems.

5.2 Discussion

In this section, we discuss the originality of our work, the relevance of our findings for industrial applications, the significance of our contributions, and the generalizability of our results.

In this paper, we applied the Simulation-driven FMEA approach to a case study in the e-Bike domain — the e-Bike motor controller component. This contribution is *original*: Simulation-driven FMEA is a recent technology [54,39] that has never been applied to the e-Bike domain. Therefore, it improves the current state of the practice in the e-Bike industrial context.

In addition, our results are *relevant* to the e-Bike industry, as e-Bikes are software-intensive systems [64]. These systems are safety-critical and must comply with safety regulations and requirements [58,59]. Our results can also be potentially generalizable to other industrial domains (see Section 5.1).

Further, this work provided *significant* contributions. Compared with previous work assessing Simulation-driven FMEA on a robotic [45] and avionic [54] case studies, this work provides significant Simulink®-specific and Simulink®-agnostic lessons learned that can support the usage of Simulation-driven FMEA in practical scenarios. These lessons learned have been considered valuable by Simulink® experts we interacted with.

Finally, our work provides significant *generalizable* lessons learned. We discussed how our results on fault modeling and simulation apply to contexts beyond the specific industrial context (e-Bikes) of our paper.

5.3 Threats to Validity

The fault models and triggers we designed threaten the *internal validity* of our results; other models and triggers could lead to different results. However, the fact that all models and triggers provided by the Simulink® Fault Analyzer™ have been used mitigates this threat since it ensures that each of them has been considered by our evaluation.

We do not claim that *all* our results can necessarily be generalized to study subjects from other domains. We acknowledge that the selection of our study subject (a model from the e-Bike domain) and the faults could threaten the *external validity* of our results, as it affects their generalizability. We only considered transient and permanent faults, without considering byzantine or intermittent faults. However, the fact that we validated them through an interview with the engineer who developed the model mitigates this threat since it ensures that the faults are representative (at least) for this domain. While we interacted with just one domain expert, the fact that it was the developer of the model under test mitigates this threat since it ensures that he possessed the required knowledge on the system. Moreover, architecture of our case study is representative of common patterns in CPSs including motor control components. Furthermore, our lessons learned result from meetings with Simulink® experts who possess a comprehensive understanding of many CPS domains and needs.

The process we applied in our study is general and can be potentially applied to other study subjects. Future studies will assess if and how our results generalize to other domains and confirm or refute our hypotheses.

6 Related Work

This section (a) summarizes other techniques that support engineers in analyzing the safety of their systems and justifies the choice of Simulation-driven FMEA, and (b) presents other works that analyze the software of e-Bikes.

Support for safety analysis. FMEA [44] is a widely used reliability analysis tool for identifying and mitigating failures in systems, designs, and processes [68]. Simulation-driven FMEA [54] integrates the simulation capabilities of existing tools within FMEA. This technique was initially demonstrated by considering a flight control system of an unmanned ultralight helicopter [54]. Unlike the original work [54], which focuses on presenting the proposed solution, this paper empirically evaluates the effectiveness of Simulation-driven FMEA in an e-Bike case study to provide practitioners with lessons learned.

There are many techniques and approaches similar to FMEA that support engineers in risk evaluation and reliability checks. For example, data-driven

FMEA [18] relies on historical data and system metrics to evaluate and prioritize risks, life cost-based FMEA [53] measures risks for the system life cycle costs, model-based safety analysis [29] extends a shared system model with faults and physical elements to enable automation, and neuro-fuzzy techniques [27] manage the uncertainty and the subjectivity of risk evaluations. Other studies integrate Monte Carlo simulations to manage uncertainty in complex scenarios, integrate FMEA with a widespread reliability and safety model technique (GO methodology) [34], and propose a multiperspective FMEA method based on rough number projection [4] to obtain more accurate and coherent safety evaluations [4]. There are also solutions (e.g., [32,22,23]) that automatically identify failure causes using testing techniques. In our study, we decided to assess Simulation-driven FMEA since it automates the fault analysis and identifies its effects on the system and also because it is integrated with industrial solutions (Simulink® Fault Analyzer™). In addition, recent studies [12,63] advocate a more extensive use of FMEA to analyze software failures, as safety analysis typically overlooks software failure because system designers usually (erroneously) assume that the software does not fail. Our study considers both the cyber (software) and physical failures of the CPS (lower and upper parts of Table 3).

E-Bike software analysis. Software plays a critical role in modern e-Bikes. A recent article [2] clarifies that while most riders "*think the e-Bike difference has to do with the frame, motor, or battery, its usually all in the code*", developing software for eBikes is costly [2]. To design their software, engineers need to have a holistic view of the system. Acquiring this knowledge is complex and time-consuming. We experienced these factors in our project and had to invest significant time acquiring the know-how to work within this domain.

The e-Bike market has a large number of players (over 10,000 companies and a 27.15 USD billion market in 2022 [25]) that typically develop proprietary software. Nevertheless, several open-source e-bike projects exist. For example, the OpenSource project [16] provides software to help users build their e-Bikes.

Recent studies confirm that recent changes in electric vehicles have introduced new security threats and additional software safety concerns [10]. Standards have been developed to regulate the development of e-Bike software systems: The ISO 26262 standard (Part 6) [26] specifies software safety requirements for road vehicles (including e-Bikes), EN 15194 [19] is dedicated to e-Bikes. Furthermore, safety breaches were found in e-Bikes. In 2020, VanMoof updated their app since customers could increase their pedal-assisted power beyond the EU limit of 25 km/h by switching to the US country setting in their app: in the US, e-Bikes are generally capped at 32 km/h (20 mph) [55]. Despite these safety concerns, limited research has considered software engineering techniques for e-Bikes. A recent study considers the problem of automatically generating test cases for e-Bikes [35]. It assessed the effectiveness of existing test case generation solutions (HECATE [22]) in identifying bugs on Simulink models from the e-Bike domain. Our work is significantly different in its scope and objective (supporting the safety analysis of the system), technological support (Simulink® Fault Analyzer™), and evaluation methodology.

7 Conclusions and Future Work

In this paper, we applied Simulation-driven FMEA on an industrial case study in the e-Bike domain. We used Simulink® Fault Analyzer™ as a tool to evaluate FMEA. Our objective was to assess the effectiveness and practicality of Simulation-driven FMEA for assessing and improving software safety in CPSs. We identified 13 realistic faults involving both cyber and physical parts, modeled them using Simulink® fault injection features, and evaluated their effects through simulation. Our results, which we evaluated with a domain expert and Simulink® experts, show that Simulink® Fault Analyzer™ effectively supports fault modeling and effect analysis. For 38% of the cases, simulation results deviated from the engineers initial expectations, revealing unexpected fault impacts, enabling meaningful safety insights and design refinements, and allowing deeper engineering understanding and model improvement. We identified a set of lessons learned, which involved both Simulink®-specific and Simulink®-agnostic considerations, and we presented them to Simulink® experts. Our findings are useful for software engineers who work as Simulink® engineers, use the Simulink® Fault Analyzer™, or work as safety analysts. In future work, we plan to extend our study to other CPSs to investigate the generalization of our conclusion.

Data Availability

The original Simulink® model, the model extended with the faults, the results of the simulation, and the transcripts of our interviews are available online [1].

References

1. Replication Package. https://github.com/foselab/SimulationDrivenFMEA_Bikes (2025), accessed: July 21, 2025
2. Software Takes eBikes to New Heights (2025), https://www.eetimes.eu/software-takes-ebikes-to-new-heights/
3. Ali, S., Briand, L.C., Hemmati, H., Panesar-Walawege, R.K.: A Systematic Review of the Application and Empirical Investigation of Search-Based Test Case Generation. IEEE Transactions on Software Engineering **36**(6), 742–762 (2010). https://doi.org/10.1109/TSE.2009.52
4. An, H., Xu, G., Sun, Z., Chen, W., Pan, J.: Multi-perspective failure mode and effects analysis based on rough number projection. Engineering Failure Analysis **169**, 109192 (2025). https://doi.org/https://doi.org/10.1016/j.engfailanal.2024.109192
5. Badreddin, O., Lethbridge, T.C., Elassar, M.: Modeling Practices in Open Source Software. In: Open Source Software: Quality Verification. pp. 127–139. Springer (2013)
6. Bartocci, E., Mariani, L., Ničković, D., Yadav, D.: FIM: fault injection and mutation for Simulink. In: Joint European Software Engineering Conference and Symposium on the Foundations of Software Engineering. p. 17161720. ESEC/FSE, ACM (2022). https://doi.org/10.1145/3540250.3558932

7. Boll, A., Brokhausen, F., Amorim, T., Kehrer, T., Vogelsang, A.: Characteristics, Potentials, and Limitations of Open-Source Simulink Projects for Empirical Research. Software and Systems Modeling **20**(6), 2111–2130 (2021)
8. Boll, A., Kehrer, T.: On the Replicability of Experimental Tool Evaluations in Model-Based Development: Lessons Learnt from a Systematic Literature Review Focusing on MATLAB/Simulink. In: Systems Modelling and Management. p. 111130. Springer (2020). https://doi.org/10.1007/978-3-030-58167-1_9
9. Boll, A., Vieregg, N., Kehrer, T.: Replicability of Experimental Tool Evaluations in Model-Based Software and Systems Engineering With MATLAB/Simulink. Innovations in Systems and Software Engineering **20**(3), 209–224 (2024)
10. Chakraborty, S., Jha, S., Samii, S., Mundhenk, P.: Introduction to the Special Issue on Automotive CPS Safety & Security: Part 2. ACM Trans. Cyber-Phys. Syst. **8**(2) (May 2024). https://doi.org/10.1145/3650210
11. Chechik, M.: On safety, assurance, and reliability: a software engineering perspective (keynote). In: Proceedings of the 30th ACM Joint European Software Engineering Conference and Symposium on the Foundations of Software Engineering. p. 2. ESEC/FSE 2022, Association for Computing Machinery, New York, NY, USA (2022). https://doi.org/10.1145/3540250.3569443
12. Cherry, C.R., MacArthur, J.H.: E-bike safety. A review of Empirical European and North American Studies. Light Electric Vehicle Education and Research Initiative (2019)
13. Dialynas, G., Christoforidis, C., Happee, R., Schwab, A.: Rider control identification in cycling taking into account steering torque feedback and sensory delays. Vehicle System Dynamics **61**(1), 200–224 (2023). https://doi.org/10.1080/00423114.2022.2048865
14. Ding, W., Liang, P., Tang, A., Vliet, H.v., Shahin, M.: How Do Open Source Communities Document Software Architecture: An Exploratory Survey. In: International Conference on Engineering of Complex Computer Systems. p. 136145. ICECCS, IEEE Computer Society (2014). https://doi.org/10.1109/ICECCS.2014.26
15. Dyba, T., Kitchenham, B.A., Jorgensen, M.: Evidence-Based Software Engineering for Practitioners. IEEE Software **22**(1), 58–65 (2005)
16. EBike, O.: EBike / EScooter modular DIY OpenSource electronics and software. https://github.com/openSourceEBike (2024), accessed: July 21, 2025
17. Engström, E., Petersen, K.: Mapping Software Testing Practice With Software Testing Research SERP-Test taxonomy. In: IEEE International Conference on Software Testing, Verification and Validation Workshops (ICSTW). pp. 1–4 (2015). https://doi.org/10.1109/ICSTW.2015.7107470
18. Ervural, B., Ayaz, H.I.: A fully data-driven FMEA framework for risk assessment on manufacturing processes using a hybrid approach. Engineering Failure Analysis **152**, 107525 (2023). https://doi.org/https://doi.org/10.1016/j.engfailanal.2023.107525
19. European Standard: EN 15194 Cycles — Electrically power assisted cycles — EPAC Bicycles (2023), https://www.en-standard.eu/ilnas-en-15194-cycles-electrically-power-assisted-cycles-epac-bicycles/?srsltid=AfmBOorJ582mAq4zKCiFsLYUqBxriXM6OvYdcDctOTdRM26dr1eGDz9d, accessed: 21 July 2025
20. European Union: Regulation (EU) No 168/2013 of the European Parliament and of the Council of 15 January 2013 on the approval and market surveillance of two- or three-wheel vehicles and quadricycles Text with EEA relevance. https://eur-lex.europa.eu/legal-content/EN/TXT/HTML/?uri=CELEX:02013R0168-20241127 (2024), accessed: July 21, 2025

21. Ford Motor Company: Ford Motor Company Customer-specific Requirements, for Use with ISO/TS 16949: 2002 (2003)
22. Formica, F., Fan, T., Rajhans, A., Pantelic, V., Lawford, M., Menghi, C.: Simulation-based testing of simulink models with test sequence and test assessment blocks. IEEE Transactions on Software Engineering **50**(2), 239–257 (2023)
23. Formica, F., Petrunti, N., Bruck, L., Pantelic, V., Lawford, M., Menghi, C.: Test Case Generation for Drivability Requirements of an Automotive Cruise Controller: An Experience with an Industrial Simulator. In: Joint European Software Engineering Conference and Symposium on the Foundations of Software Engineering. p. 19491960. ESEC/FSE 2023, Association for Computing Machinery (2023). https://doi.org/10.1145/3611643.3613894
24. Goddard, P.: Software FMEA techniques. In: Annual Reliability and Maintainability Symposium. International Symposium on Product Quality and Integrity (Cat. No.00CH37055). pp. 118–123 (2000). https://doi.org/10.1109/RAMS.2000.816294
25. Insights, F.B.: E-Bike Drive Unit Market Size, Share & COVID-19 Impact Analysis, By Product Type (Mid-drive Motors and Hub Motors), By Application (OEM and Aftermarket), and Regional Forecasts, 2023-2030. https://www.fortunebusinessinsights.com/e-bike-drive-unit-market-107520 (2024), accessed: July 21, 2025
26. International Standard Organization: ISO 26262-6:2018 — Road vehicles — Functional safety — Part 6: Product development at the software level (2024), https://www.iso.org/standard/68388.html, accessed: 21 July 2025
27. Ivanan, J., Lisjak, D., Pavleti, D., Kolar, D.: Improvement of Failure Mode and Effects Analysis Using Fuzzy and Adaptive Neuro-Fuzzy Inference System. Machines **11**(7) (2023). https://doi.org/10.3390/machines11070739
28. Joshi, A., Heimdahl, M.P., Miller, S.P., Whalen, M.W.: Model-based safety analysis. Tech. rep. (2006)
29. Joshi, A., Whalen, M.: Model-based safety analysis final report (02 2006)
30. Kitchenham, B., Dyba, T., Jorgensen, M.: Evidence-Based Software Engineering. In: International Conference on Software Engineering. pp. 273–281 (2004). https://doi.org/10.1109/ICSE.2004.1317449
31. Krishnan, R., Bhada, S.V.: An Integrated System Design and Safety Framework for Model-Based Safety Analysis. IEEE Access **8**, 146483–146497 (2020). https://doi.org/10.1109/ACCESS.2020.3015151
32. Le Tolguenec, P.A., Rachelson, E., Besse, Y., Teichteil-Koenigsbuch, F., Schneider, N., Waeselynck, H., Wilson, D.: Exploration-Driven Reinforcement Learning for Avionic System Fault Detection (Experience Paper). In: SIGSOFT International Symposium on Software Testing and Analysis. p. 920931. ISSTA, ACM (2024). https://doi.org/10.1145/3650212.3680331
33. Lisagor, O., Kelly, T., Niu, R.: Model-based safety assessment: Review of the discipline and its challenges. In: International Conference on Reliability, Maintainability and Safety. pp. 625–632. IEEE (2011)
34. Liu, L., Fan, D., Wang, Z., Yang, D., Cui, J., Ma, X., Ren, Y.: Enhanced GO methodology to support failure mode, effects and criticality analysis. Journal of Intelligent Manufacturing **30**, 1451–1468 (2019). https://doi.org/10.1007/s10845-017-1336-0
35. Marzella, M., Bombarda, A., Minervini, M., Bisceglia, N.M., Gargantini, A., Menghi, C.: Test Case Generation for Simulink Models: An Experience from the E-Bike Domain. In: Search-Based Software Engineering. Springer Nature Switzerland, Cham (2025)

36. MathWorks: Blocks that Support Fault Modeling, https://www.mathworks.com/help/simscape/ug/block-support.html, accessed: June 22, 2025
37. MathWorks: Simscape Model and simulate multidomain physical systems, https://www.mathworks.com/products/simscape.html, accessed: July 21, 2025
38. MathWorks: Simulate Models with Faults by Using the Multiple Simulations Panel, https://www.mathworks.com/help/fault-analyzer/ug/simulate-models-with-faults.html, accessed: July 21, 2025
39. Mathworks: Simulink Fault Analyzer (2003), https://www.mathworks.com/products/simulink-fault-analyzer.html
40. MathWorks: How Acceleration Modes Work. https://www.mathworks.com/help/simulink/ug/how-the-acceleration-modes-work.html (2024), accessed: July 21, 2025
41. MathWorks: Variable Resistor. https://www.mathworks.com/help/simscape/ref/variableresistor.html (2024), accessed: July 21, 2025
42. Melo, S.M., Carver, J.C., Souza, P.S., Souza, S.R.: Empirical Research on Concurrent Software Testing: A Systematic Mapping Study. Information and Software Technology **105**, 226–251 (2019)
43. Mezhuyev, V., Al-Emran, M., Ismail, M.A., Benedicenti, L., Chandran, D.A.P.: The Acceptance of Search-Based Software Engineering Techniques: An Empirical Evaluation Using the Technology Acceptance Model. IEEE Access **7**, 101073–101085 (2019). https://doi.org/10.1109/ACCESS.2019.2917913
44. MILP1629: Procedures for Performing a Failure Mode Effects and Criticality Analysis. U.S. Department of Defense. (1949)
45. Miraglia, G., Bimbi, M., Nanjundappa, M.: Enhancing Mobile Robot Safety Evaluation with Simulation-Driven Model-Based Safety Analysis. In: RSS Safe Autonomy Workshop (2024), https://sites.google.com/view/rss2024-safe-autonomy/home
46. Mode, F.: Effects and Criticality Analysis (FMECA). Reliability Analysis Center (1993)
47. Modelwise: Automatic assessment of an industrial safety-critical system (2025), https://modelwise.ai/automatic-assessment-of-an-industrial-safety-critical-system/
48. Murgano, E., Caponetto, R., Pappalardo, G., Cafiso, S.D., Severino, A.: A Novel Acceleration Signal Processing Procedure for Cycling Safety Assessment. Sensors **21**(12) (2021). https://doi.org/10.3390/s21124183
49. Office of manned space flight, Apollo program, Apollo Reliability and Quality Assurance Office: Procedure for Failure Mode, Effects and Criticality Analysis (FMECA) (1966)
50. Panichella, A., Kifetew, F.M., Tonella, P.: A large scale empirical comparison of state-of-the-art search-based test case generators. Information and Software Technology **104**, 236–256 (2018)
51. Rebello, S., Goyal, N.K.: Software system reliability and safety assessment: an extended FMEA approach. International Journal of Reliability and Safety **4**(4), 366 (2010). https://doi.org/10.1504/ijrs.2010.035575
52. Reifer, D.J.: Software Failure Modes and Effects Analysis. IEEE Transactions on Reliability **R-28**(3), 247–249 (1979). https://doi.org/10.1109/TR.1979.5220578
53. Rhee, S.J., Ishii, K.: Using cost based FMEA to enhance reliability and serviceability. Advanced Engineering Informatics **17**(3), 179–188 (2003). https://doi.org/https://doi.org/10.1016/j.aei.2004.07.002

54. Rhein, J., Bimbi, M., Miraglia, G., Holzapfel, F.: Simulation-Driven Failure Modes and Effects Analysis of Flight Control System Architectures. In: Digital Avionics Systems Conference (DASC). pp. 1–10. IEEE (2024)
55. Ricker, T.: Cheating VanMoof e-bikes will be slowed outside the US. https://www.theverge.com/2020/11/10/21558235/vanmoof-slows-s3-x3-europe-japan-speed-limit (2024), accessed: November 7, 2024
56. Rodriguez, A.D., Newman, T., Dearstyne, K.R., Cleland-Huang, J.: SAFA: A Tool for Supporting Safety Analysis in Evolving Software Systems. In: Proceedings of the 37th IEEE/ACM International Conference on Automated Software Engineering. ASE '22, Association for Computing Machinery, New York, NY, USA (2023). https://doi.org/10.1145/3551349.3559535
57. Sayyad, A.S., Goseva-Popstojanova, K., Menzies, T., Ammar, H.: On Parameter Tuning in Search Based Software Engineering: A Replicated Empirical Study. In: International Workshop on Replication in Empirical Software Engineering Research. p. 8490. RESER, IEEE (2013). https://doi.org/10.1109/RESER.2013.6
58. Schepers, P., Wolt, K.K., Fishman, E.: The safety of e-bikes in The Netherlands. International Transport Forum Discussion Paper 2018-02, Paris (2018). https://doi.org/10.1787/21de1ffa-en
59. Schleinitz, K., Petzoldt, T., Franke-Bartholdt, L., Krems, J.F., Gehlert, T.: The German Naturalistic Cycling Study — Comparing cycling speed of riders of different e-bikes and conventional bicycles. Safety Science **92**, 290297 (2017). https://doi.org/10.1016/j.ssci.2015.07.027
60. Shrestha, S.L., Chowdhury, S.A., Csallner, C.: Replicability Study: Corpora For Understanding Simulink Models & Projects. In: ACM/IEEE International Symposium on Empirical Software Engineering and Measurement (ESEM). pp. 1–12. IEEE (2023). https://doi.org/10.1109/ESEM56168.2023.10304867
61. SKYbrary: Deceleration on the Runway. https://skybrary.aero/articles/deceleration-runway (2025)
62. Stories, M.C.: Bosch eBike Systems Develops Electric Bike Controller with Model-Based Design. https://www.mathworks.com/company/user_stories/bosch-ebike-systems-develops-electric-bike-controller-with-model-based-design.html (2024), accessed: November 7, 2024
63. Thieme, C.A., Mosleh, A., Utne, I.B., Hegde, J.: Incorporating software failure in risk analysis. Reliability Engineering & System Safety **198**, 106804 (2020)
64. Times, E.: Software Takes eBikes to New Heights. https://www.eetimes.eu/software-takes-ebikes-to-new-heights/ (2025), accessed: July 21, 2025
65. Tran, C.D., Kuchar, M., Sobek, M., Sotola, V., Dinh, B.H.: Sensor Fault Diagnosis Method Based on Rotor Slip Applied to Induction Motor Drive. Sensors **22**(22) (2022). https://doi.org/10.3390/s22228636
66. Valle, P., Riccio, V., Arrieta, A., Tonella, P., Arratibel, M.: An industrial experience report on applying search-based boundary input generation to cyber-physical systems. Empirical Software Engineering **30**(4), 112 (2025)
67. Valyayev, D., Mukasheva, A., Yedilkhan, D., Aigerim, B., Mukhammejanova, D.: FMEA variables of software failure risks based on journals and metrics. In: 2024 IEEE 4th International Conference on Smart Information Systems and Technologies (SIST). pp. 302–307 (2024). https://doi.org/10.1109/SIST61555.2024.10629469
68. Wang, Z., Gao, J.M., Wang, R.X., Chen, K., Gao, Z.Y., Zheng, W.: Failure Mode and Effects Analysis by Using the House of Reliability-Based Rough VIKOR Approach. IEEE Transactions on Reliability **67**(1), 230–248 (2018). https://doi.org/10.1109/TR.2017.2778316

69. Zhu, J., Wang, L., Han, X.: Safety and Performance, Why not Both? Bi-Objective Optimized Model Compression toward AI Software Deployment. In: Proceedings of the 37th IEEE/ACM International Conference on Automated Software Engineering. ASE '22, Association for Computing Machinery, New York, NY, USA (2023). https://doi.org/10.1145/3551349.3556906

Causal Liability in Autonomous Systems

Kaveh Aryan[1], Hana Chockler[1], and Mohammad Reza Mousavi[1]

King's College London, London, UK
{kaveh.aryan,hana.chockler,mohammad.mousavi}@kcl.ac.uk

Abstract. With the widespread use of autonomous systems, liability often shifts towards the manufacturers and part suppliers, especially when various system components, sourced from different suppliers, contribute to a failure. This necessitates a framework for automatic liability apportionment which can be embedded in manufacturer-supplier contracts and minimise legal disputes. To this end, we propose a formal framework based on the notion of actual causality in structural causal models and the robustness semantics of logical specifications. We prove several desirable properties of this framework. Moreover, we formalise the notion of causal non-interaction, give sufficient conditions for it to hold, and demonstrate its utility in deriving upper bounds for liability analysis. Furthermore, we relate our definition to the existing notion of harm, empirically evaluate our framework to demonstrate its efficacy, and release a software package implementing our approach. We extend our framework to handle interval specifications.

Keywords: formal methods · causality · liability

1 Introduction [1]

The widespread adoption of autonomous systems, including autonomous vehicles (AVs) and service robots, significantly reshapes the insurance landscape [2]. Traditionally, liability rested primarily with system users and owners; in the case of reckless driving, the driver is typically held legally liable and is covered by personal auto insurance that provides protection against such risks [1]. In contrast, autonomous systems aim to function safely and reliably on their own, increasingly shifting liability toward manufacturers and their suppliers of mechanical, electronic, and software components. Manufacturers, even after indemnifying suppliers externally, still need effective means to recoup costs associated with system faults.

To fairly and automatically apportion liability within complex multi-supplier ecosystems, we propose a framework based on structural causal models (SCMs) [26] and robustness semantics of logical specifications [13]. Our method systematically apportions liability among components, allowing integration into contracts between manufacturers and suppliers so that they incorporate both component

[1] We gratefully acknowledge and appreciate Prof. Özlem Gürses, Dickson Poon School of Law, King's College London for their valuable insights.

E. Albert and C. Pasareanu (Eds.): FASE 2026, LNCS 16504, pp. 283–303, 2026.
https://doi.org/10.1007/978-3-032-22774-4_15

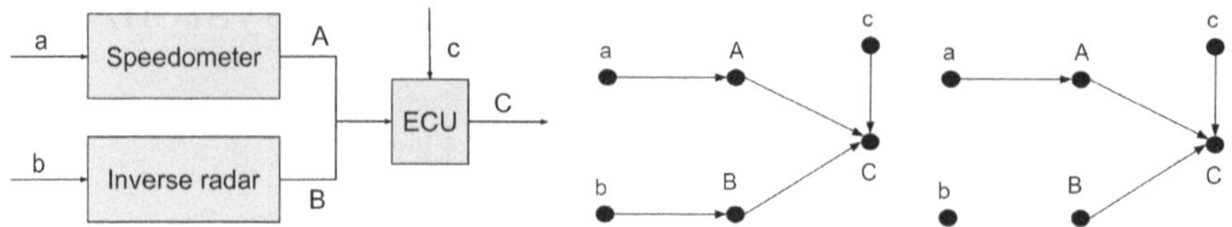

Fig. 1: Simplified AEB system in Examples 1 and 6. System (left), graph without intervention (middle), and with intervention (right). An *intervention* forces the value of a component to a fixed value, overriding its normal functional dependencies.

specifications as well as the rules for liability apportionment in cases of failure. Incorporating formal causality into contractual terms minimises legal disputes and enhances the insurability of advanced autonomous technologies [22].

A key challenge is ensuring the framework remains meaningful and tractable in complex systems with interacting faults. This issue is prominently manifest in existing approaches such as Shapley values [12]. To address this, we introduce the concept of *causal non-interaction*, provide conditions for its application, and demonstrate its utility for bounding liability calculations.

We also show that our framework relates to existing literature, specifically aligning with harm quantification by Beckers, Chockler, and Halpern (BCH) [6]. We empirically evaluate our model to underscore its practical applicability in facilitating precise and fair liability apportionment. We offer a Python toolbox implementing our liability measure (DOI: `https://doi.org/10.5281/zenodo.18175468`).

We illustrate our approach using an Automatic Emergency Braking (AEB) system example:

Example 1. Consider an AEB system comprising a speedometer, radar, and an Electronic Control Unit (ECU) calculating the braking force (Fig. 1 (left)). In the event of a failure–such as those documented in high-profile autonomous vehicle (AV) crashes[2], our framework identifies which component failures cause malfunctions, quantifies respective liabilities, and enables embedding these apportionments into manufacturer-supplier contracts.

While motivated by AV liability, our framework addresses the broader problem of attributing responsibilities in any component-based system. Our framework focuses on apportioning liability among system components conditional on a system-level failure having occurred. External or unavoidable causes, such as extreme environmental conditions or third-party actions, can be naturally modeled in our framework as exogenous variables in the causal model. If such factors alone suffice to cause the failure, no internal component forms a cause and the resulting liabilities are zero

[2] e.g., `https://www.ntsb.gov/investigations/Pages/HWY18MH010.aspx`

The paper proceeds as follows: Section 2 reviews the related literature; Section 3 reviews the preliminaries, i.e., component model, failure quantification, structural causal models, and actual causality; Section 4 defines liability formally and explores its properties and the notion of causal non-interaction; Section 5 extends our framework to handle interval specifications; Section 6 establishes the formal relation of our work to the BCH notion of harm; Section 7 presents the empirical studies; and Section 8 concludes.

2 Related Work

2.1 Actual causality

Liability inherently involves causal reasoning [21]. There are two types of causal relations: *type causality*, relating general phenomena (e.g., smoking and lung cancer), and *actual causality*, concerning specific events (e.g., a particular radar defect causing a crash) [15,33]. Actual causality is pertinent for liability apportionment.

The simplest explication of actual causality is *but-for* causality [25]—an event without which the effect wouldn't occur. There are also more sophisticated definitions like Halpern-Pearl (HP) [16,18] definitions, which, although influential, are computationally demanding—HP is D_2^P [3] or D_1^P based on the version of the definition [16]. We base our efficient approach on but-for causality, although our framework is general and accommodates any reasonable notion of actual causality.

2.2 Causality in liability law

Actual causality (cause in fact) underpins liability law (criminal, tort, insurance) [21]. Liability apportionment typically involves: (i) dividing damages into indivisible causal components and (ii) apportioning each component, often using subjective rules based on fault [19]. Recent principled yet abstract methods (i.e., Shapley values) are emerging [12,14,20]. These works are abstract because they do not address how one can measure the contribution of a component in the overall system failure. Our approach retains this two-step process, contributing a principled, concrete, and computationally efficient liability definition.

2.3 Liability in autonomous systems

The rise of autonomous vehicle functions necessitates new insurance frameworks. Two notable examples are Manufacturer Enterprise Liability [2] and the UK's Automated & Electric Vehicles Act 2018, which faces legal criticism [11]. Manufacturer Enterprise Liability exclusively burdens manufacturers, regardless of fault. Our paper provides a formal approach enabling manufacturers to distribute liability among suppliers, supporting broader insurance adoption.

2.4 Quantification of causality

Although causality is typically binary, liability apportionment requires quantified causality measures [17]. Three prominent quantified causality approaches are responsibility, harm, and Shapley values.

Responsibility and harm Responsibility [8], developed from HP causality, quantifies actual causality as inversely proportional to the number of causes in a causal set [9,30]. Unlike our method, responsibility addresses actual implementation systems without relying on formal specifications and is computationally expensive. Harm quantifies causality by looking at the outcome differences with and without an event [6]. Our work is a generalisation of the notion of the harm where component interactions are taken into account and failure is quantified by robustness of the system wrt a general failure formula.

Game theoretic approaches Shapley values apportion payoffs in cooperative games based on fairness axioms [7]. They are applied to liability by modelling tortfeasors as game players [12,14,20]. Unlike abstract Shapley approaches, we propose a concrete structural causal model-based method with polynomial-time complexity, avoiding Shapley values' exponential complexity.

Remark 1. Type causality quantification significantly differs from actual causality. For example, Pearl's graphical approach employs probability distributions and interventions [26,27], unlike actual causality focused on individual events.

2.5 Risk assessment

Reliability engineering methods, such as Failure Mode and Effects Analysis (FMEA) [29] and Fault Tree Analysis (FTA) [31], focus on risk identification and modelling *failure propagation* via logical gates. Our method, in contrast, mathematically models causal structures and assigns liability after failures, differing fundamentally in both approach and purpose.

3 Preliminaries

3.1 Component Model

As we are dealing with systems with multiple components, we define formal abstractions for components, systems, and their specifications and implementations, inspired by a similar architecture for software liability [24].

Definition 1. *A* component *is a tuple* $X = (\mathcal{I}, O, \mathcal{P}, R, f)$ *in which* $\mathcal{I}$ *is a set of variables called* input variables, O *is a single variable not in* $\mathcal{I}$ *called the* output variable, $\mathcal{P}$ *is a set of* types, $R : \mathcal{I} \cup \{O\} \to \mathcal{P}$ *is a function that determines the* types *of the input and output variables, and* $f : \prod_{Y \in \mathcal{I}} R(Y) \to R(O)$ *is the* component's function. *As a notational convenience, when it is clear from the context, we use the component's output variable and the component's name interchangeably. A component is an* implementation *of another component (labelled as* specification*) if they vary only in their functions. A* system *is a set of components* $\mathcal{S} = \{(\mathcal{I}_i, O_i, \mathcal{P}_i, R_i, f_i)\}_{i=1}^{N}$ *subject to the condition that the output variables of the components are distinct. An* implementation system *consists of the implementations of the components in a* specification system.

As evident from the definition, a component is an entity characterised by one or several input variables with specified types, an output variable with a specified type, and a mechanism to transform the inputs into the output. The decision to have a single output variable is primarily driven by notational convenience. However, this choice is not restrictive, as there is always the option to combine multiple variables into a vector.

Example 2. In the context of the AEB system of Example 1, the speedometer component is defined as $X_A = (\{a\}, A, \{\mathbb{R}\}, R_A, f_A)$ in which $R_A(a) = R_A(A) = \mathbb{R}$ and $f_A(a) = a + 10$, where a denotes the actual speed of the vehicle in meters per second and f_A reflects the sensor error in our model. The (inverse) radar component is defined as $X_B = (\{b\}, B, \{\mathbb{R}\}, R_B, f_B)$ in which $R_B(b) = R_B(B) = \mathbb{R}$ and $f_B(b) = b + 1$, where b represents actual inverse distance of the vehicle to an impending obstacle in reciprocal meter. The ECU component is defined as $X_C = (\{A, B, c\}, C, \{\mathbb{R}\}, R_C, f_C)$ in which $R_C(A) = R_C(B) = R_C(c) = R_C(C) = \mathbb{R}$ and $f_C(A, B, c) = AB + c$, where c represents a calibrating constant set at construction time. The term AB shows that the magnitude of the braking force is proportional to the speed of the speedometer and inversely proportional to the distance to the obstacle. Assuming that X_C is a component specification, there can be many different implementations thereof which differ only in their functions. The system consisting of these components is $\mathcal{T} = \{X_A, X_B, X_C\}$. As mentioned earlier, when clear, we use output variables to denote components, so a more succinct notation is $\mathcal{T} = \{A, B, C\}$.

Note that while we present algebraic definitions of specifications and implementations for the purpose of formal reasoning, the proposed framework treats components as black boxes in practice: it only requires query access to component outputs for given inputs, and does not rely on symbolic representations of their internal functions.

It is useful to define the notion of a replacement system, a system in which one or more components is replaced with others.

Definition 2. *If $\mathcal{S}$ is a system, $\mathcal{X} = \{(\mathcal{I}_i, O_i, \mathcal{P}_i, R_i, f_i)\}_{i=1}^{k} \subseteq \mathcal{S}$ is any set of components in $\mathcal{S}$, and $\mathcal{X}' = \{(\mathcal{I}_i, O_i, \mathcal{P}_i, R_i, g_i)\}_{i=1}^{k}$ is another set of components, then the* replacement system *$\mathcal{S}_{\mathcal{X} \to \mathcal{X}'}$ is defined as $(\mathcal{S} - \mathcal{X}) \cup \mathcal{X}'$. If $\mathcal{X} = \{X\}$ and $\mathcal{X}' = \{X'\}$ are singleton sets, we conveniently denote $\mathcal{S}_{\mathcal{X} \to \mathcal{X}'} = \mathcal{S}_{\{X\} \to \{X'\}}$ by $\mathcal{S}_{X \to X'}$. If one or more implementation components are replaced with their corresponding specifications, the replacement is called a* fix.

Example 3. Consider the AEB system $\mathcal{T}$ defined in Example 2. Suppose there is a specification radar component $X'_B = (\{b\}, B, \{\mathbb{R}\}, R_B, g_B(b) = b)$. The replacement system $\mathcal{T}_{X_B \to X'_B}$ is the system $\mathcal{T}$ in which the radar component is replaced with the specification one, that is $\mathcal{T}_{X_B \to X'_B} = \{X_A, X'_B, X_C\}$.

3.2 Quantification of Failure

Two final definitions concern the characterisation and quantification of the extent of failure. Failure is characterised as a quantifier-free first-order formula over the system variables. The extent of failure is quantified by how much these variables need to change to no longer satisfy the failure formula.

Definition 3. *If P is a quantifier-free first-order formula over a set of variables $\mathcal{V}$, the* extension *of P, denoted by $ext(P)$, is the set of points in the $\mathcal{V}$-space that satisfy P. If P characterises a system's failure, it is called a* failure formula *and $\mathcal{F}=ext(P)$ is called a* failure set.

Example 4. Following Example 2, suppose $P(A,B,C)=B\geq 10\wedge C\leq 1$, that is, a failure happens if the detected distance is less than 0.1 meters and the generated braking force is less than 1 units. Then the failure set is $\mathcal{F}=ext(P)=\{(A,B,C)\in \mathbb{R}^3 : B\geq 10\wedge C\leq 1\}$.

To simplify the presentation, we usually refer to failure sets such as $\mathcal{F}$, implicitly assuming suitable quantifier-free first-order formulas, such as P, for which $\mathcal{F}=ext(P)$.

We quantify the extent of a failure in a system, aka its *robustness*, by measuring the distance of the state of the system to the boundary of the failure set, along the same lines of the robustness semantics for logical specifications [13]. Assuming the reader is familiar with the concept of a metric space [34], we recall the definition of the depth of a point in a set:

Definition 4. *Consider a metric space, $(\mathcal{G},d)$, a point in the space, $x\in\mathcal{G}$, and a subset of the space, $\mathcal{H}\subseteq\mathcal{G}$, then*

- *The* distance *from x to $\mathcal{H}$ is defined as $dist_d(x,\mathcal{H})=\inf\{d(x,y):y\in\bar{\mathcal{H}}\}$, where $\bar{\mathcal{H}}$ is the closure of $\mathcal{H}$, that is the intersection of all closed sets containing $\mathcal{H}$; and*
- *The* depth *of x in $\mathcal{H}$ is defined as $depth_d(x,\mathcal{H})=dist_d(x,\mathcal{G}-\mathcal{H})$.*

The subscript d denotes the distance metric, d, in the metric space, which will be the Euclidean distance throughout the paper. Also, $dist_d$ and $depth_d$ are non-negative numbers; for all $x\in\mathcal{H}$, $dist_d(x,\mathcal{H})=0$; and for all $x\notin\mathcal{H}$, $depth_d(x,\mathcal{H})=0$.

Example 5. In Example 4, $dist_d((100,5,1),\mathcal{F})=5$ and $depth_d((100,5,1),\mathcal{F})=0$.

In practice, the failure formula (hence, the failure set) is usually a function of only a few system variables. For instance, in our running example, a reasonable failure formula could be a proposition about the impact velocity (e.g, $P: M_{\text{vehicle}}v\geq 1$) where M_{vehicle} is the vehicle's mass. In such cases, the causal models maps inputs in different dimensions to the same output space through the robustness quantity, making them comparable through the robustness of the variables in the failure formula. This is one of the benefits of our approach, which facilitates straightforward comparisons across different variables and units of measurement.

In the rest of this section we define structural causal models [17, 26] and use them to define a notion of actual causality.

3.3 Structural Causal Models

Our work is based on *structural causal models*, which serve both as a basis for the notion of causality and for our proposed apportionment of liabilities.

Definition 5. *A* structural causal model (SCM) *is a tuple* $\mathcal{M}=(\mathcal{U},\mathcal{V},\mathcal{P},R,\mathcal{E})$ *in which* $\mathcal{U}$ *and* $\mathcal{V}$ *are two disjoint sets of variables called* exogenous *and* endogenous *variables, respectively,* $\mathcal{P}$ *is a set of* types, $R:\mathcal{U}\cup\mathcal{V}\rightarrow\mathcal{P}$ *is a function that determines the* types *of variables in* $\mathcal{U}$ *and* $\mathcal{V}$, *and* $\mathcal{E}$ *is the set of* structural equations $\{X=f_X(Y_1,Y_2,Y_3,...,Y_n)\}_{X\in V}$ *where* $Y_i\in(\mathcal{U}\cup\mathcal{V})-\{X\}$ *for all* $X\in\mathcal{V}$.

Notation 1 *If* $\mathcal{M}=(\mathcal{U},\mathcal{V},\mathcal{P},R,\mathcal{E})$ *is an SCM, we denote members of each set by non-calligraphic face with an integer index, such as* U_i. *Elements in* $\mathcal{V}$, $\mathcal{R}$, *and* $\mathcal{E}$ *that share the same index are assumed to correspond. For example,* R_i *and* E_i *denote the type and structural equation of variable* V_i, *respectively.*

The motivation for differentiating between exogenous and endogenous variables is to distinguish between variables that are the inputs of the system and those that are influenced by the inputs, respectively. Structural *equations* (or *assignments*, more precisely) specify how each endogenous variable is influenced by the exogenous and other endogenous variables.

Example 6. In the AEB system in Example 2, each component (causally) determines the value of its output based on its inputs. The whole system corresponds to the following structural causal model: $\mathcal{M}=(\{a,b,c\},\{A,B,C\},\mathbb{R},R_A\cup R_B\cup R_C,\{A=f_A(a),B=f_B(b),C=f_C(A,B,c)\})$.

In line with our focus on particular events and actual causality, we are interested in the particular values, called *state*, that variables of the system take:

Definition 6. *If* $\mathcal{M}=(\mathcal{U},\mathcal{V},\mathcal{P},R,\mathcal{E})$ *is an SCM, a* context $\boldsymbol{u}$ *is a setting of (i.e., a vector assignment to) variables in* $\mathcal{U}$. *Similarly, a* state $\boldsymbol{v}$ *is a setting of variables in* $\mathcal{V}$. *The* state space *of* $\mathcal{M}$, *denoted by* $SS(\mathcal{M})$, *is the set of all states of* $\mathcal{M}$. *Moreover, if* $\boldsymbol{x}$ *is a setting of variables in* $\mathcal{X}\subseteq\mathcal{U}\cup\mathcal{V}$, *the value of the variable* $X\in\mathcal{X}$ *under* $\boldsymbol{x}$ *is denoted by* $\boldsymbol{x}[X]$.

An SCM can be visualised through a graph where each variable in $\mathcal{U}\cup\mathcal{V}$ is represented by a node, and a directed edge from X to Y exists iff the value of Y depends, in at least one state and context, on the value of X. Fig. 1 (middle) shows the graph corresponding to the SCM in Example 6. An SCM is acyclic if its corresponding graph is acyclic. If $\mathcal{M}$ is an acyclic SCM, a given context u uniquely determines the state of $\mathcal{M}$. This state is denoted by $\boldsymbol{v}=M[\boldsymbol{u}]$. For the purpose of this paper, we align with existing literature and focus on acyclic SCMs.

Example 7. In the SCM in Example 6, one possible context is $\boldsymbol{u}=(a,b,c)=(80,4,1)$. The resulting state is $\mathcal{M}[\boldsymbol{u}]=(90,5,451)$. The state space of the system is $\{(A=f_A(a),B=f_B(b),f_C(A,B,c)):a,b,c\in\mathbb{R}\}=\{(a+10,b+1,(a+10)(b+1)+c): a,b,c\in\mathbb{R}\}$. Also, $\boldsymbol{u}[a]=80$ and $\mathcal{M}[\boldsymbol{u}][A]=90$.

As suggested by Example 6, there is a close connection between our component model and SCMs. As formalised in the following definition, for each system there exists a corresponding SCM:

Definition 7. *Suppose* $\mathcal{S} = \{(\mathcal{I}_i, O_i, \mathcal{P}_i, R_i, f_i)\}_{i=1}^N$ *is a system with* N *components. The* corresponding structural causal model (SCM) *is defined as* $SCM(\mathcal{S}) = (\mathcal{U}, \mathcal{V}, \mathcal{P}, R, \mathcal{E})$ *in which* $\mathcal{V} = \cup_{i=1}^N \{O_i\}$ *is the set of endogenous variables,* $\mathcal{U} = (\cup_{i=1}^N \mathcal{I}_i) - \mathcal{V}$ *is the set of exogenous variables,* $\mathcal{P} = \cup_{i=1}^N \mathcal{P}_i$ *is the set of types,* $R = \cup_{i=1}^N R_i$ *is the function that determines the type of the variables, and* $\mathcal{E} = \{O_i = f_i(a_i)\}_{i=1}^N$ *is the set of structural equations where* a_i *denotes the arguments of* f_i.

Example 8. The corresponding SCM of the system in Example 2 is identical to the SCM presented in Example 6: $SCM(\mathcal{T}) = \mathcal{M}$.

Another important notion for defining and quantifying causal effects is that of an *intervention*. An intervention refers to deliberately changing the value of a variable to observe its subsequent effects on the other variables. By conducting interventions, we gain insights into the causal relationships and assess the impact of specific variables.

Definition 8. *If* $\mathcal{M} = (\mathcal{U}, \mathcal{V}, \mathcal{P}, R, \mathcal{E})$ *is an SCM,* $X \in \mathcal{V}$*, and* $x \in R(X)$*, then the* intervention model $\mathcal{M}[X = x]$ *is the SCM* $(\mathcal{U}, \mathcal{V}, \mathcal{P}, R, \mathcal{E}')$ *in which* $\mathcal{F} = \mathcal{F}'$ *except that the equation* $X = f_X(Y_1, Y_2, Y_3, ..., Y_n), Y_i \in (\mathcal{U} \cup \mathcal{V}) - \{X\}$*, is replaced with* $f_X(Y_1, Y_2, Y_3, ..., Y_n) = x$.

Example 9. If we intervene on the SCM in Example 6 by replacing the equation for B with $B = b_0$ where $b_0 \in R_B$ is a fixed inversed distance to an obstacle, the resulting intervention model will be $\mathcal{M}[B = b_0] = (\{a, b, c\}, \{A, B, C\}, \mathbb{R}, R_A \cup R_B \cup R_C, \{A = f_A(a), B = b_0, C = f_C(A, B, c)\})$. The corresponding graph is shown in Fig. 1 (right).

There is a similarity between the concept of intervention (Definition 8) and replacement (Definition 2). However, they have a significant difference as well: in a replacement, a component is replaced with an arbitrary component and function (with the same arguments, because the replacing component should be the same as the replaced one in its input and output variables). In contrast, in an intervention, the replacing function is a constant function.

Notation 2 *If* S *and* T *are specification and implementation systems, respectively, and* $\boldsymbol{u}$ *is a context, then the state of the systems under* $\boldsymbol{u}$ *is denoted by* $\mathbf{s}[\boldsymbol{u}]$ *and* $\mathbf{t}[\boldsymbol{u}]$*, or simply,* $\mathbf{s}$ *and* $\mathbf{t}$*, respectively. If* X *is a component or a set of components, the state of the replacement system where* X *is fixed to* X'*, i.e.,* $SCM(\mathcal{T}_{X \to X'})[\boldsymbol{u}]$ *is denoted by* $\mathbf{t}+X$.

3.4 Actual Causality

We conclude this section with our definition of actual causality, which is based on the notion of but-for causality. We define *a set* of implementation components as a cause of failure if replacing them with their specifications moves the state of the system out of the failure region.

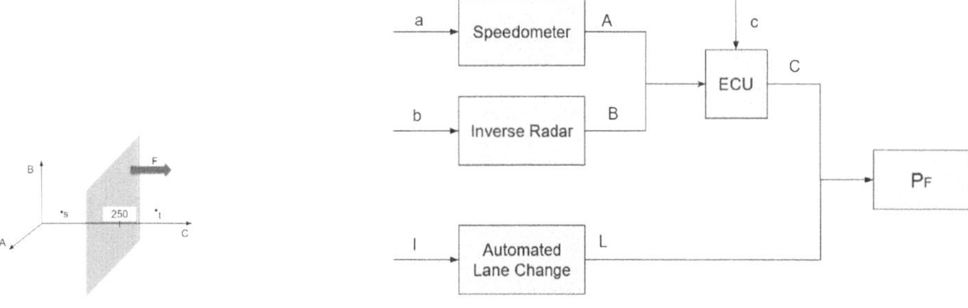

Fig. 2: Failure set in Example 10 (left) and component diagram in Example 12 (right).

Definition 9. *Suppose $\mathcal{S}$ is a specification system, $\mathcal{T}$ is an implementation of $\mathcal{S}$, $\mathcal{F}$ is a failure set, $\boldsymbol{u}$ is a context, $\mathcal{X} \subseteq \mathcal{T}$, and $\mathcal{X}'$ is the corresponding components in $\mathcal{S}$. The components in $\mathcal{X}$ are a* but-for (BF) cause *of $\mathcal{T}$ ending up in $\mathcal{F}$, denoted by $BF(\mathcal{T},\mathcal{X},\boldsymbol{u},\mathcal{F})$, iff the following conditions hold:*

- *BF1. $SCM(\mathcal{T})[\boldsymbol{u}] \in \mathcal{F}$;*
- *BF2. $SCM(\mathcal{T}_{\mathcal{X} \to \mathcal{X}'})[\boldsymbol{u}] \notin \mathcal{F}$; and*
- *BF3. $\mathcal{X}$ is minimal, in the sense that none of its subsets satisfies BF1 and BF2.*

We define the *degree of interaction* between the components of a system as the maximum size of a causal set for the system's failure. That is, every causal set has a cardinality less than or equal to the system's degree of interaction where no "higher order" interaction exists in the system.

Definition 10. *Suppose $\mathcal{S}$ is a specification system, $\mathcal{T}$ is an implementation of $\mathcal{S}$, $\mathcal{F}$ is a failure set, and $\boldsymbol{u}$ is a context. The* degree of interaction *between the components of $\mathcal{T}$ is defined as:*

$$deg_{int}(\mathcal{T},\boldsymbol{u},\mathcal{F}) = max\{|\mathcal{X}| : BF(\mathcal{T},\mathcal{X},\boldsymbol{u},\mathcal{F})\} \tag{1}$$

Example 10. Suppose $\mathcal{S}$ and $\mathcal{T}$ are a pair of specification and implementation AEB system similar to the one in Examples 1, respectively. Suppose $\mathcal{M}_{\mathcal{S}}$ and $\mathcal{M}_{\mathcal{T}}$ are the corresponding SCMs characterised by $\mathcal{U} = \{a,b,c\}$, $\mathcal{V} = \{A,B,C\}$, and the equations shown in Table 1 (left). Suppose $\boldsymbol{u} = (a,b,c) = (10,10,10)$, resulting into specification and implementation states, $\boldsymbol{s} = (A,B,C) = (10,10,110)$ and $\boldsymbol{t} = (A,B,C) = (20,20,420)$, respectively. Suppose $\mathcal{F} = \{(A,B,C) \in \mathbb{R}^3 : C \geq 250\}$, representing braking forces beyond the tolerance of the vehicle's actuators. Fig. 2 (left) depicts this situation.

Under $\boldsymbol{u}$, the states of the specification, implementation, and fixed systems are shown in Table 1 (right). It can be seen that $\{A\}$ and $\{B\}$ are a cause of $\mathcal{T}$ ending up in $\mathcal{F}$, while $\{C\}$ is not. The degree of interaction in this system is 1 for the specified context.

As stated below, if a component is not faulty, it is not a member of a cause of the failure:

Theorem 1. *Suppose $\mathcal{S}$ is a specification system, $\mathcal{T}$ is an implementation of $\mathcal{S}$, $\mathcal{F}$ is the failure set, u is a context, $X \in \mathcal{T}$, and X' is the corresponding component in $\mathcal{S}$. If $X = X'$, there is no set $\mathcal{X} \subseteq \mathcal{T}$ where $X \in \mathcal{X}$ and $BF(\mathcal{T}, \mathcal{X}, \boldsymbol{u}, \mathcal{F})$.*

Proof by contradiction. For space considerations, we provide missing proofs in [4].

4 The Liability Framework

In this section, we explain our method of apportionment of liabilities. In line with the legal procedures for determining liabilities (Section 2), we propose a two-step procedure: (i) identification of the causal components, and (ii) apportionment of liabilities. Step (i) is done in accordance with Definition 9. Step (ii) is carried out by measuring the effect of fixing each component X. To this end, we start by identifying all causal sets that include the component X. Within each causal set, we measure the effect of X by fixing all components within the set including X, and then again, without fixing X. We calculate the difference to measure the effect. We then average these differences across all causal sets that include X, to determine the average effect of fixing X. This procedure is repeated for all other components, and the resulting values are normalised to sum to one.

To keep the liability computation tractable, we restrict our causal sets to a fixed maximum cardinality, k. This is justified from both a theoretical and an empirical perspective: theoretically, we show how the assumption about the degree of interaction can be efficiently checked, in Section 4.2. Additionally, there is empirical evidence showing that higher degrees of interaction (beyond 3) rarely occur in practice [10, 28, 32].

Definition 11. *Suppose $\mathcal{S}$ is a specification system, $\mathcal{T}$ is an implementation of $\mathcal{S}$, $\mathcal{F}$ is the failure set, $\boldsymbol{u}$ is a context, $\boldsymbol{s}$ and $\boldsymbol{t}$ are specification and implementation states under $\boldsymbol{u}$, respectively, and $k \leq |\mathcal{T}|$ is a fixed number, then the* k-leg liability *of X, denoted by ϕ_X^k, is defined as:*

$$\phi_X^k(\mathcal{T}, \mathcal{S}, \boldsymbol{u}, \mathcal{F}, k, X) = \omega \frac{1}{|\mathcal{B}_X|} \sum_{\mathcal{K} \in \mathcal{B}_X} max(0, depth_d(\boldsymbol{t} + \mathcal{K}, \mathcal{F})) \tag{2}$$

Table 1: System equations (left) and states (right) in Example 10.

Component	Spec.	Impl.
A	a	$a+10$
B	b	$b+10$
C	$c+AB$	$c+AB+10$

State name	State value	$BF(\mathcal{T},\{X\},u,\mathcal{F})$
$\boldsymbol{s}$	(10,10,110)	
$\boldsymbol{t}$	(20,20,420)	
$\boldsymbol{t}+A$	(10,20,220)	*True*
$\boldsymbol{t}+B$	(20,10,220)	*True*
$\boldsymbol{t}+C$	(20,20,410)	*False*

in which $\mathcal{B}_X = \{\mathcal{K} \subseteq \mathcal{T} : BF(\mathcal{T}, \mathcal{K} \cup \{X\}, \boldsymbol{u}, \mathcal{F}) \wedge |\mathcal{K}| < k\}$, $\boldsymbol{t} + \mathcal{K}$ *is defined as in Notation 2, and:*

$$\omega = \left[\sum_{X \in \mathcal{T}} \sum_{\mathcal{K} \in \mathcal{B}_X} \frac{1}{|\mathcal{B}_X|} max(0, depth_d(\boldsymbol{t} + \mathcal{K}, \mathcal{F})) \right]^{-1} \quad (3)$$

The normalizing coefficient ω *is chosen so that* $\sum_X \phi_X^k = 1$.

According to this definition, to measure the liability of the implementation component X, we first create the set $\mathcal{B}$ of all component sets of maximum size k, that include X and are causal for $\mathcal{T}$ ending up in $\mathcal{F}$. For each causal set, we measure the effect of X, as the difference in system robustness between fixing the entire causal set and fixing the causal set without X. We then average these differences across all such causal sets. The following example shows several desirable properties of our definition which are formalised and proved afterwards.

Example 11. Consider the AEB system shown in Table 2. In this example, A and B are interpreted as before, C represents a braking coefficient, and D is the final braking force. Assuming $\boldsymbol{u} = (10,10,10,10)$, state of the specification and implementation systems are $\boldsymbol{s} = (A,B,C,D) = (10,10,10,110)$ and $\boldsymbol{t} = (A,B,C,D) = (20,20,20,420)$, respectively. Suppose $\mathcal{F} = \{(A,B,C,D) \in \mathbb{R}^4 : D \geq 250\}$ represents the braking forces beyond the tolerance of the vehicle's actuators.

The states of the specification, implementation, and replacement systems are shown in Table 3. It is evident from the table that rows containing D are not a cause for $\mathcal{T}$ ending up in $\mathcal{F}$, because for these rows $D = 410 \geq 250$. Fixing D, even in combination with other components, does not fix the problem. Therefore, intuitively, D should not be held liable. Moreover, the error—i.e., the distance between

Table 2: System equations in Example 11.

Cm.	**Spec.**	**Impl.**
A	a	$a+10$
B	b	$b+10$
C	c	$c+8$
D^{sp}	$d+\max(AB,AC,BC)$	
$D^{im.}$	$d+\max(AB,AC,BC)+10$	

Table 3: System states in Example 11.

St.	A	B	C	D	**Value**	**St.**	A	B	C	D	**Value**
$\boldsymbol{s}$					(10,10,10,110)	$t+AB$	*	*			(10,10,20,220)
$\boldsymbol{t}$					(20,20,20,420)	$t+AC$	*		*		(10,20,10,220)
$t+A$	*				(10,20,18,380)	$t+AD$	*			*	(10,20,20,410)
$t+B$		*			(20,10,18,380)	$t+BC$		*	*		(20,10,10,220)
$t+C$			*		(20,20,10,420)	$t+BD$		*		*	(20,10,20,410)
$t+D$				*	(20,20,18,410)	$t+CD$			*	*	(20,20,10,410)

specification and implementation in this context—in C is 8, which is less than the error in A and B which is 10. As these errors symmetrically contribute to the failure as mediated by D, C should be apportioned less liability followed by A and B, and A and B should be held equally liable. The 2-leg liability follows these intuitions:

$$\begin{aligned}\phi_A^2 &= \omega\frac{1}{2}((depth_d(\mathbf{t}+B,\mathcal{F}) - depth_d(\mathbf{t}+AB,\mathcal{F})) + (depth_d(\mathbf{t}+C,\mathcal{F}) - depth_d(\mathbf{t}+AC,\mathcal{F}))) \\ &= \omega\frac{1}{2}((130-0)+(170-0)) = \omega 150 = 0.348\end{aligned}$$

Similarly, $\phi_B^2 = 0.348$, $\phi_C^2 = 0.302$, and $\phi_D^2 = 0$. In this example the degree of interaction is at least $k=2$, because any single variable's effect on the output could be masked by other variables. However, two variables together are able to affect the output.

4.1 Properties of Liability

Now, we formalise several desirable properties of k-leg liability, which serve as an axiomatic justification of our definition.

Consistency Consistency states that k-leg liability remains constant beyond the system's degree of interaction (see Definition 10):

Theorem 2. *Suppose $\mathcal{S}$ is a specification system, $\mathcal{T}$ is an implementation of $\mathcal{S}$, $\mathcal{F}$ is the failure set, and $\boldsymbol{u}$ is a context. If $k = deg_{int}(\mathcal{T},\boldsymbol{u},\mathcal{F})$, then for all component $X \in \mathcal{T}$, $\phi_X^k = \phi_X^{k+1}$.*

This justifies the relevance of a fixed k in k-leg liability. In the next section, we show that if the system can be partitioned into non-interacting subsets, the degree of interaction is bounded accordingly. We also prove sufficient conditions for such decomposability.

Dummy component This property posits that components not causal for the failure receive no liability:

Theorem 3. *Suppose $\mathcal{S}$ is a specification system, $\mathcal{T}$ is an implementation of $\mathcal{S}$, $\mathcal{F}$ is the failure set, u is a context, and $X \in \mathcal{T}$ is a component. If no subset of $\mathcal{T}$ that includes X is a BF cause of $\mathcal{T}$ ending up in $\mathcal{F}$, then $\phi_X^k = 0$ for $k = 1,2,3,...,|\mathcal{T}|$.*

In particular, non-faulty components receive no liability, because, by Theorem 1, if a component is not faulty, it cannot be a member of a but-for cause of the failure. Therefore, its k-leg liability is zero.

Polynomial Complexity

Proposition 1. *Suppose $\mathcal{S}$ is a specification system, $\mathcal{T}$ is an implementation of $\mathcal{S}$, $\mathcal{F}$ is the failure set, and $\boldsymbol{u}$ is a context. Calculating k-leg liability of each component $X \in \mathcal{T}$ is $O(2^k|\mathcal{T}|^{k+1})$. As k is a fixed number, it is $O(|\mathcal{T}|^{k+1})$.*

4.2 Causal Non-Interaction

In this section, we examine conditions for bounding the parameter k in k-leg liability. For this purpose, we start with a characterisation of the notion of *non-interaction.*

Definition 12. *Suppose* $\mathcal{M} = (\mathcal{U}, \mathcal{V}, \mathcal{P}, R, \mathcal{E})$ *is an SCM;* $A, B,$ *and* $H \in \mathcal{V}$*;* $h \in R(H)$*;* $\boldsymbol{u}$ *is a context; and* $\boldsymbol{v}$ *is the corresponding state. Two variables* A *and* B *are* causally non-interacting *wrt the event* $H = h$ *iff there is no set* $\mathcal{C} \subseteq \mathcal{V}$ *for which* $C = \boldsymbol{v}$ *is a cause of* $H = h$ *and* $\{A,B\} \subseteq \mathcal{C}$*. Two sets of variables* $\mathcal{A} \subseteq V$ *and* $\mathcal{B} \subseteq V$ *are* causally non-interacting *iff for all* $A \in \mathcal{A}$ *and* $B \in \mathcal{B}$*,* A *and* B *are causally non-interacting. These definitions are generalised to more than two variables and sets in a straightforward manner.*

The following theorem shows a sufficient condition for causal non-interaction:

Theorem 4. *Suppose* $\mathcal{M} = (\mathcal{U}, \mathcal{V}, \mathcal{P}, R, \mathcal{E})$ *is an SCM. If* P *is a failure formula in the form* $P(\mathcal{A}) = \bigwedge_i^n f_i(\mathcal{A}_i)$*, where* $\mathcal{A}_i \subseteq \mathcal{A}$*, for* $i = 1, \ldots, n$*, and* $\mathcal{A}_i$*s are disjoint, then under any context* $\boldsymbol{u}$ *for which* P*,* $\mathcal{A}_i$*s are causally non-interacting wrt* P*.*

This condition mirrors a common way the output of different subsystems contribute to a failure: when both subsystems fail [35]. Now, if we know that system variables are causally non-interacting, we can use the following corollary to bound k in k-leg liability.

Corollary 1. *Suppose* $\mathcal{M} = (\mathcal{U}, \mathcal{V}, \mathcal{P}, R, \mathcal{E})$ *is an SCM and* P *is a failure formula. If* $\mathcal{V}$ *is partitioned into sets* $\mathcal{A}_1, \ldots, \mathcal{A}_n$ *that are causally non-interacting wrt* P *under a context* $\boldsymbol{u}$*, then* $\deg_{int}(\mathcal{M}, \boldsymbol{u}, \mathcal{F}) \leq \max\{|\mathcal{A}_i|\}$.

The utility of these results is illustrated in the following example.

Example 12. Consider the AV, shown in Fig. 2 (right), that includes two subsystems: one is an AEB system described in Example 10, and the other is an Automated Lane Change (ALC) subsystem consisting of three more components, that is $|ALC| = 3$. If an obstacle is detected, the vehicle will crash if neither the AEB is able to brake nor the ALC is able to change lanes to avoid the obstacle. In this case, P_F is a conjunction of the failure condition of the AEB and the failure condition of the ALC. Therefore, according to Theorem 4, AEB and ALC are causally non-interacting with respect to P_F. By Corollary 1, the maximum k of k-leg liability is given by $\max(|AEB|, |ALC|) = 3$. Thus, we need to search for causal sets of size at most 3, not 6 (the total number of components). Furthermore, this search is conducted only within each separate subsystem, without considering potential causal sets that have elements from both subsystems.

5 Extension to Interval Models

Our liability framework can be extended to handle various real-world complexities beyond the basic deterministic point-value models. In this section, we present one key extension in detail. In many real-world systems, specifications define acceptable ranges rather than exact values. For instance, a temperature sensor might be specified to operate within ś2řC of the true temperature. We extend our framework to handle such interval specifications.

Definition 13. *An* interval component *is a component* $X=(\mathcal{I},O,\mathcal{P},R,f)$ *where the specification function* $f'_X:\prod_{Y\in\mathcal{I}}R(Y)\to\mathcal{P}([l,u])$ *returns an interval* $[l,u]\subseteq\mathbb{R}$ *rather than a point value. That is, for inputs* $(y_1,\ldots,y_n)$ *where* $y_i\in R(Y_i)$ *for each* $Y_i\in\mathcal{I}$*, we have* $f'_X(y_1,\cdots,y_n)=[l(y_1,\cdots,y_n),u(y_1,\cdots,y_n)]$*. The implementation function* f_X *returns a point value that may or may not lie within this interval.*

For interval models, we need to redefine the notion of fixing a component:

Definition 14. *When fixing a component* X *to its interval specification* X'*, the resulting system projects the implementation value onto the specification interval. For a system* $\mathcal{T}$ *with interval specification* $\mathcal{S}$ *and context* $\boldsymbol{u}$*, the state of the fixed system* $SCM(\mathcal{T}_{X\to X'})[\boldsymbol{u}]$ *has the value of* X *computed as:*

$$X=\begin{cases} l(\boldsymbol{y}) & \text{if } f_X(\boldsymbol{y})<l(\boldsymbol{y})\\ f_X(\boldsymbol{y}) & \text{if } f_X(\boldsymbol{y})\in[l(\boldsymbol{y}),u(\boldsymbol{y})]\\ u(\boldsymbol{y}) & \text{if } f_X(\boldsymbol{y})>u(\boldsymbol{y})\end{cases}$$

where $\boldsymbol{y}=(y_1,\ldots,y_n)$ *are the values of* X*'s input variables in state* $SCM(\mathcal{T})[\boldsymbol{u}]$*, and* $[l(\boldsymbol{y}),u(\boldsymbol{y})]=f'_X(\boldsymbol{y})$ *is the specification interval.*

The next example illustrates the interval extension of our liability framework.

Example 13. Consider an AEB system where:

- Speedometer spec: $f'_A(a)=[a-1,a+1]$ (ś1 m/s tolerance)
- Speedometer impl: $f_A(a)=a+5$ (5 m/s bias error)
- Radar spec: $f'_B(b)=[b-0.5,b+0.5]$ (ś0.5 1/m tolerance)
- Radar impl: $f_B(b)=b+2$ (2 1/m bias error)
- ECU spec: $f'_C(A,B,c)=[AB+c-1,AB+c+1]$ (ś1 unit tolerance)
- ECU impl: $f_C(A,B,c)=AB+c+10$ (10 unit bias error)

Given context $\boldsymbol{u}=(14,14,12)$ and failure set $\mathcal{F}=\{(A,B,C):C\geq 250\}$, the implementation state is $\boldsymbol{t}=(19,16,326)$ where $A=f_A(14)=19$, $B=f_B(14)=16$, $C=f_C(19,16,12)=326$. Since $C=326\geq 250$, the system is in failure.

To calculate 2-leg liability, we examine how fixing components affects the depth in failure:

- $\boldsymbol{t}+A$: Projects $A=19$ onto $[13,15]$ yielding $A=15$, state $(15,16,262)$, $depth=12$
- $\boldsymbol{t}+B$: Projects $B=16$ onto $[13.5,14.5]$ yielding $B=14.5$, state $(19,14.5,297.5)$, $depth=46.5$
- $\boldsymbol{t}+C$: Projects $C=324$ onto $[315,317]$ yielding $C=317$, state $(19,16,317)$, $depth=67$
- $\boldsymbol{t}+\{A,B\}$: $A=15$ (projected), $B=14.5$ (projected), $C=f_C(15,14.5,12)=15\cdot 14.5+12+10=239.5$, state $(15,14.5,239.5)$, $depth=0$ (since $238.5<250$)

- $\boldsymbol{t}+\{A,C\}$: $A=15$ (projected), $C=f_C(15,16,12)=15\cdot16+10+12=261$, projection of C onto $[251,253]$ since $f'_C(15,16,12)=[15\cdot16+12-1,15\cdot16+12+1]=[251,253]$, yielding $C=253$, state $(15,16,253)$, $depth=3$
- $\boldsymbol{t}+\{B,C\}$: $B=14.5$ (projected), $C=f_C(19,14.5,12)=19\cdot14.5+12+10=297.5$, projection of C onto $[286.5,288.75]$, yielding $C=288.5$, state $(19,14.5,288.5)$, $depth=38.5$

The only causal set is $\{A,B\}$ since fixing both A and B brings the system out of failure. The 2-leg liability calculation proceeds as follows:

- For component A: $\phi_A^2=\omega\cdot\frac{1}{1}\cdot\max(0,depth_d(\boldsymbol{t}+B,\mathcal{F})-depth_d(\boldsymbol{t}+\{A,B\},\mathcal{F}))=\omega\cdot(46.5-0)=46.5\omega$
- Similarly, for component B: $\phi_B^2=12\omega$
- For components C: $\phi_C^2=0$ (not part of any causal set)

With normalization $\omega=(46.5+12)^{-1}=1/58.5$, the final liabilities are: $\phi_A^2=0.795$, $\phi_B^2=0.205$, $\phi_C^2=0$, which is expected because of the symmetric roles of A and B in causing failure, while A having larger deviation from its specification results in higher liability.

This demonstrates how interval specifications naturally handle tolerance-based engineering requirements. The following theorem confirms that the key properties of our framework are preserved under this extension.

Theorem 5. *For systems with interval specifications, the k-leg liability framework preserves all key properties of* ***Consistency*** *(Theorem 2),* ***Dummy component*** *(Theorem 3), and* ***Polynomial complexity*** *(Proposition 1).*

Proof. The projection operation during fixing, only changes the values of fixed components, not the causal dependencies. Therefore, the proofs of the original theorems apply directly, as they rely on the structure of causal sets and distance calculations, which remain unaffected by interval specifications.

6 Comparison with Harm

Beckers, Chockler, and Halpern (BCH) proposed a qualitative and quantitative definition of harm [5, 6]. Any definition of harm involves an event *causing* a loss for an agent. The causal mechanism is characterised by an SCM that includes a designated outcome variable. This outcome variable is directly linked to the utility of the agent. Quantitative harm is defined as the following:

Definition 15. *If $\mathcal{M}=(\mathcal{U},\mathcal{V},\mathcal{P},R,\mathcal{E})$ is an SCM, $O\in\mathcal{V}$ is a certain endogenous variable called the* outcome variable, *$ut: R(O)\rightarrow[0,1]$ is a function called the utility function, and $d\in[0,1]$ is a number called* default utility, *then $C=(\mathcal{M},ut,d)$ is called causal utility model.*

Definition 16. *If $\mathcal{M}=(\mathcal{U},\mathcal{V},\mathcal{P},R,\mathcal{E})$ is an SCM and $\mathcal{C}=(\mathcal{M},ut,d)$ is a causal utility model, and $X=x$ instead of $X=x'$ causes $O=o$ rather than $O=o'$ in $(\mathcal{C},\boldsymbol{u})$, then the (quantitative) harm to agent ag relative to $(X=x,X=x',O=o,O=o')$ is defined as $QH(\mathcal{C},\boldsymbol{u},X=x,x',o,o')=max(0,min(d,ut(o'))-ut(o))$. The quantitative harm to agent ag caused by $X=x$ in $(\mathcal{C},\boldsymbol{u})$ is defined as $QH(\mathcal{C},\boldsymbol{u},X=x)=max_{x',o'}QH(\mathcal{C},\boldsymbol{u},X=x,x',o,o')$ if there is some x' and o' such that $X=x$ instead of $X=x'$ causes $O=o$ instead of $O=o'$; if there is no such x' and o', then the quantitative harm is taken to be 0.*

Both harm and the 1-leg liability (i.e., k-leg liability with $k=1$) measure the difference between the utility of an actual and an expected outcome. In 1-leg liability, the utility of a state is the depth of the state within the set of failure states $\mathcal{F}$. The following theorem formalises this relationship:

Theorem 6. *Suppose $\mathcal{S}$ is a specification system, $\mathcal{T}$ is an implementation of $\mathcal{S}$, $\mathcal{M}=SCM(\mathcal{S})$, $\mathcal{N}=SCM(\mathcal{T})$, $\mathcal{F}$ is the failure set, u is a context, $X\in\mathcal{T}$, X' is the corresponding component in $\mathcal{S}$, and $\{X\}$ is a BF cause of $\mathcal{T}$ ending up in $\mathcal{F}$. Suppose $\mathcal{W}=\mathcal{T}_{X\to X'}$ and $\mathcal{P}=SCM(\mathcal{W})$. Define $x=\mathcal{N}[\boldsymbol{u}][X']$ and $x'=\mathcal{P}[\boldsymbol{u}][X]$. Also define the utility function $ut(s)=depth_d(s,\mathcal{F})$, loosening its normalisation condition. Define $\mathcal{M}'$ as an SCM identical with $\mathcal{M}$ with the additional (vector) endogenous variable $\boldsymbol{O}=\mathcal{V}(\mathcal{M})$ where $\mathcal{V}(\mathcal{M})$ denotes the set of endogenous variables of $\mathcal{M}$. Then we have:*

$$\phi_X^1=\alpha QH(\mathcal{M}',ut,\infty,X=x,x',\mathcal{P}[\boldsymbol{u}],\mathcal{N}[\boldsymbol{u}])$$

where α is constant.

7 Implementation and Empirical Evaluation

In this section, we aim to assess the effectiveness and efficiency of our proposed k-leg approach for liability apportionment compared to the widely accepted Shapley value method. We use the Shapley values as the baseline because it is considered the standard apportionment approach [7, 12, 14, 20]. Our research questions are:

- **RQ1 (Accuracy)**. Is there a meaningful difference between liabilities calculated via the k-leg approach and Shapley values?
- **RQ2 (Efficiency)**. Is there a meaningful difference between computational time of the k-leg approach and Shapley values?

7.1 Methodology

In our experiments, each subject consists of a random linear system of M components representing the specification system, re-randomisation of the specification to act as the implementation, a random failure quantifier-free first-order formula, and a context: (i) To randomly generate a specification system, we first generate a random DAG; for each DAG node (corresponding to a system components) the output is defined as a random linear function of its direct children. The linear function coefficients are real numbers uniformly sampled from $[-100,+100)$. (ii) The first-order failure formula is of the form $\bigwedge(x_i \leq | \geq a_i)$ where at most $\lfloor|\mathcal{V}|/3\rfloor$ of endogenous variables are randomly selected for x_is and a_is are real numbers uniformly sampled from $[-90,+90)$. (ii) Generation of a suitable experimental context is intricate, because we are interested in the contexts leading to a failure in implementation, but not a failure in the specification. To this end, we use Z3 SMT solver [23] to find a suitable context. If no context satisfies the constraints, we discard the generated systems and the failure and try again.

To answer RQ1, we compute the liability of the components in a subject with both Shapley and k-leg methods ($k = 1,2,3$). This gives us two vectors $\boldsymbol{s}$ and $\boldsymbol{l}$, each summing to one. We get the sum of the absolute value of the difference of the vectors (i.e., $\sum_i |s_i - l_i|$), which is a number between 0 and 2. We repeat this process $N = 1000$ times for each pair of $M = 5-14$ and $k = 1,2,3$. Similarly, for RQ2, we find the difference between Shapley and k-leg computation times (in seconds), for $N = 1000$ random subjects, and repeat this for each pair of $M = 5-14$ and $k = 1,2,3$. We developed a Python package for quantitative liability analysis within causal models which will be made available after acceptance.

7.2 Results

RQ1. For each (M,k) pair, we generated $N = 1000$ data points representing the difference between Shapley and k-leg values. Figure 3 (left) shows these differences as box plots. The 1st, 2nd, and 3rd quartiles are always 0, indicating the methods typically agree. To assess significance, we computed the percentage of cases where the L_1 norm difference exceeds 0.4 (maximum possible difference: 2). The resulting p-values are reported in Table 4. For $k = 3$, all p-values are below 0.1, showing no significant difference for systems with up to 9 components and supporting the k-leg method's efficacy.

RQ2. For each pair of (M,k) we have $N = 1000$ data points that represent the time difference between Shapley and k-leg values. The results are plotted on Fig. 3 (right). The exponential time difference is in line with the complexity results stated earlier.

Table 4: p-values for the difference between k-leg and Shapley liabilities for $M = 5-14$ and $k = 1,2,3$.

M	k=1	k=2	k=3
5	**0.021**	**0.004**	**0.000**
6	**0.028**	**0.018**	**0.000**
7	**0.027**	**0.034**	**0.002**
8	**0.033**	0.121	**0.039**
9	**0.028**	0.101	**0.041**

M	k=1	k=2	k=3
10	**0.007**	0.183	0.062
11	**0.037**	0.094	0.050
12	**0.036**	0.093	0.061
13	**0.029**	0.085	0.073
14	**0.040**	0.079	0.071

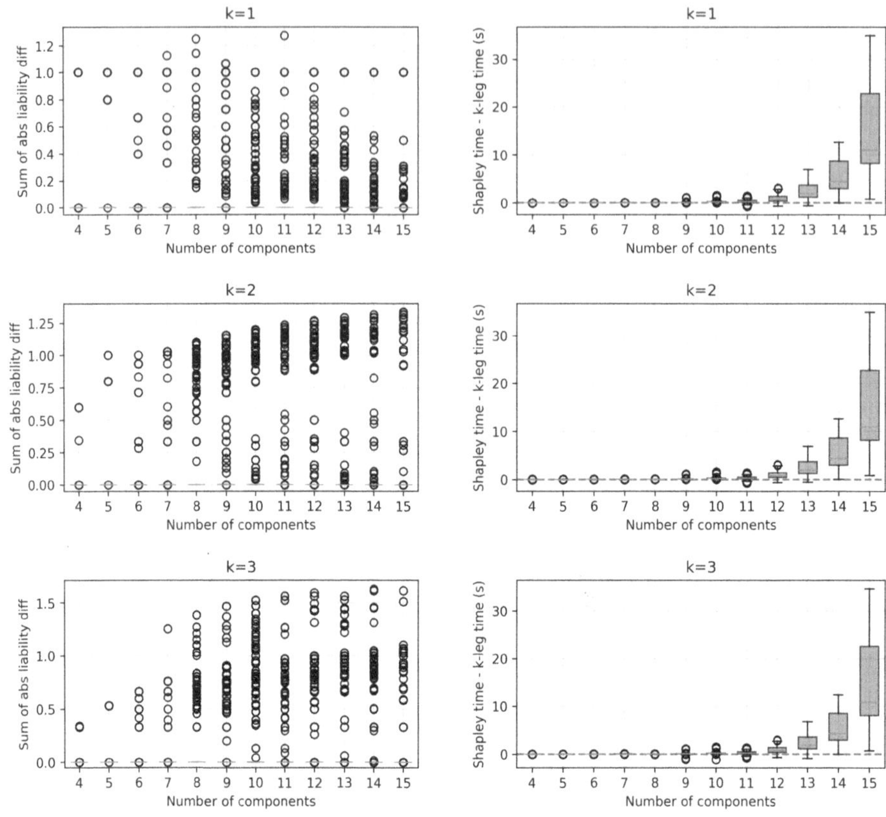

Fig. 3: Comparison of Shapley and k-leg methods in terms of liability difference (left) and computational time (right).

7.3 Discussion

(RQ1) The experimental results indicate that the k-leg approach provides liability apportionments that are closely aligned with the Shapley values, particularly for smaller k values such as $k = 3$, with p-values < 0.05, suggesting no significant difference between the methods for systems with up to nine components. This implies that the k-leg method effectively approximates the Shapley value, maintaining fairness while simplifying computations. **(RQ2)** Additionally, the computational efficiency of the k-leg approach is evident from the significant reduction in execution time compared to the Shapley method, especially as the number of components M increases (see Fig. 3 (right)). Therefore, the k-leg method offers a practical and efficient alternative for liability assessment in complex systems without compromising accuracy.

8 Conclusion and Future Work

We proposed a formal framework for automatically apportioning liabilities, illustrated its desirable features through examples, and established its formal properties. We introduced the concept of causal non-interaction and identified sufficient conditions for its validity. Furthermore, we illustrate that our framework handles real-world complexities such as interval specifications.

Future research directions include applying the k-leg liability concept directly to definitions of actual causality, extending the framework to incorporate manufacturer design flaws, and formally connecting k-leg liability with Shapley-based apportionment methods, including fairness axioms. Additionally, exploring formal semantic definitions of component interactions and identifying syntactic conditions that entail them present promising avenues for further research.

Acknowledgments

Mohammad Reza Mousavi has been partially supported by the UKRI Trustworthy Autonomous Systems Node in Verifiability, Grant Award Reference EP/V026801/2, EPSRC project on Verified Simulation for Large Quantum Systems (VSL-Q), grant reference EP/Y005244/1 and the EPSRC project on Robust and Reliable Quantum Computing (RoaRQ), Investigation 009 Model-based monitoring and calibration of quantum computations (ModeMCQ), grant reference EP/W032635/1, ITEA/InnovateUK projects GENIUS, grant reference 600642, and ITEA/InnovateUK GreenCode, grant reference 600643.

References

1. Reducing driver error accidents – orsa.org.uk, https://www.orsa.org.uk/reducing-occupational-road-risk/reducing-driver-error-accidents/
2. Abraham, K.S., Rabin, R.L.: Automated vehicles and manufacturer responsibility for accidents: a new legal regime for a new era. Virginia Law Review **105**(1), 127–171 (2018)
3. Aleksandrowicz, G., Chockler, H., Halpern, J.Y., Ivrii, A.: The computational complexity of structure-based causality. Journal of Artificial Intelligence Research **58**, 431–451 (2017)
4. Aryan, K., Chockler, H., Mousavi, M.R.: Artifact for the paper "causal liability in autonomous systems" (Jan 2026). https://doi.org/10.5281/zenodo.18393980
5. Beckers, S., Chockler, H., Halpern, J.Y.: A causal analysis of harm. In: Advances in Neural Information Processing Systems. vol. 35 (2022)
6. Beckers, S., Chockler, H., Halpern, J.Y.: Quantifying harm. In: Proceedings of Thirty-Second International Joint Conference on Artificial Intelligence (2023)
7. Chakravarty, S.R., Mitra, M., Sarkar, P.: A course on cooperative game theory. Cambridge University Press (2015)
8. Chockler, H., Halpern, J.Y.: Responsibility and blame: a structural-model approach. Journal of Artificial Intelligence Research **22**, 93–115 (2004)
9. Chockler, H., Kroening, D., Sun, Y.: Explanations for occluded images. In: Proceedings of the IEEE/CVF International Conference on Computer Vision (2021)

10. Damasceno, C.D.N., Mousavi, M.R., Simao, A.d.S.: Learning by sampling: learning behavioral family models from software product lines. Empirical Software Engineering **26**(1), 4 (2021)
11. Davey, J.: By insurers, for insurers: the UK's liability regime for autonomous vehicles. Journal of Tort Law **13**(2), 163–188 (2020)
12. Dehez, P., Ferey, S.: How to share joint liability: a cooperative game approach. Mathematical Social Sciences **66**(1), 44–50 (2013)
13. Fainekos, G.E.: Robustness of Temporal Logic Specifications. Ph.D. thesis, University of Pennsylvania (2008)
14. Ferey, S., Dehez, P.: Multiple causation, apportionment, and the shapley value. The Journal of Legal Studies **45**(1), 143–171 (2016)
15. Gallow, J.D.: The metaphysics of causation. In: Zalta, E.N., Nodelman, U. (eds.) The Stanford Encyclopedia of Philosophy. Metaphysics Research Lab, Stanford University, fall 2022 edn. (2022)
16. Halpern, J.Y.: A modification of the Halpern-Pearl definition of causality. In: Proceedings of the 24th International Conference on Artificial Intelligence. pp. 3022–3033. IJCAI'15, AAAI Press (Jul 2015)
17. Halpern, J.Y.: Actual causality. MIT Press (2016)
18. Halpern, J.Y., Pearl, J.: Causes and explanations: a structural-model approach. part i: causes. The British Journal for the Philosophy of Science **56**(4), 843–887 (2005)
19. Institute, A.L.: Restatement of the law third, torts: apportionment of liability, as adopted and promulgated. American Law Institute Publishers (2000)
20. Kim, J.Y., Lee, S.: Joint liability and stochastic shapley value. International Review of Law and Economics **60** (2019)
21. Moore, M.: Causation in the law. In: Zalta, E.N. (ed.) The Stanford Encyclopedia of Philosophy. Metaphysics Research Lab, Stanford University, winter 2019 edn. (2019)
22. Morgan, P.: Tort and Autonomous Vehicle Accidents - The Automated and Electric Vehicles Act 2018 and the Insurance Solution? In: Soyer, B., Gurses, O. (eds.) Insurability of Emerging Risks: Law, Theory and Practice, p. Chapter 10. Bloomsbury Publishing, Hart Publishing, 1st edn. (2025)
23. de Moura, L., Bj∅rner, N.: Z3: an efficient smt solver. In: Ramakrishnan, C.R., Rehof, J. (eds.) Tools and Algorithms for the Construction and Analysis of Systems. pp. 337–340. Springer (2008)
24. Métayer, D., Maarek, M., Mazza, E., Potet, M.L., Frenot, S., Viet Triem Tong, V., Craipeau, N., Hardouin, R., Alleaune, C., Benabou, V.L., Beras, D., Bidan, C., Goessler, G., Clainche, J., Mé, L., Steer, S.: Liability in software engineering overview of the LISE approach and illustration on a case study. ACM/IEEE 32nd International Conf. on Software Engineering (ICSE 2010) **1** (May 2010)
25. Norton, D.F., Norton, M.J.: David Hume: A Treatise of Human Nature: Volume 1: Texts. OUP Oxford (Jan 2011)
26. Pearl, J.: Causality: models, reasoning, and inference. Cambridge University Press (Sep 2009)
27. Pearl, J., Glymour, M., Jewell, N.P.: Causal inference in statistics: a primer. John Wiley & Sons (2016)
28. Petke, J., Yoo, S., Cohen, M.B., Harman, M.: Efficiency and early fault detection with lower and higher strength combinatorial interaction testing. In: Proceedings of the 2013 9th Joint Meeting on Foundations of Software Engineering. pp. 26–36. Association for Computing Machinery (2013)
29. Rausand, M., Barros, A., Hoyland, A.: System Reliability Theory: Models, Statistical Methods, and Applications. John Wiley & Sons (2020)

30. Sarda Gou, M., Lakatos, G., Holthaus, P., Robins, B., Moros, S., Jai Wood, L., Da Silva Araujo, H., deGraft Hanson, C., Mousavi, M., Amirabdollahian, F.: Kaspar explains: the effect of causal explanations on visual perspective taking skills in children with autism spectrum disorder. In: Proceedings of the 32nd IEEE International Conference on Robot and Human Interactive Communication (RO-MAN 2023). IEEE (2023)
31. Signoret, J.P., Leroy, A.: Reliability assessment of safety and production systems: analysis, modelling, calculations and case studies. Springer series in reliability engineering, Springer (2021)
32. Steffens, M., Oster, S., Lochau, M., Fogdal, T.: Industrial evaluation of pairwise SPL testing with MoSo-PoLiTe. In: Proceedings of the 6th International Workshop on Variability Modeling of Software-Intensive Systems. pp. 55–62. VaMoS '12, Association for Computing Machinery, New York, NY, USA (Jan 2012)
33. Wetzel, L.: Types and tokens. In: Zalta, E.N. (ed.) The Stanford Encyclopedia of Philosophy. Metaphysics Research Lab, Stanford University, fall 2018 edn. (2018)
34. Willard, S.: General topology. Courier Corporation (2012)
35. Xiang, J., Ogata, K.: Formal Fault Tree Analysis of State Transition Systems. In: Fifth International Conference on Quality Software (QSIC'05). IEEE Computer Society (2005)

Search-based Software Testing for Drone Applications: An Experience with the Simulink Environment

Annalisa Sergi[1], Yousef Ahmed Abdel Rahman Shoeib[1], Andrea Bombarda[1], Nunzio Marco Bisceglia[1], and Claudio Menghi[1,2]

[1] University of Bergamo, Bergamo, Italy
{a.sergi2,y.shoeib,n.bisceglia1}@studenti.unibg.it
{andrea.bombarda,claudio.menghi}@.unibg.it
[2] McMaster University, Hamilton, Canada

Abstract. Unmanned aerial vehicles (UAVs) are frequently used in monitoring and inspection of large and isolated areas, and often use line following techniques to guide their movement. The successful execution of this task greatly depends on the correct design of the software controller. Search-based software testing (SBST) is a widely used technique to check for software defects. It iteratively generates test cases until either violations of the system requirements are detected or the time budget is exceeded. However, the effectiveness of SBST strongly depends on the application domain. This empirical evaluation paper assesses the effectiveness of SBST in supporting the design of UAV applications by considering a rigorous case study. It considers three different versions of a drone software controller. It assesses the capability of SBST in generating failure-revealing test cases and the usefulness of the test cases. Our results confirm the effectiveness of SBST and the usefulness of the generated test cases.

Keywords: Drone Controller, Model Development, Simulink, Search-based Software Testing

1 Introduction

Unmanned aerial vehicles (UAVs), a.k.a. drones, obtained significant attention in recent years due to their wide range of applications [35]. Drones are cyber-physical systems used for aerial inspection, delivery services, defense [19], environmental monitoring, and search-and-rescue missions [51]. Many application scenarios where drones are employed are safety-critical or mission-critical: The development of reliable and adaptable control systems for such vehicles is crucial, particularly when operating in dynamic or partially structured environments.

Autonomous flying is a desirable feature for drones, as they are frequently used in monitoring and inspection of large and isolated areas [9, 54]. In such situations, the GPS signal is not guaranteed; hence, other methods of local position

E. Albert and C. Pasareanu (Eds.): FASE 2026, LNCS 16504, pp. 304–326, 2026.
https://doi.org/10.1007/978-3-032-22774-4_16

feedback are required. One of the most adopted position feedback methods is the line following [10, 5]: A line represents the track to be followed by the drone, which exploits cameras or sensors to track it and controls its motors as needed. Line-following is important benchmark for evaluating autonomous navigation capabilities [44, 45], sensor integration, and control software robustness.

Assuring the dependability and reliability of drones during line following is a critical research concern, as demonstrated by the existence of UAV testing competitions (e.g., [46]). The successful execution of this task is highly dependent on the correct design of the software controller and on the interaction between software components and their environmental conditions, making it particularly susceptible to subtle faults and performance degradation. For this reason, several testing techniques have been applied to drone software testing, such as simulation-based [31], metamorphic [23], and model-based [47] testing.

Search-Based Software Testing (SBST) employs metaheuristic optimization to generate test cases that aim at detecting failure-revealing test cases. It is widely applied to CPSs development [3, 28] in various domains, such as real-time, concurrent, distributed, embedded, and safety-critical systems [1]. SBST iteratively generates test cases until violations of the system requirements are detected [26] or the time budget for testing is exceeded. Despite being widely recognized as useful tools, the effectiveness and applicability of SBST test generators are strongly affected by their application domain [25]. An SBST tool that is effective in one domain may be less effective in another, or may require customizations that are not easily implementable.

To increase the use of SBST for drone design, engineers require precise indications of its efficiency and effectiveness in this domain. Practitioners need guidelines and lessons learned that discuss if, how, and when SBST is useful. They also need studies that assess different tools to understand their level of maturity [1]. The assessment of the efficiency of tools and the replication of experiments in different domains is widely recognized as a need by the research and industrial communities [1, 13, 34, 42, 48, 38, 14, 41]. This need is particularly relevant in the context of CPS model-driven development [6, 49, 7, 8], where models are typically created and maintained in an industrial contexts and not publicly available due to confidentiality agreements or license restrictions [4, 11].

In this empirical evaluation paper, we evaluate the effectiveness of SBST in the context of drone applications via a rigorous case study. We consider `S-TaLiRo` [2] as an SBST tool. It searches for test inputs violating a requirement of interest by applying evolutionary algorithms and/or stochastic optimization techniques (e.g., Monte-Carlo, Ant-Colony optimization, and Simulated Annealing). Our case study is the Parrot minidrone software controller we have been developing for the MathWorks Minidrone Competition [50]. More specifically, we iteratively and incrementally developed a line following controller for the drone under study. We assess how SBST supports testing our controllers.

We extensively used the SBST framework for testing three different versions of the drone controllers, including the last one that successfully participated in the MathWorks Minidrone Competition, obtaining remarkable results. By run-

Fig. 1: Parrot SA Mambo Fly Minidrone.

ning software-in-the-loop (SIL) experiments, we assessed (RQ1) how effective SBST is in generating failure-revealing test cases, and how different search algorithms compare, and (RQ2) how useful the failure-revealing test cases produced by SBST are. For RQ1, our results confirm the effectiveness of SBST in generating failure-revealing test cases and that Uniform Random (UR) is more effective than Simulated Annealing (SA) for version V3 of the controller and comparable for the other two versions. For RQ2, our results confirmed the usefulness of the failure-revealing test cases: All the behaviors identified by the framework were violating the requirements and helped identify weaknesses in the controller. Surprisingly, SBST identified requirements violations for version V3 of the controller, which was considered correct during manual validation. Finally, we present our reflections and lessons learned on applying SBST (and `S-TaLiRo`) to a new and significantly different problem.

This work is organized as follows. Section 2 describes our drone case study and introduces the development of control software. Section 3 presents SBST and describes how we have extended `S-TaLiRo` to support track generation. Section 4 reports our evaluation methodology and results. Section 5 discusses results, lessons learned, and the improvement of the state of practice. Section 6 presents related works. Section 7 concludes the work.

2 Drone Study Subject

This section presents our drone case study subject: The controlled system (Section 2.1), its requirements (Section 2.2), and the models of its controller we developed and tested (Section 2.3).

2.1 Controlled System

The controlled system is the Parrot SA Mambo Fly Minidrone from Figure 1. It is a drone platform produced by Parrot SA [43] and used in the MathWorks Minidrone Competition [50]. This competition offers a standardized environment in which participants design and implement control algorithms for a simulated or physical drone vehicle. The drone is modeled as a nonlinear dynamic system with six degrees of freedom. The drone actuators consist of four rotors. The thrust forces generated by the four rotors collectively determine translational movement along the three spatial axes as well as angular orientation through roll, pitch, and

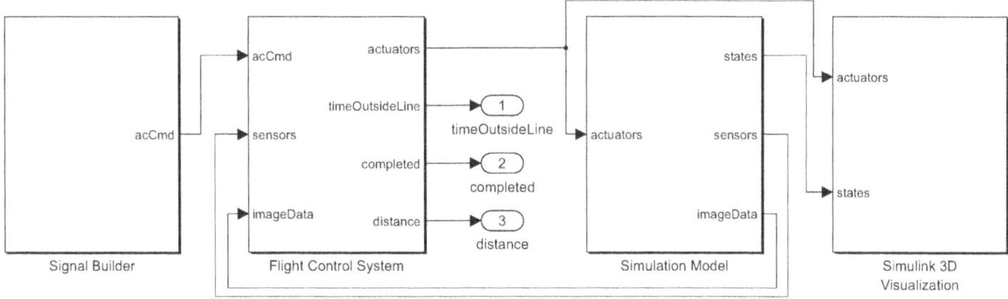

Fig. 2: The `Simulink` model.

yaw. Additionally, the controlled system possesses a downward-facing camera that can be used to gather information from the environment. Figure 2 shows the `Simulink` model of the drone used in the competition. The model consists of four components. The *Signal Builder* component is responsible for providing input commands for the simulation (*acCmd*) to the *Flight Control System* component. The *Flight Control System* component contains the flight control algorithm and has three input ports. It receives input from the cameras (*imageData*) for image processing, input commands (*acCmd*) from the *Signal Builder* component, and a signal (*sensors*) from the *Simulation Model* component for the path planning logic. Furthermore, the *Flight Control System* has four output ports. It sends commands to the actuators in the *Simulation Model* component (*actuators*), and provides three outputs used by our SBST framework: the current time the drone is off the line (*timeOutsideLine*), the track completion status (*completed*), and the current distance between the center of the drone and the closest border of the line (*distance*). The *Simulation Model* component encapsulates the models of the drone, the sensors, and the environment. It has one input port (*actuators*) for the commands to the actuators from the *Flight Control System* component, and three output ports: the data from the different sensors (*imageData* and *sensors*) is sent to the *Flight Control System* component, and a state signal (*states*) is sent to the *Simulink 3D Visualization* component, which also takes the actuator signal from the *Flight Control System* component to visualize the drone in the simulation environment.

2.2 Requirements

The competition requires participants to develop a line-following navigation algorithm on a track. The drone is tested across different unknown tracks (e.g., the one track from Figure 3). The track is represented by a 10 *cm* wide red line, and the drone is requested to land when the line ends on a circular marker having its center 25 *cm* from the end of the line and with a 10 *cm* radius. The number of sections that compose each track is always between 2 and 13. The angles between two contiguous sections are between 15 and 345 degrees. Intersections or very close (parallel) sections are not enabled in the competition.

The performance of the controllers is assessed by considering:

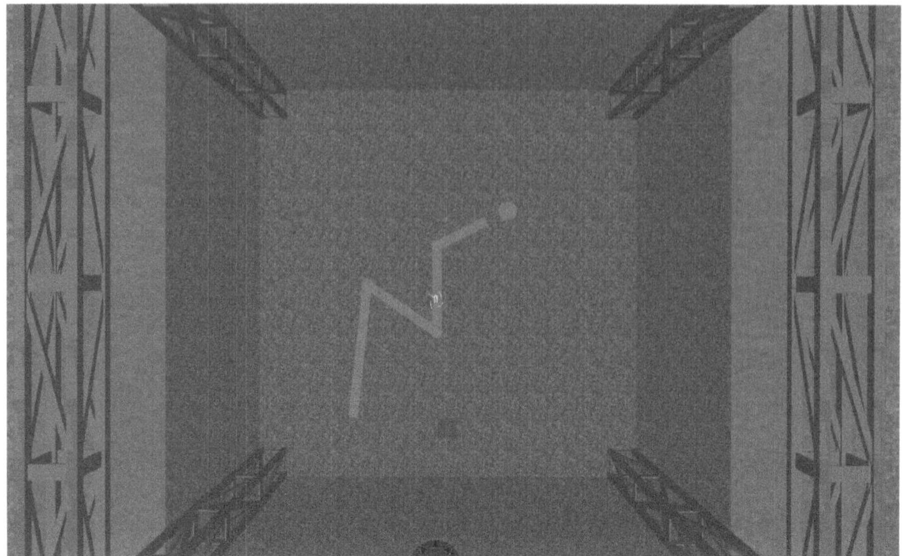

Fig. 3: The MathWorks Minidrone Competition arena.

1. the capability of the model to generate code to be uploaded to the drone,
2. the capability of the controller to land accurately and "softly": A landing is considered soft if the altitude is reduced gradually, and accurate if the drone lands within the circle with at least 20% of its total body, and
3. the accuracy of the drone following the track, measured with the number of straight sections completed (1 point per section).

In case of a tie between two or more teams, the deciding factor will be time (fastest wins).

To design the controller for our drone, we consider the requirements from Table 1. Specifically, Requirement R1 mandates the drone to be out of track for at most 1.25 seconds. This requirement is not explicitly mentioned in the competition rules: Adding this requirement helps distinguish between the accuracy of different versions of the controller. Requirement R2 mandates the drone to always land in the circular marker at the end of the track. Requirement R3 mandates the maximum horizontal distance between the center of the drone and the closest border of the track to be less than or equal to 12.5 cm. Indeed, since the drone is 13.21 cm wide, the distance of 12.5 cm is the one assuring an acceptable overlap between the drone and the track (both on the left or on the right).

2.3 Controller

The drone controller was developed by two of the authors, both undergraduate students in computer science engineering. It is embedded in the *Flight Control System* subsystem from Figure 2. The controller uses the camera to detect the

Table 1: Requirements considered for designing the controller of our drone.

ID	Description
R1	The drone shall be out of the track for at most 1.25 seconds.
R2	The drone shall always land in the circular marker at the end of the track.
R3	The distance between the drone and the track shall not exceed 12.5 *cm*.

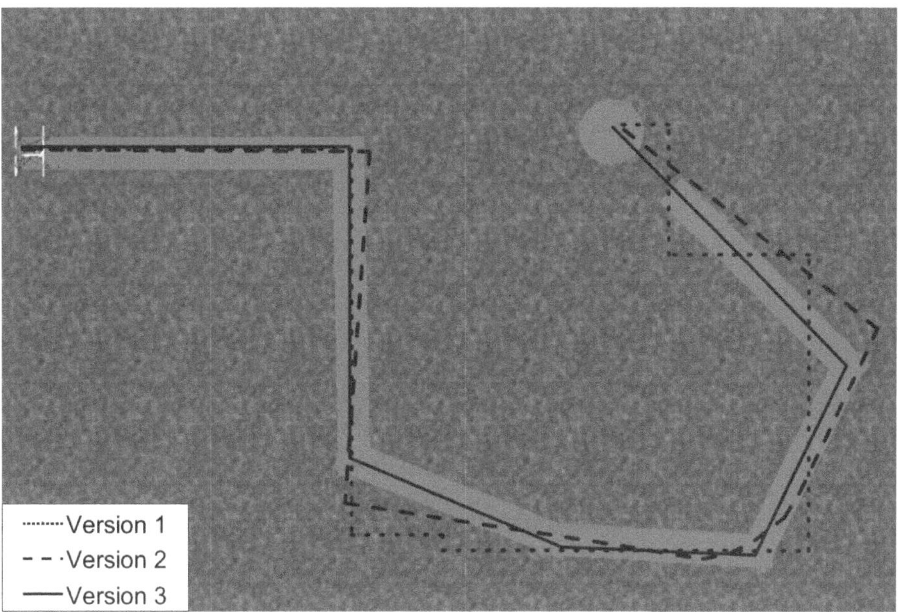

Fig. 4: Examples of paths for the versions V1, V2, and V3 of the controller.

position and orientation of the track relative to the drone's body frame. The input received by the camera is processed by the control algorithm, which computes appropriate rotor commands to maintain alignment with the track while ensuring stability of flight. Thus, the controlled system is a closed-loop interaction between the drone's motors, the environment, including the track, and the line-following control logic.

Table 2 summarizes the versions of the controller developed by the students. The development activity required approximately 400 hours. This time includes the time required for developing the different controllers and the time needed to test them. Figure 4 shows a track and three examples of paths obtained with the three different versions of the drone controller we have designed. The paths for versions V1, V2, and V3 are depicted in yellow, green, and blue.

The versions of the controller we developed are as follows:

- **Version V1**. Divides the input image from the camera into four portions (i.e., top, bottom, left, and right). For each portion, the number of pixels

Table 2: Identifier (ID), number of blocks (#B), and description and supported tracks for the controllers developed in this work.

ID	#B	Description and supported tracks
V1	47	Checks for the line in each of the 4 directions: forward, back, left, and right. Supports tracks with long segments and ideally 90-degree angles aligned with the x and y axes.
V2	44	Checks for the line in front of the drone until the end of the current segment is identified. Then, it rotates the image acquired by the drone until the next segment is in front of it. Supports tracks with medium-length segments and angles above 60 degrees.
V3	44	Checks in the section in front for the end of the current segment and the sides to know which direction to turn next. Turns the drone at the end of the segment until the next segment is in front of the drone. Supports the competition advanced tracks with a minimum distance between lines of 20 *cm* and a minimum angle of 15 degrees.

corresponding to the color of the line is computed. The drone uses this information to maintain or adjust its current direction and proceed exclusively along the X and Y axes, resulting in step-like trajectories and non-straight paths.

- **Version V2**. Divides the input image from the camera into three portions: two lateral portions (i.e., left and right) and a smaller area located at the front of the drone. The drone alternates between linear trajectories along the X and Y axes and rotations along the Z axis.
  This controller makes the drone follow a linear trajectory when the computed number of pixels in a 5×5 control matrix corresponding to the line color in the front portion is higher than a threshold of 4 pixels. When the number of pixels is lower than the threshold, the drone is approaching a corner: it stops, computes the number of pixels for the line color in the lateral portions (i.e., left and right), and performs a rotation of the image around the Z axis (i.e, counterclockwise and clockwise, respectively) depending on the pixels in the two areas. The rotation ends when a new line is revealed in the front portion, and the drone resumes a linear motion along the new direction.
  The controller regulates the flight speed based on the number of pixels corresponding to the line color revealed at the front, slowing down in proximity of a corner. Compared with version V1, the track navigation is smoother.
- **Version V3 (final)**. Relies on a finite-state machine with four states, as reported in Figure 5 and described in the following:
  - **State 0 (Take-off)**. The controller checks whether the drone is aligned with the line, counting the number of pixels in a 29×27 matrix sensed by the onboard camera under the center of the drone. If the number of pixels is between 324 and 360 pixels, the controller transitions to State 1; otherwise, it transitions to State 2.

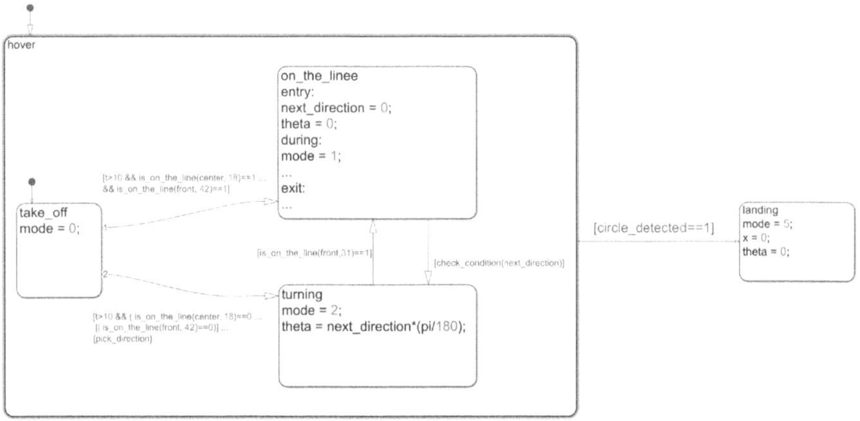

Fig. 5: State machine.

- **State 1 (On-the-line)**. The drone is facing the right direction and proceeds until the end of the current segment, using a matrix that checks the number of pixels corresponding to the line color revealed by the front drone's onboard camera. Furthermore, the new direction to follow is computed using lateral matrices. The idea of using a matrix in the front and lateral matrices comes from the previous version (V2) of the controller. Size and positions of the matrices are not the same since this controller can stay within the line more precisely: It splits the central matrix into 2 halves (left and right) and performs micro adjustments to stay exactly in the middle of the line.
- **State 2 (Turning)**. The drone is not facing the right direction or has reached the end of a segment, and no circle is detected. The end of a segment is detected when the pixels corresponding to the line color revealed at the front of the drone are zero, and the pixels with the color of the line detected by the lateral matrices are more than zero. The lateral matrix control was added since there is a break in the track between the landing spot and the end of the last segment. If this situation is detected, the controller should transition to State 3. Otherwise, the drone stops, rotates along the Z axis until it aligns with the new line, and transitions to State 1.
- **State 3 (Landing)**. Lands the drone.

We extensively used SBST to search for software behaviors of the versions V1, V2, and V3 of the controller that violate the specification from requirements R1, R2, and R3 as detailed in the next section. We emphasize that we employed SBST during development to uncover issues or vulnerabilities in the controller and to address them in the next version.

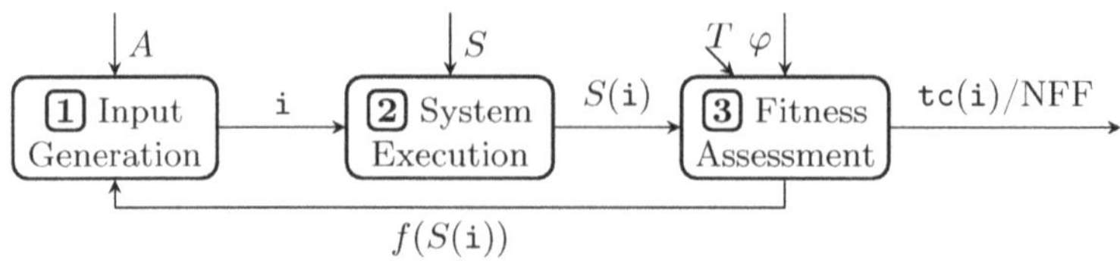

Fig. 6: SBST: An Overview.

3 Testing the Controller with SBST

SBST aims at generating failure-revealing inputs for the system under test. An overview of the SBST process is provided by Figure 6. Each box represents a step of SBST. Incoming and outgoing arrows represent inputs and outputs. Arrows with no source or destination represent inputs and outputs of the SBST framework.

When using SBST frameworks, users must provide a model of the system to be tested (S), an assumption on its inputs (A), a time budget (T), and a requirement (φ). SBST provides as output a failure-revealing test case ($\texttt{tc(i)}$) or an indication that no failure-revealing test case was found (NFF — No Failure Found) within the time budget.

To produce this output, SBST iteratively performs the steps from Figure 6:

- *Input Generation* (1). The SBST framework generates an input ($\texttt{i}$) for the model (S) compliant with the assumption (A);
- *System Execution* (2). The SBST framework runs the system model (S) by providing the generated input ($\texttt{i}$) and obtaining a system execution ($S(\texttt{i})$);
- *Fitness Assessment* (3). The fitness value ($f(S(\texttt{i}))$) associated with the system execution ($S(\texttt{i})$) is evaluated by the SBST framework that assesses whether the fitness value is below a threshold value.

For each input ($\texttt{i}$), the SBST framework evaluates whether the associated test case ($\texttt{tc(i)}$) is failure-revealing, i.e., (a) the input satisfies the assumption (A), and (b) the fitness value ($f(S(\texttt{i}))$) is smaller than a threshold value (typically the value 0). The fitness value is negative if the property is violated and positive otherwise. In addition, the higher the positive fitness value, the further the system is from violating its requirement; the lower negative values indicate that the system is further from satisfying its requirement [18, 17, 52, 40, 15].

The fitness value ($f(S(\texttt{i}))$) guides the search algorithm used by the SBST framework, which searches for an input associated with a negative fitness value. Specifically, SBST uses the fitness value computed in step 3 to drive the generation of the next input (1). The SBST framework terminates when a failure-revealing test case is detected or when the available time budget (T) expires and no failure-revealing test case is found. For the former case, SBST returns the failure-revealing test case. Note that, while many failure revealing test cases may exist for the S, SBST returns only one of them. For the latter case, SBST returns the NFF value.

The *Input Generation*, *System Execution*, and *Fitness Assessment* components are shared and implemented by many SBST tools, e.g., ARIsTEO [39], ATheNA [20], S-TaLiRo [2], Breach [12], HECATE [21], FalStar [16], FalCAuN [52], falsify [53], FalStar [16], and ForeSee [55].

SBST can be instantiated by considering different modeling formalisms. In this work, we assume that the CPS is modeled as a reactive system that receives inputs (produced by the *Input Generation* component) and produces outputs that can be monitored (used by the *Fitness Assessment* component). Alternative instances of SBST differ in the implementation of the *Input Generation*, *System Execution*, and *Fitness Assessment* components. In this work, we consider S-TaLiRo [2] as our SBST framework. S-TaLiRo is a toolbox for temporal logic falsification within the MATLAB environment. It searches for counterexamples to Metric Temporal Logic (MTL) properties in Simulink/Stateflow diagrams, minimizing a robustness metric. It uses stochastic optimization techniques, including Monte-Carlo methods and Ant-Colony Optimization, to perform a random walk over the initial states, controls, and disturbances of the system. The search returns the simulation trace with the smallest robustness value that was found. The lower the value of robustness, the closer the property is to being falsified by the tool. A simulation trace with a negative robustness indicates that the temporal logic properties were falsified.

To use S-TaLiRo, we customized the *Input Generation* (1) component to generate tracks for the drones. This was done as follows.

3.1 Track Generation

We modified the *Input Generation* (1) component to generate different tracks according to the competition rules, as specified in Algorithm 1.

Algorithm 1 takes inpRanges and prevSample as input for the GENERATE-TRACK function. The first defines the minimum and maximum coordinates for each point that connect the track segments, and the latter is the previously generated track. Algorithm 1 behaves as follows. Line 2 generates a new track. Line 3 checks if the track is compliant with the rules of the competition. In particular, a track will be discarded if (a) the angle between two consecutive sections is lower than 15 degrees or higher than 345 degrees, (b) the distance between two segments is lower than 20 cm, and (c) the track has one or more intersections. If the track is compliant, Line 6 calls the INTERPOLATE function from Algorithm 2 and the track is returned (Line 7). Otherwise, Line 4 generates a new sample. In the first iteration, prevSample is null and the sample is randomly generated. From the second iteration, S-TaLiRo slightly updates the prevSample, while still complying with the possible input range (inpRange).

Once the coordinates of the track satisfy the constraints, the set of coordinates (curSample) is passed as input (Line 6) to the custom interpolation function INTERPOLATE from Algorithm 2. Indeed, S-TaLiRo allows users to pass a function pointer as the interpolation method. Algorithm 2 behaves as follows. Line 2 transforms the 10-coordinate array into a matrix with each row representing a point. Line 3 generates the coordinates of the points composing the track (tiles)

Algorithm 1 Input Generation component.

```
1: function GENERATETRACK(inpRanges,prevSample)
2:     curSample=GETNEWSAMPLE(inpRanges,prevSample);
3:     while CHECKTRACK(curSample) == 0 do
4:         curSample =GETNEWSAMPLE(inpRanges,prevSample);
5:     end while
6:     track=INTERPOLATE(curSample)
7:     return track
8: end function
```

Algorithm 2 Track Interpolation.

```
1: function INTERPOLATE(curSample)
2:     points = ARRTOPOINTSMATRIX(curSample);
3:     [tiles,land] = LINEPATCHES(points);
4:     LINES2WRL(tiles,land);
5: end function
```

and the center of the landing circle (land) from the points previously generated. Line 4 updates the virtual world of the competition arena using the function LINES2WRL, receiving as parameters the lines and the final circular marker in simulation.

4 Evaluation

Our evaluation assesses the usefulness of SBST in testing drone control software, considering the following research questions:

RQ1: How *effective* is SBST in generating failure-revealing test cases, and how do different search algorithms compare? (Section 4.2)
RQ2: How *useful* are the failure-revealing test cases produced by SBST? (Section 4.3)

RQ1 assesses the performance of two different algorithms to assess how the choice of the algorithm influences the effectiveness of SBST within drone scenarios. RQ2 assesses the usefulness of SBST in detecting model failures.

4.1 Experimental Setup

To run our experiments, we formalized our requirements in MTL/STL as

$$\psi := \square(timeOutsideLine \leq 250) \wedge \lozenge(completed = 1) \wedge \square(distance \leq 25).$$

The symbols $\square$ and $\lozenge$ represent the *always* and *eventually* temporal logic operators. The first part of the specification ($r_1 := \square(timeOutsideLine \leq 250)$) encodes requirement R1 from Table 1 and requires that the time the drone is

Table 3: Configuration parameters for S-TaLiRo.

Parameter	Value
Search algorithms	UR, SA
Number of runs	10
Maximum number of iterations per run	1500
Time budget (T)	300 s

Table 4: Experimental results for the Drone case study.

	UR			SA		
Controller	**FR**	$\bar{S}$	$\hat{S}$	**FR**	$\bar{S}$	$\hat{S}$
Version 1	10/10	1.0	1.2	10/10	1.0	3.5
Version 2	10/10	1.0	1.4	10/10	1.0	1.5
Version 3	10/10	45.0	69.1	10/10	122.0	132.6

out of the track is less than 250 iterations. Since there are 200 iterations in a second, 250 iterations are equivalent to 1.25 seconds. The second part of the specification ($r_2 := \Diamond(completed = 1)$) encodes requirement R2 from Table 1 and requires the drone to always land in the circular marker at the end of the track. If *completed* equals 1, the drone successfully landed; otherwise, *completed* is equal to 0. The third part of the formula ($r_3 := \Box(distance \leq 25)$) encodes requirement R3 from Table 1 and requires that the maximum distance between the drone and the line shall always be less than or equal to 25 pixels (12.5 cm). The specification ψ is automatically mapped to a fitness function by S-Taliro [2].

We assume that the arena considered to generate the tracks is a 4 m × 4 m. We generated tracks with five points represented by (X, Y) coordinates, which must be within the boundaries of the arena.

Table 3 reports the configuration parameters considered for our experiments. We considered two search algorithms: Uniform Random (UR) and Simulated Annealing (SA). To evaluate the effectiveness of our SBST framework implementation in generating failure-revealing test cases, we performed six (3 models × 2 search algorithms) experiments, each obtained by considering one version of the three controllers from Section 2.3 and one of the search algorithms.

We ran our SBST framework for 10 runs to account for the nondeterminism of the search algorithms. The experiments were executed on a personal laptop.[3]

4.2 Effectiveness and Comparison (RQ1)

Table 4 shows our experimental results. Each row represents the version of the drone controller. The table is divided into two parts related to the UR and SA search algorithms. For each experiment, the table outlines the falsification rate (FR), i.e., the number of times our SBST framework found failure-revealing

[3] Intel(R) Core(TM) i7-13700K 3.4 GHz CPU, 16 cores, 32 GB of RAM

test cases within the given time, and the average ($\hat{S}$) and the median number ($\bar{S}$) of iterations required to find the test cases. Note that `S-TaLiRo` does not indicate which specific requirement (e.g., r_1, r_2, or r_3) was violated and caused the falsification of ψ.

For all versions of the controller, our SBST framework could generate a failure-revealing test case. Therefore, all versions of the controller may cause the drone to violate one of the three requirements of Table 1. This confirms the effectiveness of SBST in generating failure-revealing test cases.

Both Uniform Random (UR) and Simulated Annealing (SA) showed a 10/10 falsification rate in all the experiments. While comparing the number of iterations required by UR and SA for versions V1 and V2 is meaningless since they both require a very limited number of iterations, the comparison is relevant for version V3. Surprisingly, UR performed better than SA for version V3 of the drone controller. The average ($\hat{S}$) and the median number ($\bar{S}$) of iterations required to identify the failure-revealing test case show that for version V3 of the controller, UR required fewer iterations (69.1 vs 132.6 for the average, and 45.0 vs 122.0 for the median) to identify the failure-revealing test cases than SA. This result is caused by our current definition of the fitness function, which cannot efficiently guide the search procedure employed by SA. This behavior is due to the improvements made to version V3 of the controller, which reduces the MTL specification to just the predicate R2, because the requirements R1 and R3 are always satisfied. In particular, the drone is always able to follow the track, so the time outside the line is always less than 250 iterations, meaning that R1 is always true. Furthermore, the distance between the drone and the line is always less than 25 pixels, meaning that R3 is always true. The only unsatisfied predicate remains R2, which, however, is not a good metric to efficiently guide the search because it remains false until the track is completed. This behavior makes the uniform random algorithm a better solution than using a fitness function.

Across all our experiments, the SBST framework took on average $32'\,38''$ ($min{=}20''$, $max{=}4h\,3'\,59''$, $StdDev{=}59'\,34''$) and 34.88 iterations ($min{=}1$, $max{=}235$, $StdDev{=}63.80$) to detect failure-revealing test cases.

RQ1: Effectiveness

Our results confirm the effectiveness of SBST in generating failure-revealing test cases. They also show that, for version V3 of the controller, UR is more effective than SA, while for versions V1 and V2, the results are comparable.

4.3 Usefulness (RQ2)

We manually inspected the failure-revealing test cases returned by our SBST framework to analyze our software failures. In the following, we summarize our findings for each version of the controller.

Version V1. Version V1 could execute diagonal segments by proceeding exclusively along the X and Y axes, resulting in step-like trajectories. Therefore, the drone was unable to complete the entire track due to its inability to navigate

(a) Failure for Version V1.

(b) Failure for Version V2

Fig. 7: Failures for versions V1 and V2 of the controller.

non-right angles, resulting in the drone getting stuck in corners and failing the requirements R1 and R2. As shown in Figure 7a, the drone is not able to find the next direction and is stuck in the corner.

Version 2. The problem from version V1 was fixed by rotating the image depending on the number of colored pixels in the left and right front (and lateral) sides of the drone. However, it was unable to navigate acute corners under 60 degrees due to reaching a position where there were no colored pixels in the left and right front (and lateral), i.e., the drone shall navigate "backwards". Figure 7b shows an example of such a track.

Version 3. Surprisingly, our SBST framework was effective in finding a failure-revealing test case also for this version. Table 5 summarizes the four failures identified by our test cases. For each failure, it reports the number of the experiment (Experiment) in which the failure was identified and describes the failure (Description). When the same failure is identified by multiple experiments, the ID of each experiment is reported in the first column. Figure 8 outlines examples of tracks that lead to the violation of the requirements. For example, experiments 1, 3, 4, 6, 7, 9, and 10 show that version V3 of the controller was unable to overcome two short segments that were very close to each other (see Figure 8a), i.e., connected by a very acute angle. However, the problem was not the angle but the length of the segments. The drone turned too much during the corner, treating the current segment as the next one, and returning to the start point. Thus, it failed to find the final circular marker. However, the rules of the competition did not specify any minimum length of the segments. The problem would be solved with longer segments.

RQ2: Usefulness

The manual inspection confirmed the usefulness of the failure-revealing test cases: All the behaviors identified by the framework were violating the requirements and helped identify weaknesses in the controller. Surprisingly,

Table 5: Description of the failure identified by each SBST experiment.

ID	Experiments	Description
F1	1, 3, 4, 6, 7, 9, 10	The controller fails on a track with a very short last segment and a tight angle between the last segment and the previous one, such as in Figure 8a. The drone reaches the last turn and starts to turn to align with the track. However, it aligns itself with the previous segment due to the limited length of the last one and the tight angle.
F2	2	The controller fails on the track in Figure 8b on the second segment, where the drone was not able to align itself properly before starting to turn towards the next segment. This results in losing the line and going back to the start of the track without being able to finish.
F3	5	The controller fails on the track in Figure 8c because of an artifact on the last turn, which results from the way the track is created between points by simply overlapping segments of the right width. The areas of the image acquired by the drone camera and used to check if the drone is turning in the right direction intersect that artifact on the right edge. This mistakenly makes the drone turn right and go back on the same segment it came from, thus failing to complete the track.
F4	8	The controller fails on the turn between the second and the third segment due to the fourth segment being very close to the end of the second one, as shown in Figure 8d.

SBST identified requirements violations for version V3 of the controller, which was considered correct.

5 Discussion

We discuss lessons learned (Section 5.1) and threats to validity (Section 5.2).

5.1 Lessons Learned

Competition regulation. The SBST framework we established could identify a failure-revealing test case also for the final version (i.e., version V3) of our implementation of the Parrot minidrone software controller, which obtained remarkable results in the MathWorks Minidrone Competition. In Section 4.3, we discussed that the issue with the controller was the presence of very short segments connected by a very acute angle. The competition rules did not specify any minimum length of the segments or any other constraints, except for the minimum distance between two lines. We contacted MathWorks for clarification. Our objective is to understand if there is missing information in the competition rules, or if we should consider these test cases as failure-revealing. From

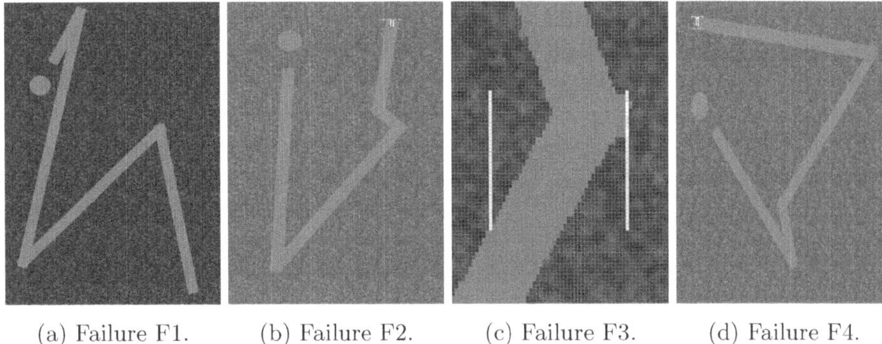

(a) Failure F1. (b) Failure F2. (c) Failure F3. (d) Failure F4.

Fig. 8: Failures for version V3 of the controller.

this experience, we learned that SBST is useful to identify failure-revealing test cases. However, in some cases, its usage can also pinpoint other problems (e.g., underspecified requirements or missing assumptions).

SBST effectiveness. We were confident about the drone's ability to follow any track for the last version of the controller. However, our experimental results showed that our SBST framework was effective in finding a failure-revealing test case (with a 10/10 falsification rate) for each experiment, identifying paths that do not allow the drone to reach the end of the track. From this result, we learned that engineers may be overconfident about their product. After investing a long time and significant effort in their design activity, they may overlook certain situations, configurations, and behaviors that lead to failures. Using SBST helps identify these behaviors and corner cases. Therefore, we expect similar SBST-based approaches to benefit all other competition participants. Since all competition participants develop within the same environment and under the same set of requirements, adapting the methodology presented in this paper to other drone controllers should be straightforward.

Tool customization. There are many SBST tools within the research literature (e.g., ARIsTEO [39], `ATheNA` [20], `S-TaLiRo` [2], `Breach` [12], `HECATE` [21], `FalStar` [16], `FalCAuN` [52], `falsify` [53], `FalStar` [16], and `ForeSee` [55]). However, applying these tools in different domains requires customization. For example, in our case, we had to modify the *Input Generation* (1) component to generate tracks (see Section 3.1). `S-TaLiRo` easily supports the customization of the *Input Generation*. However, track generation wasn't trivial and required considerable time to design a component that correctly generates tracks that satisfy the rules of the competitions. From this experience, we learned that while the high-level behavior of SBST is common and shared across many applications, different applications have peculiar needs that may require (non-trivial) customizations that can affect the effectiveness and efficiency of SBST. Similarly, we observed that tailoring SBST tools to different application scenarios can be labor-intensive, which may restrict the set of tools that can reasonably be considered in analyses such as the one presented in this paper.

SBST during development. In our case study, we implemented three versions of the Parrot minidrone software controller and assessed their ability to follow the lines using our SBST framework. The use of SBST during the development phase would have been beneficial in discovering different paths that lead the drone to fail to follow the track, improving the quality of the controller. For example, they would have been useful to identify the problem with version V3 of the controller. From this experience, we learned that using SBST during development can be beneficial to identify bugs and problems.

Fitness function design. Our results show that our fitness function could not efficiently guide the search procedure employed by SA. From this result, we learned that a proper definition of the fitness function is crucial for the effectiveness of the search process. The use of techniques such as fitness-landscape analysis could help this process. These techniques evaluate how the fitness value changes over the search space and usually support the fitness function design, helping understand the search process and its probability of success [20]. However, the fitness function design remains a complex activity and may require a combination of automated and manually defined fitness functions to guide the search of the input domain in order to increase the probability of finding failures.

5.2 Threats to Validity

The requirements we considered in this study subject could threaten the *external validity* of our results since it influences how our they can extend to other study subjects. However, the fact that the requirements were defined following the MathWorks Minidrone Competition mitigates this threat.

Our conclusions are specific to the competition environment and its regulations and may not generalize to other settings in which drones are used but no equivalent line-following task, or the same requirements, exists. However, the approach presented in this paper is general, and alternative requirements can be encoded to accommodate different use cases.

The values assigned to the fitness function and other configuration parameters in `S-TaLiRo` could threaten the *internal validity* of our results: Other values may lead to different results. However, the fact that we made a replication package publicly available mitigates this threat as it helps replicate the experiments with different parameters.

6 Related Work

Recent advancements in drone technology, driven by progress in areas such as artificial intelligence, computer science, and obstacle avoidance, have significantly expanded the capabilities of drones and opened new possibilities across various industries [35]. However, given the criticality of these systems, ensuring their reliability and safety is paramount.

Khatiri *et al.* [31, 32] implemented a search-based approach that replicates real drone flights and generates simulation-based test cases by analyzing the field test logs and created an experimental platform designed to automate various aspects of UAV system testing (e.g., test generation) in a simulation environment. This platform was adopted during the first UAV Testing Competition [33]. However, we developed our drone by participating in the MathWorks Minidrone Competition with particular focus on generating challenging tracks that the drone may fail to follow, rather than realistic ones.

Vierhauser *et al.* [51] created an approach that defines structured and reusable field test scenarios for drone missions, executes field tests, and collects data for processing and analysis. Javed *et al.* [29] proposed a hybrid approach that combines model-based testing and SBST of unmanned aircraft system (UAS) software to automate the generation and execution of test cases, improving fault detection. Lindvall *et al.* [36] developed a framework that combines metamorphic testing and model-based testing to automatically generate test cases from models that encode testing scenarios of autonomous drones in simulation. Hildebrandt *et al.* [27] proposed a world-in-the-loop (WIL) approach to reduce the gap between simulation and reality, integrating real sensor and simulation data into a running UAV. Our work differs from these contributions, focusing on the falsification of the STL specification using `S-TaLiRo` to generate trajectories that violate line following requirements, rather than deriving test cases from models, logs, or sensor integration.

Search-based techniques are widely used in the automotive domain. Gambi *et al.* [24] proposed an approach that combines SBST and procedural content generation to generate virtual roads to test autonomous cars. Kendall *et al.* [30] proposed a framework based on deep reinforcement learning to generate random roads for autonomous driving. Similarly, SBST is used by Marzella *et al.* [37] to test the controller of an e-bike. Compared to their work, our systems under test are drones, and our aim is to evaluate different versions of the drone controller in both simulated and competition environments.

7 Conclusion

This paper evaluates search-based software testing (SBST) for drone control software applications. We considered `S-TaLiRo`, a well-known SBST tool. We customized `S-TaLiRo` for track generation and assessing three software controllers against three requirements, capturing off-track time, lateral distance, and track completion status. We considered two search strategies (Uniform Random and Simulated Annealing). SBST consistently produced failure-revealing test cases (10/10 runs), uncovering subtle violations even in the final, competition-ready controller (V3) that manual validation had previously accepted. The generated failure-revealing test cases exposed controller limitations on short segments with acute angles, alignment/turning edge cases, and artifacts from track construction. Our results show that (a) domain-tailored input generation is required to make SBST applicable in different CPS domains, and (b) integrating SBST throughout development mitigates overconfidence in manual testing. As future work, we plan to improve fitness functions for landing (e.g., by considering the distance between the coordinates where the simulation stops and the landing point), compare additional SBST tools and algorithms, and perform hardware-in-the-loop testing to study the consistency between results from in vitro simulations and real-world experimentation. Additionally, we plan to conduct further experiments with other SBST tools to assess the effort needed to adapt them to scenarios involving drones, as the one we used in this paper.

Data Availability A replication package containing all of our data, test results, and scripts is publicly available [22]. An additional artifact is available at `https://doi.org/10.5281/zenodo.18173673`.

References

1. Ali, S., Briand, L.C., Hemmati, H., Panesar-Walawege, R.K.: A systematic review of the application and empirical investigation of search-based test case generation. IEEE Transactions on Software Engineering **36**(6), 742–762 (2010). https://doi.org/10.1109/TSE.2009.52
2. Annpureddy, Y., Liu, C., Fainekos, G., Sankaranarayanan, S.: S-TaLiRo: A Tool for Temporal Logic Falsification for Hybrid Systems. In: International Conference on Tools and Algorithms for the Construction and Analysis of Systems. pp. 254–257. Springer (2011)
3. Arrieta, A., Wang, S., Markiegi, U., Sagardui, G., Etxeberria, L.: Search-based test case generation for cyber-physical systems. In: IEEE Congress on Evolutionary Computation (CEC). p. 688–697. IEEE Press (2017). https://doi.org/10.1109/CEC.2017.7969377
4. Badreddin, O., Lethbridge, T.C., Elassar, M.: Modeling practices in open source software. In: Open Source Software: Quality Verification. pp. 127–139. Springer (2013)
5. Basso, M., Pignaton de Freitas, E.: A UAV guidance system using crop row detection and line follower algorithms. J. Intell. Robot. Syst. **97**(3-4), 605–621 (Mar 2020)
6. Boll, A., Brokhausen, F., Amorim, T., Kehrer, T., Vogelsang, A.: Characteristics, potentials, and limitations of open-source simulink projects for empirical research. Software and Systems Modeling **20**(6), 2111–2130 (2021)
7. Boll, A., Kehrer, T.: On the replicability of experimental tool evaluations in model-based development: Lessons learnt from a systematic literature review focusing on matlab/simulink. In: Systems Modelling and Management. p. 111–130. Springer (2020). https://doi.org/10.1007/978-3-030-58167-1_9
8. Boll, A., Vieregg, N., Kehrer, T.: Replicability of experimental tool evaluations in model-based software and systems engineering with matlab/simulink. Innovations in Systems and Software Engineering **20**(3), 209–224 (2024)
9. Bollard, B., Doshi, A., Gilbert, N., Poirot, C., Gillman, L.: Drone technology for monitoring protected areas in remote and fragile environments. Drones **6**(2) (2022). https://doi.org/10.3390/drones6020042
10. Brandão, A.S., Martins, F.N., Soneguetti, H.B.: A vision-based line following strategy for an autonomous uav. In: 2015 12th International Conference on Informatics in Control, Automation and Robotics (ICINCO). vol. 02, pp. 314–319 (2015)
11. Ding, W., Liang, P., Tang, A., Vliet, H.v., Shahin, M.: How do open source communities document software architecture: An exploratory survey. In: International Conference on Engineering of Complex Computer Systems. p. 136–145. ICECCS, IEEE Computer Society (2014). https://doi.org/10.1109/ICECCS.2014.26

12. Donzé, A.: Breach, a toolbox for verification and parameter synthesis of hybrid systems. In: Touili, T., Cook, B., Jackson, P.B. (eds.) Computer Aided Verification. pp. 167–170. Springer, Berlin, Heidelberg (2010)
13. Dyba, T., Kitchenham, B.A., Jorgensen, M.: Evidence-based software engineering for practitioners. IEEE software **22**(1), 58–65 (2005)
14. Engström, E., Petersen, K.: Mapping software testing practice with software testing research — serp-test taxonomy. In: IEEE International Conference on Software Testing, Verification and Validation Workshops (ICSTW). pp. 1–4 (2015). https://doi.org/10.1109/ICSTW.2015.7107470
15. Ernst, G., Arcaini, P., Fainekos, G., Formica, F., Inoue, J., Khandait, T., Mahboob, M.M., Menghi, C., Pedrielli, G., Waga, M., Yamagata, Y., Zhang, Z.: ARCH-COMP 2022 Category Report: Falsification with Ubounded Resources. In: Frehse, G., Althoff, M., Schoitsch, E., Guiochet, J. (eds.) International Workshop on Applied Verification of Continuous and Hybrid Systems (ARCH22). EPiC Series in Computing, vol. 90, pp. 204–221. EasyChair, Bramhall, Stockport (2022)
16. Ernst, G., Sedwards, S., Zhang, Z., Hasuo, I.: Fast falsification of hybrid systems using probabilistically adaptive input. In: Parker, D., Wolf, V. (eds.) International Conference on Quantitative Evaluation of Systems: (QEST). pp. 165–181. Springer, Cham (2019)
17. Fainekos, G., Hoxha, B., Sankaranarayanan, S.: Robustness of specifications and its applications to falsification, parameter mining, and runtime monitoring with s-taliro. In: Finkbeiner, B., Mariani, L. (eds.) International Conference on Runtime Verification. pp. 27–47. Springer, Cham (2019)
18. Fainekos, G.E., Pappas, G.J.: Robustness of temporal logic specifications. In: Formal Approaches to Software Testing and Runtime Verification, pp. 178–192. Springer (2006)
19. Foreman, V.L., Favaró, F.M., Saleh, J.H., Johnson, C.W.: Software in military aviation and drone mishaps: Analysis and recommendations for the investigation process. Reliability Engineering & System Safety **137**, 101–111 (2015). https://doi.org/10.1016/j.ress.2015.01.006
20. Formica, F., Fan, T., Menghi, C.: Search-based software testing driven by automatically generated and manually defined fitness functions. ACM Transactions on Software Engineering and Methodology (TOSEM) (2023)
21. Formica, F., Fan, T., Rajhans, A., Pantelic, V., Lawford, M., Menghi, C.: Simulation-based testing of simulink models with test sequence and test assessment blocks. IEEE Transactions on Software Engineering (2023)
22. FOSELAB: Replication package for the paper "Search-based Software Testing for Drone Applications: An Experience with the Simulink Environment". `https://github.com/foselab/ParrotMinidroneCompetition` (2025), accessed: August 8, 2025
23. Fredericks, E.M., Jacobs, M., DeVries, B.: Towards a metamorphic testing architecture for software-defined drone systems. In: 2024 11th International Conference on Software Defined Systems (SDS). pp. 170–177 (2024). https://doi.org/10.1109/SDS64317.2024.10883896
24. Gambi, A., Mueller, M., Fraser, G.: Automatically testing self-driving cars with search-based procedural content generation. In: Proceedings of the 28th ACM SIGSOFT International Symposium on Software Testing and Analysis. pp. 318–328 (2019)
25. Harman, M., Jia, Y., Zhang, Y.: Achievements, open problems and challenges for search based software testing. In: IEEE International Conference

on Software Testing, Verification and Validation (ICST). pp. 1–12 (2015). https://doi.org/10.1109/ICST.2015.7102580
26. Harman, M., Jones, B.F.: Search-Based Software Engineering. Information and Software Technology **43**(14), 833–839 (2001). https://doi.org/10.1016/s0950-5849(01)00189-6
27. Hildebrandt, C., Elbaum, S.: World-in-the-loop simulation for autonomous systems validation. In: 2021 IEEE International Conference on Robotics and Automation (ICRA). pp. 10912–10919. IEEE (2021)
28. Humeniuk, D., Khomh, F., Antoniol, G.: A search-based framework for automatic generation of testing environments for cyber–physical systems. Information and Software Technology **149**, 106936 (Sep 2022). https://doi.org/10.1016/j.infsof.2022.106936
29. Javed, Z., Iqbal, M.Z., Khan, M.U., Usman, M., Jilani, A.A.A.: A hybrid search and model-based approach for testing the self-adaptive unmanned aircraft system software. Computer Standards & Interfaces **93**, 103959 (2025). https://doi.org/10.1016/j.csi.2024.103959
30. Kendall, A., Hawke, J., Janz, D., Mazur, P., Reda, D., Allen, J.M., Lam, V.D., Bewley, A., Shah, A.: Learning to drive in a day. In: 2019 international conference on robotics and automation (ICRA). pp. 8248–8254. IEEE (2019)
31. Khatiri, S., Panichella, S., Tonella, P.: Simulation-based test case generation for unmanned aerial vehicles in the neighborhood of real flights. In: 2023 IEEE Conference on Software Testing, Verification and Validation (ICST). pp. 281–292 (2023). https://doi.org/10.1109/ICST57152.2023.00034
32. Khatiri, S., Panichella, S., Tonella, P.: Simulation-based testing of unmanned aerial vehicles with aerialist. In: Proceedings of the 2024 IEEE/ACM 46th International Conference on Software Engineering: Companion Proceedings. p. 134–138. ICSE-Companion '24, Association for Computing Machinery, New York, NY, USA (2024). https://doi.org/10.1145/3639478.3640031
33. Khatiri, S., Saurabh, P., Zimmermann, T., Munasinghe, C., Birchler, C., Panichella, S.: Sbft tool competition 2024-cps-uav test case generation track. In: Proceedings of the 17th ACM/IEEE International Workshop on Search-Based and Fuzz Testing. pp. 29–32 (2024)
34. Kitchenham, B., Dyba, T., Jorgensen, M.: Evidence-based software engineering. In: International Conference on Software Engineering. pp. 273–281 (2004). https://doi.org/10.1109/ICSE.2004.1317449
35. Le, N.B.v., Thai, H.D., Yoon, C.W., Huh, J.H.: Recent development of drone technology software engineering: A systematic survey. IEEE Access **12**, 128729–128751 (2024). https://doi.org/10.1109/ACCESS.2024.3454546
36. Lindvall, M., Porter, A., Magnusson, G., Schulze, C.: Metamorphic model-based testing of autonomous systems. In: 2017 IEEE/ACM 2nd International Workshop on Metamorphic Testing (MET). pp. 35–41. IEEE (2017)
37. Marzella, M., Bombarda, A., Minervini, M., Bisceglia, N.M., Gargantini, A., Menghi, C.: Test case generation for simulink models: An experience from the e-bike domain. In: Search-Based Software Engineering. pp. 1–15. Springer Nature Switzerland, Cham (2025)
38. Melo, S.M., Carver, J.C., Souza, P.S., Souza, S.R.: Empirical Research on Concurrent Software Testing: A Systematic Mapping Study. Information and Software Technology **105**, 226–251 (2019)
39. Menghi, C., Nejati, S., Briand, L.C., Parache, Y.I.: Approximation-refinement testing of compute-intensive cyber-physical models: An approach based on system

identification. In: Proceedings of the ACM/IEEE 42nd International Conference on Software Engineering. pp. 372–384 (2020)
40. Menghi, C., Nejati, S., Gaaloul, K., Briand, L.C.: Generating automated and online test oracles for simulink models with continuous and uncertain behaviors. In: European software engineering conference and symposium on the foundations of software engineering. pp. 27–38. ACM (2019)
41. Mezhuyev, V., Al-Emran, M., Ismail, M.A., Benedicenti, L., Chandran, D.A.P.: The acceptance of search-based software engineering techniques: An empirical evaluation using the technology acceptance model. IEEE Access **7**, 101073–101085 (2019). https://doi.org/10.1109/ACCESS.2019.2917913
42. Panichella, A., Kifetew, F.M., Tonella, P.: A large scale empirical comparison of state-of-the-art search-based test case generators. Information and Software Technology **104**, 236–256 (2018)
43. Parrot SA: Parrot sa. `https://www.parrot.com/en/drones` (2025), accessed: August 8, 2025
44. Rihem Farkh, K.A.: Vision navigation based pid control for line tracking robot. Intelligent Automation & Soft Computing **35**(1), 901–911 (2023). https://doi.org/10.32604/iasc.2023.027614
45. Roy, A., Noel, M.M.: Design of a high-speed line following robot that smoothly follows tight curves. Computers & Electrical Engineering **56**, 732–747 (2016). https://doi.org/10.1016/j.compeleceng.2015.06.014
46. Sajad Khatiri: UAV Testing Competition. `https://github.com/skhatiri/UAV-Testing-Competition?tab=readme-ov-file` (2025), accessed: August 8, 2025
47. Sartaj, H., Muqeet, A., Iqbal, M.Z., Khan, M.U.: Automated system-level testing of unmanned aerial systems. Automated Software Engineering **31**(2) (Aug 2024). https://doi.org/10.1007/s10515-024-00462-9
48. Sayyad, A.S., Goseva-Popstojanova, K., Menzies, T., Ammar, H.: On parameter tuning in search based software engineering: A replicated empirical study. In: International Workshop on Replication in Empirical Software Engineering Research. p. 84–90. RESER, IEEE (2013). https://doi.org/10.1109/RESER.2013.6
49. Shrestha, S.L., Chowdhury, S.A., Csallner, C.: Replicability Study: Corpora For Understanding Simulink Models & Projects . In: ACM/IEEE International Symposium on Empirical Software Engineering and Measurement (ESEM). pp. 1–12. IEEE (2023). https://doi.org/10.1109/ESEM56168.2023.10304867
50. The Mathworks Inc: Minidrone competitions. `https://www.mathworks.com/academia/students/competitions/minidrones.html` (2025), accessed: August 8, 2025
51. Vierhauser, M., Meixner, K., Biffl, S.: Scenario-based field testing of drone missions. In: 2024 50th Euromicro Conference on Software Engineering and Advanced Applications (SEAA). pp. 10–17 (2024). https://doi.org/10.1109/SEAA64295.2024.00012
52. Waga, M.: Falsification of cyber-physical systems with robustness-guided black-box checking. In: International Conference on Hybrid Systems: Computation and Control. ACM (2020)
53. Yamagata, Y., Liu, S., Akazaki, T., Duan, Y., Hao, J.: Falsification of cyber-physical systems using deep reinforcement learning. IEEE Transactions on Software Engineering **47**(12), 2823–2840 (2021). https://doi.org/10.1109/TSE.2020.2969178
54. Zhang, M., Li, X.: Drone-enabled internet-of-things relay for environmental monitoring in remote areas without public networks. IEEE Internet of Things Journal **7**(8), 7648–7662 (2020). https://doi.org/10.1109/JIOT.2020.2988249

55. Zhang, Z., Lyu, D., Arcaini, P., Ma, L., Hasuo, I., Zhao, J.: Effective hybrid system falsification using Monte Carlo Tree Search guided by QB-robustness. In: Silva, A., Leino, K.R.M. (eds.) Computer Aided Verification. pp. 1–24. Springer, Cham (2021)

Modeling and Analyzing Planning-Aware Distributed Cyber-Physical Systems with Timed Graph Transformation Systems

Mustafa Ghani ✉ and Holger Giese

Hasso Plattner Institute, University of Potsdam, Potsdam, Germany
{mustafa.ghani,holger.giese}@hpi.de

Abstract. Distributed Cyber-Physical Systems are often safety-critical and, therefore, establishing their safety is of paramount importance. High-level models like timed graph transformation systems have been developed to cover the complex context-aware and self-aware behavior formally and enable to often verify safety at this level. To cover the communication delays inherent in Distributed Cyber-Physical Systems, also adding delay-robustness to these models has been studied. However, ensuring safety by design is often in conflict with other relevant goals like, for example, high throughput, as oftentimes the need for a delay-robust design leads to an overcautious behavior. By incorporating planning-awareness into the design such that Distributed Cyber-Physical Systems agents share their planning information, one can avoid the need to sacrifice throughput to ensure safety, compared to a design that is limited to context and self-awareness alone.
In this paper, we develop an approach employing timed graph transformation systems for Distributed Cyber-Physical Systems (i) to model planning-awareness without compromising verifiability, (ii) to derive such a model systematically from a non-planning-aware model, and (iii) to analyze for the derived model whether it compromises throughput to establish safety less often than the employed non-planning-aware model. As a running example, we consider a Distributed Cyber-Physical Systems in which multiple autonomous shuttles locally coordinate their movement on a track topology to avoid collisions while maximizing throughput.

Keywords: Cyber-Physical Systems · Model-driven Systems Engineering · Planning-Awareness · Delay-Robustness

1 Introduction

For safety-critical **D**istributed **C**yber-**P**hysical **S**ystems (DCPS), it is of paramount importance to ensure safe operation. High-level modeling formalisms have been developed to formally capture complex context-aware and self-aware behaviors, and they often allow verifying safety properties at this level of abstraction (see [2, 18, 17, 29] among others).

E. Albert and C. Pasareanu (Eds.): FASE 2026, LNCS 16504, pp. 327–347, 2026.
https://doi.org/10.1007/978-3-032-22774-4_17

To account for the communication delays inherent in DCPS, arising from transmission, propagation, queuing, and processing times (cf. [13, 40]), the addition of *delay robustness* to such models has also been investigated [16, 15]. Delays in inter-agent communication may cause agents to form incorrect assumptions about information received from others. In safety-critical environments, delayed messages may result in inaccurate estimates of other agents' positions, thereby increasing the risk of safety violations. Consequently, DCPS models must explicitly distinguish between local, immediate observations (occurring with zero delay) and remote, δ-delayed observations (subject to delays of up to δ time units). A system model is then considered *δ-delay robust* if it remains safe and functional even when remote observations are delayed by up to δ time units.

The authors proposed an approach for deriving δ-delay robust models from given zero-delay models in [16]. However, ensuring safety by design often conflicts with other key objectives such as maintaining high throughput, as achieving delay robustness frequently results in overcautious system behavior. In this mentioned approach, for example, safety reactions must be triggered whenever a potential future unsafe state cannot be excluded under all possible behaviors. Consequently, agents must take premature safety measures and halt operation to avoid potential unsafe states, leading to a reduction in throughput.

To address this limitation, we propose a planning-aware modeling approach in which agents share their planned future steps. This additional information allows agents to maintain safety without compromising throughput, outperforming purely context- and self-aware designs. Specifically, each agent is required to plan its next n steps in advance, covering at least Δ time units, where $\Delta > \delta$, and to communicate this plan to other agents, enabling them to coordinate their behavior accordingly. Even if parts of the exchanged plans are delayed by up to δ time units, agents can still make less overcautious decisions because reliable information remains available for at least $\Delta - \delta$ time units.

We developed this approach using *Timed Graph Transformation Systems (TGTSs)* [32], an extension of *Graph Transformation Systems (GTSs)* [12], to model planning-aware designs for DCPS. GTSs provide a powerful modeling formalism for systems whose states can be represented as graphs and whose state transitions are described by rule-based graph transformations. By integrating timing constraints such as clocks, guards, invariants, and resets, TGTSs offer a suitable framework for formally modeling autonomous agents in DCPS. Moreover, by encoding the agents' context within the graph and allowing rules to access not only local information but also contextual and other agents' states, TGTSs enable the formal specification of complex context-aware and self-aware behaviors under a non-zero-delay assumption [18]. To model planning-aware agents, the agents' next n steps are incorporated into the overall graph, allowing other agents to observe them as well. To this end, we propose an algorithm that determines the minimal required length n of the planning horizon. In particular, our presented approach supports

(i) modeling planning-aware DCPS without compromising verifiability,
(ii) deriving a planning-aware model with a corresponding planning horizon sys-

tematically from a non-planning-aware model, and (iii) analyzing for the derived model whether it compromises throughput to establish safety less often than the employed non-planning-aware model.
As a running example, we consider a DCPS in which multiple autonomous shuttles locally coordinate their movement on a shared track topology to avoid collisions. Our goal is to maximize throughput (i.e., to minimize braking) while ensuring that all shuttles safely reach their terminal tracks. To highlight our approach and simplify the exposition, we focus on a core behavioral and interaction pattern in which two shuttles independently approach a shared track segment from different predecessor tracks. We demonstrate the effectiveness of our approach through a series of experiments using various track topologies.

This paper is structured as follows: Section 2 establish the necessary foundations. In Section 3, we present our main contributions to model planning-aware designs without compromising verifiability (see Section 3.2), to derive most of such a model for a planning-aware designs systematically from a non-planning-aware model (see Section 3.3), and to analyze for the derived model whether it less often compromise throughput to establish safety than the employed not planning-aware model (see Section 4). Section 5 discusses related work, positioning our approach within the broader research landscape. Finally, Section 6 concludes the paper and outlines potential directions for future research.

2 Background

We employ typed attributed graphs (graphs) [12] and injective graph morphism $m : G_1 \hookrightarrow G_2$ between them. For our running example, we rely on the type graph TG (see Figure 1a and the Start Graph G_0 from Figure 4). Here and subsequently, we use an abbreviated notation for graphs in which (a) node types are indicated by the node names (S, T, and M indicating shuttles, tracks, and markers (whose purpose we explain in the next section)), (b) edge types are omitted as edge types can be derived uniquely for TG, (c) node attributes and their values are, if present, given behind the node name (e.g., $S_1(c1, \mathit{drive})$ in G_0 is a shuttle node with a *clock* attribute $c1$ of unspecified value and *mode* attribute of value *drive*).

Following the Double Pushout (DPO) approach in [12], graph transformation (GT) steps are derived by applying GT rules $\rho = (\ell : K \hookrightarrow L, r : K \hookrightarrow R)$ (where we assume ℓ and r to be inclusions) for a match $m : L \hookrightarrow G_1$. The morphisms ℓ and r capture elements to be preserved in K, deleted in $L - \ell(K)$, and created in $R - r(K)$. When depicting GT rules as in Figure 1b, we use a standard integrated notation for ℓ and r, providing a single graph where $\ominus$ and $\oplus$ indicate the elements to be deleted and created. As in Figure 2a, we depict the change of an attribute as $v1 \rightsquigarrow v2$ for values $v1$ and $v2$.

TGTSs employ clocks and clock constraints (CCs) thereon. For a set of clock variables C, CCs $\psi \in \mathbf{CC}(C)$ are finite conjunctions of clock comparisons of the form $c1 \sim r$ and $c1 - c2 \sim r$ where $c1, c2 \in C$, $\sim \in \{<, >, \leq, \geq\}$, and $r \in \mathbb{N} \cup \{\infty\}$. Clock valuations $cv : C \rightarrow \mathbb{R}_0^+$ satisfy CCs ψ, written $cv \models \psi$, as expected.

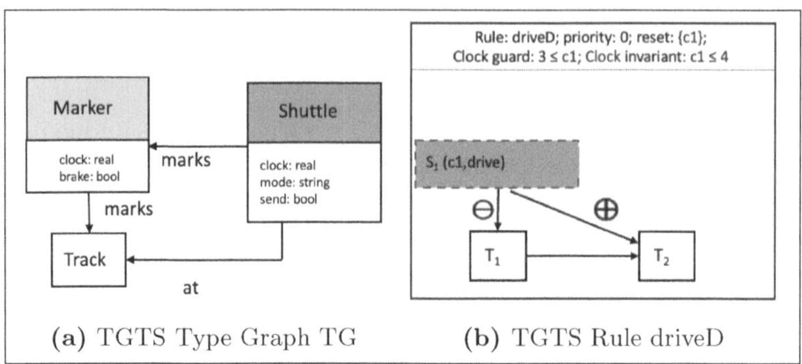

(a) TGTS Type Graph TG (b) TGTS Rule driveD

Fig. 1. TGTS Type Graph TG and TGTS Rule driveD

For a clock valuation cv and a set of clocks C', $cv[C' := 0]$ is the clock valuation mapping the clocks from C' to 0 and all other clocks according to cv. For a clock valuation cv and a duration $\delta \in \mathbb{R}_0^+$, $cv + \delta$ is the clock valuation mapping each clock x to $cv(x) + \delta$. We now discuss the syntax and semantics of TGTS with agent-based priorities, and present the TGTS model of our running example based on clock-based timing constraints. Each TGTS employs a type graph and contains a single start graph (for our running example, see again Figure 1a for TG and Figure 4 for G_0). In our running example, shuttles S_1 and S_2 are initially in mode *drive* and will advance on the track topology. TGTSs identify for each graph G a set of clock attributes $CA(G)$.

For our running example, these are the *clock* attributes of shuttle and marker nodes. TGTS states (G, cv) contain a graph G and for the clocks $CA(\mathrm{G})$ of G, a clock valuation $cv : CA(\mathrm{G}) \rightarrow \mathbb{R}_0^+$. The start state of a TGTS consists of the start graph and the clock valuation mapping all clocks to 0. TGTS invariants (I, ψ) contain a graph I and a CC $\psi \in \mathbf{CC}(CA(I))$ They are used to state clock constraints based on graph patterns that must be satisfied by all traversable TGTS states. A TGTS state (G, cv) satisfies a TGTS invariant (I, ψ), if $cv \circ m \models \psi$ for every match $m : I \hookrightarrow G$. TGTS Atomic Propositions (AP) are given by graphs; each TGTS state (G, cv) is labeled with the TGTS AP A for which a match m: $A \rightarrow G$ exists.

In our running example, we employ the TGTS AP from Figure 2b capturing states, where two shuttles are located on a common track. The shuttles' clocks are reset to 0 upon each advancement and the TGTS invariant then prevents timed steps when a shuttle in mode *drive* has a clock value of 4 time units, capturing that such a shuttle must advance.

TGTS rules describe how discrete steps between TGTS states are to be derived. Rules $\sigma = (\rho, a, \psi, CR, \mathrm{p})$ consist of a GT rule $\rho = (\ell : K \hookrightarrow \mathrm{L}, \mathrm{r}: \mathrm{K} \hookrightarrow \mathrm{R})$, an actor embedding $a : A \hookrightarrow L$, a clock guard $\psi \in \mathbf{CC}(CA(L))$ over the clocks of L, a reset set $CR \subseteq CA(\mathrm{R})$ of clocks to be reset,and a priority $\mathrm{p} \in \mathbb{N}$.

For our running example, see Figure 1b, Figure 2a, Figure 3a, and Figure 3b for the visualizations of the rules employed where we depict the actor subgraph A (consisting of a shuttle node with its attributes each time) using a red, dashed

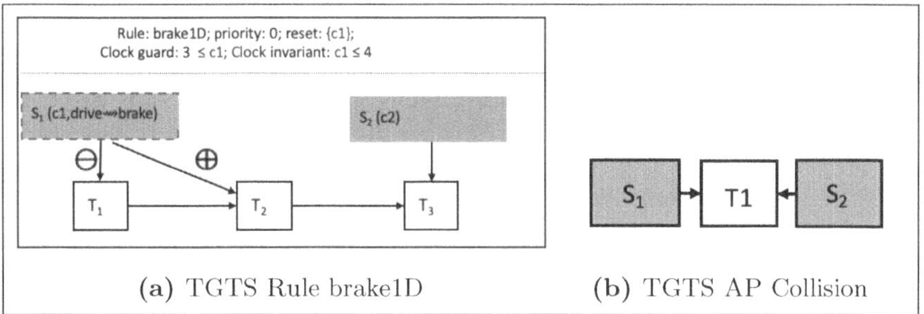

(a) TGTS Rule brake1D (b) TGTS AP Collision

Fig. 2. TGTS Rule brake1D and TGTS AP Collision

border: Rule driveD represents the advancement of a shuttle from Track T_1 to T_2 after at least 3 time units. Rule brake1D, brake2D, and brake3D change the mode from *drive* to *brake* to avoid potential subsequent collision with a potential nearby shuttle with varying distances.

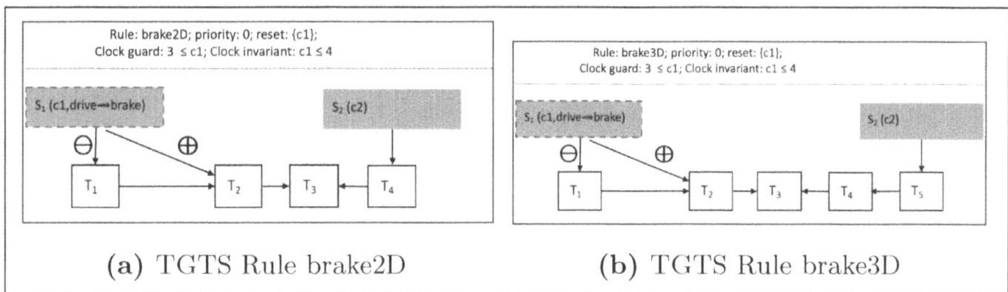

(a) TGTS Rule brake2D (b) TGTS Rule brake3D

Fig. 3. TGTS Rule brake2D and brake3D

We refer to the local agent-based priority concept proposed in [16]. The standard GT rule priority concept is insufficient for TGTS modeling multi-agent systems because a high priority step $s1$ for an actor A_1 prevents a lower priority step s_2 of another actor A_2, which can lead to the modeling error of timelocks when A_2 must perform s_2 before A_1 can perform s_1 (for our running example, a shuttle that needs to brake using the brake rule prevents a step using drive to be executed by all other shuttles). To evaluate priorities for agents separately, we rely on the actor embedding $a : A \hookrightarrow L$ in the rules. Local agent-based priorities can be encoded using application conditions.

A TGTS S $=(\mathrm{G}_0, \mathcal{P}, \mathcal{I}, \mathcal{AP})$ consists of a start graph G_0, a set of rules $\mathcal{P}$, a set of TGTS invariants $\mathcal{I}$, and a set of TGTS AP $\mathcal{AP}$. For such a TGTS S, we use TGTS $states(\mathrm{S})$ to capture its TGTS states satisfying all its TGTS invariants $\mathcal{I}$.

The single step relation of a TGTS S on TGTS states (G, cv) defines timed steps in which time elapses by adding the same delay to all clocks requiring that the implicitly traversed steps are TGTS states as well, and discrete steps where a rule is applied by applying its underlying GT rule and resetting the clocks in the reset set to 0 requiring that the clock guard of the rule is satisfied and that no rule of S with an overlapping actor-embedding and higher priority is applicable. Consequently, the passage of time competes with possibly multiple rule applications of possibly multiple actors, resulting in non-determinism. Finally, we define the two types of steps of a TGTS.

Definition 1 (TGTS Steps). TGTS $S = (G_0, \mathcal{P}, \mathcal{I}, \mathcal{AP})$ *defines a set of timed and discrete labeled steps* $\mathrm{steps}(S)$ *among TGTS states of* S.

- *Timed Step:* $((G_1, cv_1), \delta, (G_1, cv_1 + \delta)) \in \mathrm{steps}(S)$ *if* $(G_1, cv_1) \in \mathrm{states}(S)$, $\delta \in \mathbb{R}^+$, *and* $(G_1, cv_1 + \delta') \in \mathrm{states}(S)$ *for each delay* $\delta' \in [0, \delta]$.
- *Discrete Step:* $((G_1, cv_1), (\sigma, m), (G_2, cv_2)) \in \mathrm{steps}(S)$ *if* $(G_1, cv_1), (G_2, cv_2) \in \mathrm{states}(S)$, $\sigma = (\rho, a : A \hookrightarrow L, \psi, CR, p) \in \mathcal{P}$, $\rho = (\ell : K \hookrightarrow L, r : K \hookrightarrow R)$, $m : L \hookrightarrow G_1$ *(match)*, $(G_1, (\rho, m, k, \bar{m}, \ell', r'), G_2) \in \mathit{GTsteps}$ *(GT step)*, $cv_1 \models \psi$ *(clock guard satisfaction)*, $cv_2 = cv_1[\bar{m}(CR) := 0]$ *(reset of clocks)*, *and* $\nexists \sigma' = (\rho', a' : A' \hookrightarrow L', \psi', CR', p') \in \mathcal{P}$ $((G_1, cv_1), (\sigma', m'), \_) \in \mathrm{steps}(S) \wedge (m \circ a)(A)$ *and* $(m' \circ a')(A')$ *overlap* $\wedge\, p' > p$ *(priorities)*.

The states of the (forward constructed) symbolic state space are of the form (G, ψ) representing TGTS states (G, cv) where $cv \models \psi$. The syntactic restrictions of CCs are sufficient to ensure the finiteness of the symbolic state space when a finite number of discrete state components can be reached.

3 Modeling

3.1 Problem Statement

As demonstrated by our previous work [16], the presence of δ-delayed inter-agent messages disrupts synchronization among agents within a multi-agent system, as agents may base their decisions on outdated information. Such synchronization disruptions pose significant risks to the system's safety requirements. To address this problem, we proposed a methodology to derive TGTS rules that guarantee robustness with respect to δ-delayed messages (with $\delta = 1$ time unit, an assumption we also adopt in this paper) while ensuring safety. However, this approach tends to result in overcautious configurations, consequently restricting overall system efficiency by limiting throughput. In this section, we illustrate the limitations of this approach through the provided running example. The example involves multiple autonomous shuttles that locally coordinate their movements on a shared track topology. See Figure 4 for the topology, and Figures 1b, 2a, 3a, 3b for the corresponding TGTS rule set, which we denote as *Comparison Model*, in short: CM.

In [16], we considered the track topology without the green labeled tracks (i.e., excluding tracks T_7 and T_G). Consider the initial state of this topology, where S_1 is at T_1, and S_2 at T_A. Moreover, we consider T_F as a potential conflict track since the location of two shuttles at this track simultaneously leads to a collision. (Recall that we consider a collision (see Figure 2b) as a safety violation.)

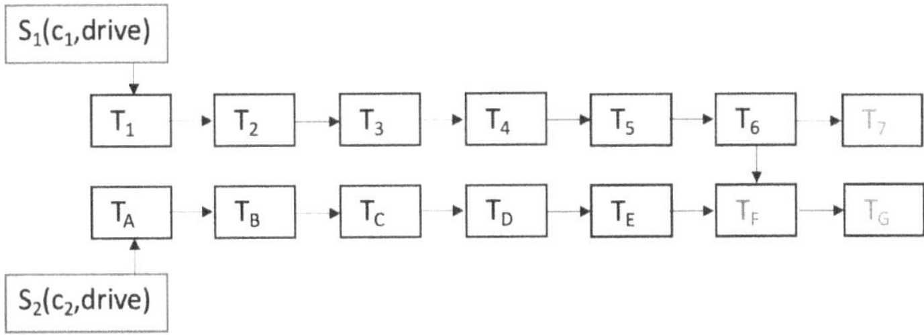

Fig. 4. TGTS Start Graph G_0

The application of this proposed solution (i.e., CM) to this topology leads to a state in which shuttle S_1 terminates at T_6 and S_2 at T_E. This is realized since S_1 brakes at T_5 and S_2 brakes at T_D to avoid a collision at T_F.

However, if we consider the topology with the green labeled tracks (called extended topology), then the application of CM causes both shuttles to brake for every trace of this model. This also holds if S_1 aims to traverse track T_7 instead of T_F, where a collision is obviously not possible because both shuttles are not located at a common track at the same time since they do not share a common track, and, thus, safety is preserved. Hence, due to overcautious braking behavior, the shuttles of CM brake in every trace for this given topology. We consider this behavior as a throughput limitation. To address this limitation, we propose an approach (see Section 3.2) to minimize braking. We employ the running example of CM to ease comparison between the two solutions.

3.2 Planning-Aware DCPS Models

In this section, we introduce the notion of planning awareness for DCPS models. Such models are characterized by the explicit integration of an agent's planned steps. In the following, we formally define a planned state and a planned step, and illustrate their application using our running example.

Definition 2 (Planned State). *A planned TGTS state ps consists of graph(ps), which is the planned graph, which contains all present and planned graph elements. Moreover, v(ps): graph(ps)→* $\mathbf{R}_0^+$ *is the current valuation of all present and planned graph clocks.*

Definition 3 (Planned Step).

- *Timed Step: Let* $[ts] = (G_c, v_c)$ *with* $v_c = v(ps)$*. Then,* $([ts], \theta + v_c, [ts]')$ *is a planned timed TGTS step, where* $\theta \in \mathbf{R}_0^+$ *models the elapse of time.*
- Discrete Step: *Let* $[ds] = (G_p, v_p)$ *with with* $v_p = v(ps)$*. Let* $(\sigma = (\rho, a : A \hookrightarrow L, \psi, CR, p) \in \mathcal{P}$, $\rho = (\ell : K \hookrightarrow L, r : K \hookrightarrow R)$, $m : L \hookrightarrow G_1$ *(match))* *according to Definition 1. Then,* $(ds, \delta + v_p, \sigma, ds')$ *is a planned discrete TGTS step.*

In general, we create a planning-aware model (PM) based on our algorithm (see Section 3.3) that takes as input a non-planning-aware model. The algorithm computes the planning horizon length for a given TGTS rule. Thus, a planning-aware TGTS rule is formed by the integration of a planning horizon into a non-planning-aware TGTS rule.

To construct the PM for our running example, we revisit CM, which serves as input to derive the planning horizon. By integrating the derived planning horizon into CM, we obtain PM. (Recall, CM is the solution proposed in [16].)

The createPlan rule (see Figure 5) with priority 1 represent the notion of a planning rule, where shuttle S_1 marks track segment T_2 and marks by the application of the rule T_3 as the planned step while its mode remains in *drive*. Its application is independent of clock valuations and depends exclusively on the current graph structure. Consequently, it uses an unconditional guard (i.e., Guard: true) and involves no invariants or clock resets. Intuitively, the createPlan rule is enabled as soon as an agent is connected by a directed edge to exactly one marker node. Once enabled, it is immediately applied (i.e., without any time elapse), linking the existing marker node to the newly generated marker node via a directed edge, thereby maintaining the planning horizon of two (which we describe in Section 3.3).

The PM of our running example incorporates the TGTS rules *brakeR*, *driveR*, and *createPlan* (see Figure 6b, 6a, and 5). Recall, we construct driveR and brakeR based on the brake1D (see Figure 2a) and driveD (see Figure 1b) automatically by means of our proposed algorithm, which equips each shuttle with two marker nodes representing its planning horizon.

Rule driveR (see Figure 6a) ensures the movement of a shuttle from the currently located track to the next track. The application of this rule deletes the marker node of the target track, while it creates an edge to the marker node of the next track.

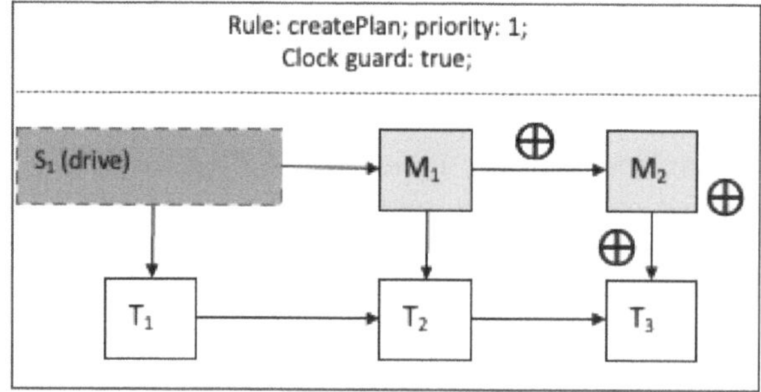

Fig. 5. TGTS Rule createPlan

Rule brakeR (see Figure 6b) changes the mode of a shuttle from drive to brake since T_3 is marked by the marker node M_2 of a remote agent. This is visible due to the existence of M_2 without an incoming edge from M_1. Rule brakeR ensures

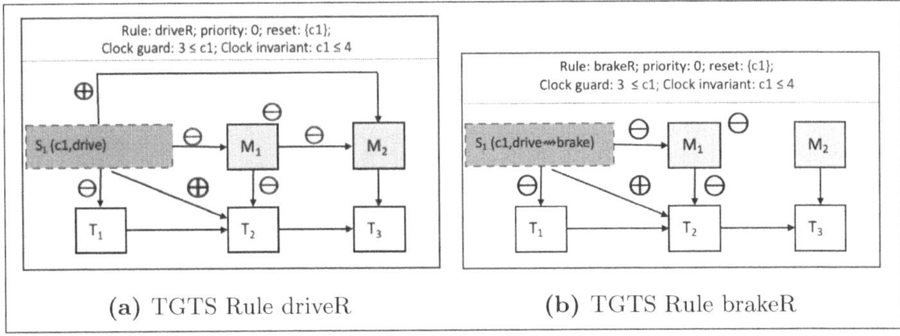

(a) TGTS Rule driveR (b) TGTS Rule brakeR

Fig. 6. TGTS Rule driveR and brakeR

the advancement from the current location to the next track, where the last marker node M_1 of S_1 is located. Moreover, it deletes this marker node located at the targeted track and causes the shuttle to terminate at the newly occupied track (i.e., T_2). The application of the TGTS rule createPlan (see Figure 5) generates an additional marker node representing the step after next. Note, the createPlan rule generates a marker node with a corresponding edge from the existing marker node during execution. This rule ensures that each shuttle is equipped with marker nodes permanently.

The generic scheme for deriving TGTS rules for PM is as follows. We extract the behavioural model of PM from the behavioural model of CM. We then integrate a planning horizon into PM so that it captures not only the current but also the planned behaviour. This is achieved by introducing a planning horizon via a corresponding TGTS rule, which ensures that the length of the planning horizon remains constant. Since collisions are guaranteed not to occur in PM, we exploit this property by executing PM through CM.

In the following, we use the tool [22] to simulate situations using PM. To this end, we employ the extended topology of Figure 7. Consider for the initial state S_1 with $M_{1,1}$ and $M_{1,2}$ indicating the traversal of T_2 and T_3, while S_2 with $M_{2,1}$ and $M_{2,2}$ for the traversal of T_B and T_C. Note, for brevity, we omit the TGTS rule for the generation of the two initial planning nodes for each agent. For the same reason, we omit the visualization of (a) clock attributes from the marker nodes and (b) the δ-delayed inter-agent message passing.

We now discuss Situation 1, where we construct a planning conflict, i.e., two agents intend to mark a common location at the same time leading potentially to an unsafe state.

Situation 1: Both Shuttles plan to traverse the conflict track T_F at the same time Starting from this initial state, both shuttles traverse locations by processing their marked locations using the driveR rule and subsequently marking additional locations through the application of the createPlan rule, leading to the state depicted by Figure 8.

Assume S_1 marks T_F first. This leads to a planning conflict as S_2 intends to mark/ traverse this conflict track as well. Since S_1 marks this conflict track

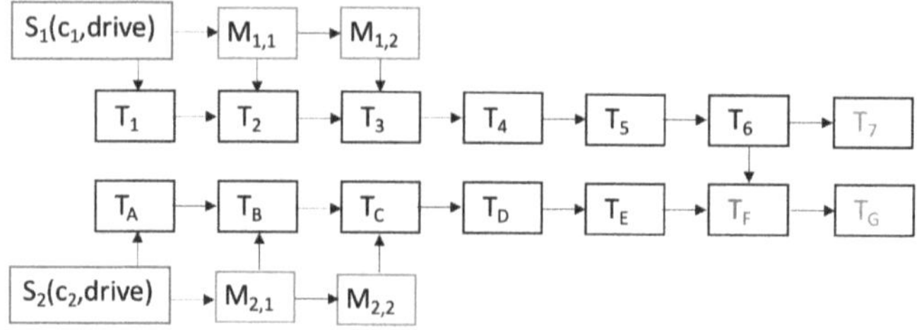

Fig. 7. TGTS Extended Topology with Initial State

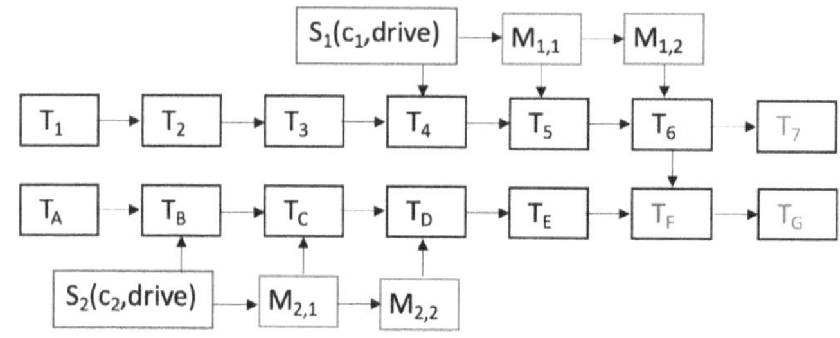

Fig. 8. TGTS Extended Topology with S_1 on the verge to plan further steps leading to a potential conflict with S_2 at T_F

first implying that S_2 is not allowed to mark/ traverse that track, S_2 performs the rule brakeR to stop at T_E to avoid a collision. Recall that we assume for the running example an inter-agent message passing delay of up to one time unit (inherited from [16]). Therefore, S_1 is required to communicate its two planned steps (which includes the conflict point) while locating at T_5, such that S_2 obtains this message (documenting the planned steps of S_1) during its stay at T_D.

As a result, S_2 performs brakeR at T_D to stop at T_E. Eventually, S_1 traverses the conflict point to terminate at T_G. Note if S_2 marks first the conflict track, then S_1 is not required to brake since T_7 is then an option to traverse while preserving the system safety.

Situation 2: One shuttle plans to traverse the conflict track T_F at a time Given Figure 8, if S_1 marks as next step T_7, while locating at T_5, then S_2 traverses T_F. Since S_1 transmits his remote plan at T_5, S_2 obtains this message at the latest while located at T_D (due to the δ-delayed message exchange). Therefore, S_2 eventually traverse T_F and S_1 T_7 and both shuttles terminate at a terminal track without braking.

From these two situations, we conclude the following. In CM, both shuttles brake and terminate before reaching the terminal tracks. This also holds for Situation 2, where both shuttles intend to traverse different tracks and therefore a collision is not possible. Still, both shuttles brake and terminate before their desired terminal track. We consider this braking behavior as a limitation of throughput. This limitation occurs due to overcautious configurations to manage delayed inter-agent messages while preserving safety, and resulting in reduced overall throughput. In contrast, by employing PM, either one shuttle or no shuttle brakes. Recall that we consider braking as limiting throughput.

3.3 Construction Scheme of Planning Horizon

In the previous section, we presented the notion of PM. In this section, we discuss Algorithm 1 to construct the planning horizon of a PM. Given the solution of CM (see Figures 1b, 2a, 3a, and 3b) as input, we calculate the length of the planning horizon using this algorithm.

To enable collaborative planning by means of a PM, an agent exchanges its remote plan with remote agents. In a remote plan, an agent documents its current location, fixates its planned steps, and shares this plan with remote agents. Once an agent processes a planned step, it updates and transmits its current remote plan, such that remote agents are informed regarding its updated planned steps, and updated location. If a location is marked (i.e., included in an agent's remote plan), no other agent is permitted to mark or traverse this marked location. The traversal of a marked location is only permitted by an agent whose remote plan contains this marked location as a next immediate step. Therefore, remote agents are required to stop at the latest at the preceding location before reaching that marked location (or select another location to traverse if possible).

Given the inter-agent message delay (i.e., $\delta = 1$ time unit), parts of the remote plan may be outdated upon reception for remote agents since the message-sending agent may directly perform a step (i.e., change location) after sending his remote plan, which, as a result, incorrectly states the previous location as the latest one. Hence, the remote plan must contain the number of planned steps (i.e., planning horizon) such that parts of the remote plan are not outdated upon reception for the remote message-receiving agents to ensure collaboration. To address this, we quantify the number of steps of a remote plan may be become outdated.

In particular, we calculate the number of steps that are possible during δ-delayed messages. Then, we over-approximate (i.e., either round up or increase it by one) this number, which serves as the length of the planning horizon. By doing this, we ensure that parts of the remote plan are not outdated upon reception since the length of the planning horizon is greater than the number of possible steps during δ-delayed messages. Intuitively, agents must plan their planned steps such that at least Δ time units are covered and communicate this remote plan to remote agents. Given the remote plan, remote agents can coordinate their behavior based on the received information. Even when parts of the exchanged plans are delayed up to δ time units, remote agents can make less overcautious decisions as proper information for the next $\Delta - \delta$ time units is always available.

Algorithm 1 determines the length of the *Planning Horizon* (represented by the variable PH) based on the numerical value of *Guard* and *Invariant*. After computing temp = Invariant − Guard, four cases are identified to ensure that the length of the planning horizon is greater than the number of possible steps being

Algorithm 1 Calculation of the length of the Planning Horizon

Require: Guard, Invariant, $\delta = 1$. Precondition: $1 <$ Guard $<$ Invariant ≤ 15.
Ensure: PH, where $2 \leq$ PH ≤ 15 represents the length of the Planning Horizon.

1: temp $\leftarrow$ Invariant $-$ Guard
2: **if** temp $=$ Guard **then**
3: PH $\leftarrow \delta + 1$
4: **else if** temp $<$ Guard **and** temp $= \delta$ **then**
5: PH $\leftarrow \delta + 1$
6: **else if** temp $>$ Guard **then**
7: PH $\leftarrow \left\lceil \frac{\text{temp}}{\text{Guard}} \right\rceil$
8: **else**
9: PH $\leftarrow \left\lceil \frac{\text{Invariant}}{\text{Guard}} \right\rceil$
10: **end if**
11: **return** PH

outdated in the remote plan. If temp $=$ Guard, then it is possible that at most one step is outdated if this potentially outdated step happens immediately after being enabled due to temp $=$ Guard and Invariant $-$ Guard $=$ temp causing inaccuracy in the remote plan. Therefore, PH is set to $\delta + 1$ to exceed the system delay ($\delta = 1$). If temp $<$ Guard and equals δ, then it is also possible to have a deviation of maximally one step if (temp$+\delta$) $=$ Guard. Hence, PH is assigned ($\delta + 1$). For temp $>$ Guard, PH is computed by $\lceil \frac{\text{temp}}{\text{Guard}} \rceil$. Also, for $1 <$ temp $<$ Guard, PH is computed by $\lceil \frac{\text{Invariant}}{\text{Guard}} \rceil$. In both branches, we cover cases, where either temp or Invariant is many times greater than Guard. Therefore, we divide either temp or Invariant by Guard to calculate how many times the guard fits into temp or Invariant. To ensure $\Delta > \delta$, we round up the quotient, which we then use as (a bounded) length of the planning horizon.

Recent works in the field of motion planning [14, 23] assume a maximum of 15 steps as a planning horizon. Hence, while we require PH to be 15 at most, our objective is to compute the minimal required number for the planning horizon to ensure safety and throughput.

In the following, we apply the algorithm to our running example. Consider the case where Guard $= 3$ and Invariant $= 4$. (Recall, we inherited these valuations from CM.) First, we calculate temp: temp $=$ Invariant - Guard $=$ 4 - 3 $=$ 1. Next, we check the conditions of the algorithm:

- temp $=$ Guard is false, since $1 \neq 3$.
- temp $<$ Guard and temp $= \delta = 1$ is true, because $1 < 3$ and $\delta = 1$.

Therefore, the second branch applies, we compute PH $=$ temp $+ 1 = 1 + 1 = 2$. Thus, for Guard $= 3$ and Invariant $= 4$, the length of the planning horizon is 2. During the transmission of a remote plan, a shuttle traverses one track segment at most due to the guard ($= 3$ time units) and invariant ($= 4$ time units) of the rules driveR and brakeR. This causes the location deviation in a remote plan by one track segment exactly. To compensate for this deviation, we calculate a planning horizon of two track segments (by the operation $(\delta + 1)$, resulting in PH $= 2$) such that parts of the remote plan are not outdated upon reception. Therefore, we define two marker nodes, M_1 and M_2, as the planning horizon in the running example.

In the following, we prove termination and correctness of our algorithm.

Theorem 1 (Termination). *The Planning Horizon Algorithm terminates for all inputs g and n satisfying* $1 < g < n \leq 15$.

Proof. The algorithm consists of a finite sequence of arithmetic operations and a fixed conditional (if–else) structure. It contains no loops or recursive calls. Consequently, for any valid input, the algorithm reaches its return statement after a finite number of steps. Therefore, the algorithm always terminates.

Theorem 2 (Correctness). *Let g and n be integers satisfying* $1 < g < n \leq 15$, *and set* $\delta = 1$. *Define* $\text{temp} = n - g > 0$, *and let* PH *be the value returned by the Planning Horizon Algorithm. Then*

$$\text{PH} = \max\bigl(2, \lceil \text{temp}/g \rceil\bigr).$$

Proof. The value of temp determines four mutually exclusive and exhaustive cases corresponding to the branches of the conditional structure.

(I) Case $\text{temp} = g$. The algorithm returns $\delta + 1 = 2$. Since $\text{temp}/g = 1$, we have $\lceil \text{temp}/g \rceil = 1$, and hence $\max(2, 1) = 2$.

(II) Case $\text{temp} < g$ *and* $\text{temp} = \delta = 1$. The algorithm returns $\text{temp} + 1 = 2$, which equals $\max(2, \lceil \text{temp}/g \rceil)$ because $0 < 1/g < 1$ implies $\lceil \text{temp}/g \rceil = 1$.

(III) Case $\text{temp} > g$. The algorithm returns $\lceil \text{temp}/g \rceil$. Since $\text{temp}/g > 1$, the ceiling value is at least 2, and therefore matches the formula.

(IV) Case $1 < \text{temp} < g$. Here $n = g + \text{temp}$ gives

$$1 + \frac{1}{g} < \frac{n}{g} < 2,$$

so $\lceil n/g \rceil = 2$. Moreover, $0 < \text{temp}/g < 1$ implies $\lceil \text{temp}/g \rceil = 1$, and thus $\max(2, 1) = 2$, which coincides with the algorithm's output.

These four cases cover all possibilities for $\text{temp} > 0$. In each case, the algorithm returns exactly $\max\bigl(2, \lceil \text{temp}/g \rceil\bigr)$. Therefore, the algorithm works correctly.

4 Evaluation

We evaluate our approach in an experimental setting regarding three different objectives. First, we evaluate whether our approach violates the safety-critical requirement. Then, we evaluate the throughput, and the scalability of our approach. The latter includes three further experiments, where we incrementally add two conflict tracks per experiment in the used topologies (see Figure 9).

This topology contains seven highlighted conflict points: T_F, T_7, T_G, T_8, T_H, T_9, and T_I. For the second experiment, we employ the topology without the tracks T_8, T_H, T_9, T_I. Hence, T_7 and T_G are the predecessor tracks of T_{10} and T_J. We extend the topology with track segments T_8 and T_H but still exclude T_9 and T_I for the second experiment. Lastly, we extend this topology with track segments T_9 and T_I. Track segments T_{10} and T_J have no impact, since they are not connected and are used solely for diagnostic purposes, as they are terminal tracks.

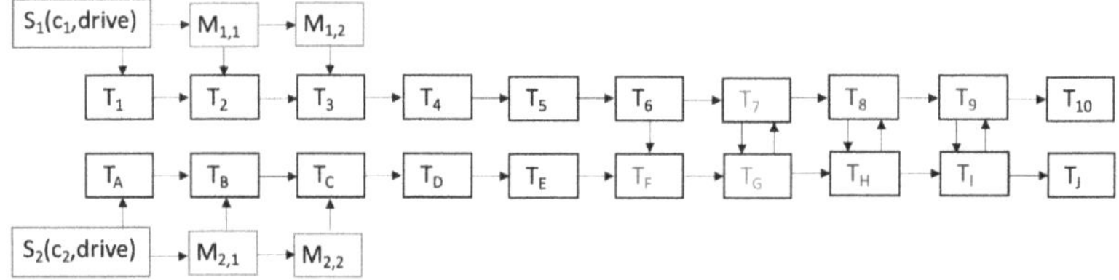

Fig. 9. TGTS Topology used for the Evaluation

Comparison Based on the given input model (i.e., CM), we automatically generated PM. Once we obtain PM, we conduct a series of Experiments (see results in Figure 11): (a) We generate the state space of PM and CM for all four topologies, and (b) we measure the state space efforts of CM and PM for all four topologies.To compute the state space for the above cases, we used Henshin [22]. For the state space generation of PM, we used the corresponding model PM. Similarly, for CM. We compared both state spaces in terms of identical traces (see Figure 10, which we used for the evaluation.

Note that CM never traversed the first conflict track. Therefore, the state space remains similar to the first experiment (Exp1), see situations 1 and 2 of section 3.2.

	PM	CM
Identical Trace	Number of Brakes	Number of Brakes
1	2	2
2	1	2
3	1	2
4	0	2
5	0	2

Fig. 10. Number of Brakes of PM and CM per identical Trace

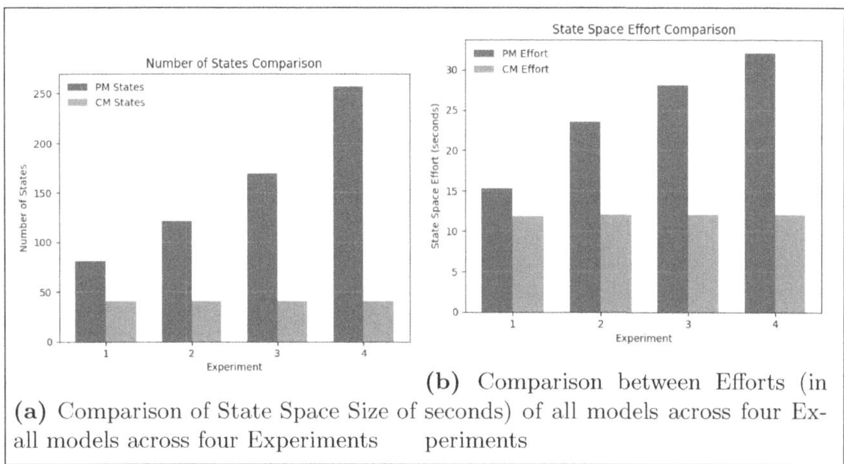

(a) Comparison of State Space Size of all models across four Experiments

(b) Comparison between Efforts (in seconds) of all models across four Experiments

Fig. 11. Experimental Results comparing Planning-aware Model (PM) and Comparison Model (CM)

Results Both models, PM and CM, preserve safety based on our experiments. This can be checked in Henshin using AP collision (see Figure 2b) with the highest priority detecting a collision by marking configurations in the state space, where the AP can be matched. We observe that this AP labels no state. Moreover, we analyzed the state space through PRISM, a model checker tool [24], where safety and real-time behaviour are formally verified. Hence, no additional analysis is required, and safety is guaranteed.

CM exhibits overcautious behavior in scenarios where a collision may happen. Therefore, both shuttles always brake and terminate at T_6 and T_E. This also holds for the case where both shuttles aim to traverse different tracks (i.e., T_7 and T_G), in which a collision is not possible. Consequently, in each of its five traces, both shuttles of CM brake. Moreover, none of the seven highlighted conflict tracks were reached in any trace. As a result of this, the generated state space of CM remains unchanged and consists of 41 states with a state space effort of 11.8 seconds (see Figure 11).

In comparison, while PM has a state space with 81 states and efforts of 15.3 seconds for its first experiment, it has 257 states with efforts of 32.1 seconds for the last experiment. PM exhibits different behavior in the context of the five identical traces. In two traces, one shuttle brakes, respectively. While in one trace both shuttles brake, in two remaining traces, neither shuttle brakes. An overview of the results is shown in Figure 10. Figure 11b illustrates the quantitative results of PM across four experiments. We conclude that PM outperforms CM since it minimizes braking while ensuring safety with manageable efforts under δ-delayed messages.

5 State-of-the-Art and Related Work

The idea of planning is not new. In the context of multi-agent systems, Daun et al. [10] proposed a framework where planning is realized through runtime models, based on individual agent goals.

A formal approach modeling the next immediate planned steps was introduced in [9]. The authors presented the Sonar-Formalism, based on Petri Nets, where distributed planning is implemented through "tasks." If two agents need to execute the same task, they synchronize their next intermediate steps. This approach restricts the planning horizon to a single next step.

Petri Nets, specifically fuzzy Petri Nets, were also employed in [8] to model sequence planning for a single agent robotic system guaranting preservation of properties such as safety.

Timed Automata have been applied to model multi-robot systems, as demonstrated in [34]. Here, collaboration is achieved via synchronization channels, and agents are constrained within a predefined movement radius represented as a planar grid.

Graph transformations have also been explored for architectural reconfiguration. In [38], the authors demonstrated how to transform graph transformation rules into actions for the Planning Domain Definition Language (PDDL), allowing off-the-shelf tools to compute self-adaptation plans.

In [20], the authors presented a different version of Timed Graph Transformation Systems not supporting quantitative analysis and not considering delay-robustness.

Another adaptation-based approach was presented in [26], where adaptation plans were derived based on a given system state model and a desired state model. These adaptation plans were then used to control the behavior of runtime models using the Unified Modeling Language [4].

Automated planning in the context of self-adaptive systems was proposed in [31]. The hybrid planning approach introduced in this work aims to balance potentially conflicting requirements of timeliness and optimality in adaptation plans.

Regarding the modeling of timing constraints, GTS have been extended to variations of TGTS in [19, 21, 33, 3, 35] without relying on clocks as in Timed Automata (TA) [1] and to variations based on clocks in [27, 28, 30]. Distribution aspects complicating design solutions as considered for our context in 3 have been surveyed in [15], and in [41] listing further aspects of general relevance.

Clock-related effects such as clock drifts and imprecise clock measurements (jittering) have been investigated thoroughly in the fundamental setting of TA [1] as surveyed in [5, 7, 6] but also for Hybrid Automata [37, 11, 39]. In particular, in [28] shuttle convoy establishment was analyzed where message delays have been implicitly considered (by limiting the number communications per time) in the context of probabilistic communication failures.

In [36, 25], similar examples on self-driving cars employing delayed unreliable wireless communication is considered where cars communicate information on current or future locations and are manually designed at a concrete, explicit level to adjust information from received messages based on delay estimates.

In a discrete time setting, delay-robustness of timed distributed system has been investigated in [43] in the context of supervisory control theory.

Lastly, in [42] design-time and run-time analysis are integrated whereby symbolic paths to violations are derived (backwards as in k-induction) at design-time to increase the look-ahead towards such violations at run-time. However, this approach considers untimed systems and attempts to disable steps leading to unsafe states.

While these works contribute to planning and adaptation in distributed systems, they do not comprehensively integrate real-time constraints, such as inter-agent message passing delays and corresponding countermeasure techniques in safety-critical environments to maximize throughput. Our approach addresses this gap by introducing a framework that supports formal reasoning with a planning horizon algorithm tailored to multi-agent systems (such as DCPS) with δ-delayed message exchanges in real-time. Moreover, in this work, we benefit from modeling planning-aware designs without compromising verifiability. Thereby, we derive a planning-aware design systematically from a non-planning-aware model to ensure safety and maximize throughput.

6 Conclusion and Future Work

In this work, we addressed the challenge of ensuring safety in DCPS while avoiding throughput limitations caused by overcautious δ-delay-robust designs. We introduced a planning-aware modeling approach based on TGTS that enables agents to share their future plans to enhance coordination under δ-delayed messages. The presented algorithm determines the minimal required planning horizon length ensuring that sufficient future information is always available for remote agents to maintain safety, throughput, and verifiability. Already for our running example, we conclude that our automatic rule derivation approach can ease model-driven engineering for DCPS. As future work, we aim to extend our approach to more complex track topologies with more than two agents and varying delay conditions. To further enhance system adaptability, we plan to consider dynamic adjustments to planning horizons.

References

[1] R. Alur and D. L. Dill. "A Theory of Timed Automata". In: *Theor. Comput. Sci.* 126.2 (1994), pp. 183–235. DOI: 10.1016/0304-3975(94)90010-8.

[2] B. Becker, D. Beyer, H. Giese, F. Klein, and D. Schilling. "Symbolic invariant verification for systems with dynamic structural adaptation". In: *28th International Conference on Software Engineering (ICSE 2006), Shanghai, China, May 20-28, 2006*. Ed. by L. J. Osterweil, H. D. Rombach, and M. L. Soffa. ACM, 2006, pp. 72–81. DOI: 10.1145/1134285.1134297.

[3] B. Becker and H. Giese. "On Safe Service-Oriented Real-Time Coordination for Autonomous Vehicles". In: *11th IEEE International Symposium on Object-Oriented Real-Time Distributed Computing (ISORC 2008), 5-7 May 2008, Orlando, Florida, USA*. IEEE Computer Society, 2008, pp. 203–210. ISBN: 978-0-7695-3132-8. DOI: 10.1109/ISORC.2008.13. URL: https://ieeexplore.ieee.org/xpl/mostRecentIssue.jsp?punumber=4519543.

[4] G. Booch. *The unified modeling language user guide*. Pearson Education India, 2005.

[5] P. Bouyer. "Timed automata". In: *Handbook of Automata Theory*. Ed. by J. Pin. European Mathematical Society Publishing House, Zürich, Switzerland, 2021, pp. 1261–1294. DOI: 10.4171/Automata-2/12.

[6] P. Bouyer, P. Gastin, F. Herbreteau, O. Sankur, and B. Srivathsan. "Zone-Based Verification of Timed Automata: Extrapolations, Simulations and What Next?" In: *FORMATS 2022*. Ed. by S. Bogomolov and D. Parker. Vol. 13465. Lecture Notes in Computer Science. Springer, 2022, pp. 16–42. DOI: 10.1007/978-3-031-15839-1_2.

[7] P. Bouyer, O. Kupferman, N. Markey, B. Maubert, A. Murano, and G. Perelli. "Reasoning about Quality and Fuzziness of Strategic Behaviours". In: *IJCAI 2019*. Ed. by S. Kraus. ijcai.org, 2019, pp. 1588–1594. DOI: 10.24963/ijcai.2019/220.

[8] T. Cao and A. Sanderson. "Task sequence planning using fuzzy Petri nets". In: *IEEE Transactions on Systems, Man, and Cybernetics* 25.5 (1995), pp. 755–768. DOI: 10.1109/21.376489.

[9] L. Capra, M. Kohler-Bussmeier, H. Rolke, J. Sudeikat, et al. "Petri Nets as Run-Time Models for Self-Adaptive Cyber-Physical Systems Cost-Benefit Analysis of Structural Transformations". In: *CEUR WORKSHOP PROCEEDINGS*. Vol. 3730. CEUR Workshop Proceedings. 2024, pp. 164–181.

[10] M. Daun, V. Stenkova, L. Krajinski, J. Brings, T. Bandyszak, and T. Weyer. "Goal modeling for collaborative groups of cyber-physical systems with GRL: reflections on applicability and limitations based on two studies conducted in industry". In: *Proceedings of the 34th ACM/SIGAPP Symposium on Applied Computing* (2019). URL: https://api.semanticscholar.org/CorpusID:142503523.

[11] B. Denis, J. Lesage, and Z. Juárez-Orozco. "Performance Verification of discrete Event Systems using Hybrid Model-Checking". In: *ADHS 2006*. Ed. by C. G. Cassandras, A. Giua, C. Seatzu, and J. Zaytoon. Vol. 39. IFAC Proceedings Volumes 5. Elsevier, 2006, pp. 365–370. DOI: 10.3182/20060607-3-IT-3902.00067.

[12] H. Ehrig, K. Ehrig, U. Prange, and G. Taentzer. "Fundamentals of Algebraic Graph Transformation. 2006". In: *EATCS Monographs in Theoretical Computer Science* (2006).

[13] B. A. Forouzan. *Data communications and networking*. Huga Media, 2007.

[14] A. Gautam, Y. He, and X. Lin. "Motion Planning for Autonomous Driving in Unsignalized Intersections Using Combined Multi-Modal GNN Predictor and MPC Planner". In: *Machines* 13.9 (2025). DOI: 10.3390/machines13090760.

[15] M. Ghani and H. Giese. "Towards Model Consistency between abstract and explicit Delay-Robustness in Timed Graph Transformation System". In: *ZEUS 2025* (2025), p. 12.

[16] M. Ghani, S. Schneider, M. Maximova, and H. Giese. "Deriving Delay-Robust Timed Graph Transformation System Models". In: *International Conference on Graph Transformation*. Springer. 2024, pp. 158–179.

[17] H. Giese. "Formal Models and Analysis for Self-adaptive Cyber-physical Systems". In: *Formal Aspects of Component Software*. Ed. by O. Kouchnarenko and R. Khosravi. Cham: Springer International Publishing, 2017, pp. 3–9.

[18] H. Giese, T. Vogel, and S. Wätzoldt. "Towards Smart Systems of Systems". In: *Proceedings of the 6th International Conference on Fundamentals of Software Engineering (FSEN '15)*. Ed. by M. Dastani and M. Sirjani. Vol. 9392. Lecture Notes in Computer Science (LNCS). (invited paper). Springer, 2015, pp. 1–29. DOI: 10.1007/978-3-319-24644-4_1.

[19] S. Gyapay, R. Heckel, and D. Varró. "Graph Transformation with Time: Causality and Logical Clocks". In: *ICGT 2002*. Ed. by A. Corradini, H. Ehrig, H. Kreowski, and G. Rozenberg. Vol. 2505. Lecture Notes in Computer Science. Springer, 2002, pp. 120–134. DOI: 10.1007/3-540-45832-8_11.

[20] S. Gyapay, R. Heckel, and D. Varró. "Graph transformation with time: Causality and logical clocks". In: *Graph Transformation: First International Conference, ICGT 2002 Barcelona, Spain, October 7–12, 2002 Proceedings 1*. Springer. 2002, pp. 120–134.

[21] S. Gyapay, D. Varró, and R. Heckel. "Graph Transformation with Time". In: *Fundam. Inform.* 58.1 (2003), pp. 1–22. URL: https://content.iospress.com/articles/fundamenta-informaticae/fi58-1-02.

[22] E. Henshin. "The Eclipse Foundation (2013)". In: *URL http://www. eclipse. org/-modeling/emft/henshin* ().

[23] S. Khaitan, Q. Lin, and J. M. Dolan. "Safe Planning and Control Under Uncertainty for Self-Driving". In: *IEEE Transactions on Vehicular Technology* 70.10 (2021), pp. 9826–9837. DOI: 10.1109/TVT.2021.3108525.

[24] M. Kwiatkowska, G. Norman, and D. Parker. "PRISM: Probabilistic symbolic model checker". In: *International Conference on Modelling Techniques and Tools for Computer Performance Evaluation*. Springer. 2002, pp. 200–204.

[25] G. Lee and J. Jung. "Decentralized Platoon Join-in-Middle Protocol Considering Communication Delay for Connected and Automated Vehicle". In: *Sensors* 21.21 (2021), p. 7126. DOI: 10.3390/s21217126.

[26] M. Lushpenko, N. Ferry, H. Song, F. Chauvel, and A. Solberg. "Using Adaptation Plans to Control the Behavior of Models@ runtime." In: *Models@ run. time*. 2015, pp. 11–20.

[27] M. Maximova, H. Giese, and C. Krause. "Probabilistic Timed Graph Transformation Systems". In: *Graph Transformation - 10th International Conference, ICGT 2017, Held as Part of STAF 2017, Marburg, Germany, July 18-19, 2017, Proceedings*. Ed. by J. de Lara and D. Plump. Vol. 10373. Lecture Notes in Computer Science. Springer, 2017, pp. 159–175. ISBN: 978-3-319-61469-4. DOI: 10.1007/978-3-319-61470-0_10.

[28] M. Maximova, H. Giese, and C. Krause. "Probabilistic timed graph transformation systems". In: *J. Log. Algebr. Meth. Program.* 101 (2018), pp. 110–131. DOI: 10.1016/j.jlamp.2018.09.003.

[29] M. Maximova, S. Schneider, and H. Giese. "Compositional Analysis of Probabilistic Timed Graph Transformation Systems". In: *Formal Aspects Comput.* 35.3 (2023), 16:1–16:79. URL: https://doi.org/10.1145/3572782.

[30] M. Maximova, S. Schneider, and H. Giese. "Interval Probabilistic Timed Graph Transformation Systems". In: *ICGT 2021*. Ed. by F. Gadducci and T. Kehrer. Vol. 12741. Lecture Notes in Computer Science. Springer, 2021, pp. 221–239. DOI: 10.1007/978-3-030-78946-6_12.

[31] G. A. Moreno, J. Cámara, D. Garlan, and B. R. Schmerl. "Proactive self-adaptation under uncertainty: a probabilistic model checking approach". In: *ESEC/FSE 2015*. Ed. by E. D. Nitto, M. Harman, and P. Heymans. ACM, 2015, pp. 1–12. DOI: 10.1145/2786805.2786853.

[32] S. Neumann. "Modellierung und Verifikation zeitbehafteter Graphtransformationssysteme mittels GROOVE". Master's thesis, University of Paderborn, 2007.

[33] S. Neumann. "Modellierung und Verifikation zeitbehafteter Graphtransformationssysteme mittels GROOVE". MA thesis. University of Paderborn, 2007.

[34] M. M. Quottrup, T. Bak, and R. Zamanabadi. "Multi-robot planning: A timed automata approach". In: *IEEE International Conference on Robotics and Automation, 2004. Proceedings. ICRA'04. 2004.* Vol. 5. IEEE. 2004, pp. 4417–4422.

[35] S. Schneider, M. Maximova, L. Sakizloglou, and H. Giese. "Formal testing of timed graph transformation systems using metric temporal graph logic". In: *Int. J. Softw. Tools Technol. Transf.* 23.3 (2021), pp. 411–488. DOI: 10.1007/s10009-020-00585-w.

[36] D. Shin and K. Yi. "Compensation of wireless communication delay for integrated risk management of automated vehicle". In: *2015 IEEE Intelligent Vehicles Symposium, IV 2015, Seoul, South Korea, June 28 - July 1, 2015.* IEEE, 2015, pp. 1355–1360. DOI: 10.1109/IVS.2015.7225904.

[37] B. I. Silva and B. H. Krogh. "Modeling and verification of hybrid systems with clocked and unclocked events". In: *CDC 2001*. IEEE, 2001, pp. 762–767. DOI: 10.1109/.2001.980198.

[38] M. Tichy and B. Klöpper. "Planning self-adaption with graph transformations". In: *AGTIVE 2011, Revised Selected and Invited Papers*. Springer. 2012, pp. 137–152.

[39] Y. Tsuchie and T. Ushio. "Control-invariance of Sampleddata Hybrid Systems with periodically Clocked Events and jitter". In: *ADHS 2006*. Ed. by C. G. Cassandras, A. Giua, C. Seatzu, and J. Zaytoon. Vol. 39. IFAC Proceedings Volumes 5. Elsevier, 2006, pp. 417–422. DOI: 10.3182/20060607-3-IT-3902.00075.

[40] M. Van Steen and A. S. Tanenbaum. "A brief introduction to distributed systems". In: *Computing* 98 (2016), pp. 967–1009.

[41] D. Weyns, H. V. D. Parunak, F. Michel, T. Holvoet, and J. Ferber. "Environments for Multiagent Systems State-of-the-Art and Research Challenges". In: *E4MAS 2004, Revised Selected Papers*. Ed. by D. Weyns, H. V. D. Parunak, and F. Michel. Vol. 3374. Lecture Notes in Computer Science. Springer, 2004, pp. 1–47. DOI: 10.1007/978-3-540-32259-7_1.

[42] H. Xu, S. Schneider, and H. Giese. "Integrating Look-ahead Design-time and Run-time Control-synthesis for Graph Transformation Systems". In: *FASE 2024, ETAPS 2024. Proceedings*. Ed. by D. Beyer and A. Cavalcanti. (accepted). 2024.

[43] R. Zhang, K. Cai, Y. Gan, and W. M. Wonham. "Delay-robustness in distributed control of timed discrete-event systems based on supervisor localisation". In: *Int. J. Control* 89.10 (2016), pp. 2055–2072. DOI: 10.1080/00207179.2016.1147606.

Composing Clinical Activity Guidance for Multimorbidity via Bounded Relational Analysis ⋆

Artur Boronat

School of Computing and Mathematical Sciences, University of Leicester, UK
artur.boronat@leicester.ac.uk

Abstract. Patients with multiple long-term conditions (LTCs) often face physical-activity recommendations that were authored for single conditions, yet such recommendations quite often conflict. We present a lightweight, design-time methodology to formally compose and analyse LTC-specific physical-activity guidelines for multimorbidity. Each guideline is encoded as a named set of Object Constraint Language (OCL) invariants over a shared Unified Modeling Language (UML) schema capturing weekly activity programmes, environment, and patient safety state. Composition is defined as the conjunction of invariant sets and checked for bounded satisfiability using the USE (UML-based Specification Environment)↔Kodkod relational pipeline. When satisfiable, the analysis synthesizes concrete, symmetry-reduced weekly programmes; when unsatisfiable, it produces a minimal set of inconsistent guidelines, expressed at the level of named clinical rules, to explain incompatibilities. We instantiate the approach with modules for type 2 diabetes, atrial fibrillation, asthma, and an early post-event recovery policy, and evaluate it on three scenarios: compatible, parameter-sensitive, and intrinsically incompatible. The results demonstrate how relational model finding yields interpretable artifacts—satisfiability frontiers, minimal contradiction sets, and concrete programme exemplars—that are auditable by clinicians and exportable as explainable test cases for health decision support.

1 Introduction

Mobile health (mHealth) applications increasingly embed AI-enabled components to support physical activity self-management for long-term conditions (LTCs) [12,5]. A significant challenge arises, however, because clinical guidance is typically authored for a *single LTC*, specifying distinct targets for activity frequency, intensity, time (duration) and type (FITT). For example, a guideline for type 2 diabetes (T2D) might recommend a minimum weekly exercise dose [10]. In practice, many patients present with *multiple LTCs*, such as T2D, atrial fibrillation (AF) [21], and asthma [18]. When recommendations for each LTC are independently encoded and integrated into an mHealth application without formal compatibility checks, their underlying constraints may become

⋆ This work was supported by the European Space Agency under ESA Contract 4000133105/20/NL/AF (P-STEP project).

E. Albert and C. Pasareanu (Eds.): FASE 2026, LNCS 16504, pp. 348–367, 2026.
https://doi.org/10.1007/978-3-032-22774-4_18

contradictory. Evidence from chronic respiratory disease shows that comorbidity burden modifies outcomes, reinforcing the need for explicit, auditable reconciliation when translating guideline texts into activity recommendations [16]. This explicit, auditable reconciliation is particularly critical in multimorbidity, where interacting LTCs and risk thresholds alter outcomes and tolerances [1]. Such conflicts—ranging from direct contradictions to temporal and context-dependent interactions—are often handled ad-hoc or post-hoc rather than by principled design-time analysis [2,19]. This can collapse the feasible space of safe programmes or silently bias recommendations, a phenomenon observed when narrative guidance is digitised without precise, auditable semantics [4,2]. Because computerisation without standardized structure yields brittle, non-portable logic, we adopt a shared UML schema with named OCL invariants to align with calls for standardized care-process specifications prior to automation [17].

This paper proposes a design-time, formal methodology to compose disease-specific physical-activity guidance for patients with multiple LTCs. We represent each guideline as a *LTC module* encapsulating clinical constraints (dose targets, intensity zones, environmental guards, and conditional rules such as "if rate-controlled" or "if well-controlled") over a shared schema of weekly activity programmes, outdoor environment, and patient clinical state. Composition of two or more guideline modules is interpreted as their *intersection*: a weekly programme is acceptable if and only if it satisfies every contributing LTC module. Under bounded semantics, we leverage a SAT-based relational solver (USE/Kodkod [22]) to decide whether a composed LTC module is satisfiable (yielding concrete weekly witness timetables) or unsatisfiable (in which case we compute the smallest subset of named constraints whose conjunction is unsatisfiable—and, optionally, enumerate clinician-defined minimal repairs that restore satisfiability). Each LTC module constraint is a named OCL invariant traceable to a specific guideline sentence (Section 2), making both witnesses and cores clinically interpretable.

Our approach contributes (i) a proof-of-concept, domain-grounded formalization of walking-focused guidance, realized as provenance-tagged OCL invariants over a shared UML schema, with exemplar modules for type 2 diabetes, atrial fibrillation, and asthma aligned with FITT, conditional rules, and risk stratification [20,21]; (ii) a composition method based on LTC module conjunction with formal guarantees of soundness and scope-completeness under bounded semantics that returns either symmetry-reduced witnesses or bounded subset-minimal contradiction sets (UNSAT cores), and suggests minimal repairs to reconcile incompatibilities; (iii) a synthesis toolkit with OCL-level traceability that exports the above artifacts—programme enumeration, partial completion, delta witnesses, and sanity checks—for clinician validation, together with a module-parametric implementation on USE↔Kodkod; and (iv) a *context-sweep* operator that systematically explores discretized patient and environment discrete domains (bands) to chart the satisfiability frontier—i.e., the boundary between contexts where the composed guidance is satisfiable and where it is not—and to produce flip certificates, namely subset-minimal context changes that switch the result, thereby localizing incompatibilities and suggesting concrete repairs.

We instantiate the methodology through three canonical scenarios. First, *compatible compositions* (T2D $\wedge$ AF) that are satisfiable under default parameters and yield diverse witness programmes, demonstrating baseline feasibility. Second, *parameter-sensitive compositions* (AF $\wedge$ asthma) that remain satisfiable under lenient environmental thresholds but become unsatisfiable under strict settings, illustrating how satisfiability frontiers inform safe parameterization. Third, *intrinsically incompatible compositions* (T2D $\wedge$ RecoveryCap) that are unsatisfiable due to conflicting dose constraints, requiring minimal unsatisfiable cores to localize the contradiction and counterfactual repairs to propose clinically grounded reconciliations.

Our implementation builds on the *USE↔Kodkod* relational validation pipeline and is *schema- and module-parametric*: new guideline sets or domains can be analyzed by swapping the shared UML schema and the named OCL invariant modules, while the composition, sweep, and core-extraction machinery remain unchanged.

The rest of the paper is structured as follows. Section 2 introduces the clinical modeling foundations, including the shared UML schema and the disease-specific OCL modules used in the study. Section 3 formalizes the composition and compatibility analysis, detailing the bounded relational semantics and the USE↔Kodkod pipeline that underpins our implementation. Section 4 describes the validation workflow for synthesized programmes, ensuring traceable evidence at the OCL level. Section 5 presents three representative compositions—compatible, parameter-sensitive, and intrinsically incompatible—illustrating how the analysis surfaces witnesses, satisfiability frontiers, and contradiction sets. Section 6 positions our contribution within solver-based guideline analysis and model validation research, and Section 7 concludes with future directions.

2 Clinical Modeling and Data Sources

We formalize physical-activity guidance as a typed domain model (UML class diagram) with named constraints (OCL invariants), enabling explicit traceability from guideline sentences to formal specifications. The bounded semantics and discrete domains justify scope-complete SAT checking and support the synthesis capabilities described in Section 3.

To make the problem concrete, we encode guideline text as named OCL invariants over a compact walking/outdoor schema and study three representative compositions: (i) *compatible* (type 2 diabetes $\wedge$ atrial fibrillation), (ii) *compatible but parameter-sensitive* (atrial fibrillation $\wedge$ asthma), and (iii) *intrinsically incompatible* (type 2 diabetes $\wedge$ an early-recovery cap). We now summarise the shared data model at a high level and the guideline modules that constrain it, before turning to the three case studies.

2.1 Domain Model and Bounded Semantics

Figure 1 presents a compact schema with three roles: `Programme` (the weekly walking prescription), `Environment` (ambient conditions relevant to safe outdoor

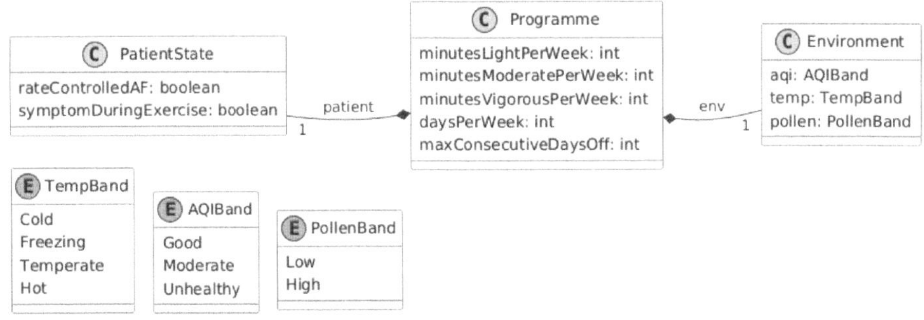

Fig. 1. Shared schema PPE

activity), and `PatientState` (flags for per-condition safety assumptions). A `Programme` aggregates dose (light/moderate/vigorous minutes per week) and spread (e.g., days per week, allowable gaps), and is linked to exactly one `Environment` and one `PatientState`. In the following we will refer to this schema as PPE.

Environmental attributes are encoded as *finite discrete domains (bands)* that clinicians recognize at a glance: air quality index band ∈ `Good`, `Moderate`, `Unhealthy`; pollen band ∈ `Low`, `High`; and temperature band ∈ `Hot`, `Temperate`, `Cold`, `Freezing`. Patient-state guards are represented as explicit booleans (e.g., `rateControlledAF`, `symptomDuringExercise`). Time-related quantities use small discrete bins suitable for a one-week planning horizon. This discretization keeps the model readable for domain experts while enabling scope-bounded, complete analysis within the declared categories.

2.2 Guideline Modules and OCL Constraints

Each disease-specific guideline is encoded as an *LTC module*: a named set of OCL invariants over the shared schema PPE. Names follow the pattern `MODULE_Purpose`, so that both valid programmes and inconsistent constraints are traceable and clinician-readable. In the following, a `Programme` is a one-week activity plan (dose and spread) linked to an `Environment` and a `PatientState`; a *module* M is a pair $(\text{name}(M), \Phi_M)$, where Φ_M is a finite set of named OCL invariants (optionally augmented with provenance metadata linking invariants to guideline sentences).

Type 2 diabetes (T2D). We formalize the recommendation for at least 150 minutes per week of moderate-equivalent activity (vigorous counts double), plus a spread constraint (at least three days, with no more than two consecutive days off) [10]:

```
context Programme inv T2D_Dose:
self.minutesModeratePerWeek + 2 * self.minutesVigorousPerWeek >= 150

context Programme inv T2D_Spread:
self.daysPerWeek >= 3 and self.maxConsecutiveDaysOff <= 2
```

Atrial fibrillation (AF). Dose aligns with the general aerobic recommendation; we add two safety guards: vigorous minutes are permitted only when AF is rate-controlled, and programmes assume no symptoms during exercise [21,20]:

```
context Programme inv AF_VigorousGuard:
self.minutesVigorousPerWeek = 0 or self.patient.rateControlledAF

context Programme inv AF_SymptomGuard:
not self.patient.symptomDuringExercise
```

Asthma. We encode a conservative environmental guard using bands. Outdoor activity is allowed only when air quality is not `Unhealthy`, pollen is `Low`, and temperature is not `Freezing`; otherwise, the programme may be empty (rest) [18]:

```
context Programme inv ASTHMA_EnvGuard:
(self.env.aqi <> AQIBand::Unhealthy
and self.env.pollen = PollenBand::Low
and self.env.temp <> TempBand::Freezing)
or
(self.minutesLightPerWeek = 0
and self.minutesModeratePerWeek = 0
and self.minutesVigorousPerWeek = 0)
```

Recovery cap (policy variant). To illustrate intrinsic incompatibility, we include an early-recovery policy that caps weekly moderate-equivalent minutes:

```
context Programme inv RECOVERY_Cap:
self.minutesModeratePerWeek + 2 * self.minutesVigorousPerWeek <= 60
```

The combination T2D $\wedge$ AF is satisfiable under the default bands and dose bins and yields diverse witnesses. AF $\wedge$ asthma is satisfiable under `Good/Moderate` air, `Low` pollen, and `Temperate` conditions but becomes unsatisfiable when any guard is violated (e.g., `Unhealthy` AQI, `High` pollen, or `Freezing` temperature), producing single-constraint cores that are easily audited. Finally, T2D $\wedge$ RecoveryCap is unsatisfiable; the identified core isolates the intended contradiction between `T2D_Dose` and `RECOVERY_Cap`, which then guides targeted repairs.

3 Method: Composition and Decision Procedure

We propose a formal, lightweight, design-time methodology that captures clinical guidance as OCL invariants over a shared planning schema, decides guideline compatibility by bounded satisfiability of the conjunction, and returns interpretable artifacts—either witness programmes or bounded UNSAT cores. Technically, modules are authored in USE/OCL and compiled to relational logic; the USE model validator provides an OCL$\leftrightarrow$Kodkod translation that preserves the front–back mapping between OCL snapshots and relational instances [15]. Kodkod compiles the relational instance to propositional SAT with symmetry breaking and compact encodings; a SAT solver then returns either a programme within the declared bounds or a refutation [22]. In this setting, concrete SAT models are rendered back as object diagrams satisfying the OCL constraints [13].

We write B for a fixed *bound configuration* consisting of (i) object scopes (maximum numbers of objects per class and links per association) and (ii) finite attribute domains (integers, enumerations, and Booleans). All satisfiable/unsatisfiable verdicts and derived artifacts (witnesses, cores, and sweeps) are relative to B. We keep B fixed within each study/sweep.

3.1 Compositional Encoding and the Compatibility Judgement

We treat each guideline as a small, named *contract* over the shared class diagram vocabulary. Composition then amounts to *accumulating* the selected contracts into a single analysis instance: we take the invariants exactly as authored, keep their identifiers intact, and analyse the result under a fixed set of bounds B. Two lightweight assumptions keep the story predictable: (i) every LTC module speaks only the shared types and attributes; (ii) no LTC module rewrites another's constraints. Intuitively, adding a LTC module tightens the space of admissible programmes without changing the language in which requirements are expressed.

Composition of modules. Given a selection of modules $M_1, \ldots, M_k$ with named invariant sets $\Phi_{M_1}, \ldots, \Phi_{M_k}$, the *composed LTC module* is the set-theoretic union:

$$\Phi = \mathsf{Compose}(M_1, \ldots, M_k) = \Phi_{M_1} \cup \cdots \cup \Phi_{M_k}.$$

Semantically, LTC module composition corresponds to the *intersection* (logical conjunction) of their denotations: a programme p satisfies Φ iff $p \in [\![\varphi]\!]$ for every $\varphi \in \Phi$, equivalently $p \in \bigcap_{i=1}^{k} \bigcap_{\varphi \in \Phi_{M_i}} [\![\varphi]\!]$. Thus, composition tightens the space of admissible plans—adding a LTC module narrows the solution set—while preserving the shared vocabulary over which constraints are expressed.

In the implementation, composition is realized by concatenating the selected modules' OCL into a single USE specification (a textual UML class model together with its OCL constraints, as accepted by the USE validator) *without* schema merging. That is, we analyse all modules against the fixed shared schema PPEand compose only their invariant sets. Invariant identifiers are carried through unchanged so that front–back mappings (OCL $\leftrightarrow$ relational formulas $\leftrightarrow$ object diagrams) remain intact [13,15]. Because no rewriting occurs, the mapping from OCL invariant names to relational formulas (and back to model elements) remains intact, which is crucial for subsequent explanation of findings in clinician terms.

3.2 Compatibility as a Decision Problem

For a set of modules $S = \{M_1, \ldots, M_k\}$, we say that S is *compatible under B* iff

$$\mathsf{Compatible}_B(S) \overset{\text{def}}{\iff} \mathsf{SAT}_B\Big(\bigcup_{M \in S} \Phi_M\Big).$$

Otherwise S is *incompatible under* B. The decision procedure returns one of two interpretable artifacts:

- a *compatibility witness* (a concrete weekly `Programme` with its `Environment` and `PatientState`) when $\mathsf{SAT}_B(\Phi)$ holds, rendered back as an object diagram [13] —and can enumerate a small number of symmetry-reduced variants by re-invocation at the same scope [15];
- a *compatibility core* $C \subseteq \{\text{invariant names}\}$ when $\neg\mathsf{SAT}_B(\Phi)$ holds, obtained via assumption-labelled solving; we report the resulting core at the level of named OCL invariants [14,22].

Bounded satisfiability and the Kodkod pipeline. The composed LTC module Φ is checked by invoking the SAT-based decision procedure $\mathsf{DecideSAT}(\Phi, B)$, which performs model finding (with UNSAT cores) over the finite universe defined by bounds B. Operationally, Kodkod translates Φ into a propositional formula over a bounded set of relations and domains, then delegates to a SAT solver to determine whether any assignment exists within those bounds [22].

Three technical properties of Kodkod's relational backend are essential to the clinical validation workflow. First, *scope-completeness* guarantees that the solver exhaustively searches the bounded space: if $\mathsf{SAT}_B(\Phi)$ is returned, a witness provably exists within B; if $\neg\mathsf{SAT}_B(\Phi)$, no instance within B can satisfy Φ [15]. This bounded-exhaustive property ensures that compatibility verdicts are definitive within the declared universe, avoiding false negatives due to incomplete search. Second, *symmetry breaking* applies predicates and compact encodings to prune isomorphic solutions during search [22]. By eliminating redundant permutations of structurally identical programmes, symmetry breaking accelerates solving and—crucially for our use case—enables efficient enumeration of *symmetry-reduced* witnesses when multiple feasible programmes exist. Third, when unsatisfiable, *assumption-labeled solving* allows Kodkod to extract a bounded minimal core $C \subseteq \Phi$ as described below, enabling targeted diagnosis at the constraint level [14]. Together, these properties make the SAT phase not merely a yes/no oracle but a source of interpretable, actionable artifacts—witness diversity for validation, minimal cores for debugging, and exhaustive guarantees for certification—all phrased at the level of the relational model rather than low-level clauses.

Crucially, the SAT phase operates entirely at the *logical* level: it reasons about the structure of the constraint system without materializing concrete object graphs until a valid assignment is found. The returned SAT model is a *relational instance*—a binding of relation signatures to tuples—that the USE model validator then renders as a typed object diagram [13]. This separation between logical reasoning (SAT) and instance materialization (USE) allows us to distinguish bounded satisfiability checking from post-synthesis instance validation, as detailed in Section 4.

UNSAT core extraction. We instrument the composed LTC module $\Phi = \{\varphi_1, \ldots, \varphi_n\}$ with a fresh *assumption literal* a_i per top-level invariant, and invoke Kodkod under the assumption set $A = \{a_1, \ldots, a_n\}$. Operationally, each assumption literal a_i acts as a Boolean *selector* guarding its invariant: we encode $a_i \Rightarrow [\![\varphi_i]\!]$, so that assuming a_i enforces φ_i and dropping a_i disables it. Solving under the assumption set $A = \{a_1, \ldots, a_n\}$ therefore means "check all invariants simultaneously"; if the instance is unsatisfiable, then the solver can identify the smallest subset of assumptions that must remain true for the conflict to persist.

In our case the universe of candidate assumptions is precisely the set of named OCL invariants, so the returned core $C_A \subseteq A$ corresponds to a minimal subset of invariants whose guarded forms cannot be jointly satisfied under the fixed finite bounds B. When $\neg\mathsf{SAT}_B(\Phi)$, the SAT backend returns an *unsat core* $C \subseteq A$; Kodkod's assumption interface lets us *trim* C to a subset-minimal unsatisfiable set of invariants relative to the declared bounds B (hence "bounded minimality"). We say that a set $C \subseteq \{\varphi_1, \ldots, \varphi_n\}$ is a *bounded subset-minimal core* iff:

$$\neg\mathsf{SAT}_B(C) \ \wedge \ \forall \psi \in C : \ \mathsf{SAT}_B(C \setminus \{\psi\}).$$

Typing/multiplicity constraints and the encoding of bounds are treated as background and are not reported in C by default (an "include-structural" mode is available in the artifact).

Each a_i is maintained in a one-to-one map to the *named* USE/OCL invariant φ_i, so the core is lifted back from propositional clauses to invariant identifiers. This relies on the USE model validator's OCL↔relational translation and back-translation that preserve the front–back correspondence between OCL constraints, their relational encodings, and rendered model elements, allowing us to trace unsatisfiability to specific invariants rather than opaque clauses [13,15]. The compilation to SAT with symmetry breaking and compact encodings is handled by Kodkod; the unsatisfiable core we obtain is therefore minimal only with respect to the chosen finite universe and bounds B, which is the granularity appropriate to design-time satisfiability checks in UML/OCL validation [22]. In practice, our assumption-tagging works uniformly across the OCL fragment we use (including collections), because the validator's translation keeps a stable mapping from invariant names to the relational constraints they generate [14].

3.3 Reporting and Interpretability

We report an UNSAT explanation as a compact, ordered list of *named* OCL invariants. Each item is a direct mapping `id` ↦ `invariant`: we display the stable identifier (e.g., `T2D_Dose`, `RECOVERY_Cap`) together with the exact OCL body as authored—the invariants are written in the shared clinical vocabulary and are intended to be readable as-is. For reproducibility, the report also records the bounds B (scopes/discrete domains), the active LTC module set, and solver metadata (backend, seed, wall-clock time). Because the USE↔Kodkod path preserves front–back mappings between OCL formulas, their relational encodings, and rendered model elements, each core entry remains traceable to its source invariant and to the corresponding model fragments, yielding clinician-facing explanations at the invariant level rather than low-level SAT clauses [15,13].

In practice, reporting a subset-minimal set of named invariants that is jointly infeasible provides clinicians and implementers with a small, actionable diagnostic: (1) it localizes the conflict to a few human-readable rules rather than opaque solver clauses; (2) it reduces cognitive load during multidisciplinary review by minimizing the number of items to inspect; (3) it suggests targeted repair strategies (e.g., relax a numeric threshold, weaken a guard, or mark a conditional as patient-specific) that can be validated clinically; (4) because each invariant is named and provenance-tagged, the core supports traceability and reproducibility of design-time decisions; and (5) the same cores can be exported as explainable test-cases for downstream verification, clinician training, or safety-monitoring of mHealth recommenders. These pragmatic benefits make bounded minimal cores a lightweight yet powerful bridge between formal analysis and clinical decision-making.

3.4 Context Sweep (Bounded)

Beyond a yes/no compatibility verdict, we often want to understand how that verdict varies with a small set of *context parameters* while keeping the LTC modules and bounds fixed. We therefore provide a bounded, declarative *context sweep* that systematically explores how satisfiability varies across clinically meaningful *contexts* while holding the composed LTC module Φ and bounds B fixed. A programme π is internally represented as a finite UML object diagram that is an instance of the shared PPEclass diagram (a witness instance produced by the solver), where attribute–value pairs are part of the object graph itself. Bounds B determine a finite universe of objects, links, and finite attribute domains.

Let $\mathbb{P}_B$ denote the set of (possibly) *partial* programmes within bounds B (typed object diagrams that may omit objects or leave attributes unassigned, while respecting the schema), and let $\mathbb{P}_B^\bullet \subseteq \mathbb{P}_B$ denote the *ground* (complete) programmes, i.e., total object diagrams with all required links/multiplicities satisfied and all attributes assigned concrete values.

Valid programmes. For a composed LTC module Φ, the *valid programmes* are

$$\mathbb{P}_B(\Phi) \;=\; \{\, \pi \in \mathbb{P}_B^\bullet \mid \pi \models \Phi \,\}.$$

Context slices and satisfiability. A projection $\tau : \mathbb{P}_B \longrightarrow \mathcal{C}$ maps (partial or ground) programmes to a finite *context* domain $\mathcal{C} = \tau(\mathbb{P}_B)$, obtained by reading selected attributes that are assigned concrete finite-domain values (or Boolean truth values) (e.g., `aqiBand`, `pollenHigh?`, `tempBand`, `rateControlledAF?`).

Two programmes $\pi_1, \pi_2 \in \mathbb{P}_B$ are *context-equivalent* under τ when their projections coincide, $\tau(\pi_1) = \tau(\pi_2)$. This equivalence relation induces a family of *slices* indexed by projected contexts:

$$\mathsf{Slice}(c) \;=\; \{\, \pi \in \mathbb{P}_B \mid \tau(\pi) = c \,\}$$

Each slice collects all (possibly partial) programmes that share the same contextual projection c. When restricted to the valid set $\mathbb{P}_B(\Phi)$, these slices identify the feasible partial contexts:

$$c \text{ feasible} \iff \exists \pi^\bullet \in \mathbb{P}_B^\bullet : \tau(\pi^\bullet) = c \wedge \pi^\bullet \models \Phi.$$

That is, the partial context c admits at least one completion to a ground programme that is valid for Φ within bounds B. Otherwise c is infeasible, and we return a *named*, bounded subset-minimal UNSAT core pinpointing the smallest set of invariant names that preclude satisfiability within B.

Witnesses and cores. If c is feasible, we may present up to $1+k$ ground witnesses with $\tau(\pi^\bullet) = c$ (symmetry broken at scope B). If c is infeasible, we enforce c by a tiny OCL selection predicate $\mathsf{Select}(c)$ and extract a bounded subset-minimal core over invariant names. Formally, let $\mathcal{I}$ be the finite set of invariant identifiers and $\iota : \Phi \to \mathcal{I}$ the name map. A core is a set $C \subseteq \mathcal{I}$ such that

$$\neg\exists \pi \in \mathbb{P}_B^\bullet : \pi \models \Big(\bigwedge_{\psi \in \Phi,\ \iota(\psi) \in C} \psi \wedge \mathsf{Select}(c) \Big),$$

and for every $\iota(\psi) \in C$, satisfiability is restored when ψ is dropped (subset-minimality within B). Here, $\mathsf{Select}(c)$ holds exactly for programmes whose projection under τ is c.

Frontier and flip certificates. To move from per-context verdicts to *structure*, we separate the sweep domain into feasible and infeasible regions:

$$\begin{aligned} \mathsf{SAT\_set}_B(\Phi, \tau) &= \Big\{ c \in \mathcal{C} \;\Big|\; \exists \pi^\bullet \in \mathbb{P}_B^\bullet : \tau(\pi^\bullet) = c \wedge \pi^\bullet \models \Phi \Big\}, \\ \mathsf{UNSAT\_set}_B(\Phi, \tau) &= \mathcal{C} \setminus \mathsf{SAT\_set}_B(\Phi, \tau). \end{aligned}$$

Here, satisfiability means "there exists a concrete, ground weekly programme at c." We then make locality explicit: change exactly one context coordinate (one band) at a time and ask whether satisfiability survives. Let the chosen context coordinates be $\boldsymbol{\Gamma} = (\gamma_1, \ldots, \gamma_m)$ with finite discrete domains (bands) $D_1, \ldots, D_m$ (from the modeling vocabulary and bounds B), so that $\mathcal{C} \subseteq D_1 \times \cdots \times D_m$. For $c = (v_1, \ldots, v_m) \in \mathcal{C}$, define its Hamming-1 neighbourhood (single-band flips)

$$N(c) = \bigcup_{i=1}^{m} \{(v_1, \ldots, v_{i-1}, v_i', v_{i+1}, \ldots, v_m) \mid v_i' \in D_i,\ v_i' \neq v_i\}.$$

The *bounded satisfiability frontier* captures the crisp boundary where a one-step band change breaks satisfiability:

$$\mathcal{F}_B(\Phi, \tau) = \{ c \in \mathsf{SAT\_set}_B(\Phi, \tau) \mid N(c) \cap \mathsf{UNSAT\_set}_B(\Phi, \tau) \neq \emptyset \}.$$

For each $c \in \mathcal{F}_B(\Phi, \tau)$ and neighbour $c' \in N(c) \cap \mathsf{UNSAT\_set}_B(\Phi, \tau)$ we record a *flip certificate* $(c,\ c',\ \mathsf{Core}_B(c'))$, i.e., a local counterfactual showing *what to change* (one band), *what breaks* (unsatisfiability at c'), and *why* (the named core). Here $\mathsf{Core}_B(c')$ is the bounded subset-minimal core computed under the selection $\mathsf{Select}(c')$.

Context sweep: signature and return. Putting the pieces together, the sweep exposes a simple interface:

$$\mathsf{Sweep}_B(\Phi,\tau,k) \;=\; \big(\ \mathsf{Outcome}_B(\Phi,\tau,k),\ \mathcal{F}_B(\Phi,\tau),\ \mathcal{X}_B(\Phi,\tau)\ \big).$$

Intuitively, $\mathsf{Outcome}_B$ is the *map* (per-context labels with witnesses or cores); $\mathcal{F}_B$ is the *edge* where satisfiability tips; and $\mathcal{X}_B$ lists actionable *explanations* for each tip as $(c, c', \mathsf{Core}_B(c'))$. Witness sets use Pick_k and are quotiented by $\simeq_B$ to avoid duplicates.

Design parameters and trade-offs. The analysis exposes three explicit design parameters. (i) The bounds B fix object scopes and finite attribute domains, controlling both completeness guarantees and solver cost. (ii) The projection τ selects which discrete context parameters (bands and Booleans) are swept, determining $|\mathcal{C}|$ and hence sweep cost. (iii) The witness quota k controls how many symmetry-reduced programme exemplars are returned per feasible context. Finer discretization increases interpretability only if the added bands are clinically meaningful; otherwise it increases $|\mathcal{C}|$ without improving actionability. Symmetry breaking reduces redundant (isomorphic) programmes at fixed B, improving enumeration efficiency for small k.

Programmes with clinician input. A pre-committed part of a programme (e.g., clinician-specified rate control or already-scheduled days) is a *partial programme* as defined above. Let $c_{\text{partial}} = \tau(\pi_{\text{partial}}) \in \mathcal{C}$ be the context induced by the clinician input. A *valid programme given* π_{partial} is precisely a *ground* programme that lies in the slice of this context and satisfies Φ:

$$\pi^\bullet \text{ valid given } \pi_{\text{partial}} \quad\Longleftrightarrow\quad \pi^\bullet \in \mathbb{P}^\bullet_B \,\cap\, \mathsf{Slice}(c_{\text{partial}}) \;\wedge\; \pi^\bullet \models \Phi.$$

Conceptually, clinician input fixes a point in $\mathcal{C}$; satisfiability then asks for concrete completions in that slice, preserving the same decision procedure and explanations.

Remarks. (i) *Exhaustiveness within B.* Every context in $\mathcal{C}$ is classified, and each frontier point has an explicit neighbouring infeasible context with a named core. (ii) *Evidence in domain terms.* Witnesses are ground object diagrams (weekly programmes); cores are lists of named OCL invariants traceable to clinical rules. (iii) *Cost vs. granularity.* Complexity scales with $|\mathcal{C}|$ and scope (sizes of $\mathbb{P}_B$ and $\mathbb{P}^\bullet_B$); using clinically meaningful finite discrete domains (bands)—and, when available, a partial programme to anchor interpretation—keeps the sweep tractable without changing semantics.

Caveats. The context sweep is an exact analysis under the finite discrete domains induced by the chosen projection and bounds B; as usual for bounded exhaustive methods, its cost depends on the size of that discretized space, so we apply it to small, clinically meaningful partitions. For larger spaces, the same USE↔Kodkod decision procedure can be used in a more targeted way, for example by iteratively requesting additional non-isomorphic witnesses or by characterizing context regions for fixed programmes; we do not pursue these engineering optimizations here. On unsatisfiable instances, we report one bounded subset-minimal UNSAT core per run (at the level of named clinical rules), which is sufficient for localizing contradictions in our case studies; alternative cores and minimum-cardinality explanations can be obtained with additional solver queries when needed. Finally, we report representative outcome statistics and illustrate the impact of discretization and integer-domain width on translation size; exploring substantially longer horizons or much finer discretizations is orthogonal to the present contribution.

4 Validation of Synthesized Programmes

The sweep establishes existence within the declared bounds B; what clinicians and implementers need next is a checked, inspectable programme that realizes that existence claim. We therefore validate each synthesized ground witness by interpreting the *original* OCL invariants over the obtained activity programmes, keeping evidence and explanations in the modeling vocabulary rather than the solver's propositional encoding.

Concretely, an activity programme is represented as a typed object diagram with concrete attribute values and links [13]. Formally, each witness is a ground instance of the shared schema PPEwhose attributes take values from the finite domains induced by B (bands and integer bins). The USE validator then evaluates every authored invariant $\varphi \in \Phi$ on the same diagram; we write $\pi^{\bullet} \models \Phi$ when all evaluate to `true`. The resulting per-invariant verdicts and violation traces are expressed in domain terms (dose, spread, environment bands, guards), which makes the artifact directly auditable.

The same step serves two further purposes. First, it certifies the sweep's outputs: every witness attached to a feasible context in the outcome map/frontier is a ground programme that has been evaluated against Φ. Second, it acts as a gate for external candidates—programmes proposed by clinicians or generated by recommenders can be loaded and checked without re-solving, with named violations pinpointing precisely which rule fails. In short, bounded solving establishes that compatible programmes exist within B; validation turns that claim into concrete, provenance-preserving evidence suitable for clinical review and reuse.

To support process-level applicability, we aligned the modeling vocabulary and solver artifacts with the P-STEP content-development and algorithm specifications that define the intended app workflow. In particular, the shared schema variables (weekly minutes and days, symptom flags, and discretised environment bands) were selected to coincide with the baseline assessment and week-by-week goal setting logic, including the step-count algorithm and the interaction for confirming or editing weekly goals and distributing minutes across selected days. This specification-conformance check ensures that each SAT witness can be rendered directly as a concrete weekly recommendation in the same terms used by the workflow, and that each UNSAT core can be reviewed as a small set of

Study	$\|\mathcal{C}\|$	SAT	UNSAT	Frontier / flips
S1 base	1	1	0	n/a
S1 flags	2	1	1	1 / 1
S1 prog	3	3	0	n/a
S2 env	24	6	18	6 / 18
S3 base	1	0	1	n/a
S3 prog	4	0	4	n/a

Table 1. Sweep sizes and frontier structure under fixed bounds B

named, provenance-tagged rules that supports targeted, design-time reconciliation without re-authoring the overall guideline logic.

5 Evaluation on Three Compositional Scenarios

We evaluate the approach on three compositions that progressively exercise satisfiable, parameter-sensitive, and intrinsically incompatible behaviours. In all cases, modules are authored as named OCL invariants over the shared schema PPE, composed by set union, and analysed under fixed bounds B using the SAT-based pipeline described in Section 3. For interpretability, all results are reported in domain terms: concrete `Programme` instances (witnesses) or bounded subset-minimal sets of named invariants (cores). We also expose a bounded *context sweep* (Section 3.4) over environment bands and patient safety flags, returning per-context feasibility verdicts, frontier structure, and *flip certificates* with named cores.

Sweep coordinates and bounds. Unless noted otherwise, the sweep projects onto the environment bands

$$\begin{aligned}&\texttt{aqi} \in \{\texttt{Good}, \texttt{Moderate}, \texttt{Unhealthy}\},\\&\texttt{pollen} \in \{\texttt{Low}, \texttt{High}\},\\&\texttt{temp} \in \{\texttt{Hot}, \texttt{Temperate}, \texttt{Cold}, \texttt{Freezing}\}.\end{aligned}$$

Patient guards (e.g., `rateControlledAF`, `symptomDuringExercise`) are toggled explicitly in scenarios where they matter. Minutes and days are discretized to small integer domains (one-week horizon); witnesses and cores are therefore *scope-complete* within B. To complement the worked examples with a compact quantitative summary, Table 1 reports the explored configuration counts, SAT/UNSAT split, and frontier structure for the scenario analyses under fixed bounds B. We then discuss representative witnesses and cores for each scenario in the remainder of this section.

In the table, we report configuration counts together with representative outcome statistics from the logs. Across all runs, the overall cost is dominated by the OCL-to-relational-to-CNF translation step, while SAT solving is negligible under the fixed bounds B. As expected, widening integer domains increases the size of the propositional encoding and the translation time, whereas the satisfiability phase remains fast for the scenario sizes considered here.

5.1 Scenario 1: Compatible Composition (T2D $\wedge$ AF)

We compose `T2D_Dose` and `T2D_Spread` with AF safety guards `AF_Vigorous-Guard` (vigorous minutes allowed only if `rateControlledAF`) and `AF_Symptom-Guard` (no symptoms during exercise).

We additionally exercised a small *patient-state sweep* that toggles `rateControlledAF` (with `symptomDuringExercise=false`) under a fixed safe environment (`aqi=Good`, `pollen=Low`, `temp=Temperate`). The sweep has two configurations and yields one SAT point (`rateControlledAF=true`) and one UNSAT point (`rateControlledAF=false`), producing a single frontier flip certificate that localizes satisfiability to the rate-control assumption. This shows that the sweep operator applies to patient flags, not only to environmental bands.

At the SAT configuration (`rateControlledAF=true`), the solver yields multiple symmetry-reduced weekly programmes that satisfy the T2D dose floor and spread while respecting AF guards. In our runs, the generated witnesses differ in clinically relevant aspects such as dose allocation across intensity bands and the distribution of activity over the week. Invoking Pick_k with $k{=}2$ returns up to $1{+}k$ symmetry-distinct witnesses, supporting clinician review while avoiding isomorphic duplicates.[1]

5.2 Scenario 2: Parameter-Sensitive Composition (AF $\wedge$ Asthma)

Here we study how satisfiability depends on environmental bands when AF guards must hold *and* a minimal weekly dose is desired. The asthma module permits outdoor activity only when air quality is not `Unhealthy`, pollen is `Low`, and temperature is not `Freezing`; otherwise the programme must be (clinically) suspended. To rule out trivial "rest" solutions in parameter-sensitive analyses, we include a lightweight module that requires a non-zero weekly exercise dose:

```
context Programme inv MinExercise:
  self.minutesModeratePerWeek + 2 * self.minutesVigorousPerWeek >= 30
```

This *moderate-equivalent* floor (30 min/week) is intentionally conservative; it serves as a simple clinical design choice to prefer minimal activity over complete suspension *when safety permits*. We compose `AF_*`, `ASTHMA_EnvGuard`, and `MinExercise`. We then sweep the $3{\times}2{\times}4 = 24$ environment contexts where air-quality index (`aqi`) is Good, Moderate, or Unhealthy; pollen (`pollen`) is Low or High; and temperature (`temp`) is Temperate, Cold, Hot, or Freezing; holding AF flags at `rateControlledAF=true`, `symptomDuringExercise=false`.

The outcome is crisp and interpretable:

[1] Witness sets are quotiented by $\simeq_B$ to avoid isomorphic variants; see Section 3.

- Exactly the *six* contexts that satisfy asthma's guard are feasible:

$$\{\texttt{Good}, \texttt{Moderate}\} \times \{\texttt{Low}\} \times \{\texttt{Temperate}, \texttt{Cold}, \texttt{Hot}\}.$$

  Each admits symmetry-reduced witnesses meeting the 30-minute floor while respecting AF guards.
- The remaining *eighteen* contexts are UNSAT because `ASTHMA_EnvGuard` enforces rest (0 minutes) while `MinExercise` forbids it. In our runs, the bounded subset-minimal core reported at these neighbours consistently includes

$$\{\texttt{Fix\_Environment}, \texttt{AF\_VigorousGuard}, \texttt{MinExercise}, \texttt{ASTHMA\_EnvGuard}\},$$

  where `Fix_Environment` is the sweep's context selector that pins the tested bands.[2]

The *satisfiability frontier* coincides with these six SAT points: each has three Hamming-1 neighbours that flip to UNSAT by changing exactly one band (e.g.

$$\texttt{pollen:Low} \to \texttt{High},$$
$$\texttt{aqi:Good/Moderate} \to \texttt{Unhealthy},$$
$$\texttt{temp:Temperate/Cold/Hot} \to \texttt{Freezing}.$$

We obtain *18* flip certificates in total (all Hamming-1; distance distribution $\{1 \mapsto 18\}$; parameter flip counts balanced: $\texttt{aqi} = 6$, $\texttt{pollen} = 6$, $\texttt{temp} = 6$). Each certificate $(c,\ c',\ \mathsf{Core}_B(c'))$ makes the sensitivity local and actionable ("which single band breaks satisfiability and why"). Moreover, for any infeasible context we compute a *nearest feasible* one (Hamming-1 in this sweep), offering concrete counterfactuals such as

$$\texttt{Good,High,Temperate} \to \texttt{Good,Low,Temperate},$$
$$\texttt{Good,Low,Freezing} \to \texttt{Good,Low,Cold},$$
$$\texttt{Unhealthy,Low,Hot} \to \texttt{Moderate,Low,Hot}.$$

5.3 Scenario 3: Intrinsic Incompatibility (T2D ∧ RecoveryCap)

We compose the T2D dose floor with an early-recovery policy that caps weekly moderate-equivalent minutes:

```
context Programme inv RECOVERY_Cap:
  self.minutesModeratePerWeek + 2 * self.minutesVigorousPerWeek <= 60
```

The conjunction $\{\texttt{T2D\_Dose}, \texttt{RECOVERY\_Cap}\}$ is UNSAT within B. Assumption-labelled solving returns a bounded subset-minimal core equal to these two named invariants; structural typing/multiplicity constraints remain in the background (not reported). This core pinpoints the intended clinical contradiction and directly suggests repair options (e.g., relaxing the T2D floor for early recovery; staging the cap; parameterising by rate-control status), each of which can be re-checked by re-solving.

[2] Clinically, the essential contradiction is the pair $\{\texttt{ASTHMA\_EnvGuard}, \texttt{MinExercise}\}$; `Fix_Environment` anchors the counterfactual context, and `AF_VigorousGuard` persists under assumption-labelled solving, though it is not causal when AF is rate-controlled.

5.4 Micro-Studies Exercising Additional Parameters

Beyond the three main scenario compositions (S1 base, S2 env, S3 base), Table 1 includes three micro-studies that exercise additional parameters already supported by the implementation. S1 flags is a two-point sweep that fixes a safe environment and `symptomDuringExercise=false` while toggling `rateControlledAF`, yielding one SAT point and one UNSAT point (one flip certificate). S1 prog is a single-parameter programme sweep that pins `Programme.minutesModeratePerWeek` to {100,150,200} under the T2D module; environment and patient-state attributes are not projected in this micro-study, so they remain unconstrained. S3 prog pins `Programme.minutesModeratePerWeek` to {100,150,200,250} under T2D $\wedge$ RecoveryCap; all points remain UNSAT and the reported core is stable across the sweep. In S1 flags and S3 prog, the core includes the corresponding sweep selector (e.g., `Fix_PatientState` or `Fix_Programme`) because the tested assignment is pinned.

Validation in the scenarios. For every synthesized programme we perform post-synthesis *validation* by evaluating the original OCL invariants on the returned object diagram (Section 4): each witness is checked against all composed invariants and reported as `true`/`false` per name, preserving the front–back mapping from OCL to the rendered model elements.[3] For UNSAT contexts, we validate explanations by inspecting the named cores reported by the solver; in Scenario 2 (unsafe bands) the core consistently contains `ASTHMA_EnvGuard` and `MinExercise`, while in Scenario 3 it is exactly {`T2D_Dose`, `RECOVERY_Cap`}. External candidate programmes (e.g., clinician-proposed timetables) can be loaded and checked the same way, without re-solving, with violations pinpointed at the level of named invariants.

6 Related Work

Solver-based composition of multiple guidelines for individual patients has been studied in pharmacotherapy. Bowles et al. translate BPMN pathways into Labelled Event Structures and, combining Isabelle/HOL with Z3, detect conflicts and synthesize temporally coherent executions by optimizing an objective that trades off interaction severities and timing [3]. While this provides well-founded, temporally aware reasoning with interactive visualization, the focus is medication pathways and the computational task is cast as optimization under conflict rather than design-time diagnosis of unsatisfiability with rule-level explanations. In a similar vein, Kovalov et al. encode pharmaceutical graphs and use optimization-capable SMT to select one path per disease that minimises drug–drug and drug–disease interactions while rewarding efficacy [11]. Their approach yields concrete regimens with good performance on moderate instances but abstracts

[3] Because solving is bounded and symmetry-broken, validation certifies concrete instances rather than re-proving satisfiability; this keeps explanations in the domain vocabulary (dose, spread, bands, guards).

dosing and temporal co-existence and, like Bowles et al., does not provide bounded UNSAT cores or facilities for synthesizing diverse programmes. In contrast, we target *activity* planning, treat composition as pure conjunction over a shared UML/OCL schema, and use bounded relational analysis to either enumerate symmetry-reduced weekly programmes or return subset-minimal contradiction sets that localize incompatibility.

We favour a SAT-first, relational backend (USE$\leftrightarrow$Kodkod) because our domain is intrinsically bounded and relational—weekly schedules (7 days), discretised minutes, and finite environment bands. Within fixed scopes this affords: (i) symmetry-aware enumeration of distinct weekly programmes; (ii) completion from clinician-specified partial programmes; and (iii) scope-bounded context sweeps that chart satisfiability frontiers with flip certificates (minimal explanations) [22,13,14]. On top of this, we add a scope-bounded satisfiability-frontier analysis over discrete environment/patient bands with flip certificates that pair boundary changes with their minimal explanations. Within the USE ecosystem, MaxUSE [6,25] and QMaxUSE[24] route OCL to SMT back ends with query-driven checking and solver-reported UNSAT cores for large constraint sets. While SMT-backed USE pipelines are viable, they typically require extra machinery for isomorphism control and iterative enumeration.

Alloy/Kodkod provides an alternative path: pure relational modeling with symmetry breaking, instance generation, and core extraction [9,8,22]. A pure Alloy encoding would also be viable; we chose UML/OCL in USE to preserve provenance at the OCL level for clinician-readable reports without re-expressing constraints in Alloy's syntax. In particular, Alloy has been applied to healthcare modelling for bounded verification tasks. Wang and Rutle encode healthcare workflow models into Alloy (including an Alloy-level account of workflow semantics) to check behavioural properties such as loop-related properties and to generate counterexamples when properties fail [23]. Haraty and Naous model the Clinical Information Systems security policy in Alloy and use the Alloy Analyzer to check the policy model for consistency, focusing on integrity and access-control constraints [7]. Compared with these works, we focus on design-time composition of disease-specific activity guidance via conjunction of named constraints, and we emphasise rule-level explanations (bounded subset-minimal cores) and parameter sweeps that expose satisfiability frontiers for multimorbidity.

7 Conclusions and Future Work

We introduced a lightweight, design-time methodology for composing disease-specific physical-activity guidance for multimorbidity. By encoding guidelines as *named* OCL invariants over a shared UML schema and interpreting composition as conjunction, the USE$\leftrightarrow$Kodkod pipeline yields interpretable artefacts: concrete symmetry-reduced weekly programmes when satisfiable, and bounded subset-minimal UNSAT cores when unsatisfiable. A scope-bounded context sweep further exposes satisfiability frontiers with flip certificates, making boundary failures explicit and auditable. Across three scenarios—compatible, parameter-sensitive, and intrinsically incompatible—we showed that relational model finding can surface clinically meaningful explanations and export witnesses/cores as explainable test assets for activity recommender validation.

Future work. We plan to extend the schema to richer activities and physiological guards, and to multi-week horizons; incorporate preference- and sensor-aware personalization and clinician-guided partial-programme completion; automate guideline-to-OCL extraction with provenance; and, in parallel, run a small formative clinician review of the generated witnesses and named cores to assess interpretability and to refine the reporting artifacts and modeling vocabulary; and explore hybrid back ends (e.g., MaxUSE/QMaxUSE or optimization layers) while preserving OCL-level traceability.

References

1. Aramrat, C., , Choksomngam, Y., Jiraporncharoen, W., Jirapornchaoren, W., Wiwatkunupakarn, N., Pinyopornpanish, K., Mallinson, P.A.C., Kinra, S., Angkurawaranon, C.: Advancing multimorbidity management in primary care: a narrative review. Primary Health Care Research & Development **23**, e36–e36 (July 2022). https://doi.org/10.1017/s1463423622000238, mAG ID: 4283768528
2. Bilici, E., Despotou, G., Arvanitis, T.N.: The use of computer-interpretable clinical guidelines to manage care complexities of patients with multimorbid conditions: A review. Digital Health **4**, 2055207618804927 (October 2018). https://doi.org/10.1177/2055207618804927
3. Bowles, J., Caminati, M.B., Cha, S., Mendoza, J.: A framework for automated conflict detection and resolution in medical guidelines. Science of Computer Programming **182**, 42–63 (August 2019). https://doi.org/10.1016/j.scico.2019.07.002
4. Fenella Beynon, Frédérique Guérin, Riccardo Lampariello, Torsten Schmitz, Rainer Tan, Natschja Ratanaprayul, Tigest Tamrat, Karell G. Pellé, Gaud Catho, Kristina Keitel, Irene Masanja, Clotilde Rambaud-Althaus: Digitalizing Clinical Guidelines: Experiences in the Development of Clinical Decision Support Algorithms for Management of Childhood Illness in Resource-Constrained Settings **11**(4), e2200439–e2200439 (July 2023). https://doi.org/10.9745/ghsp-d-22-00439, mAG ID: 4385356748
5. Hamine, S., Gerth-Guyette, E., Faulx, D., Green, B.B., Ginsburg, A.S.: Impact of mHealth Chronic Disease Management on Treatment Adherence and Patient Outcomes: A Systematic Review. Journal of Medical Internet Research **17**(2), e52 (February 2015). https://doi.org/10.2196/jmir.3951
6. Hao Wu, Wu, H.: MaxUSE: A Tool for Finding Achievable Constraints and Conflicts for Inconsistent UML Class Diagrams pp. 348–356 (September 2017). https://doi.org/10.1007/978-3-319-66845-1_23, mAG ID: 2749804820
7. Haraty, R.A., Naous, M.: Modeling and Validating the Clinical Information Systems Policy Using Alloy. In: Huang, G., Liu, X., He, J., Klawonn, F., Yao, G. (eds.) Health Information Science. pp. 1–17. Springer, Berlin, Heidelberg (2013). https://doi.org/10.1007/978-3-642-37899-7_1
8. Jackson, D.: Towards a theory of conceptual design for software. In: 2015 ACM International Symposium on New Ideas, New Paradigms, and Reflections on Programming and Software (Onward!). pp. 282–296. Onward! 2015, Association for Computing Machinery, New York, NY, USA (October 2015). https://doi.org/10.1145/2814228.2814248

9. Jackson, E.K., Levendovszky, T., Balasubramanian, D.: Reasoning about Metamodeling with Formal Specifications and Automatic Proofs. In: Whittle, J., Clark, T., Kühne, T. (eds.) Model Driven Engineering Languages and Systems. pp. 653–667. Springer, Berlin, Heidelberg (2011). https://doi.org/10.1007/978-3-642-24485-8_48
10. Kanaley, J.A., Colberg, S.R., Corcoran, M.H., Malin, S.K., Rodriguez, N.R., Crespo, C.J., Kirwan, J.P., Zierath, J.R.: Exercise/Physical Activity in Individuals with Type 2 Diabetes: A Consensus Statement from the American College of Sports Medicine. Medicine and science in sports and exercise **54**(2), 353–368 (February 2022). https://doi.org/10.1249/MSS.0000000000002800
11. Kovalov, A., Bowles, J.K.F.: Avoiding Medication Conflicts for Patients with Multimorbidities. In: Ábrahám, E., Huisman, M. (eds.) Integrated Formal Methods. pp. 376–390. Springer International Publishing, Cham (2016). https://doi.org/10.1007/978-3-319-33693-0_24
12. Ku, J.P., Sim, I.: Mobile Health: making the leap to research and clinics. NPJ Digital Medicine **4**, 83 (May 2021). https://doi.org/10.1038/s41746-021-00454-z
13. Kuhlmann, M., Gogolla, M.: From UML and OCL to Relational Logic and Back. In: France, R.B., Kazmeier, J., Breu, R., Atkinson, C. (eds.) Model Driven Engineering Languages and Systems. pp. 415–431. Springer, Berlin, Heidelberg (2012). https://doi.org/10.1007/978-3-642-33666-9_27
14. Kuhlmann, M., Gogolla, M.: Strengthening SAT-Based Validation of UML/OCL Models by Representing Collections as Relations. In: Vallecillo, A., Tolvanen, J.P., Kindler, E., Störrle, H., Kolovos, D. (eds.) Modelling Foundations and Applications. pp. 32–48. Springer, Berlin, Heidelberg (2012). https://doi.org/10.1007/978-3-642-31491-9_5
15. Kuhlmann, M., Hamann, L., Gogolla, M.: Extensive Validation of OCL Models by Integrating SAT Solving into USE. In: Bishop, J., Vallecillo, A. (eds.) Objects, Models, Components, Patterns. pp. 290–306. Springer, Berlin, Heidelberg (2011). https://doi.org/10.1007/978-3-642-21952-8_21
16. Lin, C.H., Li, Y.R., Cheng, S.L., Wang, H.C., Lin, H.I., Lee, K.Y., Chong, I.W., Chan, P.C., Chen, H.W., Yu, C.J.: Prognostic risk profiling in COPD using Global Initiative for Chronic Obstructive Lung Disease 2023 ABE and comorbidity assessment: evidence from a register-based COPD cohort. Journal of Global Health **15**, 04152. https://doi.org/10.7189/jogh.15.04152
17. McLachlan, S., Kyrimi, E., Dube, K., , Hitman, G.A., Simmonds, J.A., Fenton, N.: Towards standardisation of evidence-based clinical care process specifications. Health Informatics Journal **26**(4), 2512–2537 (Mar 2020). https://doi.org/10.1177/1460458220906069, mAG ID: 3011724853
18. National Institute for Health and Care Excellence (NICE): Asthma: diagnosis, monitoring and chronic asthma management. NICE Guideline, No. 80 (Mar 2021), https://www.ncbi.nlm.nih.gov/books/NBK560178/, published 22 March 2021. Available from: https://www.ncbi.nlm.nih.gov/books/NBK560178/
19. Peleg, M.: Computer-interpretable clinical guidelines: A methodological review. Journal of Biomedical Informatics **46**(4), 744–763 (August 2013). https://doi.org/10.1016/j.jbi.2013.06.009
20. Pelliccia, A., Sharma, S., Gati, S., Bäck, M., Börjesson, M., Caselli, S., Collet, J.P., Corrado, D., Drezner, J.A., Halle, M., Hansen, D., Heidbuchel, H., Myers, J., Niebauer, J., Papadakis, M., Piepoli, M.F., Prescott, E., Roos-Hesselink, J.W., Graham Stuart, A., Taylor, R.S., Thompson, P.D., Tiberi, M., Vanhees, L., Wilhelm, M., ESC Scientific Document, G.: 2020 ESC Guidelines on sports cardiology and

exercise in patients with cardiovascular disease. European Heart Journal **42**(1) (January 2021). https://doi.org/10.1093/eurheartj/ehaa605, publisher: Oxford University Press

21. Ripoll, J.G., Chang, M.G., Bittner, E.A., Ortoleva, J., Khromava, M., Bradley, D.T., Griffin, E.K., Diaz Soto, J.C., Wieruszewski, P.M., Chang, K., Nabzdyk, C.S., Ramakrishna, H.: Analysis of The 2024 ESC/EACTS Guidelines For The Management Of Atrial Fibrillation. Journal of Cardiothoracic and Vascular Anesthesia **39**(3), 818–835 (March 2025). https://doi.org/10.1053/j.jvca.2024.11.020
22. Torlak, E., Jackson, D.: Kodkod: A Relational Model Finder. In: Grumberg, O., Huth, M. (eds.) Tools and Algorithms for the Construction and Analysis of Systems. pp. 632–647. Springer, Berlin, Heidelberg (2007). https://doi.org/10.1007/978-3-540-71209-1_49
23. Wang, X., Rutle, A.: Model Checking Healthcare Workflows Using Alloy. Procedia Computer Science **37**, 481–488 (Jan 2014). https://doi.org/10.1016/j.procs.2014.08.072, https://www.sciencedirect.com/science/article/pii/S1877050914010370
24. Wu, H.: QMaxUSE: A new tool for verifying UML class diagrams and OCL invariants. Science of Computer Programming **228**, 102955 (June 2023). https://doi.org/10.1016/j.scico.2023.102955
25. Wu, H., Farrell, M.: A formal approach to finding inconsistencies in a metamodel. Software and Systems Modeling **20**(4), 1271–1298 (August 2021). https://doi.org/10.1007/s10270-020-00849-8

Testing and Verification

Abstract Symbolic Finite Automata for Algorithmic Game Semantics

Aleksandar S. Dimovski[1]

Faculty of Informatics, Mother Teresa University, Skopje, North Macedonia
aleksandar.dimovski@unt.edu.mk https://aleksdimovski.github.io/

Abstract. Game semantics provides fully abstract (sound and complete) models for open program fragments containing calls to undefined identifiers (e.g., library functions). The standard regular-language representation for algorithmic game semantics of open programs with unbounded integers yields infinite-state automata. By employing symbolic instead of concrete values for integers, we obtain symbolic finite automata (SFA) representation that is amenable to automatic reasoning if the predicates labelling transitions of the given SFA are from a decidable first-order theory, like the linear integer arithmetic. Otherwise, no automatic analysis can be performed.
In this paper, we employ abstract interpretation techniques to define over-approximations of the SFAs representing game models by applying abstractions on symbolic (predicate) level. As a result, we obtain *abstract symbolic finite automata* (ASFA) that can be automatically analyzed, and so they can be applied to prove safety (assertion validity) of open programs. That is, provided that the abstraction preserves the safety property, the analysis of smaller ASFA suffices to decide the safety of the input open programs. This way, we enable efficient automatic verification of open programs containing various constraint formulae, like polynomial and exponential constraints from the non-linear integer arithmetic.

Keywords: Algorithmic Game Semantics, Abstract Model Checking, Abstract Symbolic Finite Automata, Program Verification

1 Introduction

Game semantics [1] is a technique for building models of program fragments (open programs) that are *fully abstract*, i.e. sound and complete, with respect to observational equivalence. The notion of observational equivalence relies on comparing the outcomes of placing program fragments in all possible syntactic contexts. The algorithmic game semantics [18,19,31] aims to apply the inferred game models to software verification by providing concrete automata-based representations for them. However, in the presence of unbounded (infinite) integers, the obtained (concrete) automata become infinite state, thus losing their algorithmic properties. The symbolic representation of algorithmic game semantics [7,8], where symbolic data values are used instead of concrete ones for integers, enable

E. Albert and C. Pasareanu (Eds.): FASE 2026, LNCS 16504, pp. 371–391, 2026.
https://doi.org/10.1007/978-3-032-22774-4_19

to obtain compact models of program fragments with infinite integers. The game models are represented by so-called symbolic finite-state automata (SFA), which can model languages with potentially infinite alphabets. Transitions in SFAs contain symbolic predicates, so that by providing the semantic interpretation of predicates we obtain the concrete (standard) game models [19]. Each *complete symbolic play* (accepting word) in the game model (SFA) represents one possible execution path of the program fragment. It is guarded by a conjunction of constraints on the symbols, known as *play condition*, which indicate under what conditions this symbolic play is feasible. Therefore, a symbolic play represents the potentially infinite set of concrete plays (executions) in the standard (concrete) game model [19]. We say that a program fragment is *safe* if no program execution violates an assertion. Hence, we can employ the symbolic game models (SFAs) to efficiently verify safety of program fragments.

However, SFAs introduce their own limitations: namely, that they can be automatically verified if the predicates (constraints) labelling their transitions are limited to those from a fixed, supported (decidable) first-order theory, such as linear integer arithmetic (LIA). This limitation has created a gap in verifying programs with semantics outside of a supported theory. Moreover, if the SFA representing the game model of a program fragment contains many predicates from a supported but less efficient theory, e.g. polynomial constraints from the non-linear integer arithmetic (NIA), it would be also beneficial to generate an over-approximation of the SFA that contains fewer predicates from a more efficient theory, thus enabling more feasible verification task. That is, the idea is to trade the use of computationally expensive (NIA) solvers (for polynomial constraints) for much less expensive (LIA) solvers.

Abstract model checking represents a research area that uses abstraction and reduction techniques to address the complexity originating from the model [3,5,23,28]. The generation of the abstract model is often based on abstract interpretation theory [4,29]: the semantics of the concrete model is related with the semantics of its abstract version by using Galois connections. Provided that the abstraction preserves the property to check, the analysis of the abstract model suffices to decide the satisfaction of the property on the concrete model.

In this work, we define abstract model checking in the settings of symbolic game semantics. In particular, we introduce the notion of *abstract symbolic finite-state automaton* (ASFA) for representing game models, where the approximation is made by abstract interpretation of the standard SFA representation. Abstraction acts at symbolic (predicates and constraint formulae) level, resulting in an ASFA whose recognized language is an over-approximation of the language of the standard SFA. The aim is to reduce instances of complex constraints into problems that can be straightforwardly handled by existing efficient SMT solvers like (LIA). The inferred ASFA is sound, which means that the safety of the ASFA implies the safety of the standard SFA representation. Thus, we can use the ASFA of game models for efficient verification of program fragments.

We have implemented our approach in the `Symbolic GameChecker` tool [7,8], which is used for generating and verifying the SFA representation of game models of program fragments. It also calls the Z3 tool for solving (symbolic) constraints in various SMT theories, such as (LIA), polynomial (NIA), etc. We have shown how the combination of abstraction, symbolic techniques, and algorithmic game semantics can be used for efficiently verifying several interesting examples.

The main contributions of this paper are:

(1) We define the ASFA for representing the game models of program fragments;
(2) We show the soundness of the ASFA for verifying safety of program fragments;
(3) We demonstrate the practicality of our approach on several examples.

1.1 Related Work

Algorithmic Game Semantics. Game semantics for full Idealized Algol (IA) has been defined by Abramsky and McCusker [1]. Algorithmic game semantics for second-order IA with finite integers has been proposed by Ghica and McCusker [19], and several model checking tools based on this representation have been developed [17,18]. Subsequently, algorithmic game semantics has been introduced for third-order (finite) IA by representing the game models by visibly pushdown automata [31], for parallel (finite) IA that contains shared-variable concurrency and binary semaphores [20], etc. Algorithmic game semantics has also been defined for nondeterministic (finite) IA that is fully abstract with respect to may-termination and must-termination [30], for probabilistic (finite) IA [24], etc.

Symbolic Game Semantics. Symbolic representation of algorithmic game semantics was first proposed in [7] to generate SFAs for second-order Idealized Algol with infinite integers. Subsequently, symbolic game models have been used for lifted (SPL) verification [13,14,16] of program families implemented by `#ifdef` directives [8], as well as for finding the weakest specifications of unknown identifiers that ensure the safety of the open program calling those identifiers [12]. Moreover, symbolic execution game semantics [27], which extends operational game semantics [21,26] with symbolic values, was introduced to verify open higher-order programs. Symbolic execution game semantics combined with bisimulation up-to techniques and state invariant annotations have been also applied for verifying contextual equivalence of open higher-order programs [25].

Abstract Model Checking. Model checking [2] is a well-known technique for automatic verification of systems: a model of the system is constructed over which temporal logic formulae are checked for satisfaction. Abstract interpretation [4,29,9] is a general theory for approximating the semantics of systems (models), so it can be used to reduce the size of a possibly infinite model. Clarke, Grumberg and Long [3] introduce abstract model checking as a technique for abstracting data in a complex circuit design via definition of an abstraction function α. The theoretical foundation of abstract model checking is introduced in [5,28] as a property preserving abstraction technique for various models and temporal logics. Graf and Saidi propose the predicate abstraction [23] as a technique that maps concrete states of a model to abstract states according to their evaluation under a finite set of predicates.

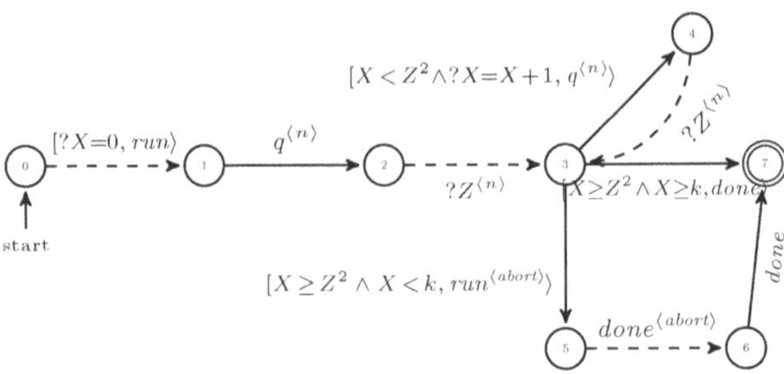

Fig. 1. The SFA A_{M_k}.

2 Motivating Example

Consider the following program term M_k ($k \geq 0$ is a parameter):

$$n : \mathsf{expint}^{\langle n \rangle}, abort : \mathsf{com}^{\langle abort \rangle} \vdash \mathsf{new_{int}}\ x := 0\ \mathsf{in}\\ \mathsf{while}\ (!x < n^2)\ \mathsf{do}\ x :=!x + 1;\\ \mathsf{assert}\ (!x \geq k) : \mathsf{com}$$

where undefined identifiers are integer expression n and command $abort$, which is executed when the assertion fails, and $!x$ is a de-referencing operation for reading the value stored in the local variable x.

The SFA A_{M_k} representing the *game model* of M_k is given in Fig. 1. The dashed edges indicate moves of the environment (Opponent, **O**) and solid edges moves of the term (Player, **P**). Accepting state is designated by an interior circle. Every letter (label of transition) $[b, \delta\rangle$, also called a *guarded move*, contains a (symbolic) move δ and a Boolean condition b that represents a constraint over symbols that needs to be satisfied in order the corresponding move δ to be performed. We write only δ for $[\text{true}, \delta\rangle$. A *play* in the game model is a sequence of moves played by two players **O** and **P** in turns. The moves for commands are: '*run*' and '*done*' to initiate a command and to signal termination of a command respectively, whereas the moves for expressions are: 'q' and 'v' to ask for a value of an expression and to provide a concrete value for an expression, respectively. The term communicates with its environment using undefined identifiers n and *abort*, and so in the game model are only visible actions associated with n and *abort* (which are syntactically tagged with $\langle n \rangle$ and $\langle abort \rangle$ to indicate the origin of moves) as well as with the top-level type com of M_k. The symbol X is used to keep track of the current value of the local variable x, while the symbol Z is used to denote the value read from the undefined expression n. Note that symbol X occurs only in conditional parts of moves, and symbols X and Z can take on any value from integers $\mathbb{Z}$.

The environment (Opponent, **O**) starts the execution of the term M_k by playing the move *run* under condition that the initial value of variable x is 0 (transition ⓪ → ①). Each time when the term (Player, **P**) asks for a value of undefined expression n with the move $q^{\langle n \rangle}$ (transition ① → ②), the environment (Opponent, **O**) provides a new fresh value for it via the symbol $Z^{\langle n \rangle}$ (transition

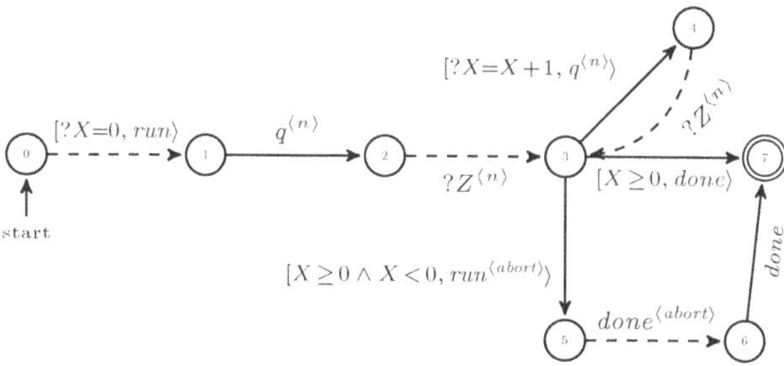

Fig. 2. The ASFA $\alpha_0(A_{M_0})$.

② → ③). Whenever a new value Z for undefined expression n is provided, the term has three possible options depending on the current values of symbols Z and X: (1) it can run the assignment $x := !x + 1$ and ask for a new value of n, when $X < Z^2$ (transition ③ → ④); (2) it can terminate successfully with *done* (i.e., assertion holds), when $X \geq Z^2 \wedge X \geq k$ (transition ③ → ⑦); and (3) it can execute *abort* (i.e., assertion fails) and terminate, when $X \geq Z^2 \wedge X < k$ (transition ③ → ⑤).

The set of predicates used in the SFA A_{M_k} corresponding to the guards in M_k are $\Psi_{A_{M_k}} = \{X < Z^2, X \geq k\}$. We want to abstract some of the predicates in $\Psi_{A_{M_k}}$, thus obtaining an abstract SFA $\alpha_k(A_{M_k})$ that recognizes an over-approximation of the language recognized by the original A_{M_k}. Assume that we want to abstract from the value Z read from the undefined expression n. Hence, we define the predicate abstraction α_k of any predicate ψ occurring in A_{M_k} induced by the new abstract predicate set $\{X \geq k\}$ as:

(1) $\alpha_k(\psi) = (X \geq k)$, if $\psi \models (X \geq k)$;
(2) $\alpha_k(\psi) = \neg(X \geq k)$, if $\psi \models \neg(X \geq k)$; and
(3) $\alpha_k(\psi) = \text{true}$, otherwise

Consider the term M_0 with the assertion assert$(!x \geq 0)$. We obtain $\alpha_0(X \geq Z^2) = (X \geq 0)$ since $X \geq Z^2 \models X \geq 0$; and $\alpha_0(X < Z^2) = \text{true}$ since both `isSat`$(X < Z^2 \wedge X \geq 0)$ and `isSat`$(X < Z^2 \wedge X < 0)$ hold. That is, $(X < Z^2)$ is abstracted to true since it has a non-empty intersection with both $(X \geq 0)$ and $\neg(X \geq 0)$. α_0 is the identity on the predicates $(X \geq 0)$ and $(X < 0)$. The ASFA $\alpha_0(A_{M_0})$, shown in Fig. 2, is obtained by replacing predicates (and their negations) from $\Psi_{A_{M_k}}$ with their abstracted predicates according to α_0, which leads to more non-deterministic symbolic plays. Due to the soundness of the abstraction α_0, every concrete play (execution) from the concrete game model of M_0 [19] is represented by some abstract symbolic play (path) in the ASFA $\alpha_0(A_{M_0})$. The unsafe plays, which designate the assertion failure, contain *abort* moves. In $\alpha_0(A_{M_0})$, the unsafe plays are:

$$[?X{=}0, run\rangle \cdot q^{\langle n\rangle} \cdot ?Z^{\langle n\rangle} \cdot ([?X{=}X{+}1, q^{\langle n\rangle}\rangle \cdot ?Z^{\langle n\rangle})^* \cdot [X{\geq}0 \wedge X{<}0, run^{\langle abort\rangle}\rangle \cdot done^{\langle abort\rangle} \cdot done$$

They are all inconsistent plays since the play condition contains an unsatisfiable constraint $(X \geq 0 \wedge X < 0)$. Therefore $\alpha_0(A_{M_0})$ is safe, and we thus conclude the safety of A_{M_0} and the term M_0.

Consider the term M_2 with the assertion $\mathsf{assert}\,(!x \geq 2)$. In this case, we obtain $\alpha_2(X \geq Z^2) = \alpha_2(X < Z^2) = \text{true}$ since they have non-empty intersection with both $(X \geq 2)$ and $(X < 2)$, and α_2 is the identity on the predicates $(X \geq 2)$ and $(X < 2)$. The shortest unsafe play in $\alpha_2(A_{M_2})$ is:

$$[?X = 0, run\rangle \cdot q^{\langle n \rangle} \cdot ?Z^{\langle n \rangle} \cdot [X < 2, run^{\langle abort \rangle}\rangle \cdot done^{\langle abort \rangle} \cdot done$$

which is consistent play as $(X = 0 \wedge X < 2)$ is satisfiable. We can construct a concrete play from the above symbolic play: $run \cdot q^{\langle n \rangle} \cdot 0^{\langle n \rangle} \cdot run^{\langle abort \rangle} \cdot done^{\langle abort \rangle} \cdot done$, which can be classified as a genuine counter-example by simulating it through the SFA A_{M_2}. This play corresponds to the execution that uses value 0 for undefined expression n so it does not run the while-body as the while-guard $(0 < 0)$ evaluates to false. This way, the assertion $(!x \geq 2)$ fails since x has value 0 at the assertion location.

3 Symbolic Game Semantics

The Language. In this work, we consider Idealized Algol (IA) [1], a well studied meta-language in semantics community, that enables functional (typed call-by-name λ-calculus) and imperative programming. For the aim of constructing algorithmic game semantics (AGS), we consider its second-order recursion-free fragment (IA_2 for short), where only first-order functions are allowed. Types are: $D ::= \mathsf{int} \mid \mathsf{bool}$, $B ::= \mathsf{exp}D \mid \mathsf{com} \mid \mathsf{var}D$, and $T ::= B \mid B \rightarrow T$, where D, B, and T are data types, base types, and first-order function types. The *syntax* is:

$$\begin{aligned} M ::= & \, x \mid v \mid \mathsf{skip} \mid \mathsf{diverge} \mid M \,\mathsf{op}_D\, M \mid M;M \mid \mathsf{if}\, M \,\mathsf{then}\, M \,\mathsf{else}\, M \mid \mathsf{while}\, M \,\mathsf{do}\, M \\ & \mid M := M \mid !M \mid \mathsf{new}_D\, x{:=}v \,\mathsf{in}\, M \mid \mathsf{mkvar}_D MM \mid \lambda x.M \mid MM \end{aligned}$$

where x ranges over a countable set of identifiers, v ranges over constants of type D, which includes integers $(n \in \mathbb{Z})$ and booleans $(\text{true}, \text{false})$, and op_D are the usual arithmetic-logic operations of type D. *Well-typed terms* (terms-in-context) are given by typing judgements of the form $\Gamma \vdash M : T$, where $\Gamma = x_1 : T_1, \ldots, x_k : T_k$ is a type *context* consisting of a finite number of typed free identifiers. *Typing rules* and *operational semantics* of IA are standard and can be found in [1].

Symbolic Representation of AGS. We now present an overview of symbolic representation of the AGS for IA_2 [7]. Let Sym be a countable set of symbolic names, ranged over by upper case letters X, Y, Z. For any finite $W \subseteq Sym$, the function $new(W)$ returns a minimal symbolic name which does not occur in W, and sets $W := W \cup \{new(W)\}$. The set of symbolic expressions of type D, $SExp^D$, is generated by:

$$se^D ::= v \in D \mid X^D \mid ?X^D \mid se^D \,\mathsf{op}_D\, se^D$$

We omit to write the superscript D when clear from the context. The input symbols $?X$ represent a mechanism for dynamically generating new symbolic names. More specifically, $?X$ creates a stream of fresh symbolic names, binding X to the next symbol from its stream, $new(W)$, whenever $?X$ is evaluated.

For each type T, we define alphabet $\mathcal{A}_{[\![T]\!]}$ as follows:

$$\mathcal{A}_{[\![\mathsf{int}]\!]} = \mathbb{Z},\ \mathcal{A}_{[\![\mathsf{bool}]\!]} = \{\text{true}, \text{false}\},\ \mathcal{A}_{[\![\mathsf{exp}D]\!]} = \{q\} \cup \mathcal{A}_{[\![D]\!]},\ \mathcal{A}_{[\![\mathsf{com}]\!]} = \{run, done\},$$
$$\mathcal{A}_{[\![\mathsf{var}D]\!]} = \{write(a), read, ok, a \mid a \in \mathcal{A}_{[\![D]\!]}\},\ \mathcal{A}_{[\![B_1^{\langle 1\rangle} \to \ldots \to B_k^{\langle k\rangle} \to B]\!]} = \sum_{1 \leq i \leq k} \mathcal{A}^{\langle i\rangle}_{[\![B_i]\!]} + \mathcal{A}_{[\![B]\!]}$$

where $+$ denotes a disjoint union of alphabets. Function types are syntactically tagged by a superscript $\langle i\rangle$ to keep record from which type, i.e. which component of the disjoint union, each move comes from. The letters in the alphabet $\mathcal{A}_{[\![T]\!]}$ represent the *moves*, i.e. observable actions that a term of type T can perform. Each move is either a *question* (a demand for information) or an *answer* (a supply of information). For expressions in $\mathcal{A}_{[\![\mathsf{exp}D]\!]}$, there is a *question* move q to ask for the value of the expression, and values from $\mathcal{A}_{[\![D]\!]}$ to *answer* the question. For commands, there is a *question* move *run* to initiate a command, and an *answer* move *done* to signal successful termination of a command. For variables, there are *question* moves for writing to the variable, $write(a)$, which are acknowledged by the *answer* move *ok*; and a *question* move *read* for reading from the variable, which is *answered* by a value from $\mathcal{A}_{[\![D]\!]}$.

The guarded alphabet $\mathcal{A}^{gu}_{[\![T]\!]}$, induced by $\mathcal{A}_{[\![T]\!]}$, is a set of guarded letters $[b, \delta\rangle$ where $b \in SExp^{\mathsf{bool}}$ is a Boolean condition and δ is a symbolic letter that represents a move from $\mathcal{A}_{[\![T]\!]}$ in which all data values $v \in D$ are replaced with symbolic expressions $se \in SExp^D$. For example, $\mathcal{A}^{gu}_{[\![\mathsf{exp}D]\!]} = \{[b, q\rangle, [b, se\rangle \mid b \in SExp^{\mathsf{bool}}, se \in SExp^D\}$ and $\mathcal{A}^{gu}_{[\![\mathsf{com}]\!]} = \{[b, run\rangle, [b, done\rangle \mid b \in SExp^{\mathsf{bool}}\}$. A guarded letter $[b, \delta\rangle$ is δ only if b evaluates to true otherwise it is the constant $\emptyset$. We will often write only δ for $[\text{true}, \delta\rangle$. A word $[b_1, \delta_1\rangle \cdot [b_2, \delta_2\rangle \ldots [b_n, \delta_n\rangle$ can be represented as a pair $[b, w\rangle$, where $b = b_1 \wedge b_2 \wedge \ldots \wedge b_n$ and $w = \delta_1 \cdot \delta_2 \ldots \delta_n$.

For any (β-normal) IA_2 term, we define a (symbolic) regular-language which represents its game semantics, i.e. its set of complete symbolic plays. A *play* is a sequence of moves played by two players in turns: **P** (Player) which represents the term being modeled, and **O** (Opponent) which represents its environment. Every complete symbolic play represents the observable effects of a completed execution path of the given term. It is given as a guarded word $[b, w\rangle$, where b is also called the *play condition*. Assumptions about a symbolic play to be feasible are recorded in its play condition. For infeasible plays, the play condition is unsatisfiable. For any term $\Gamma \vdash M : T$, we define the regular expression $[\![\Gamma \vdash M : T]\!]$ by recursion on the syntax over the guarded alphabet:

$$\mathcal{A}^{gu}_{[\![\Gamma \vdash T]\!]} = \Big(\sum_{x:T' \in \Gamma} \mathcal{A}^{gu\,\langle x\rangle}_{[\![T']\!]}\Big) + \mathcal{A}^{gu}_{[\![T]\!]}$$

where we syntactically tag moves corresponding to types of free identifiers with their names. Hence, $[\![\Gamma \vdash M : T]\!]$ contains only moves associated with types of free identifiers from Γ and moves of the top-level type T of M.

Free identifiers $x : B_1^{\langle 1\rangle} \to \ldots B_k^{\langle k\rangle} \to B$ are represented by the so-called copy-cat regular expressions which contain all possible behaviours of terms of

$$
\begin{aligned}
&[\![\Gamma, x:\mathsf{exp}D \vdash x : \mathsf{exp}D]\!] = q \cdot q^{\langle x\rangle}\cdot ?N^{\langle x\rangle} \cdot N \\
&[\![\Gamma, x:\mathsf{com} \vdash x : \mathsf{com}]\!] = run \cdot run^{\langle x\rangle} \cdot done^{\langle x\rangle} \cdot done \\
&[\![\Gamma, x:\mathsf{var}D \vdash x : \mathsf{var}D]\!] = \big(read \cdot read^{\langle x\rangle}\cdot ?N^{\langle x\rangle} \cdot N\big) + \big(write(?N) \cdot write(N)^{\langle x\rangle} \cdot ok^{\langle x\rangle} \cdot ok\big) \\
&[\![\Gamma, x:B_1^{\langle 1\rangle} \to \ldots B_k^{\langle k\rangle} \to \mathsf{exp}D \vdash x : B_1^{\langle 1\rangle} \ldots B_k^{\langle k\rangle} \to \mathsf{exp}D]\!] = q \cdot q^{\langle x\rangle} \cdot \big(\textstyle\sum_{1\leq i\leq k} R_{B_i}^{\langle x,i\rangle}\big)^{*} ?N^{\langle x\rangle} \cdot N \\
&[\![\Gamma, x:B_1^{\langle 1\rangle} \to \ldots B_k^{\langle k\rangle} \to \mathsf{com} \vdash x : B_1^{\langle 1\rangle} \ldots B_k^{\langle k\rangle} \to \mathsf{com}]\!] = \\
&\qquad\qquad run \cdot run^{\langle x\rangle} \cdot \big(\textstyle\sum_{1\leq i\leq k} R_{B_i}^{\langle x,i\rangle}\big)^{*} \cdot done^{\langle x\rangle} \cdot done \\
&[\![\Gamma, x:B_1^{\langle 1\rangle} \to \ldots B_k^{\langle k\rangle} \to \mathsf{var}D \vdash x : B_1^{\langle 1\rangle} \ldots B_k^{\langle k\rangle} \to \mathsf{var}D]\!] = \\
&\big(read \cdot read^{\langle x\rangle} \cdot \big(\textstyle\sum_{1\leq i\leq k} R_{B_i}^{\langle x,i\rangle}\big)^{*} ?N^{\langle x\rangle} \cdot N\big) + \big(write(?N) \cdot write(N)^{\langle x\rangle} \cdot \big(\textstyle\sum_{1\leq i\leq k} R_{B_i}^{\langle x,i\rangle}\big)^{*} \cdot ok^{\langle x\rangle} \cdot ok\big) \\
&R_{\mathsf{exp}D}^{\langle x,i\rangle} = q^{\langle x,i\rangle} \cdot q^{\langle i\rangle}\cdot ?Z^{\langle i\rangle} \cdot Z^{\langle x,i\rangle} \\
&R_{\mathsf{com}}^{\langle x,i\rangle} = run^{\langle x,i\rangle} \cdot run^{\langle i\rangle} \cdot done^{\langle i\rangle} \cdot done^{\langle x,i\rangle} \\
&R_{\mathsf{var}D}^{\langle x,i\rangle} = (read^{\langle x,i\rangle} \cdot read^{\langle i\rangle}\cdot ?Z^{\langle i\rangle} \cdot Z^{\langle x,i\rangle}) + (write(?Z')^{\langle x,i\rangle} \cdot write(Z')^{\langle i\rangle} \cdot ok^{\langle i\rangle} \cdot ok^{\langle x,i\rangle})
\end{aligned}
$$

Table 1. The game models for free identifiers

$$
\begin{aligned}
&[\![\mathsf{op} : \mathsf{exp}D_1^{\langle 1\rangle} \times \mathsf{exp}D_2^{\langle 2\rangle} \to \mathsf{exp}D]\!] = q \cdot q^{\langle 1\rangle}\cdot ?Z^{\langle 1\rangle} \cdot q^{\langle 2\rangle}\cdot ?Z'^{\langle 2\rangle} \cdot (Z \,\mathsf{op}\, Z') \\
&[\![; : \mathsf{com}^{\langle 1\rangle} \times \mathsf{com}^{\langle 2\rangle} \to \mathsf{com}]\!] = run \cdot run^{\langle 1\rangle} \cdot done^{\langle 1\rangle} \cdot run^{\langle 2\rangle} \cdot done^{\langle 2\rangle} \cdot done \\
&[\![\mathsf{if} : \mathsf{expbool}^{\langle 1\rangle} \times \mathsf{com}^{\langle 2\rangle} \times \mathsf{com}^{\langle 3\rangle} \to \mathsf{com}]\!] = run \cdot q^{\langle 1\rangle}\cdot ?Z^{\langle 1\rangle} \cdot \big([Z, run^{\langle 2\rangle}\rangle \cdot done^{\langle 2\rangle} + [\neg Z, run^{\langle 3\rangle}\rangle \cdot done^{\langle 3\rangle}\big) \cdot done \\
&[\![\mathsf{while} : \mathsf{expbool}^{\langle 1\rangle} \times \mathsf{com}^{\langle 2\rangle} \to \mathsf{com}]\!] = run \cdot q^{\langle 1\rangle}\cdot ?Z^{\langle 1\rangle} \cdot \big([Z, run^{\langle 2\rangle}\rangle \cdot done^{\langle 2\rangle} \cdot q^{\langle 1\rangle}\cdot ?Z^{\langle 1\rangle}\big)^{*} \cdot [\neg Z, done\rangle \\
&[\![:= : \mathsf{var}D^{\langle 1\rangle} \times \mathsf{exp}D^{\langle 2\rangle} \to \mathsf{com}]\!] = run \cdot q^{\langle 2\rangle}\cdot ?Z^{\langle 2\rangle} \cdot write(Z)^{\langle 1\rangle} \cdot ok^{\langle 1\rangle} \cdot done \\
&[\![! : \mathsf{var}D^{\langle 1\rangle} \to \mathsf{exp}D]\!] = q \cdot read^{\langle 1\rangle}\cdot ?Z^{\langle 1\rangle} \cdot Z \\
&\mathsf{cell}_v^{\langle x\rangle} = ([?X{=}v, read^{\langle x\rangle}\rangle \cdot X^{\langle x\rangle})^{*} \cdot \big(write(?X)^{\langle x\rangle} \cdot ok^{\langle x\rangle} \cdot (read^{\langle x\rangle} \cdot X^{\langle x\rangle})^{*}\big)^{*}
\end{aligned}
$$

Table 2. Symbolic representations of some language constructs

that type, thus providing the most general environment for an open term. For any free identifier $x : B_1^{\langle 1\rangle} \to \ldots B_k^{\langle k\rangle} \to B$, the corresponding game model is defined in Table 1. For example, we have:

$$
\begin{aligned}
&[\![\Gamma, x:\mathsf{exp}D_1^{\langle x,1\rangle} \to \ldots \mathsf{exp}D_k^{\langle x,k\rangle} \to \mathsf{exp}D^{\langle x\rangle} \vdash x:\mathsf{exp}D_1^{\langle 1\rangle} \to \ldots \mathsf{exp}D_k^{\langle k\rangle} \to \mathsf{exp}D]\!] = \\
&\qquad\qquad q \cdot q^{\langle x\rangle} \cdot \big(\textstyle\sum_{1\leq i\leq k} q^{\langle x,i\rangle} \cdot q^{\langle i\rangle}\cdot ?Z^{\langle i\rangle} \cdot Z^{\langle x,i\rangle}\big)^{*} \cdot ?X^{\langle x\rangle} \cdot X
\end{aligned}
$$

When a call-by-name undefined function x with k arguments is called, it may evaluate any of its arguments, zero or more times, in an arbitrary order (hence, the Kleene closure *) and then it returns any allowable answer (symbol X^D) from its result type $\mathsf{exp}D$.

The representation of constants is standard: $[\![\Gamma \vdash v:\mathsf{exp}D]\!] = q \cdot v$, $[\![\Gamma \vdash \mathsf{skip}:\mathsf{com}]\!] = run \cdot done$, $[\![\Gamma \vdash \mathsf{diverge}:\mathsf{com}]\!] = \emptyset$. For example, a constant v is modeled by a play where the initial question q that asks for the value of this expression is answered by the constant value v.

The representations of some language constructs "c" are given in Table 2. Note that language constructs can be also given in a functional form, e.g. we have "$:=(M,N) \equiv M{:=}N$", "$\mathsf{if}(B,M,M') \equiv \mathsf{if}\,(B)\,\mathsf{then}\,M\,\mathsf{else}\,M'$", etc. In the case of "if" construct, when the value of the first argument (if-guard) given by the symbol Z is true then its second argument (then-command) is run, otherwise if $\neg Z$ is true then its third argument (else-command) is run. In the case of "while" construct, the while-guard produces the symbol Z as answer, so the model is an iteration of plays consisting of the while-guard producing Z as true concatenated with complete plays of the body (moves $[Z, run^{\langle 2\rangle}\rangle$ and $done^{\langle 2\rangle}$), followed by one single play of the while-guard producing $\neg Z$ as true (move $[\neg Z, done\rangle$). A composite term $\mathsf{c}(M_1, \ldots, M_k)$ built out of a language construct "c" and subterms $M_1, \ldots, M_k$ is interpreted by composing the regular expressions for $M_1, \ldots, M_k$ and the regular expression for "c". For example,

$$[\![\Gamma \vdash M{:=}N : \mathsf{com}]\!] = [\![\Gamma \vdash M : \mathsf{var}D^{\langle 1\rangle}]\!] \circ [\![\Gamma \vdash N : \mathsf{exp}D^{\langle 2\rangle}]\!] \circ [\![:= : \mathsf{var}D^{\langle 1\rangle} \times \mathsf{exp}D^{\langle 2\rangle} \to \mathsf{com}]\!]$$

where $[\![:= : \mathsf{var}D^{\langle 1\rangle} \times \mathsf{exp}D^{\langle 2\rangle} \to \mathsf{com}]\!]$ is defined in Table 2. Composition of regular expressions ($\circ$) is defined as "parallel composition followed by hiding" in CSP style [1]. The parallel composition is matching (synchronizing) of the moves in the shared types, whereas hiding is deleting of all moves from the shared types [7]. Conditions of the shared (interacting) moves in the composition are conjoined, along with the condition that their symbolic letters are equal [7]. E.g., the shared types in the above composition are $\mathsf{var}D^{\langle 1\rangle}$ and $\mathsf{exp}D^{\langle 2\rangle}$. The $\mathsf{cell}_v^{\langle x\rangle}$ regular expression in Table 2 is used to impose the good variable behaviour on a local variable x introduced using $\mathsf{new}_D\ x{:=}v \ \mathsf{in}\ M$. Note that X is a symbol used to track the current value of x. The $\mathsf{cell}_v^{\langle x\rangle}$ behaves as a storage cell and plays the most recently written value in x in response to *read*, or if no value has been written yet then answers *read* with the initial value v. Hence, we have $[\![\Gamma \vdash \mathsf{new}_D\ x{:=}v \ \mathsf{in}\ M]\!]$ is obtained by constraining $[\![\Gamma, x : \mathsf{varD} \vdash M]\!]$ to only those plays where x exhibits good variable behaviour described by $\mathsf{cell}_v^{\langle x\rangle}$, and then by hiding all moves of the local variable x since local variables are not visible outside of their binding scope [7].

Formal Results. The following formal results are proved in [7].

Proposition 1 ([7]). *For any IA_2 term, $[\![\Gamma \vdash M : T]\!]$ is a (symbolic) regular-language without infinite summations defined over its effective alphabet. Moreover, a symbolic finite-state automata (SFA) $\mathcal{A}_{[\![\Gamma \vdash M:T]\!]}$ is effectively constructible.*

Given a complete *symbolic* play $[b, w\rangle \in \mathcal{L}([\![\Gamma \vdash M : T]\!])$, we now show how to generate the corresponding complete *concrete* plays, in which concrete values are used instead of symbols for integers. Whenever $?Z$ is met in a symbolic play, the mechanism for fresh symbol generation is used to dynamically instantiate it with a new fresh symbolic name from its stream. This symbolic name binds all occurrences of Z that follow in the play until a new $?Z$ is met which overrides the previous symbolic name with the next symbolic name taken from its stream. For example, the unsafe play corresponding to execution path of the term M_0 from Section 2 where while-body is executed once is:

$$[?X{=}0, run\rangle \cdot q^{\langle n\rangle}\cdot ?Z^{\langle n\rangle} \cdot [?X{=}X{+}1, q^{\langle n\rangle}\rangle \cdot ?Z^{\langle n\rangle} \cdot [X{\geq} Z^2 \wedge X{<}0, run^{\langle abort\rangle}\rangle \cdot done^{\langle abort\rangle} \cdot done$$

After instantiating its input symbols $?X$ and $?Z$, we obtain the play:

$$[X_0{=}0, run\rangle \cdot q^{\langle n\rangle} \cdot Z_0^{\langle n\rangle} \cdot [X_1{=}X_0{+}1, q^{\langle n\rangle}\rangle \cdot Z_1^{\langle n\rangle} \cdot [X_1{\geq} Z_1^2 \wedge X_1{<}0, run^{\langle abort\rangle}\rangle \cdot done^{\langle abort\rangle} \cdot done$$

where X_0, X_1, Z_0 and Z_1 are different symbolic names generated by $?X$ and $?Z$. We write $[\![b, w\rangle\!\rangle$ for play obtained after instantiating all input symbols in $[b, w\rangle$.

Let *Eval* be the set of evaluations, i.e. the set of total functions from W to $\mathcal{A}_{[\![\mathsf{int}]\!]} \cup \mathcal{A}_{[\![\mathsf{bool}]\!]}$. We use ρ to range over *Eval*. Given a word of symbolic letters w, let $\rho(w)$ be the word where every symbol X is replaced by the concrete value $\rho(X)$. We define $\rho([\![b, w\rangle\!\rangle) = \rho(w)$ if $\rho(b) =$ true; otherwise $\rho([\![b, w\rangle\!\rangle) = \emptyset$ if $\rho(b) =$ false. The concretization of a symbolic regular-language is defined as: $\texttt{concretize}(\mathcal{L}(R)) = \{\rho[\![b, w\rangle\!\rangle \mid [b, w\rangle \in \mathcal{L}(R), \rho \in Eval\}$. Let $[\![\Gamma \vdash M : T]\!]^{CR}$ denote the set of all complete concrete plays for a term $\Gamma \vdash M : T$ [19], where concrete values for integers in words are used.

Proposition 2 ([7]). $\mathit{concretize}([\![\Gamma \vdash M : T]\!]) = [\![\Gamma \vdash M : T]\!]^{CR}$.

We are interested here in proving safety properties. Suppose that there is a special free identifier *abort* : com. We define an assertion as a function that takes one boolean expression as argument and calls *abort* if the argument is false: assert $= \lambda b : \mathsf{expbool}.\mathsf{if}\ \neg b\ \mathsf{then}\ abort\ \mathsf{else}\ \mathsf{skip}$. A term is *safe* iff it has no execution that leads to running *abort*. A play is *safe* if it contains no moves from $\mathcal{A}_{[\![\mathsf{com}]\!]}^{\langle abort \rangle}$; otherwise the play is *unsafe*.

Proposition 3 ([7]). *$\Gamma \vdash M : T$ is safe iff all plays in $[\![\Gamma \vdash M : T]\!]$ are safe.*

4 Abstract Symbolic Game Semantics

Complete Boolean Lattices. Let Ψ be a set of predicates defined over symbols from $W \subseteq Sym$. The interpretations of the predicates in Ψ have the domain $\mathcal{D}$ that is a tuple of n copies of values of type D (integers $\mathbb{Z}$ or Booleans $\{\text{true}, \text{false}\}$), one for each symbol in Ψ. Given a predicate ψ defined over symbols in W, the denotation function $[\![\psi]\!] \in 2^{\mathcal{D}}$ is the set of all interpretations from $\mathcal{D}$ under which ψ evaluates to true. Thus, $[\![\text{false}]\!] = \emptyset$, $[\![\text{true}]\!] = \mathcal{D}$, $[\![\psi \vee \psi']\!] = [\![\psi]\!] \cup [\![\psi']\!]$, $[\![\psi \wedge \psi']\!] = [\![\psi]\!] \cap [\![\psi']\!]$, and $[\![\neg\psi]\!] = \mathcal{D} \backslash [\![\psi]\!]$. We build a *complete lattice* induced by the set of predicates Ψ as follows.

We define a *minterm* [6,32] to be a minimal satisfiable Boolean combination of all predicates in Ψ. Thus, minterms provide a minimal and univocal representation of the predicates in a given set Ψ. The procedure for generating minterms from a set of predicates Ψ is given in Algorithm 1. It uses a binary tree whose leaves define the partition of the domain $\mathcal{D}$. Initially, the binary tree is $\top \equiv$ true. Each time a predicate $\psi \in \Psi$ is used to refine the tree, it may cause splitting of its leaves into finer predicates.

Example 1. Consider the predicate sets $\Psi_{A_{M_0}} = \{X < Z^2, X \geq 0\}$ and $\Psi'_{A_{M_0}} = \{X \geq 0\}$ from the running example in Section 2. The domain is $\mathcal{D}_{A_{M_0}} = \mathbb{Z} \times \mathbb{Z}$. The binary trees generated by $\texttt{Minterms}(\Psi_{A_{M_0}})$ are shown in Fig. 3 when $(X < Z^2)$ is selected first in the forall loop in line 2 of Algorithm 1 and in Fig. 4 when $(X \geq 0)$ is selected first in the forall loop in line 2 of Algorithm 1, whereas the binary tree generated by $\texttt{Minterms}(\Psi'_{A_{M_0}})$ is shown in Fig. 5.

Algorithm 1 `Minterms`(Ψ)

Require: Set of predicates Ψ
Ensure: All minterms
1: $t :=$ `new Tree`$(\top, \texttt{null}, \texttt{null})$
2: **for all** $\psi \in \Psi$ **do**
3: $\quad t.\texttt{Refine}(\psi)$
4: **end for**
5: **return** `Leaves`(t)
6:
7: **class Tree**
8: `Predicate` ϕ; `Tree` $left$; `Tree` $right$
9: `Refine`$(\psi) =$
10: **if** $(\texttt{isSat}(\phi \wedge \psi) \wedge \texttt{isSat}(\phi \wedge \neg\psi))$ **then**
11: $\quad$ **if** $(left = \texttt{null})$ **then**
12: $\quad\quad left :=$ `new Tree`$(\phi \wedge \psi, \texttt{null}, \texttt{null})$
13: $\quad\quad right :=$ `new Tree`$(\phi \wedge \neg\psi, \texttt{null}, \texttt{null})$
14: $\quad$ **else**
15: $\quad\quad left.\texttt{Refine}(\psi)$; $right.\texttt{Refine}(\psi)$
16: $\quad$ **end if**
17: **end if**

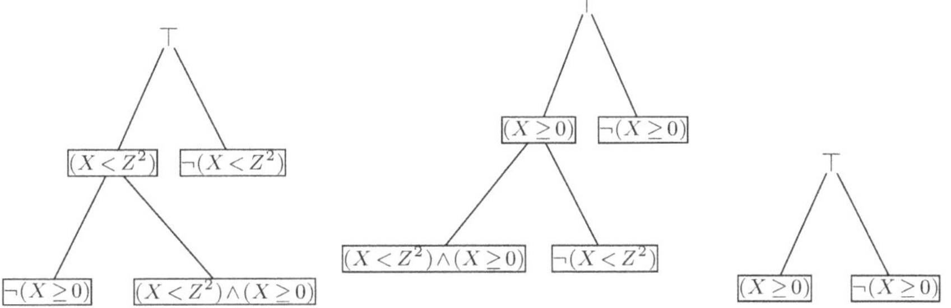

Fig. 3. `Minterms`$(\Psi_{A_{M_0}})$. **Fig. 4.** `Minterms`$(\Psi_{A_{M_0}})$. **Fig. 5.** `Minterms`$(\Psi'_{A_{M_0}})$.

Thus, the minterms returned by `Minterms`$(\Psi_{A_{M_0}})$ (resp., `Minterms`$(\Psi'_{A_{M_0}})$) are the leaves: $\neg(X \geq 0)$, $(X < Z^2) \wedge (X \geq 0)$, and $\neg(X < Z^2)$ (resp., $(X \geq 0)$ and $\neg(X \geq 0)$). Note that $[\![X < 0]\!] \subset [\![X < Z^2]\!]$, so $(X < Z^2) \wedge \neg(X \geq 0) \equiv \neg(X \geq 0)$; and $[\![X \geq Z^2]\!] \subset [\![X \geq 0]\!]$, so $\neg(X < Z^2) \wedge (X \geq 0) \equiv \neg(X < Z^2)$. Both sets of minterms represent a partition of the domain $\mathcal{D}_{A_{M_0}} = \mathbb{Z} \times \mathbb{Z}$. The same minterms will be returned by `Minterms`$(\Psi_{A_{M_0}})$ in the case when the predicate $(X < 0)$ is selected first in the loop in line 2.

Let T_Ψ be the tree built during the minterm generation from a set Ψ. Given $\psi \in \Psi$, let T_ψ be the subtree of T_Ψ having ψ as root (when ψ is the first selected predicate in the forall loop of Algorithm 1). The following properties hold [6,32]:

(1) Let `Leaves`$(T_\psi) = \{\phi_1, \ldots, \phi_k\}$, then $\psi \equiv (\phi_1 \vee \ldots \vee \phi_k)$.
(2) For all $\psi_1, \psi_2 \in \Psi$, $\psi_1 \wedge \psi_2$ is satisfiable iff `Leaves`$(T_{\psi_1}) \cap$ `Leaves`$(T_{\psi_2}) \neq \emptyset$.

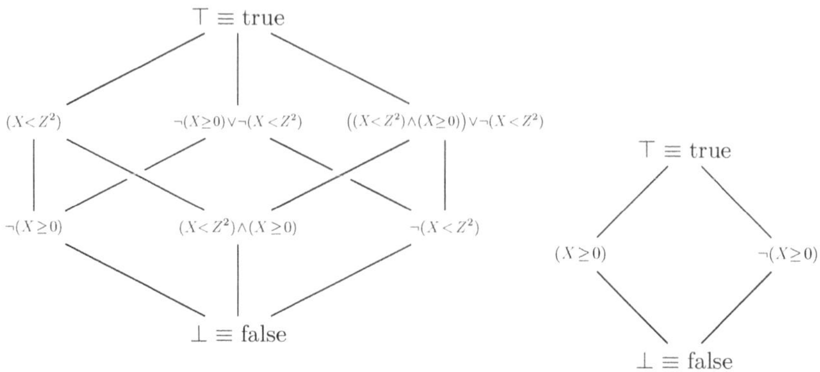

Fig. 6. $(\mathcal{B}(\texttt{Minterms}(\Psi_{A_{M_0}})), \models)$.

Fig. 7. $(\mathcal{B}(\texttt{Minterms}(\Psi'_{A_{M_0}})), \models)$.

(3) For all $\psi_1, \psi_2 \in \Psi$, $\psi_1 \implies \psi_2$ is valid with ψ_1 satisfiable iff $\texttt{Leaves}(T_{\psi_1}) \subseteq \texttt{Leaves}(T_{\psi_2})$.

Given a predicate $\psi \in \Psi$, the property (1) means that ψ can be written as a disjunction of minterms from $\texttt{Minterms}(\Psi)$. The semantics of minterms is a partition of the domain $\mathcal{D}$.

Proposition 4 ([6,32]). *$\{[\![\phi]\!] \mid \phi \in \texttt{Minterms}(\Psi)\}$ is a partition of $\mathcal{D}$.*

The *complete Boolean lattice* induced by the set Ψ is: $(\mathcal{B}(\texttt{Minterms}(\Psi)), \models, \vee, \wedge, \text{false}, \text{true})$, where $\mathcal{B}(\texttt{Minterms}(\Psi))$ are elements of the lattice in which $\texttt{Minterms}(\Psi)$ are atoms (the least elements covering $\bot$) [22]. The ordering relation $\models$ is defined as the satisfaction relation from predicate logic, the join is $\vee$, the meet is $\wedge$, the least element is $\bot = \text{false}$, and the greatest element is $\top = \text{true}$.

Example 2. Reconsider the predicate sets $\Psi_{A_{M_0}} = \{X < Z^2, X \geq 0\}$ and $\Psi'_{A_{M_0}} = \{X \geq 0\}$ from the running example in Section 2. The Hasse diagrams for the complete latices $(\mathcal{B}(\texttt{Minterms}(\Psi_{A_{M_0}})), \models)$ and $(\mathcal{B}(\texttt{Minterms}(\Psi'_{A_{M_0}})), \models)$ are shown in Figs. 6 and 7, respectively.

Alternatively, we could work with the set-theoretic definition of predicates and consider an isomorphic complete lattice: $(\mathcal{P}(\{[\![\phi]\!] \mid \phi \in \texttt{Minterms}(\Psi)\}), \subseteq, \cup, \cap, \bot, \top)$, where $\mathcal{P}(S)$ is the powerset of S. The ordering is $\subseteq$, the join is $\cup$, the meet is $\cap$, the least element is $\bot = [\![\text{false}]\!] = \emptyset$, and the greatest element is $\top = [\![\text{true}]\!] = \mathcal{D}$.

Galois Connections. Sometimes the computational task on a *concrete* complete lattice (domain) may be too costly or even uncomputable and this motivates replacing it with a simpler *abstract* lattice. A *Galois connection* is a pair of total functions, $\alpha : C \to A$ and $\gamma : A \to C$, known as the *abstraction* and *concretization* functions, connecting two complete lattices, $\langle C, \leqslant_C \rangle$ and $\langle A, \leqslant_A \rangle$, (often called the *concrete* and *abstract* domain, respectively), such that:

$$\alpha(c) \leqslant_A a \iff c \leqslant_C \gamma(a) \text{ for all } c \in C, a \in A$$

written $\langle C, \leqslant_C \rangle \xrightleftharpoons[\alpha]{\gamma} \langle A, \leqslant_A \rangle$. Note that $\leqslant_C$ and $\leqslant_A$ are the pre-order relations for C and A, respectively.

Given two partitions Π_1 and Π_2 of the domain $\mathcal{D}$, we say that Π_1 is a *refinement* of Π_2, denoted $\Pi_1 \sqsubseteq \Pi_2$, if for every partitioning $\pi_1 \in \Pi_1$, there exists a unique partitioning $\pi_2 \in \Pi_2$, such that $\pi_1 \subseteq \pi_2$. Let Ψ_C and Ψ_A be sets of predicates such that the partition of $\mathcal{D}$ induced by $\texttt{Minterms}(\Psi_C)$ is a refinement of the partition of $\mathcal{D}$ induced by $\texttt{Minterms}(\Psi_A)$, i.e. we have that $\Psi_C \sqsubseteq \Psi_A$. We now define a *Galois connection* between complete Boolean lattices $(\mathcal{B}(\texttt{Minterms}(\Psi_C)), \models)$ and $(\mathcal{B}(\texttt{Minterms}(\Psi_A)), \models)$. First, we define extraction function $\beta : \texttt{Minterms}(\Psi_C) \to \texttt{Minterms}(\Psi_A)$ as:

$$\beta(\phi) = \phi' \text{ if } \phi \models \phi', \text{ for } \phi \in \texttt{Minterms}(\Psi_C), \phi' \in \texttt{Minterms}(\Psi_A)$$

Note that by definition of $\Psi_C \sqsubseteq \Psi_A$, for each $\phi \in \texttt{Minterms}(\Psi_C)$ (let π_1 be the corresponding partitioning of $\mathcal{D}$), there exists an unique $\phi' \in \texttt{Minterms}(\Psi_A)$ (let π_2 be the corresponding partitioning of $\mathcal{D}$) such that $\phi \models \phi'$ (i.e., $\pi_1 \subseteq \pi_2$). Thus, β is a total function. We define $\beta^{-1}(\phi') = \cup\{\phi \mid \phi \models \phi'\}$. Any predicate $\varphi \in \mathcal{B}(\texttt{Minterms}(\Psi))$ can be written as a disjunction of minterms by definition. Let $\mu(\varphi)$ be the set of such minterms. The abstraction and concretization functions between $\mathcal{B}(\texttt{Minterms}(\Psi_C))$ and $\mathcal{B}(\texttt{Minterms}(\Psi_A))$ are defined as follows:

$$\alpha(\varphi) = \vee_{\phi \in \mu(\varphi)} \beta(\phi), \quad \gamma(\varphi') = \vee_{\beta(\phi) \in \mu(\varphi')} \phi$$

Theorem 1. *$\langle \mathcal{B}(\texttt{Minterms}(\Psi_C)), \models \rangle \xrightleftharpoons[\alpha]{\gamma} \langle \mathcal{B}(\texttt{Minterms}(\Psi_A)), \models \rangle$ is a Galois connection.*

Proof. Let $\varphi \in \mathcal{B}(\texttt{Minterms}(\Psi_C))$ and $\varphi' \in \mathcal{B}(\texttt{Minterms}(\Psi_A))$.

$$\begin{aligned}
&\alpha(\varphi) \models \varphi' \\
&\iff \vee_{\phi \in \mu(\varphi)} \beta(\phi) \models \varphi' && \text{(by def. of } \alpha) \\
&\iff \vee_{\phi \in \mu(\varphi)} \beta(\phi) \models \vee_{\phi' \in \mu(\varphi')} \phi' && \text{(by def. of } \mu) \\
&\iff \vee_{\phi \in \mu(\varphi)} \phi \models \vee_{\phi' \in \mu(\varphi')} \beta^{-1}(\phi') && \text{(by def. of } \beta) \\
&\iff \vee_{\phi \in \mu(\varphi)} \phi \models \vee_{\beta(\phi) \in \mu(\varphi')} \phi && \text{(by def. of } \models) \\
&\iff \varphi \models \gamma(\varphi') && \text{(by def. of } \gamma)
\end{aligned}$$

We write $\texttt{literals}(\Psi)$ to denote the set of all predicates in Ψ and their negations. Let ψ be a predicate from the set $\texttt{literals}(\Psi_C)$. It can be represented as disjunction of minterms from $\texttt{Leaves}(T_\psi)$, so $\psi \in \mathcal{B}(\texttt{Minterms}(\Psi_C))$. Thus, we can use the abstraction function α to translate any $\psi \in \texttt{literals}(\Psi_C)$ to a predicate that is a disjunction of minterms from $\texttt{Minterms}(\Psi_A)$.

Abstracting SFA.

Definition 1. *A symbolic finite automaton (SFA) $\mathcal{A}_{[\![\Gamma \vdash M:T]\!]}$ represents a tuple $(\Psi_C, Q, q_0, F, \Delta)$, where Ψ_C is the set of predicates occurring in guards of the term M, Q is a finite set of states, $q_0 \in Q$ is the initial state, $F \subseteq Q$ is the set of final states, and $\Delta \subseteq Q \times \mathcal{A}^{gu}_{[\![\Gamma \vdash T]\!]} \times Q$ is a finite set of transitions.*

A transition $(p, [b(\psi), \delta\rangle, q) \in \Delta$, where $b(\psi)$ means that b is a Boolean symbolic expression containing a predicate $\psi \in \texttt{literals}(\Psi_C)$ as sub-expression, means that there is a transition from state p to q labelled by $[b(\psi), \delta\rangle \in \mathcal{A}^{gu}_{[\![\Gamma \vdash T]\!]}$.

By approximating the predicates in $\texttt{literals}(\Psi_C)$, we want to approximate the given SFA by building different automaton that recognizes an over-approximation of the original recognized language. Given a Galois connection $\langle \mathcal{B}(\texttt{Minterms}(\Psi_C)), \models\rangle \overset{\gamma}{\underset{\alpha}{\leftrightarrows}} \langle \mathcal{B}(\texttt{Minterms}(\Psi_A)), \models\rangle$, let $\alpha(A^{gu}_{[\![\Gamma \vdash T]\!]})$ be the abstract guarded alphabet, where for each $[b(\psi), \delta\rangle \in A^{gu}_{[\![\Gamma \vdash T]\!]}$, $[b(\alpha(\psi)), \delta\rangle \in \alpha(A^{gu}_{[\![\Gamma \vdash T]\!]})$.

Definition 2. *Given the SFA $\mathcal{A}_{[\![\Gamma \vdash M:T]\!]} = (\Psi_C, Q, q_0, F, \Delta)$ and the Galois connection $\langle \mathcal{B}(\texttt{Minterms}(\Psi_C)), \models\rangle \overset{\gamma}{\underset{\alpha}{\leftrightarrows}} \langle \mathcal{B}(\texttt{Minterms}(\Psi_A)), \models\rangle$, we define the abstract SFA (ASFA) $\alpha(\mathcal{A}_{[\![\Gamma \vdash M:T]\!]}) = (\Psi_A, Q, q_0, F, \Delta^\alpha)$, where $\Delta^\alpha \subseteq Q \times \alpha(\mathcal{A}^{gu}_{[\![\Gamma \vdash T]\!]}) \times Q$ is defined: $\Delta^\alpha = \{(p, [b(\alpha(\psi)), \delta\rangle, q) \mid (p, [b(\psi), \delta\rangle, q) \in \Delta\}$.*

Example 3. Consider the SFA A_{M_0} shown in Fig. 1, where $k = 0$ and $\Psi_C = \{X < Z^2, X \geq 0\}$. Assume that $\Psi_A = \{X \geq 0\}$. By definition of α, we have $\alpha(X < Z^2) = \beta(\neg(X \geq 0)) \vee \beta((X < Z^2) \wedge (X \geq 0)) = \neg(X \geq 0) \vee (X \geq 0) = \text{true}$, whereas $\alpha(\neg(X < Z^2)) = \beta(\neg(X < Z^2)) = (X \geq 0)$. We also have $\alpha(X \geq 0) = \beta((X < Z^2) \wedge (X \geq 0)) \vee \beta(\neg(X < Z^2)) = (X \geq 0)$, whereas $\alpha(\neg(X \geq 0)) = \beta(\neg(X \geq 0)) = \neg(X \geq 0)$. The ASFA $\alpha(A_{M_0})$ is shown in Fig. 2.

Soundness. We now show that the safety of the ASFA implies the safety of the corresponding SFA. We prove that if we abstract the underlying set of predicates of an SFA, then we over-approximate the recognized language of concrete plays (words) in the sense of abstract interpretation.

Theorem 2. *$\texttt{concretize}(\mathcal{A}_{[\![\Gamma \vdash M:T]\!]}) \subseteq \texttt{concretize}(\alpha(\mathcal{A}_{[\![\Gamma \vdash M:T]\!]}))$.*

Proof. The abstraction α does not influence the topological structure of the SFA $\mathcal{A}_{[\![\Gamma \vdash M:T]\!]}$, but only simplifies the conditional parts of its transition labels. Thus, for any $[b, w\rangle \in \mathcal{A}_{[\![\Gamma \vdash M:T]\!]}$, we have $[\alpha(b), w\rangle \in \alpha(\mathcal{A}_{[\![\Gamma \vdash M:T]\!]})$. We want to show that any concrete play $\rho([\![b, w\rangle\!\rangle)$, which is derived from the symbolic play $[b, w\rangle$ and evaluation $\rho \in Eval$, can be also derived from the corresponding abstract symbolic play $[\alpha(b), w\rangle$.

Let $\rho([\![b, w\rangle\!\rangle) \in \texttt{concretize}(\mathcal{A}_{[\![\Gamma \vdash M:T]\!]})$, such that $[b, w\rangle \in \mathcal{A}_{[\![\Gamma \vdash M:T]\!]}$, $\rho \in Eval$, and $\rho(b) = \text{true}$. The play condition b is of the form $b_1(\psi_1) \wedge \ldots \wedge b_n(\psi_n)$, where $\psi_1, \ldots, \psi_n \in \texttt{literals}(\Psi_C)$. Since $\rho(b) = \text{true}$, it follows that $\rho(b_i(\psi_i)) = \text{true}$ for all $i = 1, \ldots, n$. Since $\Psi_C \sqsubseteq \Psi_A$, we have that $\psi_i \models \alpha(\psi_i)$ (by definition of α and the fact that $\beta(\phi) = \phi'$ when $\phi \models \phi'$ for minterms ϕ, ϕ'). Therefore, we have that $\rho(b_i(\alpha(\psi_i))) = \text{true}$ for all $i = 1, \ldots, n$, and so $\rho(\alpha(b)) = \text{true}$. Therefore, $\rho([\![\alpha(b), w\rangle\!\rangle) \in \texttt{concretize}(\alpha(\mathcal{A}_{[\![\Gamma \vdash M:T]\!]}))$.

By using Theorem 2, we can prove the following soundness result.

Theorem 3. *If $\alpha(\mathcal{A}_{[\![\Gamma \vdash M:T]\!]})$ is safe then $\mathcal{A}_{[\![\Gamma \vdash M:T]\!]}$ is also safe.*

Proof. We proceed by contraposition. Assume that $\mathcal{A}_{[\![\Gamma \vdash M:T]\!]}$ is not safe. There exists an unsafe concrete play $\rho([\![b, w\rangle\!\rangle) \in \texttt{concretize}(\mathcal{A}_{[\![\Gamma \vdash M:T]\!]})$, such that $[b, w\rangle \in \mathcal{A}_{[\![\Gamma \vdash M:T]\!]}$, $\rho \in Eval$, and $\rho(b) = \text{true}$. By Theorem 2, we have that $\rho([\![b, w\rangle\!\rangle) \in \texttt{concretize}(\alpha(\mathcal{A}_{[\![\Gamma \vdash M:T]\!]}))$. So it follows $\alpha(\mathcal{A}_{[\![\Gamma \vdash M:T]\!]})$ is not safe.

If a counter-example (unsafe symbolic play) is found in the ASFA $\alpha(\mathcal{A}_{[\![\Gamma \vdash M:T]\!]})$, then any concrete play inferred from it may be either spurious (introduced due to the abstraction) or genuine (i.e., it also belongs to $\texttt{concretize}(\mathcal{A}_{[\![\Gamma \vdash M:T]\!]})$). This can be established by simulating the concrete play through the SFA $\mathcal{A}_{[\![\Gamma \vdash M:T]\!]}$.

Example 4. The ASFA $\alpha(A_{M_0})$ in Fig. 2 is safe, since any unsafe play in it contains the unsatisfiable condition $(X \geq 0 \wedge X < 0)$. By the soundness result, it follows that the SFA A_{M_0} in Fig. 1 and the term M_0 are safe as well.

On the other hand, the ASFA $\alpha(A_{M_2})$ described in Section 2 is not safe. Still, from the found unsafe symbolic play in $\alpha(A_{M_2})$ we can construct a concrete play that belongs to $\texttt{concretize}(\mathcal{A}_{M_2})$. We conclude that A_{M_2} and M_2 are not safe.

5 Evaluation

We have extended the `Symbolic GameChecker` tool [7,8] to develop a proof-of-concept implementation of our abstraction-based approach for verifying safety of open terms with various constraints. `Symbolic GameChecker` converts any IA_2 term into a SFA representing its game semantics. To verify its safety, the tool performs bounded exploration of the SFA for feasible unsafe traces (plays). The numeric bound d is placed on the number of iterations of the while-loop and on the number of times an undefined function can call its arguments. The tool uses the breadth-first search (BFS) algorithm to visit all states in the SFA that are reachable from the initial state and check whether one of visited states in the SFA is unsafe (i.e., it has an outgoing transition labelled with run^{abort}). Finally, when an unsafe play within the given bound d is detected, the external Z3 SMT solver is called to check the consistency (i.e., satisfiability modulo the background theories) of its play condition. The extended tool applies a given abstraction on the SFA, and verifies the safety of the obtained ASFA. We now illustrate the tool with an example.

Linear search. Consider the linear search algorithm `Linear`:

$$
\begin{array}{l}
x[k] : \mathsf{varint}^{\langle x[-]\rangle},\ y : \mathsf{expint}^{\langle y\rangle},\ \mathsf{abort} : \mathsf{com}^{\langle abort\rangle} \vdash \\
\qquad \mathsf{new_{int}}\ i := 0\ \mathsf{in}\ \mathsf{new_{int}}\ p := !y\ \mathsf{in} \\
\qquad \mathsf{while}\ (!i < k)\ \mathsf{do}\ \{ \\
\qquad\quad \mathsf{new_{int}}\ z := !x[!i]\ \mathsf{in} \\
\qquad\quad \mathsf{if}\ (!p \geq 0)\ \mathsf{then\ assert}\ (!z < 2^{!p}); \\
\qquad\qquad\qquad \mathsf{else\ assert}\ (!z \leq !p^2 - !p + 1\ \mathsf{or}\ !z \geq -2); \\
\qquad\quad i := i + 1; \}\ : \mathsf{com}
\end{array}
$$

where the meta variable $k > 0$ represents the size of array x. In the above term, the input expression y is first copied into the local variable p. Then the non local

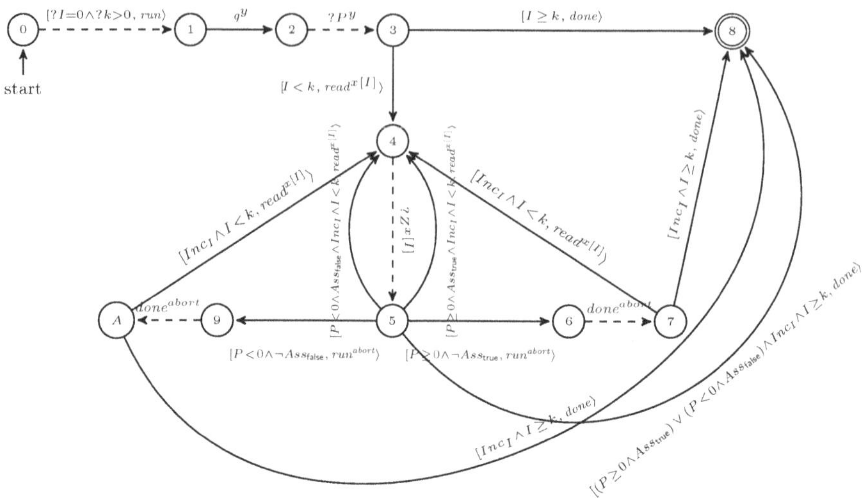

Fig. 8. The game model for the `Linear` term. For readability reasons we use predicates: $Ass_{\mathsf{true}} \equiv (Z < 2^P)$, $Ass_{\mathsf{false}} \equiv (Z \leq P^2 - P + 1 \vee Z \geq -2)$, $Inc_I \equiv (?I = I + 1)$.

array x is examined linearly to check all its elements against two assertions: if the value stored in p is positive, we check whether the array element stored in z is less than 2^p; otherwise we check whether the array element stored in z is less or equal to $(p^2 - p+1)$ or it is greater or equal to -2. If one of the above facts is not true, the assertion will fail and the `abort` command will be executed.

The SFA $\mathcal{A}_{\mathtt{Linear}}$ (suitably adapted for readability) for the term `Linear` is given in Fig. 8. The array $x[k]$ is given a symbolic representation [7], where the array size k and the index of the array elements represent symbols. The symbol I is used to track the current values of local variable i and to represent the index of an array element. The value read from the environment $\mathbf{O}$ for some undefined array element $X[I]$, where $0 \leq I < k$, is represented by symbol Z, and the value read from the environment $\mathbf{O}$ for undefined expression y is represented by symbol P. The `then` assertion is valid when $(P \geq 0) \wedge (Z < 2^P)$, while the `else` assertion is valid when $(P < 0) \wedge (Z \leq P^2 - P + 1 \vee Z \geq -2)$. Otherwise, the corresponding assertion fails and an unsafe behaviour can be found. To successfully analyze `Linear`, we need to have a bounded exploration with the bound d.

However, the SFA $\mathcal{A}_{\mathtt{Linear}}$ contains complex (polynomial and exponential) symbolic constraints, $\Psi_C = \{Z < 2^P, Z \leq P^2 - P + 1, Z \geq -2, P \geq 0\}$, so that their satisfiability cannot be determined by an SMT solver. Therefore, we cannot automatically verify the SFA $\mathcal{A}_{\mathtt{Linear}}$ for safety. To enable the automatic verification of the `Linear` term, we use the following set of abstract predicates $\Psi_A = \{Z \geq 0, P \geq 0\}$. By calculating $\mathtt{Minterms}(\Psi_C)$ and $\mathtt{Minterms}(\Psi_A)$, and by defining the extraction function $\beta : \mathtt{Minterms}(\Psi_C) \rightarrow$

Bench.	d	Abs+SFA			SFA		
		Max-Model	Fin-Model	Time	Max-Model	Fin-Model	Time
$\mathtt{M}_0$	4	23	8	0.214	23	8	0.288
$\mathtt{M}_0$	8	23	8	0.253	23	8	0.361
$\mathtt{M}_2$	4	23	8	0.183	23	8	0.205
Linear	4	29	10	0.280	29	10	infeasible
$\mathtt{Linear}_{tt}$	4	25	8	0.220	25	8	infeasible
$\mathtt{Linear}_{ff}$	4	25	8	0.274	25	8	0.308
$\mathtt{Linear}_{ff}$	8	25	8	0.321	25	8	0.377

Table 3. Performance results of Abs+SFA vs. SFA. Times are in seconds.

$\mathtt{Minterms}(\Psi_A)$, we generate the abstraction and concretization functions α and γ, such that $\langle\mathcal{B}(\mathtt{Minterms}(\Psi_C)),\models\rangle \underset{\alpha}{\overset{\gamma}{\leftrightarrows}} \langle\mathcal{B}(\mathtt{Minterms}(\Psi_A)),\models\rangle$. In particular, we obtain $\alpha(Z < 2^P) = \text{true}$, $\alpha(Z \geq 2^P) = (Z \geq 0)$, $\alpha(Z \leq P^2 - P + 1) = \text{true}$, $\alpha(Z > P^2 - P + 1) = (Z \geq 0)$, $\alpha(Z \geq -2) = \text{true}$, $\alpha(Z < -2) = \neg(Z \geq 0)$, $\alpha(P \geq 0) = P \geq 0$, $\alpha(P < 0) = \neg(P \geq 0)$. The ASFA $\alpha(\mathcal{A}_{\mathtt{Linear}})$ is obtained by replacing all predicates $\psi \in \mathtt{literals}(\Psi_C)$ that occur in transitions of $\mathcal{A}_{\mathtt{Linear}}$ with the corresponding abstract predicate $\alpha(\psi)$.

We first analyze the then assertion $(!z < 2^{!p})$. We obtain a feasible unsafe play where $x[0]$ (symbol Z) is ≥ 0. The shortest unsafe (instantiated) play is:

$$[I_0 = 0 \wedge k > 0, run\rangle \cdot q^{\langle y\rangle} \cdot P_0^{\langle y\rangle} \cdot [I_0 < k, read^{\langle x[I]\rangle}\rangle \cdot Z_0^{\langle x[I]\rangle} \cdot \\ [P_0 \geq 0 \wedge Z_0 \geq 0, run^{\langle abort\rangle}\rangle \cdot done^{\langle abort\rangle} \cdot [I_1 = I_0 + 1 \wedge I_1 \geq k, done\rangle$$

The following concrete play can be constructed from the above symbolic play (by replacing symbols P_0 and Z_0 with concrete integers): $run \cdot q^{\langle y\rangle} \cdot 0^{\langle y\rangle} \cdot read^{\langle x[0]\rangle} \cdot 1^{\langle x[0]\rangle} \cdot run^{\langle abort\rangle} \cdot done^{\langle abort\rangle} \cdot done$. By simulating the above concrete play through the SFA $\mathcal{A}_{\mathtt{Linear}}$, we can see that it belongs to $\mathtt{concretize}(\mathcal{A}_{\mathtt{Linear}})$. Thus, it represents a genuine counter-example corresponding to the execution where the values read from y and $x[0]$ are 0 and 1, thus making assertion $(!z < 2^{!p})$ to fail.

We now analyze the else assertion $(!z < !p^2 - !p + 1 \vee !z \geq -2)$. The shortest unsafe (instantiated) play reported by the tool is:

$$[I_0 = 0 \wedge k > 0, run\rangle \cdot q^{\langle y\rangle} \cdot P_0^{\langle y\rangle} \cdot [I_0 < k, read^{\langle x[I]\rangle}\rangle \cdot Z_0^{\langle x[I]\rangle} \cdot \\ [P_0 < 0 \wedge Z_0 \geq 0 \wedge \neg(Z_0 \geq 0), run^{\langle abort\rangle}\rangle \cdot done^{\langle abort\rangle} \cdot [I_1 = I_0 + 1 \wedge I_1 \geq k, done\rangle$$

All other unsafe plays related with the violation of the else assertion also contain the unsatisfiable constraint $(Z_0 \geq 0) \wedge \neg(Z_0 \geq 0)$, so they are all inconsistent. Therefore, this assertion is valid in $\alpha(\mathcal{A}_{\mathtt{Linear}})$, and so we can conclude that it is valid in the SFA $\mathcal{A}_{\mathtt{Linear}}$ and the term Linear.

Performance results. All experiments are run on a 64-bit Intel®Core^{TM} i7-1165G7 CPU@2.80GHz, VM Ubuntu 18.04 LTS, with 8 GB memory. All times are reported as average over five independent executions. For the aim of evaluation, we ran: (1) the extended `Symbolic GameChecker` based on ASFAs, denoted Abs+SFA; and (2) the basic `Symbolic GameChecker` based on SFAs, denoted SFA. We analyze the motivating example M_k from Section 2 and the linear search term `Linear`. Two additional versions of the `Linear` term are also considered, namely $\texttt{Linear}_{tt}$ where only the then assertion is present and the else assertion is replaced with skip, as well as $\texttt{Linear}_{ff}$ where only the else assertion is present and the then assertion is replaced with skip. For both approaches, we report the exploration bound d, the size of the biggest game model generated `Max-Model`, the size of the final game model `Fin-Model`, and the total time to analyze a term `Time`. The safe terms, M_0 and $\texttt{Linear}_{ff}$, are analyzed with two exploration bounds $d = 4$ and $d = 8$. For the safe terms, M_0 and $\texttt{Linear}_{ff}$, the tools first generate d infeasible unsafe plays before they are reported as safe. So, we analyze them with two exploration bounds $d = 4$ and $d = 8$, while all other terms are analyzed with the default exploration bound $d = 4$.

Table 3 shows the performance results of analyzing our examples. While the Abs+SFA approach successfully analyzes all examples, the SFA approach cannot handle terms that contain exponential non-linear constraints since they are not supported by the SMT solvers. The Abs+SFA approach also outperforms SFA for all other terms, and the achieved speed-up grows with the number of checked polynomial non-linear constraints during the verification task. For safe terms M_0 and $\texttt{Linear}_{ff}$, we need to check the satisfiability of d constraints (including polynomial ones) before they are reported as safe. Thus, Abs+SFA achieves bigger runtime speed-ups compared to SFA for these two examples. To conclude, the experiments demonstrate that our abstraction-based approach Abs+SFA outperforms SFA for all examples, and moreover also turns some previously infeasible tasks into feasible.

6 Conclusion

In this work, we have explored the techniques to weaken the SFAs representing game models by abstract interpretation. This way, we can generate approximated SFAs parametric on the chosen set of abstracted predicates. Provided the abstraction is sound, the approximated SFAs represent over-approximations of the behaviours of the original open program, so they can be used for efficient verification of the safety properties of open programs. We demonstrate the effectiveness of this approach by verifying several interesting open programs.

The game model considered here contains only convergent behaviours of terms, which makes it suitable for analyzing safety properties. If we want to take into account liveness properties, such as termination, then the game model should be enriched to contain divergent behaviors as well [30]. For such game models, we can also employ abstractions to enable efficient verification. In the future, we would also like to explore the possibilities of applying symbolic game models in program synthesis [10,11,15].

References

1. Abramsky, S., McCusker, G.: Linearity, sharing and state: a fully abstract game semantics for idealized algol with active expressions. Electr. Notes Theor. Comput. Sci. **3**, 2–14 (1996). https://doi.org/10.1016/S1571-0661(05)80398-6
2. Baier, C., Katoen, J.: Principles of model checking. MIT Press (2008)
3. Clarke, E.M., Grumberg, O., Long, D.E.: Model checking and abstraction. ACM Trans. Program. Lang. Syst. **16**(5), 1512–1542 (1994). https://doi.org/10.1145/186025.186051, http://doi.acm.org/10.1145/186025.186051
4. Cousot, P., Cousot, R.: Abstract interpretation: A unified lattice model for static analysis of programs by construction or approximation of fixpoints. In: Conf. Record of the Fourth ACM Symposium on POPL. pp. 238–252. ACM (1977). https://doi.org/10.1145/512950.512973, http://doi.acm.org/10.1145/512950.512973
5. Dams, D., Gerth, R., Grumberg, O.: Abstract interpretation of reactive systems. ACM Trans. Program. Lang. Syst. **19**(2), 253–291 (1997). https://doi.org/10.1145/244795.244800, http://doi.acm.org/10.1145/244795.244800
6. D'Antoni, L., Veanes, M.: Minimization of symbolic automata. In: The 41st Annual ACM SIGPLAN-SIGACT Symposium on Principles of Programming Languages, POPL '14. pp. 541–554. ACM (2014). https://doi.org/10.1145/2535838.2535849, https://doi.org/10.1145/2535838.2535849
7. Dimovski, A.S.: Program verification using symbolic game semantics. Theor. Comput. Sci. **560**, 364–379 (2014). https://doi.org/10.1016/j.tcs.2014.01.016
8. Dimovski, A.S.: Verifying annotated program families using symbolic game semantics. Theor. Comput. Sci. **706**, 35–53 (2018). https://doi.org/10.1016/j.tcs.2017.09.029
9. Dimovski, A.S.: Fault localization by abstract interpretation and its applications. J. Comput. Lang. **80**, 101288 (2024). https://doi.org/10.1016/J.COLA.2024.101288, https://doi.org/10.1016/j.cola.2024.101288
10. Dimovski, A.S.: Imperative program synthesis by abstract static analysis and SMT mutations. In: Proceedings of the 24th ACM SIGPLAN International Conference on Generative Programming: Concepts and Experiences, GPCE 2025. pp. 27–40. ACM (2025). https://doi.org/10.1145/3742876.3742884, https://doi.org/10.1145/3742876.3742884
11. Dimovski, A.S.: On synthesizing presence conditions in numerical software product lines. In: Proceedings of the 29th ACM International Systems and Software Product Line Conference - Volume A, SPLC 2025. pp. 161–171. ACM (2025). https://doi.org/10.1145/3744915.3748474, https://doi.org/10.1145/3744915.3748474
12. Dimovski, A.S.: Weakest safe context synthesis by symbolic game semantics and logical abduction. In: Proceedings of the 40th ACM/SIGAPP Symposium on Applied Computing, SAC 2025. pp. 1990–1997. ACM (2025). https://doi.org/10.1145/3672608.3707849, https://doi.org/10.1145/3672608.3707849
13. Dimovski, A.S., Apel, S.: Lifted static analysis of dynamic program families by abstract interpretation. In: 35th European Conference on Object-Oriented Programming, ECOOP 2021. LIPIcs, vol. 194, pp. 14:1–14:28. Schloss Dagstuhl - Leibniz-Zentrum für Informatik (2021). https://doi.org/10.4230/LIPIcs.ECOOP.2021.14, https://doi.org/10.4230/LIPIcs.ECOOP.2021.14
14. Dimovski, A.S., Apel, S., Legay, A.: A decision tree lifted domain for analyzing program families with numerical features. In: Fundamental Approaches to Software Engineering - 24th International Conference, FASE 2021, Proceedings. LNCS, vol. 12649, pp. 67–86. Springer (2021), https://arxiv.org/abs/2012.05863

15. Dimovski, A.S., Apel, S., Legay, A.: Program sketching using lifted analysis for numerical program families. In: NASA Formal Methods - 13th International Symposium, NFM 2021, Proceedings. LNCS, vol. 12673, pp. 95–112. Springer (2021). https://doi.org/10.1007/978-3-030-76384-8_7, https://doi.org/10.1007/978-3-030-76384-8_7
16. Dimovski, A.S., Brabrand, C., Wasowski, A.: Finding suitable variability abstractions for family-based analysis. In: FM 2016: Formal Methods - 21st International Symposium, Proceedings. LNCS, vol. 9995, pp. 217–234. Springer (2016). https://doi.org/10.1007/978-3-319-48989-6_14, https://doi.org/10.1007/978-3-319-48989-6_14
17. Dimovski, A.S., Ghica, D.R., Lazic, R.: A counterexample-guided refinement tool for open procedural programs. In: Model Checking Software, 13th International SPIN Workshop, 2006, Proceedings. LNCS, vol. 3925, pp. 288–292. Springer (2006). https://doi.org/10.1007/11691617_17, https://doi.org/10.1007/11691617_17
18. Dimovski, A.S., Lazic, R.: Compositional software verification based on game semantics and process algebra. Int. J. Softw. Tools Technol. Transf. **9**(1), 37–51 (2007). https://doi.org/10.1007/S10009-006-0005-Y, https://doi.org/10.1007/s10009-006-0005-y
19. Ghica, D.R., McCusker, G.: The regular-language semantics of second-order idealized algol. Theor. Comput. Sci. **309**(1-3), 469–502 (2003). https://doi.org/10.1016/S0304-3975(03)00315-3
20. Ghica, D.R., Murawski, A.S.: Compositional model extraction for higher-order concurrent programs. In: 12th International Conference TACAS 2006. LNCS, vol. 3920, pp. 303–317. Springer (2006). https://doi.org/10.1007/11691372_20, http://dx.doi.org/10.1007/11691372_20
21. Ghica, D.R., Tzevelekos, N.: A system-level game semantics. In: Proceedings of the 28th Conference on the Mathematical Foundations of Programming Semantics, MFPS 2012. Electronic Notes in Theoretical Computer Science, vol. 286, pp. 191–211. Elsevier (2012). https://doi.org/10.1016/j.entcs.2012.08.013, https://doi.org/10.1016/j.entcs.2012.08.013
22. Giacobazzi, R., Ranzato, F., Scozzari, F.: Making abstract interpretations complete. J. ACM **47**(2), 361–416 (2000). https://doi.org/10.1145/333979.333989, https://doi.org/10.1145/333979.333989
23. Graf, S., Saïdi, H.: Construction of abstract state graphs with PVS. In: Computer Aided Verification, 9th International Conference, CAV '97, Proceedings. LNCS, vol. 1254, pp. 72–83. Springer (1997). https://doi.org/10.1007/3-540-63166-6_10, https://doi.org/10.1007/3-540-63166-6_10
24. Kiefer, S., Murawski, A.S., Ouaknine, J., Wachter, B., Worrell, J.: Algorithmic probabilistic game semantics - playing games with automata. Formal Methods in System Design **43**(2), 285–312 (2013). https://doi.org/10.1007/s10703-012-0173-1
25. Koutavas, V., Lin, Y., Tzevelekos, N.: From bounded checking to verification of equivalence via symbolic up-to techniques. In: 28th International Conference, TACAS 2022. LNCS, vol. 13244, pp. 178–195. Springer (2022). https://doi.org/10.1007/978-3-030-99527-0_10, https://doi.org/10.1007/978-3-030-99527-0_10
26. Laird, J.: A fully abstract trace semantics for general references. In: Automata, Languages and Programming, 34th International Colloquium, ICALP 2007, Proceedings. LNCS, vol. 4596, pp. 667–679. Springer (2007). https://doi.org/10.1007/978-3-540-73420-8_58, https://doi.org/10.1007/978-3-540-73420-8_58
27. Lin, Y., Tzevelekos, N.: Symbolic execution game semantics. In: 5th International Conference on FSCD 2020. LIPIcs, vol. 167, pp. 27:1–27:24. Schloss Dagstuhl -

Leibniz-Zentrum für Informatik (2020). https://doi.org/10.4230/LIPIcs.FSCD.2020.27, https://doi.org/10.4230/LIPIcs.FSCD.2020.27
28. Loiseaux, C., Graf, S., Sifakis, J., Bouajjani, A., Bensalem, S.: Property preserving abstractions for the verification of concurrent systems. Formal Methods in System Design **6**(1), 11–44 (1995). https://doi.org/10.1007/BF01384313, http://dx.doi.org/10.1007/BF01384313
29. Miné, A.: Tutorial on static inference of numeric invariants by abstract interpretation. Foundations and Trends in Programming Languages **4**(3-4), 120–372 (2017). https://doi.org/10.1561/2500000034, https://doi.org/10.1561/2500000034
30. Murawski, A.S.: Reachability games and game semantics: Comparing nondeterministic programs. In: Proceedings of the Twenty-Third Annual IEEE Symposium on Logic in Computer Science, LICS 2008. pp. 353–363. IEEE Computer Society (2008). https://doi.org/10.1109/LICS.2008.24, http://dx.doi.org/10.1109/LICS.2008.24
31. Murawski, A.S., Walukiewicz, I.: Third-order idealized algol with iteration is decidable. In: 8th International Conference, FOSSACS 2005. LNCS, vol. 3441, pp. 202–218. Springer (2005). https://doi.org/10.1007/978-3-540-31982-5_13, http://dx.doi.org/10.1007/978-3-540-31982-5_13
32. Preda, M.D., Giacobazzi, R., Lakhotia, A., Mastroeni, I.: Abstract symbolic automata: Mixed syntactic/semantic similarity analysis of executables. In: Proceedings of the 42nd Annual ACM SIGPLAN-SIGACT Symposium POPL 2015. pp. 329–341. ACM (2015). https://doi.org/10.1145/2676726.2676986, https://doi.org/10.1145/2676726.2676986

Timed Contract Automata*

Bernhard Beckert, Andreas Bremer(✉), and Alexander Weigl

Institute for Information Security and Dependability
Karlsruhe Institute of Technology
{beckert,bremer,weigl}@kit.edu

Abstract. Real-time systems are ubiquitous today and are often employed in safety-critical environments. Therefore, formally specifying and verifying the correctness of real-time systems is crucial. We introduce *Timed Contract Automata* to specify the functional and timing behavior of systems that are strong enough to formalize common real-time requirements. Timed Contract Automata model possible situations using modes and specify the expected inputs, outputs, and the timing of their arrival with formulae. Timed Contract Automata combine Contract Automata, which specify the allowed stimuli and system responses using assume-guarantee contracts, with the clocks of Timed Automata to specify the expected real-time behavior. We define the syntax and the game-based semantics of Timed Contract Automata. To validate system conformance, we have implemented a method for automatic runtime monitor generation. We demonstrate the feasibility and expressive power of Timed Contract Automata and validate the generated runtime monitor through multiple implemented case studies. From these case studies, we derive specification patterns for common real-time requirements.

Keywords: Program Verification, Real-time, Formal Contracts, Runtime Verification, Timed Automata

1 Introduction

Real-time systems are ubiquitous today and control safety- and mission-critical processes, e.g., in the automotive, aviation, and medical domains. Malfunctions or failures of these systems can have severe consequences, including financial losses or even loss of life. The correct reaction of real-time systems is crucial, but the correctness does not only depend on producing the valid output for the current input stimuli, but also on the correct timing [16]. For the verification of real-time systems we need to formally specify their required real-time properties. Static analysis of real-time systems is possible if the timing can be statically modeled. Runtime verification is an approach of validating the compliance with formal properties in real time by using a runtime monitor that checks the behavior of the system during its execution against the specification. This allows

* This work was supported by KiKIT—the Helmholtz pilot program for core informatics research at the KIT and by the DFG - project number 508985913.

E. Albert and C. Pasareanu (Eds.): FASE 2026, LNCS 16504, pp. 392–411, 2026.
https://doi.org/10.1007/978-3-032-22774-4_20

the detection of errors that cannot be discovered through static analysis, as the real-time behavior may depend on environmental factors or system internal processes. The monitor can report errors resulting from incorrect assumptions about the system's environment behavior (e.g., hardware malfunction).

We build on Contract Automata [18], which are automata over the alphabet of contracts, where a contract formally specifies assumptions about the stimuli from the environment and guarantees about the response from the system.

Contribution. We introduce *Timed Contract Automata* (TCA), an extension of Contract Automata [18] for real-time systems, to enable comprehensive specification of real-time properties. We define the syntax of TCAs as automata to provide an intuitive approach to system specification. Additionally, TCAs make use of the well established concept of clocks to specify real-time properties. We formally define the semantics of TCAs using a two-party game between the system and its environment (Sect. 2). We use runtime verification to check system compliance based on observed inputs, outputs, and timing. To facilitate runtime verification, we define and implement a general automatic transformation of TCAs into a runtime monitor for offline and online monitoring (Sect. 3). We show how real-time requirements of systems with event-based and sample-based [15] operation can be formalized as TCAs. The specification with TCAs allows differentiating between assumptions about the behavior of the environment and requirements for the running system. We present case studies to evaluate the feasibility and expressive power of TCAs and to validate the usability of the implementation (Sect. 4). We present real-time specification patterns for common real-time properties collected from the case studies.

2 Foundations of TCAs

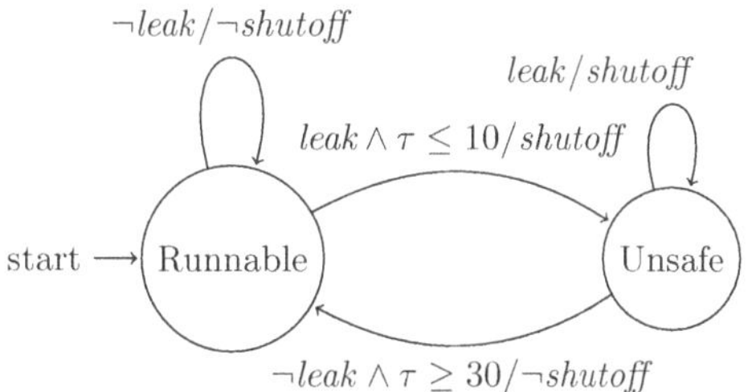

Fig. 1: Event based automaton GB_1 for the gas burner example. Contracts are written "*assume/guarantee*".

Introductory Example. We extend the gas burner example from [4], considering an emergency shutoff if a sensor observes a leak, where unignited gas flows out of the burner's nozzle. To ensure safe operation, gas leakage should not last more than 10 ms. The operation resumes after 30 ms to allow the gas to dissipate. Fig. 1 shows a specification with two modes. The system operates by repeatedly reading inputs, performing computations and updating the internal state, and setting outputs. We refer to each execution of this sequence as one system iteration. In each system iteration, some time elapses, and the transition with a satisfied contract is used. A contract "*assume/guarantee*" consists of two formulae, assumption and guarantee, divided by "/". The environment is responsible for satisfying the assumption and the system is responsible for satisfying the guarantee.

The input variable *leak* of the system denotes the information given by the sensor and is used in the assumption to select the corresponding transition, whereas the output variable *shutoff* controls the actuator for shutting down the safety valve to prevent gas flow. We specify the timing constraints for each mode using the variable τ, which represents the elapsed time of the current system iteration. This TCA is written for an event-based operation in which the system iteration is triggered on events (compare to samples-based operation [15]): This specification assumes that an input is only received when an event occurs, which happens when a leak of at least 10 ms or a non-leaking phase of at least 30 ms starts. Implementing this requires filtering stuttering steps to ignore sampled inputs that do not designate an event. We revisit this example after defining how to measure time across multiple transitions to create a specification that can handle sampled inputs at any time points.

2.1 Time and Variables

TCAs have a set of *modes* and have *transitions* between these modes. Each transition has a *contract*, that consists of an *assume*-formula and a *guarantee*-formula, and can be taken if both formulae are satisfied. During each system iteration, some amount of time elapses. This duration of elapsed time is partitioned into an environment time and a system time, which add up to the total amount of time elapsed during the system iteration. The environment time is the time that has elapsed until the inputs were made available to the system. The system time is the time used by the system to compute its output after receiving the inputs. This separation for example allows specifying that the system must react promptly to any given inputs, regardless of the time taken before the inputs were available, or constraining the amount of time the environment may take to generate inputs to establish that meeting some deadline is out of the scope of the required system behavior when the inputs were given too late. We use *clocks* to reference the elapsed time. Each clock can be reset upon taking a transition, and represents the duration of elapsed time since its last reset. To allow measuring the elapsed environment time and system time separately, we differentiate between environment clocks and system clocks. All clocks run synchronously, meaning the same amount of environment or system time elapses in each iteration for every environment or system clock, respectively; They only differ in their last reset point. Initially, all clocks are reset, and represent the time since the start of the run of the automaton.

Definition 1 (Contract Signature). *A contract signature basis is a tuple $\Sigma_B = (I, O, X^e, X^s)$, with the finite sets of input variables I, output variables O, environment clocks X^e and system clocks X^s. From Σ_B we derive the contract signature Σ, the set of all variables that can occur in a contract, as $\Sigma = I \cup O \cup X^e \cup X^s$*

We write X for the set of all clocks $X = X^e \cup X^s$. To reset clocks, every transition contains a set $X_R \subseteq X$ of clocks that are reset to 0 when taking that transition. In the gas burner example, we used τ to express the elapsed time duration of the current system iteration. This is specifiable with a clock that is reset on every transition. For the remaining, we assume that every TCA has clocks $\tau^e \in X^e$ and $\tau^s \in X^s$ that are reset on every transition, and do not explicitly write their clock resets. Therefore, the variable τ^e always denotes the last iteration's environment time and τ^s its system time. Requirements are commonly expressed in terms of the total elapsed time since some previous event, which can be specified by adding the respective elapsed environment and system time. For readability, we write the name of a clock x in a contract formula to refer to the total duration of elapsed time $x = x^e + x^s$ for $x^e \in X^e$ and $x^s \in X^s$ that are always reset simultaneously, $x^e \in X_R$ iff $x^s \in X_R$. In Fig. 1 the name τ therefore represents a combined clock that refers to $\tau^e + \tau^s$. For such clocks, we write the name x once in a reset set to specify that both clocks x^e and x^s are reset.

2.2 Syntax

Let $Term_\Sigma$ be the set of terms, Fml_Σ the set of formulae and $C_\Sigma = {Fml_\Sigma}^2$ the set of contracts over the variables in Σ. A contract consists of an *assume*-formula and a *guarantee*-formula, that can each use *all* variables in Σ – inputs, outputs and clocks. This allows environment and system clocks, such as τ^e and τ^s, to be used in both the assumption and guarantee of a contract. This is not just done for consistency, but also for expressive power. It allows formalizing requirements for the system based on the time usage of the environment, and vice versa, which is essential to be able to specify certain real-time properties in a reactive system. For example, we can specify that the system may never use more time than the environment took to provide its inputs, or that the available time for the system to compute its result depends on how much time was left after the inputs were set. To enable referring to the previous values of variables, we define the function *old* such that *old*$(v, -n)$ for a variable $v \in \Sigma$ and $n \in \mathbb{N}$ denotes the value that v held n iterations ago.

Definition 2 (Timed Contract Automaton (TCA)). *A TCA* $A = (\Sigma_B, M, M_0, \delta)$ *consists of*

1. $\Sigma_B = (I, O, X^e, X^s)$ *the contract signature basis, consisting of the input and output variables and environment and system clocks,*
2. M *the nonempty finite set of modes,*
3. $M_0 \subseteq M$ *the nonempty set of starting modes,*
4. $\delta \subseteq M \times C_\Sigma \times M \times 2^X$ *the finite transition relation. A transition* $e \in \delta$ *with* $e = (m, c, m', X_R)$ *goes from mode* m *to* m' *with contract* c*, resetting all clocks* $x \in X_R$ *of the reset set* $X_R \subseteq X$*.*

2.3 Semantics: Evaluation of Formulae

Since on every system iteration, each variable should denote a value, we define one input and output of the monitored system to assign a value to each input and output variable respectively. $\mathcal{I}$ is the set of input values where an input $i \in \mathcal{I}$ assigns a value of the respective domain to each of the input variables in I. Analogously, $\mathcal{O}$ is the set of output values for the output variables in O.

Let $\mathcal{T} = \mathbb{R}_{\geq 0}$ be the set of values for the clocks in X. The value of a clock represents the length of the time interval starting at the clock's last reset point, i.e. a time duration. Representing time durations as real numbers is common practice for real-time systems [9, 4, 7]. $(\mathbb{R}_{\geq 0}, +, 0)$ also fulfills the requirement of being a totally ordered monoid. We use this to define the empty time duration 0 as the value of a clock after a reset and addition to compute the passing of time. We compute the new value of a clock by increasing its old value by the current system iteration's time duration, like $x^s = \mathit{old}(x^s, -1) + \tau^s$. The associativity of addition is required to ensure the elapsed time $\tau = \tau^e + \tau^s$ during a system iteration can be partitioned into adding τ^e followed by τ^s, with $(x + \tau^e) + \tau^s = x + \tau$.

We model the behavior of a system S as successive invocations of a function $\mathcal{S}$, that represents the system's computation. This models the fact that the runtime monitor treats the running system as a black box, and only receives information about the inputs and outputs of the system, as well as the time used by the environment and the system.

Definition 3. *The function $\mathcal{S} : \mathcal{I} \times \mathcal{T} \to \mathcal{O} \times \mathcal{T}$ for a given system S with input values $\mathcal{I}$ and output values $\mathcal{O}$ models the computation done by S in the current system iteration.*

$$\mathcal{S}(i, \tau^e) = (o, \tau^s)$$

calculates the output $o \in \mathcal{O}$ of S in its current state and provides the system time τ^s used for this calculation, based on the input $i \in \mathcal{I}$ and environment time τ^e, and updates the internal state of S accordingly.

The behavior $\mathcal{B}(\mathcal{S}) \subset (\mathcal{I} \times \mathcal{T} \times \mathcal{O} \times \mathcal{T})^*$ of the system S is the set of finite timed input-output traces (TIO-traces), which are defined as sequences of tuples containing input and output of $\mathcal{S}$:

$$\mathcal{B}(\mathcal{S}) = \left\{ \langle (i_0, \tau_0^e, o_0, \tau_0^s), ..., (i_n, \tau_n^e, o_n, \tau_n^s) \rangle \mid (o_k, \tau_k^s) = \mathcal{S}(i_k, \tau_k^e) \text{ for } 0 \leq k \leq n \right\}$$

When evaluating a formula $f \in \mathit{Fml}_\Sigma$, the values of its input and output variables $\mathit{var} \in I \cup O$ are obtained from the given TIO-trace. The values of clocks depend on the taken transitions and their corresponding clock resets, which are not present in the TIO-trace, but instead depend on the TCA. We use *clock valuations* (CVs) to define the values of clocks, where $\mathcal{V} = \{\nu : X \to \mathcal{T}\}$ is the set of CVs. A CV $\nu \in \mathcal{V}$ assigns a time $\nu(x)$ to every clock $x \in X$. A clock x can occur inside $\mathit{old}(x, -k)$ expressions, which requires keeping a trace of previous CVs. This CV-trace must also satisfy the condition that in each iteration the same amount of time elapsed for each environment or system clock, namely τ^e and τ^s respectively.

Definition 4. *A CV-trace $\bar{\nu}$ is a sequence $\bar{\nu} \in \mathcal{V}^*$ with $\bar{\nu} = \langle \nu_1, ..., \nu_n \rangle$ for some length $n > 0$ where for every clock $x \in X$*

$$\nu_1(x) = \nu_1(\tau^i)$$

and for every $j \in \{2, ..., n\}$

$$\nu_j(x) = \underbrace{\nu_j(\tau^i)}_{(reset)} \vee \underbrace{\nu_j(x) = \nu_{j-1}(x) + \nu_j(\tau^i)}_{(not\ reset)}$$

holds, with $\tau^i = \tau^e$ if $x \in X^e$ and $\tau^i = \tau^s$ if $x \in X^s$.

The clocks' elapsed time for each iteration according to the CV-trace must be equal to the elapsed time according to the TIO-trace. We then call the CV-trace *compatible* to the TIO-trace.

Definition 5. *A CV-trace $\bar{\nu} = \langle \nu_1, ..., \nu_n \rangle \in \mathcal{V}^*$ is compatible to a TIO-trace $\bar{\sigma} = \langle (i_1, \tau_1^e, o_1, \tau_1^s), ..., (i_n, \tau_n^e, o_n, \tau_n^s) \rangle \in \mathcal{B}(\mathcal{S})$ of the same length n if for all $j \in \{1, ..., n\}$ the condition $\nu_j(\tau^e) = \tau_j^e \wedge \nu_j(\tau^s) = \tau_j^s$ holds.*

We write $\bar{\sigma}, \bar{\nu} \models f$ to denote that the formula $f \in Fml_\Sigma$ is satisfied by the finite TIO-trace $\bar{\sigma} = \langle \sigma_1, ..., \sigma_n \rangle \in \mathcal{B}(\mathcal{S})$ with the compatible CV-trace $\bar{\nu} = \langle \nu_1, ..., \nu_n \rangle \in \mathcal{V}^n$. The value of a variable $var \in I \cup O$ is taken from the last element $\sigma_n = (i_n, \tau_n^e, o_n, \tau_n^s)$ of the trace $\bar{\sigma}$, where i_n and o_n provide the values of the input and output variables respectively. The value of a clock $x \in X$ is given by $\nu_n(x)$. The previous variable values $old(var, -k)$ for all variables $var \in \Sigma$ are obtained analogously from ν_{n-k} and σ_{n-k} or defaulted to 0 if $n \leq k$.

2.4 Semantics: Compliance of Systems

The compliance of a real-time system S to a TCA A is defined via a two-party game between the environment and the system, depicted in Algorithm 1, where each loop iteration corresponds to one system iteration of S. In each iteration, the environment Env provides an input $i \in \mathcal{I}$ nondeterministically from the possible input values using time τ^e, which must satisfy the assumption of some outgoing transition in any of the currently possible modes. The system then computes its output $o \in \mathcal{O}$ using time τ^s, which must satisfy the guarantee of at least one of the transitions with a satisfied assumption. If the environment fails to provide an input that would satisfy any checked assumption, the environment loses. If the output computed by the system does not satisfy any checked guarantee, the system loses.

The variable k represents the current iteration number and $\bar{\sigma}$ tracks the TIO-trace of the play up to the current iteration. We separate the TIO-trace, which stores observed inputs, outputs and timing of S, from the CV-traces, which store possible clock values given A. While $\bar{\sigma}$ is equal for all possible modes, the CV-traces might differ, depending on which transitions where taken and what clocks these reset. We store a set of possible *traced modes* $\hat{N} \subseteq (M \times \mathcal{V}^*)$, each

Algorithm 1 Algorithmic representation of the round-based game between the system S and its environment Env for a given TCA $A = (\Sigma_B, M, M_0, \delta)$.

Input: System S, Environment Env, TCA $A = (\Sigma_B, M, M_0, \delta)$
Output: Returns the winner (System / Environment)
1: $\bar{\sigma} \leftarrow \langle\rangle$
2: $\hat{N} \leftarrow \{(m, \langle\nu_0\rangle) \mid m \in M_0 \ \wedge \ \nu_0 = \{x \longmapsto 0 \ \text{ for all } x \in X\}\}$
3: $k \leftarrow 0$
4: **while** true **do**
5: $\quad (i, \tau^e) \leftarrow Env()$
6: $\quad (o, \tau^s) \leftarrow \mathcal{S}(i, \tau^e)$
7: $\quad \bar{\sigma} \leftarrow \bar{\sigma} \cdot (i, \tau^e, o, \tau^s)$
8: $\quad \hat{N} \leftarrow \{(m, \bar{\nu}') \mid (m, \bar{\nu}) \in \hat{N} \wedge \bar{\nu}' = advance(\bar{\nu}, \tau^e, \tau^s)\}$
9: $\quad \hat{E} \leftarrow \Big\{((m, c, m', X_R), \bar{\nu}') \mid (m, c, m', X_R) \in \delta \ \wedge (m, \bar{\nu}') \in \hat{N} \ \wedge \ \bar{\sigma}, \bar{\nu}' \models assume(c)\Big\}$
10: $\quad$ **if** $\hat{E} = \emptyset$ **then return** System wins
11: $\quad \hat{N} \leftarrow \Big\{(m', \bar{\nu}'') \mid ((m, c, m', X_R), \bar{\nu}') \in \hat{E} \ \wedge \bar{\sigma}, \bar{\nu}' \models guarantee(c) \ \wedge \ \bar{\nu}'' = reset(\bar{\nu}', X_R)\Big\}$
12: $\quad$ **if** $\hat{N} = \emptyset$ **then return** Environment wins
13: $\quad k \leftarrow k + 1$

consisting of a mode $m \in M$ and the CV-trace $\bar{\nu} \in \mathcal{V}^*$ that resulted in reaching m. There might be different CV-traces that result in reaching the same mode, and each is represented as a distinct traced mode. The TCA's nondeterminism is modeled by keeping track of the set of traced modes, and checking all outgoing transitions for each traced mode. Initially, $\hat{N}$ contains the initial modes M_0 and all clocks are reset. In each iteration, all clocks are first advanced by the current τ^e or τ^s (Algorithm 1, line 8), before evaluating the respective mode's contracts. $\hat{E}$ is the set of transitions with satisfied assumption and their corresponding CV-trace (line 9). $\hat{N}$ is updated to the next set of possible traced modes (line 11), by taking the transitions of $\hat{E}$ with satisfied guarantee and appending the initial CVs for the next iteration. The next iteration's initial CVs are obtained by applying the used transition's clock resets. Since clocks are only reset after the contract formulae are evaluated, the last iteration's system and environment time are included in the clocks' measurements. This ensures that clocks may be used on transitions with a corresponding reset instead of evaluating to zero. This also enables clocks to refer to the current iteration's time duration. The updates of the CV-traces are defined by the functions *advance* and *reset*.

Definition 6. *$advance(\bar{\nu}, \tau^e, \tau^s)$ increments the last CV ν_k of the CV-trace $\bar{\nu} = \langle\nu_1, ..., \nu_k\rangle$ for all environment and system clocks by τ^e and τ^s respectively:*

$$advance(\langle\nu_1, ..., \nu_{k-1}, \nu_k\rangle, \tau^e, \tau^s) = \langle\nu_1, ..., \nu_{k-1}, \nu_A\rangle$$

$$\text{for } \nu_A(x) = \nu_k(x) + \begin{cases} \tau^e & \text{if } x \in X^e \\ \tau^s & \text{if } x \in X^s \end{cases}$$

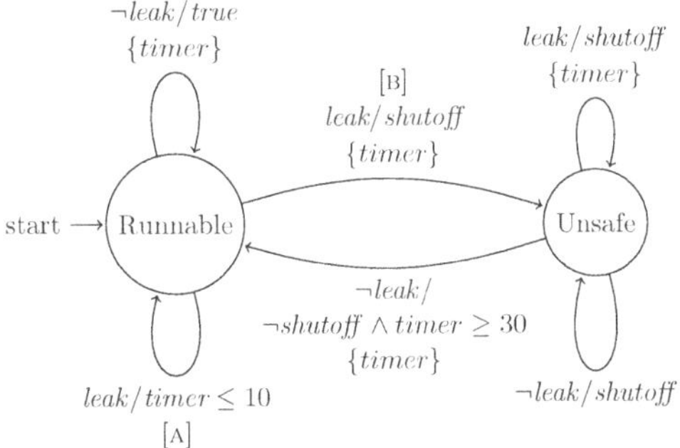

Fig. 2: Gas Burner TCA GB_2 with clock

Definition 7. *$reset(\bar{\nu}, X_R)$ adds a new element to the CV-trace $\bar{\nu} = \langle \nu_1, ..., \nu_{k-1}, \nu_k \rangle$, where the last CV is reset for every clock $x \in X_R$ and keeps the last iteration's value for every clock $x \notin X_R$:*

$$reset(\langle \nu_1, ..., \nu_k \rangle, X_R) = \langle \nu_1, ..., \nu_k, \nu_R \rangle, \text{ for } \nu_R(x) = \begin{cases} 0 & \text{if } x \in X_R \\ \nu_k(x) & \text{if } x \notin X_R \end{cases}$$

Definition 8 (TCA Compliance). *A system S is compliant to a TCA A if no play of the game in Algorithm 1 for S with regard to $A = (\Sigma_B, M, M_0, \delta)$ terminates with* Environment wins.

Gas Burner Example. We extend the example automaton GB_1 introduced in Fig. 1 to illustrate the use of clocks and their resets. GB_1 requires the environment to start a new system iteration when an event occurs. This allows a simple specification that only refers to τ to express timing constraints. The automaton GB_2 given in Fig. 2 measures time across multiple transitions with the clock *timer*, using the introduced shorthand for combining $timer^e$ and $timer^s$. If no leak of over 10 ms occurs, the system may continue running (mode *Runnable*). Otherwise, the transition to the *Unsafe* mode is taken and the system must send the *shutoff* signal until no leak was detected for 30 ms. In the event-based TCA the environment is responsible for sending events at the correct time. In this sampling-based TCA the system is responsible for meeting the real-time requirements. While GB_1 requires filtering out stuttering steps from the traces, GB_2 correctly handles updates from a sampling-based system, with sensor inputs that do not designate an event. Additional constraints could be placed on τ^e or τ^s to specify a sampling rate or upper bound on the reaction time.

Consider an example iteration, where a leak is detected, but the elapsed time does not exceed 10 ms, e.g. $\tau^e = 5$, $\tau^s = 3$. In this case a compliant system may continue to run until 10 ms elapsed (A) or already send the shutoff signal (B), specified in GB_2 using nondeterministic choice of the taken transition. In Algorithm 1, at the beginning of the loop iteration (line 4), *Runnable* is active and *timer* is reset: $\hat{N} = \{(Runnable, \bar{\nu})\}$ with $\bar{\nu}_k(timer^e) = \bar{\nu}_k(timer^s) = 0$. The environment provides input i with $leak = true$ after $\tau^e = 5$ (line 5). Assume the system responds with *shutoff* = *true* after $\tau^s = 3$ (line 6). The TIO-trace $\bar{\sigma}$ is updated (line 7) and the clocks advanced (line 8): $\hat{N} = \{(Runnable, \bar{\nu}')\}$ with $\bar{\nu}'_k(timer^e) = 5$, $\bar{\nu}'_k(timer^s) = 3\}$. $\hat{E}$ contains the transitions from *Runnable* with satisfied assumption, A and B (line 9): $\hat{E} = \{(\text{A}, \bar{\nu}'), (\text{B}, \bar{\nu}')\}$. $\hat{N}$ is updated (line 11), contains both modes, as both transitions' guarantees are satisfied, and resets the clocks on B: $\hat{N} = \{(Runnable, \bar{\nu}^{\text{A}}), (Unsafe, \bar{\nu}^{\text{B}})\}$, where $\bar{\nu}^{\text{A}}_{k+1} = \bar{\nu}'_k$ and $\bar{\nu}^{\text{B}}_{k+1}(timer^e) = \bar{\nu}^{\text{B}}_{k+1}(timer^s) = 0$.

3 Towards Runtime Verification

Token automata. To implement runtime monitoring, we introduce an intermediate structure, the token automaton, that models the nondeterminism of the TCA using tokens and replaces the algorithm's set constructions by a function to update the tokens. The token automaton simulates the runtime monitor during its execution, tracks possible active modes as tokens, and determines the outcome of the play. A token automaton has *places* and *transitions* between those, similar to a Petri net [14]. A marking assigns a set of tokens to each place, and tokens are transferred via transitions. Every mode in the modeled TCA has a corresponding place in the token automaton. Each token carries a CV-trace and represents one possible traced mode. A token t on place p states that during the simulated play of the game (algorithm 1), that $(m, \bar{\nu}) \in \hat{N}$ exists where place p corresponds to mode m, and the token's CV-trace reflects $\bar{\nu}$. Every transition has a guard formula that restricts when the transition can be taken based on the current TIO-trace and the token's CV-trace. Additionally, every transition has an assignment $\gamma \in \Gamma$, with $\Gamma \subset \{\gamma : X \to Term_\Sigma\}$, to provide the new value of each clock after taking the transition. The term $\gamma(x)$ is τ^i if the clock is reset and otherwise $x + \tau^i$, with $\tau^i = \tau^e$ if $x \in X^e$ and $\tau^i = \tau^s$ if $x \in X^s$. For a set of clocks $X_R \subseteq X$, $\gamma_{X_R} \in \Gamma$ resets a clock $x \in X$ if and only if $x \in X_R$.

Evaluating a contract formula requires a TIO-trace and a CV-trace. In the token automaton, the CV-trace is given by the token's carried trace; the current TIO-trace is stored as one trace $\bar{\sigma}$ separate from the individual tokens. To model the fact that in a TCA all satisfied transitions from a possible current mode can be taken, every token uses all outgoing transitions from its current place whose guard is satisfied. Neither transitions nor tokens have a capacity: All satisfied transitions are taken by duplicating the token. The result is a new marking of tokens to places within the token automaton with updated CV-traces. For a token to stay in its current place, a satisfied self-transition to its current place is required.

Definition 9. *A token automaton is a 4-tuple* $T = (\Sigma_B, P, \delta, P_0)$, *where*

- Σ_B *is a contract signature basis,*
- $P \neq \emptyset$ *is a finite set of places,*
- $\delta \subseteq P \times P \times Fml_\Sigma \times \Gamma$ *is a set of transitions, where a transition* $(p, p', g, \gamma) \in \delta$ *goes from place* p *to* p' *with guard* g *and uses the assignment* $\gamma \in \Gamma$ *to change the transferred token's CV-trace,*

– $P_0 \subseteq P$ *is the nonempty set of initially marked places.*

Please note that the token automaton does not operate on contracts anymore. Contracts are compiled down to the transition guard and assignment (Def. 10).

Let $\mathbb{V} = \mathcal{V}^*$ be the set of token values (identical to the set of CV-traces), then a marking $s\colon P \to 2^{\mathbb{V}}$ assigns a finite set of token values to each place. The set of all markings is $\mathbb{S} = \{s\colon P \to 2^{\mathbb{V}}\}$. Note, equal tokens at the same place are automatically collapsed into one token.

We say a token $\bar{\nu}$ is on place p if $\bar{\nu} \in s(p)$ given the current marking $s \in \mathbb{S}$. The initial marking $s_0 \in \mathbb{S}$ is given by

$$s_0(p) = \begin{cases} \{\langle \nu_0 \rangle\} & \text{if } p \in P_0, \text{ where } \nu_0 = \{x \longmapsto 0 \text{ for all } x \in X\} \\ \emptyset & \text{if } p \notin P_0, \end{cases}$$

for all $p \in P$. The initial marking s_0 places one token at each initial place with an *all-zero* clock valuation. On each system iteration, the marking is updated. The updated marking s' is computed based on the current marking s and the updated TIO-trace $\bar{\sigma}$, with the environment time τ^e and system time τ^s from the last element of $\bar{\sigma}$:

$$s'(p) = \{\bar{\nu} \cdot \nu_n \mid (q, p, g, \gamma) \in T \;\; \wedge \;\; \bar{\nu} \in s(q) \;\; \wedge \\ \bar{\sigma}, \mathit{advance}(\bar{\nu}, \tau^e, \tau^s) \models g \;\; \wedge \;\; \nu_n(x) = [\![\gamma(x)]\!]_{\bar{\sigma},\bar{\nu}}\}$$

for all $p \in P$. Here, variable $\bar{\nu}$ represents the previous clock valuations on place q, variable ν_n is the the new clock valuation and $[\![\gamma(x)]\!]_{\bar{\sigma},\bar{\nu}}$ denotes the time value obtained by evaluating the term $\gamma(x)$ using the variables from $\bar{\sigma}, \bar{\nu}$.

Construction. We provide a transformation to construct a token automaton $T(A)$ for any given TCA $A = (\Sigma_B, M, M_0, \delta)$.

Definition 10. *Given a TCA* $A = (\Sigma_B, M, M_0, \delta)$, *the corresponding token automaton* $T(A)$ *is*

$$T(A) = (\Sigma_B, \{p_m \mid m \in M\} \cup \{p_\top, p_\bot\}, \Delta, \{p_m \mid m \in M_0\}),$$

with

$$\Delta = \{(p_m, p_{m'}, \mathit{assume}(c) \wedge \mathit{guarantee}(c), \gamma_{X_R}) \mid e = (m, c, m', X_R) \in \delta\} \cup \\ \{(p_m, p_\bot, \mathit{assume}(c) \wedge \neg \mathit{guarantee}(c), \gamma_{X_R}) \mid e = (m, c, m', X_R) \in \delta\} \cup \\ \{(p_m, p_\top, \neg \mathit{assume}(c), \gamma_{X_R}) \mid e = (m, c, m', X_R) \in \delta\}$$

Every mode $m \in M$ has a corresponding place p_m in $T(A)$. Additionally, every transition $e = (m, c, m', X_R) \in \delta$ has a corresponding transition $\hat{e} = (p_m, p_{m'}, \mathit{assume}(c) \wedge \mathit{guarantee}(c), \gamma_{X_R}) \in \Delta$. To model the outcome of the play, two additional places $p_\top$ and $p_\bot$ are added, where $p_\top$ signals that the system wins the play and $p_\bot$ signals that the environment wins. If a token's trace satisfies the assumption, but not the guarantee, of a transition from the

TCA's corresponding mode, the token is transferred to $p_\bot$. Analogously, if it does not satisfy the assumption, it is transferred to $p_\top$.

If all contracts are violated during an update, only the places $p_\top$ and $p_\bot$ hold tokens. This signals that the play is terminated. The marking determines the outcome of the play: If any tokens are on $p_\bot$, the environment wins. If all tokens are on $p_\top$, the system wins (including the case where no tokens are on any place).

Theorem 1. *Given a TCA A, the token automaton $T(A)$ models the game faithfully for all plays; meaning given any play with TIO-trace $\bar{\sigma}$, the outcome of the game (Algorithm 1) and $T(A)$ are identical.*

The proof is done by induction, where each update of the marking s of the token automaton corresponds to one loop iteration in Algorithm 1, using the same TIO-trace $\bar{\sigma}$. We maintain the invariant that each token in s corresponds to one possible traced mode in the algorithm, evaluated in every iteration (line 4 in Algorithm 1):

$$(m, \bar{\nu}) \in \hat{N} \textbf{ iff } \bar{\nu} \in s(p_m)$$

Initially, the invariant is satisfied, as $\hat{N}$ contains the initial modes with a zero-initialized trace each, and s places equivalent tokens on the respective places. On each iteration one of the following cases occurs: If all traced modes have no outgoing transition, then in the algorithm $\hat{E} = \emptyset$ and the system wins. The updated marking s' contains no tokens, which represents the system winning, as there are no tokens on $p_\bot$. Otherwise, there is at least one outgoing transition for some traced mode, and contract formulae are evaluated. $\bar{\sigma}$ is equivalent by the induction hypothesis. The CV-traces are equivalent by design, using $advance(\bar{\nu}, \tau^e, \tau^s)$ with τ^e, τ^s from the last element of $\bar{\sigma}$. If no token satisfies any assume-formula, then s' places all tokens on $p_\top$, which represents the system winning. In the algorithm $\hat{E} = \emptyset$ and the system wins. If some token satisfies an assume-formula, but none satisfy a contract, then s' places at least one token on $p_\bot$, and no tokens on any p_m. This represents the environment winning. In the algorithm $\hat{E} \neq \emptyset = \hat{N}$ and the environment wins. If any token satisfies a contract, then (except for tokens on $p_\top$ and $p_\bot$ – which are removed on the next iteration) s' contains exactly the tokens that correspond to $\hat{N}$, because:

1. For every $\hat{n} \in \hat{N}$ and each taken transition the corresponding token satisfies the guard $assume(c) \wedge guarantee(c)$ on the transition to the corresponding place. γ_{X_R} is evaluated using the token's CV-trace and clocks are updated according to the corresponding transition's reset set.
2. No other tokens are on any mode m's corresponding place p_m.

Implementation. We provide a prototype implementation that generates a monitor in C++17 based on an interface description of the system and the TCAs given in a domain-specific language. [1] The resulting monitor accepts new input

[1] Implementation artifact https://doi.org/10.5281/zenodo.18175317

and output values with timings, updates the internal state (maintaining the tokens and TIO-trace), and determines the outcome of the play. It is able to receive updates and track information from a running system (online monitoring), or to analyze the TIO-trace constructed from an existing execution log (offline monitoring). Internally, the runtime monitor follows the token automaton, but also has additional optimizations: The length of the TIO-trace $\bar{\sigma}$ is limited by the maximal lookbehind access given syntactically in any $old(var, -n)$ (as n is fixed to be a literal). Since the maximal lookbehind distance differs per variable, the traces of each variable are stored separately, and irrelevant trace prefixes are discarded. Applying this also to CV-traces reduces the token's memory size and leads to more frequent deduplication of tokens. Each variable's trace is implemented as a ring buffer using a fixed-size array, avoiding any memory allocation and allowing accessing by index, appending, and discarding an element in constant time. The number of tokens on $p_\top$ and $p_\bot$ and their carried CV-trace do not affect the outcome a marking represents. Their representation is therefore optimized to a single `bool`, which states, whether there are any tokens on the corresponding place. The transitions also reuse formula evaluation results from identical formulae in other transitions.

On the first n iterations, evaluating an $old(var, -n)$ expression would access an invalid variable value. The monitor checks these accesses and allows using a default value (as defined in Sect. 2.3) or treating the assume- or guarantee-formula as violated by the environment or system, respectively. This is done lazily, supports short-circuiting conjunctions and disjunctions, and short-circuits guarantee-formula evaluation using its assumption.

Time is measured using `std::chrono::steady_clock` to obtain monotonically increasing time point values using an implementation-defined precision. Time points are fetched before and after each system update and subtracted to compute the elapsed time. Duration values are stored in a C++ built-in type, by default an integer type representing milliseconds. We decided against using a multi-precision rational number type, because of its runtime performance impact, and because precision of time measurements, depending on the operating system is limited enough, which in our case was unable to represent sub-nanosecond durations. The risk of overflow using a fixed-width integer type is low, as storing nanoseconds in a 64-bit integer allows representing an approximately 585-year duration.

4 Specification Patterns from Case Studies

We implemented case studies to evaluate the expressiveness of TCAs and to validate the implementation of the runtime monitor.

The first case study is a floodgate controller, based on a real-world case study presented in [13]. The controller receives sensor inputs to determine the water levels inside and outside of the floodgate, and reacts to changing sea levels by sending signals to operate the gate. The second case study is a system that controls a pump and alarm based on measured water and gas levels in a mine,

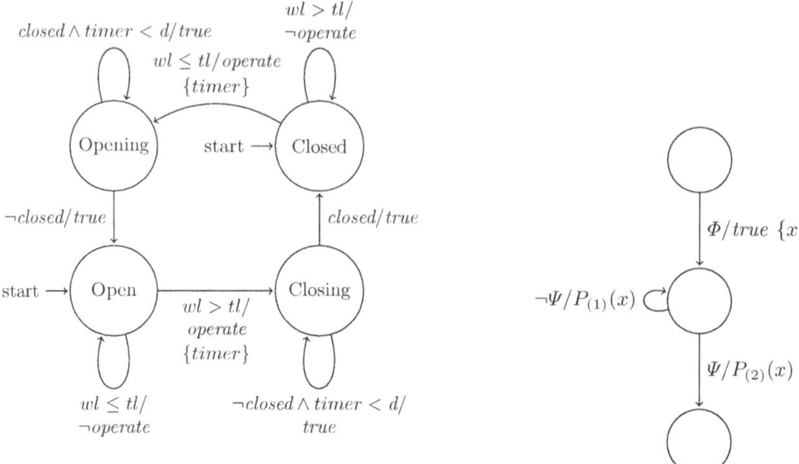

Fig. 3: The TCA specifies the floodgate control system based on water level wl and trigger level tl.

Fig. 4: The TCA specifies a time duration constraint for a process.

based on an example presented in [7]. The pump must be activated when a sufficient amount of water has accumulated in the mine's sump, but must be turned off when a gas leak is detected. If the measured gas or water levels pose a threat to the workers, the system activates an alarm to evacuate the mine. We illustrate the extraction of a specification pattern using a TCA for the floodgate control system, and present other specification patterns for different kinds of requirements extracted from the case studies.

Example: Sequential Control of the Floodgate. Fig. 3 shows a TCA specifying the operation stages of the floodgate. The floodgate control system operates the floodgates based on measured water levels, ensuring that the gates close to prevent flooding when the outside water level rises. The system continuously monitors the water levels on both sides of the gates. When the outside water level wl rises above the trigger level tl, the system must respond by sending the *operate* signal to initiate the closing of the floodgates. After this signal is sent, the gates should be closed within the duration d, measured by the clock *timer*. This specification only imposes an upper bound on the duration of the gate closing. A compliant environment can produce the *closed* signal already on the first iteration after the system issued the *operate* command. The system is responsible for sending the signal, and the environment is responsible for changing and detecting the state of the gate. This distinction between assume and guarantee enables differentiating between program errors and malfunctioning sensors or actuators. Note, when the monitoring begins, it is unclear whether the gates are closed or open. Therefore, the monitoring starts in both states.

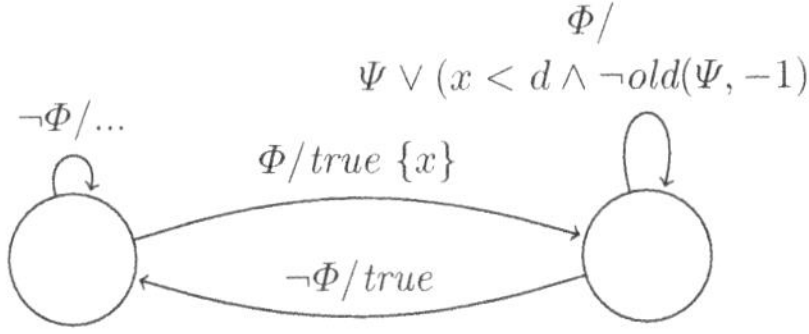

Fig. 5: The TCA specifies that the system reacts within duration d.

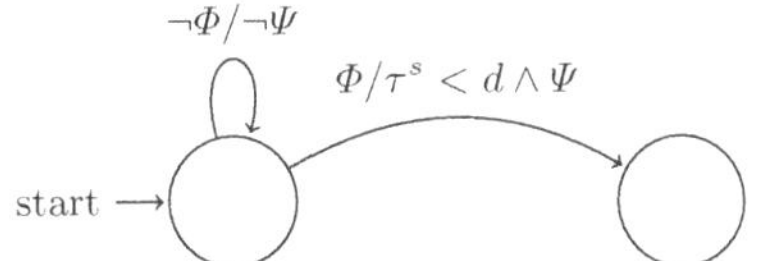

Fig. 6: The TCA specifies that the system reacts quickly to some condition Φ.

Duration Constraint on Operation Sequence. From the floodgate TCA, we extract the specification pattern in Fig. 4 for expressing a time bound for a process. The process is represented as a sequence of modes with one or more intermediate waiting modes. The sequence is initiated when the begin condition Φ (the water exceeds the trigger level) is met, and terminated by the end condition Ψ (the gate is closed). The time constraint condition $P(x)$ uses the clock x, and can be checked on intermediate transitions ($P_{(1)}$) and on the process terminating transition ($P_{(2)}$). A minimum duration constraint only uses $P_{(2)}$. A maximum duration constraint uses $P_{(1)}$, and optionally $P_{(2)}$. The floodgate does not specify $P_{(2)}$ at the transition to *Closed*, to allow terminating the closing process when the deadline is reached, if the environment provides the necessary input immediately. The previously introduced gas burner uses the same pattern for specifying minimum and maximum duration, and checks the maximum duration constraint in $P_{(1)}$ and $P_{(2)}$. This is the most common real-time specification pattern found in our case studies.

Delayed Reaction. Fig. 5 shows a pattern allowing some delay before reacting to a condition. The "..." formula can specify other requirements not essential to the pattern. When condition Φ is detected, the system should set the outputs to satisfy Ψ within duration d. A guarantee-formula Ψ would require the output to be set immediately when the condition Φ is true. Using $\Psi \vee x < d$ enforces the output to be set within duration d after Φ becomes true, but allows the value of the outputs to fluctuate freely within that duration, so we add $\neg old(\Psi, -1)$ to ensure that Ψ stays true once activated.

Immediate Reaction. Fig. 6 shows the specification of an immediate reaction to some condition Φ. When Φ is detected, the system must ensure the output satisfies Ψ in the same iteration and takes at most some duration d to compute the required output. We use this in the alarm specification to specify that when the system detects a dangerous condition, it activates the alarm without stalling.

Computation-Aware Timeout. Consider a system that should set outputs satisfying Ψ for duration d. When d has elapsed, Ψ should no longer hold. Assume the implementation checks the current time t_C once during its computation, and sets the output based on that time measurement. In a system iteration with

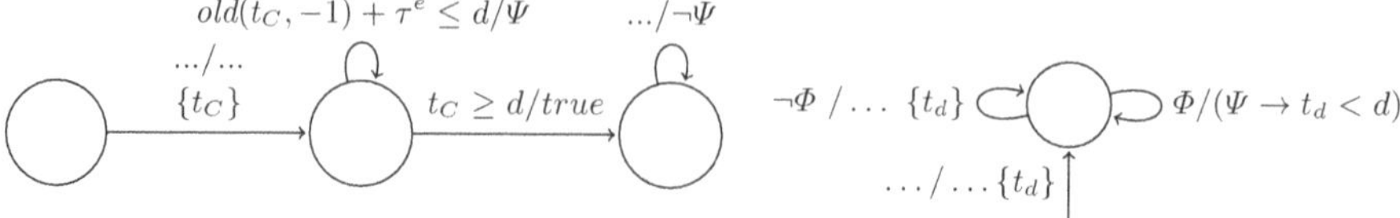

Fig. 7: The TCA permits the system to react to deadline d based on current time t_C measured during the system's computation.

Fig. 8: The TCA constrains the validity of Φ to the first d time units after Ψ became true.

$t_C - \tau^s < d < t_C$, the system may read the current time just before the deadline is reached. The system computes its outputs accordingly, but the deadline is exceeded during that computation. The system then violates $t_C > d \to \neg\Psi$ at the end of the system iteration. To permit such an implementation, we allow the system to set the respective output if the deadline was not exceeded at the start of its computation in the current iteration (Fig. 7). The system adheres to this specification regardless of when during its computation it measures t_C.

Condition-Gated Response Time. The next pattern (Fig. 8) specifies whether a condition Ψ holds depending on how long some other condition Φ was satisfied. In any interval in which Φ holds continuously, Ψ is only allowed to be valid for the first duration d of that interval. After the duration d has elapsed, Ψ must no longer hold, until $\neg\Phi$ resets the interval. This pattern is also used to specify that a condition must hold for some initial duration (using the converse $t_d < d \to \Psi$), or may only hold after some initial duration has elapsed ($\Psi \to t_d > d$).

Experimental Validation. We used the generated runtime monitor of the constructed TCAs for runtime verification of systems constructed from the provided TCAs. For the floodgate control system, we implemented additional environments and systems, with various (compliant and violating) behaviors for setting inputs/outputs, response durations, and computation delays. The monitor correctly tracks the tokens when given a conforming TIO-trace, detects specification violations of environment and system, and reports the outcome of the play, as well as diagnostics about invalid accesses. It can display the received inputs/outputs, measured time points, information about existing tokens, and their traces. While creating multiple tokens is necessary to track the nondeterminism, it affects the memory usage and runtime performance of the generated monitors. Eager resetting of unused clocks mitigates the resource consumption by enabling further token deduplication.

5 Related Work

Runtime verification is used for the verification of real-time systems with different real-time specification languages. Multiple approaches use extensions of Linear Temporal Logic (LTL) for real-time specification. Bauer et al. [3] show an approach to runtime verification of LTL formulae that generates an optimal runtime monitor for a given LTL formula, and demonstrate how this work can be extended to generate a runtime monitor for Timed Linear Temporal Logic (TLTL), which adds time bounds to the temporal operators of LTL to express real-time properties. Their monitor interprets the given trace as a finite prefix of an infinite trace using a three-valued semantics, where the processed finite word is classified to express whether no/every/some continuation satisfies the LTL formula. This approach is similar to the semantics of the runtime monitor for TCAs, where the marking differentiates between the environment winning/system winning/continuing play. Havelund and Rosu [6] propose an algorithm to construct a runtime monitor for past-time linear temporal logic formulae and its embedding into Java code, including error reporting. Building on Metric Temporal Logic (MTL), de Matos Pedro et al. [12] define a restricted decidable subset of MTL with durations (MTL-$\int$, defined in [10]) for which they introduce algorithms to enable runtime verification. They define an offline simplification algorithm for quantifier removal and an online evaluation algorithm for runtime verification, which uses a three-valued interpretation to evaluate the simplified formulae. The authors show the feasibility of scaling the algorithm for runtime verification of hard real-time systems, where using incremental evaluation allows handling large input samples and specification formulae.

There also exist automata-based approaches to express real-time properties. UPPAAL is a model-checking tool used to design, simulate, and verify real-time systems [11]. It is based on timed automata and provides additional capabilities for the synchronization of multiple automata, to model a system as a network of automata. While UPPAAL is primarily used for modeling and static program verification, Truscan et al. [17] implement runtime verification for UPPAAL models. Their monitor selects messages matching specified patterns from the process's execution log, similar to our approach of checking a TIO-trace. A similarity to our approach is the automaton-based structure with clocks of the specification. A difference lies in the semantics of the specification. UPPAAL's timed automata reason about events, whereas TCAs make use of formal contracts with assumptions and guarantees, which allows using the game-based semantics to define each player's obligations depending on the values provided by the other player. A TCA that only uses combined clocks in contracts and resets, does not use *old* expressions and only uses UPPAAL's clock constraint conditions could be expressed in UPPAAL by splitting the obligations of environment and system into separate synchronized timed automata. The environment automaton uses the guard *assume* and the system automaton $\mathit{assume} \rightarrow \mathit{guarantee}$ for each contract. Checking compliance requires evaluating transitions for environment and system in alternating order, mapping specification violations to the respective player, and classifying infinite runs as compliant (Büchi acceptance condition for all states).

Interface Automata[1] provide a light-weight formalism for describing software-component interfaces and their interactions. While interface automata specify component interactions, a similarity to TCAs is their approach to define the relation of a component with its environment using a game based on assumptions for the environment and guarantees of system outputs. An interface automaton specifies the order of observable method calls using actions: Input actions encode assumptions about the environment (the permitted order in which the environment may invoke the component's methods), while output actions express the component's guarantees about the order in which it calls out to other components. They extend this to the specification of timing expectations [2]. Their approach allows checking interface compatibility and computing the composition interface.

Duration Calculus (DC) is an interval temporal logic [4]. Colombo et al. [5] discuss the use of DC as a real-time specification language for runtime verification. They state that runtime monitoring slows down the monitored system, define real-time properties that are not invalidated because of the monitor's performance impact, and generalize this to classes of properties that are not affected by the system slowing down or speeding up. In our approach, when the monitored system is slowed down, it may also violate certain real-time properties because of the monitor's performance impact. A difference stems from the kind of specification affected by this. Whereas in DC, complexity arises from the evaluation of formulae, notably the necessary decision for evaluating the chop operator, the performance impact of formula evaluation for TCAs is minimal, as they are arithmetic and logical expressions without quantifiers that are compiled to fast machine code. Instead, more extensive computation is required to model non-deterministic choices for multiple possible paths in the TCA.

Kallwies et al. [8] present the runtime verification framework TeSSLa. They focus on the tools associated with the TeSSLa ecosystem, give an overview of the used stream runtime verification language and discuss typical challenges for runtime verification. A runtime monitor must be able to be synthesized for a changed specification and should minimize the performance impact on the monitored system, as discussed above, to avoid incorrect verdicts as well as not interfere with the working system. Additionally, they mention the use-case of runtime verification for long-term observations or life-long supervision of a system. This necessitates the monitor to be able to efficiently handle many consecutive updates. In our tool this is addressed by the design of the monitor that only tracks a bounded amount of necessary information for deciding specification compliance. The problem when dealing with specifications that require creating large amounts of tokens over time is addressed by deduplicating tokens using their trace suffixes.

6 Conclusion

We introduce Timed Contract Automata (TCA) as a combination of contract automata [18] and timed automata which allows formal specification of the behavior of a real-time system in terms of functional contracts (relation of input and output) and real-time behavior using clocks. The semantics are based on a two-party game between the environment and the systems. The environment and system have their own set of clocks, similar to the separation of constraints (assumption vs. guarantees). The clocks allow the specification of duration spent in a single or a group of modes. We fully implemented the runtime monitor generation for C++ for offline and online monitors. We show how specifications can be formalized using existing case studies and generalize the occurred real-time requirements into specification patterns.

We show the feasibility of expressing real-time properties using TCAs, however, it can be tedious or error-prone to write TCAs. To make them useful for specifications in real-world applications and enable scaling to larger and more complex systems, another higher level of abstraction specification language could be built on top of TCAs. This would allow expressing common requirements using simple higher level formulae or graphical structures and then be automatically lowered into the equivalent TCA to make use of the defined semantics and translation to a runtime monitor. This approach could also make use of the composition of the resulting TCAs and allow refinement checking specifications. In our case studies we compose TCAs using logical conjunction or disjunction of the specified requirements. As the generated TCAs resulting from the combination of different requirements can grow multiplicative, an algorithm to minimize TCAs might help. Additionally, a formal definition of composition with regard to the compliance of a system to the respective TCAs would be useful.

7 Data Availability

The artifact is archived on https://doi.org/10.5281/zenodo.18175317.

References

1. de Alfaro, L., Henzinger, T.A.: Interface automata. In: ESEC / SIGSOFT FSE, pp. 109–120 (2001), https://doi.org/10.1145/503209.503226
2. de Alfaro, L., Henzinger, T.A., Stoelinga, M.: Timed interfaces. In: EMSOFT, pp. 108–122 (2002), https://doi.org/10.1007/3-540-45828-X_9
3. Bauer, A., Leucker, M., Schallhart, C.: Runtime verification for LTL and TLTL. ACM Trans. Softw. Eng. Methodol. **20**(4), 14:1–14:64 (2011), https://doi.org/10.1145/2000799.2000800
4. Chaochen, Z., Hoare, C.A.R., Ravn, A.P.: A calculus of durations. Inf. Process. Lett. **40**(5), 269–276 (1991), https://doi.org/10.1016/0020-0190(91)90122-X
5. Colombo, C., Pace, G.J., Schneider, G.: Safe runtime verification of real-time properties. In: Ouaknine, J., Vaandrager, F.W. (eds.) Formal Modeling and Analysis of Timed Systems, FORMATS 2009, Lecture Notes in Computer Science, vol. 5813, pp. 103–117, Springer (2009), https://doi.org/10.1007/978-3-642-04368-0_10
6. Havelund, K., Rosu, G.: Synthesizing monitors for safety properties. In: Katoen, J., Stevens, P. (eds.) Tools and Algorithms for the Construction and Analysis of Systems, TACAS 2002, Held as Part of the Joint European Conference on Theory and Practice of Software, ETAPS 2002, Proceedings, Lecture Notes in Computer Science, vol. 2280, pp. 342–356, Springer (2002), https://doi.org/10.1007/3-540-46002-0_24
7. Joseph, M.: Real-time systems - specification, verification and analysis. Prentice Hall International series in computer science, Prentice Hall (1996), ISBN 978-0-13-455297-2
8. Kallwies, H., Leucker, M., Schmitz, M., Schulz, A., Thoma, D., Weiss, A.: Tessla - an ecosystem for runtime verification. In: Runtime Verification - 22nd International Conference, RV 2022, Tbilisi, Georgia, September 28-30, 2022, Proceedings, Lecture Notes in Computer Science, vol. 13498, pp. 314–324, Springer (2022), https://doi.org/10.1007/978-3-031-17196-3_20
9. Koymans, R.: Specifying real-time properties with metric temporal logic. Real Time Syst. **2**(4), 255–299 (1990), https://doi.org/10.1007/BF01995674
10. Lakhnech, Y., Hooman, J.: Metric temporal logic with durations. Theor. Comput. Sci. **138**(1), 169–199 (1995), https://doi.org/10.1016/0304-3975(94)00151-8
11. Larsen, K.G., Pettersson, P., Yi, W.: Uppaal in a nutshell. Int. J. Softw. Tools Technol. Transf. **1**(1-2), 134–152 (1997), https://doi.org/10.1007/S100090050010
12. de Matos Pedro, A., Pereira, D., Pinho, L.M., Pinto, J.S.: Monitoring for a decidable fragment of mtl-d. In: Bartocci, E., Majumdar, R. (eds.) Runtime

Verification, RV 2015 Vienna, Austria, September 22-25, 2015. Proceedings, Lecture Notes in Computer Science, vol. 9333, pp. 169–184, Springer (2015), https://doi.org/10.1007/978-3-319-23820-3_11
13. Rock, G.: Formal methods for real-time requirements engineering. Ph.D. thesis, Saarland University, Saarbrücken, Germany (2004)
14. Rozenberg, G., Engelfriet, J.: Elementary net systems. In: Reisig, W., Rozenberg, G. (eds.) Lectures on Petri Nets I: Basic Models, Advances in Petri Nets, Lecture Notes in Computer Science, vol. 1491, pp. 12–121, Springer (1996), https://doi.org/10.1007/3-540-65306-6_14
15. Sánchez, J., Guarnes, M.Á., Dormido, S.: On the application of different event-based sampling strategies to the control of a simple industrial process. Sensors **9**(9), 6795–6818 (2009), https://doi.org/10.3390/S90906795
16. Shin, K.G., Ramanathan, P.: Real-time computing: a new discipline of computer science and engineering. Proc. IEEE **82**(1), 6–24 (1994), https://doi.org/10.1109/5.259423
17. Truscan, D., Ahmad, T., Siavashi, F., Tuuttila, P.: A practical application of UPPAAL and DTRON for runtime verification. In: Shukla, R., Sen, S., Shull, F., Bishop, J. (eds.) 2nd IEEE/ACM International Workshop on Software Engineering Research and Industrial Practice, SER&IP 2015, pp. 39–45, IEEE (2015), https://doi.org/10.1109/SERIP.2015.15
18. Weigl, A., Bachmeier, J., Beckert, B., Ulbrich, M.: Contract automata: A specification language for mode-based systems. In: Proceedings of the 2024 IEEE/ACM 12th International Conference on Formal Methods in Software Engineering (FormaliSE), p. 1–11, FormaliSE '24, Association for Computing Machinery, New York, NY, USA (2024), ISBN 9798400705892, https://doi.org/10.1145/3644033.3644381

Unified Timing-Aware Program Verification

Dóra Cziborová, Mihály Dobos-Kovács,
Kristóf Marussy, and András Vörös

Department of Artificial Intelligence and Systems Engineering, Faculty of Electrical Engineering and Informatics, Budapest University of Technology and Economics
{cziborova,mdobosko,marussy,vori}@mit.bme.hu

Abstract. Three complementary verification approaches exist for real-time concurrent programs: (i) Timed Automata (TA) model checkers reason rigorously about timing but cannot express C's memory model and synchronization primitives. (ii) Program verifiers handle advanced language features but ignore timing, producing spurious errors when timing makes races impossible. (iii) Worst-Case Execution Time (WCET) analyzers bound execution time but cannot verify safety properties.
We present a vision for timing-aware program verification and propose a workflow that integrates: (i) TA semantics, (ii) existing C program verifier capabilities, and (iii) WCET timing estimates. We identify three key research challenges and demonstrate feasibility through a prototype implementation in a state-of-the-art software model checker.
Our prototype demonstrates the potential to eliminate false positives from timing-infeasible scenarios and verify real-time properties previously impossible to express in C program verifiers.

Keywords: Program verification · Concurrency · Timed automata.

1 Introduction

Temporal behavior fundamentally affects the correctness of concurrent and embedded systems. Hard real-time systems require an upper bound on execution time. In multi-core systems and lock-free algorithms, safe access to a shared resource might be ensured by separation in time.

Software model checkers have become increasingly capable of efficiently verifying the functional correctness of complex source code. For example, the SV-COMP verification competition [15] contains benchmark cases for recursive functions [13], multi-threading [5,7,27,28,47], arrays and memory operations [24]. It is also possible to analyze the behavior of programs under hardware-specific aspects like weak memory models [24]. Nevertheless, these verifiers are *unsuitable for analyzing timing-related properties* and *may output spurious error traces for safety properties* which are excluded by timing.

Timed Automata (TA) model checkers [12,17] can reason about timing and scheduling through dedicated clock variables and can verify properties such as schedulability and deadline satisfaction. However, they *lack support for many C*

E. Albert and C. Pasareanu (Eds.): FASE 2026, LNCS 16504, pp. 412–423, 2026.
https://doi.org/10.1007/978-3-032-22774-4_21

language features (e.g., including pointer arithmetic, dynamic memory allocation, and weak memory models) requiring developers to manually abstract programs into automata models. This abstraction loses the precise language semantics needed to verify concurrent C code. *Worst-Case Execution Time (WCET) analyzers* [3,8,39] have accurate low-level models of instruction timing, but focus entirely on bounding execution time and *cannot verify safety properties.*

In this paper, we present a vision for *unified timing-aware program verification* to formalize and verify properties concerning both the functional behavior and scheduling. We leverage existing software model checker capabilities for a large coverage of language and runtime environment features.

In particular, we (i) propose a C language extension incorporating *first-class clock variables and timing constraints* inspired by TA; (ii) present a *verification workflow*; and (iii) identify three *key research directions and challenges*: (Ch1) integrating WCET bounds into program representations, (Ch2) extending verifiable semantics with clocks and scheduling, and (Ch3) achieving scalable model checking. Our prototype implemented in the Theta [7] program verification framework shows the feasibility of the vision.

This approach enables verification of properties currently inexpressible in existing program verifiers, including (a) safety properties ensured by timing constraints, such as races eliminated by execution time separation; (b) real-time properties including deadline satisfaction and schedulability [38]; and (c) timing-dependent security properties, such as timing side channels [19,43,44]. For the first time, these properties can be verified directly on C programs while preserving full language semantics.

2 Motivating example

Spurious error traces. Consider the C23 program in Fig. 1c. We use functions and annotations similar to the *ConcurrencySafety* category of the SV-COMP [15] software verification competition (shown in *`italics`*). The function *`__VERIFIER_nondet32`* reads an arbitrary input (32-bit integer), while calling *`reach_error`* indicates an unsafe condition. SV-COMP assumes that threads can be scheduled arbitrarily and any operation performed by the program can take any amount of time, including exactly 0 units of time.

The `main` function starts two threads, `thr1` and `thr2`. In `thr1`, we write nondeterministic values to x (lines 5 and 9). Lines 12 and 13 of `thr2` may read distinct values, which sets *ERR* to `1` (line 15). This triggers the dangerous condition `reach_error` (line 27). Fig. 1a illustrates this error trace. However, further assumptions about the schedule and timing of the instructions may constrain the behavior of the program. The error trace is excluded if (i) all threads execute simultaneously without preemption (ii) `do_work` takes much longer time than the two reads in lines 12–13.

Existing program verification tools *cannot encode these assumptions nor use them during analysis, which leads to spurious error traces.*

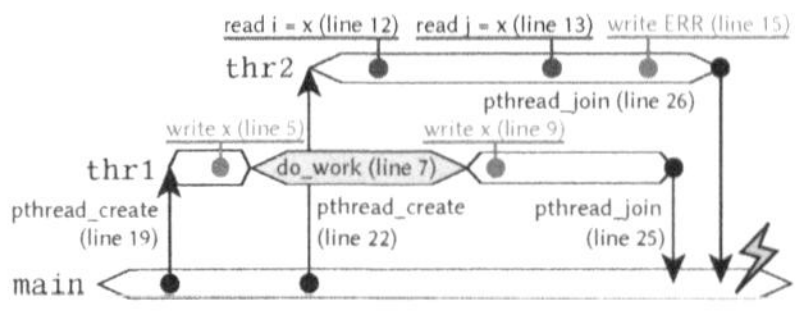

(a) Possible error trace without timing

(b) Execution trace with timing constraints

```
1  _Thread_local __cpu_clock tc;
2  _Atomic int x = 0, ERR = 0;
3  void *thr1(void *arg) {
4    __VERIFIER_elapsed(tc, 5, 5);
5    x = __VERIFIER_nondet32();
6    __VERIFIER_elapsed(tc, 0, 5);
7    do_work();
8    __VERIFIER_elapsed(tc, 1000, 2000);
9    x = __VERIFIER_nondet32();
10 }
11 void *thr2(void *arg) {
12   int i = x;
13   int j = x;
14   __VERIFIER_elapsed(tc, 15, 20);
15   if (i != j) { ERR = 1; }
16 }
17 int main() {
18   pthread_t t1, t2;
19   pthread_create(&t1, 0, thr1, 0);
20   __VERIFIER_elapsed(tc, 100, 120);
21   __VERIFIER_elapsed(tc, 80, 100);
22   pthread_create(&t2, 0, thr2, 0);
23   __VERIFIER_elapsed(tc, 100, 120);
24   __VERIFIER_elapsed(tc, 80, 100);
25   pthread_join(t1, 0);
26   pthread_join(t2, 0);
27   if (ERR) { reach_error(); }
28 }
```

(c) Program listing

Fig. 1: Example C program with a spurious race condition

Encoding timing information in C programs. We propose to extend the input programming language with first-class *clock variable* support similarly to Timed Automata (TA) verification [12]. In contrast with ordinary (data) variables, clock variables increase spontaneously during program execution. Hence, they allow formulating assumptions and assertions about timed behaviors. We introduce new annotations for such additions; in Fig. 1c they are dimmed.

In our example, the thread-local clock variable *tc* tracks the CPU time of each thread. The `__VERIFIER_elapsed(C,L,U)` macro encodes the assumption that the time elapsed on the clock C since the last assumption satisfies $L \leq C \leq U$ (corresponding to two guards and a reset in TA), which *enables describing the timings of individual instructions.* Individual assumptions can also be used, e.g., diagonal clock constraints for relative ordering. The function prologue of `thr1` takes exactly 5 units of time (line 4), while `__VERIFIER_nondet32` and `do_work` calls take 0–5 (line 6) and 1000–2000 units (line 8), respectively.

Multiple effects in a block. Timed semantics also enable reasoning about executions with less granular timing information. This is often the case with Worst-Case Execution Time (WCET) analysis tools [2], which partition programs into (branchless) Basic Blocks (BBs), and provide estimates on the BB level. In our example, line 14 annotates that the first BB of `thr2` takes 15–20 units of time. More permissive timing annotations can preserve the soundness of the analysis even if the OS or hardware provides fewer guarantees.

Multiple effects visible to other threads in a single block make the resulting semantics more complex. Ordering of global memory operations has been extensively studied in program verification [5,7,27,28,47], including ordering consistency [1,4,33] and weak memory models [24], but, to our best knowledge, *there*

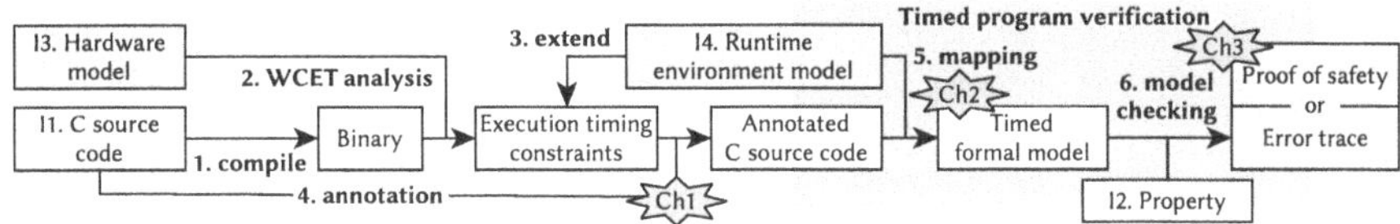

Fig. 2: Workflow for timed program verification. Section 4 discusses Ch1–3

is no existing technique that can incorporate timing constraints. In our example, we assume that the two reads happen in the thread `thr1` sequentially, but at arbitrary points in time within the interval marked with `__VERIFIER_elapsed`.

Runtime environment. Software model checkers for multithreaded code have to model the runtime environment [7,13,38], including atomic operations, thread start (`pthread_create`) and joining (`pthread_join`), and synchronization primitives like locks and mutexes. *It is crucial to leverage these existing models to endow C programs with accurate timed semantics.* For example, in lines 20–21 and 23–24, we add two `__VERIFIER_elapsed` annotations for each `pthread_create` call. The first assumes that the global effect (thread start) happens in a given interval (100–120 units), while the second assumes an additional interval (80–100 units) before execution is yielded back to the `main` function.

As illustrated in Fig. 1b, the aforementioned timing annotations restrict the memory reads in `thr2` to occur while the long-running `do_work` function is executing in `thr1`. This shows that the error trace in Fig. 1a is spurious and the program is *free of unsafe conditions under the provided timing assumptions.*

3 Proposed analysis workflow

We propose an analysis workflow for verifying timed multi-threaded C programs. The main inputs of the workflow are the **(I1) C source code**; and the **(I2) property** to be verified, which is usually a timing invariant, or a reachability property stating that there exists a run to some distinguished state (e.g., an unsafe `reach_error` state). Additional inputs specify the timing behavior of the target platform: the **(I3) hardware model** is used by the WCET analysis to provide accurate timing constraints (containing the execution times of instructions, caches, pipelines, etc. of the given hardware); and the **(I4) runtime environment model** describes timing of synchronization primitives and I/O, as well as the scheduling of threads. Both the hardware and runtime environment models must contain safe overapproximations of timing to preserve soundness, and re-running with different models can adapt the analysis to another target platform. The output of the workflow is a **proof** of the program satisfying the property or an **error trace**, taking into consideration the timed semantics.

Steps of the analysis. In the proposed workflow, the timing constraints of the input C program are acquired by WCET analysis. Since WCET analysis tools require machine code to estimate time bounds, the source code is first

```c
1 #define __VERIFIER_elapsed(C, L, U) \
2   __VERIFIER_assume(C >= L && C <= U); \
3   __VERIFIER_reset(C)
```

(a) The **__VERIFIER_elapsed** macro

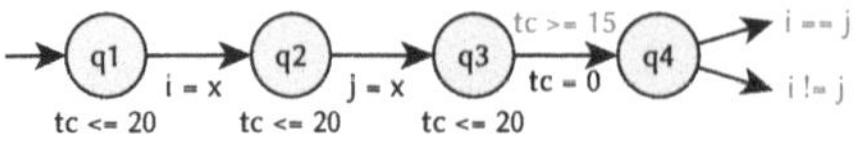

(b) XTA fragment for lines 12–14 of Fig. 1c

Fig. 3: TA semantics for elapsed time

```c
_Thread_local __cpu_clock tc;                      1
pthread_mutex_t mutex;                             2
void *thr3(void *arg) {                            3
    __wall_clock taken;                            4
    __VERIFIER_reset(taken);                       5
    pthread_mutex_lock(&mutex);                    6
    do_work();                                     7
    __VERIFIER_elapsed(tc, 1000, 2000);            8
    pthread_mutex_unlock(&mutex);                  9
    __VERIFIER_assert(taken <= 2100);              10
}                                                  11
```

Fig. 4: Verifiable timing properties

(1) compiled into a binary. To produce accurate bounds, the cross-compilation and optimization settings must match the intended target environment. Then, the **(2) WCET analysis** provides estimates for the timing of BBs in the binary on the given hardware model. These timing constraints of the execution are **(3) extended** by timing constraints from the runtime environment, e.g., time needed to start a thread or to yield back execution. The obtained timing constraints are used to **(4) back-annotate** the original C source code, as shown, e.g., in lines 8, 14 and 20–21 of Fig. 1c, where the program is annotated with the **__VERIFIER_elapsed** macro. We propose to **(5) map** the source code to a *timed* formal model. We must turn operations specific to the runtime environment, like threading and synchronizations, to corresponding formal constructs. Lastly, the formally specified input property is checked against the timed formal model by **(6) model checking**, which produces either a formal proof that the program satisfies the property or an error trace.

Timed semantics for C programs. In the proposed workflow, the formal model produced by the (5) mapping step must be able to express timing constraints and concurrency. We will adapt TA as a semantics basis, as they are well-established in concurrent timed verification. Clock variables are incremented equally on time *delays*. They may be *reset* to set their values to 0, and they may appear in *clock guards* and *invariants* to restrict state transition.

Our proposed semantics couples the elapse of time with the execution of specific program instructions on active threads. Fig. 3a shows a translation of the **__VERIFIER_elapsed** annotation in terms of TA semantics. We first create a clock guard to assume that the value of the clock variable C is between the bounds $L \leq C \leq U$ (lines 2), then reset C (line 3) to start measuring the elapsed time again until the next **__VERIFIER_elapsed** annotation. Fig. 3b illustrates such semantics as a TA fragment for lines 12–14 of Fig. 1c. Outgoing transitions from locations q_1 and q_2 realize the two atomic reads, while the transition from q_2 enforces the guard $tc \geq 15$ and resets tc. This ensures that the block can be only left if at least 15 units of time have elapsed. The TA translation enforces the upper bound $tc \leq 20$ as location invariants.

However, *modeling timed code execution accurately demands semantics beyond standard TAs.* To this end, we propose (i) clock variables as first-class entities, which can be declared in the same manner as ordinary (data) variables and (ii) distinct `cpu_clock` and `wall_clock` variables. CPU clock variables only increase if the corresponding thread is active. Wall clock variables allow reasoning about the observable delays in a program. As an example, Fig. 4 measures time spent acquiring `mutex` and in the following critical section with the local `__wall_clock` variable *taken*. It asserts the deadline $taken \leq 2100$ at the end of the function `thr3`. Separate calls to `thr3` shall have their own *taken* clock variable, ensuring that the asserted properties do not conflict with each other.

4 Challenges and related work

4.1 Challenge 1: WCET annotations for program verification

Static WCET analysis methods estimate WCET without program execution, providing sound results [2]. Traditional WCET analysis utilizes the Implicit Path Enumeration (IPET) [37] to model program control flow with integer linear programming constrained by flow facts like loop limits and infeasible paths. Abstract interpretation [48] is often applied to further restrict executable paths or derive more flow facts. Techniques also exist for multi-core analysis [21,42].

A major challenge is the semantic gap between formal verification and WCET analysis tools. Advanced software verification tools use various methods to address C's complexity [6]. Some parse C code directly, while others parse a precompiled intermediary representation (e.g., LLVM). Bajczi et al. [6] demonstrated that different verification algorithms favor different inputs: (i) Bmc benefits from LLVM's low-level optimizations, (ii) while abstraction-based algorithms like Cegar require detailed source code information absent in low-level formats.

Back-annotating WCET results to C source code is challenging [20]. WCET tools annotate basic blocks [3,8,39] based on hardware models. Source-based WCET approaches can back-annotate timings to C code, but make broad assumptions as with the "simple processor" in Becker et al. [9,10], or assume a thread [41] or execution unit [44]. In our experience, *no solution exists for effectively annotating C source code from WCET analysis considering modern multi-threaded processors for efficient abstraction-based formal verification.*

4.2 Challenge 2: Timed formal models for runtime environments

The formal verification of multi-threaded programs is an actively researched topic. Most common verification techniques aim to reduce the state-space to handle the complexity by either some form of Partial Order Reduction (POR) [1,4,5,33] or abstraction [7,27,28,47]. Closest to our proposed TA-like semantics is [47], which suggest modeling multi-threaded software as networks of automata. Such models have been adapted to support various program constructs (like functions [13], pointers, arrays and weak memory models [24]).

Applying reductions like POR is challenging for timed systems due to the global nature of time delays [29]. Furthermore, *timed semantics for concurrent software must consider the influence of advanced language features on time:*

(i) function calls and dynamic thread initiation create and destroy clock variables on the fly, while (ii) synchronization primitives and other calls to the runtime environment may suspend threads along with their CPU clock variables. Moreover, (iii) scheduling (e.g., preemption or cooperative multitasking, number of execution units) must be modeled to obtain accurate timed behaviors [38].

Bengtsson et al. [12] presents clock operations for an efficient representation of time in TA models. Delays are expressed by the `up` operation, which preserves information about the differences of clocks. However, this operation affects all clocks and an efficient generalization is not trivial [18,25].

4.3 Challenge 3: Scalable timed program analysis

The most commonly used algorithms for software model checking [15] are Counterexample-Guided Abstraction Refinement (CEGAR) [23] and lazy abstraction [31,40]. Bounded Model Checking (BMC) [16] is also common in portfolios, but is not *complete* and cannot deliver a proof of safety on its own. Common abstraction-based verifiers for timed systems combine *zone abstraction* [12] with LU-abstraction [11,32] and a variant of lazy abstraction [32,49,45] for TA models. However, the latter has not been adapted to support program semantics. Several works apply timed model checking with efficient time abstraction to TA models with data variables [30,36,45,51], but their data operations have to be deterministic or are restricted to an explicitly enumerated domain, which limits their expressiveness. BDD-based [14,45] and SMT-based [22,26,34,35,50] approaches allow greater expressiveness on the data domain but do not use efficient time abstractions. As a result, in contrast with software model checkers, timed model checkers lack support for complex program semantics.

A new approach [46] splits the timed verification task into two parts: timed automaton verification and discrete state model checking, and solves them using different model checkers. However, the method does not scale well for a large number of different clock expressions, which is the case for timing constraints generated by WCET analysis. Therefore, *there is an algorithmic gap for combining efficient and expressive abstractions for time and data.*

5 Preliminary evaluation

We demonstrate the feasibility of the approach through a prototype implementation in the Theta model checking framework [7]. We analyzed the example C program with spurious race condition provided in Section 2.

To obtain timing constraints of the execution, we used the OTAWA WCET analysis tool [8]. We provided stub implementations for nondeterministic input and thread operations and cross-compiled the C source code of the example to an ARM Cortex A9 processor. OTAWA provides Low Time Set (LTS) and High Time Set (HTS) bounds for the BBs. After mapping each sequence of the C source code corresponding to a BB, we used the LTS and HTS as the lower and upper bounds of execution time, as also shown in Fig. 1c.

Building on Theta's existing C program semantics, we added support for clock variables and operations. We follow the SMT-based approach from [22] and transform clocks into rational variables. We used the BMC and CEGAR algorithms that Theta implements in its SV-COMP portfolio [7]. As a comparative measure, we used the UPPAAL TA model checker [12], which uses zone abstraction for clocks, and manually mapped the C code to a TA network. We also ran Theta on unaltered C code, and UPPAAL with a deterministic TA model, substituting nondeterministic assignments with (distinct) constant values. We measured the execution times of the listed approaches on our example with a time limit of 600 sec on a computer with 2.6GHz CPU and 16GB RAM.

Table 1: Execution times of analyses

Tool	T. sem.	C sem.	Compl.	Exec. time	Res.
UPPAAL	Zone	◐	■	> 600 s	TO
UPPAAL	Zone	○	■	0.01 s	Safe
Theta BMC	–	●	□	2.19 s	Unsafe
Theta CEGAR	–	●	■	2.67 s	Unsafe
Theta BMC	**Rat.**	●	□	**> 600 s**	**TO**
Theta CEGAR	**Rat.**	●	■	**171.08 s**	**Safe**

Results. The results of our experiments are summarized in Table 1. The baseline method using UPPAAL, which retains limited program semantics (◐), e.g., lacks support for dynamic thread creation, fails to verify program safety due to timeout (TO) after 600 seconds. Conversely, UPPAAL quickly verified the deterministic model's race condition absence, but erasing nondeterminism preserves only a tiny fraction of the original semantics (○). Theta preserves full C semantics (●) of our example, including threading and nondeterminism. For the untimed C code, both BMC and CEGAR algorithms generated the expected spurious unsafe outcome. These results indicate that Theta efficiently manages nondeterministic, multi-threaded C programs without timing: while not complete for reachability (□), BMC promptly identifies error traces and is supplemented by the complete (■) CEGAR algorithm. In the timed C program, BMC experienced a timeout. CEGAR was able to prove safety under timing assumptions, although it took significantly longer than finding an error trace in the untimed program.

Discussion. The results indicate that our proposed workflow effectively verifies source code using software model checkers while also taking into consideration precise scheduling and timing of instructions. However, to efficiently address timing constraints, specialized methods like zone abstraction are necessary, highlighting the need to merge software model checking with timing-focused techniques. Theta incorporates zone abstraction for timed automata verification [51], which could potentially be combined with CEGAR for verifying timed C programs. Addressing Challenge 1 to automate back-annotation of WCET bounds will enable the automatic synthesis of diverse benchmarks for timed program verification, e.g., by translating the SV-COMP concurrent benchmarks. This will enable rigorous evaluation of timed semantics for language features (Challenge 2) and the scalability of verification algorithms (Challenge 3).

Acknowledgement. The project supported by the Doctoral Excellence Fellowship Programme (DCEP) is funded by the National Research Development and Innovation Fund of the Ministry of Culture and Innovation and BME. The work of the third author was partially supported by the Department of Navy award (N629092412063) issued by the Office of Naval Research.

References

1. Abdulla, P., Aronis, S., Jonsson, B., Sagonas, K.: Optimal dynamic partial order reduction. In: POPL. p. 373–384. ACM (2014). https://doi.org/10.1145/2535838.2535845
2. Abella, J., Hernandez, C., Quiñones, E., Cazorla, F.J., Conmy, P.R., Azkarate-askasua, M., Perez, J., Mezzetti, E., Vardanega, T.: WCET analysis methods: Pitfalls and challenges on their trustworthiness. In: SIES. pp. 1–10 (2015). https://doi.org/10.1109/SIES.2015.7185039
3. AbsInt: aiT worst-case execution time analyzers. Online (2010), http://www.absint.com/ait/
4. Agarwal, P., Chatterjee, K., Pathak, S., Pavlogiannis, A., Toman, V.: Stateless model checking under a reads-value-from equivalence. In: CAV. pp. 341–366. Springer (2021). https://doi.org/10.1007/978-3-030-81685-8_16
5. Alglave, J., Kroening, D., Tautschnig, M.: Partial orders for efficient bounded model checking of concurrent software. In: CAV. pp. 141–157. Springer (2013). https://doi.org/10.1007/978-3-642-39799-8_9
6. Bajczi, L., Ádám, Z., Molnár, V.: C for yourself: comparison of front-end techniques for formal verification. In: FormaliSE. p. 1–11. ACM (2022). https://doi.org/10.1145/3524482.3527646
7. Bajczi, L., Telbisz, C., Somorjai, M., Ádám, Z., Dobos-Kovács, M., Szekeres, D., Mondok, M., Molnár, V.: Theta: Abstraction based techniques for verifying concurrency (competition contribution). In: TACAS. pp. 412–417. Springer (2024). https://doi.org/10.1007/978-3-031-57256-2_30
8. Ballabriga, C., Cassé, H., Rochange, C., Sainrat, P.: OTAWA: An open toolbox for adaptive WCET analysis. In: Software Technologies for Embedded and Ubiquitous Systems. pp. 35–46. Springer (2010). https://doi.org/10.1007/978-3-642-16256-5_6
9. Becker, M., Metta, R., Venkatesh, R., Chakraborty, S.: Scalable and precise estimation and debugging of the worst-case execution time for analysis-friendly processors: a comeback of model checking. Int. J. Softw. Tools Technol. Transf. **21**(5), 515–543 (2019). https://doi.org/10.1007/S10009-018-0497-2
10. Becker, M., Pazaj, M., Chakraborty, S.: WCET analysis meets virtual prototyping: Improving source-level timing annotations. In: SCOPES. p. 13–22. ACM (2019). https://doi.org/10.1145/3323439.3323978
11. Behrmann, G., Bouyer, P., Larsen, K.G., Pelánek, R.: Lower and upper bounds in zone-based abstractions of timed automata. Int. J. Softw. Tools Technol. Transf. **8**(3), 204–215 (2006). https://doi.org/10.1007/s10009-005-0190-0
12. Bengtsson, J., Yi, W.: Timed Automata: Semantics, Algorithms and Tools, pp. 87–124. Springer (2004). https://doi.org/10.1007/978-3-540-27755-2_3
13. Beyer, D., Friedberger, K.: Domain-independent interprocedural program analysis using block-abstraction memoization. In: ESEC/FSE. p. 50–62. ACM (2020). https://doi.org/10.1145/3368089.3409718
14. Beyer, D., Lewerentz, C., Noack, A.: Rabbit: A tool for BDD-based verification of real-time systems. In: CAC. pp. 122–125. Springer (2003). https://doi.org/10.1007/978-3-540-45069-6_13
15. Beyer, D., Strejcek, J.: Improvements in software verification and witness validation: SV-COMP 2025. In: TACAS. LNCS, vol. 15698, pp. 151–186. Springer (2025). https://doi.org/10.1007/978-3-031-90660-2_9

16. Biere, A., Cimatti, A., Clarke, E., Zhu, Y.: Symbolic model checking without BDDs. In: TACAS. pp. 193–207. Springer (1999). https://doi.org/10.1007/3-540-49059-0_14
17. Bouyer, P., Gastin, P., Herbreteau, F., Sankur, O., Srivathsan, B.: Zone-based verification of timed automata: Extrapolations, simulations and what next? In: FORMATS. LNCS, vol. 13465, pp. 16–42. Springer (2022). https://doi.org/10.1007/978-3-031-15839-1_2
18. Cassez, F., Larsen, K.G.: The impressive power of stopwatches. In: CONCUR. LNCS, vol. 1877, pp. 138–152. Springer (2000). https://doi.org/10.1007/3-540-44618-4_12
19. Cauligi, S., Soeller, G., Johannesmeyer, B., Brown, F., Wahby, R.S., Renner, J., Grégoire, B., Barthe, G., Jhala, R., Stefan, D.: FaCT: a DSL for timing-sensitive computation. In: PLDI. pp. 174–189. ACM (2019). https://doi.org/10.1145/3314221.3314605
20. Černý, P., Henzinger, T.A., Kovács, L., Radhakrishna, A., Zwirchmayr, J.: Segment abstraction for worst-case execution time analysis. In: Programming Languages and Systems. pp. 105–131. Springer (2015). https://doi.org/10.1007/978-3-662-46669-8_5
21. Chattopadhyay, S., Kee, C.L., Roychoudhury, A., Kelter, T., Marwedel, P., Falk, H.: A unified WCET analysis framework for multi-core platforms. In: RTAS. pp. 99–108 (2012). https://doi.org/10.1109/RTAS.2012.26
22. Cimatti, A., Griggio, A., Magnago, E., Roveri, M., Tonetta, S.: Extending nuXmv with timed transition systems and timed temporal properties. In: Computer Aided Verification. pp. 376–386. Springer (2019). https://doi.org/10.1007/978-3-030-25540-4_21
23. Clarke, E., Grumberg, O., Jha, S., Lu, Y., Veith, H.: Counterexample-guided abstraction refinement. In: CAV. pp. 154–169. Springer (2000). https://doi.org/10.1007/10722167_15
24. Colvin, R.J.: A fine-grained semantics for arrays and pointers under weak memory models. In: Formal Methods. pp. 301–320. Springer (2023). https://doi.org/10.1007/978-3-031-27481-7_18
25. Cortés, D., Leneutre, J., Malvone, V., Ortiz, J.J., Schobbens, P.: Extending timed automata with clock derivatives. In: iFM. LNCS, vol. 16194, pp. 99–119. Springer (2025). https://doi.org/10.1007/978-3-032-10794-7_6
26. Dutertre, B., Sorea, M.: Modeling and verification of a fault-tolerant real-time startup protocol using calendar automata. In: FORMATS. LNCS, vol. 3253, pp. 199–214. Springer (2004). https://doi.org/10.1007/978-3-540-30206-3_15
27. Eilers, M., Dardinier, T., Müller, P.: CommCSL: Proving information flow security for concurrent programs using abstract commutativity. Proc. ACM Program. Lang. **7**(PLDI) (2023). https://doi.org/10.1145/3591289
28. Farzan, A., Klumpp, D., Podelski, A.: Stratified commutativity in verification algorithms for concurrent programs. Proc. ACM Program. Lang. **7**(POPL) (2023). https://doi.org/10.1145/3571242
29. Govind, R., Herbreteau, F., Srivathsan, Walukiewicz, I.: Abstractions for the local-time semantics of timed automata: a foundation for partial-order methods. In: LICS. ACM (2022). https://doi.org/10.1145/3531130.3533343
30. Håkansson, J., Pettersson, P.: Partial order reduction for verification of real-time components. In: FORMATS. pp. 211–226. Springer (2007). https://doi.org/10.1007/978-3-540-75454-1_16
31. Henzinger, T.A., Jhala, R., Majumdar, R., Sutre, G.: Lazy abstraction. In: POPL. pp. 58–70 (2002). https://doi.org/10.1145/503272.503279

32. Herbreteau, F., Srivathsan, B., Walukiewicz, I.: Lazy abstractions for timed automata. In: CAV. LNCS, vol. 8044, pp. 990–1005. Springer (2013). https://doi.org/10.1007/978-3-642-39799-8_71
33. Huang, J.: Stateless model checking concurrent programs with maximal causality reduction. In: PLDI. p. 165–174. ACM (2015). https://doi.org/10.1145/2737924.2737975
34. Isenberg, T., Wehrheim, H.: Timed automata verification via IC3 with zones. In: ICFEM. LNCS, vol. 8829, pp. 203–218. Springer (2014). https://doi.org/10.1007/978-3-319-11737-9_14
35. Kindermann, R., Junttila, T., Niemelä, I.: SMT-based induction methods for timed systems. In: FORMATS. pp. 171–187. Springer (2012). https://doi.org/10.1007/978-3-642-33365-1_13
36. Larsen, K.G., Mikučionis, M., Muñiz, M., Srba, J.: Urgent partial order reduction for extended timed automata. In: Automated Technology for Verification and Analysis. pp. 179–195. Springer (2020). https://doi.org/10.1007/978-3-030-59152-6_10
37. Li, Y.T.S., Malik, S.: Performance analysis of embedded software using implicit path enumeration. SIGPLAN Not. **30**(11), 88–98 (1995). https://doi.org/10.1145/216633.216666
38. Lin, S., Jellum, E., Theile, M., Tanneberger, T., Sun, B., Jerad, C., Xu, Y., Feng, G., Mæhlum, M., Chen, J.J., Schoeberl, M., Phan, L.T.X., Castrillon, J., Seshia, S.A., Lee, E.A.: Quasi-static scheduling for deterministic timed concurrent models on multi-core hardware. ACM Trans. Embed. Comput. Syst. **24**(5s) (2025). https://doi.org/10.1145/3762653
39. Lisper, B.: Sweet – a tool for WCET flow analysis (extended abstract). In: Leveraging Applications of Formal Methods, Verification and Validation. Specialized Techniques and Applications. pp. 482–485. Springer (2014). https://doi.org/10.1007/978-3-662-45231-8_38
40. McMillan, K.L.: Lazy abstraction with interpolants. In: CAV. pp. 123–136. Springer (2006). https://doi.org/10.1007/11817963_14
41. Metta, R., Becker, M., Bokil, P., Chakraborty, S., Venkatesh, R.: TIC: a scalable model checking based approach to WCET estimation. SIGPLAN Not. **51**(5), 72–81 (2016). https://doi.org/10.1145/2980930.2907961
42. Nowotsch, J., Paulitsch, M., Bühler, D., Theiling, H., Wegener, S., Schmidt, M.: Multi-core interference-sensitive WCET analysis leveraging runtime resource capacity enforcement. In: Euromicro Conference on Real-Time Systems. pp. 109–118 (2014). https://doi.org/10.1109/ECRTS.2014.20
43. Pasareanu, C.S.: Symbolic Execution and Quantitative Reasoning: Applications to Software Safety and Security. Synthesis Lectures on Software Engineering, Morgan & Claypool Publishers (2020). https://doi.org/10.2200/S01010ED2V01Y202005SWE006
44. Pasareanu, C.S., Phan, Q., Malacaria, P.: Multi-run side-channel analysis using symbolic execution and max-smt. In: CSF. pp. 387–400. IEEE (2016). https://doi.org/10.1109/CSF.2016.34
45. Roussanaly, V., Sankur, O., Markey, N.: Abstraction refinement algorithms for timed automata. In: CAV. LNCS, vol. 11561, pp. 22–40. Springer (2019). https://doi.org/10.1007/978-3-030-25540-4_2
46. Sankur, O.: Timed automata verification and synthesis via finite automata learning. In: TACAS. LNCS, vol. 13994, pp. 329–349. Springer (2023). https://doi.org/10.1007/978-3-031-30820-8_21

47. Telbisz, C., Bajczi, L., Szekeres, D., Vörös, A.: On-the-fly cone-of-influence reduction for model checking concurrent software. In: SPIN. LNCS, vol. 15945, pp. 161–181. Springer (2025). https://doi.org/10.1007/978-3-032-06847-7_9
48. Theiling, H., Ferdinand, C., Wilhelm, R.: Fast and precise WCET prediction by separated cache and path analyses. Real Time Syst. **18**(2/3), 157–179 (2000). https://doi.org/10.1023/A:1008141130870
49. Tóth, T., Majzik, I.: Lazy reachability checking for timed automata using interpolants. In: FORMATS. LNCS, vol. 10419, pp. 264–280. Springer (2017). https://doi.org/10.1007/978-3-319-65765-3_15
50. Tóth, T., Vörös, A., Majzik, I.: K-induction based verification of real-time safety critical systems. In: DEPCOS. Advances in Intelligent Systems and Computing, vol. 224, pp. 469–478. Springer (2013). https://doi.org/10.1007/978-3-319-00945-2_43
51. Tóth, T., Majzik, I.: Configurable verification of timed automata with discrete variables. Acta Informatica (2020). https://doi.org/10.1007/s00236-020-00393-4

Testing in Formal Verification via Witness Generation (Empirical Evaluation)

Dirk Beyer, Thomas Lemberger, and Henrik Wachowitz

LMU Munich, Munich, Germany

Abstract. The communities surrounding formal software verifiers and automatic test generators have developed different formats to describe a path to an error. Test generators export a test case whose execution makes the error observable, while verifiers produce a violation witness, an abstract description of the error path. To leverage potential synergies between both communities, transformations between these formats are necessary. Previous work transformed violation witnesses to test cases, and improved test generation with formal verification techniques. But the other direction is not considered so far: Test cases are not yet transformed to violation witnesses, and there is no empirical evaluation for the application of test generators in formal verification. We change both. We present a transformation that allows the use of test generators in verification scenarios like the Competition on Software Verification (SV-COMP), both directly and as parts of bigger verification systems. In a large empirical evaluation we examine the improvements this can add to formal verifiers.

1 Introduction

Automated formal software verification and test generation are two complementary approaches to ensure software quality. Formal verification aims to either find program errors or prove their absence, while test generation focuses on finding error-triggering inputs. Despite potential synergies, the communities surrounding verifiers and test generators have developed different formats to describe a path to a found error. Test generators export a test case whose execution makes the error observable, while verifiers produce a *violation witness*, an abstract description of the error path. Previous work [1, 2] turned violation witnesses into test cases, and many other works [3, 4, 5, 6, 7, 8, 9, 10, 11] showed that the adaption of formal techniques can improve the effectiveness of test generation. By now, participants of Test-Comp use formal methods extensively [12]. But the application of test generation may be valuable for formal verification, as well: A previous study [12] on SV-COMP [13] and Test-Comp [14] indicates that current test generators are more effective in bug finding than formal verifiers. Still only two [11, 15] SV-COMP participants use dynamic approaches for automated software verification.

This paper closes the gap: We evaluate the off-the-shelf use of test generators in formal verification on the largest available benchmark set for software verification, SV-Benchmarks [16], in the well-established ecosystem of SV-COMP [17]. To make

E. Albert and C. Pasareanu (Eds.): FASE 2026, LNCS 16504, pp. 424–446, 2026.
https://doi.org/10.1007/978-3-032-22774-4_22

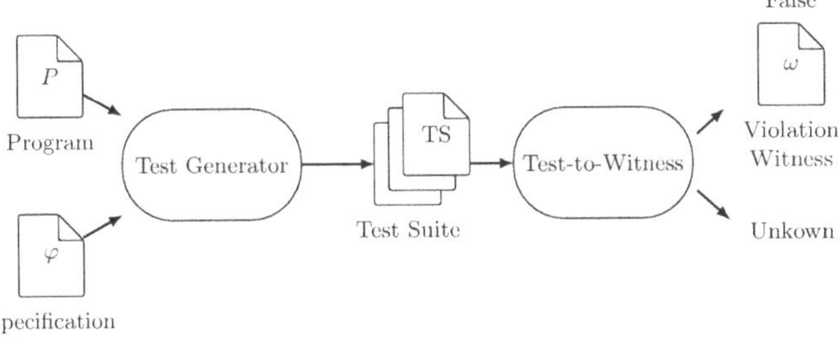

Fig. 1: Integrating test generators in the ecosystem of formal software verification

this possible, test generators need to speak the same language as verifiers, i.e., provide violation witnesses instead of test cases. Our approach, Test-to-Witness, performs this transformation for test generators. Figure 1 shows the overall idea: We couple an off-the-shelf tester with Test-to-Witness to create, from the generated test suite, a violation witness; as long as the test suite contains at least one test case that triggers the error. This tool-chain can then be used in the ecosystem of formal software verification—we use it to evaluate potential gains.

We base Test-to-Witness on the uniform test-suite format of Test-Comp [18] to support a wide range of test generators. Unfortunately, no standalone fuzzer participated in the latest editions of Test-Comp [14, 18, 19, 20, 21, 22, 23]. To include fuzzers in our evaluation, we introduce AFL-to-Test-Case (AFL-TC) [24], which transforms the tests produced by AFL-fuzz [25, 26] into test cases in the Test-Comp format. From there we can apply Test-to-Witness. Our work answers the following research questions:

RQ 1 Can test cases be reliably transformed into violation witnesses?
Evaluation design: We use Test-to-Witness to generate violation witnesses from the existing test suites created in Test-Comp 2025.We check that the created witnesses can also be understood and confirmed by witness validators that participate in SV-COMP.

RQ 2 Does the standalone use of test generators yield competitive results in the falsification category of SV-COMP?
Evaluation design: The violation witnesses created in RQ 1 represent the results in error finding of Test-Comp 2025 participants in the SV-COMP setting. We directly compare this to the results of SV-COMP 2025.

RQ 3 What is the impact on overall efficiency if we combine test generators with formal verifiers?
Evaluation design: We compare the consumption of CPU time per verification task between the parallel portfolios and the corresponding standalone formal verifiers.

RQ 4 Does it improve the overall effectiveness if we combine test generators with formal verifiers?
Evaluation design: We create pairwise parallel-portfolio combinations of six test generators and six formal verifiers, and compare the number of solved tasks between the parallel portfolios and the standalone formal verifiers.

This extensive evaluation shows that the addition of test generators to formal verifiers can offer a significant increase in their bug-finding capabilities.

Related Work. Our work belongs into the ecosystem of automatic tools for verifying and testing software programs. A list of actively participating and well-maintained tools is available in the competition reports for SV-COMP [17] and Test-Comp [18]. Information and literature about most of the openly available verifiers and testers that participate in the competitions can be found online at `https://fm-tools.sosy-lab.org/`.

There are several surveys that describe the technology of tools for software testing [27, 28, 29, 30, 31, 32, 33] and software verification [34, 35, 36, 37]. Modern software testers and verifiers usually combine different techniques [38, 39, 40].

Another line of work is to use verification witnesses and test suites as exchange between different tools. For example, WITNESS2TEST takes as input a program and a violation witness and produces a test case that leads the program execution to the specification violation. The approach that we propose in this paper works in the opposite direction: It uses a program and a test case, runs the (instrumented) program and produces a witness that can be used for further analysis, such as visualization. There are several works concerned with explaining the results of software analysis [41, 42, 43, 44, 45, 46, 47].

2 Background

Program Representation. For the sake of presentation[1] we consider imperative, sequential programs over integers. A program $P = (L, \ell_0, E)$ consists of its program locations L, the initial program location $\ell_0 \in L$, and a set of program edges $E \subseteq L \times \text{Ops} \times L$. Each program edge $(\ell, op, \ell') \in E$ represents a control-flow transition from program location ℓ to ℓ' by evaluating operation $op \in \text{Ops}$. We consider three types of program operations: expression assignments, input assignments, and assumptions. An expression assignment $x \leftarrow expr$ assigns the value of expression $expr$ to program variable x. Expression $expr$ is an arithmetic expression over integers. An input assignment $x \leftarrow \circ$ receives an integer value from outside the program (e.g. sensor inputs, user inputs) and assigns it to program variable x. An assumption $[p]$ evaluates the Boolean expression p over program variables. Control-flow continues only if p evaluates to true. A program state $c : X \mapsto \mathbb{Z}$ is a mapping from variables to their assigned integer value.

An execution $[\![P]\!] = (\ell_0, c_0) \xrightarrow{op_0} (\ell_1, c_1) \ldots \xrightarrow{op_{m-1}} (\ell_m, c_m)$ of program P is a sequence where each step $(\ell_{i-1}, c_{i-1}) \xrightarrow{op_{i-1}} (\ell_i, c_i)$ corresponds to a program edge $(\ell_{i-1}, op_{i-1}, \ell_i) \in E$, and the program state c_i is the result of applying operation op_{i-1} to program state c_{i-1}.

Test Case. A test case $\boldsymbol{t} = \langle v_0, \ldots, v_{n-1} \rangle$ is a vector of input values v_i. The length n of a test case $\boldsymbol{t} = \langle v_0, \ldots, v_{n-1} \rangle$ is its number of input values. During program execution, whenever an input assignment $x \leftarrow \circ$ is evaluated, variable x is assigned the next input value from the test case.

[1] Our implementation works on C programs.

```
<testcase>
  <input>1</input>
  <input>0</input>
  <input>0</input>
</testcase>
```

Fig. 2: Test case in XML format that describes the test vector $\langle 1, 0, 0\rangle$

```
- segment:
  - waypoint:
      action: "follow"
      location:
        file_name: "prog.c"
        line: 5
        column: 35
      type: "function_return"
      constraint:
        format: "acsl_expression"
        value: "\\result == 0"
- segment:
  - waypoint:
      action: "follow"
      location:
        file_name: "prog.c"
        line: 14
        column: 5
      type: "target"
```

Fig. 3: Segments of a violation witness

Test-Comp requires participants to produce test cases in XML format. Each test case is a separate XML file with a sequence of **<input>** elements. Figure 2 shows the test case in XML format for test vector $\langle 1, 0, 0\rangle$. A Test-Comp test suite is a collection of test cases together with a metadata file. A test suite is *successful* if it contains at least one test case that induces a program execution that reaches a call to `reach_error()`.

Competitions. Competitions are a scientific method for comparative evaluation, in which participants submit their tools together with instructions how to execute them, and an organizer executes all experiments under the same conditions. The competition on software verification SV-COMP annually evaluates verifiers, which take as input a program and a safety or liveness specification and produce as output a result *true* (together with a correctness witness), `false` (together with a violation witness), or *unknown* (if the verifier cannot determine the result). The competition on software testing Test-Comp annually evaluates testers, which take as input a program and a coverage specification and produce as output a test suite. SV-COMP validates the quality of a reported verification result through witness validation: A verifier only receives points for a correct verification result if it also produced a witness that can be validated.

Both SV-COMP and Test-Comp use the SV-Benchmarks collection of verification and test tasks, which is the largest and most diverse benchmark set of testing and verification tasks for the languages C and Java. The benchmark set contains verification tasks for properties such as reachability, memory safety, termination, no-overflows, and no-data-races, which are used by SV-COMP. Test-Comp uses tasks with coverage specification `cover-branches` and `cover-error`. Tasks with coverage specification `cover-error` must fulfill the following conditions: (a) the program contains at least one call to an input method `__VERIFIER_nondet_X`, (b) the program always terminates, (c) the program compiles successfully, and (d) the program has a reachability property with expected verdict `false` (i.e., it can reach a call to function `reach_error`). In consequence, the tasks that are used in Test-Comp with coverage specification `cover-error` are a subset of the tasks that are used in SV-COMP for reachability verification.

Violation Witnesses 2.0. A decade ago, violation witnesses [48] were introduced in the area of software verification and adopted by SV-COMP. Later, witnesses for correctness [49], non-termination, and other properties were introduced. While the first generation of witnesses were based on an XML format, the more recent witnesses in version 2.0 [50] are based on the YAML format. In this paper we use violation witnesses in version 2.0. Their aim is to support validation of the verification verdict `false`; that is, there is a path through the program that violates a safety specification.

A violation witness describes a set of program executions, of which at least one must reach a violation of the specification. The set of executions is described as a sequence of segments (cf. Fig. 3). Each segment consists of at least one waypoint `follow` and multiple optional waypoints `avoid`. Each waypoint is anchored to a program location (line number and column), and can hold assumptions over program variables, describe branching decisions or function-return values, or signal a function entry. The last segment of a violation witness contains a waypoint `target`, which indicates that the violation of the specification is reached. Figure 3 shows two example segments: The first segment contains a waypoint `follow` of type `function_return` that matches some function call at line 15, column 33 of file `prog.c`. This function call's constraint `\\result == 0` expresses that the call's return value must be 0 for the path to be valid. The second segment contains a waypoint `follow` of type `target`. This claims that the path should reach line 8, column 5 of file `prog.c`, where a specification violation occurs.

A validator for violation witnesses can re-play the described paths to show that one of the paths is feasible and indeed violates the specification. For a described path to be feasible, there must be a program execution that passes all waypoints, satisfies all assumptions along the way, and reaches the target. There is broad support for witness format version 2.0, but only two validators in SV-COMP 2025 support function-return assumptions: CPAchecker and Witch.

3 Test-to-Witness

Consider the example program in Fig. 4, and two test cases that both trigger the error at ℓ_8: $\mathrm{tc}_1 = \langle 0, 0 \rangle$ and $\mathrm{tc}_2 = \langle 1, 0, 0 \rangle$. Program execution with test case tc_1 introduces the first input value 0 at ℓ_6 and the second input value 0 at ℓ_{12}, while program execution with test case tc_2 introduces the first input value 1 at ℓ_6, but then assigns the second input value at ℓ_7 before the third input value 0 is assigned at ℓ_{12}. This shows the key challenge in converting a test case to a violation witness: the test case lists the sequence of input values to give to a program execution, but it has no information on *where* in the program an input value is used. This information is strictly necessary to describe waypoints in witnesses. Because the control flow of two program executions can lead to a different order of calls to input methods, pattern matching on the program code is not sufficient. Instead, it is necessary to consider the program semantics to reliably match which input method consumes which input value. Input methods within loops (as induced by ℓ_9) may also create test cases of dynamic length.

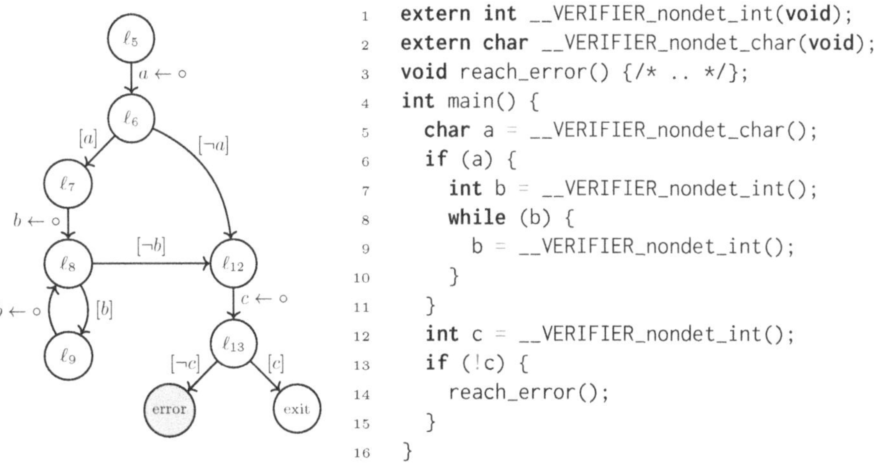

Fig. 4: Program in graph representation (left) and corresponding C code (right)

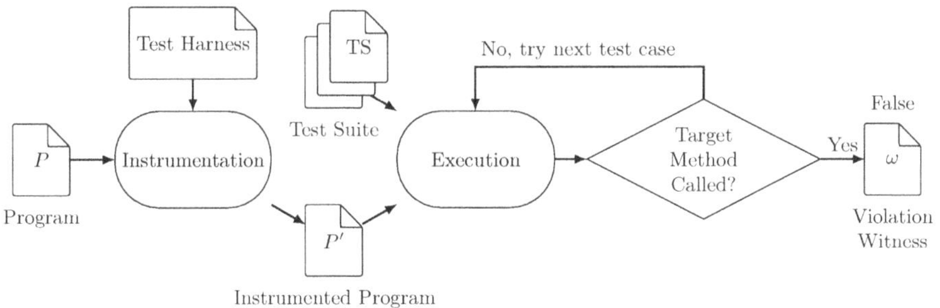

Fig. 5: Workflow of Test-to-Witness

Test-to-Witness solves this issue through a projection of the program execution trace: Given a program P and a test case $\boldsymbol{t} = \langle v_0, \ldots, v_{n-1} \rangle$, Test-to-Witness executes P with $\boldsymbol{t}$ to obtain a finite execution trace $[\![P]\!]_{\boldsymbol{t}} = (\ell_0, c_0) \xrightarrow{\text{op}_0} (\ell_1, c_1) \ldots$ for $\boldsymbol{t}$. To receive a violation witness from this trace, Test-to-Witness projects $[\![P]\!]_{\boldsymbol{t}}$ onto input operations $\text{op}_j = w_j \leftarrow \circ$ and the valuation $c_j(w_j)$:

$$vs = \langle (\ell_{i_1}, c_{i_1}(w_{i_1})), (\ell_{i_2}, c_{i_2}(w_{i_2})), \ldots, (\ell_{i_k}, c_{i_k}(w_{i_k})) \rangle$$

where $\{i_1, i_2, \ldots, i_k\} = \{j \mid \text{op}_{j-1} = w_j \leftarrow \circ\}$ and $i_1 < i_2 < \ldots < i_k$. Sequence vs describes that at program location ℓ_{i_j}, variable w_{i_j} is assigned the test input value $c_{i_j}(w_{i_j}) = \boldsymbol{t}_{i_j}$. Each tuple in vs is then translated to its corresponding segment in the violation witness, specifying the program location through source-code line and column, and the input value to assume as constraint. A formalization of the segments can be found in the SV-COMP witness format specification [51].

Our implementation of Test-to-Witness works on C programs. It realizes the projection through a program instrumentation that, when executed with a test

```
1  extern int __VERIFIER_nondet_int();
2  extern char __VERIFIER_nondet_char();
3  void reach_error() {/* .. */};
4  int __VERIFIER_nondet_int_log(int line, int column) {
5    int val = __VERIFIER_nondet_int();
6    /* .. print violation-witness segment for line, column,
7       with assumption '\result = {val}' */
8    return val;
9  }
10 char __VERIFIER_nondet_char_log(int line, int column) {
11   char val = __VERIFIER_nondet_char();
12   /* .. print violation-witness segment for line, column,
13      with assumption '\result = {val}' */
14   return val;
15 }
16 void reach_error_log(int line, int column) {
17   /* .. print violation-witness segment with target waypoint
18         for line, column */
19   reach_error();
20 }
21 int main() {
22   char a = __VERIFIER_nondet_char_log(5, 35);
23   if (a) {
24     int b = __VERIFIER_nondet_int_log(7, 35);
25     while (b) {
26       b = __VERIFIER_nondet_int_log(9, 33);
27     }
28   }
29   int c = __VERIFIER_nondet_int_log(12, 33);
30   if (!c)
31   {
32     reach_error_log(14, 5);
33   }
34 }
```

Fig. 6: Instrumented version of Fig. 4

case, directly writes a violation witness with the correct location information. Figure 5 shows this workflow. Test-to-Witness first instruments the program P and compiles it against a test harness. To represent input assignments, it relies on the SV-COMP convention of using input methods `__VERIFIER_nondet_X`, where X is the type of the returned value. It considers calls to method `reach_error(void)` as specification violations. This property can be reduced to other reachability properties, like failing assertions.

After compilation, Test-to-Witness executes the resulting binary with all test cases of the test suite until one test case reaches the target method. If this happens, the violation witness produced by this execution is returned.

Program Instrumentation. For each input method, Test-to-Witness defines a new variant that (1) receives its call location in the program file as two parameters `line` and `column`, (2) calls the original input method and stores the returned value in a local variable `val`, (3) prints a fragment of the violation witness that describes that the return value of the input method must be equal to `val`, and (4) returns `val` to the caller. For each target method, Test-to-Witness defines a variant that first prints the fragment of the violation witness and then calls the original target method. Figure 6 shows these method definitions for Fig. 4 in lines 4–34. Test-to-Witness then replaces all calls to input methods and target methods with the new variants, passing the appropriate line and column numbers

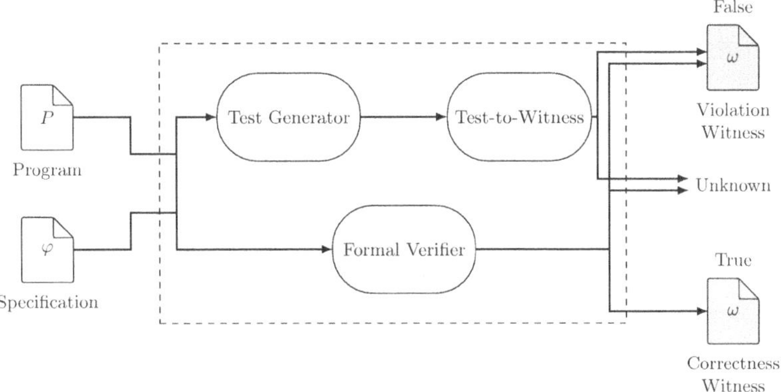

Fig. 7: Architecture of our Parallel Portfolio

for each original call site. To match the specific waypoint of violation witnesses, the column number is the position of the closing parenthesis of the original method call for input methods, and the position of the first character of the method call for target methods. Last, Test-to-Witness creates a test harness that defines the original input methods so that they parse input values from standard input, and compiles the instrumented program against this harness. Because the resulting binary parses input values from standard input, the same binary can be used to execute all available test cases.

Execution with Test Cases. Test-to-Witness executes the compiled binary with each test case of the test suite until one execution reaches the target method. To not be blocked by slow test executions, Test-to-Witness executes multiple test cases in parallel. Each execution's produced violation witness is captured to a separate file. As soon as one execution reaches the target method, Test-to-Witness terminates all other executions and returns the corresponding violation witness.

Testers as Falsifiers. Figure 1 shows how any off-the-shelf tester can be used with Test-to-Witness to produce violation witnesses for formal verification. Similar to a formal verifier, the tester receives the program P under analysis and a specification φ.[2] Once started, the tester tries to find a test case that violates the specification. Testers consider the given specification to various degrees: Some testers stop as soon as a test case is found that matches the test-goal specification [52, 53], while others generate test cases for internally implemented coverage criteria [54], or fully randomly [25, 55]. For the latter we can monitor the generated test cases continuously and still stop the tool as soon as one covering test case is found.

Parallel Portfolio. Testers can only find specification violations, but not proof the absence of violations. Because of this, the use of testers in formal verification is mostly useful in combination with a formal verifier. For this we propose a

[2] We do not show a possible translation of a verification specification to a test goal specification, as this is not the focus of this paper. In our context this was merely matching existing verification specifications to test goals.

parallel-portfolio approach (Fig. 7), where a tester runs concurrently to a formal verifier. Whenever the tester produces a test case, Test-to-Witness tries to convert the test case into a witness. If the conversion is successful, the portfolio terminates and returns the witness generated by Test-to-Witness. If the conversion fails, the portfolio continues. The two most common reasons for failure are: (1) the tester was aborted before it could find a violating test case and (2) the test case does not lead to a violation of the property; it is a false positive. We implement the parallel portfolio in the cooperative verification framework CoVeriTeam [56]. CoVeriTeam provides unified interfaces for both testers and formal verifiers, and allows to specify the specific tools to use through the command line. This enables us to plug-and-play different combinations of testers and verifiers easily.

AFL-TC. To enable the use of AFL-FUZZ with Test-to-Witness, we implement AFL-TC [24], a tool chain that runs AFL-FUZZ in parallel with a monitor process. It continuously monitors the test cases generated by AFL-FUZZ. Whenever a test case is produced that triggers a program crash, the monitor invokes Test-to-Witness to transform the test case to a violation witness. If this transformation is successful, the monitor terminates AFL-FUZZ and returns the violation witness.

4 Evaluation

We answer the following research questions with an experimental evaluation:

RQ 1 Transformation: Can test cases be reliably transformed into violation witnesses?
RQ 2 Viability: Are the standalone use of Test-Comp test generators competitive in the falsification category of SV-COMP?
RQ 3 Efficiency: Does the combination of Test-Comp test generators with verifiers improve the overall efficiency?
RQ 4 Effectiveness: Does the combination of Test-Comp test generators with verifiers improve the overall effectiveness?

Tool Versions. We use verification tasks from SV-Benchmarks [57] in the version used for SV-COMP 2025 [58]. We use Test-to-Witness revision c9d2a32. For the portfolio, we use CoVeriTeam [56] revision 0408cbd. For reliable resource measurement, we use BENCHEXEC [59] b07c314d. All experiments were executed on machines equipped with one Intel Xeon E3-1230 v5 (3.4 GHz, 8 processing units) and 33 GB of RAM, running Ubuntu 24.04 LTS 64 bit and GNU/Linux 6.8.0.

RQ 1: Can test cases be reliably transformed into violation witnesses?
We let Test-to-Witness transform test suites that were produced in Test-Comp 2025 into violation witnesses. We consider each test suite that was produced in the `cover-error` category and that contains at least one test case where TESTCOV [60] confirmed in Test-Comp that its execution calls the error function.

This selection consists of 10 935 test suites that were produced by 18 testers. We run Test-to-Witness on all test suites, with a timeout of 5 min per test suite.

Table 1: Summary of test cases that were transformed to violation witnesses

Total Tasks	Converted	Avg. Time (s)	Median Time (s)
10 935	10 897	0.77	0.16

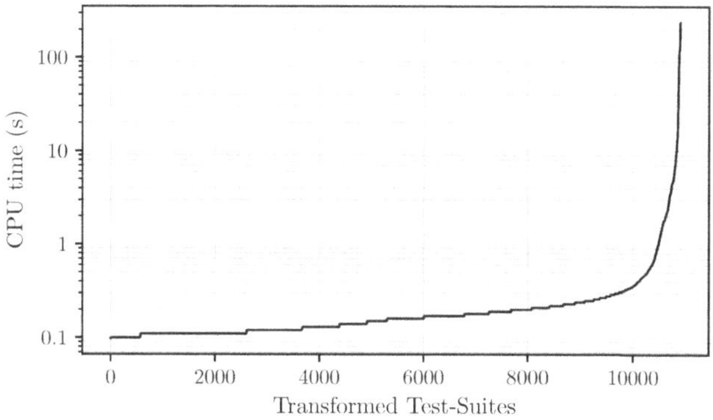

Fig. 8: Quantile plot of transformation times for test cases to violation witnesses

Table 1 shows that 10897 ($\approx$ 99.6 %) test suites were transformed successfully within the given time limit. The quantile plot in Fig. 8 shows the distribution of transformation times that Test-to-Witness requires to transform the test suites into violation witnesses. The x-axis shows the number of test suites that can be transformed within the CPU time that is given on the y-axis. For example, the graph shows that 8 069 test suites ($\approx$ 74 %) are transformed by Test-to-Witness with a run time of 0.2 s or less, and 10 490 test suites ($\approx$ 96 %) are transformed within 1 s or less. This shows that the time required to transform a test suite into a violation witness is usually so low that it is negligible.

Next we explore the impact that the size of a test suite has on the transformation time. Figure 9 shows the distribution of test-suite sizes on the left plot. The x-axis shows the size of the test suite and the y-axis is the number of test suites that have at least x amount of test cases. The median size of a test suite is 1, but we also observe significant outliers.

The scatter plot on the right side of Fig. 9 shows the effect of test-suite size on transformation time. The x-axis shows the size of a test suite and the y-axis shows the CPU time that the transformation takes. We observe a trend that the transformation of larger test suites consumes more CPU time. We expect this, since Test-to-Witness executes test cases in parallel until one is found that reaches the error location. We look at two example test suites whose transformation takes long: The test suite created by TracerX-WP for the task `list-2.yml` takes 78 s to transform. The suite consists of 20 774 test cases. Each individual test case only takes a few milliseconds to execute, but the cumulative time for all test cases quickly adds up, especially since Test-to-Witness runs as many test-cases in parallel as there are CPU cores available.

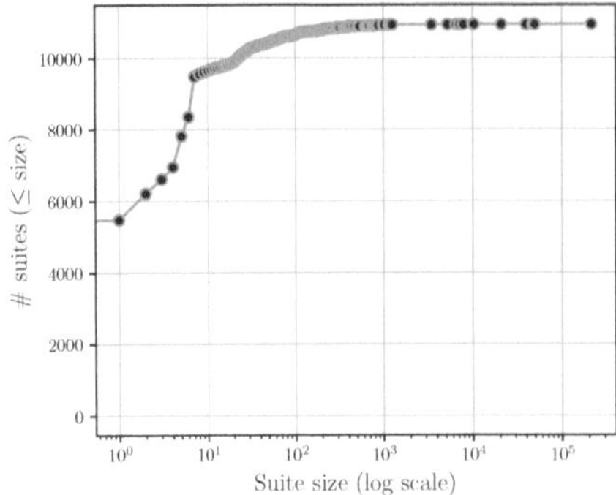

Fig. 9: Distribution of test-suite sizes

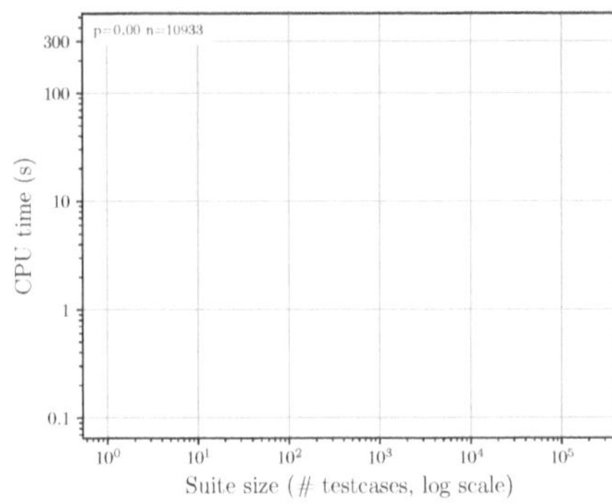

Fig. 10: Effect of test-suite size on transformation time (in CPU time)

But also test suites with few test cases can take a long time to transform: The test suite created by KLEEF for task `btor2c-lazyMod.unsafe_buggy_ridecore.yml` consists of a single test case, but takes 110 s to transform. The compilation of the instrumented program dominates this transformation time. Executing the test case itself takes less than 1 s.

We evaluate the quality of the generated violation witnesses by running the two SV-COMP validators on them that support function-return constraints: CPACHECKER and WITCH. We run both validators with a timeout of 90 s per witness, which is the limit for violation-witness validation in SV-COMP.

Table 2 shows, for each test generator, the number of test suites created by that test generator (# Suites), the number of witnesses that are successfully transformed into violation witnesses (# Converted), the number of witnesses that are confirmed by at least one validator (# Confirmed), and the percentage of considered test suites that are successfully transformed and confirmed (% Confirmed). In total, 9 739 (≈ 89 %) of the 10 935 test suites are successfully transformed and subsequently confirmed by a validator.

From these results we conclude that test cases can be reliably transformed into violation witnesses. Almost all test suites can be transformed within 1 s of CPU time, and almost 90 % of the generated witnesses are confirmed by at least one of the two validators. The extremely efficient transformation makes the approach feasible for real-time integration into test-to-verification-workflows such as the portfolio presented in Sect. 3.

RQ 2: Does the standalone use of Test-Comp test generators yield competitive results in the falsification category of SV-COMP?

Since the benchmark set of Test-Comp is a subset of the benchmark set of SV-COMP, we can compare the results of test generators in Test-Comp to the results of verifiers in SV-COMP. We achieve this by comparing the *validated* test-generator results from Test-Comp 2025 to the verifier results of SV-COMP 2025. We define a *validated* test-generator result as a test suite that was successfully transformed into violation witnesses and then confirmed by at least one validator—this is the criterion that a *tester as falsifier* would need to fulfill to score points in SV-

Table 2: Transformed and validated violation witnesses from test cases

Tester	# Suites	# Converted	# Confirmed	% Confirmed
cetfuzz	320	317	313	98
esbmc-incr	948	948	772	81
esbmc-kind	948	948	770	81
fdse	628	626	589	94
fizzer	612	608	589	96
fusebmc	979	978	826	84
fusebmc-ia	951	950	844	89
hybridtiger	428	423	421	98
klee	889	887	759	85
kleef	998	995	841	84
owic	230	227	227	99
prtest	295	290	240	81
rizzer	550	549	503	92
symbiotic	586	584	581	99
tracerx	420	419	391	93
tracerx-wp	402	400	360	90
utestgen	317	314	311	98
wasp-c	434	434	402	93
Total	10 935	10 897	9 739	89

COMP. To enable a fair comparison, we add the CPU time that Test-to-Witness takes to transform the test suites into violation witnesses to the time the test generator initially needed to generate the test suite in Test-Comp 2025. We restrict ourselves to the `ReachSafety` category of tasks, where we only consider tasks with an expected verdict of `false`; since test generators cannot find proofs.

On the entire benchmark set of tasks with an expected verdict of `false`, test generators are not competitive with verifiers. The best verifier solves 1 943 tasks, while the best test generator only solves 848 tasks. We discussed in Sect. 2 that not all tasks with an expected verdict of `false` qualify for test generation. The `ReachSafety` category of SV-COMP 2025 contains 2 929 tasks with an expected verdict of `false`. But out of those, Test-Comp 2025 restricts its benchmark set to the 1 074 tasks that qualify for test generation. We consider the results of verifiers and test generators on this subset. Figure 11 shows the quantile plot of correctly found alarms per tester and verifier. We highlight some verifiers and test generators: CPAchecker and Symbiotic as the two best performing verifiers in the `Falsification` category, and UAutomizer as the overall winner of SV-COMP 2025; FuSeBMC and Kleef as the two best performing test generators in the `cover-error` category of Test-Comp 2025. The quantile plot shows that these test generators outperform the verifiers. FuSeBMC, the winner of the `cover-error` category, is able to find 832 alarms within the time limit of 900 s, while the winning verifier of the Falsification and `ReachSafety` category, CPAchecker, finds only 706 alarms within the time limit. To get a better understanding of the potential improvements that are possible through tool combinations, we include the virtual

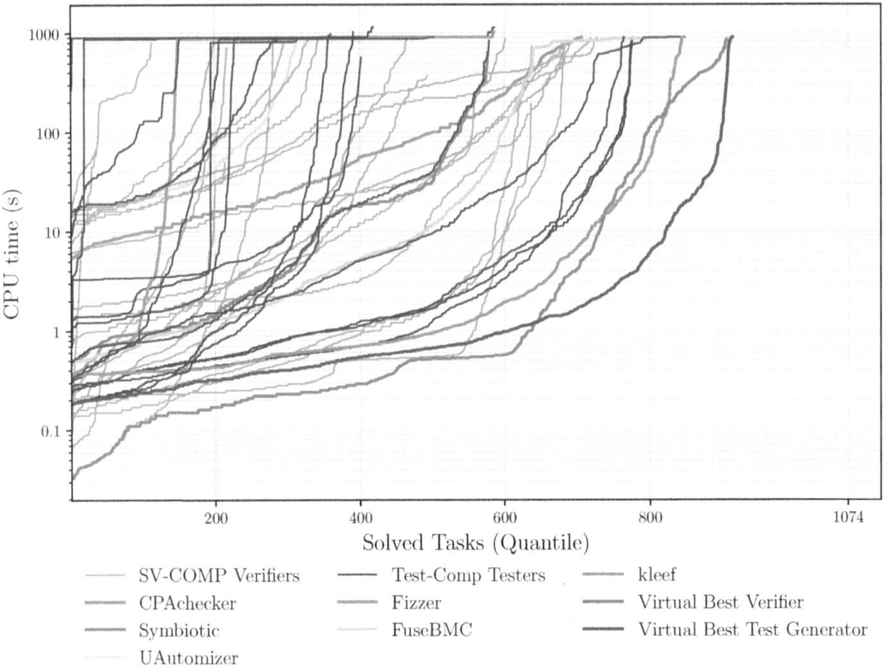

Fig. 11: Quantile plot of correctly found alarms per tester and verifier, limited to the 1 074 tasks that are suitable for test generation

best verifier and the virtual best test generator in Fig. 11. The virtual best verifier picks from all verifiers the fastest solving time per task; the virtual best test generator picks from all test generators the fastest time per task.

The results show that, if we level the playing field by restricting the benchmark set to tasks that are suitable for test generators, test generators yield competitive results in the falsification category of SV-COMP. When we create a virtual best tester and a virtual best solver, we observe only a thin advantage of test generators over verifiers.

RQ 3: Does the combination of test generators with verifiers improve the overall efficiency? We study the impact that combining test generators with formal verifiers has on the overall efficiency of verification. For this, we create a set of portfolio solvers that consist of one test generator and one verifier each, as described in Sect. 3.

We select a representative set of verifiers based on their performance in SV-COMP 2025: We select CPACHECKER as the best tool in the `Falsification` and `ReachSafety` categories, SYMBIOTIC, and BUBAAK as the runner ups in the `Falsification` category, as well as CPV, and ESBMC-KIND as the runner ups in the `ReachSafety` category. Additionally we select UAUTOMIZER as it is the overall winner of SV-COMP 2025. We select representative test generators based on their performance in Test-Comp 2025: We select FuSeBMC, Kleef, and Symbiotic as the top three test generators of the `cover-error` category. We also select Fizzer as the third place in the overall ranking of Test-Comp 2025. Finally, we select PRTest as a simple baseline tester that uses black-box random testing.

We run all combinations on the `ReachSafety` tasks contained in the SV-Benchmarks repository [16]. We limit each portfolio to a CPU time limit of 900 s, a memory limit of 15 GB and 4 CPU cores. The scatter plots in Fig. 12 show the CPU time consumption for tasks that both the combination of verifier and test generator as well as the reference alone solved correctly. The figure is structured in rows and columns, where each row represents a verifier and each column a test generator. For space reasons, we omit the test generators Symbiotic and Fizzer from the plots. The full plot is archived on Zenodo: 10.5281/zenodo.18312562. Each subplot has the same structure: the x-axis shows the CPU time needed by the reference verifier alone, while the y-axis shows the CPU time needed by the portfolio combination of verifier and test generator. Points below the diagonal line indicate that the portfolio combination was faster than the verifier alone, while points above the diagonal line indicate that the verifier alone was faster. The subplots also contain the number of considered tasks (N), and the P-Value of a Wilcoxon signed-rank test (p) [61], testing the one-sided hypothesis that the portfolio is slower than the reference. Orange dots indicate tasks that the reference was not able to solve, but that the portfolio was able to solve. Green dots indicate tasks that the portfolio was not able to solve, but that the reference was able to solve. Both orange and green dots are ignored for the statistical test. We only consider tasks that both variants solved correctly.

The addition of test generators does not improve the efficiency of verification, overall. In all considered combinations, the p-value is 0, indicating that the portfolios use significantly more CPU time than the verifiers alone. However, we can see an overall trend that the increase in CPU time is moderate. There are few outliers where the portfolio is significantly slower than the verifier alone. But we can still see improvements in the efficiency on individual tasks: fuzzing-based test generators such as AFL-TC can find violations quickly for some tasks, showing potential, e.g., in the combination with UAutomizer, CPAchecker, and CPV. The portfolios with PRTest also show potential: they have faster tasks along the 10 s line of the y-axis. This speeds up multiple tasks for every verifier, that originally takes hundreds of seconds to solve (points far right on the x-axis).

In summary, the addition of test generators to verifiers does not improve the overall efficiency. However, the increase in CPU time is moderate and does not constitute a practical limitation: in real-world usage, a moderate overhead in CPU time is acceptable when it leads to finding more bugs.

RQ 4: Does the combination of test generators with verifiers improve the overall effectiveness?

To check whether the addition of test generators to verifiers can increase the overall effectiveness, we analyze whether the combination can solve more tasks than the verifier alone. We use the same portfolio combinations as in RQ 3.

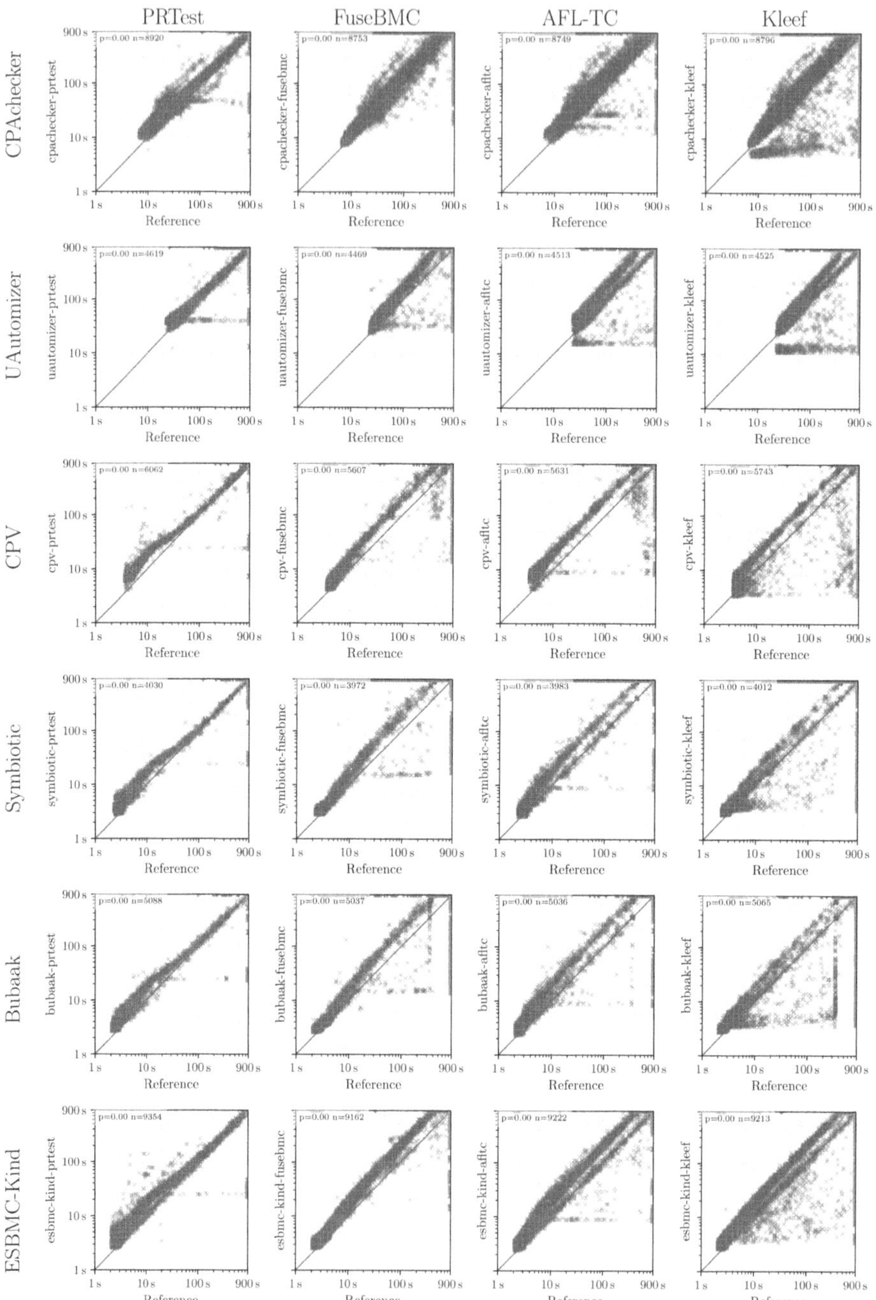

Fig. 12: Scatter plot of different verifier-test-generator-combinations

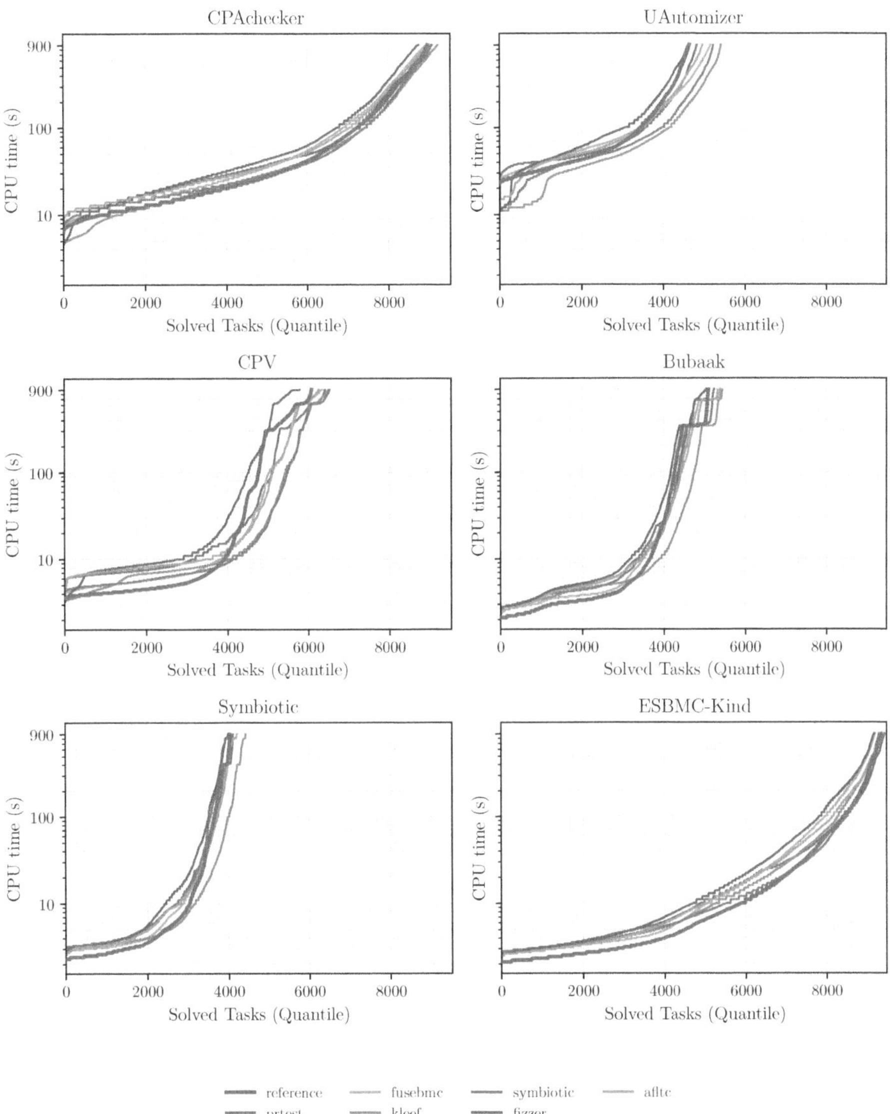

Fig. 13: Quantile plot of different verifier-test-generator combinations (number of solved tasks per configuration, out of 15 310 total tasks)

Table 3: Summary of gains and losses of verifier-test-generator-combinations; Uniquely solved (Unq) tasks are tasks that only the portfolio solved, not the reference; Timeouts (TO) and memory outs (MO) are tasks that the reference solved, but the portfolio did not due to timeout or memory out.

Verifier	PRTest			Fizzer			FuSeBMC			AFL-TC			Symbiotic			Kleef		
	Unq	TO	MO	Unq	TO	MO	Unq	TO	MO	Unq	TO	MO	Unq	TO	MO	Unq	TO	MO
CPAchecker	125	33	0	114	331	1	166	198	2	214	204	0	298	99	92	405	142	15
UAutomizer	222	21	12	153	149	40	702	172	18	457	122	23	679	27	75	893	84	48
CPV	360	6	0	372	643	0	746	460	1	631	458	0	770	56	244	774	321	3
Symbiotic	82	1	3	92	132	0	233	64	2	222	54	0	33	23	57	410	21	5
Bubaak	152	9	1	100	144	0	353	65	0	291	65	0	223	20	189	372	29	5
Esbmc-kInd	93	8	0	69	248	0	48	197	4	133	140	0	140	41	144	95	148	2

Figure 13 shows the results of all portfolio combinations. For each portfolio we also provide as reference a run of the verifier on its own, giving it the full time limit and memory limit. We observe that verifiers that excel in proving the absence of errors, such as UAutomizer and CPV, benefit more from the addition of test generators in the portfolio than verifiers that are already proficient in bug-finding (according to SV-COMP results), like CPAchecker and Esbmc-kInd. The portfolio combinations can, in some cases, end up solving less tasks than the verifier alone, indicated by the plot line ending further to the left than the reference line. But each verifier, when paired with an appropriate test generator, can improve their effectiveness, even when staying within the same CPU-time and memory limits given by SV-COMP.

We take a closer look at the gains and losses of the portfolio combinations in Table 3. One observation is that even adding plain random testing (PRTest) yields new uniquely solved tasks for all verifiers. The portfolios with more elaborate test generators have more potential for uniquely solved tasks, but also incur more losses due to timeouts and out-of-memory errors. These timeouts occur because in the CPU time limit is shared between the two tools in the portfolio, leaving less CPU time for each individual tool. In a practical setting, one could counteract these timeouts by increasing the overall CPU time limit of the portfolio. We also observe that most verifiers are not inhibited by out-of-memory errors when combined with test generators. Only UAutomizer suffers from a significant amount of out-of-memory errors when combined with test generators.

Another observation from Table 3 is that static-analysis based test generators such as Kleef and Symbiotic also yield new uniquely solved tasks for most verifiers—tools which are static analyzers themselves. As an example, both Kleef and CPAchecker implement a form of symbolic execution, yet their combination is able to solve 405 more tasks than CPAchecker alone. Even the portfolio of Symbiotic in verifier configuration with Symbiotic in test generator configuration is able to solve new tasks when compared to just Symbiotic (verifier) alone.

From the results we conclude that the addition of test generators to verifiers can significantly improve the overall effectiveness. All considered verifiers are able to solve more tasks when combined with an appropriate test generator. Most tasks that are not solved by the portfolio are due to timeouts, which can be counteracted by increasing the overall CPU time limit of the portfolio.

Threats to Validity. The validity of drawn conclusions is always limited: We consider the internal, external, and construct validity of the presented results.

Internal Validity. We evaluate combinations of tools rather than combinations of techniques in isolation, which means that observed effects may be due to specific implementations in the tools rather than the underlying techniques themselves. Many test generators use hybrid approaches [12], which prevents us from drawing conclusions about which specific techniques work well together. However, to minimize internal validity threats, we conduct our experiments on the same infrastructure as the official SV-COMP and Test-Comp competitions, ensuring consistency with the competition setting. We use BenchExec [59] for reliable resource measurements, which minimizes measurement errors and variability.

External Validity. Our evaluation is limited to the C programming language and the benchmark sets from SV-COMP and Test-Comp. However, these represent the largest publicly available benchmark set of verification tasks for C programs. Both competitions are highly concerned with precise measurements and reproducibility, lending credibility to our results. The tools we selected are proven to be good representatives of their kind, as they perform well in the respective competitions. Thus, while results may not generalize to other programming languages or entirely different domains, our findings are representative of the state-of-the-art in formal verification and testing for C.

Construct Validity. We design our experiments to evaluate whether test generators can improve verification. We measure effectiveness in terms of correctly solved tasks and efficiency in terms of CPU time, which are standard metrics in the software verification community and used by SV-COMP and Test-Comp. For witness validation, we use the two active SV-COMP validators that support the required witness features, ensuring that our results reflect the actual acceptance criteria of the competition.

5 Conclusion

We presented Test-to-Witness, a tool to convert test cases into violation witnesses. Our extensive evaluation shows that the transformation of test suites is feasible and efficient. We provided evidence that even the combination of a simple plain random tester with any state-of-the-art verifier can improve the effectiveness of bug-finding capabilities in formal verification significantly. Our experiments suggest that especially tools that focus heavily on proving programs correct benefit from a pairing with a test generator. We also show that a portfolio approach, with a small negative impact on efficiency, can improve effectiveness of all considered verifiers.

Data Availability. Test-to-Witness and AFL-TC are publicly available via our supplementary web page https://www.sosy-lab.org/research/test-to-witness/ and as reproduction package at Zenodo [62]. The reproduction package was evaluated by the artifact-evaluation committee and allows the reproduction of our experiments and contains all reported data.

Funding Statement. This project was funded by the Deutsche Forschungsgemeinschaft (DFG) – 378803395 (ConVeY) and 418257054 (Coop).

References

1. Beyer, D., Dangl, M., Lemberger, T., Tautschnig, M.: Tests from witnesses: Execution-based validation of verification results. In: Proc. TAP. pp. 3–23. LNCS 10889, Springer (2018). https://doi.org/10.1007/978-3-319-92994-1_1
2. Beyer, D., Chlipala, A.J., Henzinger, T.A., Jhala, R., Majumdar, R.: Generating tests from counterexamples. In: Proc. ICSE. pp. 326–335. IEEE (2004). https://doi.org/10.1109/ICSE.2004.1317455
3. Beyer, D., Lemberger, T.: Conditional testing: Off-the-shelf combination of test-case generators. In: Proc. ATVA. pp. 189–208. LNCS 11781, Springer (2019). https://doi.org/10.1007/978-3-030-31784-3_11
4. Alshmrany, K.M., Aldughaim, M., Bhayat, A., Cordeiro, L.C.: FuSeBMC: An energy-efficient test generator for finding security vulnerabilities in C programs. In: Proc. TAP. pp. 85–105. Springer (2021). https://doi.org/10.1007/978-3-030-79379-1_6
5. Godefroid, P., Levin, M.Y., Molnar, D.A.: Automated whitebox fuzz testing. In: Proc. NDSS. The Internet Society (2008), https://www.ndss-symposium.org/ndss2008/automated-whitebox-fuzz-testing/
6. Godefroid, P., Klarlund, N., Sen, K.: Dart: Directed automated random testing. In: Proc. PLDI. pp. 213–223. ACM (2005). https://doi.org/10.1145/1065010.1065036
7. Tillmann, N., de Halleux, J.: Pex-white box test generation for .net. In: Proc. TAP. pp. 134–153. LNCS 4966, Springer (2008). https://doi.org/10.1007/978-3-540-79124-9_10
8. Stephens, N., Grosen, J., Salls, C., Dutcher, A., Wang, R., Corbetta, J., Shoshitaishvili, Y., Kruegel, C., Vigna, G.: Driller: Augmenting fuzzing through selective symbolic execution. In: Proc. NDSS. Internet Society (2016). https://doi.org/10.14722/ndss.2016.23368
9. Chen, C., Kande, R., Nguyen, N., Andersen, F., Tyagi, A., Sadeghi, A., Rajendran, J.: Hypfuzz: Formal-assisted processor fuzzing. In: USENIX Security. pp. 1361–1378. USENIX Association (2023)
10. Cadar, C., Sen, K.: Symbolic execution for software testing: three decades later. Commun. ACM **56**(2), 82–90 (2013). https://doi.org/10.1145/2408776.2408795
11. Metta, R., Medicherla, R.K., Chakraborty, S.: BMC+Fuzz: Efficient and effective test generation. In: Proc. DATE. pp. 1419–1424. IEEE (2022). https://doi.org/10.23919/DATE54114.2022.9774672
12. Beyer, D., Lemberger, T.: Six years later: Testing vs. model checking. Int. J. Softw. Tools Technol. Transf. **26**(6), 633–646 (2024). https://doi.org/10.1007/S10009-024-00769-8
13. Beyer, D.: State of the art in software verification and witness validation: SV-COMP 2024. In: Proc. TACAS (3). pp. 299–329. LNCS 14572, Springer (2024). https://doi.org/10.1007/978-3-031-57256-2_15

14. Beyer, D.: Automatic testing of C programs: Test-Comp 2024. In: TBA. Springer (2024)
15. Afzal, M., Asia, A., Chauhan, A., Chimdyalwar, B., Darke, P., Datar, A., Kumar, S., Venkatesh, R.: VeriAbs: Verification by abstraction and test generation. In: Proc. ASE. pp. 1138–1141. IEEE (2019). https://doi.org/10.1109/ASE.2019.00121
16. Collection of verification tasks. https://gitlab.com/sosy-lab/benchmarking/sv-benchmarks, accessed: 2025-10-17
17. Beyer, D., Strejček, J.: Evaluating software verifiers for C, Java, and SV-LIB (Report on SV-COMP 2026). In: Proc. TACAS (2). pp. 461–502. LNCS 16506, Springer (2026). https://doi.org/10.1007/978-3-032-22749-2_23
18. Beyer, D.: Evaluating tools for automatic software testing (Report on Test-Comp 2026). In: Proc. FASE. pp. 449–468. LNCS 16504, Springer (2026). https://doi.org/10.1007/978-3-032-22774-4_23
19. Beyer, D.: Second competition on software testing: Test-Comp 2020. In: Proc. FASE. pp. 505–519. LNCS 12076, Springer (2020). https://doi.org/10.1007/978-3-030-45234-6_25
20. Beyer, D.: Status report on software testing: Test-Comp 2021. In: Proc. FASE. pp. 341–357. LNCS 12649, Springer (2021). https://doi.org/10.1007/978-3-030-71500-7_17
21. Beyer, D.: Advances in automatic software testing: Test-Comp 2022. In: Proc. FASE. pp. 321–335. LNCS 13241, Springer (2022). https://doi.org/10.1007/978-3-030-99429-7_18
22. Beyer, D.: Software testing: 5th comparative evaluation: Test-Comp 2023. In: Proc. FASE. pp. 309–323. LNCS 13991, Springer (2023). https://doi.org/10.1007/978-3-031-30826-0_17
23. Beyer, D.: Advances in automatic software testing: Test-Comp 2025. In: Proc. FASE. pp. 257–274. LNCS 15693, Springer (2025). https://doi.org/10.1007/978-3-031-90900-9_13
24. Lemberger, T., Wachowitz, H.: AFL-TC: Transforming fuzzer test inputs for Test-Comp (competition contribution). In: Proc. FASE. pp. 475-480. LNCS 16504, Springer (2026). https://doi.org/10.1007/978-3-032-22774-4_25
25. Google: american fuzzy lop. https://github.com/google/AFL, accessed: 2025-10-17
26. Böhme, M., Pham, V., Roychoudhury, A.: Coverage-based greybox fuzzing as markov chain. In: Proc. SIGSAC. pp. 1032–1043. ACM, New York, NY, USA (2016). https://doi.org/10.1145/2976749.2978428
27. Beyer, D., Lemberger, T.: Software verification: Testing vs. model checking. In: Proc. HVC. pp. 99–114. LNCS 10629, Springer (2017). https://doi.org/10.1007/978-3-319-70389-3_7
28. Yoo, S., Harman, M.: Regression testing minimization, selection, and prioritization: A survey. STVR **22**(2), 67–120 (2012). https://doi.org/10.1002/stvr.430
29. McMinn, P.: Search-based software test-data generation: A survey. STVR **14**(2), 105–156 (2004). https://doi.org/10.1002/stvr.294
30. Li, J., Zhao, B., Zhang, C.: Fuzzing: A survey. Cybersecurity **1**(1), 6 (June 2018). https://doi.org/10.1186/s42400-018-0002-y
31. Manès, V.J.M., Han, H., Han, C., Cha, S.K., Egele, M., Schwartz, E.J., Woo, M.: The art, science, and engineering of fuzzing: A survey. IEEE Trans. Software Eng. **47**(11), 2312–2331 (2021). https://doi.org/10.1109/TSE.2019.2946563
32. Baldoni, R., Coppa, E., D'Elia, D.C., Demetrescu, C., Finocchi, I.: A survey of symbolic-execution techniques. ACM Comput. Surv. **51**(3), 50:1–50:39 (2018). https://doi.org/10.1145/3182657

33. Anand, S., Burke, E.K., Chen, T.Y., Clark, J.A., Cohen, M.B., Grieskamp, W., Harman, M., Harrold, M.J., McMinn, P.: An orchestrated survey of methodologies for automated software test case generation. Journal of Systems and Software **86**(8), 1978–2001 (2013). https://doi.org/10.1016/j.jss.2013.02.061
34. D'Silva, V., Kröning, D., Weissenbacher, G.: A survey of automated techniques for formal software verification. IEEE Trans. on CAD of Integrated Circuits and Systems **27**(7), 1165–1178 (2008). https://doi.org/10.1109/TCAD.2008.923410
35. Jhala, R., Majumdar, R.: Software model checking. ACM Computing Surveys **41**(4) (2009). https://doi.org/10.1145/1592434.1592438
36. Garavel, H., ter Beek, M.H., van de Pol, J.: The 2020 expert survey on formal methods. In: Proc. FMICS. pp. 3–69. LNCS 12327, Springer (2020). https://doi.org/10.1007/978-3-030-58298-2_1
37. Beyer, D., Podelski, A.: Software model checking: 20 years and beyond. In: Principles of Systems Design. pp. 554–582. LNCS 13660, Springer (2022). https://doi.org/10.1007/978-3-031-22337-2_27
38. Godefroid, P., Sen, K.: Combining model checking and testing. In: Handbook of Model Checking, pp. 613–649. Springer (2018). https://doi.org/10.1007/978-3-319-10575-8_19
39. Beyer, D., Gulwani, S., Schmidt, D.: Combining model checking and data-flow analysis. In: Handbook of Model Checking, pp. 493–540. Springer (2018). https://doi.org/10.1007/978-3-319-10575-8_16
40. Fraser, G., Wotawa, F., Ammann, P.: Testing with model checkers: A survey. STVR **19**(3), 215–261 (2009). https://doi.org/10.1002/stvr.402
41. Kaleeswaran, A.P., Nordmann, A., Vogel, T., Grunske, L.: A systematic literature review on counterexample explanation. Information and Software Technology **145**, 106800 (2022). https://doi.org/10.1016/j.infsof.2021.106800
42. Beyer, D., Dangl, M.: Verification-aided debugging: An interactive web-service for exploring error witnesses. In: Proc. CAV (2). pp. 502–509. LNCS 9780, Springer (2016). https://doi.org/10.1007/978-3-319-41540-6_28
43. Novikov, E., Zakharov, I.S.: Towards automated static verification of GNU C programs. In: Proc. PSI. pp. 402–416. LNCS 10742, Springer (2017). https://doi.org/10.1007/978-3-319-74313-4_30
44. Groce, A., Kröning, D., Lerda, F.: Understanding counterexamples with explain. In: Proc. CAV'04. pp. 453–456. LNCS 3114, Springer (2004). https://doi.org/10.1007/978-3-540-27813-9_35
45. Groce, A., Visser, W.: What went wrong: Explaining counterexamples. In: Proc. SPIN. pp. 121–135. LNCS 2648, Springer (2003). https://doi.org/10.1007/3-540-44829-2_8
46. Chaki, S., Groce, A., Strichman, O.: Explaining abstract counterexamples. In: Proc. FSE. pp. 73–82. ACM (2004). https://doi.org/10.1145/1029894.1029908
47. Castaño, R., Braberman, V.A., Garbervetsky, D., Uchitel, S.: Model checker execution reports. In: Proc. ASE. pp. 200–205. IEEE (2017). https://doi.org/10.1109/ASE.2017.8115633
48. Beyer, D., Dangl, M., Dietsch, D., Heizmann, M., Stahlbauer, A.: Witness validation and stepwise testification across software verifiers. In: Proc. FSE. pp. 721–733. ACM (2015). https://doi.org/10.1145/2786805.2786867
49. Beyer, D., Dangl, M., Dietsch, D., Heizmann, M.: Correctness witnesses: Exchanging verification results between verifiers. In: Proc. FSE. pp. 326–337. ACM (2016). https://doi.org/10.1145/2950290.2950351

50. Ayaziová, P., Beyer, D., Lingsch-Rosenfeld, M., Spiessl, M., Strejček, J.: Software verification witnesses 2.0. In: Proc. SPIN. pp. 184–203. LNCS 14624, Springer (2024). https://doi.org/10.1007/978-3-031-66149-5_11
51. Beyer, D., Strejček, J.: SV-Witnesses – Format 2.1. Zenodo (2025). https://doi.org/10.5281/zenodo.17277275
52. Beyer, D., Jakobs, M.C.: Cooperative verifier-based testing with CoVeriTest. Int. J. Softw. Tools Technol. Transfer **23**(3), 313–333 (2021). https://doi.org/10.1007/s10009-020-00587-8
53. Barth, M., Jakobs, M.C.: Test-case generation with automata-based software model checking. In: Proc. SPIN. Springer (2024). https://doi.org/10.1007/978-3-031-66149-5_14
54. Cadar, C., Dunbar, D., Engler, D.R.: Klee: Unassisted and automatic generation of high-coverage tests for complex systems programs. In: Proc. OSDI. pp. 209–224. USENIX Association (2008), available at https://www.usenix.org/events/osdi08/tech/full_papers/cadar/cadar.pdf
55. Lemberger, T.: Plain random test generation with PRTest (competition contribution). Int. J. Softw. Tools Technol. Transf. **23**(6), 871–873 (December 2021). https://doi.org/10.1007/s10009-020-00568-x
56. Beyer, D., Kanav, S.: CoVeriTeam: On-demand composition of cooperative verification systems. In: Proc. TACAS. pp. 561–579. LNCS 13243, Springer (2022). https://doi.org/10.1007/978-3-030-99524-9_31
57. Beyer, D., Strejček, J.: SV-Benchmarks: Benchmark set for software verification (SV-COMP 2025). Zenodo (2025). https://doi.org/10.5281/zenodo.15012096
58. Beyer, D., Strejček, J.: Improvements in software verification and witness validation: SV-COMP 2025. In: Proc. TACAS (3). pp. 151–186. LNCS 15698, Springer (2025). https://doi.org/10.1007/978-3-031-90660-2_9
59. Beyer, D., Löwe, S., Wendler, P.: Reliable benchmarking: Requirements and solutions. Int. J. Softw. Tools Technol. Transfer **21**(1), 1–29 (2019). https://doi.org/10.1007/s10009-017-0469-y
60. Beyer, D., Lemberger, T.: TestCov: Robust test-suite execution and coverage measurement. In: Proc. ASE. pp. 1074–1077. IEEE (2019). https://doi.org/10.1109/ASE.2019.00105
61. Wilcoxon, F.: Individual comparisons by ranking methods. Biometrics Bulletin **1**(6), 80–83 (1945). https://doi.org/10.2307/3001968
62. Beyer, D., Lemberger, T., Wachowitz, H.: Artifact for the fase 26 paper: Testing in formal verification via witness generation (empirical evaluation). Zenodo (2026). https://doi.org/10.5281/zenodo.18351121

Competition on Software Testing (Test-Comp 2026)

Evaluating Tools for Automatic Software Testing (Report on Test-Comp 2026)

Dirk Beyer ✉

LMU Munich, Munich, Germany

Abstract. This report presents the results of the 8th Competition on Software Testing (Test-Comp 2026), which is an annual event to provide an overview and comparative evaluation of automatic tools for test-suite generation for C programs. The experiment setup is publicly available and suitable for reuse as a baseline when comparing newly developed approaches for test generation. The benchmark set SV-Benchmarks contains 16 217 test-generation tasks for C programs. Each test-generation task consists of a program and a test specification. The test specifications included error coverage (generate a test suite that exhibits a bug) and branch coverage (generate a test suite that executes as many program branches as possible). Test-Comp 2026 evaluated 21 software systems for test generation that are all freely available. This included 11 test-suite generators that participated with active support from teams led by 11 different representatives from 6 countries (actively maintained software systems, participation in competition jury). Test-Comp 2026 had 1 new test generator (AFL-TO-TC [new]) and 1 new test-suite validator (TestCoCa [new]). The evaluation included also 10 test-generation tools from previous years.

Keywords: Software Testing · Test-Case Generation · Competition · Program Analysis · Software Validation · Software Bugs · Test Validation · Test-Comp · Benchmarking · Test Coverage · Bug Finding · Test Suites · SV-Benchmarks · BenchExec · TestCov · FM-Weck

1 Introduction

This report explains the competition setup and presents the results of the 8th edition of the International Competition on Software Testing (Test-Comp, https://test-comp.sosy-lab.org). The competition compares automatic test-suite generators for C programs, in order to showcase the state of the art in the area of automatic software testing. Since this report is a continuation of the series of yearly competition reports, we only slightly adjust the structure of the new report,

This report extends previous reports on Test-Comp [11, 13, 14, 15, 16, 18, 19, 21] by providing new results, while the procedures and setup of the competition stay mainly unchanged. Reproduction packages are available on Zenodo (see Table 5).

✉ dirk.beyer@sosy.ifi.lmu.de

E. Albert and C. Pasareanu (Eds.): FASE 2026, LNCS 16504, pp. 449–468, 2026.
https://doi.org/10.1007/978-3-032-22774-4_23

in order to facilitate quick lookup as reference [11, 13, 14, 15, 16, 18, 19, 21]. We repeat the rules and definitions, present the competition results, and give some interesting data about the execution of the competition experiments.

Competition Goals. In summary, the goals of Test-Comp are the following [13]:

- Establish *standards* for software test generation. This means, most prominently, to develop a standard for marking input values in programs, define an exchange format for test suites, agree on a specification language for test-coverage criteria, and define how to validate the resulting test suites.
- Establish a *benchmark* set for software testing in the community. This means to create and maintain a set of programs together with coverage criteria, and to make those publicly available for researchers to be used in performance comparisons when evaluating a new technique.
- Provide an overview of *available tools* for test-case generation and a snapshot of the state-of-the-art in software testing to the community. This means to compare, independently from particular paper projects and specific techniques, different test generators in terms of effectiveness and performance.
- Increase the visibility and credits that *tool developers* receive. This means to provide a forum for presentation of tools and discussion of the latest technologies, and to give the participants the opportunity to publish about the development work that they have done.
- Educate PhD students and other participants on how to set up performance experiments, package tools in a way that supports reproduction, and how to perform *robust and accurate research experiments.*
- Provide *resources* to development teams that do not have sufficient computing resources and give them the opportunity to obtain results from experiments on large benchmark sets.

Related Competitions. In the field of formal methods, competitions are respected as an important evaluation method and there are many competitions [9, 31]. We refer to the report from Test-Comp 2020 [13] for a more detailed discussion and give here only the references to the most related competitions: Competition on Software Verification (SV-COMP) [36], Competition on Search-Based Software Testing (SBST) [62], and the DARPA Cyber Grand Challenge [65]. An overview of competitions can be found in the TOOLympics volumes [9, 31]. For the techniques used for automatic software testing, we refer to the literature [5, 47].

Quick Summary of Changes. While we keep the setup of the competition stable, we apply some consolidation and extensions to improve the quality of the competition. The following changes were made for Test-Comp 2026:

- The registration to participate and the qualification process were simplified.
- We use a more systematic way to name the categories, consisting of the language, the coverage specification, and the name of the base category.
- The number of test-generation tasks was increased from 11 226 to 16 217.
- Several new base categories were added.

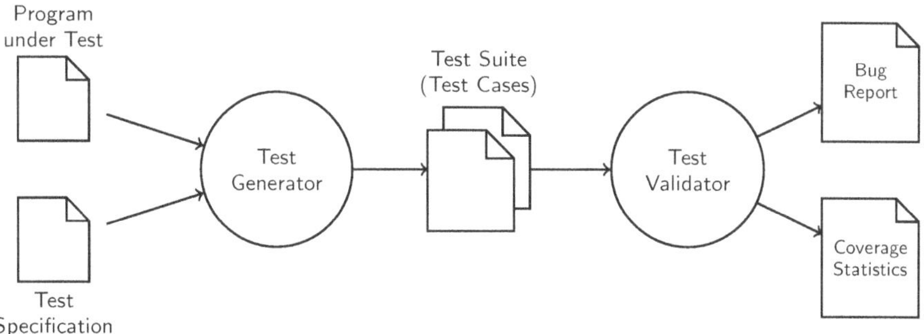

Fig. 1: Flow of the Test-Comp execution for one test generator (taken from [13])

2 Organization, Definitions, Formats, and Rules

Organizational aspects such as the classification (automatic, off-site, reproducible, jury, training) and the competition schedule is given in the initial competition definition [11]. In the following, we repeat some important definitions that are necessary to understand the results.

Organizer and Jury. The competition Test-Comp consists of an organizer, the participants, and a jury. The organizer is responsible for hosting a web site, executing the experiments, providing the results for the participants, and assembling the competition report after the competition is completed. The competition jury is responsible for overseeing the process, ensuring transparency of all components of the competition, resolving any interpretation questions regarding the rules, and reviewing the competition-contribution papers, from which a selection will be published in the FASE proceedings.

Test-Generation Task. A *test-generation task* is a pair of an input program (program under test) and a test specification. A *test-generation run* is a non-interactive execution of a test generator on a single test-generation task, in order to generate a test suite according to the test specification. A *test suite* is a sequence of test cases, given as a directory of files according to the format for exchangeable test-suites.[1]

Execution of a Test Generator. Figure 1 illustrates the process of executing one test-suite generator on one benchmark test-generation task. One test run for a test-suite generator gets as input (i) a program from the benchmark set and (ii) a test specification (cover error, or cover branches), and returns as output a test suite (i.e., a set of test cases). The test generator is contributed by a competition participant as a software archive in ZIP format on Zenodo, via a DOI entry of a version in the FM-Tools record of the test generator. All test runs are executed centrally by the competition organizer.

[1] `https://gitlab.com/sosy-lab/test-comp/test-format`

Table 1: Coverage specifications used in Test-Comp 2026 (same as 2019–2025)

Formula	Interpretation
`COVER EDGES(@CALL(reach_error))`	The test suite contains at least one test that executes function `reach_error`.
`COVER EDGES(@DECISIONEDGE)`	The test suite contains tests such that all branches of the program are executed.

Execution of the Test Validator. The test-suite validator takes as input the test suite from the test generator and validates it by executing the program on all test cases: for bug finding it checks if the bug is exposed and for coverage it reports the coverage. In Test-Comp 2026, we used the test-suite validators TestCov [34] (in four configurations as in Test-Comp 2025 [21]) and TestCoCa new (in one configuration).

Test Specification. The specification for testing a program is given to the test generator as input file (either `properties/coverage-error-call.prp` or `properties/coverage-branches.prp` for Test-Comp 2026, as previously). The definition `init(main())` is used to define the initial states of the program under test by a call of function `main` (with no parameters). The definition `FQL(f)` specifies that coverage definition `f` should be achieved. The FQL (FShell query language [51]) coverage definition `COVER EDGES(@DECISIONEDGE)` means that all branches should be covered (typically used to obtain a standard test suite for quality assurance) and `COVER EDGES(@CALL(foo))` means that a call (at least one) to function `foo` should be covered (typically used for bug finding). A complete specification looks like: `COVER(init(main()), FQL(COVER EDGES(@DECISIONEDGE)))`.

Table 1 lists the two FQL formulas that are used in test specifications of Test-Comp 2026; there was no change from 2020 (except that special function `__VERIFIER_error` does not exist anymore).

Task-Definition Format 2.1. Test-Comp 2026 used the task-definition format in version 2.1.

License and Qualification. The license of each participating test generator must allow its free use for reproduction of the competition results. The license for each tool is available in the FM-Tools entry for the tool, as well as in Table 2. Details on qualification criteria can be found in the competition report of Test-Comp 2019 [14].

Technical Setup and Infrastructure. The technical setup of the competition is based on BenchExec [35] to execute the benchmark runs, BenchCloud [29] to distribute the execution to a large and elastic set of computers, FM-Weck [37] to execute tools (even from from previous years) using a container with all their requirements fulfilled, and the FM-Tools [22] collection to look up all the information we need about the tools for test-case generation, including their versions, parameters, and jury representatives. The results are presented in tables and graphs, also on the competition web site (`https://test-comp.sosy-lab.org/2026/results`), and are available in the accompanying archives (see Table 5).

Table 2: Evaluated tools (test generators and test-suite validators) with tool references and representing jury members; [new] indicates first-time participants, [∅] indicates inactive (hors concours) participation; licenses are abbreviated, see the hyperlink or tool page at FM-Tools for the specific version of the license; TestCoCa[new] and TestCov are the test-suite validators that compute the scores for each test-suite

Tester	Ref.	License	Jury member	Affiliation
AFL-to-TC[new]	[58]	Apache	H. Wachowitz	LMU Munich, Germany
cetfuzz[∅]		Apache	–	–
CoVeriTest	[32, 53]	Apache	M.-C. Jakobs	LMU Munich, Germany
ESBMC-incr	[69]	Apache	C. Wei	U. Manchester, UK
ESBMC-kind	[48, 69]	Apache	C. Wei	U. Manchester, UK
FDSE	[71, 72]	Apache	Z. Chen	National U. Defense Techn., China
Fizzer	[54, 55]	Zlib	M. Trtík	Masaryk U., Brno, Czechia
FuSeBMC	[3, 4]	MIT	K. Alshmrany	Inst. Public Admin., Saudi Arabia
FuSeBMC-AI[∅]	[1, 2]	MIT	–	–
HybridTiger[∅]	[39, 64]	Apache	–	–
KLEE[∅]	[40, 41]	NCSA	–	–
KLEEF[∅]	[61]	NCSA	–	–
Owi[∅]		AGPL	–	–
PRTest	[33, 57]	Apache	T. Lemberger	LMU Munich, Germany
Rizzer[∅]		Zlib	–	–
Sikraken	[60]	LGPL	C. Meudec	South East Technological U., Ireland
Symbiotic	[42, 43]	MIT	M. Jonáš	Masaryk U., Brno, Czechia
TracerX[∅]	[45, 52]	Apache	–	–
TracerX-WP[∅]	[45, 52]	Apache	–	–
UTestGen	[7, 8]	LGPL	M. Barth	LMU Munich, Germany
WASP-C[∅]	[59]	Apache	–	–
TestCoCa[new]	[46]	Zlib	M. Trtík	Masaryk U., Brno, Czechia
TestCov	[34]	Apache	M. Kettl	LMU Munich, Germany

Participating Test-Suite Generators and Test-Suite Validators. We provide an overview of the participating test generators and test-suite validators in Table 2. The table lists the tool name together with a hyperlink to the FM-Tools page for the tool, references to their publications, the license of the tool, the team representatives of the jury of Test-Comp 2026, and their affiliation. (The competition jury consists of the chair and one member of each participating team.) An online table with information about all participating systems is provided on the competition web site.[2] Table 3 lists the features and technologies that are used in the test generators, as declared in the FM-Tools record for each tool.

There are test generators that did not actively participate (tester archives taken from last year) and that are not included in rankings. Those are called *inactive* participation and the tools are labeled with a symbol ([∅]). In the past, we named those inactive tools 'hors concours', but since there could be other

[2] `https://test-comp.sosy-lab.org/2026/systems.php`

Table 3: Algorithms and techniques used by the participating tools; we use the annotations $^{\varnothing}$ for inactive and ^{new} for first-time participants

Tool	Bit-Precise Analysis	Bounded Model Checking	CEGAR	Concurrency Support	Explicit-Value Analysis	Floating-Point Arithmetics	Guidance by Coverage Measures	Interpolation	k-Induction	Portfolio	Predicate Abstraction	Random Execution	Symbolic Execution	Targeted Input Generation
CoVeriTest	✓		✓		✓	✓				✓	✓	✓		
ESBMC-incr	✓	✓		✓					✓					
ESBMC-kind	✓	✓		✓	✓	✓			✓					
FDSE						✓	✓					✓	✓	
Fizzer	✓													
FuSeBMC		✓				✓	✓			✓				✓
FuSeBMC-AI$^{\varnothing}$		✓				✓	✓			✓				✓
HybridTiger$^{\varnothing}$			✓		✓	✓					✓			
KLEE$^{\varnothing}$						✓							✓	✓
KLEEF$^{\varnothing}$	✓					✓	✓						✓	✓
Owi$^{\varnothing}$	✓					✓						✓	✓	✓
PRTest						✓						✓		
Rizzer$^{\varnothing}$	✓												✓	
Sikraken													✓	
Symbiotic	✓			✓		✓	✓	✓	✓	✓	✓		✓	✓
TracerX$^{\varnothing}$		✓				✓		✓					✓	✓
TracerX-WP$^{\varnothing}$								✓						
UTestGen			✓					✓		✓				
WASP-C$^{\varnothing}$						✓						✓	✓	

reasons for hors-concours participation (for example meta tools that consist of other participating tools), we now use the more specific term 'inactive'.

3 Categories and Scoring Schema

Benchmark Programs. The input programs were taken from the largest and most diverse open-source repository of software-verification and test-generation tasks[3], which is also used by SV-COMP [20]. As in the previous editions, we selected all programs for which the following properties were satisfied (see merge

[3] `https://gitlab.com/sosy-lab/benchmarking/sv-benchmarks`

requests on GitLab for Test-Comp 2019 [4], and for Test-Comp 2026 [5], and the Test-Comp 2019 report [14]):

1. compiles with gcc, if a harness for the special methods [6] is provided,
2. should contain at least one call to a nondeterministic function,
3. does not rely on nondeterministic pointers,
4. does not have expected result 'false' for property 'termination', and
5. has expected result 'false' for property 'unreach-call' (only for category *C.Cover-Error*).

This selection yielded a total of 16 217 test-generation tasks, namely 1 895 tasks for category *C.Cover-Error* and 14 322 tasks for category *C.Cover-Branches*.

Categories. The test-generation tasks are partitioned into categories, which are listed in Tables 6 and 7 and described in detail on the competition web site.[7] Figure 2 illustrates the category composition.

Changes to Category Structure in Test-Comp 2026. In the following we outline the most important changes to the categories used for the competition:

- We use a more systematic way to name the categories, consisting of the language (always C for Test-Comp), the coverage specification (coverage-error-call or coverage-branches): ⟨*language*⟩.⟨*specification*⟩.⟨*base-category*⟩. For example, the complete name of a category looks like: *C.coverage-branches.BitVectors*.
- The previous base category *Fuzzle* was merged into base category *Recursive* in order to better balance the category structure. [8] Therefore, *Fuzzle* was removed from both *C.Cover-Error* and *C.Cover-Branches*.
- Base category *SoftwareSystems-coreutils* was added to *C.Cover-Error*.
- Base category *SoftwareSystems-Intel-TDX-Module* was added to both *C.Cover-Error* and *C.Cover-Branches*. This alone added 658 tasks to *C.Cover-Error* and 836 tasks to *C.Cover-Branches*. This category is special because it consists of security-critical firmware code from the Intel® TDX Module. More details about these verification and test tasks are available from a case-study [27, 28]. These tasks use the newly introduced competition-specific function `__VERIFIER_nondet_memory(void *, size_t)`, which havocs a given memory block of a given size.

Category C.Cover-Error. The first category is to show the abilities to discover bugs. The benchmark set consists of programs that contain a bug. We produce for every tool and every test-generation task one of the following scores: 1 point if the validator succeeds in executing the program under test on a generated test case that explores the bug (i.e., the specified function was called), and 0 points otherwise.

[4] https://gitlab.com/sosy-lab/benchmarking/sv-benchmarks/-/merge_requests/774
[5] https://gitlab.com/sosy-lab/benchmarking/sv-benchmarks/-/merge_requests/1683
[6] https://test-comp.sosy-lab.org/2026/rules.php
[7] https://test-comp.sosy-lab.org/2026/benchmarks.php
[8] https://gitlab.com/sosy-lab/benchmarking/sv-benchmarks/-/merge_requests/1599

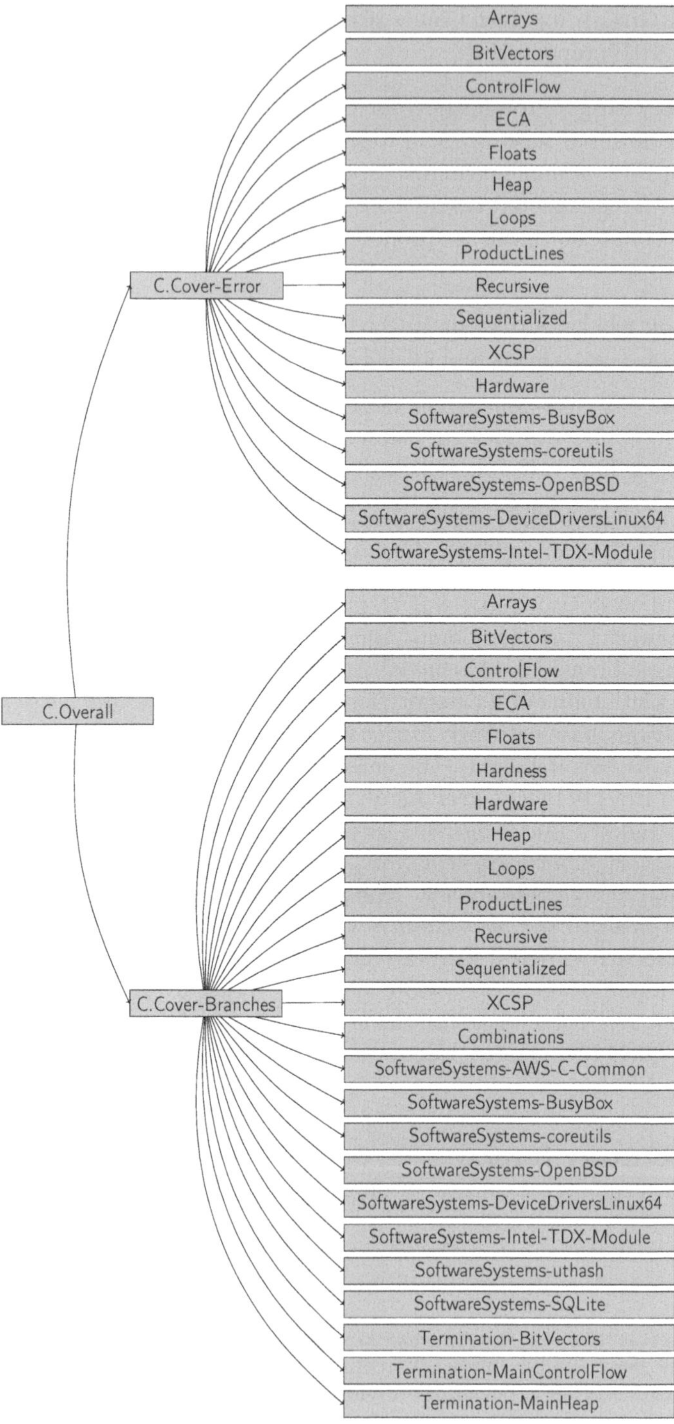

Fig. 2: Category structure for Test-Comp 2026

Category C.Cover-Branches. The second category is to cover as many branches of the program as possible. The coverage criterion was chosen because many test generators support this standard criterion by default. Other coverage criteria can be reduced to branch coverage by transformation [50]. We produce for every tool and every test-generation task the coverage of branches of the program (as reported by TestCov [34] and TestCoCa[new]; a value between 0 and 1) that are executed for the generated test cases. The score is the returned coverage.

Max Over All Validators. As mentioned before, each test-suite is validated five times: TestCov is executed four times on each test suite, using four different configurations, and TestCoCa[new] is executed once. The score of a test suite is the maximum of the five computed scores. This reduces the validation bias towards a particular technique: the five configurations together can validate more coverage then a single technique.

Ranking. The ranking was decided based on the sum of points (normalized for meta categories). In case of a tie, the ranking was decided based on the run time, which is the total CPU time over all test-generation tasks. Opt-out from categories was possible and scores for categories were normalized based on the number of tasks per category (see competition report of SV-COMP 2013 [10], page 597).

4 Reproducibility

We followed the same competition workflow that was described in detail in a previous competition report (see [15, Sect. 4]). All major components that were used for the competition were made available in public version-control repositories. An overview of the components that contribute to the reproducible setup of Test-Comp is provided in Fig. 3, and the details are given in Table 4. We refer to the report of Test-Comp 2019 [14] for a thorough description of all components of the Test-Comp organization and how we ensure that all parts are publicly available for maximal reproducibility. In order to guarantee long-term availability and immutability of the test-generation tasks, the produced competition results, and the produced test suites, we also packaged the material and published it at Zenodo (see Table 5). The competition report of SV-COMP 2022 (see [17, Sect. 3]) provides a description on reproducing individual results and on trouble-shooting.

OCI Containers. The competition used FM-Weck [37][9] again to provide participants easy execution of their tools inside the competition container. Test-Comp 2026 executed all tools (active and inactive, test-generation and test-validation tools) in containers using FM-Weck [37] (which is based on podman). In Test-Comp 2025, the container solution was used only for the inactive tools. This was necessary to include older archives in the comparative evaluation, even if the tools were made for an older distribution of Ubuntu or use packages that are not available anymore. Now, also active tools are executed in containers, and the tools can specify in their FM-Tools [22] entry a container in which they can run.

[9] `https://gitlab.com/sosy-lab/software/fm-weck`

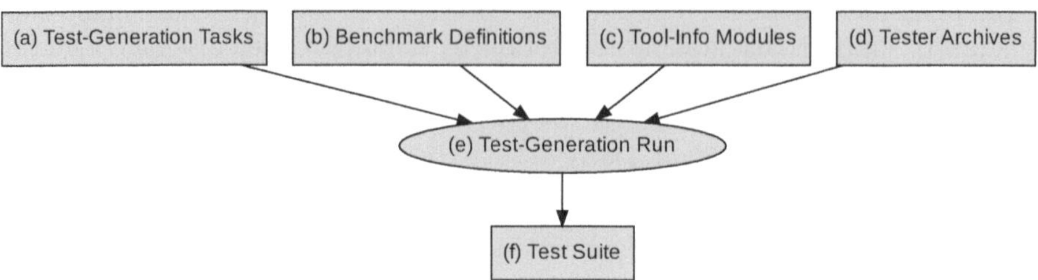

Fig. 3: Benchmarking components of Test-Comp and competition's execution flow (same as for Test-Comp 2020)

Table 4: Publicly available components for reproducing Test-Comp 2026

Component	Fig. 3	Repository at http://gitlab.com/sosy-lab/...	Version
Test-Generation Tasks	(a)	benchmarking/sv-benchmarks	testcomp26
Benchmark Definitions	(b)	test-comp/bench-defs	testcomp26
Tool-Info Modules	(c)	software/benchexec	3.34
Test-Generators	(d)	benchmarking/fm-tools	2.3
BenchExec (Benchmarking)	(e)	software/benchexec	3.34
BenchCloud (Distribution)	(e)	gitlab.com/sosy-lab/software/benchcloud	1.5.0
FM-Weck (Containers)	(e)	gitlab.com/sosy-lab/software/fm-weck	1.6.0
Test-Suite Format	(f)	test-comp/test-format	testcomp26
Processing Scripts		benchmarking/competition-scripts	testcomp26

Table 5: Artifacts published for Test-Comp 2026

Content	DOI	Reference
Test-Generation Tasks	10.5281/zenodo.18650775	[25]
Competition Results	10.5281/zenodo.18650772	[24]
Test-Suite Generators	10.5281/zenodo.18650756	[23]
Test Suites (Witnesses)	10.5281/zenodo.18650733	[26]
BenchExec	10.5281/zenodo.18455156	[70]
FM-Weck	10.5281/zenodo.18650812	[38]
BenchCloud	10.5281/zenodo.14331949	[6]

For example, consider the FM-Tools snippet in Fig. 4: Besides the version id, the DOI of the archive, and the command-line parameters, the key `full_container_images` specifies the container to be used to execute the tool. The OCI container image is long-term archived under `doi:10.5281/zenodo.18001984` at Zenodo.

Files at Zenodo not Immutable Anymore. The immutability of a uniquely identified object is of existential importance for reproducibility. The reproducibility of the experiments of the competition relies on the property that the content of a tool archive (of a test-generation tool) does not change after its registration.

```
1  versions:
2    - version: "testcomp26"
3      doi: "10.5281/zenodo.18051027"
4      benchexec_toolinfo_options: ["-s", "incr"]
5      required_ubuntu_packages: []
6      base_container_images:
7        - docker.io/ubuntu:24.04
8      full_container_images:
9        - registry.gitlab.com/sosy-lab/benchmarking/fm-tools/10.5281/zenodo.18001984
```

Fig. 4: Snippet of FM-Tools data file for FuSeBMC for the tool version (from file `fusebmc.yml`, version 2.3)

We assumed that the content for a given version-specific DOI is immutable, which was the case for Zenodo records for years.

This assumption does unfortunately not hold anymore for Zenodo DOIs since a recent upgrade of the platform and the policies [63]. Zenodo allows users to change the files that are stored for a given DOI: "You can edit the files of your records within 30 days of publishing. Once unlocked you will have 40 days to publish your changes." Even more dramatic, Zenodo now allows users to delete published content: "You can delete your records within 30 days of publishing." [Zenodo, 2026-02-21]

To fix this threat to reproducibility, we cannot use DOIs for specific versions as identifiers anymore. We need to use *content identifiers* such as cryptographic hashes (e.g., SHA-256) or hash trees (e.g., Merkle trees) of the archive files in order to uniquely identify them. The API of Zenodo provides unfortunately only MD5 hashes for the files that it stores.

Currently, the competition scripts store the version hashes for the relevant repositories of the competition environment (fm-tools, sv-benchmarks, benchexec, competition-scripts, bench-defs), the archive (name, DOI suffix, date, hash), and the container, inside the tag `<description>` under `<result>` in each results XML file that BenchExec produces. (For example, have a look at such a results file from the results artifact [12].) This description tagging was meant for humans, e.g., reproduction engineers, who want to double check the correct components. So far, it was assumed that the identifier from the DOI is sufficient to address an immutable archive, but now we should add new XML tags to store a hash or hash tree. This way, it can be (automatically) checked that an archive file is indeed the same archive file that was used for the competition experiments.

Alternatively, one could use Zenodo as long-term storage for the archive files, but address and access the files via IPFS. That is, tool archives get published at Zenodo as before, and tool archives are then specified in the FM-Tools record by the DOI *and* a content identifier.[10]

[10] Another thought was to use the Software Heritage Archive, but this archive is restricted to source code and to public version-control repositories only.

5 Results and Discussion

This section represents the results of the competition experiments. The report shall help to understand the state of the art and the advances in fully automatic test generation for whole C programs, in terms of effectiveness (test coverage, as accumulated in the score) and efficiency (resource consumption in terms of CPU time). All results mentioned in this article were inspected and approved by the participants.

Computing Resources. The computing environment and the resource limits were the same as previously [21]. Each test run was limited to 4 processing units (cores), 15 GB of memory, and 15 min of CPU time. The test-suite validation was limited to 2 processing units, 7 GB of memory, and 5 min of CPU time. The machines for running the experiments are part of a compute cluster that consists of 168 machines. Each machine had one Intel Xeon E3-1230 v5 CPU, with 8 processing units each, a frequency of 3.4 GHz, 33 GB of RAM, and a GNU/Linux operating system (x86_64-linux, Ubuntu 24.04 with Linux kernel 6.8). We used BenchExec [35] to measure and control computing resources (CPU time, reponse time), BenchCloud [29] to distribute, install, run, and clean-up test-case generation runs, and to collect the results, and FM-Weck [37] to execute the tool in the correct container according to the tool's FM-Tools [22] entry. The values for CPU time are accumulated over all cores of the CPU. Further technical parameters of the competition machines are available in the repository that contains the competition scripts. [11] The packages that were installed in the competition execution container are also specified there. [12]

One complete test-generation execution of the competition consisted of 325 560 single test-generation run executions. The total CPU time was 5.3 years for one complete competition run for test generation (without validation). Test-suite validation consisted of 1 627 523 single test-suite validation runs. The total consumed CPU time was 1.6 years. Each tool was executed several times, for training and in order to make sure no installation issues occur during the execution. Including preruns, the infrastructure managed a total of 1.1 million single test-generation runs (consuming 18 years of CPU time). The prerun test-suite validation consisted of 3.9 million single test-suite validation runs (consuming 3.1 years of CPU time).

Quantitative Results. The quantitative results are presented in the same way as last year: Table 6 presents the quantitative overview of all tools and all categories. The head row mentions the category and the number of test-generation tasks in that category. The tools are listed in alphabetical order; every table row lists the scores of one test generator. We indicate the top three candidates by formatting their scores in bold face and in larger font size. An empty table cell means that the test generator opted-out from the respective main category (perhaps participating in subcategories only, restricting the evaluation to a specific topic). More information (including interactive tables, quantile plots for every category, and also the raw data in XML format) is available on

[11] `https://gitlab.com/sosy-lab/benchmarking/competition-scripts/-/tree/svcomp26?ref_-type=tags#parameters-of-runexec`

[12] `.../benchmarking/competition-scripts/-/blob/svcomp26/test/Dockerfile.user.2026`

Table 6: Quantitative overview over all results; empty cells mark opt-outs; new indicates first-time participants, ∅ indicates hors-concours participation

Participant	**C.Cover-Error** 1895 tasks max. score 1895	**C.Cover-Branches** 14322 tasks max. score 14322	**C.Overall** 16217 tasks max. score 16217
AFL-TO-TC new	1082	6817	8488
CETFUZZ∅	556	3584	4410
CoVeriTest	853	7084	7660
ESBMC-INCR	445	1378	2685
ESBMC-KIND	472	2508	3438
FDSE	1103	**8121**	**9319**
Fizzer	**1123**	**7967**	**9317**
FuSeBMC	**1486**	**8237**	**11024**
FuSeBMC-AI∅	1338	5960	9099
HybridTiger∅	727	5688	6329
KLEE∅	1213	4476	7723
KLEEF∅	1413	8282	10735
Owi∅	383	3411	3569
PRTest	331	4443	3932
Rizzer∅	997		
Sikraken		4460	
Symbiotic	**1151**	6192	8429
TracerX∅	664	4864	5594
TracerX-WP∅	543	4679	4974
UTestGen	629	5643	5888
WASP-C∅	818	3844	5674

the competition web site [13] and in the results artifact (see Table 5). Table 7 reports the top three test generators for each category. The consumed run time (column 'CPU Time') is given in hours.

Score-Based Quantile Functions for Quality Assessment. We use score-based quantile functions [35] because these visualizations make it easier to understand the results of the comparative evaluation. The web site [13] and the results artifact (Table 5) include such a plot for each category; as example, we show the plot for category *C.Overall* (all test-generation tasks) in Fig. 5. We had

[13] `https://test-comp.sosy-lab.org/2026/results`

Table 7: Overview of the top-three test generators for each category (measurement values for CPU time rounded to two significant digits, in hours)

Rank	Tester	Score	CPU Time
C.Cover-Error (1895 tasks, max. score 1895)			
1	**FuSeBMC**	**1486**	290
2	Symbiotic	1151	160
3	Fizzer	1123	230
C.Cover-Branches (14322 tasks, max. score 14322)			
1	**FuSeBMC**	**8237**	3 500
2	FDSE	8121	3 400
3	Fizzer	7967	2 500
C.Overall (16217 tasks, max. score 16217)			
1	**FuSeBMC**	**11024**	3 800
2	FDSE	9319	3 800
3	Fizzer	9317	2 800

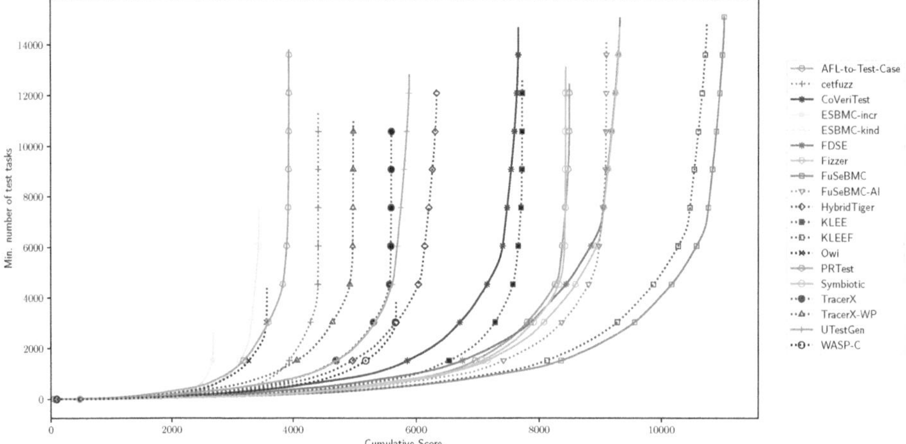

Fig. 5: Quantile functions for category *C.Overall*; each quantile function illustrates the quantile (x-coordinate) of the scores obtained by test-generation runs below a certain number of test-generation tasks (y-coordinate); more details about score-based quantile plots can be looked up in a previous report [14]; the graphs are decorated with symbols to make them better distinguishable without color

19 test generators participating in category *C.Overall*, for which the quantile plot shows the overall performance over all categories (scores for meta categories are normalized [10]). A more detailed discussion of score-based quantile plots for testing is provided in the Test-Comp 2019 competition report [14].

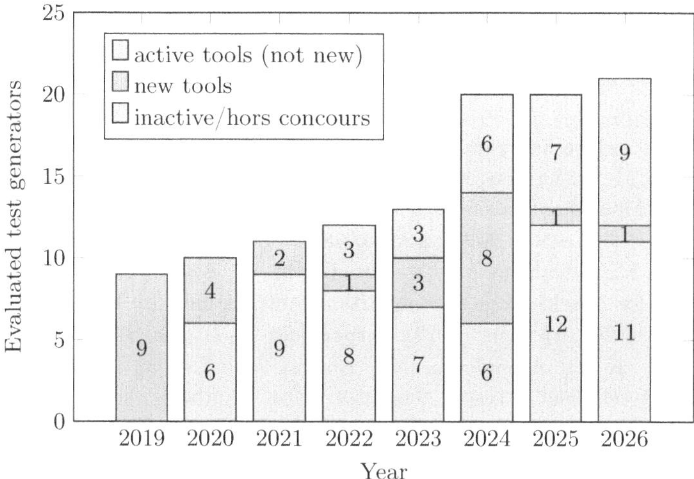

Fig. 6: Number of evaluated test generators for each year (green/bottom: active participants from previous years, orange/middle: number of first-time participants, violet/top: inactive participants from previous years)

6 Conclusion

The 8th Competition on Software Testing (Test-Comp) provides again an overview of fully-automatic test-generation tools for C programs. In total, 21 test-suite generators were compared (see Fig. 6 for the participation numbers and Table 2 for the details). This off-site competition uses a benchmark infrastructure that makes the execution of the experiments fully-automatic and reproducible. Transparency is ensured by making all components available in public repositories and by having a jury (consisting of members from each team) that oversees the process. All test suites were validated by the test-suite validator TestCov [34] and by the newly contributed test-suite validator TestCoCa new to measure the coverage. The competition used again several different validation runs for each test suite, in order to obtain the best possible coverage result, using different compiler backends and different formatting choices after instrumentation for coverage measurement. The results of the competition were presented at the 29th International Conference on Fundamental Approaches to Software Engineering (FASE) at ETAPS 2026 in Turin, Italy.

Data-Availability Statement. The test-generation tasks and results of the competition are published at Zenodo, as described in Table 5. All components and data that are necessary for reproducing the competition are available in public version repositories, as specified in Table 4. For easy access, the results are presented also online on the competition web site `https://test-comp.sosy-lab.org/2026/results`.

Funding Statement. This project was funded in part by the Deutsche Forschungsgemeinschaft (DFG) — 418257054 (Coop).

References

1. Aldughaim, M., Alshmrany, K.M., Gadelha, M.R., de Freitas, R., Cordeiro, L.C.: FuSeBMC_IA: Interval analysis and methods for test-case generation (competition contribution). In: Proc. FASE. pp. 324–329. LNCS 13991, Springer (2023). https://doi.org/10.1007/978-3-031-30826-0_18
2. Aldughaim, M., Alshmrany, K.M., Mustafa, M., Cordeiro, L.C., Stancu, A.: Bounded model checking of software using interval methods via contractors. arXiv/CoRR **2012**(11245) (December 2020). https://doi.org/10.48550/arXiv.2012.11245
3. Alshmrany, K., Aldughaim, M., Cordeiro, L., Bhayat, A.: FuSeBMC v.4: Smart seed generation for hybrid fuzzing (competition contribution). In: Proc. FASE. pp. 336–340. LNCS 13241, Springer (2022). https://doi.org/10.1007/978-3-030-99429-7_19
4. Alshmrany, K.M., Aldughaim, M., Bhayat, A., Cordeiro, L.C.: FuSeBMC: An energy-efficient test generator for finding security vulnerabilities in C programs. In: Proc. TAP. pp. 85–105. Springer (2021). https://doi.org/10.1007/978-3-030-79379-1_6
5. Anand, S., Burke, E.K., Chen, T.Y., Clark, J.A., Cohen, M.B., Grieskamp, W., Harman, M., Harrold, M.J., McMinn, P.: An orchestrated survey of methodologies for automated software test case generation. Journal of Systems and Software **86**(8), 1978–2001 (2013). https://doi.org/10.1016/j.jss.2013.02.061
6. Barth, M., Beyer, D., Chien, P.C., Jankola, M.: BenchCloud Release 1.5.0. Zenodo (2026). https://doi.org/10.5281/zenodo.18670174
7. Barth, M., Dietsch, D., Heizmann, M., Jakobs, M.C.: Ultimate TestGen: Combining parallel trace abstraction and symbolic path execution (competition contribution). In: Proc. FASE. pp. 492–496. LNCS 16504, Springer (2026). https://doi.org/10.1007/978-3-032-22774-4_28
8. Barth, M., Jakobs, M.C.: Test-case generation with automata-based software model checking. In: Proc. SPIN. Springer (2024). https://doi.org/10.1007/978-3-031-66149-5_14
9. Bartocci, E., Beyer, D., Black, P.E., Fedyukovich, G., Garavel, H., Hartmanns, A., Huisman, M., Kordon, F., Nagele, J., Sighireanu, M., Steffen, B., Suda, M., Sutcliffe, G., Weber, T., Yamada, A.: TOOLympics 2019: An overview of competitions in formal methods. In: Proc. TACAS (3). pp. 3–24. LNCS 11429, Springer (2019). https://doi.org/10.1007/978-3-030-17502-3_1
10. Beyer, D.: Second competition on software verification (Summary of SV-COMP 2013). In: Proc. TACAS. pp. 594–609. LNCS 7795, Springer (2013). https://doi.org/10.1007/978-3-642-36742-7_43
11. Beyer, D.: Competition on software testing (Test-Comp). In: Proc. TACAS (3). pp. 167–175. LNCS 11429, Springer (2019). https://doi.org/10.1007/978-3-030-17502-3_11
12. Beyer, D.: Results of the 1st International Competition on Software Testing (Test-Comp 2019). Zenodo (2020). https://doi.org/10.5281/zenodo.3856661
13. Beyer, D.: Second competition on software testing: Test-Comp 2020. In: Proc. FASE. pp. 505–519. LNCS 12076, Springer (2020). https://doi.org/10.1007/978-3-030-45234-6_25
14. Beyer, D.: First international competition on software testing (Test-Comp 2019). Int. J. Softw. Tools Technol. Transf. **23**(6), 833–846 (December 2021). https://doi.org/10.1007/s10009-021-00613-3
15. Beyer, D.: Status report on software testing: Test-Comp 2021. In: Proc. FASE. pp. 341–357. LNCS 12649, Springer (2021). https://doi.org/10.1007/978-3-030-71500-7_17

16. Beyer, D.: Advances in automatic software testing: Test-Comp 2022. In: Proc. FASE. pp. 321–335. LNCS 13241, Springer (2022). https://doi.org/10.1007/978-3-030-99429-7_18
17. Beyer, D.: Progress on software verification: SV-COMP 2022. In: Proc. TACAS (2). pp. 375–402. LNCS 13244, Springer (2022). https://doi.org/10.1007/978-3-030-99527-0_20
18. Beyer, D.: Software testing: 5th comparative evaluation: Test-Comp 2023. In: Proc. FASE. pp. 309–323. LNCS 13991, Springer (2023). https://doi.org/10.1007/978-3-031-30826-0_17
19. Beyer, D.: Automatic testing of C programs: Test-Comp 2024. Springer (2024)
20. Beyer, D.: State of the art in software verification and witness validation: SV-COMP 2024. In: Proc. TACAS (3). pp. 299–329. LNCS 14572, Springer (2024). https://doi.org/10.1007/978-3-031-57256-2_15
21. Beyer, D.: Advances in automatic software testing: Test-Comp 2025. In: Proc. FASE. pp. 257–274. LNCS 15693, Springer (2025). https://doi.org/10.1007/978-3-031-90900-9_13
22. Beyer, D.: Find, use, and conserve tools for formal methods. In: Proc. Festschrift Podelski 65th Birthday. pp. 75–91. LNCS 14765, Springer (2026). https://doi.org/10.1007/978-3-032-13711-1_5
23. Beyer, D.: FM-Tools Release 2.3: Data set of metadata about tools for formal methods (SV-COMP 2026, Test-Comp 2026). Zenodo (2026). https://doi.org/10.5281/zenodo.18650756
24. Beyer, D.: Results of the 8th Intl. Competition on Software Testing (Test-Comp 2026). Zenodo (2026). https://doi.org/10.5281/zenodo.18650772
25. Beyer, D.: SV-Benchmarks: Benchmark set for software verification and testing (SV-COMP 2026, Test-Comp 2026). Zenodo (2026). https://doi.org/10.5281/zenodo.18650775
26. Beyer, D.: Test suites from test-generation tools (Test-Comp 2026). Zenodo (2026). https://doi.org/10.5281/zenodo.18650733
27. Beyer, D., Chien, P.C., Huang, B.Y., Lee, N.Z., Lemberger, T.: A case study in firmware verification: Applying formal methods to Intel® TDX Module. In: Proc. TACAS (2). pp. 42–64. LNCS 16506, Springer (2026). https://doi.org/10.1007/978-3-032-22749-2_3
28. Beyer, D., Chien, P.C., Huang, B., Lee, N.Z., Lemberger, T.: The Intel TDX Module benchmark set. Zenodo (2025). https://doi.org/10.5281/zenodo.16547223
29. Beyer, D., Chien, P.C., Jankola, M.: BenchCloud: A platform for scalable performance benchmarking. In: Proc. ASE. pp. 2386–2389. ACM (2024). https://doi.org/10.1145/3691620.3695358
30. Beyer, D., Chlipala, A.J., Henzinger, T.A., Jhala, R., Majumdar, R.: Generating tests from counterexamples. In: Proc. ICSE. pp. 326–335. IEEE (2004). https://doi.org/10.1109/ICSE.2004.1317455
31. Beyer, D., Hartmanns, A., Kordon, F.: TOOLympics Challenge 2023: Updates, Results, Successes of the Formal-Methods Competitions. LNCS 14550, Springer (2024). https://doi.org/10.1007/978-3-031-67695-6
32. Beyer, D., Jakobs, M.C.: CoVeriTest: Cooperative verifier-based testing. In: Proc. FASE. pp. 389–408. LNCS 11424, Springer (2019). https://doi.org/10.1007/978-3-030-16722-6_23
33. Beyer, D., Lemberger, T.: Software verification: Testing vs. model checking. In: Proc. HVC. pp. 99–114. LNCS 10629, Springer (2017). https://doi.org/10.1007/978-3-319-70389-3_7

34. Beyer, D., Lemberger, T.: TestCov: Robust test-suite execution and coverage measurement. In: Proc. ASE. pp. 1074–1077. IEEE (2019). https://doi.org/10.1109/ASE.2019.00105
35. Beyer, D., Löwe, S., Wendler, P.: Reliable benchmarking: Requirements and solutions. Int. J. Softw. Tools Technol. Transfer **21**(1), 1–29 (2019). https://doi.org/10.1007/s10009-017-0469-y
36. Beyer, D., Strejček, J.: Evaluating software verifiers for C, Java, and SV-LIB (Report on SV-COMP 2026). In: Proc. TACAS (2). pp. 461–501. LNCS 16506, Springer (2026). https://doi.org/10.1007/978-3-032-22749-2_23
37. Beyer, D., Wachowitz, H.: FM-Weck: Containerized execution of formal-methods tools. In: Proc. FM. pp. 39–47. LNCS 14934, Springer (2024). https://doi.org/10.1007/978-3-031-71177-0_3
38. Beyer, D., Wachowitz, H.: Fm-weck Release 1.6.0. Zenodo (2026). https://doi.org/10.5281/zenodo.18650812
39. Bürdek, J., Lochau, M., Bauregger, S., Holzer, A., von Rhein, A., Apel, S., Beyer, D.: Facilitating reuse in multi-goal test-suite generation for software product lines. In: Proc. FASE. pp. 84–99. LNCS 9033, Springer (2015). https://doi.org/10.1007/978-3-662-46675-9_6
40. Cadar, C., Dunbar, D., Engler, D.R.: Klee: Unassisted and automatic generation of high-coverage tests for complex systems programs. In: Proc. OSDI. pp. 209–224. USENIX Association (2008)
41. Cadar, C., Nowack, M.: Klee symbolic execution engine in 2019 (competition contribution). Int. J. Softw. Tools Technol. Transf. **23**(6), 867 – 870 (December 2021). https://doi.org/10.1007/s10009-020-00570-3
42. Chalupa, M., Novák, J., Strejček, J.: Symbiotic 8: Parallel and targeted test generation (competition contribution). In: Proc. FASE. pp. 368–372. LNCS 12649, Springer (2021). https://doi.org/10.1007/978-3-030-71500-7_20
43. Chalupa, M., Strejček, J., Vitovská, M.: Joint forces for memory safety checking. In: Proc. SPIN. pp. 115–132. Springer (2018). https://doi.org/10.1007/978-3-319-94111-0_7
44. Cok, D.R., Déharbe, D., Weber, T.: The 2014 SMT competition. JSAT **9**, 207–242 (2016)
45. Dutta, A., Maghareh, R., Jaffar, J., Godboley, S., Yu, X.L.: TracerX: Pruning dynamic symbolic execution with deletion and weakest precondition interpolation (competition contribution). In: Proc. FASE. pp. 320–325. LNCS 14573, Springer (2024). https://doi.org/10.1007/978-3-031-57259-3_19
46. Ergang, M., Trtík, M.: TestCoCa: Test-suite coverage calculator (competition contribution). In: Proc. FASE. pp. 469 – 474. LNCS 16504, Springer (2026). https://doi.org/10.1007/978-3-032-22774-4_24
47. Fraser, G., Wotawa, F., Ammann, P.: Testing with model checkers: A survey. STVR **19**(3), 215–261 (2009). https://doi.org/10.1002/stvr.402
48. Gadelha, M.Y., Ismail, H.I., Cordeiro, L.C.: Handling loops in bounded model checking of C programs via k-induction. Int. J. Softw. Tools Technol. Transf. **19**(1), 97–114 (February 2017). https://doi.org/10.1007/s10009-015-0407-9
49. Godefroid, P., Sen, K.: Combining model checking and testing. In: Handbook of Model Checking, pp. 613–649. Springer (2018). https://doi.org/10.1007/978-3-319-10575-8_19
50. Harman, M., Hu, L., Hierons, R.M., Wegener, J., Sthamer, H., Baresel, A., Roper, M.: Testability transformation. IEEE Trans. Softw. Eng. **30**(1), 3–16 (2004). https://doi.org/10.1109/TSE.2004.1265732

51. Holzer, A., Schallhart, C., Tautschnig, M., Veith, H.: How did you specify your test suite. In: Proc. ASE. pp. 407–416. ACM (2010). https://doi.org/10.1145/1858996.1859084
52. Jaffar, J., Murali, V., Navas, J.A., Santosa, A.E.: TRACER: A symbolic execution tool for verification. In: Proc. CAV. pp. 758–766. LNCS 7358, Springer (2012). https://doi.org/10.1007/978-3-642-31424-7_61
53. Jakobs, M.C., Richter, C.: CoVeriTest with adaptive time scheduling (competition contribution). In: Proc. FASE. pp. 358–362. LNCS 12649, Springer (2021). https://doi.org/10.1007/978-3-030-71500-7_18
54. Jonáš, M., Strejček, J., Trtík, M.: FIZZER with local space fuzzing (competition contribution). In: Proc. FASE. pp. 275–280. LNCS 15693, Springer (2025). https://doi.org/10.1007/978-3-031-90900-9_14
55. Jonáš, M., Strejček, J., Trtík, M., Urban, L.: FIZZER: New gray-box fuzzer (competition contribution). In: Proc. FASE. pp. 309–313. LNCS 14573, Springer (2024). https://doi.org/10.1007/978-3-031-57259-3_17
56. King, J.C.: Symbolic execution and program testing. Commun. ACM **19**(7), 385–394 (1976). https://doi.org/10.1145/360248.360252
57. Lemberger, T.: Plain random test generation with PRTest (competition contribution). Int. J. Softw. Tools Technol. Transf. **23**(6), 871–873 (December 2021). https://doi.org/10.1007/s10009-020-00568-x
58. Lemberger, T., Wachowitz, H.: AFL-TC: Transforming fuzzer test inputs for Test-Comp (competition contribution). In: Proc. FASE. pp. 475 – 480 . LNCS 16504, Springer (2026). https://doi.org/10.1007/978-3-032-22774-4_25
59. Marques, F., Santos, J.F., Santos, N., Adão, P.: Concolic execution for webassembly (artifact). Dagstuhl Artifacts Series **8**(2), 20:1–20:3 (2022). https://doi.org/10.4230/DARTS.8.2.20
60. Meudec, C.: SIKRAKEN: Symbolic execution using constraint logic programming for generating test inputs (competition contribution). In: Proc. FASE. pp. 487 – 491. LNCS 16504, Springer (2026). https://doi.org/10.1007/978-3-032-22774-4_27
61. Misonizhnik, A., Morozov, S., Kostyukov, Y., Kalugin, V., Babushkin, A., Mordvinov, D., Ivanov, D.: KLEEF: Symbolic execution engine (competition contribution). In: Proc. FASE. pp. 314–319. LNCS 14573, Springer (2024). https://doi.org/10.1007/978-3-031-57259-3_18
62. Panichella, S., Gambi, A., Zampetti, F., Riccio, V.: SBST tool competition 2021. In: Proc. SBST. pp. 20–27. IEEE (2021). https://doi.org/10.1109/SBST52555.2021.00011
63. Pavlidou, A.: Zenodo introduces a new way to manage and correct published records (December 2025), available online, accessed 2026-02-21
64. Ruland, S., Lochau, M., Jakobs, M.C.: HYBRIDTIGER: Hybrid model checking and domination-based partitioning for efficient multi-goal test-suite generation (competition contribution). In: Proc. FASE. pp. 520–524. LNCS 12076, Springer (2020). https://doi.org/10.1007/978-3-030-45234-6_26
65. Song, J., Alves-Foss, J.: The DARPA cyber grand challenge: A competitor's perspective, part 2. IEEE Security and Privacy **14**(1), 76–81 (2016). https://doi.org/10.1109/MSP.2016.14
66. Stump, A., Sutcliffe, G., Tinelli, C.: STAREXEC: A cross-community infrastructure for logic solving. In: Proc. IJCAR, pp. 367–373. LNCS 8562, Springer (2014). https://doi.org/10.1007/978-3-319-08587-6_28
67. Sutcliffe, G.: The CADE ATP system competition: CASC. AI Magazine **37**(2), 99–101 (2016). https://doi.org/10.1609/aimag.v37i2.2620
68. Visser, W., Păsăreanu, C.S., Khurshid, S.: Test-input generation with Java PATHFINDER. In: Proc. ISSTA. pp. 97–107. ACM (2004). https://doi.org/10.1145/1007512.1007526

69. Wei, C., Wu, T., Menezes, R.S., Shmarov, F., Aljaafari, F., Godboley, S., Alshmrany, K., de Freitas, R., Cordeiro, L.: ESBMC v7.7: Automating branch-coverage analysis using CFG-based instrumentation and smt solving (competition contribution). In: Proc. FASE. pp. 281–286. LNCS 15693, Springer (2025). https://doi.org/10.1007/978-3-031-90900-9_15
70. Wendler, P., Beyer, D.: sosy-lab/benchexec: Release 3.34. Zenodo (2026). https://doi.org/10.5281/zenodo.18455156
71. Zhang, G., Chen, Z., Wang, J.: FDSE v2: Variable importance guided hybrid fuzzing (competition contribution). In: Proc. FASE. pp. 481–486. LNCS 16504, Springer (2026). https://doi.org/10.1007/978-3-032-22774-4_26
72. Zhang, G., Shuai, Z., Ma, K., Liu, K., Chen, Z., Wang, J.: FDSE: Enhance symbolic execution by fuzzing-based pre-analysis (competition contribution). In: Proc. FASE. pp. 304–308. LNCS 14573, Springer (2024). https://doi.org/10.1007/978-3-031-57259-3_16

TestCoCa: Test-Suite Coverage Calculator

(Competition Contribution)

Martin Ergang and Marek Trtík*

Faculty of Informatics, Masaryk University, Brno, Czechia
{524697,trtikm}@mail.muni.cz

Abstract. We present TestCoCa, a tool calculating coverage of particular location(s) in a C program (like branchings in the program or an entry block of some function) from a given test-suite. TestCoCa executes all tests in the suite and for each it accumulates the coverage of the locations. A location is covered when program execution (for input data stored in a test case) reaches that location. The tests are expected to be in the XML-based Test-Comp's format. TestCoCa has been successfully used in Test-Comp 2026 as a validator, i.e., as a tool calculating coverage from test-suites produced by competing test-generation tools. TestCoCa is implemented in C++, its source code is released under the open-source zlib license and it is freely available at https://github.com/staticafi/TestCoCa.

1 Introduction

Test generation tools competing in Test-Comp produce a test-suite for each given C program (benchmark). The tests are supposed to be generated for a goal defined in a property file passed to the tool with the benchmark. The goal is either to achieve the highest branch coverage (cumulatively from all generated test cases) in the benchmark or to generate a test case for which an "error" function (specified in the property file) is reached (called).

Performance of the competitors is measured by so called validator tools. A validator accepts a benchmark, a generated test-suite in the competition's XML-based format [8] and a property file [7] with a goal. Based on the goal, the output is either the percentage of covered branchings or an answer whether the "error" function was called or not.

TestCov [10,9] was the only validator used in previous competitions. TestCoCa [13,12] is a new validator used (together with the TestCov validator) in the Test-Comp 2026. Clearly, the use of multiple validators improves objectivity of measurements and thus also our confidence in correctness of competition results.

* Jury member and the corresponding author: trtikm@mail.muni.cz

E. Albert and C. Pasareanu (Eds.): FASE 2026, LNCS 16504, pp. 469–474, 2026.
https://doi.org/10.1007/978-3-032-22774-4_24

2 Software Architecture

TestCoCa is implemented in `C++` and uses the `CMake` [4] build system. The tool consists of three main components *Instrumenter*, *Target Libraries*, and *Driver*. The components are used by a Python script `TestCoCa.py` implementing the actual analysis pipeline of the tool. Figure 1 shows the data flow in the pipeline.

In the first stage of the pipeline, TestCoCa performs *code instrumentation*. Its purpose is to instrument (insert) TestCoCa's probes into the analyzed program. A probe is a piece of code inserted into a carefully chosen location in the program. Whenever a probe is executed (during the program's execution for an input specified in some test case), it saves the information about the execution into the *shared memory* with the Driver component. We discuss the use of shared memory later.

The instrumentation is performed by the *Instrumenter* component of the tool. It is a standalone executable and it operates on LLVM [6] bitcode. The `C` program is thus first compiled into LLVM bitcode using Clang [2] compiler before the component is called. The Instrumenter can operate in two modes, based on the goal specified in the property file:

– *Coverage*: Every basic block in LLVM bitcode, which is a target of some conditional jump, is instrumented. This mode implements the short-circuit evaluation of branching conditions as specified by the semantics of the `C` language.
– *Error function*: Rather than instrumenting program branchings, the tool instruments the entry basic block of the given "error" function, whose reachability should be checked.

It is important to mention that the Coverage mode may place probes to different program locations than TestCov does for the same goal. Even the number of probes may differ. The main reason for the difference is that TestCov treats all conditions (including conjunctions and disjunctions) atomically, i.e., short-circuit evaluation is not applied. In order to synchronize the instrumentation, TestCoCa provides an alternative instrumentation process for this goal. It is enabled by options `--format` and `--testcomp`. The instrumentation then proceeds as follows. First the Clang-Tidy [3] tool is applied on the input `C` program. It puts block brackets `{` and `}` around branches of `if-else` statements, bodies of loops, etc. It is essentially a preparation step for the Label-Adder tool of TestCov, which then iterates through branching constructs (like `if-else` statements) and inserts labels into all code blocks, where the execution can branch. TestCoCa's script then converts these labels into actual probes. Lastly, the instrumented `C` program is compiled into LLVM bitcode using Clang compiler.

The next stage of the pipeline translates the instrumented LLVM bitcode into an executable program, called the *Target*. The translation is done by calling Clang with TestCoCa's *Target Libraries* component. The libraries provide definitions of functions called by probes. These functions write information about the executed probe (in particular, the unique ID of the probe) to the shared memory. The libraries further provide definitions of `__VERIFIER_nondet_*` functions

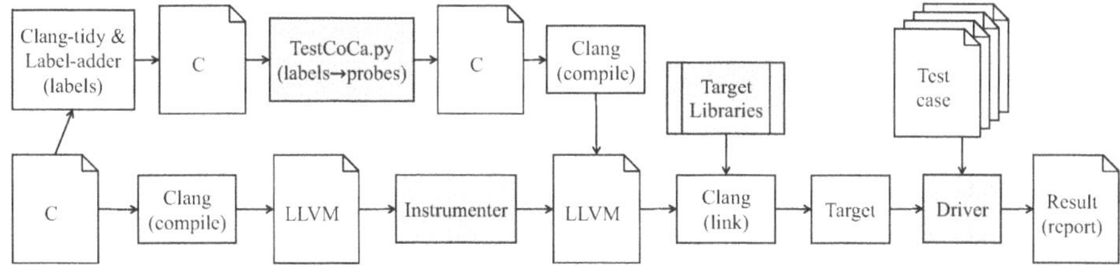

Fig. 1. Data flow in TestCoCa's pipeline. The lower path is default, the upper one must be enabled via options. Components in gray are from TestCoCa's repository.

responsible for feeding input data from the test cases to the program. They are described in the competition's rules [7].

In the last stage, the *Driver* component is called. It executes the Target program for each test case in the test-suite passed to the tool. Shared memory is created between the process of the Driver and the Target. The Driver first writes the input data from the test case into the shared memory. Then the Target reads the input data via calls to `__VERIFIER_nondet_*` functions during its execution and executed probes save their information to the shared memory. Once the execution of the Target ends (either normally or forcefully by the Driver), the Driver reads the saved information from the shared memory and updates overall statistics of branch coverage or the reachability state of the "error" function.

More details about architecture and functionality of TestCoCa can be found in Bachelor's thesis [13]. And we also note that TestCoCa's architecture is inspired by the one of the gray-box fuzzer Fizzer [14,5].

3 Strengths and Weaknesses

TestCoCa is able to handle the following two "special" situations. (1) Target's execution may crash for some test case. Since probes save their information to the shared memory which survives the Target's crash, the Driver can still read and use the information. (2) TestCoCa is supposed to execute the Target for each test case in the suite within a timeout passed to the tool. An execution of some test case may however take long time (it can even get stuck in an infinite loop). Unfortunately, execution times for test cases are not known in advance. If we executed the Target for such test case first, then there may not remain enough time for others. TestCoCa resolves the issue such that test cases are executed repeatedly in waves. Each wave defines a "wave timeout" (same for each test case in the wave). The Driver force-terminates longer executions. The timeout of the first wave is the shortest and it increases with further waves. The first wave comprises all test cases. If the Target's execution for a test case ends before the wave timeout, then the test case does not appear in future waves.

Target's execution may accidentally overwrite some parts of the shared memory, e.g., due to wrong pointer arithmetic. The Driver thus checks for consistency of information read from the shared memory and discards all corrupted entries (also prints warnings).

4 Tool Setup and Configuration

TestCoCa can be downloaded either as a binary or as a source code (links are in Section 6). For the source code, checkout the commit tagged `TESTCOMP26` in order to build the version used in the competition. The `build.py` file in the root of the repository is available for building the tool. The script provides `--help` option printing the usage. In short, the command:

```
$ python3 build.py --config Relase
```

will build the `Release` version of the tool. The built tool can then be found in `dist` directory. The content of the directory can be copied "as-is" to a target computer, i.e., no installation is necessary. The tool should be used via `TestCoCa.py` script. For the –`--testcomp` option to function, the Label-Adder utility of TestCov must be manually installed and placed in the same directory as `TestCoCa.py`. The option `--help` reveals the usage. Here is how the tool was used in the competition:

```
$ python3 TestCoCa.py --input_file <my-c-program>
    --test_suite <my-test-suite> --goal <my-prp-file>
    --max_exec_megabytes <mem-limit>
    --max_exec_milliseconds <time-limit>
    --testcomp --format
```

The memory and time limits were set to 512 and 600000, respectively. The property file [7] passed to the script with the `--goal` option determines whether to measure the branch coverage or to check whether the "error" function (whose name is specified in the file) is called. The test-suite must be in the competition's XML based format [8]. The options `--testcomp` and `--format` activate the alternative instrumentation compatible with TestCov (see Section 2 for more details).

By default the outputs are written to the current working directory. This can be overridden by passing the desired output directory with the option `--output_dir` to the tool. If the `C` program is targeted for 32-bit CPU (the default is 64-bit), then TestCoCa should also be passed the option `--m32`.

Since TestCoCa executes the Target program natively, it is highly recommended to run it within a safe environment. In the Test-Comp 2026, TestCoCa was always executed within safe environments established by BenchExec [11,1].

5 Software Project and Contributors

TestCoCa has been developed at the Faculty of Informatics of Masaryk University by Martin Ergang in his Bachelor's thesis. Marek Trtík participated in the project as the supervisor of the thesis.

6 Data-Availability Statement

TestCoCa is available in a binary form at Zenodo [12] and the source code is available at GitHub:

https://github.com/staticafi/TestCoCa

The tool is open-source and it is available under the zlib license.

Acknowledgement We would like to thank Prof. Dr. Dirk Beyer for aiding the development of the tool by performing evaluations on the Test-Comp computing infrastructure. This work has been supported by the Czech Science Foundation grant GA23-06506S.

References

1. BenchExec: tool's repository, https://github.com/sosy-lab/benchexec, Accessed: 20 December 2025
2. Clang: home page, https://clang.llvm.org/, Accessed: 20 December 2025
3. Clang-Tidy: home page, https://clang.llvm.org/extra/clang-tidy/, Accessed: 20 December 2025
4. CMake: home page, https://cmake.org/, Accessed: 20 December 2025
5. Fizzer: tool's repository, https://github.com/staticafi/fizzer, Accessed: 20 December 2025
6. LLVM: home page, https://llvm.org/, Accessed: 20 December 2025
7. Test-Comp 2026: rules page, https://test-comp.sosy-lab.org/2026/rules.php, Accessed: 20 December 2025
8. Test-Comp 2026: test format page, https://gitlab.com/sosy-lab/test-comp/test-format/blob/testcomp23/doc/Format.md, Accessed: 20 December 2025
9. TestCov: tool's repository, https://gitlab.com/sosy-lab/software/test-suite-validator, Accessed: 20 December 2025
10. Beyer, D., Lemberger, T.: Testcov: Robust test-suite execution and coverage measurement. In: 34th IEEE/ACM International Conference on Automated Software Engineering, ASE 2019, San Diego, CA, USA, November 11-15, 2019. pp. 1074–1077. IEEE (2019). https://doi.org/10.1109/ASE.2019.00105, https://doi.org/10.1109/ASE.2019.00105
11. Beyer, D., Löwe, S., Wendler, P.: Reliable benchmarking: requirements and solutions. Int. J. Softw. Tools Technol. Transf. **21**(1), 1–29 (Feb 2019). https://doi.org/10.1007/s10009-017-0469-y
12. Ergang, M.: Testcoca: binary (Dec 2025). https://doi.org/10.5281/zenodo.17819536
13. Ergang, M.: A tool for evaluation of test suites produced by participants in Test Competition. Bachelor's thesis, Masaryk University, Faculty of Informatics, Brno (May 2025), https://is.muni.cz/th/mdom3/?lang=en
14. Jonáš, M., Strejček, J., Trtík, M.: Fizzer with local space fuzzing: (competition contribution). In: FASE 2025. p. 275–280. Springer-Verlag, Berlin, Heidelberg (2025). https://doi.org/10.1007/978-3-031-90900-9_14

BY NC ND

AFL-TC: Transforming Fuzzer Test Inputs for Test-Comp (Competition Contribution)

Thomas Lemberger and Henrik Wachowitz*

LMU Munich, Munich, Germany

Abstract. AFL-TC is a tool chain that integrates AFL++ into the environment of Test-Comp. Coverage-guided greybox fuzzers like AFL++ produce raw binary data that is given to programs as input on stdin, without any knowledge of how this data is interpreted. In contrast to that, Test-Comp requires structured XML descriptions of test cases that list a sequence of individual input values, which are read whenever the program calls an input function. Previous adaptations of fuzzers used tool-specific modifications for Test-Comp. Now, AFL-TC demonstrates a flexible solution that decouples the test generation from the Test-Comp format: AFL-TC first runs AFL++ (or any other tester that produces binary input for stdin), then replays each input with a test harness that (a) records how the test input is interpreted by the program and (b) outputs the recording as corresponding XML elements. To provide test cases early, AFL-TC employs a monitor that triggers a transformation whenever new test files are discovered. AFL-TC participated in both Test-Comp categories Cover-Error and Cover-Branches. It placed 6th overall, 4th among active participants, and best in the sub-category `C.coverage-branches.Arrays`.

1 Test-Generation Approach

AFL++ [1] is a prominent coverage-guided greybox fuzzer for C. So far, two variants of AFL++ participated in Test-Comp: FairFuzz [2,3] in 2019 and cetfuzz [4] in 2024. However, the original AFL++ remained to be evaluated in Test-Comp. We change this with AFL-to-Test-Case (AFL-TC), a tool chain that combines AFL++ with the tool FUZZ-TO-TC [5]. FUZZ-TO-TC transforms binary test inputs—as produced by AFL++ and other fuzzers—into structured Test-Comp test cases.

Each test case produced by AFL++ is a file with raw binary content that is provided to the program under test via standard input. How the program reads this binary content into concrete input values is not visible from the outside. As first example, given the binary input in hex notation in Fig. 1, a program could read the first four bytes as an integer n and then read the next n bytes as a sequence of char values. This interpretation of input values is not evident from the binary content itself. As second example, consider the program in Fig. 2. Through the special Test-Comp input method `__VERIFIER_nondet_int()`, the

* Jury member

E. Albert and C. Pasareanu (Eds.): FASE 2026, LNCS 16504, pp. 475–480, 2026.
https://doi.org/10.1007/978-3-032-22774-4_25

```
ff ff ff ff 01 00 00 00
01 00 00 00 01 00 00 00
01 00 00 00 01 00 00 00
01 00 00 00 01 00 00 00
01 11 00 00 01 00 00 00
01 00 00 00 01 00 00 00
01 00 00 00 01 00 00 00
01 00 00 00 01 00 00 00
01 00 00 00 01 00 00 00 0a
```

Fig. 1: Binary input generated by AFL++, in hex notation

```
int main() {
  int x = __VERIFIER_nondet_int();
  if (x != 0) {
    reach_error();
  }
}
```

Fig. 2: C program with reachable error

```
<?xml version="1.0" [...] ?>
<!DOCTYPE testcase [...]>
<testcase>
  <input type="int">-1</input>
</testcase>
```

Fig. 3: Test-Comp test case produced by FUZZ-TO-TC by executing Fig. 2 with Fig. 1

program receives a signed 32-bit integer and stores it in variable x. If $x \neq 0$, it calls the error function `reach_error()`. When AFL++ runs on this program, it does generate the error-triggering binary input in Fig. 1 (shown in hex notation). But the program only reads the first four bytes `ff ff ff ff` and interprets them as the value -1. The remaining bytes of the generated input are superfluous.

In contrast to the raw binary format produced by AFL++, test cases in Test-Comp are represented by an XML file that describes the sequence of concrete input values in the order they are supposed to be read by the program. Whenever the program execution calls an input method, the method returns precisely the next value from the sequence.

To receive structured XML test cases from AFL++, AFL-TC executes a tool chain that consists of three steps: (1) Run AFL++ on the program under test to generate inputs in the default binary format of AFL++; (2) watch for new tests in the relevant output directories of AFL++; (3) whenever a new test is discovered, transform it to the Test-Comp format. Figure 3 shows the Test-Comp test case that this tool chain produces for Fig. 2 (by transforming Fig. 1).

To run AFL++ on Test-Comp benchmark tasks, AFL-TC compiles each program under test against a test harness that defines the Test-Comp-specific input methods. Each method (a) reads the number of bytes that match its expected return type from standard input, (b) casts the read bytes to the expected return type, and (c) returns that value. For the test transformation this harness is extended to output the expected XML element for a value before returning it. This dual-mode behavior is controlled by a compile-time macro. The original test harness without XML output originates from FairFuzz [3].

For the category Cover-Error, AFL-TC monitors only the crash directory of AFL++, and only keeps tests whose execution actually call the error function. For the category Cover-Branches, AFL-TC monitors both the crash and queue directories and keeps all generated tests.

2 Software Architecture

Figure 4 shows the workflow of AFL-TC. First, AFL-TC passes the program P and the test harness H to the AFL++ compiler `afl-clang-lto` (and, as fallback, `afl-gcc-fast`). This creates an AFL-instrumented binary. Next, AFL-TC starts

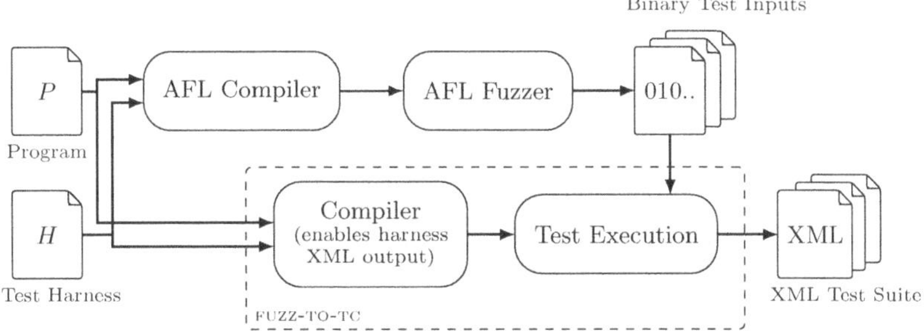

Fig. 4: Workflow of AFL-TC

an AFL++ run on the AFL-instrumented executable to generate binary test files. AFL++ writes newly created tests to an output directory `queue/`. Tests that trigger a program crash are then moved to a separate directory `crash/`. While AFL++ runs, AFL-TC enters a loop to monitor these output directories. For test goal `coverage-error` (Test-Comp category Cover-Error), it watches only the directory `crash/`. For test goal `coverage-branches` (Test-Comp category Cover-Branches), it watches both directories. Whenever the monitor discovers a new test file it passes the currently existing tests to FUZZ-TO-TC for transformation.

FUZZ-TO-TC is a standalone Go tool. It receives the coverage goal, a directory with test cases to transform, the program under test as source code, the machine model to compile the program for, and, for metadata generation, the name of the original test generator (here: AFL++). FUZZ-TO-TC first compiles the program against our test harness with enabled XML output and then runs the resulting executable once for each binary test case, using that test case as program input. For each execution, FUZZ-TO-TC captures the produced XML output and saves it as a Test-Comp-conforming test case. For `coverage-error` tasks, FUZZ-TO-TC only saves test cases that actually reach the error function during execution. FUZZ-TO-TC also creates a necessary metadata file for the test suite. To avoid duplicate tests when FUZZ-TO-TC is run multiple times, it saves each test case under the name of the SHA1 hash of its contents.

3 Strengths and Weaknesses

Strengths. AFL-TC is a tool chain that adapts AFL++ for Test-Comp, but the framework behind AFL-TC can be used with other binary-format fuzzers. The test-generation harness and FUZZ-TO-TC are tool-agnostic. AFL++ itself uses coverage-guided greybox fuzzing, which reaches broad code coverage fast [1] and has found many bugs in real-world software [6]. In Test-Comp 2026, AFL-TC reaches the 6th place overall and 4th among active participants [7]. It outperforms CETFUZZ [4], a derivative of AFL++, justifying the participation of the original AFL++ to improve the comparability of participants' performance. AFL-TC reached the highest score among participants in sub-category `C.coverage-branches.Arrays`.

Weaknesses. Greybox fuzzing struggles with complex input constraints that require specific byte sequences. Tasks where reaching the target requires navigating a complex series of branches (e.g., tasks from XCSP) are challenging for AFL-TC. Unlike symbolic-execution tools, AFL-TC does not reason about program paths on a semantic level, limiting its effectiveness on programs that require precise input sequences. We use the CmpLog instrumentation [8] to mitigate this issue. This instrumentation enables the tracing of comparison operations and better steering of mutators towards branches that are not covered yet [9].

AFL++ is not built for low CPU time usage. It runs as many threads and iterations as possible, consuming significant CPU resources. In the Test-Comp scenario, where CPU time per task is strictly limited, this leads to frequent timeouts. It also restricts the strategies we can use for test-case generation. For example, it is too resource-intensive in Test-Comp to start with deterministic test-input mutations, the default in AFL++. Instead, we directly rely on random mutations to achieve a broad exploration of the program fast.

4 Tool Setup and Configuration

AFL-TC is available open source [10]. The version used in Test-Comp is archived at Zenodo [11]. Installation is possible via FM-WECK [12] or manual setup. When fuzzing 32-bit programs on a 64-bit system, the `gcc-multilib` package is required. In manual setup, the tool requires an installation of AFL++. Our Test-Comp archive contains pre-compiled binaries of AFL++ for x64 Linux systems. To run the tools with newer versions of AFL++ or on other architectures, we recommend the official Docker container [13] that is provided by the AFL++ team.

Installation. To install AFL-TC via FM-WECK into directory `afltc/`, run:

```
fm-weck install afltc:testcomp26 -d afltc
```

Use. AFL-TC takes as input a C program (`<program>`), the machine model (`<arch>`) to compile the program under test for, and a coverage goal (`<spec>`). The command-line to run AFL-TC is:

```
afl-tc <program> <arch> <spec>
```

This produces a Test-Comp-conforming test suite in directory `output`. Supported machine models are `32bit` and `64bit`.

Configuration. The concrete AFL++ compilation and fuzzing can be customized by editing the commands `afl-clang-lto`, `afl-gcc-fast`, and `afl-fuzz` in the shell script `bin/afl-tc`. By default, the fuzzing runs with fixed seed 42 (`-s 42`) for reproducibility; uses the CmpLog instrumentation [8] (`AFL_LLVM_CMPLOG=1`) to better handle comparison operands; and lets AFL++ decide on a time limit per run automatically (`-t1000+`).

5 Software Project and Contributors

The underlying fuzzer AFL++ is maintained by Andrea Fioraldi, Dominik Maier, Heiko Eißfeldt, and Marcel Heuse. AFL-TC and FUZZ-TO-TC are maintained by Thomas Lemberger and Henrik Wachowitz at LMU Munich.

Data-Availability Statement. AFL-TC is available open source under the Apache-2.0 license at gitlab.com/sosy-lab/software/test-to-witness. The version of AFL-TC that was used in Test-Comp 2026 is archived at https://doi.org/10.5281/zenodo.18060896. All results and artifacts from Test-Comp 2026 are available in the competition report [7]. AFL++ is available open source under the Apache-2.0 license at github.com/AFLplusplus/AFLplusplus.

Funding. This work is supported by the Deutsche Forschungsgemeinschaft (DFG) – ConVeY (378803395) and IdeFix (496588242).

References

1. Fioraldi, A., Maier, D., Eißfeldt, H., Heuse, M.: AFL++: Combining incremental steps of fuzzing research. In: Proc. WOOT. USENIX Association (2020)
2. Lemieux, C., Sen, K.: FairFuzz: A targeted mutation strategy for increasing greybox fuzz testing coverage. In: Proc. ASE. pp. 475–485. ACM (2018). https://doi.org/10.1145/3238147.3238176
3. Lemieux, C., Sen, K.: FAIRFUZZ-TC: A fuzzer targeting rare branches (competition contribution). Int. J. Softw. Tools Technol. Transf. **23**(6), 863–866 (December 2021). https://doi.org/10.1007/s10009-020-00569-w
4. Krishnan, S., George, S.S., Medicherla, R.K., Divakaran, S.: Gitlab repository of cetfuzz. https://gitlab.com/Sarathkrishnan/cetfuzz, accessed: 2026-01-22
5. Beyer, D., Lemberger, T., Wachowitz, H.: Testing in formal verification via witness generation (empirical evaluation). In: Proc. FASE. pp. 424–445. LNCS, Springer (2026). https://doi.org/10.1007/978-3-032-22774-4_22
6. Zalewski, M.: American Fuzzy Lop. https://lcamtuf.coredump.cx/afl/, accessed: 2026-01-30
7. Beyer, D.: Evaluating tools for automatic software testing: Test-Comp 2026. In: Proc. FASE. pp. 449–468. LNCS 16504, Springer (2026). https://doi.org/10.1007/978-3-032-22774-4_23
8. Repository, A.G.: CmpLog instrumentation. https://github.com/AFLplusplus/AFLplusplus/blob/68b492b2c7725816068718ef9437b72b40e67519/instrumentation/README.cmplog.md, accessed: 2026-01-30
9. Aschermann, C., Schumilo, S., Blazytko, T., Gawlik, R., Holz, T.: Redqueen: Fuzzing with input-to-state correspondence. In: Symposium on Network and Distributed System Security (NDSS) (2019). https://doi.org/10.14722/ndss.2019.23371
10. Lemberger, T., Wachowitz, H.: AFL-TC: Test-to-witness translation for afl++. https://gitlab.com/sosy-lab/software/test-to-witness, accessed: 2026-01-22
11. Lemberger, T., Wachowitz, H.: AFL-TC competition participation Test-Comp 2026 (archive). Zenodo (2025). https://doi.org/10.5281/zenodo.18060896
12. Beyer, D., Wachowitz, H.: FM-WECK: Containerized execution of formal-methods tools. In: Proc. FM. pp. 39–47. LNCS 14934, Springer (2024). https://doi.org/10.1007/978-3-031-71177-0_3
13. Heuse, M., Eißfeldt, H., Fioraldi, A., Maier, D., Zalewski, M.: AFL++ docker image. https://hub.docker.com/r/aflplusplus/aflplusplus, accessed: 2026-01-30

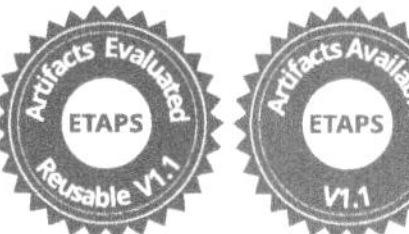

FDSE v2: Variable Importance Guided Hybrid Fuzzing

(Competition Contribution)

Guofeng Zhang [1], Zhenbang Chen [1] ⋆, and Ji Wang [1]

College of Computer Science and Technology, National University of Defense Technology, Changsha, China
{zhangguofeng16, zbchen, wj}@nudt.edu.cn

Abstract. FDSE v2 is a hybrid fuzzing tool that automatically generates high-coverage test suites for C programs. In prior work, we introduced an initial version of FDSE that used fuzzing-based pre-analysis to enhance symbolic execution. This paper presents FDSE v2, featuring a novel constraint tree component that more effectively coordinates the fuzzer and concolic execution engine, thereby reducing ineffective search in fuzzing. The constraint tree models the space of path constraints already explored by concolic execution and enables fine-grained partitioning of input variables based on their semantic relevance. During seed mutation, the fuzzer focuses only on the most important variable groups identified through this analysis. Concolic execution excels at navigating complex path conditions involving arithmetic or logical guards, while the fuzzer leverages the resulting high-quality seeds as starting points for deeper exploration under extended time budgets. By reducing redundant efforts between the two engines, FDSE v2 achieves significant improvements in both code coverage and vulnerability detection effectiveness.

Keywords: Hybrid Fuzzing · Concolic Execution · Testcase Generation.

1 Overview

Software testing remains one of the most labor-intensive phases in the software development lifecycle [1]. Automated test-case generation is therefore essential to reduce manual effort and improve software reliability. By integrating complementary automated testing techniques, such approaches can achieve both higher effectiveness and greater efficiency.

This year, we present FDSE v2, which represents a redesign and strategic shift from its predecessor FDSE [11]. While FDSE was primarily a symbolic execution tool, achieved 4th place overall in the Test-Comp 2025. FDSE v2 is now repositioned as a hybrid fuzzing framework [10,7,9] that tightly integrates symbolic execution with coverage-guided fuzzing. In Test-Comp 2026 [2], FDSE v2

[1] Also with the affiliation: State Key Laboratory of Complex & Critical Software Environment, National University of Defense Technology, Changsha, China
⋆ Jury Member and Corresponding Author

E. Albert and C. Pasareanu (Eds.): FASE 2026, LNCS 16504, pp. 481–486, 2026.
https://doi.org/10.1007/978-3-032-22774-4_26

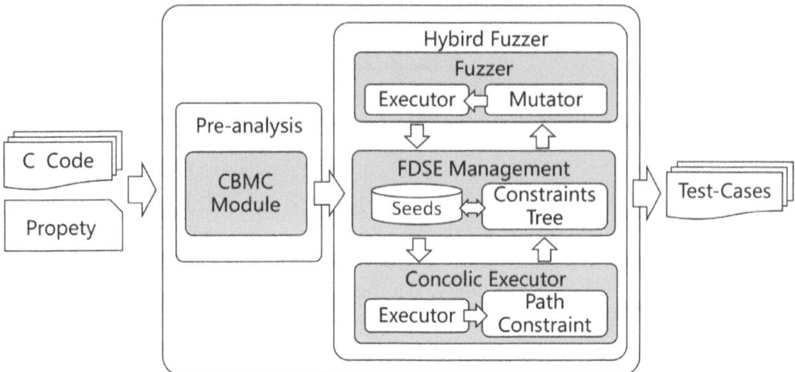

Fig. 1: FDSE v2's workflow in Test-Comp.

earned a total score of 9,319, securing 2nd place overall, and scored 8,121 in the Cover-Branches category, also ranking 2nd.

FDSE v2 demonstrates further improvements in code coverage over its predecessor. A key contribution of this work is the use of a constraint tree generated by concolic execution to identify groups of input variables that are semantically relevant to uncovered program regions, thereby guiding the seed mutation strategy of the fuzzer. During concolic execution [8], every program operation is precisely modeled, and at each branching point, an SMT solver is invoked to generate inputs that satisfy the negated branch condition, thereby producing high-quality test inputs that reach deep program states.

However, most existing hybrid fuzzing approaches interact with the concolic execution engine only superficially, for example by exchanging seeds or basic coverage information, and consequently discard the rich set of path constraints accumulated during analysis [3]. In contrast, FDSE v2 systematically collects all constraints and their corresponding concrete inputs generated across multiple runs of concolic execution. Within the central control process, these constraints are reconstructed into a persistent constraint binary tree. This structure enables precise extraction of variable groups associated with uncovered code regions, which in turn directs hybrid fuzzing toward unexplored parts of the program state space.

This architectural innovation enables FDSE v2 to mitigate redundant exploration between its constituent engines, leading to more efficient coverage growth and improved bug-finding capability.

2 Test Generation Approach

Figure 1 shows the workflow of FDSE v2 in Test-Comp. The tool takes a C program and test properties as input. The program is compiled into bytecode and instrumented separately for fuzzing and concolic execution. A key enhancement is the integration of the CBMC [4] (Bounded Model Checker) module. During

```
1  #define N 100
2  int main() {
3    int a1[N], a2[N], i;
4    for(i=0; i<N; i++) {
5      a1[i]=input();
6      a2[i]=input();
7    }
8    assume(a1[0]+a2[0]>a2[1]);
9    assume(a1[2]+a2[2]>a2[3]);
10   ......
11   if(a1[98]+a2[98]>a2[1]){
12     // Uncoverd
13   }
14   return 0;
15 }
```

Fig. 2: motivation.c

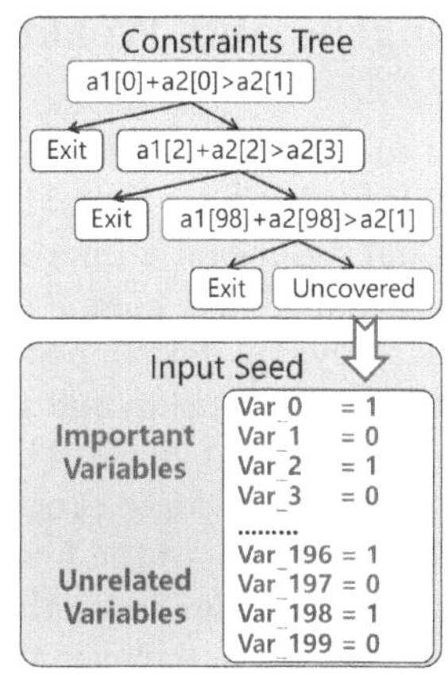

Fig. 3: Constraint tree identification of important variables

pre-analysis, CBMC unrolls loops up to a fixed bound to explore part of the program's state space and generate initial seeds that reach non-trivial paths.

The FDSE v2 manager first launches the fuzzer to collect seeds achieving new edge coverage. When progress stalls, it switches to the concolic executor, which re-executes recent high-coverage seeds to extract path constraints. These are stored in a persistent constraint binary tree maintained by the manager. The manager then identifies uncovered edges, locates corresponding nodes in the tree, and uses an SMT solver to generate high-quality seeds satisfying the target conditions. These seeds are returned to the fuzzer, which performs selective byte-level mutations guided by the key variables in the constraints. All seeds yielding new coverage are exported as test cases throughout execution.

Demonstration. We illustrate how FDSE v2 identifies important variable groups to guide fuzzing mutations through a motivating example. Figure 2 shows a program that accepts 200 integer inputs. Suppose FDSE v2 has only covered the false branch at line 11 and seeks an input that triggers the true branch. The manager invokes an SMT solver, which successfully generates a seed satisfying the condition for the true branch. To further explore the program space beyond line 12, randomly mutating this seed across all 200 input variables would be highly inefficient. Instead, FDSE v2 analyzes the constraint tree: starting from the condition at line 11, it recursively identifies semantically related constraints. For instance, the variable $a2[1]$ involved in the condition at line 8 overlaps with the condition at line 11. This important variable set $\{a1[0], a2[0], a2[1], a1[98], a2[98]\}$ of related constraints defines a reduced solution space involving only a small subset of relevant variables. The fuzzer then performs selective mutations on this improtant variable group within the subspace, using the SMT-generated seed as a starting point, as illustrated in Figure 3. This strategy avoids wasting computational effort on irrelevant inputs and enables rapid convergence toward uncovered code regions.

3 Strengths and Weaknesses

Compared to prior approaches, `FDSE v2` offers three main advantages. First, its constraint tree eliminats redundant exploration between fuzzing and symbolic execution and significantly improving coverage efficiency, especially on programs with deep or numerically complex guards that pure fuzzing struggle to penetrate. Second, by analyzing data dependencies, `FDSE v2` identifies input variables relevant to uncovered branches and guides mutations toward semantically meaningful regions of the input space. Third, unlike `FDSE`, which suffered from explosive constraint growth on some programs and placed heavy demands on the SMT solver, `FDSE v2` leverages the fuzzer's high-throughput execution. After extracting important variables from the constraint tree, `FDSE v2` performs targeted mutations. This often achieves the same coverage faster than computing exact solutions via the SMT solver, effectively prioritizing rapid guided exploration over costly precise solving.

However, `FDSE v2` has several limitations. First, constructing and maintaining the constraint tree incurs substantial memory and computational overhead, particularly for programs with extensive branching or long execution paths, which can hinder scalability. Second, the effectiveness of guided mutation relies heavily on the accuracy of constraint collection. In programs involving pointer arithmetic or calls to uninstrumented external libraries, path constraints may be lost or incomplete, preventing full identification of improtant variables and thereby reducing mutation efficiency. Finally, `FDSE v2` does not design a specialized search strategy over the constraint tree for bug-finding tasks, which limits its performance in the **Cover-Error** category.

4 Software Project

`FDSE v2` is developed by the National University of Defense Technology. More infomation is publicly available at https://github.com/zbchen/fdse-test-comp. The tool integrates two core components: a concolic executor built on `SymCC` [8], and a fuzzing engine implemented in C++ using LLVM 10.0.1 [5]. Coordination between these engines is managed by a central module that employs the Z3 SMT solver [6], while the command-line interface is implemented in Python.

`FDSE v2` participated in the **Cover-Branches** and **Cover-Error** categories in Test-Comp 2026. Integration with BenchExec is provided through the module `fdse.py`, with benchmark settings defined in `fdse.xml`. Users can invoke the tool as follows:

```
fdse -testcomp -property-file=<..> -max-time=<..> -single-file-name=<..>
```

During execution, all benchmarks are treated as 64-bit programs, and the engine prioritizes maximizing code coverage. Generated test suites are written to the directory `fdseoutput/test-suite`, with each suite containing a metadata XML file and one or more test-case XML files conforming to the Test-Comp format.

5 Data Available

The artifact of `FDSE v2` used for the Test-Comp 2026 submission is archived on Zenodo[1] and distributed under the Apache-2.0 license. To support full reproducibility, the official Test-Comp 2026 website[2] provides access to the competition benchmarks, execution environment, validation scripts, and the `FDSE v2` binaries employed during evaluation. All data necessary to replicate the reported results, including tool configuration, benchmark instances, and output formats, are publicly accessible through these resources.

This research was supported by National Key R&D Program of China (No. 2024YFF0908003) and the NSFC Program (No. 62172429, 62032024).

References

1. Anand, S., Burke, E.K., Chen, T.Y., Clark, J.A., Cohen, M.B., Grieskamp, W., Harman, M., Harrold, M.J., McMinn, P.: An orchestrated survey of methodologies for automated software test case generation. J. Syst. Softw. **86**, 1978–2001 (2013)
2. Beyer, D.: Evaluating tools for automatic software testing: Test-Comp 2026. In: Proc. FASE. LNCS 16504, Springer (2026)
3. Jiang, L., Yuan, H., Wu, M., Zhang, L., Zhang, Y.: Evaluating and improving hybrid fuzzing. In: 2023 IEEE/ACM 45th International Conference on Software Engineering (ICSE) (2023)
4. Kroening, D., Schrammel, P., Tautschnig, M.: Cbmc: The c bounded model checker. ArXiv **abs/2302.02384** (2023)
5. LLVM: Https://llvm.org
6. de Moura, L.M., Bjørner, N.S.: Z3: An efficient smt solver. In: International Conference on Tools and Algorithms for Construction and Analysis of Systems (2008)
7. Peng, C., Hao, C.: Angora: Efficient fuzzing by principled search. In: 2018 IEEE Symposium on Security and Privacy (SP). pp. 711–725 (2018)
8. Poeplau, S., Francillon, A.: Symbolic execution with symcc: Don't interpret, compile! In: USENIX Security Symposium (2020)
9. Sen, K.: Concolic testing. In: Proceedings of the 23th IEEE/ACM international conference on Automated software engineering (2007)
10. Yun, I., Lee, S., Xu, M., Jang, Y., Kim, T.: Qsym : A practical concolic execution engine tailored for hybrid fuzzing. In: USENIX Security Symposium (2018)
11. Zhang, G., Shuai, Z., Ma, K., Liu, K., Chen, Z., Wang, J.: FDSE: Enhance symbolic execution by fuzzing-based pre-analysis (competition contribution). In: Proc. FASE. pp. 304–308. LNCS 14573, Springer (2024). https://doi.org/10.1007/978-3-031-57259-3_16

[1] https://zenodo.org/records/17900875
[2] https://test-comp.sosy-lab.org/2026

BY

Sikraken: Symbolic Execution using Constraint Logic Programming for Generating Test Inputs (Competition Contribution)

Christophe Meudec*

South East Technological University, Kilkenny Road, Carlow, R93 V960, Ireland
chris.meudec@setu.ie
http://www.echancrure.eu/

Abstract. Sikraken is a novel prototype tool for generating test inputs from C source code, aiming to achieve high branch coverage. After minimal pre-processing, it performs the symbolic execution of C code using Prolog and relies on interval constraints resolution using Constraint Logic Programming (CLP) for solving arithmetic Path Conditions to generate test inputs that can achieve high branch coverage by construction. Standard Prolog backtracking is used as early as possible on sub-paths detected as infeasible, and standard instantiation techniques are used on successful test input generation. Sikraken has a relatively compact code size and has significant potential for handling more C constructs using user-defined constraints and exploring better path search strategies and input instantiation techniques.

Keywords: Automated Test Input Generation · Symbolic Execution · Prolog · Constraint Logic Programming · Software Testing

1 Overview

Sikraken employs a test generation approach based on a technique developed by the author ([10], [11]) for Ada, which has been further applied to Java Bytecode [4] and C [3]. It uses a symbolic executor based on Prolog [2] (ECLiPse [5] flavour) and solving capabilities using Constraint Logic Programming (CLP) [6]. It works at the level of the source code and only competes in Test-Comp's branch coverage meta-category.

2 Test Generation Approach

2.1 Parsing

First, the preprocessor of GCC (GNU Compiler Collection) is used to generate a single source code file free of macros [7]. Then, this C source code is parsed

* Jury Member

E. Albert and C. Pasareanu (Eds.): FASE 2026, LNCS 16504, pp. 487–491, 2026.
https://doi.org/10.1007/978-3-032-22774-4_27

using a custom-made parser implemented using Flex and Bison to generate a Prolog-readable file of terms.

Parsing industrial C code is challenging. Many improvements have been made to Sikraken's parser over the past year, primarily focusing on the correct handling of symbols due to `typedef` declarations and shadowing, which has reduced its parsing failure rate from approximately 10% of Test-Comp Benchmarks in 2025 to 29 benchmarks out of 14,376 (0.2%) for Test-Comp 2026.

The potential reward resides in the logical closeness between the human-readable C source code and Sikraken's analysis: the ease of mapping of the input and output variables between Sikraken's output and the source code should allow generic unit test frameworks to be used easily; also, it may be beneficial for applying higher-level constraints solving heuristics.

2.2 Prolog Initialisations

Using the Prolog file of terms, Sikraken processes the file-level C declarations and extracts the Control Flow Graph of the code under test. This process is very similar to the author's approach for ATGen [11] targeting Ada. After this initial parsing and global variables processing, which usually takes less than a few seconds for most Test-Comp benchmarks successfully handled by Sikraken, the symbolic execution of the main C function starts.

2.3 Symbolic Execution

The symbolic executor traverses the control flow of the C program in a logical manner, performing symbolic execution of assignments by updating the output value of the corresponding Prolog-attributed variable. These updates are automatically reverted during backtracking by Prolog's main execution engine. Sikraken relies heavily on ECLiPSe's [5] attributed variables (metaterms with attached attributes and specific Prolog unification behaviour) and coroutining (where constraints are suspended and awakened only when specific events, such as a variable instantiation event, occur) mechanisms.

Difficulties historically associated with Symbolic Execution are dealt with in a similar manner as in ATGen [11]. For example, function calls are handled by pushing copies of the argument onto a stack embedded in the parameter's name and popped on return; indexing of arrays with symbolic values is suspended using ECLiPSe's coroutining mechanism; additional Prolog predicates handle constraints not available in ECLiPSe's IC library (e.g. arithmetic shifting and bitwise operations, casting).

2.4 Constraints Resolution

When the symbolic executor encounters a branch, its associated symbolic conditions are posted to our bespoke solver, which is an extension of the ECLiPSe IC solver for resolution. ECLiPSe IC is a library that uses interval propagation to resolve linear and non-linear arithmetic constraints on integer/real variables [5]. If the constraints resolution fails, the symbolic executor backtracks immediately using Prolog's built-in Depth First Search mechanism until another suitable branch is found to be feasible. On reaching the end of a path, the labelling mechanism of ECLiPSe, which generates a suitable solution to the set of constraints posted during symbolic execution, is used to generate test inputs that satisfy the Path Conditions.

Irrespective of the outcome of the labelling strategy, the symbolic executor backtracks and restarts the process, allowing it to reuse the symbolic execution of subpaths efficiently.

2.5 Search Strategy

The current version of Sikraken has no Control Flow Graph (CFG) heuristic, so it merely keeps track of the branches already covered and faced with a binary choice opts for the branch uncovered, if any, or selects one at random otherwise; this very basic strategy allows Sikraken to exit loops at the earliest possible opportunity and to desist from generating test inputs from paths which do not contain uncovered branches.

To avoid potentially deep, fruitless searches, Prolog's default depth-first search mechanism is interrupted by a time-out: when it is triggered, the symbolic executor restarts from the main C function. The timeout is dynamic: from a small value, its value increases when triggered without producing a test vector, enabling deeper CFG exploration. Because it relies on wall-clock time, this mechanism currently leads to non-reproducible test-generation runs.

3 Strengths and Weaknesses of the Approach

Sikraken version 1.3.4, as used for Test-Comp 2026, is a prototype and has many shortcomings. Its search is essentially blind: it does not exploit the extracted Control Flow Graph for guidance—for example, it does not even detect when full branch coverage has already been achieved. Its labelling strategy, used to generate an input vector at the end of a path, is also very rudimentary, relying on ECLiPSe's default approach of labelling all integers first before attempting floating-point values. In addition, the tool is incomplete, lacking support for many fundamental C features, including pointers to non-scalar elements, pointer arithmetic, dynamic memory allocation, switch statements, static variables, some forms of goto, and numerous GCC extensions and behaviours; it also has no awareness of overflow or underflow. Finally, it is unsound: non-instantiated constraints involving bitwise shift operators are currently implemented incorrectly, and its handling of more complex data structures—such as structs containing arrays—requires significant revision, as it currently follows Ada semantics rather than C.

Sikraken, with its custom-made parser, symbolic executor using Prolog, and its customised constraints solver, is ambitious. Thus, despite being based on an idea presented more than twenty years ago [11], this entire approach is still under development and has yet to fulfil its potential.

However, its implementation is progressing. For Test-Comp 2026, the custom parser failure rate has been reduced from 10% to 0.2%, enumeration constants are fully efficiently handled, the Control Flow Graph, although still unused, is extracted correctly, and many bugs (e.g. handling of negative floating point numbers) have been retired.

For the Test-Comp sub-categories where Sikraken can handle the semantics of the C constructs used, it performs among the best tools [1]: e.g. in ReachSafety-ECA, Main-ControlFlow. It was 1st ex aequo in ReachSafety-XCSP with another tool in 2026. However, due to its incomplete state of development, Sikraken is non-competitive in categories requiring dynamic memory handling, for example. It frequently records very low scores in many sub-categories, falling short of the results achieved by even basic, randomised approaches. This deeply negatively affects its overall normalised Test-Comp's score.

4 Way Forward

As Sikraken is a work in progress, further work is necessary to allow the evaluation of its novel approach to the problem of automatic test inputs generation from C source code.

In particular, there is a need to develop an efficient algorithm, using the source code level Control Flow Graph already extracted, to guide the symbolic execution during its search towards uncovered branches or the target error branch (to allow Sikraken to compete in the Cover-Error meta-category). In addition, the C subset handled needs expanding as currently, and for example, any benchmarks using union types or dynamic memory allocation simply fail.

None of these improvements is constrained by the novel approach adopted: they are simply work that remains to be done before a deeper assessment of Sikraken and its approach can be presented.

5 Tool Setup and Configuration

Sikraken's Development and User Guide [7] describes the current best practices for using Sikraken.

For Test-Comp 2026, Sikraken was called using the command

```
./bin/sikraken.sh --testcomp
```

with BenchExec appending the data model and path to the target input file.

6 Data-Availability Statement

The source code of the specific version (v. 1.3.4) of Sikraken used for Test-Comp 2026 is available online as a Zenodo archive [9]. Sikraken is under continuous development and is available from its GitHub repository [8], and the latest version of its user and development manual [7] should be consulted.

References

1. Beyer, D.: Evaluating tools for automatic software testing: Test-Comp 2026. In: Proc. FASE. LNCS 16504, Springer (2026)
2. Clocksin, W.F., Mellish, C.S.: Programming in PROLOG. Springer Science & Business Media (2003)
3. Dillon, E., Meudec, C.: Automatic Test Data Generation from Embedded C Code. In: International Conference on Computer Safety, Reliability, and Security. pp. 180–194. Springer (2004)
4. Doyle, J., Meudec, C.: IBIS: an Interactive Bytecode Inspection System, using Symbolic Execution and Constraint Logic Programming. In: Second International Conference on the Principles and Practice of Programming in Java. vol. 42, pp. 55–58. ACM International Conference Proceeding Series (2003)
5. ECLiPSe: The ECLiPSe Constraint Programming System, https://eclipseclp.org/, [Accessed: 2026-01-21]
6. Jaffar, J., Lassez, J.L.: Constraint logic programming. In: ACM-SIGACT Symposium on Principles of Programming Languages (1987), https://api.semanticscholar.org/CorpusID:2088154
7. Meudec, C.: Sikraken Development and User Guide, https://urlr.me/CFPB4D, [Accessed: 2026-01-21]
8. Meudec, C.: Sikraken GitHub Repository, https://github.com/echancrure/Sikraken, [Accessed: 2026-01-21]
9. Meudec, C.: Sikraken Zenodo Archive, https://zenodo.org/records/18062402
10. Meudec, C.: Automatic Test Data Generation Using Constraint Logic Programming - Report V (1997), The University of York
11. Meudec, C.: ATGen: Automatic Test Data Generation using Constraint Logic Programming and Symbolic Execution. Software Testing, Verification and Reliability **11**(2), 81–96 (2001)

Ultimate TestGen: Combining Parallel Trace Abstraction and Symbolic Path Execution (Competition Contribution)*

Max Barth**[1], Daniel Dietsch[2], Matthias Heizmann[3], and Marie-Christine Jakobs[1]

[1] LMU Munich, Munich, Germany
[2] University of Freiburg, Freiburg, Germany
[3] University of Stuttgart, Stuttgart, Germany

Abstract. Prior to Test-Comp 2026, Ultimate TestGen generated test cases with a sequential software model checking approach, which is named trace abstraction and performs counterexample-guided abstraction refinement. To generate tests, Ultimate TestGen encodes test goals as property violations and generates test cases from counterexamples detected by trace abstraction. For Test-Comp 2026, we keep this general principle but make two changes. First, we adapt Ultimate TestGen to a recent parallelization of trace abstraction. Second, we extend Ultimate TestGen with a Path-Checker, which runs in parallel with parallel trace abstraction and exhaustively explores counterexamples but skips refinement.

Keywords: Ultimate Automizer · Test-case generation · Software testing · Test Coverage · Software model checking · Automata

1 Test-Case Generation Approach

Test-case generators based on verifiers, e.g., Ultimate TestGen [3], allow us to generate test cases for test goals that may only be reached with very specific inputs but they may become costly if they spend lots of time on excluding infeasible paths to test goals or even proving the unreachability of certain test goals. Also, they are often sequential and ignore today's multi-core processors.

To address the latter limitation, we adopt Ultimate TestGen's test-case generation to a recent parallelization of trace abstraction [4,1], its underlying verification procedure. To counteract the other limitations, we extend Ultimate TestGen with a new Path-Checker, which exhaustively tries to generate test cases from counterexamples but skips the costly exclusion of infeasible paths.

Figure 1 shows the workflow of Ultimate TestGen when using parallel trace abstraction in combination with the Path-Checker. Parallel trace abstraction uses a coordinator and several worker threads while we use one thread for the

* This work was partially funded by the Deutsche Forschungsgemeinschaft (DFG, German Research Foundation) - 378803395 (ConVeY) and 496852682 (ReVeriX).
** Jury Member: Max Barth

E. Albert and C. Pasareanu (Eds.): FASE 2026, LNCS 16504, pp. 492–496, 2026.
https://doi.org/10.1007/978-3-032-22774-4_28

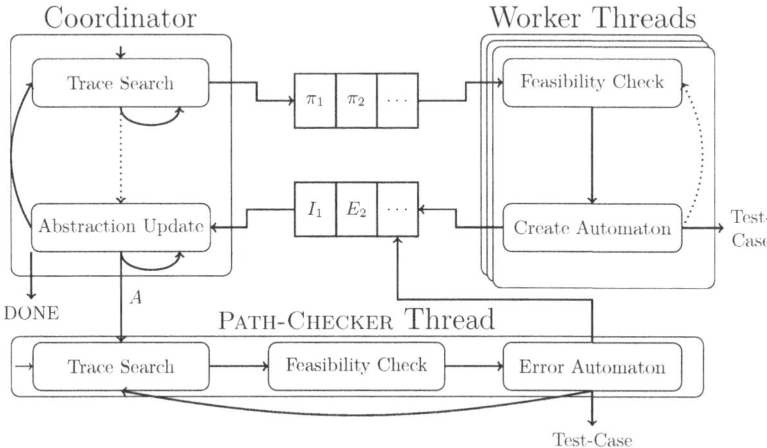

Fig. 1. Overview of the ULTIMATE TESTGEN workflow.

PATH-CHECKER. To let the two approaches cooperate, the coordinator shares its trace abstraction A with the PATH-CHECKER. The trace abstraction is an automaton that accepts all relevant error traces[4], i.e., all syntactic program paths that reach a not yet covered test goal and that are not yet shown to be semantically infeasible. The PATH-CHECKER uses the same mechanism as the worker threads to inform the coordinator about covered test goals. More concretely, the PATH-CHECKER adds an error automata E_i [3] into the input buffer of the coordinator when it covers a test goal. The error automaton accepts all error traces associated with the covered test goal and is used by the coordinator to exclude those traces from further considerations. To avoid duplicate test cases, which for instance may occur when parallel trace abstraction and the PATH-CHECKER simultaneously explore the same error trace, we name test cases by their hash value of their content. Next, we describe the general workflow for test-case generation with parallel trace abstraction and with the PATH-CHECKER and explain their common algorithm for (error) trace search.

Test-Case Generation with Parallel Trace Abstraction. To generate test-cases with parallel trace abstraction, we need to adapt how to handle feasible error traces. Like the sequential ULTIMATE TESTGEN version [3], we add the creation of test cases, the generation of error automaton, and ideally run until all reachable goals are covered. Now, let us briefly look at the resulting test-case generation procedure, which is split into a coordinator that steers the procedure and multiple worker threads that analyze error traces. The coordinator performs an iterative two step process. In the first phase, it searches diverse error traces for each idle worker and puts them into its output buffer. Then, the coordinator blocks until a worker result becomes available, i.e., its input buffer contains at least one (error or interpolant) automaton. As long as its input buffer contains

[4] Error trace is ULTIMATE TESTGEN's term for a counterexample.

an automaton, the coordinator updates its trace abstraction, i.e., it removes all traces accepted by that automaton. If the trace abstraction becomes empty, all test goals are covered, and the coordinator stops the whole process.

A worker thread iteratively analyzes error traces. As soon as it gets an error trace from the input buffer, it first analyzes the trace's semantic feasiblity using an SMT solver. If the error trace is infeasible, the worker uses interpolation to compute a refinement suggestion, i.e., an interpolant automaton I_i [6], which accepts the infeasible error trace and error traces with similar reasons for infeasibility. Otherwise, it generates a test case and an error automata E_i [3] that accepts all error traces associated with the covered test goal. In any case, it puts the generated automaton into the output buffer and starts its next iteration.

Test-Case Generation with the Path-Checker. The PATH-CHECKER iteratively explores error traces (i.e., counterexamples) exhaustively. In each iteration, the PATH-CHECKER selects an error trace for analysis, checks its semantic feasibility using an SMT solver, and exports a test-case for each semantically feasible error trace. To avoid exploring error traces known to be infeasible or error traces that do not introduce new coverage, it performs the search on the latest trace abstraction of the coordinator. Conversely, the PATH-CHECKER informs the coordinator about covered test goals. To this end, it generates an error automaton for each semantically feasible error trace it analyzed and puts this error automaton into the input buffer of the coordinator. Note that the PATH-CHECKER does not inform the coordinator about infeasible error traces because excluding a single error trace does not reduce the trace abstraction significantly but may make its representation rather large. However, the PATH-CHECKER remembers its explored error traces to avoid reexploring them again.

Since Test-Comp limits the usable CPU time, we need to distribute the CPU time between parallel trace abstraction and the PATH-CHECKER. Based on prior experimental experience, we decide to add the following Test-Comp specific sleep periods to the PATH-CHECKER. Upon initialization, the PATH-CHECKER sleeps for 30 seconds, and after the PATH-CHECKER checked the feasibility of three error traces, it sleeps for one second.

Trace Search. Both, the coordinator and the PATH-CHECKER, employ the same algorithm for their trace search [4]. The goal of the search is to find an error trace in the current trace abstraction A that is dissimilar from a set of given traces (the currently explored error traces for parallel trace abstraction and the already explored (infeasible) error traces in case of the PATH-CHECKER). The search algorithm uses the set of given traces to steer its search through the abstraction. Thereby, it incrementally constructs error traces and backtracks if a found error trace is already part of the given set. During its incremental construction, the algorithm prefers successors that are taken less often among all given traces that have the so far constructed trace as prefix.

To address the path explosion problem for the PATH-CHECKER, we dynamically restrict the number of loop unrollings that the PATH-CHECKER's search may explore to one loop iteration beyond all iterations proven infeasible. Technically, we statically bound the number of loop unrollings in the abstraction.

2 Discussion of Strengths and Weaknesses

Comparing Ultimate TestGen's approach based on a combination of parallel trace abstraction and Path-Checker against its previous version, we observe that in the `cover-error` category, we particularly profit from our combination in the subcategories `ProductLines` and `Sequentialized`. Also, our combination achieves more branch coverage in total when limiting the wall time. We observed an increase in coverage for about 30% of the test tasks. One reason is that the Path-Checker allows to generate additional test cases while the other workers perform expensive refinement (i.e., interpolant automaton) computations. Still, there is a larger number of test tasks (approximately 60% of the tasks), for which the coverage stays the same. For about 40% of these tasks, both approaches achieve the maximal coverage. Also, there is a small amount of tasks (<10%) for which the combined approach performs worse. One plausible cause is that the abstraction update is done in a different order and possible with different automata, which leads to a different (intermediate) abstraction and the detection of error traces that contribute less to the overall coverage.

While in general promising, parallelizing trace abstraction and running the Path-Checker in parallel comes at the cost of increased CPU time and memory usage. When limiting the CPU time, the fast Path-Checker may waste a lot of of CPU time when analyzing infeasible paths that could be ruled out by parallel trace analysis by analyzing one error trace. Such a waste of CPU time may decrease the overall effectiveness of the combination. To mitigate this, we force the Path-Checker to regularly pause for a short moment. In addition, parallel trace abstraction and the Path-Checker may generate redundant, duplicate test cases, which we avoid by naming test cases based on their hash values.

3 Setup and Configuration

Ultimate TestGen is part of the Ultimate framework[5], which is licensed under LGPLv3. To run Ultimate TestGen one needs Java 21 and Python 3.6. Having met these requirements, one may execute Ultimate TestGen in its Test-Comp 2026 [2] version using the following command:

```
./Ultimate.py --spec <p> --file <f> --architecture <a> --full-output .
```

Thereby, parameter `<p>` specifies a coverage property in form of a Test-Comp property file. Parameter `<f>` provides the input C file, for which test cases will be generated, and parameter `<a>` provides the architecture (`32bit` or `64bit`). To choose the number `<n>` of the worker thread, one needs to add the option

```
--traceabstraction.threadlimit.for.parallel.cegar <n> .
```

For Test-Comp 2026 [5], we use two worker threads, one of them being the Path-Checker, for which we limit its trace search to explore one loop iteration beyond all iterations proven to be infeasible.

[5] https://ultimate.informatik.uni-freiburg.de and https://github.com/ultimate-pa/ultimate

Data Availability The Test-Comp 2026 version of Ultimate TestGen is available on Zenodo [2]. Its corresponding FM-tools entry is available on GitLab[6].

References

1. Barth, M., Dietsch, D., Heizmann, M., Jakobs, M.C.: UltimateParalizer : Parallel trace abstraction (competition contribution). In: Proc. TACAS (2). pp. xx-yy. LNCS 16506, Springer (2026).https://doi.org/10.1007/978-3-032-22749-2_38
2. Barth, M.: Ultimate TestGen at Test-Comp 2026. Zenodo (2025), https://doi.org/10.5281/zenodo.17792491
3. Barth, M., Jakobs, M.C.: Test-case generation with automata-based software model checking. In: Proc. SPIN. pp. 248–267. LNCS 14624, Springer (2024), https://doi.org/10.1007/978-3-031-66149-5_14
4. Barth, M., Jakobs, M.C.: Multi-threaded software model checking via parallel trace abstraction refinement (2026), https://arxiv.org/abs/2509.13699v2
5. Beyer, D.: Evaluating tools for automatic software testing: Test-Comp 2026. In: Proc. FASE. pp. xx-yy. LNCS 16504, Springer (2026). https://doi.org/10.1007/978-3-032-22774-4_23
6. Heizmann, M., Hoenicke, J., Podelski, A.: Refinement of trace abstraction. In: Proc. SAS. pp. 69–85. LNCS 5673, Springer (2009). https://doi.org/10.1007/978-3-642-03237-0_7

[6] https://gitlab.com/sosy-lab/benchmarking/fm-tools/-/blob/main/data/utestgen.yml

Author Index

E. Albert and C. Pasareanu (Eds.): FASE 2026, LNCS 16504, pp. 497–498, 2026.
https://doi.org/10.1007/978-3-032-22774-4

The manufacturer's authorised representative in the EU is Springer Nature Customer Service Centre GmbH, Europaplatz 3, 69115 Heidelberg, Germany. If you have any concerns regarding our products, please contact ProductSafety@springernature.com

Printed and bound by CPI Group (UK) Ltd, Croydon, CR0 4YY
07/07/2026
02160913-0015